BUSINESS ACCOUNTING AND FINANCE

FOURTH EDITION

CATHERINE GOWTHORPE

KFC (SKLL. ACC)

GOW

STO

CENGAGE

Australia • Brazil • Mexico • Singapore • United Kingdom • United

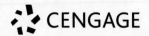

Business Accounting and Finance, 4th Edition
Catherine Gowthorpe

Publisher: Annabel Ainscow

Development Editor: Hannah Close

Content Project Manager: Phillipa Davidson-Blake

Manufacturing Manager: Eyvett Davis

Marketing Manager: Sophie Clarke

Typesetter: SPi Global

Cover Designer: Simon Levy Associates

Cover Image: © Suti Stock Photo/ Shutterstock

For product information and technology assistance, contact us at **emea.info@cengage.com**

For permission to use material from this text or product and for permission queries, email **emea.permissions@cengage.com**

British Library Cataloguing-in-Publication Data

A catalogue record for this book is available from the British Library.

ISBN: 978-1-473-74935-1

Cengage Learning, EMEA
Cheriton House, North Way
Andover, Hampshire, SP10 5BE
United Kingdom

Cengage Learning is a leading provider of customized learning solutions with employees residing in nearly 40 different countries and sales in more than 125 countries around the world. Find your local representative at: **www.cengage.co.uk**.

Cengage Learning products are represented in Canada by Nelson Education, Ltd.

For your course and learning solutions, visit **www.cengage.co.uk**.

Purchase any of our products at your local college store or at our preferred online store **www.cengagebrain.com**.

Printed in China by RR Donnelley
Print Number: 01   Print Year: 2017

Brief contents

Contents

Figures

The following figures appear in the Answers Section

Preface to the fourth edition

Who is this book aimed at?

The aim of this book is to provide an introduction to business accounting and finance. The book is suitable for students on introductory accounting courses, or on business and management courses generally, or on more specialized courses such as marketing, human resources management, tourism, hospitality management and information systems. Students outside the business area following courses in engineering, computer science, fashion and fine and applied arts will also find the book a very suitable introduction to accounting and finance.

While the principal intended audience for the book comprises students taking a formal course of instruction at college or university, it is also intended that the book should lend itself to self study by anyone who is interested in extending their knowledge of basic business accounting and finance. This could include people who are starting, or thinking of starting, their own businesses. Also, the book could be useful for people who are already engaged in business but who are aware that they do not quite understand what their accountant is telling them.

The overarching aim of the book is to develop understanding of accounting. It is not, primarily, a book about how to do accounts. Some of the chapters do, indeed, require students to prepare fairly straightforward accounting statements. However, the principal purpose of this approach is to aid understanding; it is often easier to understand how accounting figures hang together if you have had some experience of working them out for yourself.

If you are a student specializing in a non-accounting subject you may find that you are obliged, unavoidably, to study business accounting and finance. Students in this category are sometimes very unwilling to engage with a subject that they find to be alien and unhelpful. If this describes you, you may find it helpful to read the 'special notes for the suspicious' in Chapter 1 of the book.

Chapter structure

All chapters start with Aims and Learning Outcomes. Diagrams and tables aid the narrative explanations and illustrate concepts, and frequent use is made of worked examples.

Most chapters include self-test questions within the text, so that students can test their understanding as they progress through the chapter. At the end of each chapter is an extensive set of exercises so that students can test their knowledge and understanding. Students are often worried and may become demotivated if the end-of-chapter exercises are too difficult. Therefore, the exercises are designed to test the full range of learning points in the chapter, from simple to complex. If students wish to test their understanding with even more exercises, further examples are provided on the book's dedicated website (see below). About half of the end of chapter exercises contain answers within the book. Answers to the remainder are available on the lecturers' section of the book's website.

Supplementary material

In addition to the material presented in the book, a variety of supplementary material is available.

DEDICATED WEBSITE

The lecturer section of the website is password protected and the password is available free to lecturers who confirm their adoption of the book. Lecturers should complete the registration form on the website to apply for their password.

For Students and Lecturers (Open Access)

- Multiple choice questions. This contains supplementary questions for every chapter, comprising multiple choice questions (usually five or ten per chapter) and a bank of additional questions, all with answers.
    In addition, there are one or two case studies (with answers) for almost all of the chapters.
- Links to accounting and finance sites on the web, including links to the sites mentioned in the book.
- Additional questions and answers.

For Lecturers Only (Password Protected)

- Answers to the end-of-chapter questions for which answers are not provided in the book
- A downloadable Instructor's Manual including teaching notes
- PowerPoint presentations to accompany each chapter
- Testbank
- Case Studies
- Additional questions and answers
- Supplementary chapters on double-entry book-keeping.

Changes to the fourth edition

The fourth edition has been revised extensively in response to comments and suggestions from lecturers and students. Many thanks to all those who provided the useful and constructive comments and reviews on which the fourth edition is built.

The principal changes are as follows:

1 updating and/or replacement of most of the real-life examples
2 the addition of several questions on statements of cash flows in Chapter 6
3 updating of Chapter 7, and references in some other chapters, to incorporate recent developments in UK GAAP and in the IASB's Conceptual Framework.

Acknowledgements

Thanks to all the reviewers and students who have commented on earlier editions of the book, and to colleagues and students over the years who have influenced and informed the content of this book.

Reviewers whose helpful feedback has helped shape this fourth edition include the following: Tim Price, Anglia Ruskin University London; Nadia Gulko, University of Lincoln; Anwar Halari, University of Buckingham; and Alan Goodacre, University of Stirling.

Thanks to the staff at Cengage Learning who have made the production of this book possible, and especially to Annabel Ainscow, Hannah Close and Phillipa Davidson-Blake.

1 The role of accounting in business

Aim of the chapter

To introduce the most common forms of business organization and to understand the reasons why people in business need accounting information, the nature of accounting information and the role of the accountant.

Learning outcomes

After reading the chapter and completing the related exercises, students should:

- Understand the differences between the sole trader, partnership and company forms of business organizations, and know, in outline, about some of the sources of business finance available to commercial organizations.

- Know in outline about some important features of the business environment including the various ways in which tax is charged on businesses.

- Understand why accounting information is produced.

- Be able to identify the principal groups in society who need and use accounting information, and to know about the principal characteristics and features of accounting information.

- Know about the functions that accountants perform in the production of accounting information.

Introduction

Accounting information is produced, quite simply, because people need it. This chapter explains the context in which accountants produce accounting information, describes the potential users of that information and outlines the type of information that might be required. The chapter assumes no prior knowledge of accounting or finance, or indeed business in general. Students coming to these areas of knowledge for the first time are often apprehensive about them. Accounting and finance are regarded by many people as particularly difficult subjects and lecturers in accounting often face ingrained negative attitudes amongst their new students. Some of the most frequently encountered objections are considered in this introductory section of Chapter 1.

1.0.1 Special Notes for the Suspicious

If you are really looking forward to studying accounting and finance, please feel free to ignore the next few paragraphs. If, however, you are studying accounting only because of a general course requirement and if the quotations at the head of each subsection sound familiar, you might find it helpful to read the text below them.

'ACCOUNTING IS BORING AND IT'S NOT RELEVANT TO WHAT I'M DOING ANYWAY.' Some people are obliged to study accounting as part of a course in, say, marketing, engineering or a creative discipline. If you are a fashion student, for example, you are likely to be much more interested in creative outcomes and in developing your own skills. But people who are successful in making careers in fashion and other creative endeavours have to be very much alive to the business environment in which they work. People who have forged successful careers in the creative arts are often surprisingly well tuned in to the business and accounting aspects of what they do.

'ACCOUNTING SHOULD BE LEFT TO THE ACCOUNTANTS.' If you are looking forward to a career in, say, retail management or marketing, you may feel that you really should not have to bother with accounting – after all, there are plenty of accountants around to sort out the figures. One of the key messages of this book is that accounting, on the contrary, is much too important to be left to the accountants. Business managers in all disciplines owe it to themselves to be able to interpret the reports that accountants present to them; such reports are vital aids to understanding what is going on in the business. Business managers should be able to question accountants from a position of understanding the accounting information. If they are not sufficiently knowledgeable to do this, they risk being quite seriously restricted in their understanding of their business and their ability to make sound decisions.

It is important to appreciate from the outset that accounting is not an exact science. Accounting has emerged in its present-day form, after many centuries of development, because there is a need for it. It is, essentially, about communication between people and so it is vulnerable to all the impediments that hinder proper communication. For example, people sometimes tell lies, and accounting can be used, very effectively, to tell lies. Accounting is often imprecise, and its imprecision can be easily exploited by the unscrupulous. After studying this book, you should be much more aware of the strengths and limitations of accounting as a means of communication.

'ACCOUNTING IS ALL ABOUT MATHS, AND I'M NO GOOD AT MATHS.' Accounting undeniably involves dealing with numbers. However, the study of accounting rarely involves much beyond simple arithmetic. Specifically, the principal prior skills that this book requires are the ability to add, subtract, multiply, divide and to calculate a percentage. Towards the end of the book students will be required to draw simple line graphs and to calculate compound interest. There is nothing in this book that requires knowledge beyond GCSE level (in UK terms).

What the study of accounting does involve, though, is the ability to understand what the numbers signify. This is a skill that some students find relatively difficult to acquire. The book has been written with this difficulty in mind.

'I WON'T BE ABLE TO UNDERSTAND THE JARGON.' Accounting is no different from many other spheres of fairly advanced human endeavour in that it has its own terminology. Jargon is often baffling to the uninitiated but, inevitably, some of the jargon simply has to be learned. This book attempts to explain all the unfamiliar terms in the most straightforward way possible. There is a glossary towards the end of the book which collects together a lot of the most unfamiliar terminology so that students do not have to go back through the book hunting for the original explanation.

Content of this Chapter

The chapter proceeds with a brief description of different forms of business organization, and sources of finance for them. It is followed by a brief section on some important features of the business environment, including some of the ways that tax is charged on business.

The chapter then proceeds to examine the need for accounting information and the function of the accountant in providing it.

1.1 FORMS OF BUSINESS ORGANIZATION

There are three common forms of business organization: sole trader businesses, partnerships and limited companies. All three types of organization are run with a view to making profits.

1.1.1 Sole Trader Businesses

A **sole trader** operates a business himself or herself, keeping any profits which are made (after deduction of tax). This is a useful form of business for certain types of trade or profession. For example, a plumber, carpenter, financial services adviser, tax adviser, writer or nightclub singer could each operate as a sole trader business. Each of the people named offers a service to the public; each receives money in exchange for performance of the services. After deduction of the various expenses that are involved in running the business, any sum that is left over is the profit, all of which can be kept by the sole trader.

Example 1.1

Having finished his apprenticeship, Yasin sets up in business as a plumber. He pays a friend to set up a website for him, subscribes to a plumbers' trade association, and waits to be contacted by members of the public and other businesses who require plumbing services. Yasin charges fees for his services out of which he must meet business expenses.

What are Yasin's business expenses? They will typically involve: cost of tools, expenses of running a van, mobile phone bills, advertising and small amounts of administrative expense, such as paying for an accountant to sort out his tax affairs.

In order to keep his business affairs in good order, he will need to keep receipts as evidence of his expenses, copies of the bills he makes out to his customers and bank statements. It is important not to mix up the business income and expenditure with his own personal items

Yasin or his accountant will summarize all the income he has received from customers and all the expenses of running the business on an annual basis.

Income less expenses = the profit of the business

The tax authorities (Her Majesty's Revenue and Customs in the UK – HMRC for short) will naturally take an interest in Yasin's business activities. He will have to pay tax, based upon the calculation of his profit. Later in the chapter, we will examine the tax regime in a little more detail.

CHARACTERISTICS OF THE SOLE TRADER FORM OF BUSINESS The sole trader is the only person responsible for the management of the business. Although he or she may employ other people as the business gets bigger, all the decision making and risk taking involved in the business rests on the shoulders of one individual. If the business runs into financial difficulties or faces other problems, the sole trader is on his or her own in addressing them.

Sole trader businesses tend to remain fairly small. For people who are self-employed in the types of trade or profession mentioned earlier, this type of business can work very well. However, if the business is of a type that is likely to grow very much bigger, the sole trader form of organization will need to be replaced by a partnership or limited company structure which allows more than one person to act as manager.

If a sole trader overstretches himself or herself financially, perhaps by borrowing too much, or if losses rather than profits are made, he or she is liable for all the consequences as an individual. For example, a lender would be entitled to pursue repayment of a loan even to the point where the sole trader would have to sell personal property to repay it. In extreme cases, this can result in personal bankruptcy.

The sole trader business is relatively informal and easy to set up. The business does not require registration of a separate legal entity and so it is quite likely that no legal costs will arise. In the initial stages, at least, the principal administrative issues are likely to arise with the HMRC. A competent chartered accountant can mediate between the individual and the HMRC to ensure that the correct amount is paid, and that tax does not become a problem.

1.1.2 Partnerships

A partnership is a business which is run by two or more people with a view to making a profit. Typically, partnerships are fairly small businesses, but there are certain types of business activity in which very large partnerships are operated. Professional partnerships, such as those between solicitors, may develop to be very large businesses indeed. There is a legal restriction which limits the number of partners in most types of partnership to 20; however, professional partnerships (solicitors, accountants, surveyors, architects, for example) are exempt from the restriction. The very largest partnerships are such big businesses that people who may have barely met each other are in partnership together.

Many different trades and professions may be run through the medium of a partnership; apart from the professions noted above, doctors, pharmacists, business consultants, shopkeepers, builders, hairdressers and almost any other type of trade or business activity could be run via a partnership.

Example 1.2

Winston and Winona start a business selling computer games; they will rent shop premises for retail sales, but will also run a mail order service from the room behind the shop. The business is established as a partnership with a business name of WW Wizard Games. The two partners decide that, as they will both be working full-time in the new business, they will share all the profits from the business equally.

As in the case of Yasin in Example 1.1, it will be necessary to keep some records of the business activities. It makes good sense to do so, as it will contribute to good relations with the tax authorities. However, unlike the case of the sole trader, Yasin, there are some legal requirements governing the records that have to be kept by the business, and the way in which the business operates. Partnerships are covered by the Partnership Act 1890. This is a relatively straightforward piece of legislation which sets out a basic structure of legal relationships between partners, minimum record-keeping requirements, and ways of resolving disputes between partners. For example, the Partnership Act states that profits will be shared equally between partners, unless they make some other agreement between themselves. Winston and Winona have agreed in any case to share profits equally; this is a common arrangement where all partners are contributing equally to the success of the business. However, they could share profits in any way that seems appropriate.

Apart from the basic legal structure set out in the Partnership Act 1890, partners may decide to draw up a formal, legal agreement between them. Typically, this would set out the details of the financial and legal arrangements which are to operate; it might, for example, state that Partner A will receive 60% of the profits of the business while Partners B and C each receive 20%. It may also deal with the actions to be taken in the event of a dispute between the partners. Not all partnerships bother to have a formal agreement of this type set up, but it can prove to be very useful if relationships turn sour.

CHARACTERISTICS OF THE PARTNERSHIP FORM OF BUSINESS The success of a partnership depends to some extent on the quality of the relationships between partners. Sometimes, people who are friends, or who are related to each other, set up a business partnership together. The pressures of running a business can sometimes place an intolerable strain on what has previously been a good relationship. On the other hand, where partnerships work well, they can be highly productive, especially if the partners have a range of skills that complement each other. Winona, in the example above, is perhaps very good at selling over the counter, but lacks the attention to administrative detail that is required to run the mail order side of the business. If Winston is a good administrator, he will complement Winona's skills, and between them they will perhaps be able to run a successful business.

As well as sharing in the running of the business, the partners are likely to be able to command more resources to put into the business. At the start-up stage, each may have savings or other resources (such as equipment) which they can put into the business. If the partnership needs to borrow money, it may be in a better position to do so than the sole trader.

If the partnership loses money, or cannot repay loans, lenders are able to recover money owed by requiring the partners to sell items of property which they own personally. In this respect the partnership is no different from the sole trader, and the partners face the consequence of bankruptcy in the worst cases.

Each partner is liable under the law for the actions of his or her partners. If Winona makes a business decision which turns out badly and the partnership is left owing a large amount of money, both Winona and Winston are liable for the consequences of the decision. Winston could not claim that he knew nothing about the agreement; he would still be equally liable with Winona. (It really is important for partners to know and trust each other thoroughly.)

A partnership business is not difficult to set up. However, partners should be prepared to go to the additional trouble and expense of having a clear partnership agreement drawn up with the help of a solicitor. It will make the resolution of any disputes in the future easier to resolve.

1.1.3 Limited Companies

A limited company is a legal arrangement for regulating the ownership of business. A company is regarded as a separate person for the purposes of the law; so, for example, a company, unlike a partnership, can enter into a legal contract. This means that, if the other contracting person sues, he or she sues the company, not the owners of the company. The company itself becomes liable for its unpaid debts, overdrafts and so on.

This legal construction is an extremely important feature of the business world, in the UK and in many other countries. Because the company itself enters into contracts, takes out loans and so on, its owners are protected from any adverse consequences of the action. This is the concept of **limited liability**. It is an extremely useful and helpful device which protects shareholders from personal loss if the business runs into trouble.

Setting up a company (the process of **incorporation**) involves some legal formalities which must be followed strictly. It is therefore more difficult than setting up a sole trader business. However, the difficulties should not be overstated: there are specialist company registration firms which, for a modest fee, take care of all the formalities. It need cost little more than £150 to set up a company.

After the company is incorporated, there are certain regular legal formalities which must be complied with. More details are given below.

Example 1.3

Winston and Winona decide to set up their business as a limited company, rather than as a partnership. The business is registered in the name of WW Wizard Games Limited. They divide ownership of the business between them; each owns exactly 50% of the shares in the business. Winona and Winston are both **shareholders**. Both are involved in the day-to-day management of the business and, as well as being shareholders, are also **directors**.

CHARACTERISTICS OF LIMITED COMPANIES   Shareholders are liable only for the amount which they have paid into the company in exchange for shares. This is the maximum amount which they can lose if the company is, for example, sued for not repaying its loans on time.

The legal formalities involved in setting up and running a limited company are more complex than for partnerships and sole traders. The directors of a limited company are responsible for making available to the public a certain amount of financial information about the activities of the company, on a regular basis. They must do this via Companies House, an agency which is responsible for the collection of data relating to companies. Any member of the public can obtain information, including accounting information, about a limited company through the Companies House website (www.gov.uk/government/organisations/companies-house). Information which could remain private in a sole trader or partnership organization must be made public by limited companies.

In small companies, shareholders (who are the owners of the company) and directors (who are responsible for managing it) are the same people. However, in larger companies it is frequently the case that most shareholders have nothing to do with the management of the company. Day-to-day management can be left in the hands of directors who are professional managers. Shareholders in very large companies often have virtually no contact with the company or its managers.

Chapter 7 later in the book provides more detailed information about companies and their accounting.

1.2 SOLE TRADERS, PARTNERSHIPS AND LIMITED COMPANIES CONTRASTED

When setting up a business from scratch, the founder or founders must consider carefully which form of business organization is most suitable for them. Usually, it is sensible to take professional advice on the matter as it can be advantageous for tax purposes to choose one form over another. Leaving tax to one side for the time being, the following are the principal advantages and drawbacks of the three different types of organization.

1.2.1 Sole Trader – Advantages

- It is easy to start up as a sole trader.
- There are no legal formalities on start up.
- The sole trader is self-reliant; he or she does not risk the personality clashes which can occur where more than one person is managing a business.
- The sole trader does not have to share the profits from the business with anyone else.

1.2.2 Sole Trader – Drawbacks

- A sole trader bears all of the consequences of legal action against the business for unpaid debts and unfulfilled contracts. His or her personal property may have to be sold to meet business debts.
- A sole trader organization remains small-scale.
- The sole trader bears the brunt of any losses or business difficulties.
- There is no co-manager with whom problems can be shared.
- If the sole trader is weak in some aspect of business expertise (ability to sell, to manage people, to keep track of business records) the business may suffer because there is no one available with complementary skills.

1.2.3 Partnership – Advantages

- In a partnership, management is shared and the business can benefit from the complementary skills that the partners bring to it.
- Business decisions do not have to be taken alone.
- Business risks are shared, as are any losses which the business makes.

1.2.4 Partnership – Drawbacks

- Partners are responsible in law for the consequences of each other's actions.
- Partners face unlimited liability; they must bear all of the consequences of legal action against the partnership. Their personal property may have to be sold to meet unpaid business debts.
- The profits of the business are shared between all the partners whereas a sole trader keeps all the profits for himself or herself (but note that a partnership business, which combines the skills of two or more people, should be able to generate higher profits than a sole trader).

1.2.5 Limited Company – Advantages

- The most significant advantage conferred by company status is the limitation of personal liability. Shareholders can invest in a business knowing that they will not be pursued for further **contributions** once their shares have been paid for.
- The limited company legal structure allows for shareholders to appoint professional managers as directors.
- A limited company's shares can be used to spread the ownership of the business amongst many people.
- Shares can be sold and bought so that transfer of ownership is relatively easy and straightforward.

1.2.6 Limited Company – Drawbacks

- Setting up a company requires adherence to a set of strict formal legal requirements, and will sometimes require professional advice.
- Regular filing of financial information at Companies House is a legal requirement; this involves additional administration and means that members of the public have access to information which would remain strictly private in a partnership or sole trader organization.

Before moving on, make sure that you can answer the following 'true or false' questions.

a) Setting up a partnership does not involve any particular legal considerations. TRUE or FALSE?

b) A sole trader is liable personally for all losses made by the business. TRUE or FALSE?

c) A director of a company cannot hold shares in that same company. TRUE or FALSE?

d) Partners are responsible in law for the consequences of each other's actions. TRUE or FALSE?

Self-test question 1.1
(answer at the end of the book)

1.3 FINANCE FOR BUSINESS

When starting a business, the founder or founders must find a source of finance to pay for the setting up costs, any equipment that is needed and, probably, for the expenses of the business for the period during which it is getting established.

Most established businesses will also require finance from time to time to pay for such items as:

- buying major items of equipment or land and buildings.
- expanding the scope of the business (for example, opening new offices or conducting research into new product feasibility).
- helping the business through difficult periods such as temporary recessions or decreases in sales.

In this section of the chapter we will examine the principal sources of finance that may be available to a business. Some are more appropriate than others for particular purposes. Note that Chapter 20 considers the financing of businesses in much more detail than the brief summary provided below.

1.3.1 Existing Resources

When a business starts up, the founder(s) will almost certainly make an initial contribution of their own resources. This may be in the form of cash they have saved, or won or been given. It could be in the form of motor cars or vans, premises or some other item of resource. Such initial contributions are known in accounting terms as capital introduced. Where partners contribute to the setting up of a business, they may contribute unequal amounts depending on the resources they have at their disposal. In such cases, it may be decided between the partners that those who contribute more will receive an extra share of the profits to compensate.

Example 1.4

Jakes, Jones and Jessop form a partnership to conduct legal business. The total capital introduced by the partners is £190 000, constituted as follows:

Jakes: office building valued at £100 000
Jones: cash of £50 000
Jessop: cash of £30 000 plus office equipment valued at £10 000

The partners decide between them that they will allocate 10% return on each of these contributions out of the profits made by the business, before dividing the profits equally between them. The business makes £49 000 profit in its first year, which will be allocated between the partners as follows:

	Jakes £	Jones £	Jessop £
10% on Jakes's capital: £100 000 × 10%	10 000		
10% on Jones's capital: £50 000 × 10%		5 000	
10% on Jessop's capital: £40 000 × 10%			4 000
Remaining profit split equally between the partners:			
£49 000 − (10 000 + 5 000 + 4 000) = £30 000			
Split equally	10 000	10 000	10 000
TOTAL	20 000	15 000	14 000

The introduction of capital is possible at any point subsequent to the foundation of the business. Whenever the business needs more resources, the initial founders may be able to make a further contribution.

1.3.2 Retained Profits

As a business grows it makes profits. The owners of the business usually take out part of the profits as their reward for investing in it. However, they are not obliged to take out the whole of the profits. They may choose to leave some in the business to be invested to produce growth and further profits. The amount of profit left in the business is referred to as **retained profits**. This can be a very good source of funds for further investment as it is not dependent on any outside person or organization.

1.3.3 Borrowing Money

When thinking about potential sources of finance, borrowing may be one of the first possibilities that springs to mind. However, borrowing is not always the most appropriate source of finance for a business. In some circumstances it simply may not be obtainable. Many business start-ups would not be able to borrow money, because no organization would be willing to take the risk of lending it. Lenders need to know that:

- the money they lend will be paid back eventually; and
- the business will be able to pay a reasonable rate of interest on the borrowing. In order to do so the business needs to stand a good chance of being profitable.

THE COST OF BORROWING The cost of borrowing is the interest that must be paid on a regular basis to the lender of the money. Large institutional lenders may agree to lend money to the business but they will expect to receive interest payments on time and without fuss.

THE RISK/RETURN RELATIONSHIP Banks and other lenders do not always charge the same rate of interest. They make an assessment of how risky the lending is, ie how likely it is that the borrower will fail to repay. If the loan is perceived as being more risky than average, the lender will either refuse to lend, or will charge a high interest rate on the lending. Sometimes, it may only be possible to borrow at extremely high interest rates.

SECURITY Sometimes banks and other lenders will not lend unless the loan is secured. For example, a bank may make a business loan to an established sole trader business, but only on condition that it is secured on his or her house. This means that if the loan is not repaid, the bank would be able to force the sale of the house in order to ensure that funds are made available for repayment. A **mortgage** is an example of a secured loan. Businesses often take out commercial mortgages to assist in the purchase of property in the form of real estate.

OVERDRAFTS Overdraft facilities may be obtainable through the business's bank account. An overdraft is most likely to be made available to a business if it can prove that the extra funds are needed only in the short-term and that the business is fundamentally sound.

It should be noted that an overdraft is a short-term solution. It is technically repayable on demand; this means that the bank can demand immediate repayment of the overdraft at any time. In practice, however, banks rarely demand immediate repayment.

1.3.4 Leasing and Hire Purchase

When a business makes a large purchase of an item which will be used over the medium- to long-term it has to pay out a lot of cash at one time. Sometimes it makes sense to look at alternative ways of financing a major item.

Under a **leasing** arrangement, the business (the **lessee**) pays a regular amount to a **lessor** in exchange for the use of an item such as a piece of machinery. The lease often extends over a period of years. The lessor, usually a financial institution, pays for the machine which is delivered to the lessee's premises and will, typically, remain there throughout its useful productive life. The lessor organization is the legal owner of the machine but will probably never even see it. The lessee never owns the machine, but will use it, often for years, in the business.

Short-term leases are sometimes taken out on items such as photocopiers and cars. The items may be replaced regularly and each time this happens a new lease is negotiated. Again, the lessee never actually owns the item in question.

Hire purchase is a similar arrangement to the longer-term leasing described above, with the difference that, once the final agreed payment is made under the terms of the agreement ownership passes to the purchaser business.

1.3.5 Grant Finance

Businesses may be able to obtain grants from the government, local authorities or other agencies and funding bodies. Usually, grants would be awarded only in quite specific circumstances. For example, a local authority which is trying to encourage the growth of local business, might allow companies moving into the area a rent-free period in local authority business units. Although this is not a grant of cash it is a saving on the expense of rental, and it may well entice businesses into the area.

Grant finance is very advantageous in that it usually does not have to be repaid. However, there may be strings attached. In the example given above, a business taking advantage of the rent-free period might have to undertake to stay in the area for a further minimum period of time of, say, three years.

1.3.6 Financing Companies: Share Issues

A company (but not a partnership or sole trader business) can raise additional finance by issuing more shares for cash. If the company is doing well, it can offer existing and potential shareholders a sound investment opportunity.

1.3.7 Financing Companies: Venture Capital

Medium-sized companies may be able to seek finance from venture capitalists. A venture capital company invests for limited periods in growing companies, in order to give them a short-to-medium-term financial boost. Usually, the venture capitalist buys into the shares in the company, and will often provide management expertise as well.

1.4 SHORT-, MEDIUM- AND LONG-TERM FINANCE

It is important for businesses to match their needs for finance with the most appropriate form of finance. Using an overdraft to buy a new office building, for example, would be highly inappropriate. Taking out a ten-year commercial mortgage, on the other hand, would probably be the most sensible course of action.

The table below categorizes the different sources of finance discussed earlier into short-term, medium-term and long-term sources.

	Short-term	Medium-term	Long-term
Existing resources	✓	✓	✓
Retained profits	✓	✓	✓
Borrowings	✓	✓	✓
Mortgage			✓
Overdraft	✓		
Short leases	✓		
Long leases and hire purchase		✓	✓
Grant finance	✓	✓	✓
Share issues		✓	✓

Which one of the following types of finance would NOT be suitable for a sole trader business?

a) Leasing
b) Overdraft
c) Issue of share capital
d) Grants

Self-test question 1.2
(answer at the end of the book)

1.5 FUNDAMENTALS OF TAXATION

Taxation is a fact of life for most people and businesses. This section takes a brief look at the most common taxes levied on the different types of business examined earlier in the chapter.

1.5.1 Income Taxes (Personal Taxation)

Sole traders and partners in business partnerships make profits which are chargeable to tax. The tax that is levied is not a specific business tax; it is charged according to the individual's own circumstances at income tax rates.

Example 1.5

Cerise and Cherry are partners in a discounted clothing business. Under their partnership agreement Cerise takes 60% of the profits and Cherry takes 40%. In the tax year 20X2/X3 the partnership profits are £30 000. Neither partner has any other source of income.

Cerise will be entitled to 60% of the profits: £30 000 × 60% = £18 000
Cherry will be entitled to 40% of the profits: £30 000 × 40% = £12 000

Each partner will include her share of the profits in her personal tax return. Each woman will be liable for income tax on her share less any attributable personal allowances. National Insurance contributions will also be payable.

1.5.2 Corporation Tax

As the name implies, this is a tax levied on companies. Directors are paid a salary for working in the company, and they will pay tax on the amounts they earn (just like any other employee). The company itself, however, is liable to corporation tax on its profits.

The company's profit is calculated (income less expenses = profit) and then corporation tax rates are applied.

1.5.3 Capital Gains Tax

If an item such as an office building is sold at a profit, capital gains tax is likely to be charged. Capital gains tax applies to both individuals and companies, and so would be levied on sole traders, partnerships and limited companies.

1.5.4 Value Added Tax

Value added tax (VAT) is the UK's principal form of indirect tax; it is a tax on transactions in goods and services. As private individuals, we frequently pay VAT on goods and services that we purchase; we have no choice in the matter, and because prices are charged inclusive of VAT we don't usually even notice that we are paying the tax.

What about VAT from the point of view of a business? Businesses act as collectors of VAT which they pay over to the government authority which collects it (the HMRC), on a regular basis. The following example demonstrates the operation of VAT:

Example 1.6

Palfrey and Bennett Limited is a retail business which sells men's clothing from shops in several towns in the UK. The company adds a charge of 20% (the standard rate of VAT) to all the items that it sells. The company's customers pay the tax.

At the end of the three-month period ended 31 March 20X4, Palfrey and Bennett completes a VAT return. Total sales before VAT for the three-month period are £100 000. VAT at 20% is £20 000. This amount of £20 000 is known as output tax.

However, Palfrey and Bennett has itself, paid VAT on the purchases it made. During the same three-month period it has bought goods totalling £70 000 before VAT. VAT at 20% is £14 000. This amount of £14 000 is known as **input tax**. The quarterly liability to HMRC is calculated as follows:

Output tax for the quarter	£20 000
Less: Input tax for the quarter	£14 000
VAT payable	£6 000

The company must complete a VAT return immediately following each quarter. In this case, by the end of April 20X4 they must send the VAT return to HMRC together with payment of £6000. HMRC is very strict indeed about deadlines.

Each of the businesses supplying Palfrey and Bennett will also be obliged to fill in VAT returns and make payments to HMRC. People in business often complain about the large administrative burden imposed by accounting for VAT. However, once a business has set up systems to cope with VAT, filling in the VAT return is usually straightforward.

This section provides only a very general introduction to the taxation of businesses. For the purposes of this book it is regarded as general background business knowledge. Detailed knowledge of tax is not required for any part of the material which will be covered in the rest of the book. In almost all cases, the exercises ignore the effects of taxation in order to avoid adding an unnecessary layer of complication. However, students should bear in mind that the effects of taxation can be a significant factor in the real world.

A company sells a building at a profit. Which one of the following statements is correct? The profit is taxable:

a) as a capital gain.
b) under income tax rules on the company's directors.
c) as a VAT input.
d) at the end of the VAT quarter.

Self-test question 1.3 (answer at the end of the book)

1.6 THE NEED FOR ACCOUNTING INFORMATION

Quite simply, accounting information is produced because people need it. The reasons why they need it vary from one group of people to another. This section considers, for each of the main types of business organization identified earlier in the chapter, the range of accounting information that might be required, and the purposes for which it is needed.

1.6.1 Sole Trader

A sole trader business, because it usually remains small, is not complex in its organization. There is one manager, the sole trader, who may employ a few staff. The sole trader does not have to make information about his or her business profitability generally available. The HMRC may be the only external consumer of financial information about the business.

ANNUAL INFORMATION Tax returns to HMRC have to be made once a year, within the stipulated deadline. The sole trader needs to prepare simple accounting statements to accompany his or her tax return. There will be a statement showing the calculation of profit or loss for the year, and, possibly, a statement which shows the resources owned by the business. These statements are known as the **statement of profit or loss** (sometimes referred to as the income statement) and the **statement of financial position** (sometimes referred to as the balance sheet).

- The statement of profit or loss shows the revenue for the business for the year, less the business expenses. The remainder is either a profit or loss.
- The statement of financial position shows the resources owned and controlled by the business at a single point in time. It also shows any amounts owed, for example, loans taken out from the bank and payments due to suppliers of goods.

Every business has a year-end date. The statement of profit or loss is prepared for the year ended on that date, and the statement of financial position shows resources less amounts due on the same year-end date.

QUARTERLY INFORMATION If the sole trader is registered for VAT, a quarterly VAT return will have to be prepared. As explained earlier, this contains a summary of sales and purchases transactions which have taken place in the quarter, and a calculation of input and output tax, in order to arrive at the net amount payable to HMRC. Failing to meet the deadlines for submission of the return and the amounts due must be avoided at all costs. Therefore, the sole trader business has to be able to keep accounting records sufficiently well to be able to provide the required information quickly.

ACCOUNTING INFORMATION WITHIN THE BUSINESS As well as the information provided for external authorities, the sole trader needs more frequent information to help to manage the business efficiently, and to assist in decision making. At the simplest possible level this means keeping an eye on the state of the bank balance. At a slightly more sophisticated level, it is usually helpful to prepare regular accounting statements. A sole trader should keep records of sales and receipts of cash, and of the payment of expenses. From these it should be possible to prepare a simple monthly statement of profitability. This will not be used for reporting outside the business; it is an internal document for the sole trader's own use.

RECORDING AND SUMMARIZING INFORMATION In most cases, sole trader businesses do not employ an accountant. It would be far too expensive, and, besides, because accounting information needs are relatively modest, there would be little point. If the sole trader is equipped with some basic knowledge of record keeping, has the time to do it, and is sufficiently well organized to keep the records straight, the cheapest and most straightforward option is to do the job himself or herself.

Some sole traders pay a book-keeper for a few hours a week to keep the records straight. Where staff are employed it is particularly important to keep good records and to make accurate calculations of pay, income tax and National Insurance contributions due.

In almost all cases, the sole trader is well advised to use the services of a qualified accountant for assistance with preparing annual financial statements, preparing tax returns and ensuring that the correct amount of tax is paid. Unless some very complex advice is involved, this kind of service can usually be purchased for a few hundred pounds each year.

In summary, the sole trader produces financial information to be used outside the business by HMRC. No other external party can require information from the sole trader. Financial information for internal use will be produced as frequently as necessary to provide the sole trader with the information needed to run the business.

1.6.2 Partnership

A partnership, as noted earlier, does not need to make financial information generally available to the public. However, it must, in the same way as the sole trader, prepare annual financial statements which form the basis for tax calculation by HMRC. Also, quarterly financial information will probably have to be made available to HMRC in the form of summaries of sales and expenses and input and output tax totals supplied on the VAT return every quarter.

In most respects the information requirements are, so far, very similar to those of a sole trader. However, there is one important difference: in a partnership, the annual statement of profit or loss provides the profit figure which will be split between the partners in accordance with their profit-sharing arrangements. The annual financial statements, therefore, take on an additional dimension of importance in a partnership. The partners themselves need to be satisfied that the accounts have been prepared properly and that they present a reasonably accurate figure for profit.

AUDIT In some cases, the partners may decide to have an audit conducted, to ensure that the annual financial statements are properly prepared and fairly stated. There is no stipulation in the law for audit of partnership accounts, but partners may decide, in drawing up the partnership agreement, that an audit should be carried out annually.

So, what is an audit? It is an independent examination, by a properly qualified person, of the financial records and financial statements of an entity. One of the important qualities of a well-conducted audit is that the auditor should be independent of the management of the business he or she is auditing. A partnership which requires an audit would appoint a professionally qualified auditor to conduct the examination of the records and give an impartial opinion on whether or not the annual financial statements have been properly drawn up. The opinion takes the form of an audit report which is attached to the financial statements. In addition to providing reassurance to the partners themselves, the fact that an audit has been conducted may be reassuring to HMRC. However, it should be emphasized that there is no legal requirement for the audit of partnerships (or of sole traders).

ACCOUNTING INFORMATION WITHIN THE BUSINESS We saw earlier in the chapter that sole trader businesses will find it helpful in running their businesses to produce accounting information such as monthly statements of profit.

Partnership businesses tend to be larger than sole trader businesses (because more people are involved) and the need for internal accounting information may be greater because of the increased size and complexity of the business. As a business increases in size, its managers will usually find that they need more detailed information to help in decision making.

Example 1.7

Poste, Ponsonby and Peppard is a partnership of solicitors. As well as the three partners, the practice employs three other qualified solicitors and several administrative staff, including a full-time book-keeper. The partners have a monthly management meeting where they make decisions on important issues. In order to help them, they have instituted a system of internal financial reports. The book-keeper prepares the reports which are confidential, to be seen only by the partners.
The principal reports are:

- statement of profit or loss for the month
- billings summary for each solicitor for the month
- summary of hours worked by each solicitor for the month
- list of client invoices unpaid.

These reports allow the partners to see whether any of the solicitors are falling behind target in their monthly billings. They also allow for an assessment of profitability so that if, for example, monthly profits are tending to fall, the partners can take stock of the situation and decide whether action is necessary.
The list of unpaid client invoices informs the partners of any clients who are taking an excessively long time to pay. They can take action to follow up the overdue debts in order to prompt the clients to pay up.

1.6.3 Limited Company

Accounting information needs within the sole trader and partnership types of business organization are, essentially, very similar. However, the picture changes when we examine accounting for limited companies.

PROVISION OF FINANCIAL INFORMATION OUTSIDE THE BUSINESS Limited companies are required to publish financial information via Companies House. Because everyone has access to the information held at Companies House, the information is potentially available to a very large number of people. In fact, the financial information of most companies remains undisturbed because there are very few people who would be interested in it, apart from the shareholders. The company's shareholders are informed, in any case, of the financial condition of the company because they are entitled to receive a full set of annual financial statements.

However, it is possible that other groups of people, apart from the shareholders, could be interested in the information. People or organizations who have been asked to lend money to the company are likely to be interested in the financial status of the company. People who are affected by a company's existence (for example, those living near the premises of a chemical company which regularly breaches environmental legislation) may also take an interest. Later in the chapter we will consider the different categories of people who might be interested in a company's financial information.

Companies are required to submit tax returns and VAT returns, and financial reports must be made available to HMRC in the same way as in sole trader and partnership organizations.

SEPARATION OF OWNERSHIP AND MANAGEMENT In smaller companies the shareholders and directors are often the same people. Because they are engaged in the day-to-day management of the business, directors who are also shareholders really do not need annual financial information to tell them what is going on. They have access to as much internal financial information as they need.

However, the position is different for shareholders who are not directors. In large companies, most of the shareholders are remote from the activities of the business; they receive **dividends** and an invitation to the Annual General Meeting of the business, but have no other contact with it. If they are shareholders in a listed company, they will be able to follow movements in the share price by consulting the financial press, but they are not entitled to the regular detailed internal financial information which the directors use in managing the business.

The relationships between the company, the directors and the shareholders are expressed in Figure 1.1.

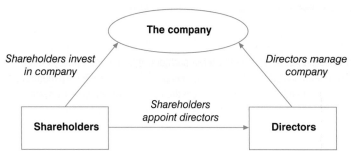

Figure 1.1
Separation of ownership and management in a limited company

The diagram demonstrates the separation between the ownership of the company and its management. Shareholders appoint directors (who in larger companies are professional managers) to manage the company on their behalf: the directors act as agents of the shareholders, or, to use an old-fashioned term, as stewards on their behalf.

The **stewardship** function requires directors to act in the best interests of the company at all times. In order to demonstrate good stewardship, they should report on a regular basis to shareholders – hence the requirement in company law that full annual financial statements are sent to shareholders. Company law also requires in some cases that financial statements are independently audited, which provides reassurance to shareholders that the financial statements present a true and fair view. The legal requirement applies only to larger companies, although there is nothing to stop smaller companies volunteering to have an audit.

Clearly, where shareholders are remote from the management of their company, there is potential for the directors to take action which benefits themselves, rather than benefiting the shareholders. This is one of the potential problems of the agency, or stewardship, relationship. For example, a current, and recurring issue, is that of directors' remuneration in very large companies. Criticisms are often voiced in the press of the very large increases in salary, and substantial bonuses which directors award themselves. Shareholders are in a position to take action if they do not approve of directors' remuneration packages (via their votes at the Annual General Meeting) but, in practice, they rarely challenge the directors.

ACCOUNTING INFORMATION WITHIN THE BUSINESS With the exception of the very large professional partnerships which are permitted by law, all larger businesses in the UK are constituted as limited companies. As a company grows in size, its management needs ever larger quantities of internally generated accounting information in order to keep control of the business, and to make good quality decisions. Larger companies, especially those involved in the complexities of say, manufacturing or banking, tend to produce highly complex and sophisticated information for use by management.

E xplain which types of business are required by law to have an annual audit of their financial statements.

Self-test question 1.4 (answer at the end of the book)

1.7 USERS OF ACCOUNTING INFORMATION

Different groups of users of financial information can be identified. In this chapter we have discussed many of them already. Table 1.1 lists the principal user groups and summarizes the most likely reasons for their interest.

Table 1.1 **Principal groups of users of financial information**

User group	Reason for interest in financial information
Shareholders	To assess the performance of management in their role as stewards of the company To use the information to make decisions on whether or not to sell the investment in the shares of the company, or perhaps whether to buy more shares in the company
Potential shareholders	To make decisions on whether or not to invest in the shares of a company
Investment analysts	To assess the performance of the company in order to be able to advise their clients on investment strategy
Lenders and potential lenders	To assess the ability of the business to make repayments and to meet regular interest payments
Employees and trade unions	To assess the viability of the business and the extent to which it is likely to be able to (a) continue to offer employment; (b) increase pay and improve employees' conditions
Suppliers	Where suppliers offer credit terms, they need to be able to assess the likelihood of being paid promptly
Special interest groups	In the case of an environmental activist group, for example: to assess the extent to which the company has set aside funds for environmental cleanup operations
Government: tax collecting agencies	To assist in the assessment and collection of taxes
Government: other agencies	To assist, for example, in the collection of national statistical information
Financial journalists	To obtain information about a company's activities and profitability which will be of interest to the journalist's readers
Academics and students	To assist in the study of business activity
Customers	To assess the likelihood of the business continuing in existence, and continuing to supply the goods or services required by the customers
The general public	Anyone, not covered by any of the categories above, who has an interest in the activities of the company

1.7.1 Access to Information

Because company financial statements are made publicly available all the above categories of users have access to them. In many cases the user groups are making important decisions on the basis of the information, answering questions such as:

- Should I sell my shares in this company?
- Should I, as a bank manager, be making an overdraft facility available to this company?
- Is the company doing well enough to make it safe for me to carry on working for it?
- How risky is it to supply goods on credit to this company?
- How well is the current management looking after my interests as a shareholder?

Company accounting information is called upon to be useful to a wide range of users in making decisions. In the next section of the chapter we look at the characteristics of useful financial information.

1.8 CHARACTERISTICS OF USEFUL FINANCIAL INFORMATION

Ideally, financial information produced by businesses would have the following key characteristics:

- *Relevance*: information should be relevant to the decisions made by stakeholders. For example, the information should be prepared shortly after the events being reported so that it is not out of date by the time it is used.
- *Faithful representation*: information should fully reflect the economic events and transactions that have taken place in the business during the financial year. Information should be complete, free from bias and free from error.

These two key characteristics are identified by the International Accounting Standards Board (IASB) as being fundamental to financial information. The IASB also identifies four further characteristics, referred to as enhancing characteristics, of useful financial information:

- *Comparability*: To be genuinely useful and reliable, it should be possible to compare financial information over time and between businesses. This means that information should be prepared using the same policies and methods.
- *Verifiability*: Information is verifiable if users would be able to agree with each other that it faithfully represents economic events and transactions that have taken place in the business.
- *Timeliness*: Information should be made available sufficiently soon after the end of a financial year to be useful to users. If there is a significant delay in issuing the information, it is likely to be too old to be of use.
- *Understandability*: Financial information is directed at those users who are sufficiently knowledgeable to understand it and who are prepared to make some effort to understand it. Provided these conditions are satisfied, financial information should be understandable.

In practice, it is not always possible to achieve information which fulfils all of the above characteristics. In large and complex businesses collecting accounting data and processing it into a set of financial statements is a time-consuming process. By the time it is published (usually three to four months after the year-end date in a very large company) circumstances may have changed and the information may be of limited use for decision making. Also, the information that is reported is all historical: ie it relates to events that have already occurred. The extent to which past events are a reliable guide to the future is questionable in a fast-changing business environment.

Accounting information should be understandable, but, again, this is not always easily achievable. The financial statements of very complex organizations tend, inevitably, to reflect that complexity. People who are reasonably knowledgeable about business matters should be able to understand financial statements, but even their ability to understand is sometimes tested by the complex financial statements of major listed companies.

1.9 FINANCIAL ACCOUNTING AND MANAGEMENT ACCOUNTING

There are two distinct strands to accounting in organizations. **Financial accounting** refers to the processes and practices involved in providing users external to the business with the information that they need. Companies, because they provide a relatively large amount of information to outside users relative to partnership and sole trader entities, tend to devote substantial resources to financial accounting. This type of accounting is also referred to as **financial reporting**, and both terms are used in this book.

Management accounting is the accounting that a business organization carries out for its own internal uses. It assists management in controlling the business and in making decisions.

Both financial and management accounting use information generated by the accounting system of the business. Clearly, the accounting systems of businesses are likely to vary enormously, depending upon the complexity and size of the business organization. However, all accounting systems have certain characteristics in common. The flow of information in an accounting system and its relationship to financial accounting and management accounting is demonstrated diagrammatically in Figure 1.2.

Data and information about events and transactions flows in and out of the business. For example, when a business makes a sale of goods supplied on credit to a customer (ie the customer is not obliged to pay cash straight away) the following events and information flows take place:

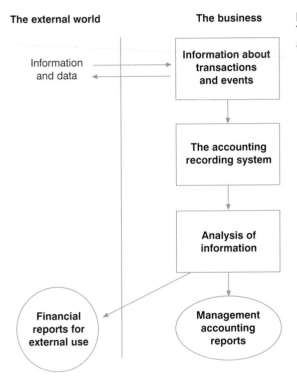

Figure 1.2
The production of financial reports and management accounting reports

At each stage details about the event are 'captured' by the accounting recording system. Periodically, data which share common characteristics (e. all sales invoices) are analyzed and the analysis is used to produce reports for both financial and management accounting purposes. See Table 1.2.

Table 1.2 Events and information flows relating to the sale of goods

Event	Information flow
An order is placed	Data about the nature and quantity of the goods required flows into the business and is recorded
Goods are assembled, packaged and sent out	A record of despatch is produced within the business and is sent out with the goods to the customer
An invoice is raised through the business recording system	The invoice is sent out from the business to the customer – information leaves the business
The customer sends payment	Information about the payment is received in the business and is recorded.

1.10 THE ROLE OF THE ACCOUNTANT IN BUSINESS ORGANIZATIONS

As we have seen, there are two separate strands in business accounting: financial reporting to user groups external to the organization, and management accounting for reporting to managers within the organization. This variation in function is reflected in the organization of the accounting profession and in the training of accountants.

1.10.1 The Accounting Profession

The accounting profession includes the following types of accountant:

* *Independent accounting practitioners:* these accountants work outside industry and business in professional practices. These are the accountants who provide taxation and accounting services to a wide range of businesses. If they are **registered auditors**, they are authorized to carry out the audits of companies and other organizations.
* *Accountants in business:* these are the accountants with whom business managers work in organizations. Broadly, they are either **financial accountants** or **management accountants**, depending upon whether they specialize in the external or the internal provision of accounting information.

Professional accountants may have one or more accounting qualifications. These days most professional accountants have a university degree, although it is not necessarily in accounting or a related subject (the author of this book for example, is a chartered accountant with a degree in Russian). After university they enter into a period of three or four years of training with an employer during which they take some very tough examinations. Not everyone who embarks on accountancy training will manage to qualify because the examinations are so demanding.

The following are the principal professional accounting bodies in the UK which have their own qualification systems:

* ICAEW: the Institute of Chartered Accountants in England and Wales (members have the letters ACA or FCA after their names).
* ICAS: the Institute of Chartered Accountants of Scotland (members have the letters CA after their names).
* ACCA: the Chartered Association of Certified Accountants (members have the letters ACCA or FCCA after their names).

The members of these organizations are found in both professional independent accounting practice and in business. Students of ICAEW and ICAS usually train in professional accountancy firms. Students of ACCA are found in both professional and business environments. Usually those who go into business specialize in financial accounting and reporting rather than in management accounting.

Finally there is CIMA: the Chartered Institute of Management Accountants (members have the letters ACMA or FCMA after their names). As the name of this organization implies, its members work principally in management accounting, and its students train exclusively in the business environment.

People who have trained as accountants are often found at the most senior levels in business organizations. It is not unusual in the UK to encounter chief executives and senior directors who started their careers as accountants before moving into more general business management.

1.11 ORGANIZATION OF THE REMAINDER OF THIS BOOK

Chapters 2 to 7 inclusive are concerned with financial statement preparation, including the fundamental principles and practices involved in preparing statement of profit or loss, statements of financial position and statements of cash flow. Chapters 8 and 9 are concerned with understanding the financial reports of businesses. Chapters 10 to 18 inclusive are concerned with the acquisition of skills and knowledge related to management accounting information. Chapters 19 and 20 explain the fundamentals of financing a business.

Chapter Summary

This chapter provides a framework of information about accounting which underpins the remainder of the book. First, the three principal types of business organization were introduced, followed by a description of the characteristics of each type. Then the chapter proceeded to examine some aspects of business financing. (This topic will be examined in much more detail in Chapter 20.) The next section was concerned with taxation because it is important to have a broad outline knowledge of how the different types of business are taxed. However, it should be noted that a detailed knowledge of taxation is not required in order to achieve the aims of this book.

The chapter then turned to accounting information. The need for accounting information was examined in the context of the three types of business organization introduced earlier in the chapter: sole trader, partnership and limited company. Each organizational type needs to make some information available to people or organizations outside the business. In addition, accounting information is needed to assist management in running the business.

The provision of information to outsiders is a much more important issue for limited companies than it is for partnership or sole trader organizations. The general public has access to company financial information through the medium of Companies House. As well as filing information at Companies House, companies are also obliged by law to make annual accounting information available to their shareholders. The chapter explained the important issue of the separation between the ownership and management of limited companies, which is especially noticeable in larger companies.

There is a long list of potential users of accounting information: shareholders, potential shareholders, investment analysts, lenders and potential lenders, employees and trade unions, suppliers, special interest groups, the government, financial journalists, academics and students, customers and the public at large.

The chapter went on to discuss some of the important characteristics of useful financial information: it should be relevant, reliable, comparable and understandable.

The distinction between financial accounting and management accounting was described and discussed, and then the role of the accountant in business organizations was described. There are several different professional accountancy qualifications and the main ones were noted.

Internet Resources

The following websites may be of use in finding out more information about certain aspects of this chapter:

www.hmrc.gov.uk – the website of Her Majesty's Revenue and Customs
www.gov.uk/government/organisations/companies-house – the Companies House website, which provides information about all UK companies.

Book's companion website

The website contains the following resources in respect of Chapter 1:

Students' section

A multiple choice quiz containing 15 questions
Four additional questions with answers

Lecturers' section

Answers to end-of-chapter exercises 1.13 to 1.18
Four additional questions with answers
Testbank
Instructor's Manual
PowerPoint presentation

Exercises: Answers at the End of the Book

1.1   Which one of the following statements about the sole trader form of business is correct?
a) A sole trader has to pay corporation tax.
b) Sole traders submit annual information to Companies House.
c) The sole trader is entirely responsible for the management of the business.
d) Because a sole trader business is simple it is not necessary to keep any records.

1.2   Which one of the following statements about the partnership form of business is correct?
a) Partnerships are always very small businesses.
b) Partners are obliged by law to put £50 000 into the business when it starts up.
c) Partnerships are very difficult to set up because of the amount of information demanded by the government.
d) Partners are personally liable for the debts of the partnership business.

1.3   Which one of the following statements about the limited company form of business is correct?
a) A limited company is a separate person in law.
b) Limited companies cannot be sued.
c) It costs a great deal of money to establish a limited company.
d) Shareholders in a limited company are obliged to act as directors.

1.4   Select from the following list the most appropriate form of finance for purchasing a new office building:
a) ten-year mortgage loan
b) loan repayable in six months time
c) overdraft
d) hire purchase.

1.5   Select from the following list the most appropriate way of financing a new office photocopier:
a) grant finance
b) issue of new share capital
c) lease
d) mortgage.

1.6   You are a small business adviser. A new client, Arnold Tapwood, has come to you for advice. Mr Tapwood explains that he is the sole proprietor of a small building business. One of his friends, Simon, who is a carpenter, has suggested that he and Arnold should join forces in a partnership. Arnold is not sure about the extra legal responsibilities which would be involved in setting up a partnership, and he asks you to explain in outline the legal formalities which would be required. What do you tell him?

1.7   Geoffrey is a keen dangerous sports enthusiast. He would like to set up in business as a sole trader organizing dangerous sports events and activities. His business idea is that people would pay an annual subscription which would allow access to his website and a range of discounts on the fees for dangerous sports events. While he expects the idea to be a winner, because there are so many like-minded enthusiasts, he feels it likely that he will need some start-up finance to equip an office, set up a website and pay for some help with administration. He estimates that he will need about £10 000 to get things up and running before the subscriptions start to appear in large numbers.

Geoffrey has just left university with accumulated debts of around £28 000 so he has no money to put into the business. His parents refuse to give him any money for the venture. He has come to you for advice on the best ways of financing the start-up. What is your advice?

1.8   Which one of the following statements about the regulations governing a sole trader business is correct?
   a) A sole trader does not need to supply any accounting information about his or her business to anyone.
   b) A sole trader must employ an accountant.
   c) Sole trader businesses are exempt from completing VAT returns.
   d) A sole trader must submit a tax return annually.

1.9   Which one of the following statements about the regulations governing partnership businesses is correct?
   a) Partnerships are obliged to have an annual audit of their financial statements.
   b) Partnerships must prepare annual financial statements as the basis for the calculation of tax.
   c) At least one of the partners is obliged to hold a book-keeping qualification.
   d) Each partner must submit his or her own VAT return.

1.10   Which one of the following statements about the regulations governing limited company businesses is correct?
   a) All limited companies are obliged by company law to have an annual audit.
   b) A limited company must send annual accounts to all of its shareholders.
   c) All shareholders have unlimited access to their company's management accounting information.
   d) The general public can access information about a company only by applying in writing to the directors.

1.11   Podgorny & Weaver Limited is involved in the wholesale of fashion goods to retailers. The company directors have a monthly meeting to discuss strategy and to make decisions. The directors are presented with the following reports prepared by the company accountant each month:

   - list of amounts owed by the retail businesses which the company supplies
   - summary of the value of fashion goods items currently held in inventory
   - summary of the orders received during the month
   - statement of profit or loss for the last month.

   Explain how the directors would be able to make use of each of the reports listed in order to improve the management of the company.

1.12   A group of environmental activists is interested in the activities of Burnip Chemicals plc, a company which has been regularly fined in the past for emitting toxic waste into the river which runs past the factory premises. What kind of information would the activist group seek about the activities of the company? To what extent are the annual financial statements likely to be helpful to them?

Exercises: Answers Available on the Lecturers' Section of the Book's Website

1.13   Which one of the following statements about the limited company form of business is correct?
   a) A limited company must submit information on a regular basis to Companies House.
   b) Directors of limited companies are always selected from amongst the shareholders.
   c) Limited companies are not eligible to apply for grants.
   d) Directors of a limited company are personally liable if the company is sued.

1.14   Select from the following list the most appropriate way of financing the accumulation of stocks of Easter eggs in a chocolate business:
   a) grant finance
   b) overdraft
   c) issue of new share capital
   d) lease.

1.15 Marie Deutsch is a fashion designer who, after graduating with a degree in fashion, obtained a very good job as a designer in a lingerie company. She has decided that she would like to leave her job and set up in business with an old friend from college who also trained as a designer. Marie has heard that it is more sensible to set up as a limited company because it would mean that she and her friend would not be personally liable for the debts of the business. However, she says she is sure that there must be some strings attached, and would like you to tell her about any disadvantages in limited company status. What do you tell her?

1.16 Which of the following statements is correct?

The stewardship function requires directors of limited companies to:

a) act at all times in the best interests of the company
b) allow shareholders to see detailed accounting records upon request
c) hold regular monthly meetings to answer shareholders' questions
d) consult the shareholders over particularly difficult management decisions.

1.17 Ponderosa & Smythe plc is a shoe manufacturing business, specializing in children's shoes. The finance director has just received the following letter from a shareholder who has recently bought some shares in the company:

'Dear Mr Pershore,

I have just read a most interesting article in the *Financial Times* about the decline in the market for children's shoes. The article suggests that, because of demographic changes, the market will decline by 3–4% each year over the next ten years. In the circumstances, I think our company should branch out into women's shoes. I would like the directors to discuss this at the next board meeting. Could you please send me a copy of the sales budget for the coming year, so that I can see whether or not you have taken the declining market properly into account?'

What are the principal points that the finance director should make in response to this letter?

1.18 Mohsin, a bank manager, is looking at an application for a loan from Boxer Burstall Limited, a local company. The company has included a copy of its most recent annual accounts which are for the year ended 31 December 20X1. The accounts show that a modest profit has been made in the year. It is now March 20X3.

i) What type of information will Mohsin be looking for from the annual accounts to help him in making a decision on whether or not to lend the money?

ii) How relevant is the accounting information which the company has provided to Mohsin's decision?

iii) Is Mohsin entitled to request any further information?

Financial Accounting and Reporting

2 The statement of financial position

Aim of the chapter

To enable students to understand how a statement of financial position is prepared, and how it assists interested parties to understand the business's position at a point in time.

Learning outcomes

After reading the chapter and completing the related exercises, students should:

- Understand how the statement of financial position relates to the other principal financial statements.

- Understand the terminology used in a statement of financial position, and some of the principal conventions used in presenting it, and in preparing financial statements in general.

- Be able to draw up a statement of financial position for a sole trader from a list of account balances and explanatory notes.

- Be able to understand and comment on the basic information conveyed by a statement of financial position.

Introduction

This chapter introduces the study of the preparation and interpretation of financial reports for external users. The first section uses a small business start-up example to explain in outline the three principal financial statements. The rest of the chapter concentrates upon one of these three statements: the statement of financial position.

The statement of financial position conveys information to people outside the business about the resources over which it has control, and which can be used in the future to generate profits. It also contains information about liabilities, that is, the amounts of obligations such as amounts owing to other businesses and individuals. It therefore produces a financial picture of the position of the business at a given point in time.

The chapter explores some of the accounting terminology that is used in a statement of financial position, and looks at the principles and conventions involved in the preparation of financial statements. All financial statements are intended to convey information to people interested in the business, and the chapter concludes with a brief examination of some of the messages transmitted by the figures in a small business statement of financial position.

2.1 BASICS OF BUSINESS ACCOUNTING: THE THREE PRINCIPAL FINANCIAL STATEMENTS

The introductory chapter to this book discussed the objective of financial statements, and the principal groups of people who might be interested in obtaining information from them. The main purpose of financial statements is to provide useful financial information to a wide range of users.

In this book we will be concerned with three principal financial statements: the statement of financial position, the statement of profit or loss and the statement of **cash flows**. (As noted in Chapter 1, two of these statements may be referred to by different names: the statement of financial position is sometimes known as the balance sheet, and the statement of profit or loss is sometimes known as the profit and loss account. This book will use the terms 'statement of financial position' and 'statement of profit or loss'.)

The statement of financial position shows readers the business's position at a particular point in time, the statement of profit or loss reports on the business's performance over the accounting period, and the **statement of cash flows** shows the movement in cash between the beginning and end of the accounting period. All businesses, regardless of size, produce a statement of profit or loss and a statement of financial position, and most also produce a statement of cash flows. The basic form of the statements is very similar from the smallest of small businesses to the largest multinational.

This chapter is principally concerned with the statement of financial position. However, as a preliminary, the relationship between the three statements is briefly explored. The example below uses a very simple business start-up to explain the outline content of the three statements, and how they interact.

Example 2.1

Jamie has decided to put his savings into starting a hairdressing business. He has saved £8700 for this purpose, and on 2 January 20X4 he opens a bank account in the name of 'JJ Hair Studio' which he has decided will be the trading name of the business. He pays £8700 into the new bank account straight away. On 8 January Jamie makes a transfer of £800 to his new landlord for the first month's rent on a salon. He also spends £3500 on equipment such as chairs, dryers, mirrors, telephone and sound systems, and so on, and opens the salon for business on 20 January. In the period up to the end of January 20X4 he receives a total of £1250 in cash from customers, and pays out £200 in various expenses such as shampoos and dyes.

There are five pieces of information about business transactions in the above scenario, and, perhaps surprisingly, this is quite enough to allow us to draw up the three financial statements for the business on 31 January 20X4, the end of Jamie's first month in business.

STATEMENT OF CASH FLOWS

Of the three statements, the statement of cash flows is probably the easiest to understand and, at this stage, to prepare. It shows the cash inflows and outflows summarized for a particular accounting period, explaining the movement in cash resources from the beginning to the end of a period of time, in this case one month. Jamie's statement of cash flows for January is as follows:

JJ Hair Studio: statement of cash flows for the month ended 31 January 20X4

	£	£
INFLOWS		
Cash introduced by proprietor		8 700
Receipts of cash from sales		1 250
		9 950
OUTFLOWS		
Payment for rental	800	
Payment for equipment	3 500	
Payment for expenses	200	(4 500)
Balance of cash on 31 January		5 450

This financial statement provides information about cash inflow and outflow. Statements of cash flows will be examined in more detail in Chapter 6.

STATEMENT OF PROFIT OR LOSS

The statement of profit or loss shows the profitability of the business for a period; it compares revenue (sometimes referred to as sales) with the expenses incurred in order to achieve that revenue. In the case of Jamie's business, revenue for the month amounts to a total of £1250. Expenses include two items: the salon rental of £800 and the other expenses of £200. Note that these items are all the same as the cash inflows or outflows. This is partly to keep the example simple, but it is also fairly realistic in the case of sales in a hairdressing business. Later in the book, we will examine the more complex situation where revenue and expenses are made on credit terms (ie. they do not have to be paid for straight away).

Jamie's statement of profit or loss for the month is as follows:

**JJ Hair Studio: Statement of profit or loss
for the month ended 31 January 20X4**

	£
Revenue	1 250
Expenses (800 + 200)	(1 000)
Profit for the period	250

Comparing the two statements prepared so far, we can see that certain items of cash inflow and outflow do not appear in the statement of profit or loss. This is because they represent resources that will be used in the business over more than one accounting period. Resources like cash and equipment used on a long-term basis, are reflected instead in the business's statement of financial position.

THE STATEMENT OF FINANCIAL POSITION

The statement of financial position shows the position of a business at a single point in time. The items shown in the statement of financial position can be categorized into three elements: assets, liabilities and capital. Jamie's statement of financial position is shown below, followed by a section of the chapter that explains the three elements in detail.

**JJ Hair Studio: Statement of financial position at
31 January 20X4**

	£	£
ASSETS		
Non-current assets: equipment		3 500
Current assets: cash (from the statement of cash flows)		5 450
		8 950
CAPITAL AND LIABILITIES		
Capital introduced by Jamie	8 700	
Add: profit for the month	250	
Liabilities	0	
		8 950

The total of resources available for use in Jamie's business is £8950. This total, or 'balance', is the same as the total of Jamie's capital invested in the business. This comprises the original amount of £8700 input into the business, plus the profit for the month of January. A helpful way of thinking about this is to reflect that £8950 is the amount that Jamie as an individual is 'owed' by the business. Thinking about it in this way emphasizes the fact that the business and Jamie are different entities. This is known as the business entity concept of accounting, and it is underlined by the fact that the business has a different name (JJ Hair Studio).

The figure for liabilities in JJ Hair Studio's statement of financial position is £0, reflecting the fact that, on 31 January 20X4, the business owes no money.

2.2 THE STATEMENT OF FINANCIAL POSITION: DEFINITIONS OF ELEMENTS

This section of the chapter examines the three elements (assets, liabilities and capital) in detail.

2.2.1 Assets

Assets are resources under the control of a business, which it will use in order to generate a profit in the future. Examples of such resources include:

- cash in the form of notes, and coins, and cash kept in bank accounts
- amounts of money that people or organizations owe to the business. Such amounts are described in accounting terminology as **trade receivables**
- items bought by the business to sell on to somebody else, or to process or transform in some way to make saleable goods. Such items are known as **inventory** (or inventories).

Cash, trade receivables and inventory are categorized as **current assets**.

This description reflects the fact that they do not remain static for long. For example, trade receivables are usually turned into cash within a short period of time, inventory is sold, and then replaced, and the business bank account balance changes very frequently.

Items bought (or sometimes leased) by the business that will be used over a long period of time are known in accounting terminology as **non-current assets**. 'Non-current' means that the assets stay in the business for a long time (at least one year and possibly for much longer). Examples are buildings (and the land they stand on) that are bought to house the activities of the business, vans and lorries that can be used for transporting goods and people, and computer hardware and software.

2.2.2 Liabilities

Liabilities are amounts that the business is obliged to pay to other people or organizations. Examples of liabilities include:

- amounts owing to people or organizations that have provided goods or services on credit (ie they provide the goods or services without requiring immediate payment for them); these amounts are known as **trade payables**.
- amounts owing to the government in the form of taxation, for example, in the UK, corporation tax and Value Added Tax (VAT).
- loans that will have to be repaid in due course to banks or other lenders.

The convention used in drawing up statements of financial position is to subdivide liabilities into two major categories: non-current liabilities that do not have to be repaid for one year or more after the date on which the statement of financial position is drawn up; and current liabilities: amounts that are payable within one year of the statement of financial position date.

2.2.3 Capital

Capital is the amount invested by the owner(s) of the business. There may be one or more owners: as explained in Chapter 1, in a sole trader business all of the capital is invested by a single owner or proprietor. In a partnership, the ownership of capital is split between two or more individuals. In an incorporated business, shares may be owned by very large numbers of people or, indeed, by other organizations.

As explained at the end of Example 2.1, it can be helpful to think of capital as being the amount 'owed' by the business to its proprietor(s).

2.2.4 Terminology

The terminology used for the different statement of financial position elements described above (inventory, trade payables, and so on) is the standard terminology used in international accounting. Companies listed on a stock exchange within the European Union (and in many other places such as Australia and New Zealand) are obliged to use standard terminology and formats for their financial statements that are established by the International Accounting Standards Board (IASB). Smaller businesses are not obliged to use such terminology, and in the UK many unlisted businesses continue to use a slightly different set of terms; for example, trade receivables are known as debtors. An appendix at the end of the book lists the UK terms against their international equivalents.

T his question tests understanding of the descriptions of the key statement of financial position elements of assets and liabilities described above.

George's retail business sells kitchen utensils, crockery and cutlery. The following are descriptions of some of the items in his statement of financial position. For each item, fill in the adjacent box with 'ASSET' or 'LIABILITY'.

Self-test question 2.1 (answer at the end of the book)

Bank overdraft

Computer and printer used to keep the administrative records of the business

Plates and cups available for sale to customers

Cash float kept in the till: £100 in various notes and coins

Loan of £20 000 from George's brother

2.3 THE ACCOUNTING EQUATION

In the JJ Hair Studio statement of financial position in Example 2.1, the total of assets was balanced by the capital contributed by Jamie, plus the profit earned since the start of the business. At any point in time, a business should be able to provide a complete list of its assets and liabilities, each having a monetary amount.

It is possible to express the three basic elements of a statement of financial position in an equation. As shown by the JJ Hair Studio statement of financial position:

$$ASSETS = CAPITAL + LIABILITIES$$

It is also true to say that:

$$ASSETS - LIABILITIES = CAPITAL$$

Also,

$$ASSETS - CAPITAL = LIABILITIES$$

The next example will examine a slightly more complex statement of financial position than that of JJ Hair Studios in order to demonstrate the accounting equation.

2.3.1 The Statement of Financial Position Format

It was noted earlier that the IASB requires listed businesses to use standard formats for financial statements. These are illustrated in International Accounting Standard 1 (IAS 1) *Presentation of Financial Statements*. Although the content of most of the international financial reporting standards is outside the scope of this book, it is worth noting that the prescribed format is similar to that used in Example 2.2. Assets are shown first, followed immediately below by capital + liabilities. However, some businesses do adopt slightly different formats that emphasize other versions of the accounting equation. Nevertheless, it should always be possible to discern the accounting equation at work in one of its forms.

Example 2.2

Robert is a wholesaler selling garden tools to garden centres. His statement of financial position at 30 June contains details of his assets, liabilities and capital, as follows:

	£	£
ASSETS		
Non-current assets: warehouse, van and equipment		60 000
Current assets		
Inventory (gardening tools)	8 000	
Trade receivables (owed by garden centres)	4 000	
Cash in the bank account	6 000	
		18 000
		78 000
CAPITAL AND LIABILITIES		
Capital (Robert's resources tied up in the business)		64 000
Non-current liabilities: amounts owed to bank	8 000	
Current liabilities: trade payables (amounts owed to the firm that supplies Robert's business with gardening tools)	6 000	
		14 000
		78 000

In this example we have a value for each of the three elements of the accounting equation: assets, liabilities and capital. Robert's capital in the business is £64 000. Although assets come to more than that (£78 000), a total of £14 000 will have to be used to pay off the liabilities. £78 000 less £14 000 is £64 000, the amount of Robert's capital.

The accounting equation holds good, in all of its forms:

$$\text{ASSETS} = \text{CAPITAL} + \text{LIABILITIES} \ (\pounds78\ 000 = \pounds64\ 000 + \pounds14\ 000)$$
$$\text{ASSETS} - \text{LIABILITIES} = \text{CAPITAL} \ (\pounds78\ 000 - \pounds14\ 000 = \pounds64\ 000)$$
$$\text{ASSETS} - \text{CAPITAL} = \text{LIABILITIES} \ (\pounds78\ 000 - \pounds64\ 000 = \pounds14\ 000)$$

Self-test question 2.2 (answer at the end of the book)

Saqib's statement of financial position at 30 September shows the following items:

	£
Non-current assets	30 000
Inventory	5 000
Trade receivables	4 000
Cash held in business bank account	3 000
Trade payables	6 000
Saqib's capital	36 000

1 What is the total of assets in the business?
2 What is the total of liabilities in the business?
3 What is the capital of the business?
4 Write down the figures for the basic accounting equation (remember: ASSETS = CAPITAL + LIABILITIES).

So far, figures have been provided for each of the three key elements of the accounting equation. However, if we know two out of the three figures, we can work out the third. Example 2.3 demonstrates how this is done, and self-test question 2.3 tests your understanding of this point.

Example 2.3

We need to supply the missing figure in each of the following incomplete accounting equations:

1 **Capital**
   Assets are £15 000 and liabilities are £3000. What is capital? Using the accounting equation in the form of

$$\text{ASSETS} - \text{LIABILITIES} = \text{CAPITAL}$$
$$£15\ 000 - £3000 = £12\ 000$$

2 **Assets**
   Capital is £6000 and liabilities are £18 000. What is the total for assets? Use the accounting equation in the form of

$$\text{ASSETS} = \text{CAPITAL} + \text{LIABILITIES}$$
$$\text{ASSETS} = £6000 + £18\ 000$$
$$\text{Assets therefore} = £24\ 000$$

Amy's statement of financial position at 31 August contains total assets of £58 000 and total liabilities of £30 000. Use the accounting equation to find Amy's capital.

**Self-test question 2.3
(answer at the end of the book)**

2.4 DRAWING UP A STATEMENT OF FINANCIAL POSITION

This section of the chapter demonstrates the link between a set of business transactions and the statement of financial position at the end of an accounting period. Like the first example in this chapter, JJ Hair Studio, it uses a business start-up, but the range of transactions and the resultant statement of financial position are more extensive and complicated. The example will illustrate some important points about the conventions used in business accounting. Remember that we have already encountered the 'business entity' convention earlier in the chapter (and see if you can remember what it is).

Example 2.4

Salma has spent several months researching business possibilities, and decides to set up a retail business selling designer kitchenware. The business will be called 'Kitchen Kit'. She has £100 000 available to put into the new business in cash, following the sale of a previous successful business. Salma signs an agreement to rent premises from 1 February 20X6, planning to open her shop on 26 February. Rent is payable in arrears, and she will not have to pay anything until the end of March 20X6. In order to illustrate the construction of a statement of financial position containing the results of several transactions, the statement of financial position will be drawn up at regular intervals during the first few days of business. This is somewhat artificial, and is for illustrative purposes only; in real life a statement of financial position would be drawn up at periodic intervals, and almost never more often than once a month.

DAY ONE

On 1 February Salma opens a business bank account in the name of 'Kitchen Kit' depositing £100 000. Assuming no other transactions on Day 1, a statement of financial position drawn up at the end of the day would show the following:

Kitchen Kit: Statement of financial position at 1 February 20X6

	£
ASSET: bank account	100 000
CAPITAL	100 000

This single transaction creates items under two of the elements of the accounting equation. Every business transaction either adds to, or depletes, two of the elements of the statement of financial position; this is known as the 'dual aspect' convention of accounting.

CONVENTIONS OF PRESENTATION

The simple statement of financial position above follows certain simple presentational conventions which are the norm in many countries, regardless of whether IAS 1 is complied with or not.

1 The statement of financial position has a heading showing the name of the business (not the individual) and the date at which it is drawn up.
2 It is in vertical format – that is, the figures are arranged in a columnar form.
3 It is headed by a sign indicating the currency adopted – in this case the pound sterling.
4 The key totals are underlined.

DAYS TWO TO EIGHT

Salma needs to display inventory in her shop, ready for the opening on 26 February. First, she has arranged for a builder to come into the shop to install a counter and some shelving. She pays him £6500 on 8 February. What are the accounting implications of this transaction?

The counter and shelving are likely to be used in the business over a long period of time and they are therefore regarded as non-current assets. The business's cash resources have been depleted by £6500 but non-current assets increase from £0 to £6500 (note the dual aspect of the transaction – one asset is depleted, but another asset increases by the same amount). If a statement of financial position is drawn up at the end of the day on 8 February, it shows the following:

Kitchen Kit: Statement of financial position at 8 February 20X6

	£
ASSETS	
Non-current assets: counter and shelving	6 500
Current assets: bank account	93 500
	100 000
CAPITAL	100 000

Note that the balance on the bank account was £100 000 before Salma paid £6500 for the counter and shelving. After the transaction has taken place, the balance on the bank account drops to £93 500. Note also that the accounting equation remains valid: assets = capital.

DAY NINE

Salma needs to stock the shop. She has ordered various items of kitchenware that are delivered on 9 February. Because Salma has several years of experience in business and a good credit record she has been able to obtain credit terms from suppliers, and will not have to pay for the inventory until 9 March. The cost of the inventory is £72 000. What are the implications for the statement of financial position of this transaction?

The business has acquired a new type of current asset in the form of inventory. It is classified as a current asset (rather than a non-current asset) because it is not expected to remain in the business for a long period (unlike the shop counter and shelving). However, in this case there is no effect (yet) on the bank account because immediate payment for the goods is not required. So what has occurred?

A current asset of £72 000 arises, and current assets in the statement of financial position will increase by this amount. The other aspect of the transaction is that a current liability for the same amount arises.

Taking this transaction into account, the statement of financial position of the business at 9 February 20X6 is as follows:

Kitchen Kit: Statement of financial position at 9 February 20X6

	£	£
ASSETS		
Non-current assets: counter and shelving		6 500
Current assets:		
Inventory	72 000	
Bank account	93 500	
		165 500
		172 000
CAPITAL AND LIABILITIES		
Capital		100 000
Current liabilities: trade payables		72 000
		172 000

What is going on here? Why are there so many more figures in this statement of financial position compared to the previous one? There is no need to panic. Most of the changes from the previous statements of financial position have been made in order to make the statement clearer and more useful to the reader. Starting at the top of this most recent statement of financial position:

- Non-current assets are the same as before at £6500.
- Under current assets we now have the new asset of inventory. There are now two categories of current asset so it is helpful to summarize current assets by means of the total figure of £165 500. In order to make the figures easier to read and understand, the current assets figures have been pulled into a separate column, and only the total is shown in the column at the right of the page. Once the reader gets accustomed to this convention of presentation it makes it much easier to understand what is going on.
- The bottom part of the statement of financial position now comprises both capital and current liabilities. The new category of current liabilities arises because of the amount of £72 000 owing for inventory.

Note that the accounting equation remains valid, but that it is now slightly more complicated because of the introduction of liabilities:

$$\text{Assets } (£172\ 000) = \text{Capital } (£100\ 000) + \text{Liabilities } (£72\ 000)$$

DAY TEN

Salma has invested in inventory to sell in the shop. When she pays for it in one month's time she will have a bank balance, assuming no other transactions in the meantime, of £21 500 (£93 500 − 72 000). She realizes that there will be many further demands on her cash in the short-term, for example, advertising, more purchases of inventory, buying a cash register, installation of a burglar alarm, and so on. She is likely to need more cash, but does not want to draw any further on her personal resources. She borrows £20 000 from her mother. This is a loan without a fixed repayment date, but her mother is happy for it to be a long-term arrangement. On 10 February Salma pays the £20 000 into the business bank account. What are the accounting implications of this transaction?

The business's cash resources have increased by £20 000. On the other hand, there is now a non-current liability. A statement of financial position drawn up on 10 February will be as follows:

Kitchen Kit: Statement of financial position at 10 February 20X6

	£	£
ASSETS		
Non-current assets: counter and shelving		6 500
Current assets:		
Inventory	72 000	
Bank account	113 500	
		185 500
		192 000
CAPITAL AND LIABILITIES		
Capital		100 000
Non-current liabilities: loan		20 000
Current liabilities: trade payables		72 000
		192 000

Each transaction that we have examined makes the statement of financial position a little more complicated – and by 10 February, when the example ends, the business has yet to make a sale. It should be emphasized that the frequent drawing up of statements of financial position as in the example would be very unusual – it is done here for the purposes of illustration and explanation. Statements of financial position are drawn up on a periodic basis – at least once a year and sometimes more often, but practically never on a daily basis.

2.4.1 Changing the Value of Capital

What would it take to alter the amount at which capital is stated in Kitchen Kit's statement of financial position? An increase could occur in two situations:

1 The owner of the business might put in some more of their personal resources. In Salma's case she might, for example, sell her house or her car and put the proceeds into the business. The dual aspects of this transaction would be to increase the amount of capital in the statement of financial position, and to increase cash by the same amount.

2 The business can increase the amount of capital by making a profit. In Salma's case she will do this by selling kitchenware at prices greater than the price she paid for the goods. The difference between selling and cost price must be sufficiently large to cover all categories of expense, such as rent, rates, advertising and administration.

Alternatively, the value of capital could decrease. This could happen in two ways:

1 The owner (or owners) of the business take out some of the resources they have put into it. Where the owner wants or needs to remove some part of the assets, the total of assets decreases, and so does the amount of capital in the statement of financial position. The removal of assets (usually cash, but it could be other types of asset) by the owner is traditionally known as **drawings**.

2 The business decreases its net assets by making a loss. If goods or services are sold for amounts that do not, overall, cover the costs of the business, a loss will be made and net assets, and capital, will be depleted.

2.5 MORE PRACTICE WITH STATEMENTS OF FINANCIAL POSITION

The example of Salma in the previous section of the chapter examined a new business start-up to illustrate the basics of statement of financial position preparation. This section applies the knowledge gained from the chapter so far to established businesses that are preparing statements of financial position at the end of an accounting period.

Each business – whether a company, partnership or sole trader – has a year-end date at which point it prepares its annual accounts. Conventionally, year-ends tend to be end of month dates (31 December, 31 March etc.) although there is no strict rule about this. It would be quite acceptable to have a year-end of 5 April, for example, which coincides with the end of the tax year in the UK. The next example deals with the preparation of a statement of financial position for an established business.

Example 2.5

Dipak has been established in business for several years in a business selling computers for home and small business use. As well as selling standard systems he also builds computer systems to customers' specifications and sells a limited range of software packages and printers. He runs the business from shop premises that he owns on a freehold basis. The business, which trades as Computers2Go, has the following balances at its year-end on 31 August 20X7:

	£
Freehold premises	53 000
Shop fittings and equipment	6 300
Cash	60
Loan from brother (no fixed repayment date)	8 000
Inventory of computers	48 000
Graphics and sound cards, cables, etc.	9 650
Bank overdraft	13 750
Trade receivables (amounts owed by customers)	5 250
Owner's capital	99 130
Inventory of software	15 000
Trade payables (amounts owed to suppliers)	16 380

First, we need to establish which categories each of the balances fall into – asset, liability or capital:

	£	Category
Freehold premises	53 000	Asset
Shop fittings and equipment	6 300	Asset
Cash	60	Asset
Loan from brother (no fixed repayment date)	8 000	Liability
Inventory of computers	48 000	Asset
Graphics and sound cards, cables, etc.	9 650	Asset
Bank overdraft	13 750	Liability
Trade receivables (amounts owed by customers)	5 250	Asset
Owner's capital	99 130	Capital
Inventory of software	15 000	Asset
Trade payables (amounts owed to suppliers)	16 380	Liability

CLASSIFYING ASSETS

Seven of the items on the list are classified as assets. Which are current and which are non-current? Remember that inventory, trade receivables and cash are categorized as current assets. The first two items on the list are non-current assets – ie freehold premises and the shop fittings and equipment; these have been, and will continue to be, used for a long time in the business.

There are three categories of inventory on the list: inventory of computers, graphics cards, etc. and software. These three are added together to give a total for inventory:

	£
Computers	48 000
Graphics cards etc.	9 650
Software	15 000
Total inventory	72 650

As well as non-current assets and inventory, Dipak's business has trade receivables of £5250 and cash of £60, which are also current assets.

DRAWING UP THE STATEMENT OF FINANCIAL POSITION

Having done the preliminary work on classification, preparing the statement of financial position should be a relatively straightforward exercise:

Computers2Go: Statement of financial position at 31 August 20X7

	£	£
ASSETS		
Non-current assets:		
Freehold premises	53 000	
Shop fittings and equipment	6 300	
		59 300
Current assets:		
Inventory	72 650	
Trade receivables	5 250	
Bank account	60	
		77 960
		137 260
CAPITAL AND LIABILITIES		
Capital		99 130
Non-current liabilities (loan from brother)		8 000
Current liabilities		
Bank overdraft	13 750	
Trade payables	16 380	
		30 130
		137 260

2.6 COMMUNICATING MEANING: WHAT DOES THE STATEMENT OF FINANCIAL POSITION SAY?

Remember that the basic function of financial statements is to be useful to a range of users. When involved in the difficulties of fitting the figures together and getting the statement of financial position to balance it is easy to forget that the point of the exercise is to communicate a message.

What does the statement of financial position of Computers2Go in Example 2.5 tell us? We know that the business sells computers, and therefore needs an inventory of computers, software, and so on. But does the business need to have quite so much inventory? Let's say that the average price that Dipak has paid for a computer is £300. This would mean that he holds approximately 160 computers (£48 000 divided by £300) in inventory. How long will it take to sell these items, and will they be out of date soon? Similar questions could be asked about the other items of inventory.

The business owes its suppliers more than £16 000. Presumably they will expect to be paid very soon. How are they to be paid? The business has a comparatively large overdraft. Will the bank allow further borrowings on overdraft? Even if the customers who owe money were to pay up straight away, there would still be a problem. Could Dipak contribute money from his own resources to help the business meet its liabilities?

Trying to understand the messages conveyed by this statement of financial position involves asking a lot of questions that cannot be easily answered. We need a lot more information.

It is important to remember at all times that the purpose of statements of financial position (and accounting in general) is not to provide number puzzles for business students, but to provide information that actually means something in the context of the real world.

2.6.1 Characteristics of Useful Financial Information

Reminder: Chapter 1 identified two key characteristics of financial information:

- relevance to decisions made by users of the information
- faithful representation of economic events and transactions.

Four further characteristics improve the quality of financial information:

- comparability, so that users can compare financial information between accounting periods and between companies
- verifiability, so that a range of different users could agree that the financial statements are a fair representation of economic events and transactions
- timeliness, which means that the financial information is made available to users within a reasonable and realistic timeframe
- understandability, so that reasonably well-informed and educated users are able to understand the financial information provided.

2.7 FINANCIAL REPORTING BY LARGE COMPANIES

The examples used in this chapter are all of very small businesses. This is done deliberately so that the figures remain small and straightforward in nature. Obviously, the financial statements of large, complex businesses such as the companies listed on the London Stock Exchange, are much more complicated. However even at this stage in your studies, you can begin to understand the statements of financial position of major businesses: see the real-life Example 2.6.

Example 2.6 (Real-Life)

Tate & Lyle plc, 2016 Annual Report

Tate & Lyle plc is a company listed on the London Stock Exchange. The principal statement of financial position headings used in the company's statement of financial position at 31 March 2016 are as follows:

> ASSETS
> Non-current assets
> Current assets
> EQUITY
> Capital and reserves
> LIABILITIES
> Non-current liabilities
> Current liabilities

The only term that is likely to be unfamiliar after studying this chapter is 'Equity'. However, the sub-description of 'Capital and reserves' suggests that this is the equivalent of what we have so far referred to simply as 'Capital' in this chapter. So, even at this stage in your studies, it is becoming possible to read the statement of financial position of a major company in an informed way.

The financial statements of companies will be covered at greater length in Chapter 7.

Self-test question 2.4

Identify a large company in which you are interested for some reason (e.g. you are a customer of it, you have worked for it, or you have a family member or a friend who works for it). Look up the company's website and find its most recent statement of financial position. You will probably find this in the Annual Report document which can run to well over 100 pages, and which will often be found under the section of the website devoted to 'Investor Information' or 'Corporate Information' or similar. Identify the statement of financial position headings and the extent to which you recognize the terminology used. It is quite likely that you will recognize most, if not all, of the main headings. Look also at the subheadings and see if you can find familiar elements such as 'trade payables', 'inventory', and so on.

(Note: there is no specific solution to this self-test question, but you may be able to discuss your findings in class.)

Chapter Summary

The statement of financial position is a statement of a business's position at a given point in time. At this stage, you should be able to prepare a statement of financial position for a small business from a given list of balances, and you should understand in outline how the statement of position interacts with the other principal financial statements.

It is important to understand from an early stage the conventions of presentation and preparation that are commonly used in preparing financial statements. Before moving on, be sure that you understand the 'business entity' concept, and the 'dual aspect' concept. Other concepts will be introduced over the next few chapters. Finally, remember that the purpose of all this accounting is to convey information and to be useful to people who are interested in the performance and position of the business. Even at this early stage in your studies it is always worth trying to discern the messages conveyed by the figures.

Internet Resources

Tate & Lyle's website is at www.tateandlyle.com, and its Annual Report can be found under the 'Investor Relations' tab.

Book's companion website

The website contains the following resources in respect of Chapter 2:

Students' section

A multiple choice quiz containing ten questions
Six additional questions with answers

Lecturers' section

Answers to end-of-chapter exercises 2.16 to 2.23
Four additional questions with answers
Chapter on double-entry book-keeping
Testbank
Instructor's Manual
PowerPoint presentation

Exercises: Answers at the End of the Book

2.1   Alexander's business manufactures and sells biscuits to supermarkets and grocery shops. Below are descriptions of some of the items in his statement of financial position. For each item fill in the adjacent box with ASSET or LIABILITY.

Cash kept in a tin in the office

Oven

Bank loan, repayable over five years

Plastic packaging for biscuits

Flour and sugar

Amounts payable to supplier of dried fruit

2.2   Amir has a consultancy business which he runs from rented offices. The following are descriptions of some of the items in his statement of financial position. For each item fill in the adjacent box with NON-CURRENT ASSET, CURRENT ASSET, NON-CURRENT LIABILITY or CURRENT LIABILITY.

Value Added Tax (VAT) payable to HMRC

Office computer

Amount due from Lomax plc for consultancy work carried out by Amir

Bank overdraft

Bank loan to be repaid in three years' time

Amount payable to stationery supplier

2.3   Brian's statement of financial position shows totals for assets of £83 000 and £36 500 for liabilities. Use the accounting equation to find the total for Brian's capital.

2.4   Basil's capital in his business is £43 650. Business assets total £188 365. Use the accounting equation to find the total for liabilities.

2.5   Brenda's business has non-current assets of £12 000, current assets of £8500 and total liabilities of £17 300. What is Brenda's capital?

2.6   Brigitte's business has non-current assets of £27 000, current assets of £16 000, current liabilities of £12 000 and non-current liabilities of £10 000. What is her capital in the business?

2.7   Bryony's statement of financial position shows the following totals:

	£
Non-current assets	35 840
Current assets	16 500
Current liabilities	12 000
Non-current liabilities	6 000

What is Bryony's capital in the business?

a) £70 340

b) £1340

c) £46 340

d) £34 340

2.8   Benito's statement of financial position shows the following totals:

	£
Non-current assets	39 497
Current assets	26 004
Current liabilities	16 777
Capital	33 058

Work out the missing figure for non-current liabilities. (Hint: first, work out total liabilities using the accounting equation.)

2.9   Blanche's statement of financial position shows the following totals:

	£
Non-current assets	36 609
Current assets	38 444
Current liabilities	26 300
Capital	39 477

What is the missing figure for non-current liabilities?

a) £61 876

b) £9276

c) £15 012

d) £67 612

2.10   Callum's statement of financial position at 31 July shows the following:

	£
Non-current assets	18 337
Inventory	12 018
Trade receivables	365
Cash	63
Bank overdraft	3 686
Trade payables	2 999

i) What is the total of assets in the business?

ii) What is the total of current assets?

iii) What is the total for liabilities?

iv) What is Callum's capital?

2.11 Ciera's business has the following balances at 31 December 20X1:

	£
Inventory	18 600
Trade payables	23 700
Cash in bank account	13 000
Long-term loan	20 000
Non-current assets: premises	39 000
Trade receivables	6 500
Amounts owed to HMRC	3 800
Ciera's capital	29 600

Prepare Ciera's statement of financial position at 31 December 20X1. Use the format shown in the chapter examples. Remember to line up columns of figures neatly, and to use a proper heading for the statement of financial position.

2.12 Dan's statement of financial position at 1 May 20X3 was as follows:

	£	£
ASSETS		
Non-current assets		30 000
Current assets		
Inventory	15 000	
Trade receivables	5 000	
Bank account	18 000	
		38 000
		68 000
CAPITAL AND LIABILITIES		
Capital		52 000
Current liabilities		
Trade payables		16 000
		68 000

On 2 May Dan paid £1500 for an office computer to help him keep the business accounts.
On 3 May Dan paid a supplier £3000.
Explain how his statement of financial position was affected and show the new statement of financial position at 3 May 20X3 after taking account of both transactions.

2.13 Ernest runs an art gallery. He organizes exhibitions at which painters and sculptors show their work. If a piece of artwork is sold, Ernest takes a commission of 50% of the selling price. He banks the cash and then pays out what is due to the artists. He held a successful exhibition in November, and is planning the next one for January. Each time he holds an exhibition he pays for advertising and sending out leaflets to people on his mailing list, as well as wine and soft drinks on the opening night of the exhibition. Putting on the exhibition in January will cost him around £4000.

Ernest has the following assets and liabilities at 31 December:

	£
Gallery premises	68 000
Cash at bank	18 600
Amounts payable to artists	16 560
Office equipment	2 260
Amounts payable to printers for publicity material for recent exhibition	1 600
Capital	70 700

1   Prepare Ernest's statement of financial position at 31 December.

2   Write a brief assessment of Ernest's business position as shown by the statement of financial position.

2.14   Explain the business entity concept of accounting.

2.15   With reference to financial statement information, briefly explain the enhancing characteristic of timeliness.

Exercises: Answers Available on the Lecturers' Section of the Book's Website

2.16   Adrian owns and runs a restaurant. The following are descriptions of some of the items in his statement of financial position. For each item fill in the adjacent box with NON-CURRENT ASSET, CURRENT ASSET, NON-CURRENT LIABILITY or CURRENT LIABILITY

Restaurant tables

Wages owed to waiter

Bank account containing £3850

Tax bill due to HMRC

Restaurant premises

Mortgage (ie loan) from bank to buy restaurant premises

Food supplies in kitchen fridges

Amounts due to baker for bread supplied over the last month

2.17   Bernie's business has liabilities of £63 000. His capital is £28 000. What is the total for assets?

2.18   Bjork's capital in her business is £97 000. The total for current liabilities is £31 000. There are no non-current liabilities. What is the total for assets?

2.19 Bashir's statement of financial position shows the following totals:

	£
Capital	68 350
Non-current assets	79 403
Current assets	16 276

What are the liabilities in Bashir's business?

a) £131 477
b) £27 329
c) £5223
d) £164 029

2.20 Benedict's statement of financial position shows the following totals:

	£
Current assets	716 237
Current liabilities	426 663
Non-current liabilities	100 000
Capital	1 373 424

What is the total for non-current assets?

2.21 Carmela's business has the following balances at 18 October 20X6:

	£
Amounts due from customers	16 303
Non-current assets: machinery	12 722
Amounts payable to suppliers for materials	6 868
Bank balance	6 993
Cash on the premises	120
Amounts payable to the HMRC	396
Long-term loan from sister	1 800
Non-current assets: office computer	1 060
Inventory of goods	17 721

Prepare the statement of financial position for Carmela at 18 October 20X6.
NB: no figure is given for Carmela's capital – it has to be calculated from the information given above.

2.22 Diana's statement of financial position at 28 August 20X1 is as follows:

	£	£
ASSETS		
Non-current assets		13 500
Current assets		
Inventory	10 300	
Trade receivables	1 200	
Bank account	1 000	
Petty cash	600	
		13 100
		26 600

	£	£
CAPITAL AND LIABILITIES		
Capital		20 200
Current liabilities		
Trade payables		<u>6 400</u>
		<u>26 600</u>

1   Diana has saved up some money for her holiday, but decides to put it into the business instead. She pays a cheque for £2000 into the business bank account on 29 August.

2   On 30 August, the business receives a cheque for £600 from one of its customers.

Explain how her statement of financial position will be affected and show the new statement of financial position at 30 August 20X1 after taking account of both transactions.

2.23   Erik has a retail business selling china and glass ornaments from a small shop in a town centre. He has the following balances at his year-end of 30 November:

	£
Freehold premises	16 800
Shop fittings, computer, till, etc.	8 300
Cash: float in till	600
Loan from mother (no fixed repayment date)	2 000
Inventory	10 300
Bank overdraft	3 800
Trade payables	3 200
Payables: due to HMRC for VAT	800
Capital	26 200

NB: the trade payables include £2200 owed to one company, Ornamental Glass Products Ltd. The company has been waiting for payment for this amount since August and Erik has been rung up on several occasions by the company's chief accountant requesting immediate payment. Erik has an overdraft limit of £4000.

1   Prepare Erik's statement of financial position at 30 November.

2   Erik has asked you to advise him on whether he should ask the bank manager for an increase in his overdraft limit. Assess Erik's position at 30 November as shown by the statement of financial position and advise Erik.

3 The statement of profit or loss

Aim of the chapter

To enable students to understand how a statement of profit or loss is prepared and how it fits together with the statement of financial position.

Learning outcomes

After reading the chapter and completing the exercises at the end, students should:

- Understand the terminology used in a statement of profit or loss, and some of the principal conventions used in presenting it.

- Be able to draw up a statement of profit or loss for a sole trader from a list of account balances and explanatory notes.

- Be able to understand and comment on the basic information conveyed by a statement of profit or loss.

- Combine skills gained as a result of studying Chapters 2 and 3 to draw up a set of financial statements comprising a statement of profit or loss and a statement of financial position.

Introduction

An organization run on a commercial basis will attempt to make profits. In straightforward terms, it does this by selling goods and/or services at prices which will allow it to cover all the expenses of the business, with a surplus remaining. Any surplus can be distributed to the owner(s) or retained in the business to fund expansion.

The statement of profit or loss reports on the performance of the business to interested parties. As noted in Chapter 1, interested parties include, for example, investors and potential investors in the business, lenders, employees and HMRC.

This chapter first explores some of the accounting terminology used in the statement of profit or loss. The appearance and content of the statement of profit or loss is influenced to some extent by the nature of the business being conducted, and so the terminology section is followed by a brief review of the broad categories of commercial activity. The chapter then proceeds to explain the techniques involved in drawing up a statement of profit or loss for a trading business, and then introduces some techniques of financial analysis which allow the user of the financial statements to understand the messages conveyed by the statement of profit or loss. This section builds upon the sole trader example, but also covers the analysis of statement of profit or loss information published by a large business.

The chapter then explains statement of profit or loss accounting for a service business. It concludes with a longer example which demonstrates the procedures involved in drawing up both a statement of profit or loss and a statement of financial position for a sole trader business.

3.1 THE STATEMENT OF PROFIT OR LOSS: TERMINOLOGY

Revenue (also referred to as 'sales' or 'turnover') is the amount of goods and/or services sold, expressed in monetary terms.

Expenses are the amounts incurred by the business in purchasing or manufacturing the goods sold, and other expenditure on items like rent and telephone charges.

Profit is the surplus remaining when revenue exceeds expenditure (a desirable state of affairs in a commercial organization).

Loss is the deficit which occurs when expenditure exceeds revenue (a state of affairs which cannot persist for a long period in a commercial organization).

The statement of profit or loss summarizes the revenue and expenses of an organization over a period of time, showing the performance of the business over the period. It gives the reader information which shows how well or how badly the business is doing.

3.2 CATEGORIES OF COMMERCIAL ACTIVITY

Commercial activities can be broadly classified into three types, as follows:

- trading
- manufacturing
- service.

Trading organizations operate as 'middlemen'. Typically, they buy in goods that have been manufactured by another individual or organization and then sell them on at a higher price to someone else.

Manufacturing organizations are often complex operations. They manufacture goods which are either sold directly to the public or to trading organizations which then sell them on. For example, a factory manufactures woollen coats which it sells to fashion shops. The factory business sells at prices which cover the various costs of manufacture plus a profit. The shop owners sell at a higher price than they are charged by the factory business, and so they, too, make a profit. By the time the customer in the shop buys the coat at least two organizations have made a profit on the transaction.

Service organizations sell services rather than goods. For example, a solicitor is not concerned at all with the sale of goods. He or she makes a surplus out of the provision of professional services.

Some organizations have a mixture of activities. Take, for example, a commercial tennis club. It sells annual subscriptions to a range of services such as use of tennis courts and tennis coaching. It also sells a range of shoes and clothing which it buys in from all the well-known sports clothing manufacturers. The club, therefore, operates both trading and service activities.

3.3 STATEMENT OF PROFIT OR LOSS FOR A SOLE TRADER

The early part of Chapter 2 explained the outline content of the three main accounting statements, including the statement of profit or loss, using the example of the first month of trading for JJ Hair Studio, a business engaged in providing a service. In this chapter we build upon that very basic example, firstly examining the statement of profit or loss of a trading business.

The statement of profit or loss of a trading business splits into two parts: firstly the profitability of the buying and selling processes are shown in the trading account, to arrive at a figure of **gross profit**, and then all the other expenses of the business are deducted to arrive at a **net profit**.

The basic layout of the statement of profit or loss is as follows:

	£
Revenue	–
Less: cost of sales	(–)
Gross profit	–
Various expenses	(–)
Net profit	–

First, we will look at the calculation and presentation of the upper part of the statement of profit or loss to arrive at gross profit. This part of the financial statement is known as the **trading account**.

Example 3.1

Mary has a shop that sells cookers. For the sake of simplicity, we will assume that she sells only one type of cooker at a price of £195 each. She buys all the cookers from one manufacturer at a cost of £135 each. Each cooker therefore produces a profit of £60 (£195 less £135). If Mary bought and sold only one cooker the basic trading account information would be as follows:

Mary: Trading account

	£
Sale of cooker	195
Less: cost of cooker	135
Profit	60

The standard terminology used in drawing up a trading account is to describe the deduction for the cost of the goods as cost of sales, and the profit shown in the trading account as gross profit. We can restate Mary's trading account using this standard terminology:

Mary: Trading account

	£
Revenue	195
Less: cost of sales	135
Gross profit	60

Naturally, if Mary is trying to make a profit out of her business she will hope and expect to sell more than one cooker. If she sells 100 cookers during the course of the month of May 20X3 her trading account will be as follows:

Mary: Trading account for the month ended 31 May 20X3

	£
Revenue: 100 cookers @ £195	19 500
Less: cost of sales: 100 cookers @ £135	13 500
Gross profit	6 000

Note that this trading account statement has a proper heading showing Mary's name and the period covered by the statement. It is necessary to show this information so that the reader of the financial statement can be quite sure about the scope of the information covered. Note also the use of the terminology: revenue, cost of sales and gross profit.

This question tests the understanding of the key elements of the trading account.

Jules sells leather bags from his market stall. The bags are all to the same design but are produced in a range of different colours with slightly different fastenings. During the month of December 20X4 he sells 66 bags at £23 each. He has bought the bags for £14.50 each. Show Jules's trading account for the month.

Self-test question 3.1
(answer at the end of the book)

3.4 MOVEMENTS IN INVENTORY

In most trading businesses an inventory of goods has to be held at all times, so that goods can be displayed and so that there are enough items available to satisfy potential demand. For example, in the cooker business outlined above, Mary has found that she needs to have at least five cookers on display at any time in order to demonstrate minor differences in styling and colours to her potential customers. Also, she needs to have a further 20 cookers available to cope with potential demand. Inventory is replaced when necessary in order to ensure that there are always at least 25 cookers on the premises. The factory from which she orders guarantees rapid delivery so Mary does not have to keep a large amount of inventory on the premises.

Example 3.2

We can explore this example further by looking at some transactions during the month of June 20X3. At 1 June Mary has 30 cookers in inventory. During June she sells 76 cookers. She orders 35 cookers which are delivered on 10 June and a further 40, delivered on 24 June.

How many cookers does Mary have in inventory at 30 June? In order to answer this question we can construct an inventory movement account:

	Units	£
Opening inventory: 30 cookers @ £135	30	4 050
Add purchases: (35 + 40) 75 cookers @ £135	75	10 125
Less: items of inventory sold: 76 cookers @ £135	(76)	(10 260)
Closing inventory: 29 cookers @ £135	29	3 915

Note that items sold are expressed in terms of the price Mary pays, so that like is compared with like. This account would form part of Mary's business record keeping but would not be shown as part of the financial statements.

We can use the information about inventory movements to draw up a more informative trading account for Mary for the month of June 20X3.

Mary: Trading account for the month ended 30 June 20X3

	Units	£	£
Revenue: 76 cookers @ £195	76		14 820
Cost of sales:			
Opening inventory: 30 cookers @ £135	30	4 050	
Add: purchases: 75 cookers @ £135	75	10 125	
	105	14 175	
Less: closing inventory: 29 cookers @ £135	(29)	(3 915)	
Cost of sales: 76 cookers @ £135	76		(10 260)
Gross profit for month			4 560

Because this is a simple example we can double check the gross profit. Mary has sold 76 cookers and we know that the gross profit on each is £60. 76 × £60 = £4560, so the answer is correct.

Note that the column containing the cost of sales calculation has been pulled to the left-hand side: this is simply to make the trading account easier to read and understand.

At 1 January 20X5 Jules has 36 handbags in inventory. Usually, January is a poor month for sales. This January is no exception and he sells only 42 bags at £23 each. However, he decides to improve the display by buying in several of each of the full range of colours. He buys in total 68 bags in January, at a cost of £14.50 each.

Prepare an inventory movement account for Jules, showing the number of units of inventory and monetary amounts. Also, prepare a full trading account for the month of January 20X5, assuming that all handbags are sold for £23.

3.5 CALCULATING COST OF SALES

The example of Mary's cooker business has been kept deliberately straightforward in order to illustrate the calculation of cost of sales. However, most businesses, even small ones, would trade in more than one product. It would become very complicated to calculate precise numbers of units in the trading account. It is also unnecessary.

Most businesses have periodic inventory counts (referred to in the UK as stocktaking), usually to coincide with the date at which the accounts are drawn up. This allows them to keep track of inventory, to identify those items that are not selling, to dispose of any damaged items found, and to generally make sure that there have not been any significant losses through inaccurate accounting or theft. Inventory counts identify the quantities of inventory, which can then be valued by reference to how much it cost. Therefore, at the date of the statement of profit or loss and statement of financial position, a valuation of inventory is established.

Purchases in the period are calculated from delivery records and from the invoices that suppliers send for payment.

Because the inventory value at the beginning and the end of the accounting period are established, and because the total purchases are known, it is easy to calculate cost of sales as follows:

	£
Opening inventory	—
+ Purchases	—
− Closing inventory	(−)
Cost of inventory	=

At this point it may be helpful to check this simplified layout against the trading account for Mary in Example 3.2. Note that it shows the same basic components.

Now we will look at Mary's trading account for a one-year period.

Example 3.3

Mary's accounting year ends on 31 October. In respect of the year to 31 October 20X3 she will need information about:

- opening inventory on 1 November 20X2
- closing inventory on 31 October 20X3
- purchases for the whole year.

At 1 November 20X2 her opening inventory value was £4725.
At 31 October 20X3 her closing inventory value was £6480.

During the year she received total purchases of cookers of £153 900. She sold 986 cookers at the normal selling price of £195 and a further 141 at £175 in a special Christmas promotion.

This is all the information that is needed to calculate Mary's gross profit for the year.

Mary: Trading account for the year ended 31 October 20X3

	£	£
Revenue: 986 cookers @ £195	192 270	
141 cookers @ £175	24 675	
		216 945
Cost of sales:		
Opening inventory at 1 November 20X2	4 725	
Add: purchases during year	153 900	
	158 625	
Less: closing inventory at 31 October 20X3	(6 480)	
		(152 145)
Gross profit for year		64 800

3.6 CALCULATING NET PROFIT

Earlier in this chapter, we looked at the basic layout of a statement of profit or loss, which was as follows:

	£
Revenue	−
Less: cost of sales	(−)
Gross profit	−
Various expenses	(−)
Net profit	=

The calculation of gross profit has now been covered comprehensively. Provided we know the expenses of the business we can deduct them from gross profit to arrive at the net profit for the period.

3.6.1 Typical Business Expenses

Expenses vary from one type of business to another, in both type and importance. For example, one of the main expenses in a road haulier's business will be the costs of fuel and other costs associated with running a fleet of haulage vehicles. By contrast, fuel and motoring costs in a business like Mary's cooker business are likely to be minor.

Expenses could include the following:

- *cost of premises*: rental, business rates, insurance, electricity, gas, water, repairs
- *selling costs and costs of distributing goods*: haulage costs, delivery services, costs of sales' staff salaries and commissions
- *administration costs*: telephone, stationery, administrative staff salaries, accountants' and legal fees, computer costs
- *finance costs*: bank charges, interest on loans.

In the next example we will continue to look at Mary's business.

Example 3.4

In the year ended 31 October 20X3 Mary's business expenses are as follows:

- *Staffing costs*: Mary works in the shop by herself on quieter days, but she employs an assistant for a few hours each day on busy days. She pays the assistant £28 per day on average and he is employed for a total of 165 days during the year to 31 October 20X3.
- *Premises costs*: Mary pays an annual rental for the shop of £17 500, including business rates, any major repair costs and service charges. In addition, in the year ended 31 October 20X3 she pays general business insurance of £1350, electricity bills of £1207 and water rates of £795.
- *Administration*: Mary does all of the basic book-keeping herself, and pays an accountant £585 to produce the final accounts and the tax computation for HMRC. She spends £103 on stationery, stamps, and so on. Her telephone and broadband bills for the year ended 31 October 20X3 come to £312, and she spends £132 on other odds and ends (usually known as 'sundry' expenses) for use in the business. The membership subscription to the trade association, the Cooker Association of Retailers and Manufacturers (CARM) costs £87 per year.
- *Finance costs*: bank charges total £85. Mary has not borrowed any money so there are no interest charges.

From this information it is possible to complete Mary's statement of profit or loss to arrive at her net profit for the year, as follows:

Mary: Statement of profit or loss for the year ended 31 October 20X3

	£	£
Revenue (detailed calculation given earlier)		216 945
Less: cost of sales (detailed calculation given earlier)		(152 145)
Gross profit		64 800
Expenses:		
Staffing costs (165 days @ £28 per day)	4 620	
Rental of premises	17 500	
Business insurance	1 350	
Electricity	1 207	
Water rates	795	
Accountant's fees	585	
Stationery	103	
Telephone and broadband	312	
Sundry expenses	132	
CARM subscription	87	
Bank charges	85	
		(26 776)
Net profit for year		38 024

Note that the expenses are set off in a separate column towards the left-hand side of the page; this is to make the statement easier to read.

Later in the chapter we will examine an example of how the statement of profit or loss and statement of financial position fit together.

3.7 WHAT DOES THE STATEMENT OF PROFIT OR LOSS MEAN?

The statement of profit or loss and other financial statements are prepared for a purpose; that purpose is to communicate information to people who need to know about the business. So, what information does Mary's statement of profit or loss communicate?

An obvious and important piece of information is that the business is profitable in the year ended 31 October 20X3. If this is a typical year, it is possible to draw the general conclusion that the business is currently successful, and may continue to be successful into the future. This general conclusion could be taken a little further by examining gross profit and net profit.

Mary is interested in assessing whether the general trend in her business profitability is upwards or downwards. She supplies the key figures from the statement of profit or loss for the previous year's trading to 31 October 20X2: sales were £197 535, gross profit was £57 300, expenses totaled £24 904 and net profit was £32 396.

This information can be summarized alongside the comparable figures for 20X3:

	20X3	20X2
	£	£
Revenue	216 945	197 535
Less: cost of sales	(152 145)	(140 235)
Gross profit	64 800	57 300
Various expenses	(26 776)	(24 904)
Net profit	38 024	32 396

3.7.1 Gross Profit Analysis

Gross profit is an important element in judging how well or badly a business has performed. However, one isolated figure has little significance on its own. We need to make comparisons between at least two figures.

COMPARING TWO CONSECUTIVE YEARS The increase in gross profit is £64 800 − £57 300 = £7500. This is sufficient information to be able to calculate the percentage increase in gross profit from 20X2 to 20X3, as follows:

20X2 gross profit	£57 300
Increase in gross profit	7 500

$$\text{Percentage increase} = \frac{£7500}{57\,300} \times 100 = 13.1\% \text{ (to nearest decimal place)}$$

If we were further informed, for example, that the Cooker Association of Retailers and Manufacturers published figures to its members showing that there had been an increase in the gross profit on cooker sales across the UK of 10% between 20X2 and 20X3, we could see that Mary's business has done rather well, and certainly better than average. Mary could achieve this better than average performance by either increasing her sales prices by a rate which is slightly above average, or by negotiating lower prices than average with the supplier, or by a combination of the two factors. As a sole trader, she may well charge higher prices than a large retailer, but customers may be prepared to pay a little more for better service and after-sales advice.

GROSS PROFIT MARGIN 'Gross profit margin' is a way of expressing, by means of a percentage, the relationship between gross profit and revenue. It simply shows gross profit as a percentage of revenue.

Two figures are needed to calculate a gross profit margin: revenue and gross profit. Mary's trading account shows both, so we can apply the following formula:

$$\frac{\text{Gross profit}}{\text{Revenue}} \times 100 = \text{Gross profit margin \%}$$

In Mary's case:

$$\frac{£64\,800}{216\,945} \times 100 = 29.9\% \text{ (to nearest decimal place)}$$

Does this tell us anything useful? Again, not unless we have more information to compare it with. Calculating the comparable ratio for 20X2 uses the gross profit and revenue figures for 20X2:

$$\frac{\text{Gross profit}}{\text{Revenue}} \times 100 = \text{Gross profit margin \%}$$

$$\frac{\text{£57 300}}{197\,535} \times 100 = 29.0\% \text{ (to nearest decimal place)}$$

To summarize, Mary's gross profit margin in 20X2 was 29.0% and in 20X3 was 29.9%. The gross profit margin in her business has improved. This means that the difference between the selling price and the cost of sales has increased. This may be as a result of selling prices increasing, cost prices reducing, or a combination of the two.

3.7.2 Net Profit Analysis

We can analyze net profit in the same way as gross profit.

COMPARING TWO CONSECUTIVE YEARS Net profit for the year is £38 024, and for 20X2 was £32 396. The fact that it has increased is good news for Mary, but we can extend the analysis further to look at the percentage increase in the same way as we did for gross profit:

The increase is £38 024 − £32 396 = £5628.

$$\text{Percentage increase} = \frac{\text{£5628}}{32\,396} \times 100 = 17.4\% \text{ (to nearest decimal place)}$$

The figures for gross profit increased by 13.1% but net profit has increased by an even greater percentage. Why? The answer lies somewhere in the figure for expenses. In 20X2 expenses totalled £24 904, increasing to £26 776 in 20X3, an increase of £1872.

$$\text{Percentage increase} = \frac{\text{£1872}}{24\,904} \times 100 = 7.5\% \text{ (to nearest decimal place)}$$

We could extend the analysis further by looking at the percentage increases and decreases in the separate categories of expense. The basic analysis shows that, although expenses have increased, the level of increase is much lower than the level of increase in gross profit. As a result net profit shows a substantial increase.

NET PROFIT MARGIN Net profit margin is a way of expressing, by means of a percentage, the relationship between net profit and revenue. It shows net profit as a percentage of revenue. In Mary's business, the net profit margin for 20X3 is as follows:

$$\frac{\text{£38 024}}{216\,945} \times 100 = 17.5\% \text{ (to nearest decimal place)}$$

The net profit margin for the previous year, 20X2, is as follows:

$$\frac{\text{£32 396}}{197\,535} \times 100 = 16.4\% \text{ (to nearest decimal place)}$$

These calculations show that net profit margin has increased. The conclusion is that, on the basis of the analysis of gross profit and net profit, Mary's business performance seems to have improved substantially.

3.8 ANALYZING FINANCIAL INFORMATION IN LARGE COMPANIES

As noted in Chapter 2, the financial statements of large businesses such as those listed on the London Stock Exchange are much more complicated than the statements of the simple, single-activity business used in the examples above. However, the analysis techniques explained in the previous section can be used productively to understand the financial statements of all types of business. Below is a real-life example.

In later chapters we will examine more closely the meaning of financial information. However, it is never too soon to start thinking about the information content of financial statements.

Example 3.5 (Real-Life)

Sainsbury plc, 2016 Annual Report (available online at www.j-sainsbury.co.uk).

Sainsbury's 2016 Annual Report contains a huge quantity of figures, facts and explanations. Extracting just four of the figures from the statement of profit or loss information in the report gives:

	2016 £ million	2015 £ million
Revenue	23 506	23 775
Operating profit*	707	81

*Operating profit is gross profit less operating expenses, but before deducting costs such as interest.

These figures show mixed messages. Revenue has decreased a little (by 1.1%). On the other hand operating profit has improved substantially. It looks likely that, even though sales have fallen, there has been a successful attempt to control costs resulting in a higher operating profit. However, interested parties would probably want more information than given here in order to fully understand the business's performance. Detailed examination of the full Annual Report would be necessary in order to find out more.

3.9 STATEMENT OF PROFIT OR LOSS ACCOUNTING IN A SERVICE BUSINESS

A service business does not trade in goods and therefore does not need to produce a trading account. In this section of the chapter we will look at the example of a business that supplies services only.

Example 3.6

Tony is a chartered surveyor who supplies property advice services to clients investing in commercial property. He also acts as a commercial property agent, handling the selling of office and retail buildings. He makes commission on any successful sales. He employs a full-time personal assistant and, in the year to 31 December 20X5 he has employed a student from the local college's estate management course on a day release basis. Other expenses incurred in his business include motor expenses for his large BMW (Tony clocks up around 50 000 miles each year in taking prospective clients to view industrial estates and business parks), entertaining, the cost of office premises, large telephone bills for office telephone and mobile, and sundries such as professional subscriptions, website maintenance and stationery.

Tony is a sole trader, trading as Aisgarth & Co. He provides the following list of income and expense items from which to draw up a statement of profit or loss for the year ended 31 December 20X5.

	£
Premises rental	12 570
Electricity bills	2 907
Personal assistant's salary	15 788
Income: commissions on commercial property sales	68 360
Motor expenses	15 370
Office and general insurance	1 003
Professional indemnity insurance (PII)*	1 880
Entertaining	9 351
Telephone charges	3 775
Income: fees for professional advice	23 333
Student's wages	1 200
Sundry office expenses	3 720

*Many qualified professionals, such as surveyors and accountants, are obliged under the regulations of their professional body, to take out special insurance against possible liabilities for professional negligence.

From this list of balances we can draw up Tony's statement of profit or loss for the year to 31 December 20X5 as follows:

Aisgarth & Co: Statement of profit or loss for the year ended 31 December 20X5

	£	£
Fees for professional services	23 333	
Commissions	68 360	
		91 693
Expenses:		
Premises rental	12 570	
Electricity	2 907	
Personal assistant's salary	15 788	
Student's wages	1 200	
Motor expenses	15 370	
Insurance	1 003	
PII	1 880	
Entertaining	9 351	
Telephone charges	3 775	
Sundry office expenses	3 720	
		67 564
Net profit for year		24 129

Note that sole traders can trade under a business name, like Tony's. It is quite common for professional businesses like accountants, solicitors and surveyors to trade as *Something & Co*, even though there is only one sole trader involved. We can work out a net profit margin figure for Tony's business:

$$\frac{£24\ 129}{91\ 693} \times 100 = 26.3\%$$

However, in a business like this, the net profit margin may fluctuate quite significantly from one year to another. Expenses are likely to be similar from year to year, but income may vary. Commercial property transactions are usually large, and the commission on a single transaction may amount to many tens of thousands of pounds. However, Tony may have to do a lot of entertaining and travel (both of which, as shown in the statement of profit or loss, cost the business significant sums) in order to bring off just one deal. Without having other years' results for comparison it is not possible to say whether 20X5 was a good, bad or middling year for Tony.

3.10 PREPARING BOTH THE STATEMENT OF PROFIT OR LOSS AND THE STATEMENT OF FINANCIAL POSITION

This final section of the chapter draws upon aspects of Chapters 2 and 3 to demonstrate how the statement of profit or loss and the statement of financial position fit together.

Example 3.7

Nellie sells boots from her market stall and also carries out a boot repair service. This activity has never made much of a profit, but some of Nellie's long-standing customers continue to expect the service. Nellie's year-end is 31 May, a time of year when boot sales are low, and when she has very little inventory on hand. She counts and values her inventory on 31 May 20X7 and arrives at a value of £2904.

You are employed in the office of Naylor & Co, Nellie's accountants. Your boss, Nasser, asks you to prepare her accounts for the year to 31 May 20X7. As well as the information about inventory you are given the following list of items as at the year-end date.

	£
Inventory at 1 June 20X6	2 672
Stall rental and service charge	3 844
Bank interest received	320
Sundry expenses	313
Saturday assistant's wages	1 200
Repairs income	1 801
Purchases	42 640
Trade payables	2 497
Accountant's fees and other administration	862
Insurance	574
Cash at bank	3 422
Drawings	14 257
Repairs expenses	1 742
Motor expenses	1 252
Revenue: sales of boots	63 060
Capital at 1 June 20X6	6 060
Non-current assets: display stands	960

Nasser will be having a meeting with Nellie next week to talk about her business. She feels that she is not doing as well as in previous years. Her gross profit for the year ended 31 May 20X6 was £22 831 on sales of £67 760. In addition to preparing the accounts, Nasser would like you to calculate the actual and percentage changes in gross profit and revenue between 20X6 and 20X7, and to compare the gross profit margins between the two years. He would also like you to make some preliminary comments on Nellie's business performance.

- *Step 1: prepare the accounts*

The first step is to prepare the statement of profit or loss and statement of financial position for Nellie's business. The list that she has provided is a jumbled mixture of items, so a useful preliminary step is to identify a category for each item depending upon whether it goes in the trading account, the rest of the statement of profit or loss or the statement of financial position. For items in the statement of financial position (referred to below as SFP) the terminology used in Chapter 2 can be used:

- non-current assets
- current assets
- current liabilities
- long-term liabilities
- capital.

	£	Category
Inventory at 1 June 20X6	2 672	Trading account
Stall rental and service charge	3 844	Statement of profit or loss
Bank interest received	320	Statement of profit or loss
Sundry expenses	313	Statement of profit or loss
Saturday assistant's wages	1 200	Statement of profit or loss
Repairs income	1 801	Statement of profit or loss
Purchases	42 640	Trading account
Trade payables	2 497	SFP: current liabilities
Accountant's fees and other administration	862	Statement of profit or loss

	£	Category
Insurance	574	Statement of profit or loss
Cash at bank	3 422	SFP: current assets
Drawings	14 257	SFP: capital
Repairs expenses	1 742	Statement of profit or loss
Motor expenses	1 252	Statement of profit or loss
Sales of boots	63 060	Statement of profit or loss
Capital at 1 June 20X6	6 060	SFP: capital
Non-current assets: display stands	960	SFP: non-current assets
Inventory at 31 May 20X7	2 904	Trading account and SFP: current assets

Note that the closing inventory always appears in both the trading account and the statement of financial position as a current asset. Inventory that remains unsold at the date of the statement of financial position is deducted, as we have seen, in arriving at the cost of sales figure. However, it is also an asset of the business, because it can be sold to make money in the following accounting period. Having categorized all the items the next stage is to pick out those that appear in the trading account, so as to be able to prepare the trading account. Then, immediately below it, the rest of the statement of profit or loss items are listed, ending with net profit. Remember that a heading with the name of the business (in this case Nellie simply uses her own name – which is common among sole traders) and a description of the financial statement are always required.

Nellie: Statement of profit or loss for the year ended 31 May 20X7

	£	£
Revenue		63 060
Less: cost of sales		
Opening inventory	2 672	
Add: purchases	42 640	
	45 312	
Less: closing inventory	(2 904)	
		(42 408)
Gross profit		20 652
Boot repairs: income	1 801	
Boot repairs: expenses	(1 742)	
		59
Other income: bank interest received		320
		21 031
Expenses		
Stall rental and service charge	3 844	
Motor expenses	1 252	
Saturday assistant's wages	1 200	
Insurance	574	
Accountant's fees and other administration	862	
Sundry expenses	313	
		(8 045)
Net profit		12 986

Once all of the balances have been put into the statement of profit or loss the remainder should all relate to the statement of financial position, which can then be prepared.

Nellie: Statement of financial position at 31 May 20X7

	£	£
ASSETS		
Non-current assets		960
Current assets		
Inventory	2 904	
Cash	3 422	
		6 326
		7 286
CAPITAL AND LIABILITIES		
Capital		
Opening capital balance 1 June 20X6	6 060	
Add: net profit for the year	12 986	
	19 046	
Less: drawings	(14 257)	
Closing capital balance 31 May 20X7		4 789
Current liabilities		
Trade payables		2 497
		7 286

The capital account shows the resources committed to the business by its owner. As explained in Chapter 2, the balance on the capital account increases or decreases in the following ways:

Capital introduced, plus Profits retained by the business, minus Drawings, minus any losses made by the business.

Nellie's capital account, as shown in the statement of financial position at 31 May 20X7, has been increased by the amount of net profit for the year (calculated in the statement of profit or loss) and has been decreased by the drawings she made from the business.

- *Step 2: calculate the actual and percentage changes in gross profit and revenue*
  Change in revenue: revenue has decreased from £67 760 to £63 060, a decrease of £4700. The percentage change is calculated as follows:

$$\frac{£4\,700}{67\,760} \times 100 = 6.9\%$$

Change in gross profit: gross profit has decreased from £22 831 to £20 652, a decrease of £2179. The percentage change is calculated as follows:

$$\frac{£2\,179}{22\,831} \times 100 = 9.5\%$$

Gross profit margins compared:

	20X7	20X6
	£	£
Gross profit margin	$\frac{£20\,652}{63\,060} \times 100 = 32.7\%$	$\frac{£22\,831}{67\,760} \times 100 = 33.7\%$

- *Step 3: comment on Nellie's accounts*
  Revenue and gross profits have both fallen between 20X6 and 20X7. The gross profit margin is poorer in 20X7 than in the previous year. We do not have net profit information available for 20X6. Nellie may be able to pinpoint reasons for the decline in trade, and Nasser needs to make some suggestions as to how she might be able to increase revenue in future. For example, a change of suppliers might improve gross profit margin. Other observations: the boot repair service is making virtually nothing. Nellie's time could perhaps be better used elsewhere and she may like to consider finally ceasing to offer the service. Nellie's drawings are in excess of the net profit generated by the business. There may be specific reasons why this level of drawings has been made during this recent financial year, but Nellie really should be considering ways of reducing drawings if possible, at least until her trade has recovered its previous levels.

Chapter Summary

By this point, if you have followed this chapter carefully, you should understand the basic procedures involved in preparing a statement of profit or loss, and should be aware of the significance of some of the revenue and cost figures that are typically included in the statement. There are many end-of-chapter exercises and website resources that you can use to consolidate your understanding.

It is very easy to access the Annual Reports of listed businesses on corporate websites. Even at this early stage it is worth making the effort to read these reports and to understand the accounting figures in them. It might be helpful to focus upon a limited number of reports to start with – perhaps a couple of competitor businesses in a sector that you find interesting. You may find it helpful to work, where possible, with other students on this exercise.

Internet Resources

Sainsbury's website is at www.j-sainsbury.co.uk. The websites of listed businesses can usually be found quite easily using Google. Alternatively, try accessing the London Stock Exchange website (www.londonstockexchange.com) which provides links to corporate websites for UK companies. Information about companies listed outside the UK is often accessible via other stock exchange websites, for example, the Australian Securities Exchange (www.asx.com.au).

Book's companion website summary

The website contains the following resources in respect of Chapter 3:

Students' section

A multiple choice quiz containing ten questions
Five additional questions with answers

Lecturers' section

Answers to end-of-chapter exercises 3.12 to 3.16
Five additional questions with answers
Case study
Testbank
Instructor's Manual
PowerPoint presentation

Exercises: Answers at the End of the Book

3.1 Jackie sells garden furniture in sets comprising a dining table and four chairs. She purchases each set for £75 from the manufacturer and retails a set for £132. At the beginning of June 20X9 Jackie had 30 sets in her inventory. At 30 June 20X9 she had 42 sets.

She sold 35 sets during the month.

i) How many sets of dining table and chairs has Jackie purchased during the month?
   a) 107
   b) 47
   c) 23
   d) 37

ii) What was Jackie's cost of sales figure for the month?
   a) £4425
   b) £4620
   c) £2625
   c) £1875

iii) What was Jackie's gross profit for June?
   a) £2745
   b) £1425
   c) £6783
   d) £1995

3.2 Jay's business is shoe retailing. He has bought in a special purchase of 1000 pairs of trainers for £8500. He sells 750 pairs quite quickly at a retail price of £15.50 per pair. Then, in order to clear the inventory out of the shop he reduces the selling price to £12.50 and clears a further 200 pairs. The remaining 50 pairs are put into a bargain bin at a price of £5 per pair and these sell during the shop's autumn sale. What is Jay's gross profit on this line of trainers? How much gross profit would he have made if he had been able to sell the whole consignment at £15.50 per pair?

3.3 During the year Jake sells 8000 units of inventory at £42.50 each. The gross profit on each unit is £17.50. He purchased inventory at a total cost of £197 300 and still had £17 400 in inventory at the year-end.

What was Jake's opening inventory?

3.4 Jethro sells an extensive range of children's toys. He likes to be well informed at all times about the performance of his business. Part of the routine work of his administrative assistant is to draw up a monthly trading account so that Jethro can check on gross profit levels. Information about revenue and purchases relating to a three-month period October to December 20X4 is as follows:

	October £	November £	December £
Revenue	39 370	48 998	56 306
Purchases	37 085	40 830	6 250

Inventory at the beginning of October was valued at £30 863.
Inventory at the end of each of the three months was as follows:

October	£43 258
November	£53 190
December	£23 980

Draw up a trading account for Jethro's business for each of October, November and December 20X4.

3.5 Leon runs a retail grocery business, dealing in luxury and delicatessen goods. In 20X7 revenue was £295 993, with cost of sales at £242 085. The equivalent figures for 20X6 were revenue of £287 300 and cost of sales of £235 920.

Calculate:

i) Leon's gross profit margin in both years.
ii) The increase in revenue.
iii) The percentage increase in revenue.
iv) The increase in gross profit.
v) The percentage increase in gross profit.

3.6 The summarized results of Louis's business for the three years to the end of 20X2 were as follows:

	20X2 £	20X1 £	20X0 £
Revenue	291 318	282 400	269 340
Cost of sales	(213 916)	(206 420)	(196 071)
Gross profit	77 402	75 980	73 269
Expenses	(52 394)	(51 720)	(49 270)
Net profit	25 008	24 260	23 999

Calculate the gross and net profit margins for each year and comment briefly on the general trends in the business trading results.

3.7 Madigan & Co is the trading name of Basil Madigan, a chartered accountant. He runs a small city-centre office, employing a part-qualified accountant as an assistant, and a part-time secretary.

In the year ended 31 March 20X8 fees from Madigan's clients totalled £95 311. The assistant's salary was £19 300 and the secretary was paid £11 150. Basil's one-room office is in a run-down office building at a comparatively low rental of £10 310 which includes energy costs and business rates. There is also an annual service charge (to cover repairs, caretaking, and so on) which amounted to £3790 in the year ended 31 March 20X8.

Basil paid general insurance of £794, plus PII of £1250. Subscriptions and professional registration charges were £952. Business travel expenses (mileage claims for use of own car by himself and his assistant) came to £1863. Entertainment was £342.

Telephone and broadband charges were £1103 for the year and other administration charges were £1575. Stationery was £761 and sundry expenses totaled £715. Basil made donations to local charities out of the business account to the sum of £120.

Prepare the statement of profit or loss for Madigan & Co for the year ended 31 March 20X8.

3.8 Norbert runs a small wholesaling business, selling imported Italian coffee machines to retailers. His business is run from a small warehouse with an office at the side on an industrial estate on the edge of a large city. The industrial estate is largely deserted at night and the crime rate is high for theft and criminal damage. Norbert has recently joined a scheme run by the local authority on behalf of tenants of its industrial units; he pays an annual contribution to a fund which pays for improved lighting and security patrols.

Norbert's accounting year-end is 31 March. He provides you with a list of figures relating to the most recent year which ended on 31 March 20X3. You are required to prepare a statement of profit or loss and a statement of financial position from the figures.

	£
Delivery vehicle	5 020
Revenue for the year	351 777
Staff costs: storeman's wages	12 090
Electricity	2 821
Cash at bank	3 444
Capital at 1 April 20X2	18 011
Administrative costs	3 810
Opening inventory at 1 April 20X2	20 762
Non-current assets in warehouse and office	3 900
Drawings	25 219
Sundry expenses	1 406
Warehouse and office rental	10 509
Insurance	3 909
Trade receivables	36 623
Water rates	1 226
Security services charge	2 937
Purchases	255 255
Bank charges	398
Trade payables	31 950
Delivery expenses	8 630
Part-time admin assistant's wages	3 779

Norbert counted and valued the coffee machines on the premises at the 31 March 20X3. The total value was £22 446. Prepare the statement of profit or loss and statement of financial position for Norbert's business for the accounting year ended 31 March 20X3.

3.9 Refer to the example of Mary's cooker business used earlier in the chapter. Briefly describe the principal groups of users of financial information who are likely to have an interest in Mary's financial statements, and the reasons for their interest. (You may find it helpful to refer back to the list of user groups provided in Chapter 1.)

3.10 Identify two listed businesses operating in the same business sector (for example, Sainsbury's and one of its competitors such as Tesco or Morrison). From the Annual Reports of the businesses, extract the revenue and profit information for the accounting year and the comparative information for the previous year. Calculate profit margins, and the year-on-year changes in the figures and compare the two businesses. Where there are differences between the businesses, use the other information in the Annual Report to see if you can identify the reasons for the differences.

3.11 Identify a company listed on a Stock Exchange outside the UK and download its Annual Report. Extract the revenue and profit information and identify whether there has been an increase or a decline in profitability.

Exercises: Answers Available on the Lecturers' Section of the Book's Website

3.12 Jin-Ming's mail-order business sells trampolines. The selling price is £400 for a standard-sized trampoline, and £550 for a large one. The opening inventory at 1 January 20X6 was six standard and five large trampolines. The cost of the trampolines to Jin-Ming is £260 (standard) and £330 (large). In the year to 31 December 20X6 Jin-Ming sold 30 standard and 17 large trampolines. He could have sold more of the large size but the manufacturer stopped making them part-way through the year. Jin-Ming's purchases for the year totalled £14 880 including the purchase of 12 large trampolines.

 i) Draw up Jin-Ming's trading account for the year ended 31 December 20X6.
 ii) Calculate the gross profit on the sale of large and standard trampolines respectively.

3.13 Jodie is a wholesaler of electrical discount goods. She buys in end-of-line and seconds quality goods from manufacturers and sells them on to small electrical retailers. She has to take advantage immediately of any special offers that manufacturers make available; if she doesn't the manufacturers will sell to one of her competitors. Therefore, her inventory levels can fluctuate substantially from one week to the next. The level of revenue is not steady from month-to-month; it depends upon what is in inventory and whether there is much demand for the items Jodie currently has in her warehouse.

At the beginning of March Jodie's inventory was valued at £93 882 and comprised principally kettles, toasters and dishwashers. An unexpected surge in demand by small retail wholesalers for these items resulted in a high level of sales in March of £89 907. By the end of March inventory dropped to £34 920. At the end of April, as the result of a special purchase of electric blankets it went up to £82 860, dropping back only slightly to £75 918 at the end of May. Jodie knows that she will find it difficult to dispose of most of this inventory before the end of the summer.

Revenue for April was £31 241 and for May, £40 270.

Purchases for each of the three months were:

March	£3 074
April	£65 747
May	£18 911

 i) Draw up trading accounts for each of the three months.
 ii) Discuss the business and financial problems Jodie would encounter in running this type of wholesaler operation.

3.14 Lulu's revenue in 20X0 was £115 399. The following year, 20X1, revenue increased by 4.3%. In 20X2 revenue was 7.8% higher than it was in 20X1. Gross profit margin in each of the three years was:

20X0: 19.3%
20X1: 21.4%
20X2: 18.7%.

Calculate cost of sales for each of the 3 years, 20X0, 20X1 and 20X2.
Work to the nearest pound sterling.

3.15 In 20X2 Lola's net profit margin fell to 9.8% from 10.2% in the previous year. Her gross profit margin, on the other hand, increased from 30.2% to 33.8%. Revenue in 20X1 was £148 360 and in 20X2 was £153 062.
From this information prepare summary statement of profit or loss for 20X1 and 20X2 showing revenue, cost of sales, gross profit, expenses and net profit.
Work to the nearest pound sterling.

3.16 Mahbub runs a recruitment agency. The agency's income is earned in the form of commissions from clients who pay a percentage of the first year's salary of new employees recruited by the agency. In the year to 31 December 20X2 the total of commission income earned was £115 900. Mahbub is very pleased with this record level of commission; it is 25% higher than total commissions in the previous year.

Expenses, however, also increased. Premises costs totalled £16 506, staff costs were £29 900 and administration costs were £15 981. In the year to 31 December 20X1 the equivalent expenses totals were:

Premises	£13 370
Staff costs	£28 807
Administration costs	£12 773

From the information given above, prepare Mahbub's statement of profit or loss for both 20X2 and 20X1. Calculate the percentage increase or decrease in net profit.

4 Applying accounting conventions

Aim of the chapter

To achieve an understanding of some further complexities in the preparation of the statement of profit or loss and the statement of financial position, and the practical application of some important conventions and principles in accounting.

Learning outcomes

After reading the chapter and completing the exercises at the end, students should:

- Understand the treatment in the statement of profit or loss of complexities such as discounts and returns of goods.

- Understand and be able to apply some of the important accounting conventions in preparing the statement of profit or loss and the statement of financial position.

- Know about the measurement of inventory and trade receivables, and the need for allowances against them, and be able to make appropriate adjustments to the statement of profit or loss and statement of financial position.

Introduction

Chapter 2 introduced the statement of financial position, and Chapter 3 the statement of profit or loss. This chapter is concerned with extending students' understanding of more complex transactions, within the framework of accounting conventions that are commonly applied in the preparation of financial statements.

The first part of Chapter 4 examines the accounting treatment of some additional types of transaction that may occur in business, and which have to be reflected in the financial statements. The principal transaction types examined here are returns of goods, discounts and delivery charges. The next section of the chapter introduces some of the principal conventions used in accounting, including the accruals assumption and **recognition** of income and expenses. Finally, the chapter turns to an examination of adjustments and allowances that may need to be made in measuring the amount of inventory and trade receivables, and the effects of these adjustments and allowances on the statement of profit or loss and statement of financial position.

4.1 RETURNS OF GOODS, DISCOUNTS AND DELIVERY CHARGES

This section of the chapter extends the knowledge gained in Chapter 3 of the statement of profit or loss, by considering three further types of transaction that affect the calculation of profit: returns, discounts and delivery charges.

4.1.1 Returns

The majority of the examples in Chapter 3 involved the purchase and sale of items of inventory, and in all cases it was assumed that the transactions were straightforward and no items were ever returned. However, while transactions are often completed without error or dispute, this is not always the case. A retail customer, for example, may buy a pair of jeans but find, on examining the jeans more carefully at home, that the zip is broken. The jeans are taken back to the shop and either a replacement is provided or a refund is paid. The same can happen, although usually on a larger scale, with the purchase and sale of items in business. The goods are not what was ordered, the quality level of the goods is insufficient, the quantity is wrong or a combination of any or all of these factors. Where purchased items are returned, there are implications for the statement of profit or loss of both the seller and the purchaser.

Example 4.1

John runs a business selling artists' easels and other art equipment. Imran purchases 30 easels from him at a cost of £45 each: total cost = £1350. The transaction is added to John's revenue, and added to Imran's purchases. Upon close examination of the easels Imran discovers that five of them are missing essential bolts and screws. He decides to return them to John. The effect of this return is that John's sales and Imran's purchases are reduced by the same amount: $5 \times £45 = £225$.

Where returns are a fairly frequent occurrence, a total of items returned is built up during the year. The returns total features in the list of balances from which the statement of profit or loss is drawn up. Sales returns must be deducted from revenue, and purchases returns must be deducted from purchases in drawing up the trading account part of the statement of profit or loss. Rather than setting these figures off against each other, it is conventional to show the total for revenue and then deduct the total amount for sales returns.

4.1.2 Discounts

TRADE DISCOUNTS A trade discount is a special kind of discount given, for example, to long-standing customers, or to customers who purchase a very high volume of goods. This type of discount is normally given via reduced prices, and results in a lower cost of purchases for the recipient. Large businesses are often able by this means to buy goods at lower unit prices than small businesses, and so can obtain a competitive advantage. If they pass on the discounts via lower prices to their customers then they may be able to gain market share at the expense of their smaller competitors.

Where discounts like this are given or received, there is no special adjustment to be made in the statement of profit or loss because the amounts invoiced already reflect the reduction. However, trade discounts may be relevant when analyzing the meaning of statements of profit or loss, especially when comparing one business with another. A business that receives discounts is more likely to be profitable than one that does not.

FINANCIAL DISCOUNTS Many businesses trade on credit, which means that they do not demand immediate payment but instead are prepared to wait for a period of time before receiving their money. The acceptable period varies from one business to another, and will depend upon the norms in that particular industry. A frequently encountered arrangement is to require payment within 30 days of invoice. For example, goods are despatched to a customer on 15 May, and an invoice is sent on 17 May. Until the invoice is paid the amount is accounted for as a trade receivable. The invoice specifies that payment should be received within 30 days; it is therefore expected that payment will be received by 16 June. Some customers will pay within the time allowed; others will take longer, and others may not pay at all (a problem we will examine in more detail later in this chapter).

Business people in most trades and professions have to accept the necessity for trading on credit. However, they will seek to minimize the length of time they have to wait for their money, and one way of actively encouraging early payment is to offer an incentive in the form of a discount. The cost of the discount has to be carefully balanced against the benefit of receiving the cash earlier than it would be received if there were no discount.

Example 4.2

Fernando runs a small business manufacturing and selling gloves. His customers are mainly retail businesses. Many of Fernando's customers do not pay within his stipulated terms of credit which are receipt of cash required within 30 days of invoice. In order to encourage earlier payment, Fernando decides to set up a discount incentive. Customers who pay within 30 days are entitled to reduce the invoiced amount by 0.5%.

On 1 October, he sends an invoice to one of his biggest customers for £3000 with a note about the discount. The value of the sale recorded in Fernando's accounting records on that day is £3000. Thirty days later, a cheque arrives for £2985, ie. £3000 less 0.5% of the invoice value. The discount is, therefore, £15. How should Fernando record it?

The discount is an expense of Fernando's business – a type of finance charge incurred in order to get the money into his bank account sooner than he would have done otherwise. Therefore, it is included as an expense in his statement of profit or loss. Where a business receives financial discounts, they are included as part of its other income, below the trading account details.

4.1.3 Delivery Charges

Some businesses incur the expense of distributing their goods to customers. Typical expenses would include road or haulage costs, handling costs and import duties. In some cases the selling business pays such costs, and they appear in the expenses section of the statement of profit or loss. Where the purchasing business pays such costs, they are added to the cost of the purchases and appear in the trading account.

Example 4.3

Brooklyn imports Brazilian footballs in cartons of 100, each carton costing £52. In addition, he must pay import duty of £5 per carton. On 15 August, he orders 16 cartons. How much is added into his total of purchases for the year?

	£
Cost of 16 cartons @ £52 per carton	832
Import duty: 16 cartons @ £5 per carton	80
Total added to purchases for the year	912

So, in summary, accounting for delivery and similar charges varies depending upon whether the selling organization or the purchasing organization is paying the cost.

Where the purchasing organization pays these costs, as noted above, they are added into the cost of purchases in the trading account. Also, they form part of the valuation of inventory. The following example shows how Sainsbury's accounts for such costs.

Example 4.4 (Real-Life)

The annual reports of large businesses always include a list of accounting policies, so that readers are able to understand the way in which certain items are accounted for. An extract from Sainsbury's annual report includes the following information about inventory valuation:

'Cost [of inventories] includes all direct expenditure and other appropriate attributable costs in bringing inventories to their present location and condition.'

The following example incorporates several of the adjustments we have examined so far in this chapter.

Example 4.5

Bennie runs an art shop that sells all kinds of artists' materials, and also items such as greetings cards, books and paper. As well as over-the-counter sales for cash, he also supplies local art colleges and schools with art materials and equipment. This type of sale is made on credit. Bennie requires payment within 30 days, but finds that colleges and schools are generally slow to pay. During the year ended 31 October 20X4 he introduces an early payment discount scheme: all credit customers paying within one month are entitled to deduct 1.25% of the invoice value from their payment. Some of Bennie's credit customers take advantage of the discount scheme, and Bennie allows total discounts of £196 during the financial year. Other relevant points are:

- Bennie himself receives discounts for early payment from some of his suppliers. The total for the year is £98.
- During the year ended 31 October 20X4 he buys in some easels from John, but finds them to be faulty. Several substandard easels have to be returned to John; the total cost of the returned easels is £853.
- One of the art colleges supplied by Bennie returns to him a large order of paint because it is infested with weevils. The value of the amount returned, at selling price, is £590.
- Generally, delivery charges are included in the price of the goods that Bennie buys. However, he imports a range of fragile pastel sticks from France. He pays a courier firm for special delivery of these items so that they are not damaged in transit. The total cost for this type of delivery for the year ended 31 October 20X4 is £150. Note that the valuation of any inventory of the pastel sticks at the business's year-end will include the cost of delivery charges.

The following is a list of all Bennie's revenue and expenses items (including those described above) for the year ended 31 October 20X4.

	£
Insurance	2 984
Discounts allowed to colleges and schools	196
Inventory at 1 November 20X3	16 037
Subscription to Chamber of Commerce	100
Delivery van expenses	760
Shop rental	18 300
Revenue	159 760
Sundry expenses	1 982
Purchases	94 736
Courier service: pastel imports	150
Returns of goods sold to college	590
Electricity and other premises costs	3 598
Assistant's wages	10 920
Discounts received for early payment	98
Returns of easels to John	853
Accountancy fees	570
Inventory at 31 October 20X4	18 006

This example is more complicated than previous examples in the book. The additional adjustments mean that more items are included in the trading account. As a first step each of the items is classified as belonging either to the trading account or to the rest of the statement of profit or loss, as follows:

	£	
Insurance	2 984	Statement of profit or loss
Discounts allowed to colleges and schools	196	Statement of profit or loss
Inventory at 1 November 20X3	16 037	Trading account
Subscription to Chamber of Commerce	100	Statement of profit or loss
Delivery van expenses	760	Statement of profit or loss
Shop rental	18 300	Statement of profit or loss
Revenue	159 760	Trading account
Sundry expenses	1 982	Statement of profit or loss
Purchases	94 736	Trading account
Courier service: pastel imports	150	Trading account
Returns of goods sold to college	590	Trading account
Electricity and other premises costs	3 598	Statement of profit or loss
Assistant's wages	10 920	Statement of profit or loss
Discounts received for early payment	98	Statement of profit or loss
Returns of easels to John	853	Trading account
Accountancy fees	570	Statement of profit or loss
Inventory at 31 October 20X4	18 006	Trading account

Several items in the above list are included in the trading account. If we separate them out, we can deal with them first:

	£	
Inventory at 1 November 20X3	16 037	Trading account
Revenue	159 760	Trading account
Purchases	94 736	Trading account
Courier service: pastel imports	150	Trading account
Returns of goods sold to college	590	Trading account
Returns of easels to John	853	Trading account
Inventory at 31 October 20X4	18 006	Trading account

Of the above seven items, two relate to sales transactions: £159 760 of revenue and £590 of sales returns. These are presented as follows:

	£
Revenue	159 760
Less: sales returns	(590)
	159 170

The remaining items relate to the cost of sales calculation. Reminder: the basic calculation is:

Opening inventory
+
Purchases
−
Closing inventory

But the calculation of purchases has become a little more complicated.

	£	£
Cost of sales:		
Opening inventory (1 November 20X3)		16 037
Add purchases:		
Purchases	94 736	
Add: courier charges	150	
Less: purchase returns	(853)	
		94 033
		110 070
Less: closing inventory (31 October 20X4)		(18 006)
Cost of sales		92 064

Note that the detail of the purchases calculation has been pulled over to the left-hand side for greater clarity.

The remainder of the profit calculation follows the same approach as in the previous chapter so should not be especially difficult. Once all the figures are put together Bennie's statement of profit or loss looks like this:

Bennie: Statement of profit or loss for the year ended 31 October 20X4

	£	£	£
Revenue			159 760
Less: sales returns			(590)
			159 170
Cost of sales:			
Opening inventory		16 037	
Add purchases:			
Purchases	94 736		
Add: courier charges	150		
Less: purchase returns	(853)		
		94 033	
		110 070	
Less: closing inventory		(18 006)	
Cost of sales			(92 064)
Gross profit			67 106
Discounts received			98
			67 204
Expenses			
Shop rental		18 300	
Electricity and other premises costs		3 598	
Assistant's wages		10 920	
Insurance		2 984	
Discounts allowed		196	
Accountancy fees		570	
Delivery van expenses		760	
Sundry expenses		1 982	
Chamber of Commerce subscription		100	
			(39 410)
Net profit			28 794

Note the following:

1 Discounts received are a type of income. However, they are not included in the trading section of the statement of profit or loss, but are added on to gross profit. This is because the level of discounts received has no bearing on the trading activities of the business; they are received as a result of good financial management.
2 Delivery van expenses are the expenses which Bennie has to pay for running a van to deliver goods to his customers. These costs are obviously not being passed on to customers and therefore have to be paid for out of the proceeds of Bennie's business.
3 Bennie's statement of profit or loss looks quite complicated because it has three columns of figures. Figures are indented like this in order to make the statement easier for the reader to understand.

Before moving on, try the following self-test question.

K onstantin's business had opening inventories valued at £35 500 on 1 April 20X6. At 31 March 20X7, the value of closing inventories was £36 600. During the financial year, purchases of £177 200 were made, and purchase returns totaled £5000. Konstantin imports some of his goods for sale, and the business incurred import duties in the year ended 31 March 20X7 of £700.
   Calculate cost of sales for Konstantin's business for the year ended 31 March 20X7.

Self-test question 4.1
(answer at the end of the book)

4.2 ACCOUNTING CONVENTIONS

Accounting conventions help to determine the amounts at which items should be stated in the financial statements, and, indeed, whether those items should be included at all. This section of the chapter explains three conventions:

- going concern
- recognition
- accruals (matching).

4.2.1 Going concern

The 'going concern' convention assumes that the business will continue in operation for the foreseeable future. The values assigned to various elements of the financial statements reflect this assumption. Conversely, if the assumption relating to going concern no longer applies because the business is about to fail, the values assigned to the financial statement elements are likely to be different. For example, a business which is a going concern values its inventory at a total of £190 000. The inventory will, in the normal course of business, be sold for amounts in excess of its cost price, and will be replaced. However, if the same business were about to fail, a valuation of £190 000 might very well be too high. If the inventory had to be sold in a hurry on the break-up of the business, a more appropriate valuation might be, say, £170 000. So, in summary, going concern values are different from break-up valuations.

4.2.2 Recognition

Recognition occurs when items such as revenue, expenses, assets and liabilities are brought into the financial statements. In this chapter, we will consider the recognition of revenue and expense items. In some cases, the point at which revenue and expenses should be recognized is straightforward. A sale made for cash is recognized at the point where the exchange of goods for cash takes place. So, for example, in the case of Bennie's art shop earlier in the chapter, all the sales he makes for cash in the year up to the close of business on 31 October 20X4 are included in his statement of profit or loss for the year.

However, Bennie makes both cash sales and sales on credit. At what point should sales on credit be recognized in the financial statements? The accounting convention on this point is that recognition takes place at the point at which the goods are supplied (or services rendered in the case of a service business). So, for example, goods delivered to an art college on 31 October 20X4 with a sales value of £366 are included in Bennie's revenue for the year. Goods delivered on the following morning (1 November 20X4) will be included in revenue for the year ended 31 October 20X5.

It is important to realize that the application of this convention means that the total recorded for sales by a business (that offers credit to its customers) in an accounting period is not usually the same amount as cash received. Referring to the example in the paragraph above, the goods that Bennie delivers to the art college on 31 October 20X4 are included in his revenue for the year ended 31 October 20X4 at their sales value of £366. However, payment for these goods will not be received until after the year-end. The amount due for payment by the art college of £366 is included in trade receivables at the year-end, and is recognized under current assets in Bennie's statement of financial position.

Similar considerations apply in respect of expenses. In Bennie's case, all goods delivered up till the close of business on 31 October 20X4 are included in his purchases for the year. At that date, Bennie has almost certainly not paid for all the purchases. Any amounts still to be paid at the year-end are trade payables, and will be recognized under current liabilities in the business's statement of financial position. So, as with sales revenue, the total for purchases and expenses recorded in the accounting period is not the same figure as cash spent.

In summary, accounting revenue is not the same figure as cash received, and accounting expenditure is not the same as cash paid.

4.2.3 Accruals (Matching)

In Chapter 3 we established the basic foundation for the calculation of profit:

$$\text{Revenue} - \text{Expenses} = \text{Profit}$$

In order to calculate profit with as much precision as possible, it is important to match revenue and expenses with each other. This means setting off against revenue for an accounting period all the expenses that have contributed to making the revenue. So, in a business such as Bennie's, which pays rent, accruals accounting requires that one year's rent is matched against one year's revenue in working out profit for the year. If only nine months' rent is included the expenses for the year will be too low, and profit will be overstated. Conversely, if fifteen months' rent is included the expenses figure will be too large, and profit will be understated.

When preparing the year-end financial statements it is important to examine the amounts recorded as expenses in detail in order to ensure that expenses and income are matched as closely as possible. The importance of accrual (matching) accounting is illustrated in the following example.

Example 4.6

Gregory runs a small business supplying leather goods on credit to small shops and market stalls. The business is run from a warehouse on a trading estate. Gregory pays rental for the warehouse, and the usual type of expenses such as insurance and telephone.

Gregory's accounting year-end is 30 June. The annual rental of the business is paid in quarterly instalments in advance. So, for example, Gregory pays rental on 29 September every year which will cover October, November and December. Any increases in rental take effect from the 1 January in the calendar year.

Gregory has the following rental arrangements with his landlord in 20X2 and 20X3: in 20X2 the total annual rental is £12 000, but in 20X3 there is a substantial increase to £14 400.

What is the total of rental expense for Gregory's business in the year ended 30 June 20X3?

Following the accruals convention in accounting, Gregory's revenue for the year ended 30 June 20X3 must be matched with the expenses that have been incurred in order to achieve that revenue. Between 1 July 20X2 and 31 December 20X3 (a period of six months) the cost of the warehouse rental was:

$$£12\,000/2 = £6\,000$$

Between 1 January 20X3 and 30 June 20X3 (a period of six months) the cost of the warehouse rental was:

$$£14\,400/2 = £7\,200$$

The total rental expense to be matched against Gregory's revenue for the year is therefore £6000 + £7200 = £13 200. The calculations may be easier to understand with the aid of a diagram (See figure 4.1).

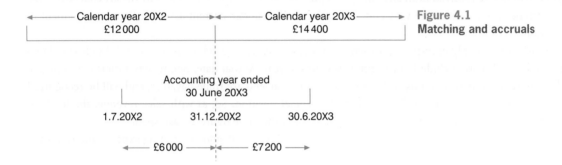

Figure 4.1
Matching and accruals

4.3 COMPREHENSIVE EXAMPLE: ACCRUALS

Example 4.7 demonstrates the adjustments that may be required to the financial statements because of the timing of expenses. Parts 1 and 2 of the example demonstrate the detailed adjustments, and then Part 3 looks at the effect on the financial statements overall.

Example 4.7

PART 1

Graham has a consultancy business with a year-end of 31 December. He receives quarterly bills for telephone call charges. At the year end 31 December 20X8 the total in his account books for his business telephone call charges is £6840. This is the total of three separate payments made during the year:

- payment on 13 April 20X8: £2175 for the bill covering 1 January to 31 March.
- payment on 30 July 20X8: £2444 for the bill covering 1 April to 30 June.
- payment on 18 October 20X8: £2221 for the bill covering 1 July to 30 September.

By 31 December 20X8 Graham has received no bill for the last quarter of the year. This is not surprising – the bill will cover the period up to and including 31 December and so Graham would not expect to receive it until several days after the year-end.

However, Graham must include the amount of the final quarter bill in his financial statements to 31 December 20X8 so that the total charge for telephone expenses reflects all of the charges for calls made in the year. If he fails to include an appropriate amount expenses will be understated and, consequently, profit will be overstated.

In drawing up the financial statements Graham must add the appropriate amount to the telephone expense. If he receives the bill before he completes the financial statements he can make an exact adjustment. If not, he must make a reasonable estimate of the likely cost. Unless the final quarter is unusual in some way, Graham could estimate based upon the previous quarters' bills. An estimate of around £2200 to £2300 would probably be appropriate.

Suppose that Graham receives the bill in good time before the financial statements are finished. The total amount of call charges is £2237 for the quarter. Graham adds this to the charges for the first three quarters:

$$£6840 + £2237 = £9077 \text{ total telephone expense for the year.}$$

There is another adjustment to be made as well, this time to the statement of financial position. The three bills already paid have depleted the bank balance. The new bill will deplete the bank balance at some point in January or February 20X9 but at the date the accounts are drawn up (31 December 20X8) the payment transaction has not yet occurred. Graham, therefore, must show the telephone bill as a liability at the year-end. This is an example of an accrual, and it is included in the statement of financial position under current liabilities.

PART 2

Telephone charges are billed after the calls have been made. The telephone company extends credit to its customers and other utilities companies commonly do the same (unless the customer is known to be very bad at paying up, in which case the companies will insist on payment in advance or via pay meters). Some types of expense, however, may be payable in advance, and matching problems may therefore occur.

Graham pays his business buildings and contents insurance on 1 July each year, in advance. The amount paid on 1 July 20X8 covers the whole year from 1 July 20X8 to 30 June 20X9. Only half of the amount paid, therefore, relates to the year to 31 December 20X8.

At 31 December 20X8 the balance on Graham's insurance account is £3901 which includes the bill paid on 1 July 20X8 for £2644. Half of this (£1322) relates to the next following accounting year (20X9). This is known in accounting terminology as a prepayment, a type of current asset. It will be included in the statement of financial position at 31 December 20X8 under current assets of the business.

The total expense for Graham's business insurance for the year comprises £1322 for the second half of the year, plus the amount relating to the first six months of the year:

Insurance expense in Graham's records at 31 December 20X8	£3 901
Less: amount relating to 20X9	1 322
Insurance expense for inclusion in the 20X8 accounts	£2 579

Because we know that the insurance expense relating to the second six months of the year was £1322 we can work out (£2579 – £1322) that the expense for the first six months of the year was £1257.

PART 3: THE FULL FINANCIAL STATEMENTS

Next, we will look at how the accrual and prepayment adjustments explained above fit into Graham's accounts for the whole year.

The following is Graham's list of balances at 31 December 20X8, before any adjustments for accrual and prepayment items. Each item is identified as to whether it belongs in the statement of profit or loss or statement of financial position.

	£	
Consultancy income	103 907	Statement of profit or loss
Secretarial assistant's salary	18 742	Statement of profit or loss
Entertaining expenses	961	Statement of profit or loss
Non-current assets	3 336	Statement of financial position
Cash at bank	12 906	Statement of financial position
Travel expenses	1 888	Statement of profit or loss
Telephone	6 840	Statement of profit or loss
Interest received	360	Statement of profit or loss
Trade receivables	14 820	Statement of financial position
Trade payables	1 793	Statement of financial position
Capital at 1 January 20X8	21 130	Statement of financial position
Office premises: rent and other expenses	23 590	Statement of profit or loss
Sundry office expenses	2 553	Statement of profit or loss
Insurance	3 901	Statement of profit or loss
Accountant's fees	772	Statement of profit or loss
Drawings	36 881	Statement of financial position

The adjustments for the accrual and the prepayment must be made before Graham's statement of profit or loss and statement of financial position are drawn up.

1 Accruals adjustment

£2237 is added to telephone expenses and an accrual for £2237 appears in the statement of financial position, included under current liabilities.

2 Prepayment adjustment

£1322 is deducted from insurance expenses and a prepayment for £1322 appears in the statement of financial position, included under current assets.

Using all of the above information Graham's financial statements can be drawn up:

Graham: Statement of profit or loss for the year ended 31 December 20X8

	£	£
Revenue: consultancy income		103 907
Interest received		360
		104 267
Expenses:		
Office premises: rent and other expenses	23 590	
Secretarial assistant's salary	18 742	
Entertaining expenses	961	
Telephone (£6840 + 2237)	9 077	
Travel expenses	1 888	
Sundry office expenses	2 553	
Insurance (£3901 − 1322)	2 579	
Accountant's fees	772	
		(60 162)
Profit for the year		44 105

Graham: Statement of financial position at 31 December 20X8

	£	£
ASSETS		
Non-current assets		3 336
Current assets		
Trade receivables	14 820	
Prepayment	1 322	
Cash at bank	12 906	
		29 048
		32 384
CAPITAL AND LIABILITIES		
Capital		
Opening capital balance 1 January 20X8	21 130	
Add: net profit for the year	44 105	
	65 235	
Less: drawings	(36 881)	
Closing capital balance 31 December 20X8		28 354
Current liabilities		
Trade payables	1 793	
Accrual	2 237	
		4 030
		32 384

Notes

1 After the adjustments are made, the statement of financial position still balances. The first adjustment, for the accrual, is an addition to expenses and a reduction in profits for the year. Consequently, the capital side of the statement of financial position is reduced. However, there is a balancing reduction in net assets because we have included a liability in the form of an accrual.

The second adjustment, for the prepayment, is a deduction from expenses and an increase in profits for the year. Consequently, the capital side of the statement of financial position is increased, but there is a balancing increase in net assets because we have included a current asset in the form of a prepayment.

2 Note the position of the new items. Prepayments are usually recorded immediately below trade receivables in the list of current assets in the statement of financial position. Accruals are recorded immediately below trade payables as part of current liabilities.

The accounting adjustments which arise because of accruals can be difficult to assimilate at first. However, there are several examples at the end of the chapter which will help to reinforce your understanding.

Before moving on, try the following self-test question.

Peter's business paid annual rental of £150 000 in advance on 1 July 20X5. The following year there was a rental increase of 10% and the amount paid on 1 July 20X6 was £165 000. Explain how these amounts are accounted for in the business's financial statements for the year ended 31 December 20X6.

Self-test question 4.2 (answer at the end of the book)

4.4 CURRENT ASSET MEASUREMENT: INVENTORY AND TRADE RECEIVABLES

This section of the chapter examines the measurement of inventory and trade receivables, including the need for allowances against their value in certain circumstances.

4.4.1 Inventory

The value of inventory at year-end is measured as follows:

Number of items in inventory × value

Where there are many different types of inventory, the valuation process can be quite complex. The number of items in inventory is usually established by means of an inventory count (sometimes referred to as 'stocktaking') carried out on the last day of the financial year. Value is generally, but not always, cost. As we saw earlier in the chapter, it may be necessary to add in certain items (such as import duties) to the cost of purchasing goods. Also, it can happen that inventory loses some part of its value before it can be sold, for example, where inventory is accidentally damaged, or where it does not hold its value for long.

The fundamental rule to be applied to inventory valuation is:

Inventory is valued at the lower of cost and net realizable value

Net realizable value is the amount for which the inventory could be sold, less any incidental expenses of sale. Where net realizable value is lower than cost, it must be applied in valuing inventory in order to avoid overstating the asset of inventory. The following example illustrates the effect of different values for cost and net realizable value.

Example 4.8

Taruni runs a wholesale business dealing in novelty items and toys. The recent winners of a massive televised talent show, the Neolithic Hamsters, have followed up their success with a tour across the UK. The tour's promoters have rushed out a range of supporting merchandise – T shirts, cuddly hamster toys, and so on. This type of merchandise presents a difficult problem for Taruni in judging just how much to keep in inventory. While the Hamsters remain popular the merchandise will sell very well and there is likely to be a strong demand for it. However, the market for such items is fickle and unreliable because relatively few talent show winners are popular for more than a few months.

The Neolithic Hamsters, it emerges, have a shorter shelf life than average and public interest disappears quickly. Taruni has miscalculated her purchasing and is now left with 3000 giant cuddly hamsters. They originally cost her £6.50 each from the manufacturer and she was able to sell them to shops for £9.50 each at the height of the interest in the Neolithic Hamsters.

In order to be able to value the hamsters still in inventory at her year-end date, 31 August, Taruni needs to know whether she will be able to sell them at a price above £6.50, the original cost to her. If so, she will value the inventory at cost price – £6.50 × 3000 = £19 500.

Taruni makes enquiries. Unfortunately, hers is not the only business trying to unload hamsters in a hurry. The tour promoters misjudged the whole merchandising promotion. Finally, in early September, Taruni finds a man who runs several street market stalls. He is prepared to take the hamsters off her hands for a price of £2 each, and he even offers to come and collect them in his van from her warehouse. In the circumstances Taruni feels she has little choice but to accept the offer.

It is clear that Taruni will make a loss on the inventory. At 31 August the inventory items were no longer worth £6.50 each. She must value at the lower of cost and net realizable value, i.e. the lower of £6.50 and £2.

Revenue for the year is £265 331. Opening inventory was £42 307, purchases amounted to £165 956 and closing inventory, apart from the hamsters, was £19 952.

As noted above, if the hamsters are valued at cost, the total value is £19 500. If they are valued at net realizable value, the total value is £2 × 3000 = £6000.

In the table below we will assess the effect on Taruni's gross profit of valuing the hamsters at cost, and at net realizable value.

	Hamsters at cost £	Hamsters at net realizable value £
Revenue	265 331	265 331
Cost of sales		
Opening inventory	42 307	42 307
Add: purchases	165 956	165 956
Less: closing inventory (19 952 + 19 500)	(39 452)	
Less: closing inventory (19 952 + 6 000)	–	(25 952)
	168 811	182 311
Gross profit	96 520	83 020
Gross profit margin	36.4%	31.3%

The difference between the two figures for gross profit is £13 500 – that is, the loss per item of £4.50 × 3000 units of inventory. This has been a very costly error in purchasing.

Businesses involved in the sale of fashionable items always face the risk that their inventory will go out of fashion before it can be sold. Purchasing in such businesses involves a high level of skill, judgement and experience. However, the risk is likely to be absorbed to some extent by charging high prices for the goods while the fashion lasts.

4.4.2 Trade Receivables

Earlier in this chapter the issue of income recognition was discussed: income from a transaction is recognized at the point where goods are despatched or when services are rendered. Where goods and services are supplied on credit, there is a time lag between the initial recognition of the transaction and the settlement of it in cash. The risk for the business supplying the goods or services is that the purchaser will fail to pay up. Businesses can take certain precautions against this happening: for example, they can use credit agencies to obtain advice on whether or not to offer credit to prospective purchasers. Larger businesses often employ their own credit control staff to make decisions about offering credit, and to chase up unpaid debts. But even in the most highly-organized businesses, unpaid invoices can become a problem.

Trade receivables in the statement of financial position represent the total value of unpaid sales invoices. If customers who owe money cannot or will not pay the amounts owed, there is an obvious problem for the business. There is also an accounting problem to be solved. In order to ensure that the statement of financial position provides information that is useful and reasonably accurate, trade receivables should be measured at their 'recoverable amount', that is, the amount that can be realistically expected to be paid within a reasonable period of time after the financial year-end.

Accounting adjustments to receivables are made to cover two eventualities:

1 Bad trade receivables: these are amounts that will almost certainly not be paid.
2 Doubtful trade receivables: these are amounts owing that may not be recoverable.

The next example illustrates the difference between these two categories, and explains the accounting adjustments required.

Example 4.9

Hilda runs a business which supplies water filter equipment. She allows customers 30 days credit. At her financial year-end, 31 May 20X5, the total of her trade receivables list is £38 384. She has problems with two of the trade receivable balances, as follows:

1 £1200 is owed by Jimbo Associates. Jimbo, head of the business, has disappeared to South America taking with him all the cash that was left in his business and leaving many angry creditors behind. It emerges that police in several countries wish to interview him. His creditors, who include Hilda, are unlikely ever to receive payment. From Hilda's point of view this is a bad trade receivable.
2 Hilda sells goods at a total price of £3985 to a firm, Bernini & Co, on her normal terms of trade which are payment within 30 days of receipt of invoice. Three months pass and by her year-end, 31 May, Hilda has still not been paid. For the last month, she has rung Bernini & Co every week, and every Monday Mr Bernini gives her his personal assurance that the cheque will be in the post by Friday. Hilda is beginning to have doubts about these assurances and intends to threaten Bernini with legal action if the receivable amount is not settled.

There is a difference between the trade receivables described above. In the first case Hilda will never receive the money. In the second case, there is a possibility that Mr Bernini will be sufficiently impressed by the threat of legal action to pay up without further fuss.

How should these receivables be recorded in Hilda's accounts?

In the first case, the receivable amount has ceased to be an asset. It is a bad trade receivable and it should be excluded from the total of trade receivables.

In the second case, it is not clear whether or not the amount can be recovered. Hilda will treat this item as a doubtful trade receivable. The appropriate accounting treatment is to make an allowance against the doubtful amount. The allowance is deducted from trade receivables in the year-end statement of financial position.

Trade receivables will be shown as follows at 31 May in Hilda's statement of financial position:

Trade receivables (£38 384 – 1200)	37 184
Less: allowance	(3 985)
	33 199

The £1200 due from Jimbo is excluded altogether. The amount due from Bernini remains in the list because it might be recovered in due course, but is deducted from the total in the form of an allowance.

The £1200 represents an actual loss of profit. The asset of trade receivables is reduced and so, consequently, is Hilda's profit.

The £3985 is a potential loss of profit. It is recognized, for the time being, as a deduction from profit for the year ended 31 May 20X5.

Next, we will look at how these adjustments fit into Hilda's accounts for the whole year. She has the following list of balances at 31 May 20X5, before making any adjustments to the trade receivables. Each item is identified as belonging in the trading account, the rest of the statement of profit or loss or the statement of financial position.

	£	
Inventory at 1 June 20X4	34 401	Trading account
Sundry administration expenses	1 270	Statement of profit or loss
Cash at bank	1 700	Statement of financial position
Drawings	38 380	Statement of financial position
Premises costs	26 670	Statement of profit or loss
Marketing expenses	2 190	Statement of profit or loss
Travelling expenses	1 630	Statement of profit or loss
Purchases	281 830	Trading account
Trade receivables	38 384	Statement of financial position
Non-current assets	18 361	Statement of financial position
Staffing costs	21 010	Statement of profit or loss
Telephone	2 620	Statement of profit or loss
Trade payables	34 600	Statement of financial position
Capital at 1 June 20X4	49 855	Statement of financial position
Revenue	389 005	Trading account
Delivery van expenses	2 967	Statement of profit or loss
Insurance	2 047	Statement of profit or loss
Inventory at 31 May 20X5	35 433	Trading account and statement of financial position

From the balances and the information about bad and doubtful trade receivables the following accounting statements can be drawn up for Hilda's business.

Hilda: Statement of profit or loss for the year ended 31 May 20X5

	£	£
Revenue		389 005
Cost of sales		
Opening inventory	34 401	
Add: purchases	281 830	
	316 231	
Less: closing inventory	(35 433)	
		(280 798)
Gross profit		108 207

Expenses

Premises costs	26 670
Staffing costs	21 010
Marketing expenses	2 190
Delivery van expenses	2 967
Travelling expenses	1 630
Telephone	2 620
Insurance	2 047
Sundry administration expenses	1 270
Bad trade receivables	1 200
Allowance for doubtful trade receivables	3 985

	(65 589)
Net profit	42 618

Hilda: Statement of financial position at 31 May 20X5

	£	£	£
ASSETS			
Non-current assets			18 361
Current assets			
Inventory		35 433	
Trade receivables	37 184		
Less: allowance	(3 985)		
		33 199	
Cash at bank		1 700	
			70 332
			88 693
CAPITAL AND LIABILITIES			
Capital			
Opening capital balance 1 June 20X4		49 855	
Add: net profit for the year		42 618	
		92 473	
Less: drawings		(38 380)	
Closing capital balance 31 May 20X5			54 093
Current liabilities			
Trade payables			34 600
			88 693

Notes:

1 After the adjustments are made in respect of trade receivables, the statement of financial position still balances. Assets are depleted by the amount of the adjustments, but so is profit. The reduced profit decreases the capital side of the statement of financial position by the same total amount.

2 The total for trade receivables includes the amount owed by Bernini & Co. The trade receivables total will continue to include this amount until either:

   a) it is paid

   b) Hilda concludes that the receivable has gone bad.

Let us look at the two possibilities in turn. If the amount is paid by Bernini & Co the asset of trade receivable (£3985) will be replaced by the asset of cash. The allowance for the doubtful receivable would no longer be necessary and it would have to be removed from the accounts. This essentially involves reversing the original adjustment. The allowance would cease to exist and profit would be increased by £3985 in the next following period.

If Hilda concludes that the receivable has gone bad, the allowance will prove to have been necessary. The amount would be removed from the list of trade receivables and the allowance would also be removed. We can see from the statement of financial position above that the net effect of this adjustment on assets would be nil.

SPECIFIC AND GENERAL ALLOWANCES AGAINST RECEIVABLES The type of allowance for doubtful receivables made by Hilda in the example above is 'specific'. That means that the allowance relates to a certain specific receivable. Sometimes, however, businesses make 'general' allowances against doubtful receivables, as illustrated in the example below.

Example 4.10

Walter sells goods on credit. Usually the invoices are for small amounts and at any time Walter has about 500 busi-nesses and traders who owe him money. He knows, on the basis of many years' experience, that a few of the trade receivables will go bad, but it is not usually possible to identify them specifically. He has calculated that, on average, about 1.5% of the value of trade receivables will not be paid.

Walter's accountant recommends that at his year-end, 30 September 20X7, he should make a general allowance for doubtful receivables. The total of trade receivables balances at that date is £52 250.

The general allowance is calculated at 1.5% of £52 250, ie. £784 to the nearest pound. Walter's accountant makes the adjustment. Profit for the year is reduced by £784, and trade receivables are shown in the year-end statement of financial position as follows:

Trade receivables	£52 250
Less: allowance	(784)
	£51 466

At 30 September 20X8 Walter's trade receivables total is £59 942, and his accountant again advises him to make a general allowance of 1.5%. 1.5% of £59 942 is £899 (to the nearest pound). What accounting adjustment is necessary for this?

Walter has £784 recorded as an allowance in his accounts. The accounting adjustment to be made at 30 September 20X8 is £899 − £784 = £115.

£115 is added to the existing allowance and is deducted from the profit for the year.

Trade receivables are shown in the year-end statement of financial position as follows:

Trade receivables	£59 942
Less: allowance	(899)
	£59 043

Chapter Summary

The earlier part of the chapter built on the content of Chapter 3 by explaining the accounting treatment of returns of goods, discounts allowed and delivery charges. The chapter also introduced the important topics of income and expense recognition and the application of the accruals convention in accounting. Some of the complexities involved in the measurement of certain current asset categories (inventory and trade receivables) were then introduced. Accountants often need to adjust current asset measurements in order to ensure that the accounting information presented to users of financial statements is as useful as possible.

A lot of quite complex material has been covered in this chapter. You should ensure that you complete as many of the end-of-chapter questions as necessary to be sure of completely understanding all the principles and practices described in the chapter.

Internet Resources

Book's companion website summary

The website contains the following resources in respect of Chapter 4:

Students' section

A multiple choice quiz containing ten questions
Eight additional questions with answers

Lecturers' section

Answers to end-of-chapter exercises 4.11 to 4.18
Six additional questions with answers
Case study
Testbank
Instructor's manual
PowerPoint presentation

Exercises: Answers at the End of the Book

4.1 Oscar's trading company prepares accounts to 31 December. In the year to 31 December 20X1 the following trading transactions occur:

	£
Revenue	72 411
Purchases	53 005
Sales returns	361
Purchases returns	1 860

Inventory at 1 January 20X1 was £4182, and at 31 December 20X1 it was £5099. What is Oscar's gross profit for the year?

a) £21 822
b) £18 102
c) £18 824
d) £22 544

4.2 Omar imports onyx picture frames from India. He prepares accounts to 30 April each year. In the year ended 30 April 20X4 he records the following totals for trading transactions:

	£
Revenue	347 348
Purchases	240 153
Import duties	6 043
Sales returns	2 971
Purchases returns	1 800

Omar's opening inventory at 1 May 20X3 was £43 730 and his closing inventory at 30 April 20X4 was £41 180.

What is Omar's gross profit for the year?

a) £97 431
b) £99 773
c) £109 517
d) £91 388

4.3 Poppy imports and sells display fireworks. She supplies her customers on credit terms, requiring payment of invoices within 30 days. In order to encourage early payment she offers customers a discount of 0.5% of invoice value for receipt of payment within 30 days.

The following is a list of Poppy's account balances for all sales and expenses items at 28 February 20X3:

	£
Staffing costs	9 777
Opening inventory at 1 March 20X2	7 140
Sales returns	3 997
Import duties	9 911
Rental	17 211
Discounts allowed	716
Telephone charges	1 227
Purchases	123 057
Insurance	8 204
Marketing	1 888
Administrative expenses	922
Electricity	1 604
Delivery van expenses	2 107
Revenue	220 713
Inventory at 28 February 20X3	7 393

Prepare Poppy's statement of profit or loss for the year ended 28 February 20X3.

4.4 Pookie's business involves telephone sales, so her business telephone bills are high. Her accounting year ends on 31 August, and in the year ended 31 August 20X2 she has received bills for telephone charges as follows:

Date received	Date paid	Period covered	Amount £
9 October 20X1	15 October 20X1	1.7.X1 – 30.9.X1	9 760
5 January 20X2	15 January 20X2	1.10.X1 – 31.12.X1	12 666
6 April 20X2	14 April 20X2	1.1.X2 – 31.3.X2	8 444
8 July 20X2	12 July 20X2	1.4.X2 – 30.6.X2	9 530

Pookie estimates that her telephone charges for July and August will be 2/12 of the total of the charges for the 12 months ended 30 June 20X2.

What is the telephone expense for inclusion in Pookie's statement of profit or loss for the year ended 31 August 20X2? (Work to the nearest pound.)

a) £40 400
b) £40 626
c) £47 133
d) £33 667

4.5 Patience pays a subscription to a business trade association annually in advance. The subscription is due on 30 September each year, to cover one year running from 1 October. Patience's accounting year runs to 28 February.

The subscriptions paid in September 20X0 and 20X1 are as follows:

20X0	£644
20X1	£796

What are the amounts included in prepayments for this expense at 28 February 20X1 and 20X2? (Work to the nearest pound.)

a) 20X1: £268   20X2: £332

b) 20X1: £376   20X2: £464.

c) 20X1: £376   20X2: £332

d) 20X1: £268   20X2: £464

4.6 Simon trades in soft furnishings from shop premises. He provides basic summaries of his transactions for his accountant, Bernie, who prepares his final accounts and tax computation. The business year-end is 31 July.

Simon's income and expense transaction totals for the year ended 31 July 20X6, before any necessary year-end adjustments, are as follows:

	£
Delivery expenses	2 490
Opening inventory at 1 August 20X5	38 888
Income from curtain-making service	6 519
Costs of curtain-making service	2 797
Shop rental	18 750
Business rates	3 510
Assistant's wages	22 379
Insurance	4 478
Electricity	2 064
Travelling expenses	603
Revenue	317 342
Telephone	1 035
Purchases	230 133
Discounts received	377
Trade subscriptions	165
Charitable donations	500
Closing inventory at 31 July 20X6	39 501

Notes:
1. Of the £4478 included above for insurance, £501 relates to the period after 1 August 20X6.
2. Simon has two very trustworthy assistants working in the shop. As well as wages, he pays each of them an annual bonus of 0.5% of total sales (not including income from the curtain-making service). An accrual needs to be made for this item.
3. Electricity charges of £377 require accrual.
4. Bernie always makes an accrual for his own fees when drawing up Simon's accounts. He estimates that the fee required for the year ended 31 July 20X6 will be £800.

5. In conversation, Simon mentions that he has been having a lot of trouble with the occupants of the shop next door who regularly leave rubbish scattered on the forecourt which serves both shops. Simon has taken legal advice to see whether he can obtain a legal injunction, but he has not yet received a bill from the solicitor for work done. At Bernie's request Simon contacts the solicitor for an estimate of the fees at 31 July 20X6. The solicitor tells Simon that time charges for consultation and correspondence amount to about £350. Bernie and Simon agree that an accrual should be made for this amount.

Prepare a statement of profit or loss for Simon for the year ended 31 July 20X6 and calculate the totals for accruals and prepayments for inclusion in the statement of financial position at that date.

4.7 Ted sells belts and accessories to fashion stores around the country, buying most of his goods from China. Long experience in the business has developed his judgement in purchasing because he needs to be able to judge fashion trends at least six months in advance. But even Ted makes mistakes.

In his accounting year ended 31 December 20X6, Ted buys in a range of coordinating accessories in hot pink. By the middle of the year Ted realises that he has misjudged the market. This year's colours are sludgy browns and greens and there is no demand for pink.

In total Ted's purchases for the year are £379 322. Of these, £21 900 related to the pink items and £17 750 of the inventory remains unsold at the year-end. Ted's revenue is £599 790 for the year. Total opening inventory (which included no pink items, and which was valued at cost) was £49 071, and total closing inventory is £62 222 including the unsold £17 750 of pink items. Ted has had an offer from a discounter of £6000 for all the pink items which remain in inventory.

Draw up a trading account which values closing inventory at the lower of cost and net realizable value. Calculate Ted's gross profit margin and compare it to the gross profit margin which would have been achieved if the whole of closing inventory were valued at cost.

4.8 Ulrich prepares his accounts to 31 July each year. At 31 July 20X5 his trade receivables list totals £397 700. Included in the list is an amount of £17 000 owing by Gayle Associates. Gayle Associates has recently ceased to trade and Ulrich has been told by Gayle's administrator that there is little likelihood of him ever recovering the £17 000 owing to him.

Ulrich is concerned that some of the other businesses that owe him money could run into difficulties. He decides to make a general allowance for doubtful debts of 1% of receivables balances that have been outstanding for more than three months at 31 July 20X5 (excluding the £17 000 owed by Gayle). He has never previously made an allowance against receivables.

An analysis of Ulrich's receivables at 31 July 20X5 shows the following:

	£
Outstanding for one month or less	169 930
Outstanding for between one month and three months	143 370
Outstanding for over three months	67 400
Gayle Associates	17 000
	397 700

How will trade receivables be presented in Ulrich's statement of financial position at 31 July 20X5? What is the effect of bad and doubtful receivables on Ulrich's profit for the year?

4.9 Ursula is a wholesaler trading in stationery supplies. She sells to offices and shops around the country and at any one time has up to 350 customers due to pay her. She allows 30 days credit but finds that her bigger customers are quite likely to exceed this limit. At 31 December 20X8 Ursula has the following balances in her accounts:

	£
Assistant's wages	10 008
Non-current assets	23 360
Opening inventory at 1 January 20X8	31 090
Discounts allowed	1 046
Trade payables	25 920
Discounts received	361
Electricity	4 850
Business and water rates	3 899
Warehouse rental	11 070
Telephone	2 663
Trade receivables	50 354
Opening capital at 1 January 20X8	70 219
Cash at bank	361
Insurance	3 414
Delivery costs	4 490
Drawings	33 988
Administration charges	3 242
Purchases	239 285
Revenue	326 620
Closing inventory at 31 December 20X8	30 048

Notes:

1. Ursula has recently been informed that a debtor of hers, Wainwright, has left the country owing large amounts of money. Ursula is advised by her accountant that the trade receivable should be treated as completely irrecoverable, and should be written off.
2. At 31 December 20X8 there are accrued charges for electricity of £338.
3. The accountant's fees in respect of the year are likely to be in the region of £700. This amount should be accrued.
4. Two trade receivables amounts are giving Ursula some cause for concern. £398 has been owed by Wilson for almost six months. Wilson assures Ursula via frequent telephone calls that the payment will be made when he gets back on his feet after a devastating fire at his offices. £700 is owed for stationery supplies to a friend of Ursula who started a new business a few months ago. The friend assures Ursula that the bill will be paid, but Ursula knows that the new venture is not going well. Ursula decides to make an allowance against both of these amounts.
5. Of the insurance balance of £3414, £622 relates to the next accounting year and should be treated as a prepayment.

Prepare a statement of profit or loss for Ursula for the year ended 31 December 20X8, and a statement of financial position at that date, incorporating all the adjustments noted.

4.10 Briefly explain the following accounting terms, providing an illustrative example in each case:

a) recognition
b) accruals
c) net realizable value
d) going concern.

Exercises: Answers Available on the Lecturers' Section of the Book's Website

4.11 Olivia's trading company prepares accounts to 31 August each year. In the year ended 31 August 20X5, the following trading transactions occur:

	£
Revenue	193 306
Purchases	144 315
Sales returns	1 836
Purchases returns	63

Opening inventory at 1 September 20X4 was £16 399 and closing inventory at 31 August 20X5 was £17 041.

What is Olivia's gross profit for the year?

a) £47 797
b) £51 469
c) £47 860
d) £51 658

4.12 Ophelia imports glass ornaments from Norway. She prepares financial statements to 30 June each year. In the year ended 30 June 20X9 she records the following totals for trading transactions:

	£
Revenue	83 722
Purchases	65 277
Special charges for safety packaging	604
Sales returns	426
Purchases returns	291

Opening inventory at 1 July 20X8 was £5799. Closing inventory at 30 June 20X9 was £5904.
What is Ophelia's gross profit for the year?

a) £18 084
b) £18 437
c) £18 663
d) £17 811

4.13 Paolo trades in promotional goods. His customers order items like pens, playing cards, golf balls, and so on, printed with their own logo. Paolo keeps an inventory of blank goods. When he receives an order from a customer he sends the plain items of inventory to a local printer who adds the customer's logo and address details. The business is run from a shed in Paolo's back garden at home. The shed is supplied with electricity; the cost of the electricity is billed together with Paolo's domestic supply. He estimates that 1/6 of the bill is attributable to electricity used in the shed. His electricity bills for the year to 31 March 20X2 total £3072.

Apart from the electricity, Paolo's records show the following items of revenue and expenses for the year:

	£
Discounts allowed to customers	88
Travelling expenses	3 914
Revenue	118 242
Opening inventory at 1 April 20X1	5 918
Cost of printing	17 291
Telephone	1 671
Mobile telephone call charges	419
Purchases	43 947
Discounts received from suppliers	133
Accountancy and tax advice	800
Office sundry expenses	977
Marketing	2 663
Interest received	204
Purchases returns	1 774
Closing inventory at 31 March 20X2	4 261

Prepare Paolo's statement of profit or loss for the year ended 31 March 20X2.

4.14 In 20X6 the gas bills for Peregrine's business are received and paid as follows:

Date received	Date paid	Period covered	Amount £
4 March 20X6	10 March 20X6	1.12.X5 – 28.2.X6	841
6 June 20X6	20 June 20X6	1.3.X6 – 31.5.X6	790
6 September 20X6	15 September 20X6	1.6.X6 – 31.8.X6	654
9 December 20X6	20 December 20X6	1.9.X6 – 30.11.X6	752

Peregrine prepares accounts to 31 December each year. He estimates that gas used in December 20X6 would be billed at about £300.

What figure for gas expense should be included in Peregrine's accounts for the year ended 31 December 20X6? (Work to the nearest pound.)

a) £2 737
b) £3 037
c) £3 057
d) £2 457

4.15 Paula's business expenses for the year ended 31 October 20X3 are summarized as follows:

Insurance	£7 280
Telephone	£2 017
Other expenses	£36 470

Examination of the detailed transactions in the insurance account shows the following:

	£
Insurance charges for seven months to 31 May 20X3	2 660
Paid 3 June for one year from 1 June 20X3 to 31 May 20X4	4 620
	7 280

Examination of the detailed transactions in the telephone account shows the following:

	£
Bill for period 1 November 20X2 – 31 January 20X3	690
Bill for period 1 February 20X3 – 30 April 20X3	627
Bill for period 1 May 20X3 – 31 July 20X3	700
	2 017

The bill for the three-month period to 31 October 20X3 was not received until after the year-end. The amount of the bill was £696.

What is the total amount of Paula's business expenses for inclusion in her statement of profit or loss for the year ended 31 October 20X3?

a) £45 767
b) £43 768
c) £43 072
d) £41 825

4.16 Sylvester runs a consultancy business, employing two members of staff as consultants and a secretarial assistant. Because he has done an accountancy course, he is able to prepare his own accounting records and statements. He consults an accountant periodically for tax advice. Sylvester's accounting year-end date is 31 January.

In the year ended 31 January 20X7 Sylvester has built up the following income and expenditure balances on his accounts:

	£
Staff consultants' salaries	47 090
Secretarial assistant's salary	14 441
Premises expenses: office rental	12 750
Premises expenses: other	4 419
Consultancy fees	239 000
Telephone: office	4 200
Mobile telephone	2 419
Entertainment	3 007
Membership subscriptions	1 136
Administration costs	3 422
Sundry expenses	1 620
Electricity	5 187

Notes:

1. Sylvester pays the two assistant consultants a basic salary plus a bonus based upon performance. The bonus for each consultant for the year ended 31 January 20X7 will be the higher of 10% of total consultancy fees billed in the year and £24 500. The bonus element of salaries must be accrued for at the year-end.

2. £366 of the membership subscriptions relate to the period after 31 January 20X7.

3. Telephone charges include bills for the ten months to 30 November 20X6. Telephone charges for the business vary very little from month to month and the charges for December and January should be in line with previous months.

4. Sylvester rings his accountant for an estimate of costs in relation to tax advice for the year. The accountant suggests that an accrual of £400 will probably be appropriate.

Prepare Sylvester's statement of profit or loss for the year ended 31 January 20X7.

4.17   Umberto makes an allowance of 1.5% against his total trade receivables each year. In the year ended 31 August 20X2 he has used up £650 of this allowance because a company has gone out of business owing him money.

Umberto's trade receivables at 31 August 20X1, before allowance, were £366 000. At 31 August 20X2 trade receivables, before any allowance is taken into account, are £390 000.

How are trade receivables presented in Umberto's statements of financial position at 31 August 20X1 and 31 August 20X2? What is the effect of the allowance for doubtful receivables on Umberto's statement of profit or loss for the year ended 31 August 20X2?

4.18   Identify and explain the fundamental rule that is applied to the valuation of inventory.

5 Depreciation and amortization

Aim of the chapter

To continue the consideration of the practical application of important conventions and principles in accounting, with specific reference to the depreciation and amortization of non-current assets.

Learning outcomes

After reading the chapter and completing the exercises at the end, students should:

- Understand the application of the accruals convention of accounting to produce adjustments for depreciation and amortization.

- Understand the distinction between tangible and intangible non-current assets.

- Be able to incorporate adjustments for depreciation and amortization into a statement of profit or loss and statement of financial position.

Introduction

Chapter 4 examined some of the important conventions used in the preparation and presentation of financial statements, including the accruals assumption and the recognition of revenue, expenses, assets and liabilities. In order to calculate a realistic and useful figure for profit, it is important to set off against sales revenue for an accounting period all the expenses which have contributed to making those sales. In Chapter 4 the adjustments for prepayments and accruals were explained; these are necessary to ensure that the calculations of expenses are realistic.

However, there is a related category of adjustment that will be examined in this chapter, in respect of the gradual using up of non-current assets. This type of adjustment is referred to as **depreciation** or amortization.

5.1 ACCOUNTING FOR THE USE OF NON-CURRENT ASSETS

Non-current assets are purchased, or sometimes leased, for use in the ordinary activities of the business in order to generate sales revenue. For example, a business that delivers goods to its customers needs delivery vans. The vans are non-current assets that will normally be expected to be used in the business over a relatively long period of time, typically for several years. (Remember that Chapter 2 explained the accounting treatment of non-current assets, which are shown in the statement of financial position of a business.) However, non-current assets such as delivery vans do not last forever; eventually they will accumulate a high mileage and will become less reliable. It is likely that before this point is reached the managers of the business will decide to dispose of them and buy new replacements.

The costs of running a fleet of delivery vehicles must be matched against the sales revenue that they help to generate in an accounting period. Some of the costs are obvious: fuel, insurance, service and repair costs. However, in addition, businesses must take into account the fact that their non-current assets are gradually being used up, and so part of the original cost of the asset must be taken into account when calculating the expenses for an accounting period. The example below explains and illustrates the practical issues involved in estimating just how much of a non-current asset has been used up in an accounting period.

Example 5.1

Quickwash is a commercial laundry service used by hotels and restaurants. Dirty towels, sheets, tablecloths, and so on, are collected in one of Quickwash's fleet of delivery vans and are taken to the laundry where they are washed, dried and pressed. The clean items are then returned to the customer, usually within 24 hours.

The delivery vans are essential to the running of the business. Experience has shown that even the high-quality vans used by the business tend to develop major faults after three or four years. The laundry business is highly competitive and Quickwash cannot afford to upset customers by being late because a van has broken down. Therefore, Quickwash's management has a policy of replacing vans every three years.

At the beginning of January 20X2, Quickwash buys a van at a cost of £20 000. Management's policy on replacement means that the van will be used for no more than three years; it will be sold and replaced at the beginning of January 20X5.

Initially, on 1 January 20X2, the van is recorded at its cost of £20 000. By the end of the first year of its life, some of that value has been used up in the course of Quickwash's business activities.

HOW DO WE CALCULATE DEPRECIATION?

It is important to realize that depreciation is an estimate, not an exact figure. The amount initially spent on buying the van is a known figure (£20 000), but no one knows exactly how much the van will be sold for at the end of three years. Suppose that, based upon past experience, it is expected that the van will be sold in January 20X5 for approximately £5000. What is the total value used up over three years?

	£
Cost of van	20 000
Expected proceeds of sale in January 20X5	(5 000)
Value of van used up over three years	15 000

£15 000 is the estimate of the van's depreciation over the three years it will be owned by Quickwash. This is a cost of running the business and the accruals convention of accounting requires that part of the cost of £15 000 is included in the statement of profit or loss in each of the three years.

HOW IS DEPRECIATION SPREAD OVER THE THREE-YEAR PERIOD?

A straightforward way of spreading depreciation is to split the total figure (sometimes referred to as 'the depreciable amount') equally over the accounting periods that benefit from the use of the non-current asset. This approach would produce an annual figure for depreciation, in respect of this van, of £5000 (£15 000/3). There are other ways of spreading the cost of depreciation, and later in the chapter another method will be explained.

The equal split of depreciation over accounting periods is known as the straight-line method of depreciation. It is the most commonly used method.

This question tests understanding of the process involved in estimating depreciation.

Salvatore runs a haulage business. The business owns two heavy goods vehicles (HGVs). Business is booming, and Salvatore decides to buy a new HGV. On 1 January 20X1 he spends £65 000 on a new HGV. He plans to use it for four years. At the end of the four years he hopes to be able to sell it for approximately £25 000.

Estimate the annual depreciation charge for the new HGV using the 'straight-line' method of depreciation.

5.2 IMPACT OF DEPRECIATION ON THE FINANCIAL STATEMENTS

In applying the accruals convention, the annual charge for depreciation must be set off against sales revenue for the accounting period. Therefore, depreciation is shown as an expense in the statement of profit or loss. Depreciation also has an impact on the value of non-current assets shown in the statement of financial position. Over time, the value of non-current assets is depleted as they are used up in the course of business. Example 5.2 below explains and illustrates the impact of depreciation on the financial statements.

Example 5.2

Using the information from example 5.1, we will examine the impact of the van's depreciation on the financial statements in each of the three years of the van's life. Quickwash's accounting year-end is 31 December.

YEAR 1

The asset is acquired on 1 January 20X2 at a cost of £20 000 paid out of the business bank account. Following the accounting equation (explained in Chapter 2) Quickwash reduces the current asset of cash at the bank, and non-current assets are increased by the same amount.

At 31 December 20X2 the van has been in use for one year. In example 5.1 we estimated an annual depreciation charge of £5000. Therefore, in Quickwash's statement of profit or loss for the year ended 31 December 20X2 a depreciation expense of £5000 is recognized. This expense reduces profit by £5000.

In the statement of financial position at 31 December 20X2, under the non-current assets heading, the van is recorded at its value after taking into account the depreciation charged:

	£
Van at cost	20 000
Less: depreciation	(5 000)
Carrying amount of van	15 000

Some points to note:

1 It is conventional to show the original cost value of non-current assets, less a deduction for depreciation.
2 Cost less depreciation is described as the 'carrying amount' of the non-current asset.
3 Quickwash owns several vans. The cost and depreciation of this particular van will be included in an overall total for vans.
4 The carrying amount of the van in the statement of financial position has been reduced from £20 000 to £15 000. At 31 December 20X2 it might be possible to sell the van on the secondhand market for more or less than £15 000. The carrying amount of a non-current asset is not the same, except by coincidence, as the market value.

YEAR 2

At 31 December 20X3 the van has been in use for two years. The statement of profit or loss should include the amount of depreciation for the year; as in Year 1 the amount of depreciation expense in respect of this van is £5000.

In the statement of financial position at 31 December 20X3 the carrying amount of the van has reduced, because more of its value has been used up in Quickwash's business activities.

	£
Van at cost	20 000
Less: depreciation	(10 000)
Carrying amount of van	10 000

Note that after each year of use in the business the carrying amount of the asset diminishes.

YEAR 3

At 31 December 20X4 the van has been in use for three years. The statement of profit or loss should include the expense of the van's depreciation for the year; this is the amount that has to be matched against sales revenue. An expense of £5000 is recognized in total expenses, reducing profit for the year by £5000.

In the statement of financial position at 31 December 20X4 the carrying amount of the van has reduced, because more of its value has been used up in Quickwash's business activities.

	£
Van at cost	20 000
Less: depreciation	(15 000)
Carrying amount of van	5 000

At this point in time the van is ready for disposal. It is shown in the statement of financial position at £5000, which is the value that Quickwash's management originally estimated it could be sold for after three years. It is unlikely that their estimate will turn out to be precisely correct. (Later in the chapter we will examine what happens when a non-current asset is sold for more or less than the original estimate.)

SUMMARY

For each year that the van is used in Quickwash's business a charge of £5000 is made to the statement of profit or loss. This charge reduces profit by £5000 and represents an estimate by management of the depletion in the van's value each year. In the statement of financial position at each year-end the following carrying amounts are shown:

	20X2	20X3	20X4
	£	£	£
Van at cost	20 000	20 000	20 000
Less: accumulated depreciation	(5 000)	(10 000)	(15 000)
Carrying amount	15 000	10 000	5 000

Note that the total for depreciation ('accumulated' depreciation) increases each year as the asset is used up. The carrying amount decreases by the same amount.

5.3 INTANGIBLE ASSETS AND AMORTIZATION

At the beginning of the chapter, the term 'amortization' was introduced. Amortization works in the same way as depreciation, but is applied to intangible non-current assets, rather than tangible non-current assets. So far the examples in this book have mostly used tangible non-current assets. 'Tangible' means capable of being touched; it is a piece of accounting terminology used to refer to assets that have a physical presence, such as the vans in the

Quickwash example earlier. 'Intangible' refers to non-current assets that are used to generate sales revenue for the business, but which do not exist physically.

Examples of tangible non-current assets include: land and buildings, machinery, office equipment, vans and cars and computer equipment. Examples of intangible non-current assets include: brands, mineral extraction rights, patents and licences, and newspaper titles.

The examples of tangible non-current assets probably require no further explanation. The intangible non-current assets are perhaps less familiar and so brief explanations follow.

BRANDS Brands can be immensely valuable to the businesses that own them. Examples of world famous brands include Coca-Cola, Microsoft, Nike and McDonalds. Brand names can be bought and sold; there are firms of specialist brand valuers who can assist in fixing an appropriate price. If a business buys a brand name it is buying an intangible non-current asset that is likely to produce income over a long period.

MINERAL EXTRACTION RIGHTS Where a piece of land contains valuable minerals, its owner may make profits by extracting the ores, processing and selling them. Alternatively, the owner may license another firm or person to extract the ores over a period of time by granting a licence over the extraction rights. The purchaser of the licence is buying a non-current asset, although it is not tangible. The asset consists of the transfer of certain rights over a piece of land, not the land itself.

PATENTS AND LICENCES The inventor of a useful and potentially money-making process may decide to set up a manufacturing business to exploit the value of the process (for example, James Dyson who invented the range of Dyson vacuum cleaners). The inventor lays claim to ownership of the knowledge by registering a patent which affirms his or her rights over the knowledge. Rather than setting up in manufacturing, however, he or she may grant the right to use the process to a manufacturer in exchange for cash. The manufacturer in this case is buying the rights of access to the inventor's knowledge; such rights are often known as patent rights.

NEWSPAPER TITLES Newspaper titles are similar to brands, and can be very valuable assets. Such titles are a type of intangible asset in that they are usually very well known, with loyal readerships and with a reputation for a particular type of journalism. It is possible to buy and sell titles (sometimes known as 'mastheads'); if such a title is bought it constitutes an intangible non-current asset.

5.3.1 What About the Staff?

For many businesses that are engaged in providing services, there are relatively few non-current assets. For example, a firm of architects succeeds or fails on the reputation of the individuals employed by the firm. There is an argument for saying that, in this type of business, the staff are the principal, sometimes the only, significant asset. If so, why are members of staff not treated as intangible assets?

Chapter 2 presented the definition of an asset as follows: **Assets** are resources under the control of a business, which it will use in order to generate a profit in the future. Using the terms of this definition in the context of the example of the firm of architects, an individual architect could certainly be expected to produce work that will generate a profit in the future. To that extent, he or she could be regarded as an asset. However, the definition requires that the asset should be controlled by the business. People can be controlled by a business only to a limited extent; they all go home at the end of the working day, and they are free to leave their jobs. A machine can be completely controlled by a business, but an individual cannot.

FOOTBALL PLAYERS – A SPECIAL CASE? Major football clubs often pay very large sums of money in transfer fees (also referred to as 'player registration fees' for talented and successful players, and this is sometimes referred to as 'buying' a player. Could this type of transaction result in a person being accounted for as a non-current asset? Although it is tempting to suppose that this is the case, the player does not meet the definition of an asset, for the same reasons as explained above in the case of the firm of architects. However, there is a difference in the two examples: firms of architects do not pay transfer fees when an architect moves from one firm to another.

How should the transfer fee be accounted for? The answer is that football clubs treat the fee as an intangible non-current asset. See the real-life example 5.3.

Example 5.3 (Real-Life)

MANCHESTER UNITED PLC

A note to Manchester United's financial statements sets out the business's accounting policy on player registrations:

'The costs associated with the acquisition of players' and key football management staff registrations are capitalized at the fair value of the consideration payable. Costs include transfer fees, FAPL levy fees, agents' fees incurred by the club and other directly attributable costs. . . . Costs are fully amortized using the straight-line method over the period covered by the player's and key football management staff contract'.

This accounting policy note explains that the cost of player registrations is recognized as intangible assets ('capitalized'). The cost is then amortized over the period covered by the employment contracts.

So, football players are not an exception to the general rule. Individual players are not treated as assets in the financial statements, but the cost of their registration, including transfer costs, is treated as an intangible non-current asset. The football club has control not over the human being but instead over the individual's contract and player registration.

5.4 ACCOUNTING FOR AMORTIZATION

The accounting procedure adopted in accounting for amortization is identical to the procedure for depreciation which we examined earlier in the chapter. Note, however, that amortization is almost invariably estimated using the straight-line method. The following example will illustrate how to account for amortization.

Example 5.4

Bright & Shoesmith is a pharmaceutical manufacturing business. It is not involved itself in pharmaceutical research and development; instead it buys rights, in the form of licences to manufacture medicines, from the large pharmaceutical development firms. On 1 January 20X4 it concludes its negotiations with Exnox Worldwide to buy a licence to manufacture Nox, a sleeping pill. The contract for the licence stipulates that it lasts for a period of four years and that a manufacturing royalty of 25.6p per packet of 20 pills will be payable over the whole period of the contract. An upfront payment of £3 600 000 will be paid by Bright & Shoesmith for the licence.

In this case, Bright & Shoesmith is acquiring an intangible non-current asset in the form of a licence, for the sum of £3 600 000. It is clearly laid down in the contract terms that the licence will last for exactly four years. After four years, the intangible asset will be completely used up and there will be no value left in it. Over that four-year period, Bright & Shoesmith will receive revenue from the sale of the sleeping pills and this is the period over which the cost of acquiring the licence must be matched (in accordance with the accruals convention).

Applying the straight-line method, amortization of the licence fee amounts to £900 000 for each of the four years (£3 600 000/4). In each of the four years, amortization of £900 000 will be charged as an expense in the statement of profit or loss of Bright & Shoesmith. The business's year-end is 31 December.

The intangible non-current asset will appear as follows in the statement of financial position of the business:

At 31 December	20X4	20X5	20X6	20X7
	£	£	£	£
Intangible non-current assets				
Licence at cost	3 600 000	3 600 000	3 600 000	3 600 000
Less: accumulated amortization	(900 000)	(1 800 000)	(2 700 000)	(3 600 000)
Carrying amount	2 700 000	1 800 000	900 000	–

After four years, the licence has no value remaining in the statement of financial position. This is correct because, by that time, Bright & Shoesmith no longer has the right to manufacture the sleeping pills.

Note that part of the deal with Exnox is that a royalty must be paid on each packet of pills manufactured. This type of arrangement is quite commonly found in licence agreements. The royalty is part of the cost of manufacturing the pills, and it will be set off against revenue in arriving at a figure for profit. It has no bearing on accounting for the amortization of the licence.

5.5 ANOTHER METHOD OF DEPRECIATION

We have examined the straight-line method of depreciation in detail in this chapter. Straight-line is the method of depreciation most often encountered in practice, and it is the method which is almost invariably adopted in accounting for amortization.

However, there are several other possible ways of estimating depreciation. The most common, apart from straight-line, is the **reducing balance method**. This method applies a given percentage to the carrying amount at each year-end to estimate the depreciation expense. This is illustrated in the following example:

Example 5.5

B oris runs a small manufacturing company which makes soft drinks and packages fruit juice for sale to supermarkets and other retailers. He runs a fleet of four delivery vehicles. On 1 April 20X1 he buys a new replacement vehicle at a cost of £15 000. Boris adopts the reducing balance method for depreciation on the vehicles, at a rate of 25% per annum. What is the depreciation expense for each of the three years to 31 March 20X2, 20X3 and 20X4, and what is the carrying amount to be included for this vehicle at each year-end?

YEAR 1

The first year of ownership is the year to 31 March 20X2.

The depreciation expense for the delivery vehicle is 25% of the original cost of the asset: $25\% \times £15\ 000 = £3750$. This will be shown as part of the expense of depreciation in the statement of profit or loss.

In the statement of financial position at 31 March 20X2 the vehicle will be recognized and presented as follows:

Vehicle at cost	£15 000
Less: depreciation	3 750
Carrying amount of vehicle	£11 250

YEAR 2

For the second year of ownership the depreciation expense for the delivery vehicle is 25% of the carrying amount at the beginning of the accounting year: $25\% \times £11\ 250 = £2813$ (to the nearest pound). This will be shown as part of the expense of depreciation in the statement of profit or loss.

In the statement of financial position at 31 March 20X3 the vehicle will be recognized and presented as follows:

Vehicle at cost	£15 000
Less: depreciation (3750 + 2813)	6 563
Carrying amount of vehicle	£ 8 437

YEAR 3

For the third year of ownership the depreciation expense for the delivery vehicle is 25% of the carrying amount at the beginning of the accounting year: 25% × £8437 = £2109 (to the nearest pound). This will be shown as part of the expense of depreciation in the statement of profit or loss.

In the statement of financial position at 31 March 20X4 the vehicle will be recognized and presented as follows:

Vehicle at cost	£15 000
Less: depreciation (3750 + 2813 + 2109)	8 672
Carrying amount of vehicle	£ 6 328

SUMMARY

The depreciation charge to the statement of profit or loss for the vehicle is as follows for each of the three years:

20X2	£3 750
20X3	£2 813
20X4	£2 109

In the statement of financial position at each year-end the following values are included:

	20X2 £	20X3 £	20X4 £
Vehicle at cost	15 000	15 000	15 000
Less: accumulated depreciation	3 750	6 563	8 672
Carrying amount	11 250	8 437	6 328

The following points should be noted:

1 Each year the depreciation charge to the statement of profit or loss falls. This may reflect the pattern of usage of the non-current asset more accurately than the straight-line method, depending upon how the asset is used up. Cars and other vehicles frequently lose a substantial amount of value in the first year of ownership from new, so the reducing balance method may be more realistic for such assets.
2 It takes many years of depreciation before the asset value is reduced to nil.
3 As with the straight-line method of depreciation it is possible to build in to the calculation the expected proceeds of sale at the end of the planned period of ownership. This requires the use of a mathematical formula. In this book none of the exercises will require use of the formula to calculate an appropriate rate of depreciation: the rate will be given in all cases.
4 Businesses may select a combination of methods for depreciating different types of non-current asset. Having selected a method, or methods, to apply to different assets it would be expected that the business would use the methods consistently. This is so that realistic comparisons between different years' results are made possible.
5 The cost in the statement of financial position of £15 000 does not change.

S ilvio runs a mobile hairdressing business. His annual mileage is high and he expects to keep his car for no more than three years. On the advice of his accountant, Silvio applies the reducing balance method of depreciation to his car over the three years of ownership at a rate of 30% per annum. He buys a new car on 1 May 20X1, the first day of his accounting year, for £17 209. Calculate the depreciation on the car for Silvio's accounts for the three years ended 30 April 20X2, 20X3 and 20X4, and show how the car will appear in Silvio's statement of financial position on each of those dates. Calculate all figures to the nearest pound.

Self-test question 5.2 (answer at the end of the book)

5.6 LAND AND BUILDINGS

In almost all cases land is not subject to depreciation, as it does not wear out. Only in exceptional cases is it necessary to charge depreciation on land. For example, land containing mineral deposits is likely to have an enhanced value. If the minerals are mined, the land will tend to lose value, and in this case it may be appropriate to reduce the value over time by charging depreciation.

Some buildings have a longer useful life than others, but all eventually wear out. Therefore, it is appropriate to charge depreciation, although it will usually be over a long period, such as 50, 75 or 100 years. The example below shows the policy that is adopted by Smith & Nephew plc (a company listed on the London Stock Exchange) in respect of its land and buildings.

Example 5.6 (Real-Life)

T he financial statements of Smith & Nephew plc, a company engaged in health care support products, for the year ended 31 December 2015 include the following depreciation policy for land and buildings:

'Freehold land is not depreciated. The estimated useful lives of items of property, plant and equipment is 3 to 20 years and for buildings is 20 to 50 years'. (Find out more about Smith & Nephew plc on the company's website: www.smith-nephew.com)

5.7 THE ROLE OF JUDGEMENT IN ESTIMATING DEPRECIATION

In each of the examples used in the chapter up to this point we have referred to the need to 'estimate' depreciation. Depreciation is one of the many areas in accounting where precision is impossible. When a non-current asset is purchased it is impossible to be precise about how long it will remain in use in the business. The longer the life of the asset the more imprecise the estimate will be. For example, a building estimated to last 75 years might last 102 years (or 78, or 93...); in any case, the people who are making the estimates will probably not be around to answer for the quality of their judgement when the building eventually falls down.

Judgement is involved in estimating both the useful lifespan of the non-current asset and any monetary value for which the asset could be eventually sold. As we have seen, depreciation has a direct impact on profitability. It is an aspect of accounting which is, consequently, subject to manipulation. A business that is going through hard times may wish to exaggerate the estimated useful lives of non-current assets so as to spread depreciation over a longer period (and thus minimize the impact on profits). It can be very difficult to challenge the judgements made by business managers in this respect.

5.8 SALE OF A NON-CURRENT ASSET

Upon sale, the non-current asset is exchanged for the asset of cash (or possibly a receivable, if it is agreed that the cash does not have to be paid straight away). If the carrying amount of the asset is the same as the price agreed for the sale, then the exchange of one type of asset for another is straightforward. However, in most cases the carrying amount of the asset will be higher or lower than the cash price. In such cases, either a profit or a loss on sale will arise. The two following examples show the calculation of profits and losses on sale.

Example 5.7

Ibrahim runs a juice bar. His business is doing well and he has decided to buy a new improved juicing machine. He advertises the old machine in the paper for sale at £750. Takis, a restaurant owner, rings up and offers him £650 in cash for the old machine, an offer which Ibrahim decides to accept. The carrying amount of the machine in Ibrahim's accounts is £475. What is Ibrahim's profit on sale, and how will the transaction be recorded in his accounts?

The profit on sale is the proceeds of £650 less the carrying amount of £475: ie. a profit of £175. Tangible non-current assets are reduced by the carrying amount (£475) and cash at the bank is increased by £650. The profit of £175 is shown in the statement of profit or loss, thus increasing Ibrahim's capital. In summary, in terms of the accounting equation, assets (overall) increase by £175, as does capital.

Note that the 'profit' is really just an adjustment reflecting the actual outcome of the judgements made about depreciation at the start of the useful life of the asset. 'Profit' in this context arises where the asset has been over-depreciated.

Example 5.8

Adebola's delivery service uses two delivery vans. Her business policy is to replace the vans every four years. One of the vans, which was bought four years ago at a cost of £12 750, is due for replacement. Adebola depreciates the vans using the reducing balance method at a rate of 25% per annum. She accepts an offer of £3650 for the van.

What is Adebola's profit or loss on sale of the van?

First, we must calculate the carrying amount of the van after four years:

	£
Van at cost	12 750
Year 1 depreciation (25% × £12 750)	3 188
Carrying amount at end of year 1	9 562
Year 2 depreciation (25% × £9562)	2 391
Carrying amount at end of year 2	7 171
Year 3 depreciation (25% × £7171)	1 793
Carrying amount at end of year 3	5 378
Year 4 depreciation (25% × £5378)	1 345
Carrying amount at end of year 4	4 033

The proceeds of the sale of the van are less than the carrying amount after four years. Therefore, Adebola makes a loss on sale of £3650 − 4033 = £383

- Tangible non-current assets are reduced by £4033 and the asset of cash is increased by the sale proceeds of £3650. The loss of £383 is included in Adebola's statement of profit or loss for the year, thus decreasing her capital.
- In terms of the accounting equation, then, assets decrease by a net amount of £383 and capital is reduced by the same amount.
- Note that the 'loss' on sale of the asset is really the amount by which the asset has been under-depreciated.

S ergio sells one of the machines from his factory for £3010. The machine was bought new exactly five years ago for £15 000, and has been depreciated using the reducing balance method at a rate of 30% per annum.
    Calculate Sergio's profit or loss on sale of the machine.

Self-test question 5.3 (answer at the end of the book)

5.9 BUYING AND SELLING ASSETS DURING THE YEAR

In all the examples in the chapter up to this point it has been assumed that non-current assets are bought on the first day of the year and are held for an exact number of years. However, businesses may buy or sell assets at any time during the accounting period. Where this happens the business must calculate the appropriate fraction of the depreciation charge for the year.

Example 5.9

A ngelina has a card shop which uses several display stands. She decides to replace all the stands at the same time as the shop frontage is refurbished, as part of a new look for the shop. She spends £8780 on new stands on 1 May 20X2. Her accounting year-end is 31 December. The stands should last for five years before they require replacement and Angelina decides to apply the straight-line method of depreciation.
    A full year's depreciation in the accounting year ended 31 December 20X2 would be:

$$\frac{£8780}{5} = £1756$$

However, the asset has been owned for only eight months out of the accounting year, and so depreciation would be charged for only eight months:

$$£1756 \times \frac{8}{12} = £1171$$

The statement of financial position at 31 December would include the following:

Display stands at cost	£8 780
Less: depreciation	1 171
Carrying amount	£7 609

Chapter Summary

This chapter shares some of the features of Chapter 4 in that both are concerned with the practical application of accounting conventions. In particular, Chapter 5 continued to examine the impact of the accruals, or matching, convention in the specific context of accounting for non-current assets.

    Non-current assets include both tangible and intangible assets, and the distinction between these two categories was explained in the chapter. Depreciation and amortization are the terms applied, respectively, to non-current tangible assets and non-current intangible assets in describing the process by which the carrying amount of non-current assets is gradually depleted. The amount of this depletion is estimated upon the original purchase of the asset, and it should be understood that the useful life of an asset and the rate at which it is depreciated or amortized are often quite imprecise.

The questions at the end of the chapter include several examples of isolated depreciation and amortization calculations, progressing to several more which demonstrate the integration of the calculations into financial statements.

Internet Resources

Book's companion website summary

The website contains the following resources in respect of Chapter 5:

Students' section

A multiple choice quiz containing ten questions
Five additional questions with answers

Lecturers' section

Answers to end of chapter exercises 5.14 to 5.23
Six additional questions with answers
Case study
Testbank
Instructor's manual
PowerPoint presentation

Exercises: Answers at the End of the Book

5.1 Valerie runs a small delivery business. She has a van which she replaces every four years. On 1 January 20X1 she sells her old van for £2000 and buys a new one for £14 460. She expects to be able to sell it for approximately £4000 in four years' time. Assuming that Valerie adopts the straight-line method of depreciation in her accounts what is her depreciation charge for the accounting year ended 31 December 20X1?

a) £2 115
b) £3 615
c) £4 615
d) £2 615

5.2 Victoria owns a gym. In her financial year to 31 August 20X5 she buys a new exercise bike for £450. The date of purchase was 1 March 20X5. Victoria aims to keep gym equipment for three years. After three years she finds that the equipment is usually well worn and worth very little. She advertises old equipment to her members, and would usually expect to receive about £30 for an old exercise bike.

Victoria charges depreciation in her accounts on the straight-line basis. What is the depreciation charge in respect of the new exercise bike in the year to 31 August 20X5?

a) £70
b) £140
c) £75
d) £150

5.3 Vinny is expanding his electrical components business. During his accounting year ended 31 December 20X8 he buys new machinery as follows:

- On 1 April, a machine costing £10 300. The estimated useful life is five years, after which point Vinny expects that it will have a nil value.
- On 1 October, a machine costing £8580. The estimated useful life is four years, and Vinny expects the machine to fetch £2000 on the second-hand market when the time comes to dispose of it.

Working to the nearest pound, what is the total depreciation charge, on the straight-line basis, for the new machines in the year ended 31 December 20X8?

a) £3 705
b) £2 081
c) £1 956
d) £2 779

5.4 Having qualified as a mining engineer, Violet decides that she would like to go into the gold mining business. She spends a considerable period of time looking for mining opportunities. Finally, she finds a piece of land in Wales which was formerly exploited for gold mining. The activity had been abandoned some years ago because the yield was insufficient. However, Violet is convinced that the mine can once more be made profitable with the help of modern equipment and technology. She enters negotiations with the owners of the land. They refuse to sell it, but agree to grant Violet the rights for a 3.5-year period from 1 January 20X5. In exchange Violet agrees to pay £273 000, plus a fixed fee per kilo of gold extracted.

How will the purchase of the mineral rights be reflected in Violet's accounts for the year to 31 December 20X5?

5.5 Vincenzo's statement of financial position at 31 August 20X3 showed the following balances in respect of non-current assets:

	£
Buildings at cost	306 000
Less: accumulated depreciation	(18 360)
Carrying amount	287 640
Motor vehicles at cost	48 770
Less: accumulated depreciation	(16 470)
Carrying amount	32 300
Fixtures and fittings at cost	12 720
Less: accumulated depreciation	(6 360)
Carrying amount	6 360

In the year ended 31 August 20X4 no purchases or sales of non-current assets were made. Vincenzo depreciates non-current assets as follows:

- Buildings: at 2% per annum on cost on the straight-line basis.
- Motor vehicles: at 25% per annum on the reducing balance basis.
- Fixtures and fittings (which were all purchased at the same time): over 10 years on the straight-line basis.

  i) Calculate the total charge to Vincenzo's statement of profit or loss in respect of depreciation for the year ended 31 August 20X4.
  ii) Show how non-current assets will be presented in Vincenzo's statement of financial position at 31 August 20X4.

5.6 Wilma runs a wedding car service. Business is expanding and she is planning to buy a new vehicle. The basic list price of a new car is £24 400, but Wilma must pay an additional £800 for it to be sprayed white. She purchases the car on 1 March in time for the main spring and summer wedding season. Her year-end is 28 February. Wilma depreciates cars on the reducing balance basis, at 15% per annum.

What will be the depreciation charge for the first year of ownership of the new car?

a) £3 660

b) £3 780

c) £3 540

d) £4 460

5.7 At 1 January 20X9 William had the following balances in his books related to the non-current asset of cars:

Cars at cost	£38 370
Less: accumulated depreciation	(15 540)
Carrying amount	22 830

He acquired a new car on the same date for £14 447. No other cars are bought or sold during the rest of the accounting period which ends on 31 December 20X9.

William depreciates cars on the reducing balance basis at 25% per year.

What is the total charge for depreciation on cars, to the nearest pound, to be included in William's statement of profit or loss for the year ended 31 December 20X9?

a) £13 204

b) £9 319

c) £5 707

d) £9 592

5.8 Xenia no longer needs a second van in her business, and so she decides to sell it. The van originally cost £8300 and by Xenia's year-end of 31 March 20X5 depreciation had accumulated of £6330. She sells the van for £2380 on 1 April 20X5.

What is the profit or loss on the sale of the van?

5.9 Xanthe runs a florist's shop. Her assistant goes out every day in the van delivering flowers. The van accumulates high mileage quickly and Xanthe usually replaces it every three years. The van cost £10 100 on 1 June 20X1 and Xanthe has depreciated it on the reducing balance basis at 30% per year for three years. She sells it on 1 June 20X4 for £3000.

What is the profit or loss on the sale of the van?

5.10 Ying runs a wholesale business supplying art equipment to retailers. She uses two computers to keep stock and other records, one in the office and one in the warehouse. In her accounting year ended 31 December 20X6 she decides to buy a new networked computer system, with terminals in both the office and warehouse. She is able to sell both of the old computers, one for £250 and the other, which is in slightly better condition, for £300. Both computers were bought on 1 January 20X4, for a total price of £3672. They have been depreciated on the straight-line basis over four years, with the assumption that their value will be nil at the end of the four-year period. Ying disposes of them on 1 July 20X6.

What is her profit or loss on the sale of the computers?

5.11 Zoe started up an independent fast food outlet at 1 January 20X2, trading as Zoe's Snacks. Her accountant advised her that she should depreciate her machinery and fixtures over a period of between four and seven years on the straight-line basis. Zoe, who is a keen amateur accountant, decided to prepare her statement of profit or loss and statement of financial position on the basis of straight-line depreciation over a four-year period. However, she is also interested to see what difference it would make to her profits if she depreciated machinery over the maximum advisable period of seven years All machinery and fixtures were bought on 1 January 20X2.

Her books show the following list of balances (before any adjustment for depreciation) at 31 December 20X2:

	£
Revenue	132 614
Staffing costs	15 030
Rental of premises	7 400
Purchases	83 430
Electricity	2 961
Phone	1 806
Insurance	1 437
Sundry expenses	981
Accountant's fees	600
Machinery and fixtures at cost	28 760
Inventory of food etc.	1 209
Cash at bank	3 406
Trade payables	1 650
Capital introduced by Zoe	20 000
Drawings	8 453

i) Prepare the statement of profit or loss and statement of financial position for Zoe's Snacks at 31 December 20X2 making adjustments for depreciation of machinery and fixtures on the basis of the straight-line method of depreciation over four years, with an estimated residual value of nil.

ii) Calculate the increase or decrease in net profit which would arise if Zoe depreciated the machinery and fixtures on the basis of the straight-line method of depreciation over seven years.

iii) Calculate the net profit margin on the basis of (a) depreciating the non-current assets over four years; and, (b) depreciating the non-current assets over seven years.

5.12 Describe the effect of a charge for depreciation upon the components of the accounting equation.

5.13 Several football clubs, both within and outside the UK, are listed companies that are required to publish their annual reports on their websites. Use a search engine to look up a football club's most recent annual report. (If the club that you support is not required to publish its financial statements, you will have to find another club that does.) Identify and read any information you can find about player registrations and transfer fees. Write a brief report that explains how the club accounts for player registrations. (If you are studying in a group, this could be done individually or in small groups, and presented in a seminar or tutorial.)

Exercises: Answers Available on the Lecturers' Section of the Book's Website

5.14 Victor adopts the straight-line method of depreciation in his accounts. He purchases a new machine on 1 June 20X1 for £13 750. He expects to keep the machine for approximately six years, at the end of which time it will have a scrap value of about £250. Victor prepares accounts to 31 May each year.

What is the first year's depreciation charge?

a) £1 125
b) £2 250
c) £2 292
d) £2 333

5.15 Virginia runs a business which supplies food for office parties and similar functions. Food is delivered to the client's premises in vans which have been specially adapted to take shallow trays of food and which contain brackets for microwave ovens. The basic cost of a new van is £9570. When a new van is purchased Virginia sends it away for modification which costs a further £1830. On 15 August 20X2 two new vans return with the modifications complete, and Virginia puts them straight into service. Virginia expects to keep the vans for a period of six years. They are subject to severe wear and tear during their useful lives and she does not expect to get more than scrap value for them after six years. Therefore, she assumes a residual value of nil.

Virginia's accounting year-end is 31 December. She charges depreciation on a straight-line basis. In the year of acquisition and disposal of non-current assets she charges depreciation for every full month of ownership in the accounting year.

What is the depreciation charge (to the nearest pound) for the two new vans in the year ended 31 December 20X2?

a) £1 267
b) £1 063
c) £1 329
d) £1 583

5.16 Valda runs a marketing agency. She prepares her own accounts and is currently working on the statement of profit or loss and statement of financial position at 31 December 20X7. She purchased the freehold of a small office building on 1 January 20X1 for £364 000. The land value included in the purchase price is estimated at £50 000. Valda depreciates the buildings element of the freehold over 100 years, the expected useful life of the building.

Apart from the building, Valda's business owns fixtures and fittings which were purchased several years ago for £16 777. The fixtures and fittings are now fully depreciated. Also, the business owns two cars which are used for staff visiting clients. One car was bought on 1 January 20X4 for £15 300 and the other on 1 January 20X5 for £17 660. Valda depreciates the cars on a straight-line basis over their estimated useful lives of four years. Both cars have an estimated residual value of £5000.

i) Calculate the total depreciation charge to Valda's statement of profit or loss in respect of depreciation for the year ended 31 December 20X7.

ii) Show how non-current assets will be presented in Valda's statement of financial position at 31 December 20X7.

5.17 Wally's business owns several machines which he depreciates on the reducing balance basis at the rate of 10% per annum.

His statement of financial position at 31 March 20X6 showed the following balances in respect of machines:

	£
Tangible non-current assets	
Machines at cost	288 994
Less: accumulated depreciation	(107 773)
Carrying amount	181 221

On 1 April 20X6 he bought a new machine for £14 800. There were no other additions or disposals of machines in the year. What is the charge for depreciation on machines (to the nearest pound) to be included in Wally's statement of profit or loss for the year ended 31 March 20X7?

a) £28 899

b) £18 122

c) £18 739

d) £19 602

5.18 Xavier depreciates his machinery over ten years using the straight-line method. On 31 December 20X8 he sold a machine which he had owned for exactly seven years. Its original cost was £73 730. The sale proceeds were £30 000.

What is the profit or loss on the sale of the machine?

5.19 Xan has a machine at carrying amount of £13 338 in his accounts. If he sells the machine for £15 000 he makes a profit on disposal of £1662. Using the accounting equation, what is the effect on his assets, liabilities and capital?

a) ASSETS increase; CAPITAL decreases; LIABILITIES no change.

b) ASSETS decrease; CAPITAL increases; LIABILITIES increase.

c) ASSETS increase; CAPITAL increases; LIABILITIES no change.

d) ASSETS decrease; CAPITAL no change; LIABILITIES decrease.

5.20 For several years Zak has run a contract office cleaning business. He employs several part-time staff who work at night and weekends. Zak has always run the business from rented premises; he has a small office to deal with the paperwork and a storage area where cleaning equipment and machinery is kept. He also runs three vans which deliver staff and their equipment to offices around the city.

Zak has the opportunity to buy the freehold office premises he currently occupies for £51 370. He would be able to obtain a commercial mortgage for £40 000 at a rate of 8% per annum. He would like some advice on whether or not to take out the mortgage to buy the premises.

Zak has the following balances in his books at 31 March 20X2:

	£
Capital at 1 April 20X1	21 410
Bank overdraft (NB overdraft limit £20 000)	10 447
Cleaning equipment at cost	6 400
Accumulated depreciation on cleaning equipment at 1 April 20X1	1 920

	£
Office fixtures and fittings at cost	1 700
Accumulated depreciation on office fixtures and fittings at 1 April 20X1	1 660
Vans at cost	22 419
Accumulated depreciation on vans at 1 April 20X1	14 490
Trade receivables	13 796
Drawings	32 479
Trade payables	1 624
Sundry inventory of cleaning materials	1 408
Revenue	107 614
Premises rental	7 462
Electricity and other premises costs	2 444
Sundry office expenses	799
Staff costs	63 491
Accountancy and tax advice	1 200
Cleaning materials	5 177
Interest paid	390

Zak has not made any accounting adjustments in respect of depreciation in the above list of figures. He charges depreciation as follows:

Cleaning equipment	Straight-line basis over ten years. None of the equipment is fully depreciated at 31 March 20X2
Office fixtures and fittings	Straight-line basis over ten years
Vans	25% on the reducing balance basis

There were no additions or disposals of non-current assets during the year ended 31 March 20X2.

i) Prepare Zak's statement of profit or loss for the year ended 31 March 20X2 and a statement of financial position at 31 March 20X2.

ii) Advise him on whether or not, in your opinion, he should take out the mortgage and buy the premises.

5.21 Explain the purpose of making adjustments for depreciation in the accounts of businesses, briefly describing the process involved in determining the appropriate amount of depreciation.

5.22 Explain the difference between depreciation and amortization.

5.23 Describe the accruals convention in accounting, and explain how it is applied to non-current assets.

6 The statement of cash flows

Aim of the chapter

To understand the distinction between profit and cash, and the principles and practices involved in preparing a statement of cash flows

Learning outcomes

After reading the chapter and completing the exercises at the end, students should:

- Understand the distinction between profit and cash.

- Be able to draw up a statement of cash flows for a small business.

- Understand some of the messages conveyed by the statement of cash flows.

Introduction

Early in Chapter 2, it was noted that this book will be concerned with 'three principal financial statements: the statement of financial position, the statement of profit or loss and the statement of cash flows'. The first two statements have been covered extensively in Chapters 2 to 5, so it is now time to turn to the third statement. The statement of cash flows provides additional important information that allows the user of the financial statements to understand the performance and position of the business. The statement of cash flows is constructed out of the same fundamental information as the other two statements, but it presents the information in a different way, which emphasizes the flows of cash in and out of the business.

This chapter first examines the distinction between profit and cash, referring back to the accounting conventions of recognition and accruals that were examined in Chapter 4. Then it turns to the mechanics of preparation of a statement of cash flows, with demonstrations based on a business start-up and then an established business. Finally, the chapter examines some of the messages and meaning conveyed by the statement of cash flows.

6.1 THE DISTINCTION BETWEEN PROFIT AND CASH

In the long run, a profitable business generates positive cash flows. Increases in cash flows can be used to buy new non-current assets for the business or to pay a return to its investors. A loss-making business in the long run produces negative cash flows, and cash inflows in the form of new investment by investors will be required to prevent it going under.

In the short term, however, profits do not necessarily equate to positive cash inflows. In Chapter 4 we examined the conventions relating to accounting recognition and to accruals and concluded that 'accounting revenue is not the same figure as cash received and accounting expenditure is not the same as cash paid'. The application of accounting conventions moves the accounting statements away from pure cash inflows and outflows by accounting for depreciation, amortization, accruals, prepayments and any other adjustment that does not represent an immediate cash flow.

It is also important to appreciate that cash can be depleted or increased by transactions that do not affect the statement of profit or loss; for example, the purchase of non-current assets. When a non-current asset is purchased, the asset of cash is replaced by, for example, an item of machinery. This transaction produces no immediate impact on profits, although over time, profits will be depleted as the asset is subject to depreciation. (But, on the other hand, it could be expected that profits will increase as a result of having the new item of machinery in effective operation).

To demonstrate these points, Table 6.1 examines the implications for cash and profits of various common transaction types. Only in the case of the fourth transaction in the list – the sale for cash of £1600 – is the impact on cash and profit identical and simultaneous. In all other cases, there is a mismatch between cash and profit.

The differences between cash and profit relate to differences in timing. For example, an outflow of cash spent on a non-current asset is likely to produce profits (and cash inflows) sooner or later, but in the meantime, there is a gap. Sometimes, if the gap between outflows and inflows is too big, the business can be at risk of going under. Later in the chapter a detailed example shows how this can occur.

Table 6.1 **The impact of transactions on cash and profits**

Transaction	Impact on cash	Impact on profits
Borrowing £10 000 at an annual interest rate of 10%. Loan to be repaid after five years	Cash and long-term liabilities are both increased in the statement of financial position by £10 000. After five years, the loan will be repaid; cash and long-term liabilities will both be reduced by £10 000	No immediate impact on profits. Each year for five years there will be an annual interest payment of £1000. This will decrease both cash and profit
Purchasing a new car for £8000. The car is to be depreciated on the straight-line basis over four years, with the assumption of no residual value at the end of four years	Cash is reduced, and non-current assets are increased by £8000	No immediate impact on profits. Each year for four years there will be a depreciation charge of £2000 (£8000/4), but this has no effect on cash
Drawings of £3500	Cash and capital are both reduced by £3500	There is no impact on profit. Effectively, the owner is taking £3500 of his/her capital out of the business
Sale for cash of £1600	Cash is increased immediately	The sale is recognized immediately, and sales in the statement of profit or loss are increased by £1600
Sale on credit for £1600	Trade receivables are increased immediately. Provided that the debtor pays up, cash will be increased at some point in the near future	The sale is recognized immediately, and sales in the statement of profit or loss are increased by £1600

W hat is the effect on cash and on profit of the following business transactions?

1 Purchase of inventory for cash of £1800.
2 Sale of old delivery van for £360.
3 Long-term loan from brother of £5000.
4 Payment of interest on bank overdraft of £150.
5 Amortization of charge of £8000 relating to patent rights.

Self-test question 6.1 (answer at the end of the book)

6.2 PREPARING A STATEMENT OF CASH FLOWS

A very simple statement of cash flows was demonstrated early in Chapter 2. This statement comprised two parts: cash inflows and cash outflows. In practice, where statements of cash flows are prepared it is usual to produce a slightly more complex statement with the cash flows classified in a way that is intended to be helpful to the reader. International Financial Reporting Standards (IAS 7 *Statements of Cash Flow*) prescribe a statement that is divided into three principal sections:

- Operating activities: cash flows arising from the business's trading activities, such as receipts of cash in respect of sales, payments for costs such as cost of sales, staff and rental. This section of the statement is concerned with inflows and outflows relating to **working capital** items: inventory, trade receivables and trade payables.
- Investing activities: cash flows in respect of payments for resources that will generate income for the business in the future. This would include payments for non-current assets and receipts from the disposal of non-current assets.
- Financing activities: cash flows in respect of capital, for example, receipt of cash invested in the business by the owner, or the repayment of loans taken out to finance business expansion.

For the very small businesses used as most of the examples in this book so far, there is no strict requirement to produce a statement of cash flows at all. However, a statement of cash flows can often provide useful information, even in small businesses, and it is easier to learn how to do them using simple business examples first. The division of cash flows into three sections, while again not mandatory for small businesses, is helpful because the terminology becomes familiar, and then it is easier to understand when it is encountered in the context of a large business.

6.2.1 Preparing a Statement of Cash Flows: a Business Start-Up

Example 6.1 describes and illustrates the procedures involved in preparing a statement of cash flows for a new business at the end of its first year of trading. This is a useful first step in learning how to prepare statements of cash flows because the starting position at the beginning of the year is zero. Subsequently, we will look at an example of a statement of cash flows in an established business, which is a little more complicated.

Example 6.1

I sobel Buchanan started up a new business on 1 April 20X1, importing and selling handmade rugs. Her business trades as Buchanan International Designs. As well as capital of her own, she borrowed money from members of her family to get the business going. In her first year of trading Isobel bought various non-current assets and items of inventory. Her sales are made partly for cash, and partly on credit.

Isobel's statement of profit or loss for the year ended 31 March 20X2 and her statement of financial position at that date were as follows:

Buchanan International Designs: Statement of profit or loss for the year ended 31 March 20X2

	£	£
Revenue		115 622
Cost of sales		(80 379)
Gross profit		35 243
Operating expenses:		
Various expenses	23 606	
Depreciation	5 351	
		(28 957)
Operating profit		6 286
Interest paid		(2 400)
Interest received		651
Net profit		4 537

The statement of profit or loss above is set out slightly differently from those used in earlier chapters. This statement isolates a figure for operating profit, from which are added or deducted amounts of interest paid or interest received, thus producing a net profit figure. (In practice, many statements of profit or loss include a figure for operating profit.)

Buchanan International Designs: Statement of financial position at 31 March 20X2

ASSETS	£	£
Non-current assets		
Cost	22 630	
Less: accumulated depreciation	(5 351)	
		17 279
Current assets		
Inventory	19 400	
Trade receivables	4 027	
Cash	13 323	
		36 750
		54 029
CAPITAL AND LIABILITIES		
Capital		
Capital introduced	10 000	
Add: profit for the year	4 537	
	14 537	
Less: drawings	(7 500)	
		7 037
Long-term liabilities		
Loan		40 000
Current liabilities		
Trade payables		6 992
		54 029

Isobel started in business on 1 April 20X1 by putting cash into a new business bank account. The total cash deposited was £50 000 comprising £40 000 she borrowed from her family, and £10 000 of her own money. One year later, we can see from the statement of financial position that, although she has made a small profit of £4537, her bank balance has fallen to £13 323, a drop of (£50 000 − £13 323) £36 677. So, although the profit figure tells a positive story, the downside is that there has been a very large outflow of cash from the business.

WHAT HAS HAPPENED TO THE CASH?

Isobel's statement of profit or loss and statement of financial position convey a great deal of useful information but are not obviously helpful in providing answers to this important question. A statement of cash flows helps to answer the question by isolating the principal cash movements.

PREPARING ISOBEL'S STATEMENT OF CASH FLOWS

Step 1: Operating cash flows

First of all, we must examine cash flows related to the business's operating activities, ie. those cash flows involved in buying and selling, and generally operating the business. The starting point is the figure for operating profit, which is £6286. This figure is calculated by deducting cost of sales and operating expenses from sales revenue. However, this amount does not represent a simple inflow of cash because it is affected by the accruals convention in accounting:

- Operating expenses include depreciation, which is a non-cash item.
- Only part of the sales revenue has actually been received in cash (we know this because there are trade receivables in the statement of financial position). The amount received in cash is the sales revenue total less trade receivables of £4027.
- Only part of the cost of sales and operating expenses have been paid for in cash (we know this because there are trade payables in the statement of financial position). The amount paid for in cash is total operating costs and expenses, less the trade payables balance of £6992.
- Outflows of cash have taken place to purchase inventory (we know this because there is a balance of inventory in the statement of financial position). This outflow is not included in cost of sales, because under the accruals convention, closing inventory is deducted from cost of sales. The amount of the cash outflow is £19 400.

The table below adjusts the totals for sales revenue and operating costs by adding or deducting, as appropriate, non-cash items and the outflow for the purchase of inventory. The final column shows the total cash inflow or outflow.

	Statement of profit or loss	Non-cash item: depreciation	Non-cash Items: trade receivables and trade payables	Cash outflow: inventory purchase	Total cash inflow (outflow)
	£	£	£	£	£
Sales revenue	115 622		(4 027)		111 595
Operating costs*	(109 336)	5 351	6 992	(19 400)	(116 393)
Operating profit/cash flow	6 286	5 351	2 965	(19 400)	(4 798)
Interest paid	(2 400)				(2 400)
Interest received	651				651
Net profit/cash flow	4 537	5 351	2 965	(19 400)	(6 547)

* Operating costs = cost of sales (£80 379) + operating expenses (£28 957)

The first part of the statement of cash flows sets out the information from the table in the following format which demonstrates the conventional layout used in practice:

	£	£
Operating profit		6 286
Depreciation		5 351
		11 637
Less: increase in inventory	(19 400)	
Less: increase in trade receivables	(4 027)	
Add: increase in trade payables	6 992	
		(16 435)
Cash generated from operations		(4 798)
Interest paid		(2 400)
Interest received		651
Net cash outflow from operating activities		(6 547)

Before progressing to the next step, make sure that you can see how the figures in the first part of the statement of cash flows relate to the figures in the table.

Step 2: Investing cash flows

Investing cash flows comprise payments for resources that will generate income for the business in the future. Investing cash flows also comprise any receipts of cash in respect of such resources, for example, cash inflows arising from the disposal of non-current assets.

In this example, there is only one amount in respect of investing cash flows: the purchase of non-current assets at cost of £22 630.

Cash outflow	(22 630)

Remember to identify the cash outflow; it is the amount *paid* for the non-current assets, *not* the year-end carrying amount.

Step 3: Financing cash flows

Financing cash flows comprise cash flows in respect of movements in capital, for example, receipt of cash invested in the business by the owner or the repayment of loans taken out to finance business expansion. The source of information about these cash flows is the capital and long-term liabilities section of the statement of financial position. In this example, the cash inflows and outflows relating to financing are as follows:

Cash inflow: capital introduced	10 000
Cash outflow: drawings (ie. capital withdrawn)	(7 500)
Cash inflow: loan	40 000

Step 4: Completing the statement of cash flows

At this point we can pull together all the information from steps 1 to 3 and produce a complete statement of cash flows. As with all financial statements, it requires a heading.

Buchanan International Designs: Statement of cash flows for the year ended 31 March 20X2

	£	£
Cash flows from operating activities		
Operating profit		6 286
Depreciation		5 351
		11 637
Less: increase in inventory	(19 400)	
Less: increase in trade receivables	(4 027)	
Add: increase in trade payables.	6 992	
		(16 435)
Cash generated from operations		(4 798)
Interest paid		(2 400)
Interest received		651
Net cash outflow from operating activities		(6 547)
Cash flows from investing activities		
Purchase of non-current assets	(22 630)	
Net cash outflow from investing activities		(22 630)
Cash flows from financing activities		
Capital introduced	10 000	
Capital returned to owner (drawings)	(7 500)	
Long-term loan	40 000	
Net cash inflow from financing activities		42 500
Net increase in cash		13 323
Cash at beginning of period		0
Cash at end of period		13 323

The final part of the statement of cash flows shows a reconciliation between the net increase or decrease in cash, and the movements in the cash balance between the opening and closing dates. In this case, the opening balance was zero, because the example deals with a new business start-up. In a continuing business, there will be cash at both the beginning and end of the period. Note that, for this purpose, 'cash' comprises all bank balances plus any cash, such as petty cash balances.

Comments on the statement of cash flows

When deeply involved in the mechanics of preparing financial statements it is easy to lose sight of the fact that their purpose is to provide useful information. The aim of a statement of cash flows is to provide explanations for the overall movement in cash in the accounting period, by isolating and describing useful categories of cash inflows and outflows.

What additional information does the statement of cash flows for Buchanan International Designs provide? We can see that operating activities produced a net cash outflow, largely because of the cash spent on building an inventory of items for sale. The other really significant items in the statement are the substantial investments in non-current assets, which will contribute to generating revenue over more than one accounting period, and inflows arising from the initial financing of the business. At the year-end, a positive balance of £13 323 remains. Further detailed analysis in the form of cash flow budgets would be required to determine whether this amount of cash would be sufficient to finance the business in its second year of trading. (Cash flow budgets are covered in detail in Chapter 16 of this book.)

Before moving on to the next section of the chapter, try this self-test question.

Self-test question 6.2
(answer at the end of
the book)

Amy Binyon started a new business on 1 January 20X2. Extracts from her statement of profit or loss for the year ended 31 December 20X2 and her statement of financial position at that date show the following information:

Revenue	89 300
Cost of sales	56 200
Operating costs, including depreciation of £4500	22 600
Interest paid	1 000
Inventory	6 900
Trade receivables	8 500
Trade payables	9 000

Prepare a table to record adjustments between profit and operating cash flows (see the table in Step 1 of Example 6.1), and then prepare the operating section of Amy Binyon's statement of cash flows for the year ended 31 December 20X2.

6.3 DIRECT AND INDIRECT APPROACHES TO CASH FLOW

There are two possible approaches to the preparation of a statement of cash flows: direct and indirect. Example 6.1 demonstrates the indirect approach: it takes the reported profit figure, and then adjusts it for non-cash items and movements in inventory, receivables and payables to calculate cash generated from operations. This requires several lines of reconciling items, as shown in the example. The direct approach to preparing a statement of cash flows is, as the name implies, more straightforward, requiring simply two lines, as follows:

- receipts from operating activities

- payments in respect of operating activities.

Example 6.2 shows how to calculate and present this information.

Example 6.2

This example uses the same information as Example 6.1. The requirement is to present a statement of cash flows for Buchanan International Designs for the year ended 31 March 20X2, but this time, using the direct method.

The table that was used to chart movements in operating items in the explanation of Example 6.1 is used again here. The upper part of the table is shown again:

	Statement of profit or loss £	Non-cash item: depreciation £	Non-cash Items: trade receivables and trade payables £	Cash outflow: inventory purchase £	Total cash inflow (outflow) £
Sales revenue	115 622		(4 027)		111 595
Operating costs*	(109 336)	5 351	6 992	(19 400)	(116 393)
Operating profit/ cash flow	6 286	5 351	2 965	(19 400)	(4 798)

The two new figures required for the direct operating cash flows can be taken from this table, and inserted into the statement of cash flows, as follows:

Buchanan International Designs: Statement of cash flows for the year ended 31 March 20X2

	£	£
Receipts from operating activities		111 595
Payments in respect of operating activities		(116 393)
Cash generated from operations		(4 798)
Interest paid		(2 400)
Interest received		651
Net cash outflow from operating activities		(6 547)
Cash flows from investing activities		
Purchase of non-current assets	(22 630)	
Net cash outflow from investing activities		(22 630)
Cash flows from financing activities		
Capital introduced	10 000	
Capital returned to owner (drawings)	(7 500)	
Long-term loan	40 000	
Net cash inflow from financing activities		42 500
Net increase in cash		13 323
Cash at beginning of period		0
Cash at end of period		13 323*

*Operating costs total = cost of sales + operating expenses

Differences between the direct and indirect approaches are confined to the operating section of the statement of cash flows. The investing and financing sections are identical in both approaches.

6.4 STATEMENTS OF CASH FLOW IN AN ESTABLISHED BUSINESS

In Example 6.1 earlier in the chapter, a statement of cash flows was prepared for the first year of trading of a new business. This meant that there were no opening balances, which simplified the example. Normally, of course, a business has both opening and closing balances. Example 6.3 demonstrates the preparation of a statement of cash flows for an established business.

Example 6.3

Horst is in business as a sole trader, trading under the name of Box Distributors. His accountant has prepared a statement of profit or loss for the business for the year ended 31 December 20X6, and a statement of financial position at that date. Horst approaches you in your capacity as a small business adviser to give him some advice. He shows you the financial statements and says:

'I cannot quite understand what has happened here. My revenue for 20X5 was £600 227, and it has increased in 20X6 to £636 636. The business is really doing quite well. I have had to replace one of the delivery vehicles during the year, because it was unreliable, but I thought I had been quite sensible about covering that spending. I got £5200 for it and extended the long-term bank loan by another £5000 which more or less covered the cost of the new van which was £10 660. I have made a big effort to control my own spending – I decided not to replace the BMW this year, and we went camping in France instead of going on that luxury cruise we had planned. So, drawings are only slightly higher than they were in 20X5. Despite all this restraint, the overdraft was almost £8000 at the year-end. Please explain to me what has happened and what I can do to reduce the overdraft.' The statement of profit or loss and statement of financial position for the 20X6 financial year are shown below:

Box Distributors: Statement of profit or loss for the year ended 31 December 20X6

	£	£
Revenue		636 636
Cost of sales		(452 483)
Gross profit		184 153
Operating expenses		
Selling and distribution expenses (excluding depreciation)	(62 466)	
Administration expenses (excluding depreciation)	(55 892)	
Depreciation of delivery vehicles	(6 313)	
Profit on disposal of delivery vehicle	336	
Depreciation of warehouse and machinery	(11 876)	
		(136 211)
Operating profit		47 942
Interest paid		(2 104)
Net profit		45 838

Box Distributors: Statements of financial position at 31 December 20X6 and 31 December 20X5

	20X6 £	20X6 £	20X5 £	20X5 £
ASSETS				
Non-current assets				
Delivery vehicles at cost	35 897		33 650	
Less: accumulated depreciation	(16 960)		(14 196)	
Carrying amount		18 937		19 454
Warehouse and machinery at cost	118 760		118 760	
Less: accumulated depreciation	(71 256)		(59 380)	
Carrying amount		47 504		59 380
		66 441		78 834
Current assets				
Inventory	52 687		45 611	
Trade receivables	78 490		65 442	
Cash at bank	–		371	
		131 177		111 424
		197 618		190 258
CAPITAL AND LIABILITIES				
Capital				
Capital brought forward	137 841		128 069	
Profit for the year	45 838		58 222	
Drawings	(49 000)		(48 450)	
		134 679		137 841
Long-term liabilities				
Loan		15 000		10 000

	20X6 £	20X6 £	20X5 £	20X5 £
Current liabilities				
Overdraft	7 996		–	
Trade payables	39 943		42 417	
		47 939		42 417
		197 618		190 258

A detailed analysis of the delivery vehicle account shows the following:

	£
Cost of delivery vehicles	
At 1 January 20X6	33 650
Disposal of vehicle	(8 413)
Addition of vehicle	10 660
At 31 December 20X6	35 897
Accumulated depreciation on delivery vehicles	
At 1 January 20X6	14 196
Accumulated depreciation on disposal	(3 549)
Depreciation for the year (to statement of profit or loss)	6 313
At 31 December 20X6	16 960

A delivery vehicle was sold for £5200 during the year.

The statement of cash flows, prepared using the indirect approach, is set out below, followed by detailed notes on its preparation.

Box Distributors: Statement of cash flows for the year ended 31 December 20X6

	£	£	Note
Cash flows from operating activities			
Operating profit		47 942	1
Depreciation		17 853	1
		65 795	
Less: increase in inventory	(7 076)		2
Less: increase in trade receivables	(13 048)		2
Less: decrease in trade payables	(2 474)		2
		(22 598)	
Cash generated from operations		43 197	
Interest paid		(2 104)	3
Net cash inflow from operating activities		41 093	
Cash flows from investing activities			
Purchase of non-current assets	(10 660)		4
Proceeds of sale of non-current asset	5 200		4
Net cash outflow from investing activities		(5 460)	
Cash flows from financing activities			
Capital returned to owner (drawings)	(49 000)		5
Increase in long-term loan	5 000		6
Net cash inflow from financing activities		(44 000)	
Net decrease in cash		(8 367)	
Cash at beginning of period		371	7
Cash at end of period – overdraft		(7 996)	7

NOTES

Note 1 The statement starts, as previously, with operating profit, and then non-cash items are added back. Depreciation does not involve any movement in cash, and nor does the profit on disposal of the delivery vehicle. Remember that a 'profit' or 'loss' on disposal of a non-current asset represents either under-depreciation or over-depreciation; neither is a cash flow. (Cash is received in exchange for the asset and this will be included further down the statement of cash flows, under the heading of 'Cash flows from investing activities'.)

	£
Depreciation of delivery vehicles	6 313
Profit on disposal of delivery vehicle	(336)
Depreciation of warehouse and machinery	11 876
Total	17 853

Note 2 In order to understand the effects on operating cash flows of the changes in inventory, receivables and payables, it may be helpful to use a table, as in Example 6.1

	Statement of profit or loss £	Non-cash Items: depreciation and profit on disposal £	Non-cash Items: trade receivables and trade payables £	Cash outflow: inventory purchase £	Total cash inflow (outflow) £
Sales revenue	636 636		(13 048)		623 588
Operating costs total*	(588 694)	17 853	(2 474)	(7 076)	(580 391)
Operating profit/cash flow	47 942	17 853	(15 522)	(7 076)	43 197

*Operating costs total = cost of sales + operating expenses (£452 483 + 136 211 = £588 694)

Inventory: there has been an increase in inventory between the two year-ends: £52 687 − 45 611 = £7076. This difference is the total additional cash outflow for the accounting period.

Trade receivables: the amount of cash received in respect of sales revenue in the period is:

	£
Opening trade receivables	65 442
Sales revenue	636 636
Less: closing trade receivables	(78 490)
Cash received	623 588

The adjustment for non-cash items is the difference between the closing and opening balances: (£78 490 − 65 442 = £13 048), ie. an increase in trade receivables.

Trade payables: the amount of cash paid in respect of operating costs and expenses in the period is:

	£
Opening trade payables	42 417
Operating costs total	588 694
Less: closing trade payables	(39 943)
	591 168

The adjustment for non-cash items is the difference between the closing and opening balances: £39 943 − 42 417 = £(2474), ie. a decrease in trade payables.

Note that adjustments in respect of inventory, trade receivables and trade payables are the net movements between the two year-ends. Once you have become accustomed to preparing statements of cash flows it is not necessary to prepare complex workings like the table above – simply insert the movement in inventory etc. into the operating cash flows section of the statement.

Note 3 The interest paid figure is taken from the statement of profit or loss.

Note 4 The cash outflow in respect of the purchase of non-current assets is taken from the detailed analysis of the delivery vehicle accounts. The cash inflow arising from the disposal of a vehicle is noted below that analysis.

Note 5 Drawings are a return of capital to the owner of the business, and so are shown under the heading of financing activities.

Note 6 We can see by comparing the two statements of financial position that the long-term liabilities figure has increased from £10 000 to £15 000. Therefore, there has been an additional cash inflow of £5000 to the business under the heading of financing activities.

Note 7 The net inflow or outflow of cash that is calculated in the statement of cash flows should equal the change in the balance of cash between the two year-end dates. In the case of Box Distributors there has been a net outflow of cash of £8367. The final section of the statement of cash flows 'proves' the figure by calculating the difference between cash at the bank on 31 December 20X5 (an asset balance of £371) and the overdraft at 31 December 20X6 (a liability balance of £7996).

The second step in the exercise is to provide Horst with some advice about his cash flow. We will analyze the situation and then make some recommendations for reducing the business's overdraft.

ANALYSIS

The overall net outflow of cash is over £8000. The principal cash inflows and outflows which have contributed to the increased overdraft are as follows:

- A substantial increase in inventory, trade receivables and trade payables of over £22 000. The total for trade receivables has increased by over £13 000, suggesting that the business has become significantly less successful at collecting money owed for credit sales. Inventories have also risen by a very significant amount. Both of these factors mean that cash in the business has been reduced.
- The net cash inflow from operating activities for the year (£41 093) is less than the total of drawings for the year (£49 000). Drawings are therefore being removed from the accumulated capital of earlier years.

Capital expenditure movements are not particularly significant in the year; the expenditure on the new vehicle is more or less covered by the proceeds of the sale of the old vehicle plus the increased borrowings from the bank.

The business is significantly less profitable in 20X6 than it was in 20X5. Net profit for 20X5 was £58 222 on sales revenue of £600 227, a margin of 9.7%. The comparable margin for 20X6 is 7.2% (£45 838/636 636 × 100). This suggests the need for better control of costs.

ACTION TO REDUCE THE OVERDRAFT

In the next accounting period the principal action points include the following:

- Control costs to improve the net profit margin.
- Reduce trade receivables by improving collection procedures.
- If possible, reduce the amount of drawings from the business.
- Reduce the amount of inventory held so that less cash is tied up.

Extracts from Amy Binyon's statement of profit or loss for the year ended 31 December 20X3 and her statement of financial position at that date (including comparative figures for 20X2) show the following information:

	£
Revenue	109 300
Cost of sales	62 700
Operating expenses, including depreciation of £5000	23 800
Interest paid	1 200

	20X3 £	20X2 £
Inventory	7 600	6 900
Trade receivables	8 700	8 500
Trade payables	9 700	9 000

Prepare a table to record adjustments between profit and operating cash flows (see the table in note 2 of Example 6.3), and then prepare the operating section of Amy Binyon's statement of cash flows for the year ended 31 December 20X3.

6.5 THE HIGH PROFIT/NO CASH PARADOX

Profitability and availability of cash do not necessarily go hand in hand in the short term. The dislocation between profits and cash can create major short-term problems even for highly profitable businesses. The final example in this chapter, 6.4, illustrates this important point.

Example 6.4

Adèle sells computer equipment, trading as Business Computer Specialist. She started in business six years ago and has done well, making a profit each year. About 18 months ago her business was the first in the UK to be granted the franchise to sell the XBS 0980, a specialist business computer system. She has become established as the principal supplier of the XBS 0980 and is likely to be supplied first with the XBS 0990 when it becomes available in the UK in the autumn of 20X8.

Despite more than doubling her sales and nearly doubling net profits, Adèle's business is short of cash. During her accounting year ended 31 December 20X7 she had to negotiate an overdraft facility of £20 000 with the bank. This was the first time since starting the business that she had needed an overdraft facility. Later in the year, the overdraft facility was increased to £40 000 and Adèle is now concerned that, if things do not improve, she will need to borrow more money. She has spent a total of £89 950 on new non-current assets during the year. Two new sales reps needed company cars, a lot of additional fixtures and fittings were required in the larger rented offices that the business moved to, and the warehouse, which is owned by the business, was extended to make space for all the additional inventory.

The business statements of profit or loss for the years ended 31 December 20X6 and 20X7are shown below, as are the statements of financial position at both dates.

Business Computer Specialist: Statements of profit or loss (summarized) for the years ended 31 December 20X7 and 20X6.

	20X7 £	20X7 £	20X6 £	20X6 £
Revenue		895 755		401 003
Less: cost of sales				
Opening inventory	35 901		32 412	
Purchases	597 136		252 499	
	633 037		284 911	
Closing inventory	(78 700)		(35 901)	
Cost of sales		(554 337)		(249 010)
Gross profit		341 418		151 993
Expenses	204 016		82 278	
Depreciation	13 700		7 796	
		(217 716)		(90 074)
Operating profit		123 702		61 919
Interest received		–		988
Interest paid		(2 709)		–
Net profit		120 993		62 907
Gross profit margin		38.1%		37.9%
Net profit margin		13.5%		15.7%

Business Computer Specialist: Statements of financial position at 31 December 20X7 and 20X6

	20X7 £	20X7 £	20X6 £	20X6 £
ASSETS				
Non-current assets				
At cost	218 420		128 470	
Less: accumulated depreciation	(44 620)		(30 920)	
Carrying amount		173 800		97 550
Current assets				
Inventory	78 700		35 901	
Trade receivables	95 514		34 996	
Cash at bank	–		12 804	
		174 214		83 701
		348 014		181 251
CAPITAL AND LIABILITIES				
Capital				
Capital brought forward	156 852		120 945	
Profit for the year	120 993		62 907	
Drawings	(29 000)		(27 000)	
		248 845		156 852
Current liabilities				
Overdraft	33 679		–	
Trade payables	65 490		24 399	
		99 169		24 399
		348 014		181 251

From this information, we can draw up a statement of cash flows for the year ended 31 December 20X7. This will help us to analyze the problems that Adèle currently faces.

	£	£
Cash flows from operating activities		
Operating profit		123 702
Depreciation		13 700
		137 402
Less: increase in inventory	(42 799)	
Less: increase in trade receivables	(60 518)	
Add: increase in trade payables	41 091	
		(62 226)
Cash generated from operations		75 176
Interest paid		(2 709)
Net cash inflow from operating activities		72 467
Cash flows from investing activities		
Purchase of non-current assets	(89 950)	
Net cash outflow from investing activities		(89 950)
Cash flows from financing activities		
Capital returned to owner (drawings)	(29 000)	
Net cash inflow from financing activities		(29 000)
Net decrease in cash		(46 483)
Cash at beginning of period		12 804
Cash at end of period: overdraft		(33 679)

Note: capital expenditure. We are told, in the introduction to the example, that Adèle has spent £89 950 on new non-current assets. It is also possible to work the figure out from the accounts, as follows:

	£
Non-current assets at carrying amount 31 December 20X6	97 550
Reduced by annual charge for depreciation in 20X7	(13 700)
	83 850
Non-current assets at carrying amount 31 December 20X7	173 800
Difference = purchases of non-current assets	89 950

The statement of cash flows shows the principal causes of the decrease in cash/increase in overdraft. The business is expanding very quickly and therefore needs new non-current assets, resulting in a cash outflow of nearly £90 000 in the year. The next largest item has been the increase in working capital (ie. inventory, trade receivables and trade payables) which is necessary to cope with the very rapid expansion in sales revenue. A greater volume of sales means that the business has to keep more inventory in hand, and trade receivables and trade payables are likely to increase as well. If the expansion continues at its present rate, the business may need further overdraft facilities and possibly longer-term loans to fund the acquisition of more non-current assets. So far Adèle has tried to meet the funding shortfall by increasing the business's overdraft, but this is not necessarily the best approach. If funding is required for long-term assets, it is usually sensible to borrow long-term rather than short-term.

It can be very difficult in practice to manage businesses that are expanding as fast as Business Computer Specialist. The problems encountered by rapidly expanding businesses include:

- the need to take on more staff very quickly. Poor quality personnel decisions may be made when management is under pressure to employ more people in a hurry.
- insufficient management time. Where small businesses grow very fast, the original proprietor is often swamped by the sheer weight and pace of decision making. Usually, in such circumstances, it is necessary to employ staff at managerial levels, but it can be difficult to get staff of the right calibre into positions quickly enough.
- loss of control over costs and inventory. A consequence of rapid expansion is often that costs get out of hand, because the business does not have systems in place to control them properly. In the case of Adèle we can see that the business's net profit margin has in fact fallen between 20X6 and 20X7, although gross profit margin has actually improved a little. The worsening of net profit margin suggests possible difficulties in controlling costs.
- failure to control receivables. Receivables should convert into cash quite easily but some debtors need chasing to make them pay up. Where management time is limited, receivables may be allowed to build up to unacceptable levels.
- chronic shortage of cash.

The case of Business Computer Specialist shows that business success can bring its own problems. Where businesses expand very rapidly they can become victims of their own success, and may even fail. In Adèle's case she needs, as a matter of urgency, to prepare budgets for the coming year, to see how much of a problem the shortage of cash is going to be. It may be time for her to consider recruiting a qualified accountant to the management team.

6.6 STATEMENTS OF CASH FLOW IN LARGE BUSINESSES

The examples in this chapter have focused upon small, simple, businesses, so as to make it easier to learn how to prepare a statement of cash flows. However, a statement of cash flows can help in understanding all types and sizes of business. Companies listed on the London Stock Exchange are required to publish a statement of cash flows in the format (prescribed by the International Accounting Standards Board) that we have used in this chapter. Therefore, if you look up the financial statements of any listed company on the internet you should be able to find a recognizable statement of cash flows in its annual report. Look at the real-life example below, and then look at other companies' annual reports on their websites, to see if you can (a) find the statement of cash flows and (b) understand the information contained in it.

Example 6.5 (Real-Life)

MAJESTIC WINE PLC

The company's annual report for the year ended 28 March 2016 included a statement of cash flows. The key figures under the principal headings were:

	2016 £000	2015 £000
Net cash generated by operating activities	14 153	27 248
Net cash (outflow) from investing activities	(44 681)	(7 481)
Net cash inflow/(outflow) from financing activities	23 365	(10 579)
Net (decrease)/increase in cash and cash equivalents	(7 163)	9 188

Comparing the two columns of figures, for 2016 and 2015, we can see that there are some very significant differences. Net cash generated by operating activities in 2016 is little more than half of what it was the previous year. Although there was a big increase in Majestic revenues (from £284 495 000 in 2015 to £402 086 000 in 2016) profitability was very much lower in 2016. Turning to the Chief Executive's report for explanation of these differences, we find that during the 2016 financial year Majestic appointed a new management team, made a very large acquisition (of Naked Wines) and undertook a major three-year transformation plan. By the end of the 2016 financial year, the three-year plan was still at an early stage and the Chief Executive reported that, although there were some encouraging early signs of success, it was too early to say conclusively that the plan was working.

The very large net cash outflow from investing activities of £44 681 000 in the 2016 financial year was mostly attributable to the acquisition of the new subsidiary, Naked Wines. This major acquisition for Majestic also explains the inflow from financing activities. In order to fund the acquisition of Naked Wines, Majestic had to take out some additional borrowings in the form of a bank loan.

The overall effect in the statement of cash flows is a net cash outflow of £7 163 000.

The figures and the explanations above are very broad summaries of some of the issues arising in Majestic Wine in its 2016 financial year. Much more detail is available in the company's full annual report, accessible at www.majesticwineplc.co.uk

Chapter Summary

This chapter started by explaining the important distinction between cash and profits. Because of the accruals (matching) convention, accounting income is not the same as cash received, and accounting expenditure is not the same as cash paid.

Most of the rest of the chapter was concerned with explaining the mechanics of preparing a third important financial statement: the statement of cash flows. The preparation of a statement of cash flows in a new business was explained, and then the chapter proceeded to explain how to prepare a statement of cash flows in an established business.

The Business Computer Specialist example demonstrated and explained the apparent paradox of a successful and profitable business running out of cash. The statement of cash flows for such a business provides answers to the very basic question: 'Where has all the cash gone?' Finally, the chapter concluded by examining the key elements of a real-life statement of cash flows.

The statement of cash flows enhances and explains some of the key elements of the two other financial statements covered in earlier chapters: the statement of financial position and the statement of profit or loss. The statement of cash flows is of equal importance to the other statements, and can be of great assistance to users in understanding the business's performance and position. Students often experience some difficulty in understanding the preparation and significance of statements of cash flow. By carefully working through the examples in the chapter and then applying their knowledge to the end-of-chapter questions, students should find they are equipped with all the necessary skills to become proficient in the preparation and understanding of the statement of cash flows.

Internet Resources

Book's companion website summary

The website contains the following resources in respect of Chapter 6:

Students' section

A multiple choice quiz containing ten questions
Four additional questions with answers

Lecturers' section

Answers to end-of-chapter exercises 6.8 to 6.14
Six additional questions with answers
Case study
Testbank
Instructor's Manual
PowerPoint presentation

Exercises: Answers at the End of the Book

6.1 Fergus's business incurred the following transactions in the year ended 31 December 20X4:

- Fergus introduced additional capital of £10 000 in cash.
- purchase on credit of goods for resale for £8000.
- payment received from customer for £1800.
- purchase of a new machine for use in the business on 1 January 20X4. The machine costs £12 000 and is to be depreciated over 10 years on the straight-line basis, assuming no residual value.
- sales returns of £1000 in exchange for a cash refund.
- drawings of £1300.

For each transaction show the impact on cash, other assets and liabilities, and the impact on profits.

6.2 Gilbert's business sells a non-current asset for cash proceeds of £1300. The asset originally cost £20 700, and accumulated depreciation at the point of sale was £18 210.

Three of the following six statements are correct:

1) Profits increase by £1190.
2) Profits decrease by £1190.
3) Cash increases by £1300.
4) Cash increases by £1190.
5) The net book value of non-current assets decreases by £2490.
6) The net book value of non-current assets decreases by £1300.

Which statements are correct?

a) 1, 3 and 6
b) 2, 3 and 5
c) 1, 4 and 5
d) 2, 4 and 6

6.3 Gregory, trading as Ketchup & Co, made an operating loss of £38 650 in the year ended 31 March 20X6, after deducting £12 750 in depreciation for the year.

At 31 March 20X6 the statement of financial position of Ketchup & Co showed inventory of £32 250, trade receivables of £26 770 and trade payables of £25 500. The corresponding figures at 31 March 20X5 were: inventory £34 400, trade receivables £25 360 and trade payables £23 380.

What is the net cash outflow from operating activities for inclusion in the statement of cash flows for Ketchup & Co for the year ended 31 March 20X6?

a) £23 040
b) £48 540
c) £28 760
d) £54 260

6.4 Gayle is preparing the statement of cash flows for her business, for the year ended 31 August 20X7. After calculating the net operating cash inflow, she is left with the following list of cashflows:

	£
Purchase of machinery	(3 688)
Proceeds of sale of computer	2 000
Drawings	(6 500)
Interest paid	(340)
Repayment of bank loan	(5 000)
Loan received from brother	1 000

What is Gayle's net cash outflow from financing activities for the year ended 31 August 20X7?

a) (12 528)
b) (4000)
c) (10 500)
d) (10 840)

6.5 Gaston's business prepares accounts to 31 December each year. In the year ended 31 December 20X2 inventory, trade receivables and trade payables are shown in the statement of financial position, with comparative figures at 31 December 20X1, as follows:

	20X2	20X1
	£	£
Inventory	37 669	31 470
Trade receivables	21 777	19 303
Trade payables	18 250	16 264

Gaston's net profit for the year ended 31 December 20X2 is £36 027, after deducting total depreciation charges of £4585.

What is the net cash inflow from operating activities for inclusion in Gaston's statement of cash flows for the year ended 31 December 20X2?

a) £47 299
b) £29 340
c) £33 925
d) £34 688

6.6 Henrietta runs a business, trading as Spicer & Co. She prepares accounts to 31 March each year. By the year-end 31 March 20X3 the business has run into overdraft. Henrietta asks you to prepare a statement of cash flows for the business for the year ended 31 March 20X3 and provides you with the following information:

Spicer & Co: Statement of profit or loss (summarized) for the year ended 31 March 20X3

	£
Revenue	598 731
Less: cost of sales	(430 131)
Gross profit	168 600
Expenses excluding depreciation	(79 633)
Depreciation	(12 471)
Operating profit	76 496
Interest paid	(230)
Net profit	76 266

Spicer & Co: Statements of financial position at 31 March 20X3 and 31 March 20X2

	20X3	20X3	20X2	20X2
	£	£	£	£
ASSETS				
Non-current assets				
At cost	175 630		128 547	
Less: accumulated depreciation	(67 248)		(54 777)	
Carrying amount		108 382		73 770

	20X3	20X3	20X2	20X2
	£	£	£	£
Current assets				
Inventory	40 747		36 600	
Trade receivables	50 661		48 730	
Cash at bank	–		7 423	
		91 408		92 753
		199 790		166 523
CAPITAL AND LIABILITIES				
Capital				
Capital brought forward	131 332		111 335	
Profit for the year	76 266		61 297	
Drawings	(45 800)		(41 300)	
		161 798		131 332
Current liabilities				
Overdraft	1 348		–	
Trade payables	36 644		35 191	
		37 992		35 191
		199 790		166 523

Note: there were no disposals of non-current assets during the year.

Prepare a statement of cash flows for Spicer & Co for the year ended 31 March 20X3.

6.7 Ishmael prepares accounts to 31 July each year. He asks you to prepare a statement of cash flows for the business for the year ended 31 July 20X5 and provides you with the following information:

Ishmael: Statement of profit or loss (summarized) for the year ended 31 July 20X5

	£
Revenue	724 450
Less: cost of sales	(586 600)
Gross profit	137 850
Expenses excluding depreciation	(83 280)
Loss on disposal of non-current asset	(627)
Depreciation	(36 900)
Operating profit	17 043
Interest paid	(3 700)
Net profit	13 343

Ishmael: Statements of financial position at 31 July 20X5 and 31 July 20X4

	20X5	20X5	20X4	20X4
	£	£	£	£
ASSETS				
Non-current assets				
At cost	543 720		501 120	
Less: accumulated depreciation	(141 120)		(107 720)	
Carrying amount		402 600		393 400

	20X5	20X5	20X4	20X4
	£	£	£	£
Current assets				
Inventory	61 650		59 900	
Trade receivables	83 360		80 410	
Cash at bank	–		12 440	
		145 010		152 750
		547 610		546 150
CAPITAL AND LIABILITIES				
Capital				
Capital brought forward	289 510		286 750	
Profit for the year	13 343		42 420	
Drawings	(53 693)		(39 660)	
		249 160		289 510
Long-term liabilities				
Bank loan		200 000		180 000
Current liabilities				
Overdraft	18 500		–	
Trade payables	79 950		76 640	
		98 450		76 640
		547 610		546 150

During the year ended 31 July 20X5 a non-current asset was sold for £1073. The asset originally cost £5200, and accumulated depreciation on this asset at the date of sale was £3500.

i) Prepare a statement of cash flows for Ishmael for the year ended 31 July 20X5

ii) Explain the principal reasons why Ishmael has an overdraft at 31 July 20X5, compared to a cash at bank balance at 31 July 20X4.

Exercises: Answers Available on the Lecturers' Section of the Book's Website

6.8   Flynn's business incurred the following transactions in the year ended 31 March 20X9:

- purchase of inventory for cash of £1300.
- sale of a non-current asset with a written down value of £300. The sale proceeds were £900.
- sale on credit for £3500.
- payment made in respect of a trade payable outstanding, for electricity bill of £6350.
- drawings of £800.
- purchase of a motor vehicle for use in the business on 1 April 20X8. The vehicle cost £10 000 and is to be depreciated at 25% per annum.

For each transaction show the impact on cash, other assets and liabilities, and the impact on profits.

6.9   Grant's business made an operating profit of £16 632 in the year ended 30 April 20X1. One of the deductions in arriving at operating profit was depreciation of £6650.

At 30 April 20X1 the statement of financial position showed inventory of £26 750, trade receivables of £12 704 and trade payables of £11 667. On 30 April 20X0 the corresponding figures were: inventory: £27 997; trade receivables: £11 940 and trade payables: £9975. There was no interest paid or interest received.

What is the net cash inflow from operating activities to be included in Grant's statement of cash flows for the year ended 30 April 20X1?

a) £21 107
b) £18 807
c) £22 073
d) £25 457

6.10 Gunter's business sells an item of machinery for £2660 on 30 June 20X4. The balances at the beginning of the accounting year (1 January 20X4) for the asset were:

Cost: £17 700
Accumulated depreciation: £15 930

Gunter charges depreciation on this class of asset at the rate of 10% per annum on cost, with a month's depreciation charged for each full month of ownership in the year of disposal. He has assumed a nil residual value for this asset.

Two of the following eight statements are correct:

1) Profits decrease by £890.
2) Profits increase by £890.
3) Profits increase by £1775.
4) Profits decrease by £1775.
5) Cash increases by £2660.
6) Cash increases by £1775.
7) Cash decreases by £2660.
8) Cash decreases by £1775.

Which statements are correct?

a) 1 and 7
b) 4 and 6
c) 2 and 8
d) 3 and 5

6.11 Gary is preparing the statement of cash flows for his business, for the year ended 31 December 20X6. After calculating the net operating cash inflow, the following list of cashflows remains:

	£
Purchase of office equipment	(5 800)
Proceeds of sale of old machine	500
Drawings	(18 600)
Interest paid	(800)
Loan received from bank	19 000
Loan repaid to sister	(4 600)

What is Gary's net cash outflow from investing activities for the year ended 31 December 20X6?

a) (5300)
b) (10 300)
c) (4200)
d) (5800)

6.12 Hamid prepares his business financial statements to 31 May each year. Because he attended an accounting course at college he knows how to prepare statements of profit or loss and statements of financial position. However, the course did not include the preparation of statements of cash flows and Hamid asks you to prepare a statement of cash flows for his business for the year ended 31 May 20X4. He supplies you with the following information:

Hamid: Statement of profit or loss (summarized) for the year ended 31 May 20X4

	£
Revenue	437 500
Less: cost of sales	(298 423)
Gross profit	139 077
Expenses excluding depreciation	(62 505)
Depreciation	(7 662)
Operating profit	68 910
Interest received	634
Interest paid	(506)
Net profit	69 038

Hamid: Statements of financial position at 31 May 20X4 and 31 May 20X3

	20X4 £	20X4 £	20X3 £	20X3 £
ASSETS				
Non-current assets				
At cost	82 610		38 750	
Less: accumulated depreciation	(21 462)		(13 800)	
		61 148		24 950
Current assets				
Inventory	26 980		27 420	
Trade receivables	44 349		42 760	
Cash at bank	5 354		6 642	
		76 683		76 822
		137 831		101 772
CAPITAL AND LIABILITIES				
Capital				
Capital brought forward	68 313		33 766	
Profit for the year	69 038		63 291	
Drawings	(23 250)		(28 744)	
		114 101		68 313
Current liabilities				
Loan	–		5 000	
Trade payables	23 730		28 459	
		23 730		33 459
		137 831		101 772

1) There were no disposals of non-current assets during the year.
2) Following your request Hamid supplies the following information relating to cash receipts and payments during the year:

Cash receipts	£435 911
Cash payments	£365 217

Prepare Hamid's statement of cash flows for the year ended 31 May 20X4 using

i) the indirect method
ii) the direct method.

6.13 India runs a business and prepares accounts to 31 December each year. India asks you to prepare a statement of cash flows for the business for the year ended 31 December 20X7 and provides you with the following information:

India: Statement of profit or loss (summarized) for the year ended 31 December 20X7

	£
Revenue	1 350 600
Less: cost of sales	(1 170 400)
Gross profit	180 200
Expenses excluding depreciation	(118 440)
Depreciation	(26 600)
Operating profit	35 160
Interest paid	(6 650)
Net profit	28 510

India: Statements of financial position at 31 December 20X7 and 31 December 20X6

	20X7 £	20X7 £	20X6 £	20X6 £
ASSETS				
Non-current assets				
At cost	342 000		275 000	
Less: accumulated depreciation	(156 600)		(130 000)	
Carrying amount		185 400		145 000
Current assets				
Inventory	144 200		138 750	
Trade receivables	155 410		140 600	
Cash at bank	–		24 400	
		299 610		303 750
		485 010		448 750
CAPITAL AND LIABILITIES				
Capital				
Capital brought forward	78 950		82 300	
Profit for the year	28 510		48 400	
Drawings	(62 200)		(51 750)	
		45 260		78 950

	20X7	20X7	20X6	20X6
	£	£	£	£
Long-term liabilities				
Bank loan		133 000		118 000
Current liabilities				
Overdraft	34 150		–	
Trade payables	272 600		251 800	
		306 750		251 800
		485 010		448 750

Note: there were no disposals of non-current assets during the year.

Prepare a statement of cash flows for India for the year ended 31 December 20X7.

6.14 Ilyas's business has the following summary statement of cash flows for the year ended 31 May 20X6:

	20X6	20X5
	£000	£000
Net cash generated by operating activities	106 700	89 950
Net cash outflow from investing activities	(60 000)	(6 600)
Net cash inflow from financing activities	20 500	50 800
Net increase in cash and cash equivalents	67 200	134 150

Analyze the cash inflows and outflows in the statement above, explaining the significance (as far as possible with such limited information) of the figures.

7 Financial reporting by limited companies

Aim of the chapter

To understand the nature of company financial reporting, including an appreciation of the accounting regulatory framework applicable to companies.

Learning outcomes

After reading the chapter and completing the related exercises, students should:

- Understand in outline the regulations relating to accounting by companies.

- Understand the roles of directors in respect of company financial reports.

- Be able to draw up a set of financial statements for a simple limited company.

- Understand the need for additional financial and non-financial reporting by listed companies.

Introduction

Chapter 1 briefly examined some of the characteristics of limited companies, including the separation between ownership and management of the company that is typical of larger limited companies. That chapter also identified the principal users of financial information, which included shareholders and potential shareholders in limited companies.

This chapter examines the nature of limited companies, and their financial reporting in more detail. The important concept of limited liability is examined, and its implications are explored in a numerical example in order to set the context for the discussion of information needs that follows. This is followed by a section on regulation related to limited companies, and then the components of a set of limited company financial statements are explained. Listed companies (those whose share capital is listed on a stock exchange such as the London Stock Exchange) are subject to additional requirements in respect of published information, both financial and non-financial, and these are briefly examined.

7.1 THE LIMITED COMPANY

The limited company has been an important form of business organization since the middle of the nineteenth century in the UK. The need for this type of organization developed as industrial organizations became larger, and as greater amounts of capital were required, for example to fund the expansion of the railway system. It is unlikely that one single individual would be wealthy enough to fund a major institution like a railway or a bank, and so a legal mechanism that allows for ownership to be shared is very useful in the development of advanced economies. Most capitalist countries have developed ownership vehicles akin to the UK limited company, and in most of Europe this development took place during the nineteenth century.

A company is a convenient form of organization in that:

● It allows for investments of differing amounts to be made by a potentially very large group of individuals or organizations.
● In the form in which it is most commonly found in the UK and elsewhere, it offers investors the protection of limited liability. This useful mechanism ensures that investors are liable for no more than their original investment.
● A company is regarded as a 'person' in law. It can sue or be sued, can hold bank accounts and other forms of assets, and it can be named as a contracting party in legal contracts. The individuals investing in it are protected by the so-called 'veil of incorporation'. This means that people or organizations with a claim against the company have no legal rights against the investors' own personal assets (Example 7.1 explains this further).
● The structure of the capital of a limited company in the form of shares lends itself to shared ownership by many parties, and, in some cases, access to markets in which share capital can be easily exchanged for cash.
● It can offer certain tax advantages over sole trader and partnership forms of organization.

7.2 LIMITED LIABILITY

Limited liability confers a great advantage upon investors in shares of companies. By contrast, a sole trader or a partner in a partnership is exposed to unlimited liability, to the extent of his or her own personal assets, in respect of business dealings.

There is, potentially, a corresponding disadvantage for the creditors of limited liability companies. Creditors of business organizations always face the risk that they will not be paid; however, if a limited company fails to pay, the creditors may have very little chance of successfully pursuing an action against the company. If it has no assets, the creditors will simply not be paid. Consider the following example:

Example 7.1

On 1 June 20X4 Elba Limited placed an order with a supplier, Tommy, to supply inventory on credit to a value of £3000. Tommy supplied the goods, but then Elba went out of business on 10 August 20X4, without having paid Tommy any of the money owing to him. Elba Limited had the following statement of financial position at 31 May 20X4:

	£	£
ASSETS		
Non-current assets		
Property, plant and equipment		8 000
Current assets		
Inventories	1 250	
Trade receivables	1 000	
		2 250
		10 250
CAPITAL AND LIABILITIES		
Equity		
Share capital		100
Retained earnings		1 300
		1 400
Current liabilities		
Trade payables	2 550	
Overdraft	6 300	
		8 850
		10 250

Note that some new terminology has appeared. Equity is another term for capital, which is used in respect of limited companies. It comprises the share capital of the business that has been issued to shareholders in exchange for their original investment plus the accumulated profits that have been retained in the business (described as retained earnings).

By 10 August 20X4 Elba's position had deteriorated. The statement of financial position at that date was as follows:

	£	£
ASSETS		
Non-current assets		
Property, plant and equipment		8 000
Current assets		
Inventories	5 250	
Trade receivables	1 600	
		6 850
		14 850
CAPITAL AND LIABILITIES		
Equity		
Share capital		100
Retained losses		(2 490)
		(2 390)
Current liabilities		
Trade payables	8 940	
Overdraft	8 300	
		17 240
		14 850

Elba's bank manager refused to extend the business overdraft any further, and the company was obliged to cease trading.

Can Tommy recover the money due to him? In this case he may recover some of his money, but probably not all of it. In total, at 10 August 20X4 Elba had current liabilities of £17 240, of which £3000 was due to Tommy. The statement of financial position showed total assets of £14 850, a shortfall of £2390. However, the asset values may not be realistic estimates of the amounts that can be recovered by selling the assets.

Non-current assets, as we know, are presented in the statement of financial position at cost less depreciation. The carrying amount in the statement of financial position may be higher than the amounts for which the assets can be sold. The trade receivables figure of £1600 may not be fully recoverable, and perhaps the inventories could not be sold for the full amount shown in the statement of financial position.

Suppose the assets of Elba could be liquidated (ie. turned into cash) as follows:

Non-current assets in a forced sale	6 000
Receivables: amounts actually receivable	1 400
Inventories in a forced sale	4 500
Total amount of cash which can be raised	£11 900

Against total liabilities of £17 240 there is a shortfall of £5340, or just over 30%. The creditors (ie. trade payables and bank overdraft) cannot be repaid in full, and are likely to receive at most about 70% of the value of the sums due to them. In practice, this proportion will be reduced by accountants' fees for doing the work of winding up the company (yes: the accountants are paid before the other 'ordinary' creditors) and by any amounts due to HMRC (who take precedence over other creditors). Note that the shareholders in Elba would lose the whole of their investment in share capital. However, the share capital amounts only to £100, and the loss is small compared to the loss which will be suffered by Tommy and other creditors.

7.3 INFORMATION NEEDS OF COMPANY CREDITORS

The situation outlined above may seem very unfair to creditors. How could Tommy have avoided losing money? Well, if he had been aware of Elba's weak position he could have either refused to trade with the company, or he could have insisted on receiving the cash in advance. Either way, he would have been protected from loss.

It is partly to protect creditors like Tommy that regulation exists to ensure that companies are obliged to make certain financial details available to the public. If creditors are in possession of accounting information they are able to make better decisions. Even so, creditors like Tommy are rarely in possession of all the relevant facts. Companies are obliged to make information available within nine months of the year-end (six months for some larger companies); by the time the information becomes available the company's position may have altered very significantly.

7.4 INFORMATION NEEDS OF COMPANY SHAREHOLDERS

As explained in Chapter 1, companies, especially larger companies, are sometimes owned and managed by different people. Where company directors and shareholders are two different groups of people (or two groups that overlap only partially), it is important that the directors are held to account for the way in which they have managed the shareholders' investments. (This accountability is known by the rather old-fashioned term **stewardship**.) Therefore, there are regulatory requirements to ensure that shareholders receive information in a standard form about the companies they have invested in. If the shareholders are unhappy about the way in which directors have managed the company, they can vote the directors out of office and replace them. Although there may be many shareholders, especially in very large companies, directors are only rarely voted out of office.

7.5 INFORMATION NEEDS OF PEOPLE OTHER THAN SHAREHOLDERS AND CREDITORS

There are other groups of people who may be interested in the information made available by companies (see Chapter 1). These include: employees, customers, financial journalists, the government, academics and the general public.

In the next section of the chapter the nature of company regulation, especially in respect of accounting, is examined in outline.

7.6 REGULATION OF COMPANY ACCOUNTING AND OTHER ISSUES

There are few regulations governing accounting by sole traders. By contrast, accounting and financial reporting by companies is subject to comparatively heavy regulation. Some of the principal sources and features of company regulation will be explained in this section.

7.6.1 Companies Acts

Since the mid-nineteenth century the conduct of companies has been subject to legal regulation in the form of Acts of Parliament. There has been a succession of Companies Acts during the period since 1844. The latest is the Companies Act 2006 (CA 2006) which supersedes all previous Companies Acts. CA 2006 is a major piece of legislation which, amongst other things, brought company law up to date in respect of issues like electronic communications with shareholders.

The CA 2006 contains many complex legal regulations relating to:

- formation of new companies and types of company
- company constitutional arrangements including the issue of shares
- role of directors
- the audit of companies
- publication and presentation of accounting information

The 1985 Companies Act, which preceded CA 2006, introduced many aspects of European company law into UK legislation; in particular, standard formats for the presentation of company financial statements were introduced. These accounting requirements were carried into the CA 2006 in general terms. The accounting requirements for companies will be examined in more detail later in the chapter.

7.6.2 Company Formation and Types of Company

Setting up a limited company is quite straightforward and is an inexpensive procedure. It is usually handled by a professionally qualified accountant or solicitor, or by one of the specialist company formation firms. Certain forms have to be registered with Companies House, and there are provisions to ensure that a company is not registered with a name identical to that of an existing company.

The private company: this has a minimum of one shareholder, and one director. The word 'limited' is attached to the name of the company (in English or Welsh).

The public limited company: this must be described in its **Memorandum of Association** (see below) as a public company, its name must end in 'public limited company' or 'plc' (or the Welsh equivalents) and it must have a share capital of at least £50 000. It must also appoint at least two directors and a company secretary.

Larger companies tend to be plcs. However, comparatively large businesses may be private companies. In order to be permitted to issue shares to the general public a company must be constituted as a plc.

7.6.3 Company Constitutional Arrangements Including the Issue of Shares

There are formal arrangements in law for company meetings. Traditionally an Annual General Meeting (AGM) had to take place and shareholders were permitted to vote democratically on resolutions at that meeting. However, under the provisions of CA 2006, private companies are no longer obliged to hold AGMs, although the obligation remains to involve shareholders in the decision making process of the company. For most normal purposes, a private company can deal with decision making via written resolutions. However, public limited companies are still obliged to hold formal AGMs.

The normal agenda for an AGM would include the following:

- acceptance of the directors' report and the financial statements
- authorization for payment of dividend (and confirmation of dividends already paid)
- election of directors
- appointment of auditors
- any other business

All companies are required to have:

- a Memorandum of Association
- Articles of Association.

The Memorandum of Association is a statement made by each of the original subscribers for shares in the company, confirming their intention to form the company and to become a shareholder in it. This document is created for incorporation purposes only and then is subsequently unchanged. The Articles of Association contain the company's internal constitution, including, for example, appropriate arrangements for appointment of directors, voting by shareholders, powers of directors and directors' expenses, pensions and remuneration.

7.6.4 Shares

The most common type of share capital is **ordinary share capital**. Each share carries the right to vote on company resolutions and the right to receive a dividend (if any). Each ordinary share has a **nominal value,** which is commonly one of the following: 5p, 10p, 25p, 50p or £1.

Decisions on the amount of ordinary dividend to be paid are made by the company's directors. Ordinary dividends for an accounting year are often paid in two or more instalments: one or more interim dividends and a final dividend.

Some companies issue preference share capital. This differs substantially from ordinary share capital, in that preference shares carry a fixed rate of dividend (and are described as, for example, 8% preference shares), and have no voting powers in decision making about issues such as the appointment of directors. Such shares are referred to as 'preference shares' because their dividends have to be paid out in preference to any dividend on the ordinary shares. Because there is a fixed rate of return on preference shares, they are really more akin to a long-term loan and in most cases **accounting standards** require that the shares are accounted for as long-term liabilities and the 'dividends' on them are accounted for as finance costs (ie. in the same way as interest paid). Some preference shares are cumulative; that is, if the company does not pay the dividend on the shares the obligation to pay is carried forward to the next following year.

Example 7.2

Pauletta Limited has ordinary share capital of £20 000, split into shares of 25 pence each. In the year ended 31 December 20X3 a dividend of 4p per share was paid. Li Ming owns 5000 shares in Pauletta Limited.

a) How many shares has Pauletta Limited issued?
b) What is the total value of the dividend paid for the year ended 31 December 20X3?
c) What is the value of Li Ming's dividend for the year ended 31 December 20X3?

Answer

a) Each £1 of ordinary share capital in Pauletta Limited is split into four shares (4 × 25p = £1). Therefore, the number of shares issued in total by Pauletta is 4 × 20 000 = 80 000.
b) The dividend is 4p per share; total value is 4p × 80 000 = £3200.
c) Li Ming's dividend is 4p × 5000 (the number of shares held by her) = £200.

The next example looks at both dividends in respect of ordinary shares and preference share dividends.

Example 7.3

Birch and Beech Limited has issued both ordinary shares and preference shares, as follows:

Ordinary share capital: 30 000 £1 shares
Preference share capital: £50 000 7% preference shares

The directors of the company decided to pay an interim dividend of 5% of nominal share value in the year ended 31 December 20X8. The preference dividend was also paid.
What is the total amount of dividend that was paid by Birch and Beech Limited for the year ended 31 December 20X8?

Answer

	£
Ordinary dividend: £30 000 × 5%	1 500
Preference dividend: £50 000 × 7%	3 500
Total	5 000

7.6.5 Role of Directors

Company directors have important responsibilities under the law, and an appointment as a director is not to be taken lightly. If a company loses money through the actions of directors, it may be able to reclaim the money from the directors, even if they acted in what they thought were the best interests of the company.

The duties of a company director under the law are as follows:

1 to comply with the company's constitution
2 to act in a way that is most likely to promote the success of the company for the benefit of its members as a whole (which may not be the same as the interests of individual shareholders). The director must have regard to all relevant matters, including the interests of the company's employees, the impact of the company's activities on the community and the environment and the reputation of the company for a high standard of business conduct.
3 to exercise independent judgement
4 to exercise reasonable skill, care and diligence
5 to avoid conflicts between his/her own interest and the interests of the company
6 not to accept benefits from third parties – this helps to avoid conflicts of interest between the director and third parties external to the company
7 to declare any interest in a transaction or arrangement proposed for the company. Again, this duty avoids conflicts of interest.

DIRECTORS' RESPONSIBILITIES IN RESPECT OF COMPANY FINANCIAL STATEMENTS Directors must ensure that adequate accounting records are kept, and they are responsible for preparing the company's annual financial statements and for ensuring that the financial statements are filed at Companies House within the time limit permitted by law. They must also ensure that the company does not trade while insolvent (the example of Elba Limited earlier demonstrates an insolvent company statement of financial position at 10 August 20X4). Breach of these rules can mean that the director is guilty of a criminal offence, and may be personally liable for a fine or imprisonment.

The financial statements of a company must present 'a true and fair view' (this is a legal term which has existed in company law since the 1940s) of the performance and state of affairs of the company. Although the directors themselves do not necessarily take part in the preparation of the financial statements (the task is often delegated to the finance director or a senior accountant in the business) they nevertheless take complete responsibility in law for the preparation and filing of financial statements. Fines are quite frequently levied on directors by Companies House in respect of late filing.

Allowing a company to trade while insolvent can have very serious consequences for individual directors. Directors may be ordered by the courts to make contributions out of their personal resources if they have allowed the company to continue trading in circumstances where there is no reasonable prospect of avoiding corporate failure. If it is proven that directors have deliberately defrauded creditors a criminal offence is involved; they may be disqualified as a director, fined or even imprisoned. It is very important that people who are appointed as directors should fully understand their responsibilities and the possible consequences of failing to meet those responsibilities. As explained earlier it is cheap and simple to set up a company in the UK and to become a director of a company, but it is important to understand the responsibilities that go with the role.

7.6.6 Publication and Presentation of Accounting Information

As illustrated by the Elba Limited example earlier in the chapter, company financial information may be important to many interested parties. After companies have filed their annual financial statements at Companies House, they are available for inspection by anyone who is interested. However, the meaning of 'annual financial statements' varies depending upon the size of the company. Small companies, as defined in law, may file 'abridged' accounts, rather than 'full' accounts. They may choose to abridge the statement of financial position (known as the 'balance sheet' in UK law) or the statement of profit or loss (known as the 'profit and loss account' in UK law), or may choose to abridge both. Micro-entities are obliged to file only an abridged statement of financial position (balance sheet) at Companies House, although they may opt to file more information.

The current criteria for micro-entities and small companies are shown in Table 7.1 below.

Table 7.1   **Criteria for micro-entities and small companies**

	Turnover	Total of assets (non-current and current)	Average number of employees
Micro-entity	Not more than £632 000	Not more than £316 000	Not more than 10
Small company	Not more than £10.2 million	Not more than £5.1 million	Not more than 50

An entity or company meets the definition if it satisfies two out of the three criteria listed.

These limits are changed from time to time. The main reason for allowing micro-entities and small companies to file a reduced amount of accounting information is to ensure that competitors do not have access to information that may harm the interests of the company. The reduced filing requirements do not save these businesses much, if anything, in costs because a full set of financial statements has to be prepared for the shareholders' use. Later in the chapter, presentation requirements for company financial statements are examined in more detail.

7.6.7 The Audit of Companies

At one time, all limited companies required a formal audit by a qualified chartered or certified accountant. The auditor examines the books and records of the business, and compares them to the final financial statements. He or she issues an **audit report** addressed to the company shareholders, which states whether or not the accounts present a true and fair view.

Gradually, over the last few years, the requirement for company audit has been progressively restricted because it was felt to be a bureaucratic burden for companies. Where there are only one or two shareholders, who are probably the company directors, it is almost always a waste of resources to have a formal audit. Currently, micro-entities and small companies (see the previous section of the chapter for the definition of a small company) are in most circumstances exempted from the audit requirement. Such businesses can, of course, choose to have an audit if they wish. Sometimes it can be useful to do so: if a small company wishes to borrow a substantial sum of money from a bank it may assist the case if there is a set of audited accounts available to show the bank manager.

In addition, the law allows shareholders the right to require an audit, provided that holders of more than 10% of the company's share capital give notice in writing that they require an audit to be carried out. This provision in the law is intended to give shareholders who hold only a minority of the share capital of the company some protection against majority holders. So, if a minority shareholder (ie. a holder of at least 10% of the share capital) in a small company suspects that directors may not be acting fairly he or she has some protection in law.

7.6.8 Accounting Standards

The Companies Act contains various requirements as to the preparation and presentation of accounting information by companies (see later section in this chapter). However, these requirements are often quite general in nature, and there is a need for additional detailed guidance on how specific accounting issues should be dealt with in the financial statements of companies and other business organizations. This guidance is published in the form of accounting standards.

In the UK accounting standards are issued by the Financial Reporting Council (FRC). At the time of writing (2017) the FRC had issued the following key Financial Reporting Standards:

FRS 100 *Application of Financial Reporting Requirements*
FRS 102 *The Financial Reporting Standard*
FRS 105 *The Financial Reporting Standard applicable to the Micro-Entities regime.*

Most unlisted companies adopt the requirements of FRS 102, *The Financial Reporting Standard*, but micro-entities are entitled to adopt FRS 105 instead.

Companies listed on the London Stock Exchange are required to adopt **International Financial Reporting Standards (IFRS)** in preparing their financial statements. IFRS and the UK standards are in most respects more or less identical, but there are some significant differences in certain areas. IFRS are considered in more detail below.

7.6.9 International Financial Reporting Standards

International accounting standards have been issued since the 1970s when the International Accounting Standards Committee (IASC) was established. In recent years international standards have become increasingly important as the volume of global trading has increased. Where, as is more and more frequently the case, companies and individuals are investing in companies based in other countries, it becomes important that financial statements should be comprehensible and comparable internationally. One means of achieving this goal is to have an internationally accepted approach to accounting so that people can invest across borders with some confidence in the financial information they are using as a basis for decision making. The international standard setting body has therefore gained in importance and stature in recent years. In 2001, the IASC was replaced by the International Accounting Standards Board (IASB) which is now responsible for setting international standards, known as IFRS.

How important are international standards? The European Union decided a few years ago that all listed companies in its member states should prepare their financial statements to comply with international standards from 2005 onwards. This meant that companies listed on the UK Stock Exchange no longer adhered to UK standards after 1 January 2005. Unlisted companies in the UK have the option of compliance with UK or international standards, an option that is permitted by the CA 2006.

Outside Europe, too, international standards are gaining in importance and many countries, such as Australia and New Zealand, have adopted them.

It is beyond the scope of this book to examine individual international standards in any detail. Some of the standards are very long and complex documents that can be fully understood only by those who are highly skilled and experienced in financial reporting. However, the financial statements prepared in accordance with IFRS can be read with understanding by those who are reasonably financially literate. The next two chapters in this book address some of the important elements in gaining an understanding of financial statements.

TERMINOLOGY Some of the terminology differs between International and UK financial statements. A glossary is provided at the end of this book.

7.7 ACCOUNTING FOR LIMITED COMPANIES

The basics of accounting remain the same, regardless of the form of organization. The accounting equation, for example, which was explained in Chapter 2, holds good whether the accounting is for a sole trader, a partnership or a limited company. However, accounting for limited companies involves the introduction of some additional complexities into the statement of profit or loss and statement of financial position.

7.7.1 Components of a Set of Limited Company Accounts

Under the law, a set of accounts for a limited company comprises the following:

- a statement of profit or loss (profit and loss account)
- a statement of financial position (balance sheet)
- notes to the accounts
- directors' report including a business review (or strategic report) for larger companies
- auditors' report (where applicable).

In addition, IAS 7 *Statements of Cash Flow* requires the inclusion of a **cash flow statement** for some businesses (cash flow was examined in detail in Chapter 6). Also, a statement of changes in equity is often included, and is a requirement in the financial statements of larger companies.

The contents of the statement of profit or loss and statement of financial position are dealt with in detail elsewhere in this chapter and in this section of the book. The statement of changes in equity has not previously been encountered; it is explained later in this chapter.

Notes to the accounts can be highly complex in practice. They contain a great deal of supporting explanatory detail about the figures in the accounts, much of which is required by law or by various accounting standards. There are extensive requirements, for example, relating to the disclosure of directors' remuneration.

The directors' report is a quite formal document which must contain explanation and comment on a range of items, including:

- description of the principal activities of the company
- review of the development of the business
- a note of political and charitable donations.

7.7.2 Presentation of Accounting Information

UK company law prescribes formats for the statement of profit or loss and statement of financial position statements. The CA 2006 permits companies to adopt either UK or international accounting. Because this textbook is based throughout on International Financial Reporting Standards and their terminology, the formats shown below use international terminology and conventions. These are based upon IAS 1 *Presentation of financial statements*. The main headings are shown, and underneath each of the headings are listed some of the items that might be included in a typical statement of financial position.

STATEMENT OF FINANCIAL POSITION

ASSETS
 Non-current assets
  Intangible assets
  Tangible assets
  Investments
 Current assets
  Inventories
  Receivables (including prepayments)
  Investments
  Cash at bank and in hand
 Total assets
EQUITY AND LIABILITIES
 Equity
  Share capital
  Retained earnings
 Non-current liabilities
  Borrowings
 Current liabilities
  Bank loans and overdrafts
  Trade payables
  Other payables, including taxation and social security
  Accruals
Total liabilities
Total equity and liabilities

The format for the statement of financial position should by now look quite familiar as it has been adopted throughout the book so far. The only section that looks a little different from the layout in previous chapters is the Equity section which, because we are now looking at companies, comprises share capital and retained earnings.

IAS 1 prescribes an additional financial reporting statement: the statement of changes in equity. This shows changes that have occurred to the components of equity, typically share capital and retained earnings. It includes transactions with owners. In previous chapters transactions with owners have comprised the commitment of owners' own resources to the capital of the business, for example, on start-up, and then drawings from the business once it is established. The statement of changes in equity (SOCIE) for a company comprises the same basic elements as in the sole trader financial statements explained in previous chapters: increases arising from new contributions by owners, and profits, and decreases arising from payments in the form of dividends, and loss. The SOCIE is usually shown in the form of a table, for example, in the case of a company with a 31 December year-end:

STATEMENT OF CHANGES IN EQUITY FOR THE YEAR ENDED 31 DECEMBER

	Share capital £	Retained earnings £	Total equity £
At 1 January	10 000	20 000	30 000
Issue of new capital	2 000		2 000
Profit for the year		5 000	5 000
Dividend		(1 200)	(1 200)
At 31 December	12 000	23 800	35 800

STATEMENT OF PROFIT OR LOSS

Revenue
Cost of sales
Gross profit or loss
Selling and distribution costs
Administrative expenses
Other operating income
Operating profit
Income from investments
Interest receivable and similar income
Finance costs [ie. interest]
Profit or loss before taxation
Tax on profit or loss
Profit or loss for the year

E xplain the current position in the UK in respect of the accounting standards applicable to companies, both listed and unlisted.

Self-test question 7.1
(answer at the end of the book)

NOTE ABOUT TAXATION In all the questions dealt with in earlier chapters in the book we have ignored the effects of taxation. Companies are subject to corporation tax; some of the examples in this chapter will include limited references to tax but no knowledge of corporation tax (or indeed any other tax) is required. In most cases, corporation tax will be a deduction from profit in the statement of profit or loss, with a corresponding liability in the statement of financial position (in the UK corporation tax is payable nine months after a company's year-end, so the liability for tax is a current liability).

Example 7.4

On 1 January 20X6 Xenophon Ltd had issued share capital comprising 8000 50p shares and retained earnings brought forward of £17 000. On 1 March 20X6, Xenophon issued a further 5000 shares of 50p each. On 31 August 20X6 the company paid a dividend of 2p per share in issue on that date. The company made a profit after tax of £5000 for the year.

Prepare Xenophon Ltd's statement of changes in equity for the year ended 31 December 20X6.

Xenophon Ltd: Statement of changes in equity for the year ended 31 December 20X6

	Share capital £	Retained earnings £	Total equity £
At 1 January 20X6	4 000	17 000	21 000
	(8 000 × 50p)		
Issue of new capital (5000 × 50p)	2 500		2 500
Profit for the year		5 000	5 000
Dividend (13 000 shares × 2p)		(260)	(260)
At 31 December 20X6	6 500	21 740	28 240

Uppingham Telephones Ltd has the following balances in its books at 31 March 20X3:

Self-test question 7.2 (answer at the end of the book)

	£
Intangible non-current assets	30 866
Premises at carrying amount	65 700
Vehicles at carrying amount	44 430
Fixtures and fittings at carrying amount	17 260
Inventories at 31 March 20X3	42 370
Receivables	82 026
Cash at bank and in hand	13 222
Trade payables	39 210
Long-term loan	15 000
Share capital: 20 000 £1 shares issued	20 000
Retained earnings at 1 April 20X2	161 479
Revenue	717 216
Cost of sales	509 582
Selling costs	63 477
Distribution costs	54 460
Administrative expenses	24 512
Dividends paid	5 000

The chief accountant must allow for a corporation tax charge for the year of £19 500. Prepare the statement of profit or loss and the statement of changes in equity for the year ended 31 March 20X3 for Uppingham Telephones Ltd, and a statement of financial position at that date.

7.8 ACCOUNTING FOR LISTED COMPANIES: ADDITIONAL REQUIREMENTS

Listed companies may have thousands of shareholders and employees, and may be of interest to a very large group of people. The nature of the information published by such companies is clearly of great public significance. Listed companies vary greatly in size – some are surprisingly small – but all are subject to additional requirements over and above Companies Act requirements.

7.8.1 Regulations for Listed Companies

Companies are described as 'listed' if they are quoted on a recognized stock exchange. Obtaining a quotation for a company opens up potentially vast sources of capital available through investment in the company's shares. The London Stock Exchange is a highly significant exchange. As well as listing UK-based companies (around 1500 of them at the end of February 2017), the London Stock Exchange has listings for many multinational companies (around 550 of them at the end of February 2017), including such well known company names as Unilever, Toyota, Banco Santander and Mitsubishi.

In order to allow investors to trade in shares with a reasonable degree of security, stock exchanges tend to be highly regulated. The London Stock Exchange is no exception; for listed companies there are additional accounting and disclosure requirements beyond those which apply to companies in general. For example, listed companies in the UK are required to issue interim reports which follow six months after the principal annual accounts. A few companies are required to report quarterly (ie. every three months). In the USA listed companies are required, as a matter of course, to produce quarterly reports. UK companies must also issue a preliminary announcement of annual results, as soon as they have been approved by the board of directors.

Listed company regulations (the 'listing rules') are overseen by the Financial Conduct Authority (FCA) (www.fca.org.uk). There are many detailed rules governing eligibility for listing and conduct for listed companies in the FCA Handbook, which can be accessed via its website.

7.8.2 The Annual Report for a Listed Company

The annual report produced by a listed company is often a very long and complex document. It contains all the minimum annual accounting requirements under company law (the statement of profit or loss, the statement of financial position, and so on) but also a great deal of additional information. Some of the additional disclosures are voluntary and some are required by other regulation. The annual report is viewed by many listed companies as an important public relations vehicle, and a great deal of care is put into design and presentation. The report is often expensive to produce because of the high quality of paper, photography and graphics used. The example below examines the content of a real-life annual report.

Example 7.5 (Real-Life)

Marks & Spencer plc is a very well known retailer, whose shares are listed in the FTSE 100 (ie. they are amongst the 100 largest companies in the UK). The company's 2016 Annual Report can be downloaded from its website (annualreport.marksandspencer.com/). This is a 132-page document, broken down as follows:

Description	Page count
Strategic report: our business review	14
Strategic report: our performance, including key performance indicators, financial review and review of risk management	16
Corporate governance: overview	12
Corporate governance: accountability	7
Corporate governance: remuneration	23
Other disclosures and auditor's report	13
Financial statements	41
Shareholder information	6
	132

The financial statements comprise just under one-third of the length of the report. Some of the items in the list are required because Marks & Spencer plc is a listed company. There are, for example, extensive additional disclosures on corporate governance and directors' remuneration. The background to these disclosures is explained below in the section below on corporate governance requirements.

It should be noted that the annual report of Marks & Spencer plc contains financial statements relating to all the companies in the Marks & Spencer group of companies. Where a company owns several others it is usually necessary in law to prepare consolidated financial statements, which bring together the results and the assets and liabilities of all companies under common control. Therefore, the statement of profit or loss in Marks & Spencer's financial statements is referred to as a 'consolidated statement of profit or loss'.

Marks & Spencer's annual report, like the annual report of most large businesses, is in part a public relations document. It is well-designed and contains photographs of the directors and of the company's products. A substantial part of the content of the report comprises disclosures required by law or other regulation, but such disclosures are combined with design elements such as pictures and graphs to make the report look as attractive as possible.

7.8.3 Corporate Governance Requirements

Corporate governance is the system by which companies are directed and controlled. In the UK, corporate governance of listed companies became the subject of much debate during the 1990s. The debate was provoked by several major company scandals which took place towards the end of the 1980s. Failures of governance were implicated in many of the scandals, and there was a general feeling that listed companies must improve the way their boards were run.

Various reports and recommendations on corporate governance were issued (the Cadbury Report in 1992, the Greenbury Report in 1995 and the Hampel Report in 1998). In 1998 the final version of the various reports combined: 'Principles of Good Governance and Code of Best Practice', usually referred to as the 'Combined Code', was published. It is currently known as the UK Corporate Governance Code and is applicable to all listed companies. The current version of the Code can be accessed on the website of the Financial Reporting Council (www.frc.org.uk).

The detailed contents of the UK Corporate Governance Code are beyond the scope of this book. Broadly, the Code addresses the following areas:

- leadership
- effectiveness
- accountability
- remuneration
- relations with shareholders.

Each listed company is required to produce, as part of its annual report, statements on its corporate governance and on directors' remuneration. The analysis of the Marks & Spencer 2016 Annual Report earlier demonstrates the importance of these statements.

7.9 ACCOUNTING FOR LISTED COMPANIES: NON-FINANCIAL INFORMATION

The annual reports of listed companies tend to be lengthy documents as we observed above in the example of the Marks & Spencer 2016 annual report. A document of well over 100 pages is quite usual, especially in the case of the largest and most publicly prominent businesses. There has been a noticeable trend in recent years towards an increase in the volume of information produced in annual reports. This is the result of a combination of factors, including the following:

- more disclosures required as a result of developments in corporate governance.
- increases in voluntary disclosures especially in respect of social, environmental and sustainability issues.
- the introduction of more complex accounting standards that require additional explanatory notes to the financial statements.

All of these factors contribute to the inclusion of much more information that is not expressed in terms of figures, ie. non-financial information. There are both advantages and drawbacks to the inclusion of this type of information.

7.9.1 Advantages of Publishing Non-financial Information

- Non-financial information can often help the less financially-knowledgeable user of financial statements to understand the performance and position of the company.
- It is quite often illustrated with photographs and graphs that can help to enhance understanding.
- The presentation of non-financial information often appears much more attractive and user-friendly when compared to the financial statement section of the report; therefore it is more likely to be read.

7.9.2 Drawbacks of Publishing Non-financial Information

- The sheer volume of information included in an annual report may be off-putting to readers.
- Non-financial information may be produced principally for public relations purposes and it may, for example, report selectively about aspects of the company's performance.
- Information in the form of graphs that accompany non-financial reports may be biased (there is academic research in this area that shows that graphs can be used to give a misleading impression).

7.9.3 The Strategic Report

A change to company law was made in 2013 which required some companies to produce a Strategic Report. The Financial Reporting Council (FRC) then produced some detailed guidance on the nature and content of the Strategic Report. It is intended to provide 'shareholders with a holistic and meaningful picture of an entity's business model, strategy, development, performance and future prospects' (FRC (2014) 'Guidance on the Strategic Report' available at www.frc.org.uk)

All companies must prepare a directors' report. All companies not defined as 'small' (see earlier in the chapter) must, in addition, prepare a Strategic Report. The FRC's guidance sets out three objectives of the report:

- to provide insight into the entity's business model and its main strategy and objectives (strategic management)
- to describe the principal risks the entity faces and how they might affect its future prospects (business environment)
- to provide an analysis of the entity's past performance (business performance).

The best way of finding out about the content of the Strategic Report is to read a few examples. In the Marks & Spencer's 2016 Annual Report (see real-life Example 7.5 earlier in the chapter), the first 30 pages comprise the Strategic Report. There is a great deal of useful narrative information about the strategic priorities of the business, the management team and some key statistics and figures.

7.10 CORPORATE REPORTING ON THE INTERNET

The Companies Act 2006 made it compulsory for listed companies to make their annual report freely available on a website and therefore it is easy to access a great deal of information about any listed company.

However, companies have to be careful about what they publish on their websites. They cannot be seen to be creating false market expectations by the publication of exaggerated or inaccurate information. In most cases, the accounting information that is published on corporate websites comprises html or pdf files containing exactly the same information as contained in the annual or half-yearly report. However, some companies use the internet in more creative ways to reach their actual and potential investors. Some examples of the type of information found on the investor section of corporate websites include the following:

- webcasts of annual general meetings and/or the analysts' meetings where directors present and discuss the financial results
- corporate videos with information about business activities

- stockbrokers' forecasts
- press releases containing, for example, the preliminary announcement of the financial results and significant events such as takeovers and share issues
- email links to corporate officers who can deal with queries about the business.

This type of information can be very useful. For example, listed companies generally hold annual meetings with the financial analysts who are interested in the activities of the company (and who often work on behalf of institutional shareholders). At one time, these meetings took place behind closed doors. However, webcasts of the meetings allow private investors and anyone else who is interested to see the directors fielding questions from analysts and discussing the financial performance and prospects of the business.

The availability of information on the internet is particularly useful for investors outside the country where the company is based.

Digital reporting of financial information has become much more important in recent years. XBRL (Extensible Business Reporting Language) is the open international standard for digital business reporting. It allows the preparers of reports to 'tag' certain items of information so that they can be readily transferred into the user's software applications. If data can be transferred in a standard format, it can then be subject to analysis, summary and comparison to suit the needs of the financial statement user. A global not-for-profit consortium, XBRL International, is responsible for managing and standardizing the use of XBRL globally. Its website (www.xbrl.org) contains a great deal of useful information.

Chapter Summary

This chapter contains information about the nature of companies in the UK, shares, directors, financial statements and the general regulatory structures surrounding financial reporting by companies. There is a great deal of very detailed regulation pertaining to companies, and this chapter provides only an outline of it. Some of the website references listed below provide more information for those students who wish to find out more.

The need for publication of accounting information by companies was explained early in the chapter as part of an introduction to the concept of limited liability. It was followed by an explanation of some of the key features of the legal requirements relating to companies.

International and UK accounting financial reporting standards form part of the overall structure of regulation. Listed companies in the UK are obliged to report under international standards, and the option of using international standards rather than UK standards is open to all other companies under the Companies Act 2006. The financial reporting sections of this book are based on international accounting standards and presentations, and so the international approach has been stressed in this chapter. However, it is worth bearing in mind that many unlisted companies continue to use UK standards for financial reporting, and so students are likely to find some financial reports in practice that look unfamiliar. The glossary will help in such cases.

The later sections of the chapter examined the additional regulation of accounting information in respect of listed companies. Students should appreciate the reasons why the requirements relating to this class of companies are so much more stringent than those that apply to smaller unlisted companies.

It may take some time to assimilate the information in this chapter. Students can increase their familiarity with corporate financial reporting by working through the exercises at the end of the chapter. However, reading the financial press will also help. Reading the *Financial Times* (FT) may present some challenges to understanding at first, but it will undoubtedly increase general business knowledge very quickly. A good way to start may be to read the FT once a week, or to start with the business pages of one of the better quality newspapers (eg. *The Guardian*, *The Times* or *The Independent*).

Internet Resources

The internet can be used to find out a great deal of information about UK companies and company law.

www.londonstockexchange.com – a very comprehensive site containing detailed information about share prices, stock exchange statistics and data relating to individual companies.
www.companieshouse.gov.uk – the website of Companies House. This provides information about all companies registered in the UK, and also, a lot of very useful and up-to-date information about the law relating to companies.
www.frc.org.uk – the website of the Financial Reporting Council which regulates corporate governance, financial reporting and auditing in the UK
www.ifrs.org – the website of the IFRS Foundation which is responsible for developing international financial reporting standards via its standard-setting body, the International Accounting Standards Board (IASB)
www.xbrl.org – the website of XBRL International which is responsible for standardizing the use of Extensible Business Reporting Language for digital reporting of financial information.

Book's companion website summary

The website contains the following resources in respect of Chapter 7:

Students' section

A multiple choice quiz containing ten questions
Five additional questions with answers

Lecturers' section

Answers to end-of-chapter exercises 7.10 to 7.14
Four additional questions with answers
Case study
Testbank
Instructor's Manual
PowerPoint presentation

Exercises: Answers at the End of the Book

7.1 Two of the following four statements are correct:

1 Directors must prepare the company's financial statements themselves.

2 Directors take complete responsibility for the preparation of financial statements.

3 Directors may be guilty of a criminal offence if the accounts do not present a true and fair view.

4 Directors may be guilty of a criminal offence if it is proven that they have defrauded creditors.

Which are the correct statements?
a) 3 and 4
b) 2 and 4
c) 1 and 2
d) 1 and 3

7.2 Bayliss Chandler Ltd has an issued share capital of £20 000, split into 50p shares. In the year ended 31 May 20X7 a dividend of 6p per share was paid.

Ambrose owns 10% of the issued shares in Bayliss Chandler Ltd. What was the value of Ambrose's dividend for the year ended 31 May 20X7?

a) £180
b) £120
c) £240
d) £360

7.3 Peachey plc has an issued share capital of £60 000 denominated in 25p shares. On 13 May 20X2 Carina, a shareholder, sold half of her total shareholding of 8000 shares to her sister Cathy. Peachey's accounting year-end is 31 December. In the year ended 31 December 20X2 the company paid dividends of 10% of nominal value. Half the dividend was paid on 31 March 20X2 and the remainder on 30 September 20X2.

What amount of dividend did Carina and Cathy receive in the year ended 31 December 20X2?

a) Carina received £600; Cathy received £200
b) Carina received £400; Cathy received £400
c) Carina received £100; Cathy received £100
d) Carina received £150; Cathy received £50

7.4 Butterthwaite plc had issued share capital on 1 January 20X3, as follows:

Ordinary share capital: 68 000 £1 ordinary shares
Preference share capital: £20 000 6% cumulative preference shares

On 31 January 20X3 the company issued a further 12 000 £1 ordinary shares. A dividend of 5p per share was paid on 31 October 20X3. In 20X2 the company failed to pay its preference dividend, but in 20X3 found that it could meet its obligations in full and paid the full amount owing on 31 December 20X3.

What is the total amount of dividend paid by Butterthwaite plc in respect of the year ended 31 December 20X3?

a) £5800
b) £5200
c) £6400
d) £4600

7.5 The directors of Solar Bubble plc, a trading company, have asked the company's chief accountant to prepare a draft statement of profit or loss for the year ended 31 January 20X8 in time for them to discuss it at their board meeting on 15th February. The directors prefer to have the information presented in the same way as in the annual financial statements.

The chief accountant identifies the following relevant balances:

	£
Administrative expenses	73 959
Opening inventory	51 240
Interest payable	1 977
Revenue	975 420
Selling and distribution costs	80 714
Purchases	603 493
Closing inventory	57 210

Notes:

1. £6000 has to be accrued in respect of sales commission for the year ended 31 January 20X8.
2. The corporation tax charge for the year is estimated at £60 625.
3. A preference dividend on the £100 000 8% preference shares was paid. The preference dividend is to be treated as a finance cost because the preference shares are treated as a liability in the statement of financial position.
4. Of the administrative expenses, £1270 relates to prepayment of insurance.

The chief accountant will be using the following format for the draft statement of profit or loss:

Revenue
Cost of sales
Gross profit or loss
Selling and distribution costs
Administrative expenses
Operating profit
Finance costs
Profit or loss before tax
Tax on profit or loss
Profit or loss for the year.

Prepare the draft statement of profit or loss for Solar Bubble plc for the year ended 31 January 20X8.

7.6   Brighton Magnets Ltd has the following balances in its books at 31 August 20X9:

	£
Closing inventories	186 420
Delivery vans at carrying amount	120 000
Secretarial costs	51 498
Electricity (administrative office)	12 491
Trade payables	219 411
Factory and plant at carrying amount	2 518 000
Retained earnings at 1 September 20X8	1 597 172
Share capital: £1 ordinary shares	800 000
Administration office: telephone charges	6 964
Finance costs	1 207
Salespersons' salaries	64 299
Delivery van depreciation	12 000
Other selling and distribution costs	5 911
Office rental	42 704
Other administrative expenses	36 075
Revenue	3 796 842
Interest receivable	644
Depreciation of office computer equipment	8 390
Salespersons' commission	12 270
Office manager's salary	21 704
Directors' remuneration	59 200
Delivery van expenses	24 470
Trade receivables	321 706

	£
Office equipment at carrying amount	151 020
Cash at bank	18 290
Cost of sales	2 712 350
Other operating income	12 900
Dividends paid	40 000

Note: corporation tax on the profits for the year is estimated at £216 470. This amount is not included in the list of balances above.

Prepare a statement of profit or loss and a statement of changes in equity for Brighton Magnets Limited for the year ended 31 August 20X9 and a statement of financial position at that date. All three financial statements are to be presented in an appropriate format.

7.7 Two of the following statements are correct:

1 Listed companies are obliged to produce a social responsibility report as part of their annual report.

2 Consolidated financial statements bring together the results and assets and liabilities of all group companies.

3 Compliance with the requirements of the UK Corporate Governance Code is compulsory for companies listed in the UK.

4 XBRL International is owned by the London Stock Exchange.

Which are the correct statements?
a) 1 and 2
b) 2 and 3
c) 3 and 4
d) 1 and 4

7.8 Explain the principal objectives of the Strategic Report.

7.9 Explain the status of UK accounting standards and International Financial Reporting Standards in financial reporting for UK companies.

Exercises: Answers Available on the Lecturers' Section of the Book's Website

7.10 Three of the following six statements are correct:

1 The audit report of a company states that the accounts are correct.

2 A private limited company does not have to make any information available to the public.

3 A public limited company must have an authorized share capital of at least £50 000.

4 The minimum number of shareholders in a private limited company is seven.

5 Each ordinary share carries the right to a vote.

6 A listed company must present its financial statements in compliance with international financial reporting standards.

Which are the correct statements?
a) 1, 3 and 5
b) 1, 2 and 4
c) 2, 4 and 6
d) 3, 5 and 6

7.11 Western Gadgets Limited has an issued share capital of £5000 denominated in 25p shares. In the year ended 30 April 20X4 an interim dividend of 2p per share and a final dividend of 2.5p per share were paid. Joan owns shares in Western Gadgets Limited with a nominal value of £1500.
What was the value of Joan's dividend for the year ended 30 April 20X4?

a) £270
b) £150
c) £225
d) £67.50

7.12 Parlabane Limited has an issued share capital of 42 500 50p shares. In the year ending 31 December 20X5 a dividend of 2p per share was paid on 1 December.
Jonah owns 13 000 shares in Parlabane Limited.
What was the total dividend paid and how much was paid to Jonah personally?

a) Total dividend paid £850; paid to Jonah £260
b) Total dividend paid £1000; paid to Jonah £260
c) Total dividend paid £425; paid to Jonah £130
d) Total dividend paid £500; paid to Jonah £130

7.13 Penge and Purley plc have in issue at 31 December 20X6:

138 000 ordinary shares of 50p each
40 000 8% preference shares of £1 each, issued on 1 July 20X6.

Derek owns 3250 ordinary shares in the company which he bought several years ago, and 1000 of the £1 preference shares which he bought on 1 July 20X6 when they were issued. An interim dividend of 2.7p per ordinary share was paid, and a final dividend of 3.7p per ordinary share was also paid, as was the preference dividend for the six months ended 31 December 20X6.
What was Derek's total dividend from the company for the year ended 31 December 20X6?

a) £184
b) £288
c) £144
d) £248

7.14 Downside Green Limited had the following balances relating to its position at 31 December 20X1:

	£
Overdraft	7 746
Share capital	100 000
Loan repayable 31 December 20X8	100 000
Trade receivables	916 278
Cash in hand	260

	£
Intangible non-current assets at carrying amount	80 000
Trade payables	868 462
Retained earnings	1 850 824
Tangible non-current assets at carrying amount	1 082 184
Inventories	841 740
Non-current asset investments	24 860
Other payables (all current liabilities)	18 290

The directors wish to see how the statement of financial position will be presented when it is sent to share-holders. Downside Green's financial controller intends to use the following statement of financial position format:

ASSETS

Non-current assets

Intangible assets

Tangible assets

Investments

Current assets

Inventories

Receivables (including prepayments)

Investments

Cash at bank and in hand

Total assets

EQUITY AND LIABILITIES

Equity

Share capital

Retained earnings

Non-current liabilities

Borrowings

Current liabilities

Bank loans and overdrafts

Trade payables

Other payables, including taxation and social security

Accruals

Total liabilities

Total equity and liabilities

Prepare the statement of financial position for Downside Green Limited for the year ended 31 December 20X1 in the format requested by the directors.

8 Understanding financial reports: trend analysis

Aim of the chapter

To develop a range of skills which assist in the understanding of financial reports for various types of business.

Learning outcomes

After reading the chapter and completing the related exercises, students should:

- Understand the potential usefulness of financial reports to various interest groups.
- Understand the principal features of the analysis of trends in financial statements.
- Be able to perform an analysis based on horizontal and/or vertical analysis of financial statements.
- Understand the problems which can arise in comparing businesses with each other.

Techniques of analysis will be developed further in Chapter 9.

Introduction

One of the most important aims of this book is to help students appreciate that financial information actually means something. The formal figures that are set out in reports may not look very interesting in themselves, but the underlying reality that the numbers symbolize is almost always fascinating, especially for those involved.

Many of the examples and exercises in Chapters 2 to 7 have emphasized the importance of accounting figures in helping people to understand what is going on in a business. However, this chapter and Chapter 9 look much more closely at the analysis of financial information as a route to understanding. The two chapters cover a range of techniques and calculations. However, those students who are less than totally confident about their numeracy skills should not be put off; none of the techniques covered in the chapters involves anything more difficult than simple arithmetical skills of the type already utilized. The important skill, in fact, lies in the interpretation of the results; this is a skill best achieved through practice.

In this chapter we will, first, briefly examine the various groups of people who are interested in accounting information, the reasons for their interest, and the aspects which might be particularly useful to them. Then the chapter proceeds to examine simple analytical techniques which compare one figure or group of figures with another.

Please note that this chapter of the book considers the analysis of the formal financial reports which we have covered in Chapters 2 to 7 inclusive. In the second section of the book (beginning with Chapter 10) attention will be turned to the type of management accounting information which is generated within a business for use by owners and managers in making plans and in controlling the business activities.

8.1 USEFULNESS OF FINANCIAL REPORTS TO VARIOUS INTEREST GROUPS

8.1.1 Owners and Investors

Previous chapters have included several examples of sole trader owners using periodic financial information to inform them about the progress of their business. However, it must be recognized that most unincorporated business owners will have available to them other, more comprehensive, sources of information about their business performance. For example, an annual financial statement does not provide any information about the state of the business's order book, but the current levels of demand for products and services would be regarded by business owners as an absolutely vital means of assessing business prospects. So, although it is not unrealistic to suggest that owners of businesses use annual financial reports as aids to understanding, it should be recognized that they have other, potentially more useful, sources of information available to them.

The situation is rather different, however, for investors in limited companies. Unless they are also directors, they do not have any privileges of access to information beyond their right to receive the annual report and accounts. An investor who buys 100 shares in Marks & Spencer plc, for example, (or any other listed company) obtains some rights (the right to receive a part of any dividend declared and the right to vote at the Annual General Meeting of the company). However, he or she does not have the right to wander in off the street to the company's head office demanding to see the monthly accounts.

Investors in companies who do not have access to information other than the annual report and accounts, are likely to be interested in the answers to some or all of the following questions:

- How is my investment doing?
- Should I buy more shares/sell the shares I already own/hold on to my current investment?
- Is the dividend likely to increase?
- What are the chances of the company going out of business?

8.1.2 Potential Investors in a Business

People who are thinking of investing in a business will usually take steps to obtain the most recent financial reports. If the company is listed on the London Stock Exchange (or a stock exchange elsewhere), access to this type of information is usually very easy; all UK listed companies are obliged by the Companies Act 2006 to have websites. These corporate websites contain the most recent published financial reports for the company and they may also contain other useful pieces of information like the preliminary announcement of results, information about directors, and more detailed information about the company's activities. Unlisted companies, as we saw in Chapter 7, are obliged to file accounting information with Companies House, and it is possible to obtain this information very easily from the Companies House website.

It may be impossible to obtain any financial information about other forms of business because sole traders and partnerships are not obliged to make information public. But if a business is interested in attracting buyers it has an incentive to provide recent, reliable financial information to potential investors.

It should be recognized, however, that financial information such as the statement of profit or loss and statement of financial position is essentially backward looking; these statements report events which have already occurred, and they may not be a reliable guide to what is going to happen in the future.

Potential investors tend to be looking for answers to some or all of the following questions:

- What are the risks involved in this business? How likely would I be to lose money? Would my investment be safe?
- How much can I make from investing in this business? Will the return be better than I could make if I were to:
  - Put the money into some other business?
  - Leave it in the bank?
  - Risk it on a bet on the horses/dogs/a card game?
- What are my chances of getting seriously rich?

8.1.3 Creditors

In Chapter 7 we looked at the example of Tommy, who supplied goods on credit to a limited company but was unable to obtain payment for them before the company became insolvent. Businesses and individuals who supply goods on credit to limited companies take the risk that they will not be paid. As noted in the discussion in Chapter 7, one of the ways of reducing the risk is to examine the financial reports of a company to assess its financial condition.

Suppliers of goods and services, like anyone else, are entitled to obtain the financial information that is filed at Companies House. Alternatively, they may prefer to use the services of a credit agency which, for a fee, supplies a detailed report on the credit-worthiness of a named company. (For example, see the range of services offered by Dun & Bradstreet – www.dnb.co.uk)

In the case of sole traders and partnerships, there is no publicly available source of financial information, and suppliers must base their decision on whether or not to offer credit on other factors (they may, for example, ask the trader or partnership to supply references from some reputable person like a bank manager).

If a bank or other financial institution lends to a business it becomes a creditor, possibly for the long term. In such cases, the bank is usually in a position to demand financial information, regardless of whether the business is a sole trader, partnership or company, and indeed, this may be part of the lending deal.

When undertaking an analysis of financial reports, creditors are interested in obtaining answers to the following questions:

- How likely is it that I will be paid?
- How likely is it that I will be paid on time?
- Will my interest (where applicable) be paid regularly?
- Is there a risk that this business will go bust before I get paid?

Financial statements, especially those produced by limited companies, tend to be principally oriented towards the information needs of investors and owners. However, other interested parties such as creditors will also find a great deal of information which is relevant to their needs.

8.2 ANALYTICAL TECHNIQUES: CHANGES IN FIGURES

The most straightforward analytical technique can be one of the most effective: comparing two or more figures with each other to assess the differences between them.

Example 8.1

Ilse is a sole trader, who runs a shop selling imported fabrics and furnishings. Her revenue figures for the three years ended 31 March 20X8 are as follows:

	20X8	20X7	20X6
	£	£	£
Revenue	217 300	209 220	204 240

It does not take a financial wizard to see that Ilse's revenue has gone up between 20X6 and 20X8. Sometimes, this kind of straightforward pointing out of the obvious is all that is needed in financial analysis. However, the analysis could be refined, without much additional difficulty, by calculating the percentage increase year on year, as follows.

BETWEEN 20X6 AND 20X7

Revenue has risen by £209 220 – 204 240 = £4980
£4980 can be calculated as a percentage of the 20X6 figure, as follows:

$$\frac{£4980}{204\ 240} \times 100 = 2.4\%$$

BETWEEN 20X7 AND 20X8

Revenue has risen by £217 300 − £209 220 = £8080

£8080 can be calculated as a percentage of the 20X7 figure, as follows:

$$\frac{£8080}{209\ 220} \times 100 = 3.9\%$$

WHAT DOES THIS MEAN?

By calculating the percentage increases, we have added a little to our slender stock of knowledge about Ilse's sales. If we know, from local Chamber of Commerce information, that traders in Ilse's part of town have experienced an average annual growth in sales of 8% between 20X6 and 20X8 it suggests that Ilse's business performance is in relative decline.

In order to increase the value of the information about Ilse's sales, we need some point of comparison. The point of comparison may come from outside the business (eg. the information provided by the Chamber of Commerce) or from inside the business. For example, suppose Ilse tells you, as her new financial adviser, that she invested a lot of additional working capital in a new line of inventory during 20X6 and 20X7, expecting to boost sales by 20% per annum, you might well conclude that her efforts to expand the business had been relatively unsuccessful.

A great deal depends upon the context of the financial information.

8.3 ANALYTICAL TECHNIQUES: HORIZONTAL AND TREND ANALYSIS

Horizontal analysis describes the type of analysis we carried out above on Ilse's sales figures. Where there is at least two years' worth of information, it is possible to conduct some type of horizontal analysis.

In some cases, several years' worth of information is available, and it becomes possible to carry out a trend analysis. This type of analysis includes figures over several years and attempts to track longer-term business trends.

Moving rapidly up the size scale from Ilse's business we will now consider the publicly available information provided by Burberry plc, a FTSE 100 listed company. (Burberry operates in the luxury fashion sector, providing expensive and exclusive clothing and accessories for men, women and children.) Listed companies commonly provide five-year summaries of information (sometimes the summaries even extend to a ten-year period). In the next example, we will examine some elements of the five-year record of information for Burberry plc.

Example 8.2 (Real-Life)

The following table shows extracts from Burberry plc's financial statements for the year ended 31 March 2016.

	2016 £m	2015 £m	2014 £m	2013 £m	2012 £m
Revenue	2 514.7	2 523.2	2 329.8	1 998.7	1 857.2
Gross profit	1 762.7	1 765.5	1 658.5	1 422.0	1 298.9
Profit before tax	415.6	444.6	444.4	350.7	366.0

This is just a small part of the information disclosed by Burberry plc in its annual financial statements. What does it tell us?

Scanning the revenue line quickly, we can tell that the business has improved its revenue each year over the period until 2016 when there was a small drop in revenue. Where revenue increases, we could expect to see a corresponding improvement in profit figures, but the trends in these figures are not consistent. Profit before tax increases substantially in 2014 from 2013, is almost identical in 2015 and then drops back in 2016.

We can extend the horizontal analysis by calculating year-on-year percentage increases, in the same way as for Ilse's business. The percentage increases/decreases) can be neatly presented in a table like this one:

Annual percentage increases (decreases) in a selection of key figures: Burberry plc

	2016	2015	2014	2013
	%	%	%	%
Revenue	0%	8.3%	16.6%	7.6%
Gross profit	0%	6.4%	15.0%	9.5%
Profit before tax	(6.5%)	0%	26.7%	(4.2%)

The horizontal analysis using percentages highlights some of the general trends in the business: impressive increases in revenue over much of the five-year period matched in part by increases in profitability. But the 2015–6 financial year was far less successful. Looking further into the information provided in the company's Annual Report, there are some explanations of the halt in sales growth. The Strategic Report for the year contains a letter to shareholders from the chairman of the board. In this letter, he notes that the luxury sector has experienced some challenges, including a slowdown of the Chinese economy, geopolitical concerns in the Middle East and Russia and uncertainty in the Eurozone. The reasons for the slowdown in revenue and profitability, therefore, appear to be attributable to macro-economic factors.

Self-test question 8.1 (answer at the end of the book)

Jamal is a sole trader selling a range of pre-packaged foods. He has a small food processing factory and employs several staff. In 20X4, he made the decision to employ a full-time sales manager. The sales manager, Jared, claimed at the interview that he would be able to achieve 15% sales increases each year.

Jared is asking for a substantial increase in his annual salary effective from the start of next year. He tells Jamal that he thinks he is worth it, because of the contribution he has made to the business since he joined. The final accounts for the year ended 31 December 20X9 have just been finished in draft form by the accountant. Jamal is now reviewing his annual sales figures which are available as far back as 20X1 when he started the business. The following table shows revenue for each year:

Year	£
20X1	250 031
20X2	347 266
20X3	441 179
20X4	531 150
20X5	523 622
20X6	545 331
20X7	590 942
20X8	679 244
20X9	771 485

Examine the horizontal trends in Jamal's revenue figures, and, briefly, advise him on whether or not Jared's claim for an increased salary appears justified.

8.3.1 Some Problems with Horizontal Analysis

There are two principal problems which are likely to arise in respect of horizontal analysis:

CHANGES IN THE BUSINESS Very rapid changes can take place in business. These may mean that figures are not really comparable over a period of years. Also, new accounting rules and standards may make a difference to the presentation of the figures. The five-year figures of Burberry plc which we examined earlier will have been adjusted for any effects of this type so that a proper and meaningful comparison can be made. In the case of unlisted companies and smaller businesses, which do not usually include five years' worth of comparative figures in their financial statements, the analyst must be careful to make any necessary adjustments.

FAILURE TO TAKE THE EFFECTS OF INFLATION INTO ACCOUNT Although it is possible to adjust accounting figures for the effects of inflation this is not usually done in UK accounting. In recent years, the general rate of inflation in the economy has not been high, and its effects are often regarded as negligible. However, this can be misleading, as the following example shows:

Example 8.3

A five-year analysis of the sales of Trevor Fine Art Productions Limited shows the following figures:

	20X7	20X6	20X5	20X4	20X3
	£	£	£	£	£
Revenue	683 084	657 469	634 868	617 576	590 530
Percentage increase on previous year	3.9%	3.6%	2.8%	4.6%	

Between 20X3 and 20X7 sales have increased in total by the following percentage:

$$\frac{£683\ 084 - 590\ 530}{590\ 530} \times 100 = 15.7\%$$

Looking at the individual years we can see that there has been an increase each year. So far, so good, but if we take inflation into account the picture changes somewhat. Suppose that in each year between 20X3 and 20X8 the average rate of inflation in the economy has been 3% per annum. We can see that in most years the sales increases were only slightly above inflation and the increase between 20X4 and 20X5 was actually a little below the rate of inflation. The sales increases are not as impressive as they first appear to be.

8.4 ANALYTICAL TECHNIQUES: VERTICAL ANALYSIS AND COMMON SIZE ANALYSIS

Vertical analysis is a simple analytical technique which can be useful and informative. It involves expressing each figure in the statement of profit or loss and statement of financial position as a percentage of one key figure (sales in the statement of profit or loss and – usually – total or net assets in the statement of financial position). The next example explains the application of vertical analysis.

Example 8.4

Bore & Hole Limited makes mining equipment. The company statement of profit or loss and statement of financial position for 20X7 are shown below, together with an extra column of percentage figures. In the statement of profit or loss, all percentages are calculated by reference to the value of sales, and in the statement of financial position, by reference to the equity total (the equity total = net assets).

Bore & Hole Limited: Statement of profit or loss for the year ended 31 December 20X7

	£	%
Revenue	4 490 370	100.0
Cost of sales	(3 521 348)	(78.4)
Gross profit	969 022	21.6
Administrative expenses	(454 432)	(10.1)
Distribution and selling costs	(407 480)	(9.1)
Other operating income	16 210	0.4
Operating profit	123 320	2.8
Finance costs	(33 900)	(0.8)
Profit before tax	89 420	2.0
Tax	(26 461)	(0.6)
Profit after tax	62 959	1.4

NB: Each item is calculated as a percentage of sales (to one decimal point):
For example:

$$\frac{\text{Administrative expenses}}{\text{Revenue}} \times 100 = \frac{£454\ 432}{4\ 490\ 370} \times 100 = 10.1\%$$

Bore & Hole Limited: Statement of financial position at 31 December 20X7

	£	£	%
ASSETS		3 975 750	99.1
Non-current assets			
Current assets			
Inventories	586 404		14.6
Trade receivables	430 580		10.7
Cash at bank	10 110		0.2
		1 027 094	
		5 002 844	
EQUITY AND LIABILITIES			
Equity			
Share capital		800 000	19.9
Retained earnings		3 213 632	80.1
		4 013 632	100.0
Long-term liabilities			
Borrowings		390 000	9.7
Current liabilities			
Trade and other payables		599 212	14.9
		5 002 844	

What does the vertical analysis statement tell us? It is a single period statement only, so its information content is limited. The percentage column is helpful in that it tends to draw attention to the relative size of the figures. For example, we can see from the statement that operating profit as a percentage of revenue is only 2.8%, and that profit after tax is a mere 1.4% of revenue. These percentages suggest that the business is not performing well.

Turning to the statement of financial position we can see that it is dominated by non-current assets; this is a manufacturing business, and non-current assets could be expected to be high. Cash is negligible and the business has long-term borrowings of almost 10% of the net asset value.

Common size analysis extends vertical analysis across more than one accounting period. In the next example, we will extend our knowledge of Bore & Hole Limited by examining the vertical analysis percentages in the company's statement of profit or loss over four years.

Example 8.5

The statement of profit or loss in Example 8.4 shows vertical analysis of all the items, based upon sales, for the year ended 31 December 20X7. Below, the comparative vertical analysis figures are repeated for the 20X7 statement of profit or loss, and are set alongside the comparative figures for the previous three years.

	20X7	20X6	20X5	20X4
	%	%	%	%
Revenue	100.0	100.0	100.0	100.0
Cost of sales	(78.4)	(78.3)	(77.2)	(77.0)
Gross profit	21.6	21.7	22.8	23.0
Administrative expenses	(10.1)	(7.3)	(7.4)	(7.2)
Selling and distribution costs	(9.1)	(10.0)	(9.3)	(9.7)
Other operating income	0.4	0.4	–	–
Operating profit	2.8	4.8	6.1	6.1
Finance costs	(0.8)	–	–	–
Profit before tax	2.0	4.8	6.1	6.1
Tax	(0.6)	(1.4)	(1.8)	(1.8)
Profit after tax	1.4	3.4	4.3	4.3

This statement is expressed entirely in percentages; it gives no indication as to the value of each component. (Revenue is the base figure and therefore is 100% in each year.) However, the statement does help understanding by presenting the trends in the figures quite clearly.

For example:

Gross profit as a percentage of revenue has fallen in each of the four years. If this trend continues the business could ultimately fail.

Administrative expenses have remained at a fairly constant level compared to revenue for three out of the four years reviewed. But in 20X7 the percentage suddenly leaps. There could be many explanations for this change; for example, perhaps there has been a change of management and the new management is not controlling costs very well. Or, there may have been a major new investment in non-current assets whose related depreciation charges are shown as part of administrative expenses.

Finance costs feature for the first time in the 20X7 statement of profit or loss, suggesting that in previous years, borrowings were either non-existent or negligible.

Overall, although we have relatively little information about the company (compared with what is available in a full set of financial statements) the common size statement of profit or loss does allow the analyst to draw some tentative conclusions about the performance of the business over time.

8.5 COMPARING BUSINESSES WITH EACH OTHER

So far in this chapter we have analyzed single businesses, generally by reference to the increases and decreases in elements of accounting information over time. However, interested parties will often need to make comparisons between businesses. They can do this by:

a) comparing the results and statements of financial position of two or more businesses.
b) comparing the results and statements of the financial position of a business with industry averages.

8.5.1 Problems in Comparison

The regulation surrounding accounting, especially accounting by limited companies, goes some way towards ensuring that financial statements are prepared to the same set of rules and in the same way. One of the four enhancing characteristics of financial information (see Chapter 1) is comparability. Information about a company is more useful if it can be validly compared with similar information about other companies.

Comparability is accorded a great deal of importance precisely in order to allow meaningful comparisons between accounting statements to be made. However, despite the best intentions of the regulators, there are often problems in ensuring that a valid comparison can be made. Some of these are briefly described below.

DIFFERENCES IN ACCOUNTING POLICIES Accounting policies are the principles of accounting applied in preparing the financial statements. Despite an extensive level of regulation, there are many areas in which a business can make legitimate choices about the amounts at which items are stated, and the way in which those items are presented. The following example will illustrate the point.

Example 8.6

Spanners Limited and Gasket Limited operate within the same business sector. A financial analyst is examining the results of the companies on behalf of a client. Extracts from their statement of profit or loss show the following information (together with vertical analysis percentages):

	Spanners Limited £	%	Gasket Limited £	%
Revenue	984 742	100.0	1 096 880	100.0
Cost of sales	673 938	68.4	756 993	69.0
Gross profit	310 804	31.6	339 887	31.0

The companies appear to be similar in size in that they generate similar levels of turnover, and the percentage of gross profit to sales is close. It seems a fair conclusion, on the face of it, that their performance is virtually identical.

However, the analyst finds out that the companies' policies on inclusion of costs in cost of sales are not the same. Specifically, Spanners Limited includes depreciation of vehicles within cost of sales, whereas Gasket Limited includes the same type of cost within selling and distribution costs. Gasket's vehicle depreciation is £28 977 for the year under review.

In order to compare like with like the analyst must make an adjustment to Gasket's cost of sales:

Adjusted cost of sales = £28 977 + 756 993 = 785 970

Building this adjusted cost into the statement of profit or loss analysis results in the following changes (vertical analysis percentages are recalculated for Gasket Limited):

	Spanners Limited £	%	Gasket Limited £	%
Revenue	984 742	100.0	1 096 880	100.0
Cost of sales	673 938	68.4	785 970	71.7
Gross profit	310 804	31.6	310 910	28.3

The recalculation makes the comparison appear in a rather different light. Gasket's gross profit is 28.3% of revenue, as compared to Spanners' at 31.6%.

Financial statement analysts have to be alert for this type of difference. As the example shows, application of different accounting policies can make a lot of difference. The example illustrates the point in relation to cost classification but there are many other potential areas of difference, including, for example, depreciation and amortization methods.

DIFFERENCES IN BUSINESS ACTIVITIES No two businesses are entirely alike. Comparison of two apparently similar businesses can lead to incorrect conclusions, if the differences between the two are not fully appreciated.

Example 8.7

A financial analyst is comparing the results of two companies for 20X9 and 20X8. Pool & Splash Limited and Dive & Float Limited are both involved in swimming pool installation and maintenance. Companies in the industry are generally performing well.

Revenue figures for the two companies for 20X9 and 20X8 are as follows:

	Pool & Splash Limited		Dive & Float Limited	
	20X9	**20X8**	**20X9**	**20X8**
	£	£	£	£
Revenue	1 662 997	1 357 549	1 842 791	1 543 360

The analyst calculates that the revenue of Pool & Splash Limited has increased by 22.5%, whereas Dive & Float Limited's revenue has increased by only 19.4%. On the face of it, Pool & Splash appear to have performed better in terms of revenue growth.

However, the picture changes when we are supplied with information about the breakdown of revenue. Pool & Splash Limited's sales and maintenance contracts are in respect of domestic sales only. Dive & Float Limited, on the other hand, undertakes contract pool maintenance for local government authorities. A breakdown of the revenue figures shows the following:

	Pool & Splash Limited		Dive & Float Limited	
	20X9	**20X8**	**20X9**	**20X8**
	£	£	£	£
Revenue: domestic				
Maintenance contracts –	1 662 997	1 357 549	1 430 111	1 135 910
Local government authorities	–	–	412 680	407 450
Total	1 662 997	1 357 549	1 842 791	1 543 360

From the more detailed figures the analyst can calculate a more meaningful comparison. Dive & Float's domestic revenue has, in fact, increased by 25.9% as compared to Pool & Splash's increase of 22.5%.

INDUSTRY AVERAGES MAY BE MISLEADING Comparison of a single company against a range of industry averages may be misleading.

Example 8.8

Wellington Burke Limited and Ashington Smith Limited are two companies operating in the same industry, but in different parts of England. According to a recent trade survey, the average increase in revenue in the industry in the year ended 31 December 20X1 was 13.8%.

The two companies show the following levels of revenue growth over that period:

| Wellington Burke Ltd | 14.2% |
| Ashington Smith Ltd | 11.6% |

It appears as though Wellington Burke Ltd is the clear leader in terms of sales growth. However, the average increase in revenue published in the trade survey masks wide regional variations.

| Average growth in the North of England | 9.7% |
| Average growth in the South of England | 17.9% |

If we know that Wellington Burke Ltd operates in the South of England, while Ashington Smith Ltd is based in the North of England, the comparison starts to look different. It appears that, in fact, Ashington Smith Ltd may have outperformed other northern-based firms in the industry, whereas, relatively speaking, Wellington Burke Ltd has under-performed in terms of revenue growth.

Comparisons between businesses, then, must be approached with caution, because apparently obvious facts may be misleading.

Self-test question 8.2 (answer at the end of the book)

Barnes & Jack Ltd and Carleen Baker Ltd are competitors in the aquarium supply business. Both companies supply, install and maintain aquariums. Revenue figures for the two companies for 20X5 and 20X4 are as follows:

	Barnes & Jack Ltd		**Carleen Baker Ltd**	
	20X5	**20X4**	**20X5**	**20X4**
	£	£	£	£
Revenue	2 044 032	1 743 906	1 850 490	1 564 774

a) Which company has produced the more impressive growth in revenue? (Calculate growth to one decimal place.)
b) Does the answer differ with the addition of the following information about revenue?

Barnes & Jack's sales are principally to the domestic and pet shop market. However, in addition, the company sells to zoos. Revenue growth in the latter area has been slow in recent years due to cuts in public funding. Carleen Baker Ltd would like to break into the zoo market, but currently supplies only the domestic and pet shop market.

Barnes & Jack's sales to zoos were £450 800 in 20X4, increasing to £488 307 in 20X5.

8.6 SEGMENT ANALYSIS

Large companies usually operate in a range of different markets and conduct varying business activities. Listed companies are required by international financial reporting standards to produce additional information about the business segments in which they operate. This can be very useful for the analyst in providing an insight into which segments of the business yield the most revenue and which are most profitable. The next example looks at some of the segment information provided by Burberry plc.

Example 8.9 (Real-Life)

Burberry plc is a luxury fashion business. It publishes information about revenue from different segments by business category and also by destination. This allows the analyst to see which product categories are dominant in the business, and which are the company's most important export markets.

Burberry plc: Revenue by product division

	2016 £m	2015 £m	2014 £m	2013 £m	2012 £m
Accessories	901.7	892.5	816.1	729.1	689.4
Womenswear	729.0	743.0	684.0	618.2	582.5
Menswear	548.4	557.5	520.8	464.2	410.5
Children's/other	90.7	77.7	78.4	72.6	66.2
Beauty	202.5	184.8	151.3	5.2	–
Licensing	42.4	67.7	79.2	109.4	108.6
Total	2 514.7	2 523.2	2 329.8	1 998.7	1 857.2

This information can be analyzed in different ways. For example, we can calculate the contribution of each of the major product categories to Burberry's overall revenue for each year:

Burberry plc: Contribution of product categories to total revenue

	2016 %	2015 %	2014 %	2013 %	2012 %
Accessories	35.9	35.4	35.0	36.5	37.1
Womenswear	29.0	29.4	29.4	30.9	31.4
Menswear	21.8	22.1	22.3	23.2	22.1
Children's/other	3.6	3.1	3.4	3.6	3.6
Beauty	8.0	7.3	6.5	0.3	–
Licensing	1.7	2.7	3.4	5.5	5.8
Total	100.0	100.0	100.0	100.0	100.0

What does this additional information tell us about Burberry's revenue for the five-year period covered by the figures? We can see from the table that the big success story over this period is the growth in beauty products which, by 2016, account for 8% of revenue. Licensing has declined, presumably as licensing contracts come to an end and are not replaced. Accessories, womenswear and menswear are the most significant product categories and all three have tended to decline a little in importance. However, by 2016, the three categories together still account for 86.7% of total revenue. We could extend the analysis by looking at the year-on-year increases or decreases in revenue in the various categories. You might find it useful to do this exercise and to read more about the various product categories in Burberry's 2016 Annual Report.

Chapter Summary

In this chapter, we first examined the usefulness of financial statements to certain interest groups: owners and investors, potential investors and creditors. The rest of the chapter was devoted to the study of a range of simple analysis techniques:

- horizontal analysis – involving analysis of the financial statements of at least two consecutive accounting periods
- trend analysis – horizontal analysis taking place over several years

- vertical analysis – expressing figures in a financial statement as a percentage of one key figure (commonly sales in the statement of profit or loss and net assets in the statement of financial position)
- common size analysis – vertical analysis taking place over more than one accounting period.

We examined some of the problems of comparability which can arise when the analyst attempts to compare accounting information from two or more businesses:

- accounting policies may be different
- there may be differences between the activities of the businesses
- industry averages may be misleading.

Finally, the chapter looked at segment analysis, which uses more detailed information about a business's activities in various business segments. It can provide very useful insights into business operations.

Internet Resources

Book's companion website summary

The website contains the following resources in respect of Chapter 8:

Students' section

A multiple choice quiz containing ten questions
Four additional questions with answers

Lecturers' section

Answers to end-of-chapter exercises 8.7 to 8.10
Four additional questions with answers
Case study
Testbank
Instructor's Manual
PowerPoint presentation

Exercises: Answers at the End of the Book

8.1 Ronald's trading business operates from a shop in a large city centre. Extracts from Ronald's most recent statements of profit or loss for 20X2 and 20X1 show the following key figures:

	20X2 £	20X1 £
Revenue	110 450	95 544
Cost of sales	(72 058)	(62 075)
Gross profit	38 392	33 469

Ronald belongs to a trade association which has recently carried out a confidential survey of its members. The survey found that between 20X1 and 20X2 the average increases in revenue and gross profitability of the membership were:

Increase in revenue	12.6%
Increase in gross profit	15.2%

Which of the following statements is correct? A horizontal analysis of Ronald's revenue and gross profit figures shows:

a) Higher than average increase in revenue, and lower than average increase in gross profit.
b) Lower than average increase in revenue, and lower than average increase in gross profit.
c) Lower than average increase in revenue, and higher than average increase in gross profit.
d) Higher than average increase in revenue, and lower than average increase in gross profit.

8.2 Rory's statements of profit or loss show the following figures for the period 20X1 to 20X4 inclusive:

	20X4	20X3	20X2	20X1
	£	£	£	£
Revenue	562 064	539 409	520 665	505 500
Cost of sales	(410 619)	(392 802)	(378 879)	(368 509)
Gross profit	151 445	146 607	141 786	136 991

Which of the following statements is correct? Analyzed horizontally, these figures show:

a) A gradually increasing percentage of revenue growth and a gradually increasing percentage of gross profit growth.
b) A gradually decreasing percentage of revenue growth and a gradually increasing percentage of gross profit growth.
c) A gradually increasing percentage of revenue growth and a gradually decreasing percentage of gross profit growth.
d) A gradually decreasing percentage of revenue growth and a gradually decreasing percentage of gross profit growth.

8.3 Inge Larsen is the principal shareholder in Larsen Locations Limited. Her company provides services to businesses that are in the process of moving from one location to another. Inge and her staff plan the moves in detail, ensuring that all arrangements are made and that the move goes smoothly. Lately, the company has itself moved into larger premises and has taken on more staff.

Tom Wilton runs The Wilton Group plc, of which he is the major shareholder; the company's principal activity is similar to Larsen's. He is considering making an offer to Inge to buy the business from her, so that he can consolidate Wilton's position as market leader in the region. He does not want Inge Larsen to know anything about his possible interest in her company until he has completed some basic financial analysis.

Tom obtains Larsen's company accounts for the last three years from Companies House. Some of the extracted statement of profit or loss information is summarized in the following table:

	20X7	20X6	20X5	20X4
	£	£	£	£
Sales of services	3 709 480	3 690 900	3 502 404	3 497 983
Administrative expenses	1 446 437	1 204 448	1 109 932	1 100 555
Operating profit	756 734	841 525	795 046	787 046

Over the period 20X4 to 20X7 The Wilton Group plc has experienced steady growth in revenue, administrative expenses and operating profits of 2–3% per year.

Analyze Larsen's revenue, administrative expenses and operating profits horizontally, reporting briefly on how the trends in these items compare with those of The Wilton Group plc.

8.4   Chapter Protection Limited is a security firm. Its statement of profit or loss for the year ended
      31 December 20X4 is as follows:

	£
Revenue	188 703
Cost of sales	(115 863)
Gross profit	72 840
Administrative expenses	(14 260)
Distribution and selling costs	(20 180)
Operating profit	38 400
Finance costs	(1 200)
Profit before tax	37 200
Tax	(7 450)
Profit after tax	29 750

Prepare a vertical analysis statement of Chapter Protection's statement of profit or loss, on the basis that
the revenue figure is 100%.

8.5   Causeway Ferguson plc is a trading company specializing in the supply of tea and coffee and related prod-
      ucts. Jason has a small shareholding in the company which was left to him by a relative. He has never taken
      much interest in the company's activities but has noticed that the company pays a regular twice-yearly
      dividend which never seems to vary much.

      Jason has recently started reading the financial press on a regular basis and one day he finds a brief
      news item about tea and coffee suppliers. Causeway Ferguson is mentioned in passing: 'Causeway
      Ferguson, a fine old name in British tea supply, is quietly withering away. Its lacklustre management team
      has failed to tackle new competitors in the market – at this rate, it starts to look like a modest takeover
      target for one of the food industry big boys.'

      Jason never throws anything away, and after a search, manages to dig out from a dusty pile of papers
      a set of unopened annual reports from Causeway Ferguson going back over four or five years. He gives
      the reports to his cousin, Jasper, who is a trainee accountant, and asks him to comment on the company's
      trading over the last few years.

      Jasper extracts the following statement of profit or loss information from the annual reports:

	20X6	20X5	20X4	20X3	20X2
	£000	£000	£000	£000	£000
Revenue	13 204	13 561	13 602	12 430	12 003
Cost of sales	(8 012)	(8 217)	(8 213)	(7 401)	(7 085)
Gross profit	5 192	5 344	5 389	5 029	4 918
Administrative expenses	(2 184)	(2 101)	(2 097)	(2 010)	(1 975)
Selling and distribution costs	(2 086)	(2 001)	(1 977)	(1 972)	(1 951)
Profit before tax	922	1 242	1 315	1 047	992
Tax	(277)	(373)	(395)	(314)	(298)
Profit after tax	645	869	920	733	694

Prepare a horizontal trend analysis statement and a common size statement of profit or loss. Comment
on the key features which emerge from the analysis of these statements. Does the newspaper report appear
credible in the light of the analysis?

8.6 The five-year financial record for Marks & Spencer plc published in the company's 2016 Annual Report includes the following information:

	2016	2015	2014	2013	2012
	£m	£m	£m	£m	£m
Revenue:					
UK	9 470.8	9 223.1	9 155.7	8 951.4	8 868.2
International	1 084.6	1 088.3	1 154.0	1 075.4	1 066.1
Total revenue	10 555.4	10 311.4	10 309.7	10 026.8	9 934.3
Operating profit/loss					
UK	627.3	640.6	600.3	632.8	658.0
International	(43.2)	60.7	94.2	120.2	88.5
Total operating profit	584.1	701.3	694.5	753.0	746.5

Write a brief report analyzing the information in the table. (Note: it will be helpful to calculate operating profit as a percentage of revenue.)

Exercises: Answers Available on the Lecturers' Section of the Book's Website

8.7 Rasheda's sales for 20X7 were £206 400, and for 20X8 were £214 656.

Her gross profit margins were: 36.3% for 20X7 and 36.4% for 20X8.

Rasheda expects sales in 20X9 to increase by the same percentage as between 20X7 and 20X9. Gross profit margin should improve to 36.5%.

What is Rasheda's expected gross profit in 20X9 (to the nearest pound)?

a) £78 349
b) £78 135
c) £81 483
d) £81 363

8.8 Reva has a jewellery business in a well-established shop. Her most recent statement of profit or loss show the following key figures:

	20X5	20X4
	£	£
Revenue	696 400	585 702
Cost of sales	(416 447)	(352 007)
Gross profit	279 953	233 695

A recent survey by the Jewellers' Guild shows that average jewellery sales increased by 17.3% in 20X5 over the previous year. Also, it was found that the average gross profit margin in 20X5 amongst the survey respondents is 38.3%.

Which of the following statements is correct? An analysis of Reva's figures shows:
a) A higher than average increase in revenue, and a higher than average gross profit margin.
b) A lower than average increase in revenue and a lower than average gross profit margin.
c) A higher than average increase in revenue, and a lower than average gross profit margin.
d) A lower than average increase in revenue, and a higher than average gross profit margin.

8.9 Isaac Prentiss Limited produce parts and components for ships' engines. The business requires a continuing investment in new machinery in order to keep production as efficient as possible. Isaac Prentiss is the founder and principal shareholder of the business, although he no longer takes an active part in management. Isaac is concerned because he feels that the business is borrowing too much.

Burgess, the managing director, assures Isaac that sales and operating profits continue to improve and that the borrowing is necessary to fund the general expansion of the business, including the acquisition of new non-current assets. In order to reassure Isaac, Burgess prepares the following statement of key extracts from the financial statements for the last five years:

	20X8	20X7	20X6	20X5	20X4
	£000	£000	£000	£000	£000
Revenue	1 635	1 421	1 254	1 181	1 133
Operating profit	303	254	223	203	199
Finance costs	(245)	(181)	(177)	(171)	(151)
Non-current assets	5 314	4 190	3 633	3 237	2 950
Borrowing	3 944	2 921	2 766	2 510	2 431

Analyze the company's figures horizontally over the five-year period, and write a brief report to Isaac on the results of the analysis. You should refer particularly to Isaac's concerns about the business borrowing.

8.10 Starkey Wilmott Limited has the following statement of financial position at 31 March 20X5:

	£	£
ASSETS		
Non-current assets		704 710
Current assets		
Inventories	369 440	
Trade receivables	416 700	
Cash at bank	81 450	
		867 590
Total assets		1 572 300
EQUITY AND LIABILITIES		
Equity		
Share capital		50 000
Retained earnings		931 400
		981 400
Long-term liabilities		200 000
Current liabilities		390 900
Total equity and liabilities		1 572 300

Prepare vertical analysis statements of Starkey Wilmott's statement of financial position at 31 March 20X5 based upon total assets = 100.0%

9 Understanding financial reports: using accounting ratios

Aim of the chapter

To add to the range of skills developed in the previous chapter in order to understand financial reports for various types of business.

Learning outcomes

After reading the chapter and completing the related exercises, students should:

- Understand the usefulness of accounting ratios in financial analysis.

- Be able to calculate a range of accounting ratios.

- Be able to use their knowledge of accounting ratios to assist in the analysis of financial statements.

Introduction

The simple analysis techniques explained in the previous chapter can be of great assistance in understanding a business. Sometimes, however, it helps to build in some ratio analysis techniques. This chapter explains how to calculate a range of useful ratios, and how to use them in analyzing a set of financial statements.

9.1 FINANCIAL RATIO ANALYSIS TECHNIQUES

There is nothing particularly remarkable about a ratio: it simply expresses the relationship between one quantity and another. Taking a very simple example: a basket of fruit contains eight apples and four oranges. The ratio of apples to oranges can be expressed in an arithmetical term such as: 8:4. It is common to reduce the smaller part of the ratio to 1, so in this example the ratio of apples to oranges is expressed as: 2:1.

Not all of the techniques and calculations commonly included under the term financial ratio analysis actually involve the calculation of a ratio of the 2:1 type calculated above. The same relationship could be expressed by a percentage (eg. '33.3% of the fruit in this basket is oranges'). However, all of the techniques result in ways of expressing the relationships between two or more figures.

A typical set of financial statements contains many figures, and it is possible to calculate almost infinite permutations expressing their relative dimensions. Some, however, are very obviously of more use than others; it is important that the figures being compared do have some genuine causal relationship between them (ie. a change in one causes a change in the other). In the rest of this chapter we will examine some of the more commonly considered relationships between items in the financial statements.

It can be helpful, when trying to understand accounting ratios, to group the various categories of financial relationships together. We will examine ratios in five principal categories:

- performance ratios – used to assess the relative success or failure of business performance
- liquidity ratios – used to assess the extent to which a business can comfortably cover its liabilities
- efficiency ratios – used to assess the extent to which items of asset and liability are well-utilized and well-managed
- investor ratios – used to assess various items of particular interest to investors
- lending ratios – used to assess the relationship between financing via loan capital and financing via equity capital.

9.1.1 A Word of Caution About Financial Ratio Analysis

Some of the ratio calculation techniques explained below may appear quite complicated, especially for students whose arithmetical skills are rusty. However, the purpose of their calculation, and the overriding purpose of this section of the book is to assist in *understanding* financial information. Students often concentrate on trying to memorize the ratio formulae and either forget, or have never properly understood, what the relationship between the figures means. Therefore, in each example, we will search for the meaning in the expression of the relationship between figures.

9.2 PERFORMANCE RATIOS

Students may be relieved to discover that they have already studied several aspects of the financial analysis of performance. Earlier chapters introduced the idea of a significant relationship between:

Revenue and gross profit

and

Revenue and net profit

In many of the examples used up to this point in the book, gross profit margins and/or net profit margins have been calculated, and students should by now be accustomed to the idea that these margin calculations can express financial relationships between revenue and profits in ways that are actually quite helpful. The rest of this section of the chapter examines a very significant and widely used ratio: return on capital employed.

9.2.1 Return on Capital Employed (ROCE)

Return on capital employed (also known as ROCE) is widely used as a means of assessing the performance of a business. ROCE looks at the level of profits generated compared to the amount of capital invested in the business. Unfortunately, although the ratio is easy to calculate, it does present problems in that it can be difficult to decide what is included in 'return' and in 'capital employed'.

An example should help to illustrate the issue.

Example 9.1

Bilton Burgess plc is a trading company, which occupies its own freehold premises. It has recently obtained a listing on a stock exchange. The company has the following summarized statement of profit or loss for the year ended 31 December 20X7 and statement of financial position at that date:

Bilton Burgess plc: Statement of profit or loss for the year ended 31 December 20X7

	£000	£000
Revenue		1 600
Cost of sales		
Opening inventories	100	

	£000	£000
Add: purchases	994	
	1 094	
Less: closing inventories	(104)	
		(990)
Gross profit		610
Various expenses		(319)
Operating profit		291
Finance costs		(80)
Profit before tax		211
Tax		(64)
Profit after tax		147

Note

A dividend of £40 000 was paid during the year ended 31 December 20X7.

Bilton Burgess plc: Statement of financial position at 31 December 20X7

	£000	£000
ASSETS		
Non-current assets		1 813
Current assets		
Inventories	104	
Trade receivables	170	
Cash at bank	10	
		284
		2 097
EQUITY AND LIABILITIES		
Equity		
Share capital		300
Retained earnings		900
		1 200
Non-current liabilities		
Borrowings		800
Current liabilities		
Trade and other payables		97
		2 097

Return on capital employed measures the profit made by the business against the capital invested:

$$\frac{\text{Profit}}{\text{Capital}}$$

Which profit figure should be used? There are several to choose from:

- gross profit (£610 000)
- operating profit (£291 000)
- profit before tax (£211 000)
- profit after tax (£147 000).

And how much has been invested? Should we include:

Total equity (£1 200 000)

or

Total equity plus non-current liabilities (£2 000 000)?

There is no definitive correct answer; it depends upon which ratio is the most useful for the analysis. For example, if the analyst is looking at a set of accounts on behalf of a shareholder, he or she will be most interested in the return made by the shareholders' investment in the business. This means comparing the amount of return that is attributable to shareholders (ie. profit after deduction of finance costs) with shareholders' equity. This version of ROCE is often referred to as 'return on equity' (ROE).

In the case of Bilton Burgess plc pre-tax ROE (return on shareholders' equity)

$$= \frac{\text{Profit (after finance costs) before tax}}{\text{Shareholders' funds}}$$

ie.

$$\frac{211}{1200} \times 100 = 17.58\%$$

£211 is the correct figure to use here because it is what is left to the shareholders after finance costs have been deducted from profit.

Post-tax ROE might also be helpful in the analysis:

$$\text{Post-tax ROE (return on shareholders' equity)} = \frac{\text{Profit after tax}}{\text{Shareholders' equity}}$$

$$\text{ie.} = \frac{147}{1200} \times 100 = 12.25\%$$

Both pre-tax and post-tax ROE could be useful to shareholders in order to compare the return on their investment in Bilton Burgess plc with other possible investments.

Another possibility is to look at the overall return against total investment in the business. Total investment in the case of Bilton Burgess plc is the total of shareholders' equity and long-term borrowings. The matching profit figure is the operating profit before any deduction for finance costs:

$$\text{ROCE (on total capital invested)} = \frac{\text{Profit before finance costs and tax}}{\text{Shareholders' equity and long-term borrowings}}$$

$$\text{ie.} = \frac{291}{2000} \times 100 = 14.55\%$$

This is a very useful measure of business performance because it focuses purely on performance rather than bringing in considerations related to the method of financing the business operations.

ROCE may seem rather confusing. Try to focus upon the objective of the analysis and, above all, ensure that, where comparisons are being made, the ratio is calculated on a consistent basis. Students sometimes want to know which of the calculations explained in the example is 'right'. The answer is that the return on capital calculations are tools to be used for the purpose of analysis. The 'right' return on capital calculation in any given situation depends upon the focus of the analysis. It is important from the outset to try to focus on the meaning of the figures and remember that accounting is an art rather than a science. Although the terminology is not always used in the same way in practice, this book will use the terms Return on Equity (ROE) to express the relationship between profit after finance costs and shareholders' equity, and Return on Capital Employed (ROCE) to express the relationship between profit before deduction of finance costs and the total of shareholders' equity and long-term borrowings.

Self-test question 9.1
(answer at the end of
the book)

The following figures are extracted from Augustus Algernon Ltd's statement of profit or loss and statement of financial position for the 20X3 financial year:

Operating profit	186 000
Finance costs	(24 000)
Profit before tax	162 000
Tax	(48 000)
Profit after tax	114 000

From the statement of financial position:

Share capital	120 000
Retained earnings	1 000 000
Long-term borrowings	480 000

Calculate pre-tax ROE, post-tax ROE and ROCE.

9.3 LIQUIDITY RATIOS

Liquidity ratios are used to assess the extent to which a business can comfortably cover its liabilities. The emphasis in this group of ratios is especially on current liabilities. Non-current liabilities, by definition, do not have to be settled in the immediate future. Current liabilities, on the other hand, have to be settled within, at most, one year of the statement of financial position date, and usually much more quickly. If the business fails to settle its current liabilities it is in danger of failing altogether.

Can the business meet its liabilities as they fall due?

Two ratios are used to provide answers to this question: the **current ratio** and the **quick ratio**. We will use data from the Bilton Burgess plc financial statements provided earlier to illustrate the calculation of these important ratios.

Example 9.2

CURRENT RATIO

The current ratio assesses the relationship between current assets and current liabilities. If current liabilities had to be settled in full, would there be sufficient current assets to cover them?

Bilton Burgess's current assets are:	£284 000
Its current liabilities are:	£97 000

The formula for the current ratio is:

$$\frac{\text{Current assets}}{\text{Current liabilities}} = \frac{284\ 000}{97\ 000} = 2.93$$

It is customary to express this relationship in the form of a ratio, ie. current assets : current liabilities, which in this case is 2.93:1, Current assets are 2.93 times as large, in total, as current liabilities. Another way of looking at this information is to say that, for every £1 of current liabilities which has to be met by the business there is £2.93 in current assets.

Does the current ratio for Bilton Burgess look reasonable? Well, the business does not appear to be in danger of going under because of inability to meet its current liabilities. If all the creditors were to arrive in a group on the company's doorstep demanding immediate payment, there is actually only £10 000 in the bank with which to pay them. However, this is an unlikely scenario. Given a month or so, many of the amounts owed to the business will be paid in cash. It is reasonable to conclude that Bilton Burgess does not have any obvious liquidity problems.

Is there any 'gold standard' figure for current ratio? Current ratios vary widely between industries, and there is no ideal figure (although some textbooks suggest that there is). It is best used as a point of comparison: for example, if we knew that the current ratio for Bilton Burgess at the previous year-end, 31 December 20X6, was 2.63, we can compare the two figures at consecutive year-ends and conclude that the current ratio has improved from 2.63 to 2.93.

QUICK (ACID TEST) RATIO

The analysis of liquidity can be further refined by examining the quick ratio, which is also referred to as the acid test ratio. This works on the assumption that it takes longer to turn inventories into cash, and so it leaves inventories out of the analysis. The formula for the quick ratio is:

$$\frac{\text{Current assets} - \text{inventories}}{\text{Current liabilities}}$$

For Bilton Burgess plc:

$$\frac{284 - 104}{97} = 1.86$$

Expressed in the form of a ratio this is 1.86:1. For every £1 of current liabilities there is £1.86 in cash or trade receivables available. If this ratio drops below 1:1 there may potentially be problems in meeting liabilities. However, it is difficult to generalize about this point. A business which generates cash quickly (like a food retailer, for example) can operate on a very low quick ratio. The quick ratio calculated for Bilton Burgess does not suggest that the company has any immediate problem in meeting its liabilities. As with the current ratio, the quick ratio is most informative when used in comparisons.

Arbus Nugent Ltd has the following figures for current assets and current liabilities in its statement of financial positions at 31 December 20X4 and 31 December 20X3:

Self-test question 9.2 (answer at the end of the book)

Current assets	20X4	20X3
Inventories	34 300	31 600
Trade receivables	42 950	42 610
Cash	10 370	640
	87 620	74 850
Current liabilities		
Trade payables	31 450	32 970

Calculate the current ratio and the quick ratio for Arbus Nugent Ltd for both years, working to one decimal place. Have the ratios improved or worsened?

9.4 EFFICIENCY RATIOS

Efficiency ratios are used to assess the extent to which items of asset and liability are well-managed and well-utilized. We will consider efficiency measurements related to four items: non-current assets, inventories, trade receivables and trade payables. The following example uses the Bilton Burgess plc data given earlier in the chapter.

Example 9.3

NON-CURRENT ASSET TURNOVER

Non-current assets are employed in the business in order to generate revenue and, ultimately, profits. It can be interesting and useful to gauge the success with which non-current assets are employed to produce turnover. The **non-current asset turnover ratio** examines the efficiency with which non-current assets have been utilized in the business.

The formula is:

$$\frac{\text{Revenue}}{\text{Non-current assets}}$$

Applying the formula to the relevant figures for Bilton Burgess plc:

$$\text{Non-current asset turnover} = \frac{\text{Revenue}}{\text{Non-current assets}}$$
$$= \frac{1600}{1813} = 0.88$$

A helpful way of looking at this result is to think of it in terms of the amount of revenue generated per pound of investment in non-current assets. Each pound invested in non-current assets in Bilton Burgess plc produces, on average, revenue of 88p.

Again, there is no 'gold standard' for this ratio. Businesses differ from each other in the extent to which they use non-current assets. Some businesses are largely people-based; because the value of people does not appear on business statements of financial position, such businesses are likely to produce a high level of revenue relative to very low investment in non-current assets. Bilton Burgess plc owns its own premises and therefore non-current assets are higher than in an equivalent business where the buildings are rented. When comparing the non-current asset turnover of two businesses caution must be exercised to ensure that like is compared with like.

INVENTORY TURNOVER

Where inventories are a significant factor in a business, it is of prime importance to manage them properly. Holding too much in inventory costs money (because of storage costs, insurance, working capital tied up); holding insufficient inventories may also lead to problems where there is a delay in supplying customer orders. The **inventory turnover ratio** gauges the average length of time that an item of inventory spends on the premises before it is sold.

There are two related calculations:

$$\text{Inventory turnover} = \frac{\text{Cost of sales}}{\text{Average inventories}}$$

$$\text{Inventory turnover in days} = \frac{\text{Average inventories}}{\text{Cost of sales}} \times 365 \text{ days}$$

Average inventories is taken as the average of opening and closing inventory. Extracting the relevant figures from Bilton Burgess's financial statements produces the following figure for average inventories:

$$\frac{\text{Opening inventories + closing inventories}}{2} = \frac{100 + 104}{2} = 102$$

The average could be more accurately calculated if more information were available; for instance, if monthly inventories figures were available, a fairly accurate average inventories figure for the year could be calculated by adding together the monthly figures and dividing by 12.

Bilton Burgess plc:

$$\text{Inventory turnover ratio} = \frac{\text{Cost of sales}}{\text{Average inventories}}$$
$$= \frac{990}{102}$$
$$= 9.7 \text{ times}$$

This means that on average inventories are replaced 9.7 times in a year. The additional calculation expresses the same information in a slightly different (possibly more helpful) way:

$$\text{Inventory turnover in days} = \frac{\text{Average inventories}}{\text{Cost of sales}} \times 365 \text{ days}$$

$$= \frac{102}{990} \times 365 \text{ days} = 37.6 \text{ days}$$

This means that, on average, an item of inventory spends 37.6 days in Bilton Burgess's warehouse.

As with previous ratio calculation results it is difficult to assess the significance of this figure without some point of comparison. If we know that in the previous year inventory turnover in days was 32.7 days, we can conclude that the inventory turnover ratio appears to have worsened. Also, much depends on the nature of the inventories. If Bilton Burgess plc is in the fresh fruit supply business, 37.6 days would appear to be an excessive inventory turnover; on the other hand, if it supplies electrical components, there is probably nothing out of the ordinary with a measure of 37.6 days.

TRADE RECEIVABLES TURNOVER RATIO

The **trade receivables turnover ratio** assesses the length of time that trade receivables take to pay. The calculation of this ratio is as follows:

$$\text{Trade receivables turnover ratio} = \frac{\text{Average trade receivables}}{\text{Revenue on credit}} \times 365 \text{ days}$$

In the case of Bilton Burgess plc we have no data available about the opening figure for trade receivables. In such cases we can use the closing figure, but it must be interpreted with some caution.

Extracting the relevant figures from the Bilton Burgess plc accounts, and assuming that all sales are made on credit (ie. there are no sales made for cash):

$$\frac{\text{Trade receivables}}{\text{Revenue on credit}} \times 365 \text{ days}$$

$$= \frac{170}{1600} \times 365 \text{ days} = 38.8 \text{ days}$$

Note: this is sometimes referred to as the trade receivables collection period.

This figure would be useful for making a comparison over time; if we had sufficient information we would be able to say whether or not this was an improvement over the previous year's figure.

The length of time it takes to collect trade receivables is related to the business's policy on offering credit. Let's suppose that Bilton Burgess's sales invoices state: 'Payment must be received within 30 days of despatch of goods'. The trade receivables turnover ratio tells us that, on average, customers exceed the credit terms by 8.8 days. It may be that, by improving its credit control procedures, Bilton Burgess plc would be able to reduce its trade receivables turnover figure.

TRADE PAYABLES TURNOVER RATIO

The **trade payables turnover ratio** measures the length of time, on average, that a business takes to settle its trade payables. Its calculation is very similar to that used for the trade receivables turnover ratio:

$$\text{Trade payables turnover ratio} = \frac{\text{Average trade payables}}{\text{Purchases}} \times 365 \text{ days}$$

In the case of Bilton Burgess plc we have no information available about the opening balance of trade payables. In such cases it is usually acceptable to use closing trade payables, but the results of the calculation need to be treated with caution.

Extracting the relevant figures from Bilton Burgess's financial statements we can calculate the ratio as follows:

$$\frac{\text{Trade payables}}{\text{Purchases}} \times 365 \text{ days}$$

$$= \frac{97}{994} \times 365 \text{ days} = 35.6 \text{ days}$$

Given that many businesses stipulate payment within 30 days, Bilton Burgess plc are probably not taking an unreasonably long time to pay their trade payables.

Where the trade payables turnover ratio is very high, or where it has risen significantly over the previous period(s), it may indicate possible liquidity problems. To some extent, it is good management practice to take advantage of this source of interest-free credit. However, it must be kept within reasonable limits. If a business takes an unreasonably long time to settle its trade payables, there may be a consequent loss of goodwill, and the business may find it difficult to obtain supplies on credit.

rmitage Horobin Ltd is a trading company which makes all its sales on credit. Its statement of profit or loss and statement of financial position for the accounting years 20X1 and 20X0 are as follows:

Self-test question 9.3 (answer at the end of the book)

Armitage Horobin Ltd: Statement of profit or loss for the years ended 31 March 20X1 and 20X0

	20X1 £000	20X1 £000	20X0 £000	20X0 £000
Revenue		283.4		271.1
Cost of sales				
Opening inventories	23.7		21.2	
Add: purchases	184.8		177.5	
	208.5		198.7	
Less: closing inventories	(25.9)		(23.7)	
		(182.6)		(175.0)
Gross profit		100.8		96.1
Various expenses		(75.9)		(73.0)
Operating profit		24.9		23.1
Tax		(4.9)		(3.7)
Profit after tax		20.0		19.4

Armitage Horobin Ltd: Statements of financial position at 31 March 20X1 and 20X0

	20X1 £000	20X1 £000	20X0 £000	20X0 £000
ASSETS				
Non-current assets		289.2		275.3
Current assets				
Inventories	25.9		23.7	
Trade receivables	33.0		28.2	
Prepayments	1.0		1.5	
Cash at bank	6.0		4.2	
		65.9		57.6
		355.1		332.9

	20X1 £000	20X1 £000	20X0 £000	20X0 £000
EQUITY AND LIABILITIES				
Equity				
Share capital		40.0		40.0
Retained earnings		289.3		269.3
		329.3		309.3
Current liabilities				
Trade payables	24.5		20.6	
Accruals	1.3		3.0	
		25.8		23.6
		355.1		332.9

Calculate the following efficiency ratios:

- non-current asset turnover
- inventory turnover
- trade receivables turnover
- trade payables turnover.

In each case state whether the ratio shows an improvement or not.

9.5 INVESTOR RATIOS

Investor ratios, as the name implies, are those ratios which are likely to be of particular interest to investors and potential investors.

In Chapter 8 we identified some of the questions investors are likely to ask:

- How is my investment doing?
- Should I buy more shares/sell the shares I've already got/hold on to the investment I've already got?
- Is the dividend likely to increase?
- What are the chances of the company going out of business?

The group of accounting ratios classified in this section under the heading 'investor ratios' may help to suggest answers to some of these questions. Although the ratios covered in this section may be of particular interest to investors, they are likely also to provide information that is useful to other people who have some reason for wanting to know more about a business.

Note that the ratios which follow in this section can be calculated only for limited companies. They are not applicable to sole trader and partnership businesses.

As with the other main groups of ratios, we will use the information given for Bilton Burgess plc earlier in the chapter to illustrate calculations.

Example 9.4

DIVIDEND PER SHARE

This ratio calculates the amount in pence of the dividend for each ordinary share:

$$\frac{\text{Dividend for the year}}{\text{Number of shares in issue}}$$

The relevant figures for Bilton Burgess plc are:

$$\frac{40}{300} = 13.3\text{p per share}$$

Note that, in this case, the number of shares is the same as the value in the statement of financial position, because the shares are of £1 each. Care must be taken where the shares are, for example, 50p shares. In this example, if the shares were of 50p nominal value there would be twice as many to take into the calculation.

DIVIDEND COVER

Dividend cover calculates the number of times the current dividend could be paid out of available profits.

$$\frac{\text{Profits after tax attributable to ordinary shareholders}}{\text{Dividend}}$$

For Bilton Burgess plc:

$$\frac{147}{40} = 3.67$$

What does this mean? Remember that the directors determine the level of dividend payout; usually they will seek to ensure that it is comfortably within available profits and that a good proportion of profits is retained in the business. The dividend cover calculated for Bilton Burgess plc tells us that the directors could pay the current level of dividend 3.67 times out of available profits.

As with all ratios the dividend cover ratio is of limited use on its own. However, it does suggest, in this case, that dividend cover is comfortable. If dividend cover = 1 it means that all available profits for the year are being paid over to shareholders in the form of dividends. This would be a matter of concern for two reasons:

- No profit is being retained in the business.
- It may not be possible to sustain this level of payout in future years.

EARNINGS PER SHARE

The dividend per share is the amount that is actually paid out per share to investors in the company. Earnings per share is the amount that is theoretically available per share. It is calculated as follows:

$$\frac{\text{Profit after tax attributable to ordinary shareholders}}{\text{Number of shares in issue}}$$

This gives earnings per share (often abbreviated to eps) in pence.
The relevant figures for Bilton Burgess plc are:

$$\frac{147}{300} = 49\text{p per share}$$

(Note that even where eps is greater than 99p the amount is always expressed in pence.) It is worth emphasizing again that the eps of 49p per share does not end up in the pockets of the Bilton Burgess plc shareholders; it is a theoretical figure which expresses the amount of earnings available to shareholders. The amount which does end up in the pockets of the shareholders is (usually) a lesser amount: the dividend.

PRICE/EARNINGS RATIO

This is a very important stock market ratio. It expresses the relationship between earnings per share (which we have just looked at) and the price of the share. Because the calculation involves a share price, it can be performed only for companies listed on a stock exchange for which a share price is available.

This ratio cannot, therefore, be calculated for most businesses, such as sole traders, partnerships and unlisted companies.

In order to calculate the ratio for Bilton Burgess plc (which, remember, is a listed company) we would need to obtain a current share price. Bilton Burgess plc is a fictional company; if it were a real UK listed company, a current share price could easily be obtained for it by looking in the companies listings in the Financial Times or by accessing the London Stock Exchange website.

Suppose that the current share price of Bilton Burgess plc is £6.40 per share. (Yes, these are £1 shares, but the value at which they are traded on the Stock Exchange depends upon the market's perception of the value and the prospects of the company.)

The price/earnings (or P/E ratio, as it is often known) for Bilton Burgess plc is:

$$\frac{\text{Price per share}}{\text{Earnings per share}}$$

$$\frac{640\text{p}}{49\text{p}} = 13.1 \text{ (to one decimal place)}$$

So what does this mean? The P/E ratio for Bilton Burgess plc tells us that investors are currently prepared to pay 13.1 × company's earnings for a single share. On its own, as with most ratios, it has little significance. However, it is very useful for making comparisons with other listed companies, and, especially, with companies in the same industry sector.

Suppose that Bilton Burgess's two main competitors are both listed companies, and that their P/E ratios are:

Abacus Casement plc	18.4
Carew Grapeshot plc	10.3

Investors are prepared to pay up to 18.4 × earnings for a share in Abacus Casement plc, which suggests that they regard the company more highly than Bilton Burgess plc. Carew Grapeshot plc, on the other hand, has a lower P/E than Bilton Burgess plc; investors are prepared to pay only 10.3 × earnings for a single share.

The P/E ratio is a measurement of the market's perception of a company's shares. A high P/E ratio suggests that the shares are regarded as highly desirable; this is often because they are perceived as relatively low risk. Low P/Es, on the other hand, suggest an unfashionable and, relatively, riskier share which is downgraded by the market.

Figure 9.1 shows a sample of real companies' P/E ratios obtained from London Stock Exchange data accessed in April 2017. All are well-known companies in the UK.

Figure 9.1 **Examples of P/E ratios of companies listed on the London Stock Exchange**

Company	P/E
Marks & Spencer	11.64
Next	15.65
BT (British Telecom)	13.27
J Sainsbury	11.29
Kingfisher	14.82

It should be noted that appearances can be deceptive. A sudden fluctuation in share price can result in a significant change to the P/E so that at any point in time, the P/E may not be representative of the general trend.

9.5.1 Market Capitalization

Market capitalization is not a ratio calculation, but it is a piece of information which is likely to be of interest to investors and potential investors in a listed company. Market capitalization is the current share price multiplied by the number of shares in issue. It provides a guide as to the market's view of the current value of the company.

For Bilton Burgess plc:

Price £6.40 × number of shares in issue 300 000 = £1 920 000

Armley Regina plc is a listed company whose current share price at 31 December 20X6 is £5.08 per share. The company has 1 000 000 50p shares in issue. In the financial year ended 31 December 20X6 the company reported profit after tax of £680 000, all of which was attributable to ordinary shareholders. Dividends of £220 000 were paid in the year.

Calculate the following:

a) Dividend per share
b) Dividend cover
c) Earnings per share
d) Price/earnings ratio
e) Market capitalization.

Self-test question 9.4 (answer at the end of the book)

9.6 LENDING RATIOS

9.6.1 Gearing

A **gearing ratio** expresses the relationship between two different types of financing of a company: (a) financing through equity, ie. ordinary shares, and (b) financing through long-term loans, ie. debt.

Equity is contributed to a company by its ordinary shareholders who have a right to a share of any ordinary dividend that is declared by the company directors. Any undistributed profits are regarded as part of equity financing.

Debt is finance in the form of loans. Lenders are usually entitled to interest at a fixed rate on the loans, but, unlike shareholders, they do not have a vote, and are not entitled to any share of the dividend.

Note: in Chapter 7 we briefly looked at another type of capital: preference share capital. This is share capital which confers the right to a fixed rate of dividend (for example, 10% preference share capital). Preference shareholders do not have any right to a share of the ordinary dividend; even if the company does really well, and distributes a lot of money to its ordinary shareholders, the preference shareholders still receive only the fixed percentage to which they are entitled. Preference share capital has characteristics more akin to debt, and so for the purposes of the **gearing** calculation, it is usually regarded as debt.

Gearing has great significance for shareholders and potential shareholders. However, it is a ratio of general importance which is likely to be significant for many interest groups.

There is more than one way of calculating gearing:

$$\frac{\text{Debt}}{\text{Equity}}$$

or

$$\frac{\text{Debt}}{\text{Debt} + \text{equity}}$$

The really important point in adopting one or other of these methods is to be consistent.

The effect of interest in the statement of profit or loss is measured by the final ratio to be considered in this chapter: interest cover.

9.6.2 Interest Cover

Interest cover is a measurement of the number of times interest (or finance costs) could be paid out of available profits. Students who have understood the idea of dividend cover will recognize that interest cover performs a similar function. It is calculated as follows:

$$\frac{\text{Profit before interest (finance costs) and taxation}}{\text{Interest (finance costs)}}$$

As for previous groups of ratios we will use the Example 9.1 from Bilton Burgess plc to illustrate the calculations.

Example 9.5

GEARING

The relevant figures for debt and equity for Bilton Burgess plc are:

- debt (assuming that amounts due after more than 1 year all relate to long-term debt) = £800 000
- equity (share capital + retained earnings) = £1 200 000.

Gearing for Bilton Burgess plc is calculated as follows:

either

$$\frac{\text{Debt}}{\text{Equity}} = \frac{800\ 000}{1\ 200\ 000} = 66.7\% \text{ (to one decimal place)}$$

or

$$\frac{\text{Debt}}{\text{Debt} + \text{equity}} = \frac{800\ 000}{800\ 000 + 1\ 200\ 000} = 40\%$$

INTEREST COVER

The relevant figures for Bilton Burgess plc are:

$$\frac{291}{80} = 3.64 \text{ times}$$

9.7 THE EFFECTS OF GEARING

9.7.1 Why are Ordinary Shareholders Interested in Gearing?

A high level of debt capital relative to equity capital (ie. a high level of gearing) means that the company faces a relatively high interest charge. Interest must be paid out of the store of available profits. If the interest profit soaks up most of the available profit there will be very little left over for the ordinary shareholders. Therefore, an investment in a highly-geared company is usually seen as relatively risky for equity shareholders. However, a great deal depends upon the level of profits generated.

The following example illustrates the potential impact of gearing.

Example 9.6

Two companies, Basket Rabbitts plc and Telford Barron plc, have very similar operations and are of very similar sizes. However, their financing varies: Basket Rabbitts plc is highly-geared, and Telford Barron plc is low-geared, as follows:

High gearing Basket Rabbitts plc	£	Low gearing Telford Barron plc	£
Long-term debt finance (10% interest)	40 000	Long-term debt finance (10% interest)	5 000
Equity finance	30 000	Equity finance	65 000
	70 000		70 000

We will look at the effects of the gearing on the return on equity ratio in these companies at three different potential levels of profit before tax:

	£
High level	12 000
Medium level	8 000
Low level	4 000

In all cases we will assume a tax rate of 30%

1 High level of profit

High gearing

Basket Rabbitts plc	£
Profit before finance costs and tax	12 000
Less: finance costs £40 000 × 10%	(4 000)
Profit before tax	8 000
Tax: £8000 × 30%	(2 400)
Profit after tax: attributable to ordinary shareholders	5 600

Post-tax return on equity (ROE):
$$\frac{5600}{30\,000} \times 100 = 18.7\%$$

Low gearing

Telford Barron plc	£
Profit before finance costs and tax	12 000
Less: finance costs £5000 × 10%	(500)
Profit before tax	11 500
Tax: £11 500 × 30%	(3 450)
Profit after tax: attributable to ordinary shareholders	8 050

Post-tax return on equity (ROE):
$$\frac{8050}{65\,000} = 12.3\%$$

2 Medium level of profit

High gearing

Basket Rabbitts plc	£
Profit before finance costs and tax	8 000
Less: finance costs £40 000 × 10%	(4 000)
Profit before tax	4 000
Tax: £4000 × 30%	(1 200)
Profit after tax: attributable to ordinary shareholders	2 800

Post-tax return on equity (ROE):
$$\frac{2800}{30\,000} \times 100 = 9.3\%$$

Low gearing

Telford Barron plc	£
Profit before finance costs and tax	8 000
Less: finance costs £5000 × 10%	(500)
Profit before tax	7 500
Tax: £7500 × 30%	(2 250)
Profit after tax: attributable to ordinary shareholders	5 250

Post-tax return on equity (ROE):
$$\frac{5250}{65\,000} = 8.1\%$$

3 Low level of profit

High gearing

Basket Rabbitts plc	£
Profit before finance costs and tax	4 000
Less: finance costs £40 000 × 10%	(4 000)
Profit before tax	–
Tax	–

Low gearing

Telford Barron plc	£
Profit before finance costs and tax	4 000
Less: finance costs £5000 × 10%	(500)
Profit before tax	3 500
Tax: £3500 × 30%	(1 050)

High gearing		Low gearing	
Basket Rabbitts plc	£	Telford Barron plc	£
Profit after tax:		Profit after tax:	
attributable to ordinary shareholders	–	attributable to ordinary shareholders	2 450
Post-tax return on equity (ROE):	0%	Post-tax return on equity (ROE):	

$$\frac{2450}{65\ 000} = 3.8\%$$

The example illustrates that returns to shareholders in a highly-geared company are more volatile than returns to shareholders in a low-geared company. Highly-geared companies are, therefore, seen by ordinary shareholders as more risky.

9.8 PREPARING AN ANALYSIS OF FINANCIAL STATEMENTS

9.8.1 Collecting the Data

This section of the chapter focuses upon the production of a written analysis of the financial statements and ratios. Some key ratios from the Bilton Burgess example calculated earlier in the chapter are tabulated below, together with average ratios for the industry in which the company operates. Gross and operating profit margins have also been calculated and added in to the performance ratio section of the table:

Ratio	Bilton Burgess 20X7	Industry average
PERFORMANCE		
Pre-tax return on equity (ROE)	17.58%	17.33%
Return on capital employed (ROCE)	14.55%	12.13%
Gross profit margin (610/1600) × 100	38.1%	36.5%
Operating profit margin (291/1600) × 100	18.2%	13.7%
LIQUIDITY RATIOS		
Current ratio	2.93	2.52
Quick (acid test) ratio	1.86	1.14
EFFICIENCY RATIOS		
Non-current asset turnover	0.88	1.13
Inventory turnover	37.6 days	52.1 days
Trade receivables turnover	38.8 days	42.3 days
Trade payables turnover	35.6 days	48.4 days
INVESTOR RATIOS		
Dividend cover	3.67	4.11
P/E ratio	13.1	10.2
LENDING RATIOS		
Gearing (debt/equity)	66.7%	33.7%
Interest cover	3.64	8.72

9.8.2 The Focus of the Analysis

The focus of the analysis varies depending upon the interests of the user. For example, an analysis prepared for a potential lender to Bilton Burgess plc is likely to focus upon the liquidity and longer-term solvency of the business, and upon its ability to pay interest and ultimately to repay the amount that the company is proposing to borrow.

In this case, however, we will assume that an investor has expressed an interest in buying a small holding of shares (less than 0.5% of the company's total issued share capital) in Bilton Burgess plc. The investor has requested an analysis of the company's performance and position in its 20X7 financial statements. The analysis should examine Bilton Burgess's key ratio figures compared to industry averages. The potential shareholder is likely to be interested in all aspects of the company's performance and position.

9.8.3 The Analysis

To: Potential Shareholder
From: Financial Analyst

Analysis of the performance and position of Bilton Burgess plc 20X7 financial statements, compared to industry averages.

Bilton Burgess plc (BB) demonstrates a strong performance compared to the industry. Gross and operating profitability, return on equity and return on capital employed are all significantly better than industry averages. The difference is particularly noticeable at operating profit margin level, suggesting that BB has excellent control over costs. However, BB's return on equity is only slightly better than industry averages, a point which is likely to be of particular interest to a potential shareholder.

BB's liquidity ratios are also superior to industry averages. A current ratio of over 2:1 usually suggests that a business will have no difficulty meeting its current obligations, and BB's current ratio is nearly at 3:1. Even once inventory is eliminated from the ratio calculation, in the quick ratio, there is no apparent liquidity problem for BB. The company's current asset and liability efficiency ratios indicate that BB has a tight control over working capital. Inventory turnover in the industry is significantly worse than BB's, as is trade payables turnover. The difference in trade receivables turnover is less marked, but BB outperforms the industry in this respect as well. The trade payables turnover comparatives suggest that there is scope for BB to take longer to pay. However, BB's management may have good reasons for its current policy over length of credit taken from suppliers.

BB's non-current asset turnover is lower than the industry average. This means that, for every £1 invested in non-current assets, BB generates less in revenue than the industry on average. Without further information, it is not possible to say whether or not this is a problem. One possible explanation is that BB's non-current assets are relatively newer. If other industry businesses are using relatively old assets this is likely to mean they have a lower value (because they have been subject to depreciation for longer) and therefore non-current asset turnover is higher.

A ratio of interest to investors in BB's ordinary shares (and to potential investors) is the gearing ratio. It is clear that BB is relatively highly-geared compared to the industry. This means that an investment in BB's ordinary shares could carry more risk. Interest cover supports the analysis; it is significantly lower in BB than in the industry as a whole. Much would depend upon the individual investor's appetite for risk. Dividend cover is lower in BB, although the dividend is covered comfortably.

Finally, the P/E ratio suggests that BB is regarded favourably by the market, and that the investment is not particularly high risk in nature.

9.8.4 Limitations of the Analysis

The quality of financial analysis depends upon the quality of the data on which it is built. A significant limitation of the BB analysis is that it is based upon only one year's figures. It would be strengthened by the inclusion of ratios for one or more comparative accounting periods. Also, although the comparison with industry averages is useful, it would be helpful to know more about the industry. As noted in Chapter 8, the analysis is valid only if the accounting figures are truly comparable. It is not possible to tell, from the industry ratios given, whether or not they can be validly used in comparison.

Example 9.7 (Real-Life)

This example uses figures extracted from the 2016 Annual Report of J Sainsbury plc (www.j-sainsbury.co.uk)

	2016 £m	2015 £m
Revenue	23 506	23 775
Cost of sales	(22 050)	(22 567)
Gross profit	1 456	1 208
Operating profit	707	81
Profit/(loss) before tax	548	(72)
Earnings/(loss) per share	23.9p	(8.7p)

Using these figures above it is possible to calculate profitability ratios as follows:

	2016 %	2015 %
Gross profit margin	6.19	5.08
Operating profit margin	3.01	0.34
Profit/(loss) before tax margin	2.33	(0.30)

Revenue has dropped in 2016 by 1.13% compared to the 2015 financial year. However, 2016 has been a more profitable year. Both gross margin and operating margin have improved significantly, and the pre-tax loss in 2015 has been converted into a pre-tax profit in 2016. From these figures and ratio calculations it is possible to state confidently that Sainsbury's performance has improved. However, more information would be needed in order to determine whether or not performance in the 2016 financial year was good in the context of the business, and also to find out about the factors which have contributed to the improved performance. A lot of relevant information on these points is available in the 2016 Annual Report. The Chief Executive's Letter in the Annual Report states that the company has changed its strategy, and that this is producing good results. Prices to consumers have been reduced and the quality of products has been improved. Also, the company has simplified its product range in 2016.

Chapter Summary

A great deal of useful material on financial ratio analysis has been covered in this chapter. The following ratios were examined within five major groups:

- **Performance ratios**
  - Gross profit margin
  - Net profit margin
  - Return on equity
  - Return on capital employed.

- **Liquidity ratios**
  - Current ratio
  - Quick (acid test) ratio.

- **Efficiency ratios**
  - Non-current asset turnover
  - Inventory turnover
  - Trade receivables turnover
  - Trade payables turnover.

- **Investor ratios**
  - Dividend per share
  - Dividend cover
  - Earnings per share
  - Price earnings ratio
  - Market capitalization.

- **Lending ratios**
  - Gearing ratio
  - Interest cover.

The final section of the chapter demonstrated the preparation of an analysis of financial statements, and briefly covered some of the limitations of the analysis.

Many small questions are included in the end of chapter questions, so that students can become accustomed to the calculation of ratios. But remember that the purpose in analyzing accounting information is to understand it better. Ratio calculations can be a useful means to an end, but the key objective is to understand the meaning of the financial statements.

Internet Resources

Book's companion website summary

The website contains the following resources in respect of Chapter 9:

Students' section

A multiple choice quiz containing ten questions
Three additional questions with answers

Lecturers' section

Answers to end-of-chapter exercises 9.21 to 9.39
Four additional questions with answers
Three case studies
Testbank
Instructor's Manual
PowerPoint presentation

Exercises: Answers at the End of the Book

The following information is relevant to questions 9.1 to 9.3 inclusive:

Extracts from Sigmund & Son Limited's financial statements for 20X8 show the following:

	£000
Gross profit	616.4
Various expenses	(313.6)
Operating profit	302.8
Finance costs	(35.0)
Profit before tax	267.8
Taxation	(80.0)
Profit after tax	187.8
Share capital	500.0
Retained earnings	1 790.0
Long-term borrowings	350.0

During the 20X8 financial year, Sigmund & Son Limited paid a dividend of £100 000 to its shareholders.

9.1 What is the pre-tax return on equity (to one decimal place)?

a) 13.2%
b) 10.1%
c) 26.9%
d) 11.7%

9.2 What is the post-tax return on equity (to one decimal place)?

a) 3.8%
b) 8.2%
c) 3.3%
d) 7.1%

9.3 What is the return on capital employed (to one decimal place)?

a) 8.2%
b) 11.5%
c) 13.2%
d) 10.1%

9.4 Shania would like to invest in a company which will give her a good rate of return on her investment. She has collected information on four companies. Extracts from their most recent financial statements are given below:

	Ambit Ltd	Bolsover Ltd	Carcan Ltd	Delphic Ltd
	£000	£000	£000	£000
Operating profit	983.6	647.8	726.8	1 061.4
Finance costs	(180.0)	(107.0)	(151.0)	(206.0)
Profit before tax	803.6	540.8	575.8	855.4
Tax	(240.0)	(160.0)	(170.0)	(250.0)
Profit after tax	563.6	380.8	405.8	605.4
Share capital	80.0	95.0	86.0	60.0

	Ambit Ltd	Bolsover Ltd	Carcan Ltd	Delphic Ltd
	£000	£000	£000	£000
Retained earnings	4 550.0	3 881.0	3 928.0	7 000.0
Long-term borrowings	2 400.0	1 250.0	1 820.0	2 500.0

Which company currently has the highest pre-tax return on shareholders' funds?

a) Ambit Limited
b) Bolsover Limited
c) Carcan Limited
d) Delphic Limited

9.5 Trixie Stores Limited has the following current asset and current liability items in its statement of financial position at 31 December 20X4:

	£
Inventory	18 370
Trade receivables	24 100
Cash in hand	70
Trade payables	15 450
Bank overdraft	6 400

What is the current ratio (working to two decimal places) for Trixie Stores Limited?

a) 1.95:1
b) 1.11:1
c) 0.51:1
d) 0.90:1

9.6 Trimester Tinker Limited has the following working capital items in its statement of financial position at 31 December 20X3:

	£
Inventory	108 770
Trade receivables	94 300
Cash in hand	1 600
Trade payables	110 650

The company belongs to a trade association which has recently published industry averages for key financial ratios based upon a survey of its members. The industry averages for current and quick ratios applicable to the business of Trimester Tinker Limited are:

Current ratio	1.62:1
Quick ratio	0.93:1

Which of the following statements is correct?
a) Trimester Tinker Limited's current ratio is higher than the industry average and its quick ratio is also higher.
b) Trimester Tinker Limited's current ratio is higher than the industry average but its quick ratio is lower.
c) Trimester Tinker Limited's current ratio is lower than the industry average and its quick ratio is also lower.
d) Trimester Tinker Limited's current ratio is lower than the industry average but its quick ratio is higher.

9.7 Upwood Sickert Limited has total revenue in the year ended 31 May 20X7 of £686 430. Extracts from the company's statement of financial position at that date show non-current assets as follows:

	Cost	Depreciation	Carrying amount
	£	£	£
Plant and machinery	200 000	30 000	170 000
Vehicles	106 640	46 655	59 985

What is the non-current asset turnover ratio for the year to two decimal places?

a) 2.24
b) 0.34
c) 0.45
d) 2.98

9.8 A sole trader's inventory at 31 December 20X1 was £405 000. By 31 December 20X2 inventory had increased in value by 10%. Cost of sales for the year ended 31 December 20X2 was £1 506 700.
    What was the business's inventory turnover in days for the year ended 31 December 20X2?

9.9 A company has trade receivables in its year-end statement of financial position of £218 603. Revenue for the year was £1 703 698. 70% of the revenue was in respect of sales made on credit. What is the trade receivables turnover in days?

a) 46.8 days
b) 32.7 days
c) 66.9 days
d) 18.3 days

9.10 The managing director (MD) of Winger Whalley Limited has just received a report from one of the accounting assistants employed by the business. The report shows key ratios and supplies explanations for any significant fluctuations. The MD is concerned to find that the trade receivables turnover period has worsened significantly in the period from 20X3 to 20X4 (it was 36.4 days at the end of 20X3 and is 41.2 days at the end of 20X4). The accounting assistant has supplied the following reasons for the fluctuations:

1   The company's credit controller did a parachute jump for charity about three months ago. The parachute failed to open properly, and because of her injuries she was away from work in the last three months of 20X4. The temporary staff agency was unable to provide a suitable replacement for her, and during most of the three-month period her work was simply not done.

2   Revenue has increased by 4% in the course of the year.

3   During 20X4 the board of directors decided to introduce a system of early settlement discounts. Trade receivables amounts paid within 30 days would receive a discount of 0.5% of the value of the invoices.

4   A new order of sales invoice stationery was received part-way through the year. Usually the sales invoice stationery is printed with 'SETTLEMENT REQUIRED WITHIN 30 DAYS', but the printers had omitted this by mistake. The office general manager decided to use the stationery anyway.

Two of these reasons could be valid explanations for the increase in the trade receivables turnover period. Which are the valid explanations?

a) 1 and 2
b) 3 and 4
c) 1 and 4
d) 2 and 3

9.11 A business has trade payables at its year-end of £206 460. Purchases for the year are £1 952 278, of which 90% were made on credit. What is the trade payables turnover period?

a) 42.9 days

b) 38.6 days

c) 34.7 days

d) 11.7 days.

The following information about Waldo Wolff plc, a company listed on the London Stock Exchange, is relevant to questions 9.12–9.15 inclusive.

Extracts from Waldo Wolff's accounts for the year ended 31 December 20X5 include the following useful information:

	£000
Operating profit	1 836.4
Finance costs	(220.0)
Profit before tax	1 616 4
Tax	(485.0)
Profit after tax	1 131.4

The company has 6 000 000 shares in issue. The shares have a nominal value of 50p each. During the financial year ended 31 December 20X5 the company paid dividends of £300 000.

The market price at 31 December 20X5 of one share in the company was £3.11.

9.12 What is the dividend per share?

a) 10p

b) 5p

c) 50p

d) 100p

9.13 What is the dividend cover ratio?

a) 3.77

b) 5.39

c) 2.77

d) 6.12

9.14 What are the earnings per share (in pence)?

a) 18.86p

b) 26.94p

c) 13.86p

d) 37.71p

9.15 What is Waldo Wolff's market capitalization at 31 December 20X5?

9.16 At 30 April 20X7 Wilson Streep plc had a market capitalization of £6 303 000 with 3 300 000 ordinary 50p shares in issue. The profit attributable to ordinary shareholders in its statement of profit or loss for the year ended 30 April 20X7 was £750 090.

What was the company's P/E ratio at 30 April 20X7?

a) 16.1

b) 4.2

c) 8.4

d) 3.8

9.17 Brazier Barkiss plc had the following capital structure at 30 April 20X4:

	£
Ordinary share capital (£1 shares)	1 000 000
Retained earnings	2 739 400
Long-term borrowings (10% interest rate)	2 000 000

Profit before interest and tax for the year ended 30 April 20X4 was £646 750 and finance costs were £200 000.

Calculate the following ratios:

i) gearing (on the basis of debt/equity)

ii) interest cover.

9.18 The directors of the Cuttlefish Biscuit Corporation Limited have calculated a set of key accounting ratios for their biscuit manufacturing business. These are set out in the following table, together with industry averages provided by the National Biscuit Manufacturers' Federation.

	Cuttlefish	Industry average
Gross profit margin	32.3%	31.6%
Operating profit margin	16.2%	17.1%
Trade receivables turnover (days)	36.0	38.4
Inventory turnover (days)	48.7	47.4
Trade payables	31.4	39.6
Gearing (debt/equity)	18.7%	29.4%

Write a brief report to the directors of Cuttlefish comparing the ratios for their company with the industry averages. Identify any areas in which you think they could make improvements.

9.19 Cryer Roussillon Limited is a trading company. At the beginning of the 20X6 accounting year (which ends on 31 December) a new managing director (MD) was appointed. He made the strategic decision to alter the company's range of products. Previously, the company had concentrated on lower margin products within its industry, but the new MD decided to move into higher quality products which produce better margins. He has made several other changes to the company. He persuaded the board of directors that the company should invest in some badly needed new non-current assets, and the company took out a long-term loan to help finance the acquisitions. He has also obtained the agreement of the other directors (all of whom are shareholders) not to propose any dividend this year, so that profits can be retained in the company to help finance future growth.

The summarized financial statements for 20X6 (with comparative figures for 20X5) are shown below.

Cryer Roussillon Limited: Statement of profit or loss for the year ended 31 December 20X6

	20X6	20X5
	£	£
Revenue	206 470	210 619
Cost of sales	(121 198)	(141 789)
Gross profit	85 272	68 830
Various expenses	(41 459)	(47 610)
Operating profit	43 813	21 220
Finance costs	(3 000)	–

	20X6	20X5
	£	£
Profit before tax	40 813	21 220
Tax	(8 100)	(3 180)
Profit after tax	32 713	18 040

In the year ended 31 December 20X5 Cryer Roussillon paid a dividend of £13 000 to its shareholders. In the year ended 31 December 20X6 it paid no dividend.

Cryer Roussillon: Statement of financial position at 31 December 20X6

	20X6	20X6	20X5	20X5
	£	£	£	£
ASSETS				
Non-current assets		129 490		68 750
Current assets				
Inventory	14 278		14 550	
Trade receivables	20 693		29 420	
Cash at bank	10 792		640	
		45 763		44 610
		175 253		113 360
EQUITY AND LIABILITIES				
Equity				
Share capital	20 000		20 000	
Retained earnings	109 783		77 070	
		129 783		97 070
Non-current liabilities				
Long-term borrowings		30 000		–
Current liabilities				
Trade payables		15 470		16 290
		175 253		113 360

The managing director has asked you, as the company's financial adviser, to write a confidential report to the board commenting upon items of significance in the accounts shown above. He would like you to calculate any key ratios which you consider to be important, and to provide an assessment of how the company is doing.

9.20   The table below presents some of the key figures from the statement of profit or loss of Tesco plc, extracted from its 2016 Annual Report.

	2016	2015
	£m	£m
Revenue	54 433	56 925
Cost of sales	(51 579)	(59 128)
Gross profit/(loss)	2 854	(2 203)
Operating profit/(loss)	1 046	(5 750)
Profit/(loss) before tax	162	(6 334)

	2016 £m	2015 £m
Profit/(loss) after tax	216	(5 664)
Earnings/(losses) per share	2.77p	(69.56p)

Write a brief report on the performance of Tesco plc in 2016, including calculations of any accounting ratios that you think are relevant.

Exercises: Answers Available on the Lecturers' Section of the Book's Website

The following information is relevant to questions 9.21 to 9.23 inclusive:
Extracts from Sinclair Salter's financial statements for 20X8 show the following:

	£000
Gross profit	896.4
Various expenses	(606.8)
Operating profit	289.6
Finance costs	(93.0)
Profit before tax	196.6
Tax	(60.0)
Profit after tax	136.6
Share capital	100.0
Retained earnings	1 170.0
Long-term borrowings	900.0

During the 20X8 financial year, Sinclair Salter Limited paid a dividend of £40 000 to its shareholders.

9.21 What is return on total capital employed (to one decimal place)?

a) 15.5%
b) 13.3%
c) 9.1%
d) 22.8%

9.22 What is pre-tax return on shareholders' equity (to one decimal place)?

a) 15.5%
b) 10.8%
c) 9.1%
d) 22.8%

9.23 What is post-tax return on shareholders' equity (to one decimal place)?

a) 15.5%
b) 9.1%
c) 10.8%
d) 6.3%

9.24 Shirley has been thinking for a while about investing some surplus cash in an unlisted company which organizes lettings of holiday properties in France. The company is run by an old friend of hers who is looking for additional investors in order to fund a planned expansion of the business.

Shirley has received financial statements for the business for 20X3 (showing comparative figures for 20X2). The statements of profit or loss and extracts from the statements of financial position are as follows:

	20X3 £000	20X2 £000
Revenue	976.9	899.6
Gross profit	377.6	360.9
Various expenses	(102.5)	(98.6)
Operating profit	275.1	262.3
Finance costs	(18.7)	(16.5)
Profit before tax	256.4	245.8
Tax	(77.0)	(74.0)
Profit after tax	179.4	171.8
Share capital	80.0	80.0
Retained earnings	1 465.0	1 285.6
Long-term borrowings	319.0	276.0

Calculate the following financial ratios for Shirley:

i) gross profit margin

ii) operating profit margin

iii) return on shareholders' equity

iv) return on total capital employed.

Work to one decimal place.
Comment briefly on any apparent changes in business performance between 20X2 and 20X3.

9.25 Tadcaster Terrier Limited has the following current assets and current liabilities in its statement of financial position at 31 May 20X7:

	£
Inventory	88 700
Trade payables	90 450
Trade receivables	85 210
Bank overdraft	16 790

What is the current ratio (working to two decimal places) for Tadcaster Terrier Limited?

a) 1.62:1

b) 0.62:1

c) 1.90:1

d) 0.79:1

9.26 Turnbull Taffy Limited's figures at 31 March 20X6 show the following working capital items:

	£
Inventory	67 400
Trade receivables	42 660
Cash at bank	6 050
Trade payables	58 760

The company's finance director is preparing a projected statement of financial position for 31 March 20X7 as part of a package of information to be presented to a bank from which the company hopes to obtain a long-term loan.

The finance director estimates that there will be the following changes to working capital between 31 March 20X6 and 31 March 20X7:

- Inventory will decrease by 10%
- Trade receivables will decrease by 15%
- Cash at bank will increase by 50%
- Trade payables will decrease by 5%

    i) Calculate (to two decimal places) the current ratio and the quick ratio at 31 March 20X6.

    ii) Calculate (to two decimal places) the expected current ratio and quick ratio at 31 March 20X7 based on the finance director's estimates.

9.27 Uriah Westwood plc is an advertising agency which operates from rented offices in the West End of London. Ulverstone Thunderbird plc is a company engaged in heavy engineering. It owns all of its plant and equipment and a small factory site in the North of England. Both companies have recently reported revenue in the region of £10 million. The non-current asset turnover ratio for one of the companies is 1.14 and for the other is 10.62.

From the brief descriptions given, which of the two companies is more likely to have the higher non-current asset turnover ratio?

9.28 A sole trader's inventory at 31 December 20X7 was £605 000. By 31 December 20X8 inventory had increased in value by 10%. Cost of sales for the year ended 31 December 20X8 was £2 560 800.

What was the business's inventory turnover in days?

9.29 The following are extracts from the statements of profit or loss of a sole trader business for the years ended 31 December 20X9 and 20X8:

	20X9	20X8
	£000	000
Opening inventory	1 605.3	1 396.4
Purchases	19 360.4	19 568.9
Closing inventory	(1 565.7)	(1 605.3)
Cost of sales	19 400.0	19 360.0

Calculate the inventory turnover in days for both years. Has it improved or worsened in 20X9?

9.30 A company has trade receivables in its year-end statement of financial position of £218 603. Revenue for the year was £1 703 698; 70% of this figure was sales on credit.

What is trade receivables turnover (in days)?

a) 46.8 days
b) 32.7 days
c) 66.9 days
d) 18.3 days

9.31 Whybird, a sole trader, has been advised by his accountant to keep an eye on the number of days it takes for his trade receivables to be settled. The accountant has explained how to calculate the trade receivables turnover period but Whybird doesn't really understand. He asks you to do the calculation for him. Extracts from the last two years of financial statements for Whybird's business show the following figures:

	20X5	20X4
	£	£
Revenue	180 630	178 440
Less: returns	(1 300)	(1 060)
	179 330	177 380
	£000	£000
Trade receivables	20 982	21 117
Less: allowance for bad trade receivables	(306)	(297)
	20 676	20 820

Calculate the trade receivables turnover period for Whybird for both years to one decimal place. Has the trade receivables turnover period improved or worsened in 20X5?

9.32 Wiswell Limited is a trading company. Its year-end financial statements for 20X3 (with comparatives for 20X2) included the following relevant details:

	20X3	20X3	20X2	20X2
	£	£	£	£
Revenue		1 936 000		1 877 200
Cost of sales				
Opening inventory	145 550		136 200	
Add: purchases	1 042 255		1 025 666	
	1 187 805		1 161 866	
Less: closing inventory	(160 370)		(145 550)	
		(1 027 435)		(1 016 316)
Gross profit		908 565		860 884
Inventory		160 370		145 550
Trade receivables		226 485		209 063
Trade payables		160 479		151 742

Calculate the following ratios for both 20X3 and 20X2:

i) inventory turnover in days

ii) trade receivables turnover in days

iii) trade payables turnover in days. Comment briefly on the significance of the changes in the ratios.

The following information about Worsley Bacup plc, a quoted company, is relevant to questions 9.33–9.36 inclusive.

Extracts from Worsley Bacup's accounts for the year ended 30 September 20X8 include the following useful information:

	£000
Operating profit	986.7
Finance costs	(106.0)
Profit before tax	880.7
Tax	(240.0)
Profit after tax	640.7

The company has 2 200 000 shares in issue. The shares have a nominal value of 25p each. During the financial year ended 30 September 20X8 a dividend of £250 800 was paid to the company's shareholders. The market price at 30 September 20X8 of a share in the company was £7.66.

9.33 What is the dividend per share?

a) 45.6p
b) 11.4p
c) 25.0p
d) 29.1p

9.34 What is the dividend cover ratio?

a) 3.51
b) 1.55
c) 3.93
d) 2.55

9.35 What are the earnings per share (in pence)?

a) 17.72p
b) 29.12p
c) 116.49p
d) 70.89p

9.36 What was Worsley Bacup plc's market capitalization at 30 September 20X8?

9.37 Watkinson Chapel plc is a listed company with a market capitalization of £3 430 000 at 31 August 20X4. It has in issue 1 000 000 £1 ordinary shares, and profits attributable to ordinary shareholders for the year ended 31 August 20X4 were £243 700. What was the company's P/E ratio at 31 August 20X4?

a) 21.4
b) 4.1
c) 3.4
d) 14.1

9.38 Better Belter Limited had the following capital structure at 31 October 20X2:

	£
Ordinary share capital (£1 shares)	80 000
Retained earnings	696 400
Long-term borrowings (8% interest rate)	300 000

Profit before interest and tax for the year ended 31 October 20X2 was £35 000, and finance costs were £24 000.

Calculate the following ratios:

i) gearing (on the basis of debt/equity)

ii) interest cover.

9.39 Refer back to question 9.20 which examined extracts from the financial information of Tesco plc in its 2016 Annual Report. By the time this book is published, Tesco will have produced subsequent Annual Reports. Using those subsequent reports (available from www.tescoplc.com) produce a table showing the key figures over a period of years. Conduct an analysis of the figures, calculating all relevant accounting ratios. Because you will have several years' worth of accounting information, you are also able to produce a horizontal analysis (see Chapter 8).

Write a brief report that summarizes your analysis.

(For obvious reasons, there is no model answer to this question.)

Management Accounting

10 Management and cost accounting information

Aim of the chapter

To explain the nature and purpose of management and cost accounting, and the principal uses of management and cost accounting information in the business environment.

Learning outcomes

After reading the chapter and completing the exercises, students should:

- Understand in principle the nature and purpose of management and cost accounting.

- Know about some of the principal features of management and cost accounting.

- Appreciate the usefulness of management and cost accounting in helping management to make decisions, and to plan, control and monitor business activity.

Introduction

This chapter sets the scene for most of the remaining chapters of the book. It first establishes some important features and characteristics of management accounting. Then it examines definitions of the key terms management accounting and **cost accounting** and explains a model of the principal steps involved in management, and a description of the management information that, in general terms, is required at each step.

10.1 WHAT IS MANAGEMENT AND COST ACCOUNTING?

As noted in the introductory Chapter 1, there are two distinct strands to accounting by organizations: management accounting and financial accounting, as set out in Figure 10.1. To recap: management accounting processes are concerned with the provision of information for use internally, within the organization, for functions such as decision making by managers, and the control of business activities.

Management accounting reports can be as abundant as necessary. For example, a small business that employs few staff and is engaged in the provision of a single service is unlikely to need a great deal of information for decision making and control purposes. Management accounting systems in such cases are likely to be rudimentary and informal. By contrast a complex multinational business engaged in a range of activities must take a much more formal and organized approach to information gathering and processing.

Although management and financial accounting are distinct from each other in terms of consumer, style and content, they often use the same sources of data, and the same accounting system may be used to produce much of the information. Figure 10.1 expresses the relationship between management and financial accounting information and reporting, showing the boundary between the organization and the external world. The consumers, or users, of

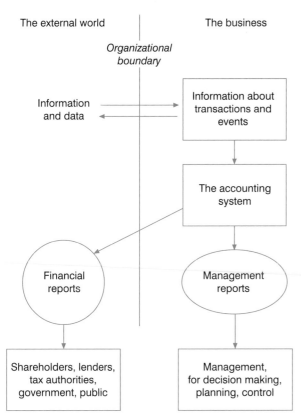

The external world | The business

Organizational boundary

Figure 10.1
The relationship between management and financial reporting

the different reports are shown at the bottom of the diagram. While there is a range of users who are interested in financial reports, management reporting information is used solely by management and is rarely distributed outside the business to anyone in the external environment.

10.1.1 Characteristics of Management Accounting Information

The typical characteristics of management accounting information, in the form of management reports, are identified in Figure 10.2, contrasting such information with the periodic financial reports that are orientated towards external users.

As the figure suggests, management information is much more flexible in nature. Financial reports tend to be highly standardized, because of regulatory requirements, but the nature of management reports is variable because managers can specify the information that they need and the frequency with which it is produced. These useful and flexible features of management accounting information are summarized and discussed further below.

FIGURE 10.2 **Characteristics of financial and management reports**

Characteristic	Financial reports	Management reports
Frequency	Usually produced annually	As frequently as necessary for management purposes
Timeliness	Usually there is a significant time lag between the period covered by the report and the date of publication	Can be produced with minimal delay, provided that appropriate systems are in place
Orientation to future or past	Summarize transactions and events that have already taken place; they are not orientated towards the future	Can be orientated towards future or past, depending upon managers' information requirements
Level of detail	The information is not detailed: transactions are summarized under a few headings	Can be as detailed or as aggregated as necessary

10.1.2 Some Useful Features of Cost and Management Accounting Information

LACK OF REGULATION Cost and management accounting, being internal to the organization, is unregulated, and can therefore be geared towards the specific needs of the organization and its managers. The cost and management accounting system can be tailored specifically to organizational own needs; information can be produced in whatever form, and in whatever quantity, is appropriate for the organization and its managers.

ORIENTATION TOWARDS PAST AND FUTURE Management accounting information draws upon past events for information but is also orientated towards the future. It considers such questions as:

- How much profit is the business likely to make next year?
- How much additional business might we pick up if we lower our prices by 5%?
- Should we close down a part of the business that is making losses?
- We need a new machine in the factory. Should we buy it or lease it?
- How much does this department cost to run?
- Which divisions in the organization are, relatively speaking, more cost-effective?

Example 10.1

Duckworths sells household alarm systems in do-it-yourself installation kits. Until recently there have been two types: the standard and the deluxe systems. This year, from 1 January, the business has introduced the super-deluxe, which has much more sophisticated circuitry and an extra alarm box for external installation. The gross margins on the three types are 38%, 40% and 46% respectively, and Duckworths' directors are keen to promote sales of the higher specification and more profitable products.

Each month the sales director holds a meeting with the sales force on about the fifth or sixth day of the month. Early in April 20X2 he discusses the sales figures (in units) for January, February and March, which are as follows:

	Standard	Deluxe	Super-Deluxe	Total
January	2 038	1 604	213	3 855
February	2 175	1 598	344	4 117
March	2 240	1 634	28	3 902

At the meeting he asks his staff why they think that sales of the super-deluxe, after a promising start in January and February, have nosedived in March. A couple of the sales reps tell him that Duckworth's principal competitor has brought out a deluxe system that is not only cheaper than Duckworth's but which also has some extra features. The Duckworths' product is more expensive and is of poorer quality.

The sales director now has quite a lot of information to take with him to the next main board meeting: concrete evidence in the form of the sales figures of problems with the super-deluxe sales, and some reasons for the drop in sales. The information he has available does not solve the problem, but the rapid provision of figures has at least allowed him to identify that a problem exists. It is then up to the board of directors to discuss the problem and possible solutions to it.

TIMELY PRODUCTION The overriding objective of the production of cost and management information is that it should be useful. Management can set up systems that produce useful information quickly. For example, in most businesses it will be useful to have monthly sales figures reported as quickly as possible. Such figures do not necessarily have to be completely accurate. Also, they do not necessarily have to be accompanied by detail of other income and expenses (because this would probably slow up the production of information). There is no reason why simple sales figures could not be available a day or two after each month end. Managers would thus be in a position to respond very quickly to changing circumstances, as illustrated in Example 10.1.

FREQUENT REPORTING In Example 10.1, sales of alarm systems were reported internally once a month. This is clearly a much more frequent basis of reporting than the annual financial reporting undertaken by businesses. It is common for businesses to organize their internal management reporting on a monthly basis, producing often quite detailed reports. However, it is possible to produce internal cost and management information as frequently as it is required. In larger businesses some important elements of internal information may be reported as frequently as once a day. For example, large retailers are likely to produce sales figures daily.

10.2 DEFINITIONS OF MANAGEMENT ACCOUNTING AND COST ACCOUNTING

The UK's premier management accounting body is the Chartered Institute of Management Accountants (CIMA). CIMA provides the following definition of management accounting: 'Management accounting is the sourcing, analysis, communication and use of decision-relevant financial and non-financial information to generate and preserve value for organizations' (www.cimaglobal.com).

CIMA emphasizes that management accounting is about much more than preparing numbers for management: 'Management accounting combines accounting, finance and management with the business skills and techniques you'll need to add real value to any organization. Management accountants are qualified to work across the business, not just in finance, advising managers on the financial implications of big decisions, formulating business strategy and monitoring risk – much more than just crunching numbers' (www.cimaglobal.com).

What about cost accounting? A CIMA definition of cost accounting is the 'Gathering of cost information and its attachment to cost objects, the establishment of budgets, standard costs and actual costs of operations, processes, activities or products; and the analysis of variances, profitability or the social use of funds.'

In practice, there is a considerable overlap in the terms 'management accounting' and 'cost accounting', and indeed they are often used together, as in this chapter's title. This book will not attempt to demarcate the terms rigorously. 'Management accounting' will be used as a general term to cover the production and uses of information within the business. 'Cost accounting' will be referred to in areas that specifically consider the identification and accumulation of costs.

10.3 THE MANAGEMENT ACCOUNTING PROCESS

The process of management, and related management information needs, can be summarized in a neat, linear form, as set out in Figure 10.3.

Figure 10.3 **The process of management**

Step	Commentary on management function	Commentary on management information needs
Set business decisions	The primary functions of management are to: a) identify the objectives of the organization; and b) direct the activities of the organization so as to meet the objectives	Information about e.g. markets, competition, availability of financing for projects
Assess alternatives and make decisions	Make a choice between available courses of action	Sufficient, relevant and reliable information to permit a rational choice to be made
Make plans	Having determined the action to be followed, develop plans to help carry out the action	Forecasts and resource allocation plans
Control activities	Exert control to ensure that the plan is followed	Short-term monitoring reports
Monitor outcomes	Assess the extent to which the plans have succeeded and the business objectives have been met	Performance reports and comparisons with forecasts and plans. Explanations of variations between planned and actual outcomes
Redefine objectives where necessary	On the basis of actual outturns amend long, medium and short-term plans as appropriate	Timely and efficient amendments to plans and budgets

10.3.1 The Objectives of the Organization

Much of the content of the forthcoming chapters is concerned with techniques and mechanisms that allow managers to make decisions and then plans, to control activities and to monitor outcomes. It is important, though, to bear in mind that these activities operate within overarching organizational objectives, and that managerial efforts should always be geared to achieving the business's objectives (note that you may sometimes see 'objective' referred to as 'vision' or 'mission'). The principal objective of a private sector business might seem obvious: to make a profit. Naturally, all businesses within an essentially capitalist system need to make a profit in order to survive: profitability is therefore important. However, business objectives and priorities go far beyond the simple desire to make money. Profitability and positive cash flow are by-products that tend to arise when a business's key objectives are met. Typical objectives might be expressed as follows:

- 'We want to be the market leader in plumbers' fittings.'
- 'This company aims to be the best in our business sector.'
- 'We aim to operate according to the highest ethical standards at all times.'

Example 10.2 (Real-Life)

Here are some real-life examples of what businesses say about their objectives:

J. Sainsbury plc: 'Our vision: To be the most trusted retailer where people love to work and shop'
GlaxoSmithKline plc: 'Our mission is to help people do more, feel better, live longer'
Kier Group plc: 'Our vision is to be a world-class, customer focused company that invests in, builds, maintains and renews the places where we live, work and play'

Public sector and not-for-profit organizations also tend to gauge their success against overarching objectives or principles. For example, the UK's National Health Service holds to the following fundamental principles: 'The provision of quality care that meets the needs of everyone, is free at the point of need, and is based on the clinical need, not ability to pay.'

10.3.2 The Effect of Uncertainty

The diagram in Figure 10.3 comprises the textbook version of how decision making, planning and control should take place. Needless to say, the process in real life is somewhat messier and less precise. Managers spend much time and effort in an attempt to anticipate future events and trends, but of course information on such matters is highly speculative. Even understanding current events and trends can present significant challenges. Managers work in rapidly changing environments beset by difficulties and uncertainties. It may be necessary to alter plans at short notice in response to unanticipated events (eg. shortage of **raw materials**, war, civil unrest, new competitors, new product inventions, and so on). The information systems that serve managers should be efficient and responsive to rapidly changing needs but in the real world this is not always the case. Management accounting systems can often, in practice, be quite inflexible and managers may have to make decisions at short notice with sub-optimal levels of information at their disposal. Luck and a favourable combination of circumstances may (or may not) subsequently validate the decisions.

Although the textbook model of management is rarely, if ever, completely reflective of reality, the model does approximate in some degree the process that intelligent managers follow. As for information, although it can rarely be complete and is always subject to uncertainties, some information is usually better than no information. The existence of information may help to give managers the confidence they need to engage in strategic planning and decision making, and will help them, at least to some degree, to follow through and monitor their decisions. It will be helpful, though, to bear in mind that the management and costing information explained in some detail in the rest of the chapters will not necessarily be complete, or sufficient or timely enough, for managers' needs.

10.4 ORGANIZATION OF THE REST OF THE BOOK

The chapters that follow will deal with many elements of management and cost accounting. A brief overview is provided below:

Chapter	Overview of the chapter content
11 Costing: overview and basic techniques	Cost accounting: • gather cost information and attach it to cost objects
12 Costing: accounting for overheads	• determine actual costs of operations, processes, activities and products.
13 Pricing	Management accounting: • inform operational decisions about pricing of products and services.
14 Marginal costing and decision making	Cost accounting: • gather cost information and attach it to cost objects. Management accounting: • plan medium- and short-run operations • inform operational decisions • ensure the efficient use of resources.
15 Capital investment decisions	Management accounting: • plan long- and medium-run operations • ensure the efficient use of resources.
16 Budgets	Cost accounting: • establish budgets. Management accounting: • plan long-, medium- and short-term operations • control operations • ensure the efficient use of resources.
17 Accounting for control	Cost accounting: • establish standard costs, and actual costs of operations, processes, activities or products • analyze variances. Management accounting: • control operations • ensure the efficient use of resources.
18 Divisional performance and transfer pricing	Management accounting: • measure and report financial and non-financial performance to management and other stakeholders.

The principal orientation of this book is towards private sector, profit-making businesses, but it should be appreciated that many of the techniques and practices discussed can be found across all sectors. Some of the examples in the chapters that follow reflect the wide applicability of management and cost accounting techniques in different sectors.

Chapter Summary

This chapter has introduced some important ideas about, and definitions of, management accounting and cost accounting.

Internet Resources

Book's companion website summary

The website contains the following resources in respect of Chapter 10:

Students' section

A multiple choice quiz containing five questions
Two additional questions with answers

Lecturers' section

Answers to end-of-chapter exercises 10.4 to 10.6
Two additional questions with answers
Case study
Testbank
Instructor's Manual
PowerPoint presentation

Exercises: Answers at the End of the Book

Note that because this chapter is a relatively short introduction to management and cost accounting, there are only a limited number of end-of-chapter exercises. The intention is that the exercises should be answered in fairly general terms, drawing upon both common sense and imagination. Students have to try to think their way into the situations described in order to specify the kind of management information that would be useful. The objective behind the questions is to get students accustomed to thinking about typical decisions that have to be made in business.

If this book is being studied as part of a taught course, any of the questions that follow could be used as a basis for class discussion.

10.1 Cueline Limited manufactures furniture at factory premises held on a lease. The lease is due to end next year, but it could probably be renegotiated. The company's directors are also considering the possibility of buying freehold premises. What items of management information would be useful to the directors in reaching a decision?

10.2 Putt plc owns several shops selling golfing and other sporting equipment. It operates principally in the area around London. The company's directors will be meeting next month to discuss a proposal for a major change in business strategy. The sales director has noted that gross margins on golf-related items are much higher than those on other stock lines, and he is proposing that the company should in future sell only golfing equipment. What items of information, financial and non-financial, are likely to be useful to the directors in assessing the pros and cons of the proposed change in strategy?

10.3 Bulstrode, Barker and Bennett is a successful firm of solicitors operating in a small town. Bulstrode died some years ago, Barker has retired, but Dexter Bennett still works in the business as senior partner. There are three junior partners, and Dexter has called a meeting of the partners to discuss the decisions they should make on the following proposals:

a) The conveyancing department is very busy. Would it make economic sense for the firm to employ another solicitor in that department?

b) The firm currently specializes in conveyancing and litigation work. The town's principal specialist in divorce work has just retired, and Bennett thinks there is an opportunity to pick up some extra business. He knows a highly experienced divorce specialist who is currently working for a large firm in London. She could be persuaded to move if she were offered a position as a junior partner.

What information are the partners likely to need (both financial and non-financial) in order to reach the right decisions on these proposals?

Exercises: Answers Available on the Lecturers' Section of the Book's Website

10.4   Cyclostyle Limited makes metal parts for bicycles. The metal press machine, which has been used in the business for several years, is now reaching the end of its useful life. The directors are looking at two replacement options. One is a German machine at a cost of £54 000. The other is a British machine at a cost of £38 500.

What items of information, financial and non-financial, are likely to be useful to the directors in deciding between the two machines?

10.5   Preedy Price Limited is a small fashion company run by two sisters, Anne Preedy and Amelia Price. They have been very successful in marketing a range of very exclusive and expensive knitwear through small specialist retail outlets. The company has been approached by a large retailer, Shield & Flagg plc, which would like to market a cut-price version of some of the sisters' exclusive designs. Shield and Flagg's buyer assures the sisters that this would be a very good opportunity for them to make high volume sales and to make a lot of money. She estimates that volumes of up to 35 000 garments per year are quite feasible. The maximum number of garments the sisters have produced and sold in one year to date is 5600.

Production could be handled by some of Shield & Flagg's regular knitwear production factories, or the sisters could set up their own large-scale production facilities. In order to make the launch of the new lines successful, however, stocks of around 20 000 items would have to be available in advance of the items going on sale in Shield & Flagg's 35 stores around the country.

What factors (both financial and non-financial) should the sisters take into consideration in deciding whether or not to take up this new opportunity?

10.6   Denver runs a restaurant business, operating from rented premises in the centre of a large town. His business has been relatively successful; he has succeeded in making a small profit each year, but he feels that he could do better if he expanded the business.

Denver is a sole trader and the only person with whom he can really discuss business strategy, in complete confidence, is his accountant, Dylan. He has arranged a meeting with Dylan to discuss possible future directions for the business. He starts the meeting by explaining some of the ideas he has had to improve the business:

'The fundamental point is that I need to expand the number of covers. I cannot do this in my current premises at Hanover Road, and I would need to move. There is a freehold building for sale on Cross Street with a restaurant on the ground floor. If I bought that I could have half as many covers again as I have now. I could sell my house and then move into the upper part of the building. That would help to keep the mortgage down to a reasonable level.

I have also been wondering about making some fairly major changes to the menu. My net profit margin, as you know from the annual accounts you have just prepared for me, is only about 6%. I would like to cut out the less profitable menu items. I think I know which ones are less profitable but I cannot be sure. As you know, I open six evenings a week at the moment. I have been wondering about starting weekend lunches as well, but I do not know whether I could make enough money to justify keeping the place open.'

Advise Denver on the type of information – financial and non-financial – he needs in order to make decisions on the three points above (the advice can be given in fairly general terms).

11 Costing: overview and basic techniques

Aim of the chapter

To achieve an understanding of how costs are gathered and attached to cost objects and knowledge of the terminology and classifications used in costing.

Learning outcomes

After reading the chapter and completing the exercises, students should:

- Recognize and understand a range of basic costing terminology.

- Be able to classify costs into direct and indirect costs.

- Understand the build-up of materials, labour and production overheads into full production costs.

Introduction

This chapter introduces some important aspects of cost and management accounting practice.

Chapter 10 introduced a definition of cost accounting, the first part of which is 'Gathering of cost information and its attachment to cost objects'.

This chapter focuses upon the processes and techniques involved in gathering the costs of production.

The first section of this chapter defines the term 'cost object' and examines the reasons why managers might find it useful to be able to identify costs. The chapter then proceeds to examine a range of relevant techniques for the costing of products.

11.1 COSTING IN BUSINESS

Costing involves the gathering of cost information and its attachment to cost objects. A **cost object** is any item or activity which requires costing; any product or service provided by a business could be a cost object. Costing can be useful to management in many aspects of its roles of planning, assessing alternatives, controlling activities and monitoring outcomes.

- Planning – in forecasting future commercial transactions it is necessary to have some idea of the cost of products and services in order to be able to estimate reliably future outflows of resources.

- Assessing alternatives and decision making – for example, when deciding on whether to produce and sell a particular product, a comparison of sales with related costs can suggest whether or not it is worthwhile to go ahead.
- Monitoring outcomes – information about expected and actual costs of a product or service is required in order to effectively monitor outcomes.

In addition, product costing has traditionally been used to provide essential inputs into financial accounting and reporting. For example, the valuation of inventories in a manufacturing business typically requires detailed information about product costs, especially where **work-in-progress** constitutes part of the value of inventories.

Section 11.2 of the chapter examines the techniques involved in costing products.

11.2 PRODUCT COSTING

In a manufacturing environment there are three basic components of cost:

- materials cost
- labour cost
- production overheads.

Direct inputs into the manufacturing process usually include both materials and labour costs. Production overheads are indirect inputs. They are costs involved in running a production facility but which are not themselves identifiable with individual items produced; they may include both indirect labour and indirect materials costs. (Production overheads and their attachment to cost objects are examined in detail in Chapter 12.)

Costs are often classified as **direct** (direct materials, direct labour and any other **direct expenses** and **indirect** (overheads). If in doubt about whether a cost is direct or indirect, ask the question: 'Can this cost be traced directly to the product?'

The following example will help to illustrate the point.

Example 11.1

GHP Limited manufactures greetings cards. The production process involves the following stages:

1 A design is produced.
2 The design is printed onto card in a run of 1000 cards per production run.
3 The card is cut and folded.
4 Other processes such as embossing, gilding and overprinting are then undertaken, depending upon the design of the card.
5 The cards are matched with envelopes of suitable size.
6 Each card and envelope is individually packaged in a cellophane wrapper.

What are the direct costs involved in this process?

DIRECT COSTS

Direct materials

Materials costs include: the cost of card, ink, possibly metal leaf, envelopes and cellophane and, perhaps, a label.

Direct labour

Labour is required to:

- set up and operate the printing machine (this is a computerized process, but it involves some input of time)
- operate the machine which cuts and folds the card
- package the card together with the envelope (at GHP Limited this is a completely manual process).

Direct expense

GHP Limited buys in designs from freelance designers. The company pays the designer £200 for the design under an agreement which allows it to produce 1000 cards of each design. The production of each card therefore includes a direct expense of 20p per card.

Indirect production costs (overheads)

Indirect production costs include all of those costs of running the production facility which cannot be directly identified with units of production. These would include such items as:

- factory rental
- production supervisor's wages
- factory cleaning costs
- maintenance and repair of factory and machinery.

Other indirect costs (overheads)

As well as indirect costs incurred in running the production facility, GHP incurs many other costs. For example:

- administration salaries
- rental of the office
- depreciation of the office computer
- salespersons' salaries.

All of the costs taken together add up to the total cost of running the business, summarized as follows:

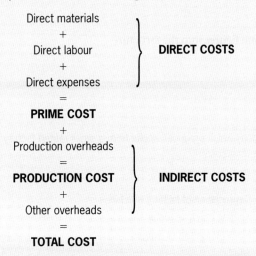

Note that the terms *'indirect costs'* and *'overheads'* mean the same thing. Either term can be used. *'Prime cost'* is a term sometimes used in practice: it simply refers to the total of direct costs (direct materials, direct labour and direct expenses).

Beeching Plumstead has a factory which produces babies' pushchairs. The following is a list of some of the costs which the company incurs:

- canvas material
- metal spokes for wheels
- spare parts for sewing machine repairs

Self-test question 11.1 (answer at the end of the book)

- advertising expenditure

- machine oil

- electricity bill for factory

- wages of assembly line workers

- wages of factory canteen staff

- wages of assembly line supervisor

- secretary's salary

- delivery vehicle depreciation.

Classify each item of expense as one of the following:

- direct labour
- direct materials
- direct expenses
- indirect production overheads
- other indirect overheads.

The next example fits some figures into the structure.

Example 11.2

Julienne Benoit is a company which produces socks from a small rented factory space. In the month ended 31 August 20X2 it incurred the following costs:

	£
Depreciation of knitting machines	420
Knitting machine repair	68
Machine operators' wages	6 330
Wool	4 850
Sticky labels for socks	93
Plastic ties for sock pairing	133
Factory rental	1 230
Electricity costs: factory	216
Electricity costs: office	38
Part-time secretary's wages	540
Office stationery and supplies	21
Factory cleaner's wages	123
Telephone: office	83
Delivery costs	436
Other office costs	214
Other factory costs	130

Rearrange the information given above into a cost statement for August 20X2.

Julienne Benoit: Cost statement for the month ended 31 August 20X2

	£	£
Direct materials		
Wool	4 850	
Sticky labels for socks	93	
Plastic ties for sock pairing	133	
		5 076
Direct labour: Machine operators' wages		6 330
Prime cost		11 406
Production overheads		
Depreciation of knitting machines	420	
Knitting machine repair	68	
Factory rental	1 230	
Electricity costs: factory	216	
Factory cleaner's wages	123	
Other factory costs	130	
		2 187
Production cost		13 593
Other overheads		
Electricity costs: office	38	
Part-time secretary's wages	540	
Office stationery and supplies	21	
Telephone: office	83	
Delivery costs	436	
Other office costs	214	
		1 332
Total costs		14 925

11.2.1 Cost Classification: Product and Period Costs

Another way of looking at costs is to classify them as product or period costs.

Product costs are those related to production of goods or services for sale by the business. Using the terminology we have already established, product costs include direct and indirect production costs.

Period costs are those costs which are incurred in the period of account, for example, salaries of sales and marketing personnel.

Note that the principle of accruals or matching operates in management accounting, just as in financial accounting. For example cost of sales used in management accounting must be adjusted for opening and closing inventories. In a manufacturing business, this means bringing forward opening inventories and carrying forward closing inventories, both valued at production cost.

11.3 APPROACHES TO COSTING

In order to keep track of costs, to be able to plan and control business activity and to be able to value work-in-progress and **finished goods** inventories, costs should be allocated to products. Work-in-progress and finished goods inventories are carried forward to the next accounting period at production cost (ie. including materials, direct labour and production overheads costs). This accumulation of costs is known as **absorption costing**.

Where the cost information relates to a single piece of work chargeable to one client or customer the accumulation of costs may help in establishing the price at which the goods or services are to be invoiced. In costing terminology this is known as **job costing**.

Often in manufacturing industries goods of a generic type are produced to replenish general inventories of finished goods. Costing information is gathered for each type of product manufactured. In costing terminology this is known as **product costing**.

Sometimes in manufacturing industries it is appropriate to produce goods in batches or production runs of convenient sizes. Costs are allocated to each batch or run. In costing terminology this is known as **batch costing**.

All product and service costing involves the allocation of costs to cost units. A **cost unit** is an item of production or a group of products or a service for which it is useful to have product cost information. Three examples of cost units follow, each illustrating a different costing method.

Example 11.3

This example illustrates **job costing**.

Clement is a sole trader who owns a small factory. He and his team of skilled workers produce high quality furniture to order. He has been given an order for 12 dining chairs by a luxury hotel chain. Clement keeps a job cost record for each order on which he records prime cost details. This order (Code ref: 3223) has had the following materials and labour booked to it:

Direct materials	Booked
Mahogany	18 pieces
Seat padding	12 pieces
Leather cloth	6 metres

Direct labour	Booked
Grade 1	115 hours
Grade 2	86 hours

Mahogany is purchased at £36 per piece, each piece of seat padding costs £3.50 and the leather cloth is £42 per metre.

Clement employs two grades of labour: grade 1 for which direct labour cost is £8.50 and grade 2, for which direct labour cost is £9.25.

The job cost record for Job No. 3223 would be as follows:

Job No. 3223

12 dining chairs	Cost	£	£
Direct materials			
Mahogany	18 @ £36	648.00	
Seat padding	12 @ £3.50	42.00	
Leather cloth	6 metres @ £42 per m.	252.00	
			942.00
Direct labour			
Grade 1	115 hours @ £8.50	977.50	
Grade 2	86 hours @ £9.25	795.50	
			1 773.00
TOTAL			2 715.00

Example 11.4

This example illustrates **product costing**.

Pierce Waterworth plc manufactures a range of components for the motor industry. The company keeps a constant inventory of its 100 or so most popular lines so that it can respond immediately to orders. For example, once inventories of component XL046, an air filter, fall to 50 units, production is scheduled to replenish the inventories of the component. The input of materials is logged, and the number of hours and minutes that people spend operating the machines. These are charged to production of the XL046 and the inventory value is built up by successive inputs of materials, labour and overheads.

Example 11.5

This example illustrates **batch costing**.

In the example of the greeting cards company used earlier (see Example 11.1), a production run of 1000 cards was assumed. This is likely to be quite a reasonable size for a cost unit. Treating each individual card as a cost unit would involve a pointlessly detailed set of calculations. Given that the 1000 cards are identical and are all produced in one run, the cost unit in this case will be the run of 1000 cards. Having established the costs for the cost unit, the cost of an individual card is easily calculated by dividing total costs by 1000.

The next two subsections of the chapter will examine the allocation of materials and labour to cost units in the context of a manufacturing environment. The allocation of overheads is covered in Chapter 12.

11.3.1 Materials Costs

Raw materials are bought in and an inventory maintained as necessary in order to ensure that shortages, which would slow up production, do not occur. Direct materials are issued to production in appropriate quantities and the cost is allocated to the appropriate cost unit.

How do we establish the cost of raw materials transferred into production?

The answer to this question is not always straightforward, especially where there is a large volume of identical items moving in and out of inventory, and where prices are changing.

There are two commonly used valuation conventions:

FIRST IN, FIRST OUT (FIFO) This convention assumes that the items which have been in inventory the longest are the first to move out into production. (Note that this is a theoretical assumption for valuation purposes only – it may not reflect the actual physical movements in inventory.)

WEIGHTED AVERAGE COST (AVCO) Under this convention the value of each individual item of inventory is a weighted average of the value of all items in inventory.

Example 11.6

Parben Ltd runs a business manufacturing pencils. These are placed in presentation boxes which hold 48 pencils. The presentation boxes are all purchased from the same supplier. The inventory record for February 20X2 shows the following details of deliveries of presentation boxes into inventory and transfers to production:

Deliveries into inventory

3 Feb	120 units purchased at £1.50 each
18 Feb	160 units purchased at £1.55 each

Transfers to production

6 Feb	95 units
21 Feb	80 units
26 Feb	70 units

Inventory at 1 February was 25 units which cost £1.50 each.

Examining each of the valuation conventions:

FIRST IN, FIRST OUT (FIFO)

Date	Deliveries into inventory Units	£	£	Transfers to production Units	£	£	Balance Units	£
1 Feb							25	37.50
3 Feb	120	1.50	180.00				145	217.50
6 Feb				95	1.50	142.50	50	75.00
18 Feb	160	1.55	248.00				210	323.00
21 Feb				50	1.50	75.00	160	248.00
				30	1.55	46.50	130	201.50
26 Feb				70	1.55	108.50	60	93.00
Total cost of transfers to production						372.50		

At the end of the month the closing balance of inventory is 60 units. Because of the assumption that the first items to enter inventory are the first to leave it, closing inventory is valued on the basis of the latest price at which inventory was purchased (in this case £1.55).

Weighted Average Cost (AVCO)

Date	Deliveries into inventory Units	£	£	Transfers to production Units	£	£	Balance Units	AVCO	£
1 Feb							25	1.50	37.50
3 Feb	120	1.50	180.00				145	1.50	217.50
6 Feb				95	1.50	142.50	50	1.50	75.00
18 Feb	160	1.55	248.00				210	1.538	323.00
21 Feb				80	1.538	123.05	130	1.538	199.95
26 Feb				70	1.538	107.67	60	1.538	92.28
Total cost of transfers to production						373.22			

At the end of the month the closing balance of inventory is 60 units (as before), but the closing inventory valuation is £92.28.

Summary

Method	Transfers to production £	Closing inventory £	Total £
FIFO	372.50	93.00	465.50
AVCO	373.22	92.28	465.50

Note that the total cost involved is identical in each case. What differs between the methods is the allocation of the total between transfers to production and closing inventory.

Why does the method of inventory valuation matter? The reason lies in the basic formula for cost of sales:

- Opening inventory
- Add: purchases
- Less: closing inventory.

If opening or closing inventory values change, cost of sales changes, and so do the figures for gross or net profit (because sales less cost of sales = gross profit).

onzalez Perez is a manufacturing company. It buys in inventories of a component, X, which it uses in production. Inventories of component X at 1 March 20X2 were 55 units at £3 each. The following movements in inventory took place in March:

10 March – 160 units of X were purchased for £3.20 each
12 March – 35 units of X were transferred to production
25 March – 70 units of X were transferred to production.

What is the closing inventory value calculated under each of the following conventions?

a) FIFO
b) AVCO

11.3.2 Labour Costs

Earlier, in Example 11.3, we looked at the example of a business booking different grades of labour time in job costing. In that example, two different types of labour were involved. The business in the example was a relatively simple sole trader enterprise. In more complex businesses, labour time booking is often an elaborate procedure involving careful observation and record-keeping. A production operative may work on a range of different cost units during a day, and a method must be found of ensuring that the work is accurately booked. If errors are made product costs will be misstated and incorrect decisions may result.

The following are some of the practical issues and complexities which may arise in respect of the identification and allocation of direct labour:

EMPLOYEE PERFORMS A COMBINATION OF DIRECT AND INDIRECT LABOUR TASKS An employee may spend part of his or her time on a production line engaged in specific aspects of production which can be allocated to cost units. However, in addition he or she may have more general tasks, such as cleaning machinery, sweeping up, engaging in routine maintenance, and so on. Therefore, it may be necessary to allocate time between direct and indirect labour tasks.

VARIATION IN METHODS OF PAYMENT There are several ways of paying employees. Usually there is a basic rate element, but in addition there may be special payments for working overtime or unsocial hours. Sometimes, for example in garment production, direct labour employees are paid piece rates for work (a fixed amount, say, for each shirt sewn); in addition they may be paid a bonus for achieving a particularly high level of output.

IDLE OR NON-PRODUCTIVE TIME If a machine breaks down or there is some other kind of hitch in the production process employees may not be able to be employed in productive activity. This is sometimes known as idle time. Employees are sometimes entitled to be paid for the time, but how should it be treated?

The management accountant takes into account all of the complexities of labour costs, averages them, and produces an hourly rate for each grade of labour, which can then be applied to all direct labour time spent in production.

Example 11.7

This example demonstrates the allocation of direct material and labour costs to a particular job.

Barker and Clyde produce machine parts for the airline industry. They have an order from an aircraft manufacturer for 150 units of component BYA570. This work is assigned Job No. V477848.

This involves the following transfers from raw materials inventories:

650 kg of material V, valued at AVCO of £3.60 per kilo
125 kg of material G, valued at AVCO of £5.50 per kilo

Three grades of direct labour are involved:

Grade 7 at a rate of £8.00 per hour
Grade 13 at a rate of £10.60 per hour
Grade 14 at a rate of £11.50 per hour.

The cost accountant collects information about direct labour time used in production and summarizes it onto a form, which identifies the job codes, labour grade and hours spent.

After completion of the job the form for this job is as follows:

<table>
<tr><td colspan="2">**Job No.: V477848**</td><td colspan="2">**Date: 12.11.X2**</td></tr>
<tr><td colspan="2">**Component No.: BYA 570**</td><td colspan="2">**Supervisor: ASHTON**</td></tr>
<tr><td colspan="2">**Quantity: 150 units**</td><td></td><td></td></tr>
<tr><td></td><td></td><td>**£**</td><td>**£**</td></tr>
<tr><td colspan="2">Direct material</td><td></td><td></td></tr>
<tr><td colspan="2">Material V (650 kg × £3.60)</td><td>2 340.00</td><td></td></tr>
<tr><td colspan="2">Material G (125 kg × £5.50)</td><td>687.50</td><td></td></tr>
<tr><td></td><td></td><td></td><td>3 027.50</td></tr>
<tr><td colspan="2">Direct labour</td><td></td><td></td></tr>
<tr><td colspan="2">Grade 7: 26.5 hours booked @ £8.00 per hour</td><td>212.00</td><td></td></tr>
<tr><td colspan="2">Grade 13: 12 hours @ £10.60 per hour</td><td>127.20</td><td></td></tr>
<tr><td colspan="2">Grade 14: 4 hours @ £11.50 per hour</td><td>46.00</td><td></td></tr>
<tr><td></td><td></td><td></td><td>385.20</td></tr>
<tr><td colspan="2">Prime cost</td><td></td><td>3 412.70</td></tr>
</table>

This information allows us to calculate prime cost per component:

$$\frac{£3412.70}{150} = £22.75$$

Self-test question 11.3 (answer at the end of the book)

Harvey & Cork produces photograph frames in batches of 500. The following materials and labour are booked to Batch No. 30453A:

- 100 kg of metal @ £4.50 per kilo
- paint: 2 litres of blue @ £6.80 per litre
- glass: 500 pieces at 30p each
- 22 hours of direct labour at A grade (charged at £8.00 per hour)
- 19 hours of direct labour at B grade (charged at £9.00 per hour).

Prepare a batch costing record to show the prime cost of Batch No. 30453A. What is the cost per picture frame?

Example 11.8 (Real-Life)

WITH MANUFACTURING IN DECLINE IN THE UK, WHY ARE WE STUDYING MANAGEMENT ACCOUNTING FROM A MANUFACTURING PERSPECTIVE?

Since the 1960s manufacturing in the UK has been in decline. The contribution of manufacturing to the UK's GDP and the percentage of people employed in manufacturing have both fallen substantially. Over the same period, the contribution of services (especially financial services) to the UK economy has risen. Similar trends are observable in other mature Western economies.

SO, SURELY, TRADITIONAL COST AND MANAGEMENT ACCOUNTING ARE NO LONGER RELEVANT AREAS OF STUDY?

There are a number of points to be made in support of the continuing relevance of cost and management accounting:

- Reports of the death of manufacturing may have been overstated. Although the provision of services has become much more important in the UK and other mature Western economies, manufacturing continues to be a significant contributor to national wealth.
- Look around you: unless you're currently afloat in an open boat or studying in a field, you are probably surrounded by stuff. Someone, somewhere, has manufactured these physical objects. Although large-scale manufacturing is less common in the UK than it used to be, it is taking place in other countries. And somebody is busy accounting for it.
- Manufacturing is not the only area in which cost and management accounting are relevant. Remember the CIMA definition of management accounting from Chapter 10: 'Management accounting is the sourcing, analysis, communication and use of decision-relevant financial and non-financial information to generate and preserve value for organizations'. There's nothing in this definition that restricts the role of management accounting to manufacturing.

As you work through the management accounting section of the book you will find examples from service industries, as well as manufacturing industries.

Chapter Summary

This chapter first established the three basic elements of product cost: materials, labour and overheads, and then proceeded to explain the techniques of costing materials and labour in the context of manufacturing industry. The application of these techniques was explained using a series of examples of costing direct labour and materials inputs. The identification of overheads with cost objects is a more complex issue and so it has been allocated a separate chapter – Chapter 12, which follows this one.

Later in the book, costs will be examined in different ways, often for different purposes. It can be confusing to students, especially those at an early stage in their studies, to be faced with different ways of looking at costs. It is important to bear in mind that all costing processes involve the use of simplifying assumptions, and that the appropriate approach to cost identification, classification and analysis depends upon context.

Internet Resources

Book's companion website summary

The website contains the following resources in respect of Chapter 11:

Students' section

A multiple choice quiz containing five questions
Three additional questions with answers

Lecturers' section

Answers to end-of-chapter exercises 11.5 to 11.8
Two additional questions with answers
Testbank
Instructor's Manual
PowerPoint presentation

11.1 Paige Peverell produces plastic casings for telephones. The following is a list of some of the costs which the company incurs:

- plastic moulding machine depreciation

- sales office fixtures and fittings depreciation

- plastic materials

- advertising expenditure

- depreciation of factory building

- electricity bill for factory

- wages of assembly line workers

- wages of factory canteen staff

- wages of assembly line supervisor

- secretary's salary

- delivery vehicle depreciation

- factory consumables

- royalty payable per item produced to telephone designer

- mobile telephone bill – sales director

- telephone designer.

Classify each item of expense as one of the following:

- direct labour
- direct materials
- direct expenses
- indirect production overheads
- other indirect overheads.

11.2 ArtKit Supplies manufactures metal paint tins for the artist's supplies industry. The company operates from a small rented factory unit. In the year ended 31 August 20X2 it incurred the following costs:

	£
Sundry factory costs	2 117
Hinge fittings for boxes	960
Secretarial and administration salaries	22 460
Delivery costs	1 920
Machine operators' wages	27 250
Machinery repair	176
Factory cleaning	980
Lacquer paint for boxes	1 600
Rental of factory	6 409
Finishing operative's wages	19 270

	£
Sundry office costs	904
Salesman's salary	28 200
Metal	18 006
Electricity: factory	1 760
Office supplies	2 411
Depreciation: machinery	1 080
Office telephone	1 630

Rearrange the information given into a cost statement for the year ended 31 August 20X2.

11.3 Porter Farrington Limited imports components for input into its production process. In November 20X2 the following deliveries into inventory and transfers to production took place in respect of component PR430:

Date	Activity	Units
1 November	Balance of inventory @ £3.00 per unit	30
2 November	Delivery of inventory @ £3.30 per unit	50
18 November	Transfer to production	(40)
30 November	Balance of inventory	40

What is the value of closing inventory at 30 November 20X2, assuming that Porter Farrington Limited adopts the FIFO convention?

a) £123

b) £126

c) £120

d) £132

11.4 Each of the following scenarios describes an approach to costing.

a) Greenaway Slipknot Limited produces high quality prints of contemporary art. Typically, a production run will involve the printing of a limited edition of 25 to 50 prints of an original piece of artwork.

b) Gracechurch Stevens Limited produces replacement components and bags for vacuum cleaners. The company keeps sufficient of each item in the range in its inventory so that it can fulfil orders within a day or two. Once inventory of a particular item falls below a certain level, a production run is scheduled so as to replenish inventory.

c) Gilligan Shoreditch Limited makes high-performance speedboats. When an order is received it is assigned its own code number and a separate record is created for it on the production department's computer. Issues of material and labour time spent on the order are booked to this record.

Apply the correct description (product costing, batch costing or job costing) to each scenario.

Exercises: Answers Available on the Lecturers' Section of the Book's Website

11.5 Xiang Products produces motherboards for PCs from a range of bought in components. The following is a list of some of the costs which the company incurs:

- depreciation of factory work benches

- bank interest charges

- administration salaries

- sundry factory expenses

  [   ]

- factory insurance

  [   ]

- supervisor's salary

  [   ]

- assembly operatives' wages

  [   ]

- managing director's salary

  [   ]

- production office computer depreciation

  [   ]

- purchase of silicone chips

  [   ]

- factory rental

  [   ]

- depreciation of sales representatives' cars

  [   ]

- purchase of circuit boards

  [   ]

- factory cleaning.

  [   ]

Classify each item of expense as one of the following:

- direct labour
- direct materials
- direct expenses
- indirect production overheads
- other indirect overheads.

11.6 Brisbane Pinker Limited manufactures a range of containers for cosmetics in metal and plastic. In the year ended 31 December 20X2 the company incurred the following costs:

	£
Selling department sundry expenses	1 899
Metal	21 444
Depreciation of factory building	1 500
Factory cleaning	6 440
Metal moulding machine: operators' wages	32 222
Factory power	8 370
Finishing operative's wages	20 240
Sales department salaries	39 434
Security guard to factory	8 290
Dyes and paint	2 490
Sundry factory expenses	4 284
Depreciation of office building	1 100
Telephone charges	4 338
Factory canteen costs	12 234
Plastics	63 570
Distribution costs	18 777
Factory insurance	6 960
Plastics machine: operators' wages	35 249
Machinery depreciation	3 950
Administrative salaries	41 496

	£
Stationery and other office admin supplies	2 937
Other admin expenses	6 422
Depreciation of office fixtures and fittings	1 929

Rearrange the information given into a cost statement for the year ended 31 December 20X2.

11.7 Wensleydale Woollen Waistcoats Limited (WWW Ltd) buys in wool to manufacture into waistcoats on its weaving machines. The inventory card for wool code 78X4A shows the following movements in June 20X2:

Date	Activity	kg
1 June	Balance of inventory @ £2 per kilo	38
2 June	Issue to production	(8)
6 June	Delivery into inventory @ £2.10 per kilo	50
20 June	Issue to production	40

There were no other transactions in the month.

What is the value of the issue to production on 20 June if WWW Ltd uses the AVCO inventory valuation convention?

a) £82.50

b) £84.00

c) £80.00

d) £81.00

11.8 Ravenna & Michele produces components to order for specialist motor manufacturers. An order for 100 components code 1187AB6 was received from one of the business's principal customers. A job code, X4721, was assigned and over the following month various items of direct material and labour were booked to the job:

Material J	21.4 kg
Material Q	3.7 kg
Grade IV labour	16 hours
Grade VIII labour	8 hours

Material J was booked out of stores on 21 September 20X2. The store card for material J contains the following details for September 20X2:

Date	Activity	kg
1 September	Balance of inventory @ £14.30 per kg	28.7
8 September	Delivery of inventory @ £14.20 per kg	30.0
18 September	Transfer to production job code X4692	(20.6)
21 September	Transfer to production job code X4721	(21.4)

Ravenna & Michele apply the FIFO method of inventory valuation.
Material Q costs £2.75 per kg.

Grade IV direct labour cost	= £8.28 per hour
Grade VIII direct labour cost	= £10.21 per hour

Produce a job cost record for Job No. X4721, calculating:

i) total prime cost

ii) prime cost per component.

12 Costing: accounting for overheads

Aim of the chapter

To build upon the previous chapter and acquire an understanding of the issues and techniques involved in attaching overheads to cost objects.

Learning outcomes

After reading the chapter and completing the exercises, students should:

- Be able to calculate and apply suitable overhead absorption rates.

- Understand some important issues in relation to the costing of services.

- Understand the nature of activity-based costing (ABC) and be able to apply its principles to straightforward costing examples.

- Be able to contrast ABC with traditional costing methods, and to understand the benefits and problems associated with ABC.

Introduction

Chapter 11 introduced the three basic components of cost in a manufacturing environment: materials, labour and production overheads. Remember that production costs are those costs involved in running a production facility but which are not themselves identifiable with individual items produced. This chapter is concerned with the techniques adopted in practice for identifying production overheads with cost objects.

The first section of the chapter explains how to allocate and apportion production overheads between the different processes involved in production. Using these methods, production overheads are divided into groups, each of which is attributable to, typically, one stage in a process. The second section of the chapter is concerned with the attribution of an amount of production overhead to a cost object, a process usually referred to as absorption.

The chapter then considers the costing of services. Many of the examples in Chapters 11 and 12 are drawn from manufacturing industry, where complex costing procedures were originally developed. However, as noted in Chapter 11, in the UK and other mature Western economies, the proportion of economic activity associated with manufacturing has been falling steadily for decades, and has been replaced by service industries. In service industries it is comparatively rare to find direct material inputs, and so the cost of services comprises only overheads and, sometimes, direct labour.

Costing is of growing importance in various public sector activities, and this aspect of costing is briefly considered later on in the chapter.

There are various drawbacks associated with traditional methods of overhead absorption, and the final part of the chapter explains an alternative to the traditional methods: activity-based costing (ABC).

12.1 PRODUCTION OVERHEADS: ALLOCATION AND APPORTIONMENT

Allocation of production overheads is one of the most difficult costing problems for the management accountant. Production overheads are part of the overall production cost, and it is usually necessary to allocate them in order to produce useful information for management and for inventory valuation. However, as we have seen, they are not directly identifiable with cost objects. Where production goes through several stages, the first step in dealing with production overheads is usually to allocate them to cost centres.

12.1.1 Allocation to Cost Centres

Often, production is organized methodically into **cost centres** to which costs can be allocated. Cost centres are functions or areas into which costs can be organized.

Example 12.1

Choremaster Ltd produces industrial cleaning machines. There are three distinct stages in the production process:

● metal machining
● brush fitting
● paint and finishing.

The metal machining department has its own full-time production supervisor. The other production supervisor employed by the company splits her time in a 60:40 ratio between the brush fitting department and the painting and finishing department. The cost of employing each production supervisor, including benefits and employer's health insurance contribution is £17 360 per year. Production supervisors' salaries are part of the company's indirect production overheads.

What is the allocation of supervisors' salaries to each of the three production areas?

Metal machining	17 360
Brush fitting (60% × £17 360)	10 416
Paint and finishing (40% × £17 360)	6 944

12.1.2 Apportionment to Cost Centres

In the above example the indirect cost of supervisors' salaries could be allocated because precise information was available about the use of the supervisors' time. Where indirect costs cannot be allocated, they must be apportioned. Cost apportionment often involves some arbitrary decisions about the split of costs between cost centres.

We will expand the Choremaster Ltd example to illustrate what is involved in cost apportionment.

Example 12.2

Choremaster Ltd incurs the following indirect production overheads in the year ended 31 December 20X4:

	£
Factory rent	33 970
Production supervisors' salaries	34 720
Canteen costs	13 440
Cleaning and other indirect labour	8 885

	£
Factory rates	12 480
Insurance	8 760
Electricity: factory	10 770
Building maintenance	2 490
Machine maintenance and repair	3 423
Depreciation of machinery	12 220
Depreciation of canteen fixtures and fittings	1 792
Total	142 950

The indirect production overheads have to be apportioned between the three production areas: metal machining, brush fitting and painting and finishing. Usually, different methods of apportionment are used depending upon the nature of the cost. Some common approaches to apportionment are listed below:

Type of cost	Typical method of apportionment
Factory rent, rates, insurance, building maintenance, electricity, indirect labour and cleaning	Floor area
Depreciation of machinery	Machinery value
Canteen costs	Number of employees
Machinery maintenance and repair	Number of call-outs
Production supervisors' salaries	Number of employees

These methods of apportionment do not constitute precise rules. Much depends upon the nature of the expense, and the amount of detail that can be collected about how it is incurred. In the case of Choremaster Ltd, for example, we know that the production supervisors' salaries can be allocated neatly across the three departments. In other companies, it might not be possible to make such an allocation, and a basis of apportionment (such as number of employees, as suggested in the table above) would be more appropriate.

We need some further information in order to be able to apportion Choremaster's costs. This is given in the table below:

		Cost centre		
	Total	Metal machining	Brush fitting	Paint and finishing
Floor area (sq. metres)	10 000	6 000	2 000	2 000
Number of employees	28	17	6	5
Machinery value	122 200	103 000	8 400	10 800
Maintenance and repair call-outs	7	6	0	1

We can now apportion costs to each cost centre, as follows:

Factory rent is apportioned to each cost centre on the basis of floor area. For example, the part of cost to be apportioned to the metal machining cost centre is:

$$\frac{6000}{10\ 000} \times £33\ 970 = £20\ 382$$

Brush fitting:

$$\frac{2000}{10\ 000} \times £33\ 970 = £6794$$

Paint and finishing:

$$\frac{2000}{10\ 000} \times £33\ 970 = £6794$$

(Note that £20 382 + 6794 + 6794 = £33 970, ie. all of the cost is apportioned.)

We can use the same approach to apportioning all the other costs:

			Cost centre		
			Metal	Brush	Paint and
		Total	machining	fitting	finishing
	Basis	£	£	£	£
Factory rent	Floor area	33 970	20 382	6 794	6 794
Production supervisors' salaries	Actual	34 720	17 360	10 416	6 944
Canteen costs	Employees	13 440	8 160	2 880	2 400
Cleaning and other indirect labour	Floor area	8 885	5 331	1 777	1 777
Factory rates	Floor area	12 480	7 488	2 496	2 496
Insurance	Floor area	8 760	5 256	1 752	1 752
Electricity: factory	Floor area	10 770	6 462	2 154	2 154
Building maintenance	Floor area	2 490	1 494	498	498
Machine maintenance and repair	Call outs	3 423	2 934	–	489
Depreciation of machinery	Machinery value	12 220	10 300	840	1 080
Depreciation: canteen	Employees	1 792	1 088	384	320
Totals		142 950	86 255	29 991	26 704

Swift Metals Ltd produces machine parts. Its factory is divided into three areas: preparation, tooling and finishing. These three functional areas are used as cost centres. Swift's management accountant has asked you to prepare a schedule showing the apportionment of the company's production overheads between the three cost centres for the year ended 31 December 20X3.

Self-test question 12.1 (answer at the end of the book)

The production overhead totals are as follows:

	£
Factory costs (rental, insurance, cleaning, etc)	700 000
Canteen costs	18 496
Machinery depreciation	17 650
Machinery maintenance and repair	2 961
Supervisory salaries	23 358
	762 465

- Factory costs are to be apportioned on the basis of floor area.
- Canteen costs and supervisory salaries are to be apportioned on the basis of number of employees.
- Machinery depreciation is to be apportioned on the basis of the value of machinery used in each cost centre.
- Machinery maintenance and repair is to be apportioned on the basis of the number of call-outs.

Relevant data is included in the following table:

		Cost centre		
	Total	Preparation	Tooling	Finishing
Floor area (sq. metres)	20 000	7 000	9 000	4 000
Number of employees	34	16	12	6
Machinery value	176 500	26 000	112 000	38 500
Maintenance and repair call-outs	9	2	6	1

Prepare the overhead apportionment schedule for the management accountant.

12.2 OVERHEAD ABSORPTION

In the previous section of this chapter we examined the allocation and apportionment of costs to cost centres. This allows us to say, for example, that overheads of £29 991 were allocated to Choremaster's brush fitting cost centre, but we are no closer to identifying the total production overhead cost of an individual cost unit.

We need to find some way of transferring overhead costs to cost units. Traditionally, the way this has been done in manufacturing industries is via **overhead absorption**, a method of allocating an appropriate portion of production overheads to cost units. A logical way of doing this might be on the basis of the number of units of production. Suppose that Choremaster Ltd produces 5400 cleaning machines in the period during which it incurred total production overheads of £142 950. The total production overhead attributable to each cleaning machine could then be calculated as:

$$\frac{£142\,950}{5400} = £26.47 \text{ (rounded)}$$

£26.47 becomes the **overhead absorption rate** applied to each machine in respect of production overhead. It would be added to the materials and direct labour costs for each cleaning machine to arrive at a total production cost per machine. Note that this is a 'blanket' overhead rate; it is appropriate where a business produces only one product. Where there is more than one product the overhead absorption procedures become more complicated.

In this example, the information could only be calculated accurately once the accounting period was over and total costs could be summed and allocated to cost centres. Management accounting information, as we have seen, needs to be produced very quickly in order to be useful and a retrospective exercise in overhead absorption is not likely to be very helpful. For this reason, overhead absorption is done in practice on the basis of figures budgeted in advance; a budgeted overhead absorption rate is calculated and then applied to production. (Note that we will examine budgeting in more detail in Chapter 16.)

The next example will demonstrate some of the techniques involved in calculating overhead absorption rates and will examine three possible approaches to overhead absorption: number of units of production, machine hours and labour hours.

Example 12.3

Stahlprodukt Limited produces large metal storage containers in one size only. The production process involves three stages:

- cutting department: large metal sheets are cut into standard sizes, and are shaped and drilled
- assembly department: the standard pieces are attached together by screwing and welding
- painting and finishing: the containers are smoothed down and spray painted.

Each department is treated as a cost centre.

The management accountant is working out appropriate overhead absorption rates for the next financial year (the year to 31 December 20X5). She estimates that total production overheads will be £136 000, allocated as follows between the cost centres:

Cutting	£56 000
Assembly	£48 000
Painting and finishing	£32 000

Total production in units for 20X5 is estimated at 16 000 containers. The management accountant has also worked out budgeted materials and labour costs per container, as follows:

Prime cost of container	£
Direct materials (metal, fixings, paint)	15.50
Direct labour:	
Cutting: 10 minutes (@ £6 per hour)	1.00
Assembly: 1 hour 30 minutes (@ £6 per hour)	9.00
Painting and finishing: 20 minutes (@ £4.50 per hour)	1.50
Total prime cost	27.00

Note that the cutting department processes are mostly mechanized; there is a relatively low input of labour. Assembly processes, by contrast, are mostly manual. The extent to which processes are labour intensive influences the choice of overhead absorption method.

The management accountant now needs to work out an overhead absorption rate to be applied to each of the three cost centres. She will use three different rates, one for each department, and each worked out on a different basis.

CUTTING DEPARTMENT: OVERHEAD RATE PER MACHINE HOUR

Where manufacturing processes depend more upon machines than upon labour input, it is usually most appropriate to work out an overhead absorption rate based upon machine hours available. The number of machine hours is estimated by reference to factory working hours and number of machines. For example, in this case, suppose that the accountant estimates that a total of 16 000 hours of machine time will be available over the next year. The cutting department overhead for the year is estimated at £56 000. The estimated overhead absorption rate for the cutting department for 20X5 will therefore be:

$$\frac{£56\ 000}{16\ 000} = £3.50 \text{ per machine hour}$$

For every machine hour used in production £3.50 will be charged in production overheads.

How many machine hours will be used to produce one container? Assuming that all of the available machine hours (16 000) are required to produce 16 000 containers, each cost unit uses up 1 machine hour. £3.50 will, therefore, be included in the production cost of a container.

ASSEMBLY DEPARTMENT: OVERHEAD RATE PER LABOUR HOUR

In this department the manufacturing processes are labour intensive. The accountant estimates that 24 000 direct labour hours will be used in this department in 20X5. The assembly cost centre overhead for the year is estimated at £48 000. The estimated overhead absorption rate for the assembly department for 20X5 will therefore be:

$$\frac{£48\ 000}{24\ 000} = £2.00 \text{ per labour hour}$$

How many assembly labour hours will be used to produce one container? Each container requires 1 hour 30 minutes in labour time. 16 000 containers would therefore require 24 000 hours (which just happens to be the number of direct labour hours available in this department). The overhead to be absorbed in respect of assembly for each cost unit will be $1.5 \times £2.00$, ie. £3.00.

PAINTING AND FINISHING: RATE PER UNIT OF PRODUCTION

The painting and finishing cost centre overhead for 20X5 is estimated at £32 000. This will be spread over an estimated 16 000 units of production (cost units). The estimated overhead absorption rate for the assembly department for 20X5 will therefore be:

$$\frac{£32\ 000}{16\ 000} = £2.00 \text{ per unit}$$

Finally, we will work out an estimated total production cost per unit, as follows:

Production cost of container	£	£
Direct materials (metal, fixings, paint)		15.50
Labour:		
Cutting: 10 minutes (@ £6 per hour)	1.00	
Assembly: 1 hour 30 minutes (@ £6 per hour)	9.00	
Painting and finishing: 20 minutes (@ £4.50 per hour)	1.50	
		11.50
Production overhead:		
Cutting	3.50	
Assembly	3.00	
Painting and finishing	2.00	
		8.50
Total production cost		35.50

12.2.1 Overhead Absorption Rates: Some Other Approaches

The example of Stahlprodukt Limited demonstrated the use of three different approaches to calculating overhead absorption rates: rate per unit, rate per machine hour and rate per labour hour. There are other possibilities:

PERCENTAGE OF DIRECT LABOUR The overhead absorption rate would be calculated as follows:

$$\frac{\text{Production overheads}}{\text{Direct labour cost}} \times 100$$

The next example explains how the overhead absorption rate is calculated and applied on this basis.

Example 12.4

The fabrications cost centre of Millom Holz uses two grades of direct labour. Grade A is paid at £9.50 per hour and Grade B is paid at £8.20 per hour. The production estimates for the 2013 accounting year require 30 000 hours of Grade A and 28 000 hours of Grade B labour. The management accountant has already carried out an allocation and apportionment exercise which resulted in estimated production overheads of £208 000 for the fabrications cost centre in 2013. What is the overhead absorption rate to be used for fabrications?

Direct labour

Grade A: 30 000 hours × £9.50	=	£285 000
Grade B: 28 000 hours × £8.20	=	£229 600
		£514 600

Overhead absorption rate for fabrications:

$$\frac{\text{Total budget production overheads}}{\text{Direct labour cost}} \times 100 = \frac{208\,000}{514\,600} = 40.4\% \text{ (to one decimal place)}$$

So, 40.4% of the direct labour charge for any batch, job or cost unit will be added to costs to represent production overheads.

Taking the example a little further:

Millom Holz manufactures components for the shipbuilding industry on a job costing basis. The job cost card for an order of 120 units of component 177Z2A is as follows:

Component No.: 177Z2A
Quantity: 120 units

	£	£
Direct materials		370.00
Direct labour		
Grade A: 25 hours @ £9.50	237.50	
Grade B: 39 hours @ £8.20	319.80	
		557.30
Prime cost		927.30
Production overheads		
40.4% × direct labour cost = 40.4% × 557.30		225.15
Total cost		1 152.45

PERCENTAGE OF DIRECT MATERIALS COST This approach to overhead absorption works in the same way as the percentage of direct labour cost. An overhead absorption rate is worked out in advance by using budget figures. Production overheads for an individual job, batch or product are then calculated by reference to the input of materials cost.

Both this method and the percentage of direct labour cost method can be particularly useful where a range of different products is made.

It must be recognized, however, that there are no fixed rules about which method to use. The ultimate test to be applied to all management accounting information is whether or not it is useful in managing the firm. Management should use the methods and techniques which they find most efficient and effective in achieving the overall objectives of the business.

12.3 COSTING OF SERVICES

Costing of services uses the same approach as costing products. But, depending upon the circumstances and nature of the business, the process of identification may be more difficult when costing services. The element of direct materials input is absent, but there may be elements of labour input that are more or less direct in nature. The problem of allocating overheads is common to both services and product costing.

Take the example of an advertising agency that works for various clients on a range of campaigns using different media. An employee may work on a single project over a long period of time in which case all of the costs associated with that employee are attributable to the project. However, some employees will be involved with the project only for brief periods, and others are likely to be employed in administrative functions that are not directly associated with any particular project. The cost object in such a case is the advertising campaign and it is a matter for debate, depending upon circumstances, whether any useful purpose is served by allocating overhead costs to it. In all cases, the benefits of a particular management accounting technique should not be outweighed by the costs associated with it.

By contrast, some services involve a large number of identical items or processes, and in such cases it may well be worth allocating overheads to them. For example, retail banking involves the processing of very large numbers of identical transactions in the form of direct debits, automated teller transactions, and so on.

Some service businesses employ job costing in order to control costs and to assist with billing of services. For example, professional firms of accountants, auditors, solicitors, surveyors, and so on, need to keep detailed records of costs associated with particular clients. This is a form of job costing as illustrated by example 12.5

Example 12.5

Gulam, a conveyancing solicitor, spends time on work for various different clients in the course of a day. Each piece of work for a client represents a cost unit. For example, Gulam's client, Maisie, is moving house and is also selling a commercial property. Each of these two matters represents a cost unit. Each of the matters Gulam deals with has its own unique code; for example, Maisie's house move is coded 0376 and her commercial property sale is coded 0375. During the day, Gulam keeps a time record of each unit of 5 minutes that he spends on each matter. On a particular day, extracts from his time records look like this:

Name: Gulam   **Date: 15 October 20X6**

Time	Time units	Client and code	Details
2.05–2.15	2	Maisie 0376	Telephone call to discuss possible completion dates
2.15–2.30	3	Bryan 0412	Dictate letter re Land Registry search
2.30–2.40	2	Maisie 0375	Dictate letter to commercial agents

The above form serves as a computer input document. At the end of the day, all the solicitors in Gulam's firm submit their time sheets, and the details are input to the computer system. In respect of the day recorded above, two time units of 5 minutes each will be logged to each of Maisie's file codes. The time is costed by the computer at Gulam's charge-out rate – so, if his charge-out rate is £60 per hour, each file will receive a charge of £10 (ie. 10 minutes at £1 per minute) in respect of the solicitor's time spent on 15 October 20X6. Other types of cost will be logged against the codes, for example, the cost of Land Registry searches and similar fees, which in this context constitute direct costs.

Once the conveyancing is successfully concluded Gulam will be able to generate an invoice to send to Maisie from the information that is logged on the computer.

Sometimes businesses avoid the complicated processes involved with controlling and costing the provision of services by outsourcing those services to suppliers outside the firm. So, for example, a business might outsource its payroll function: rather than employing clerical staff to administer the payment of salaries and wages, the business buys in those services. The supplier of services takes on the obligation to administer the payroll, in exchange for a regular fee. Until recently, outsourcing has typically involved the purchasing of services from other businesses, but lately it has become more common to outsource to workers located in their own homes. Below is a real-life example of outsourcing of services.

Example 12.6 (Real-Life)

HOMESHORING

Many large businesses locate call centres in developing countries in order to save costs. Some countries, notably India, have a resource of well-educated English speakers who can be employed at far lower labour rates than in economies such as the UK and the USA. However, this development has not been completely successful and some companies have adopted a new approach to handling calls: homeshoring (also known as homesourcing). For example, JetBlue Airways, an American low-cost airline, employs home-based call agents in the USA. The agents work in their own homes, thus eliminating the costs involved in provision of offices and computers. It is estimated that using home-based agents can cut property and IT costs by as much as 80% compared to locating call centres offshore.

From a costing perspective, outsourcing the service makes costing much more straightforward. Agents are paid an hourly rate for their work which is the basic cost of the service to the organization. Other costs of training, and employee benefits, are involved, but because many elements of service provision are devolved to the employees, far fewer overheads are involved.

12.4 COSTING OF PUBLIC SECTOR SERVICES

In many countries over the last few decades public sector organizations have adopted management accounting techniques that originated in the private sector as part of a process often referred to as New Public Management (NPM). NPM appears to have produced changes in many areas of the public sector, especially in the UK, a country which has adopted NPM more vigorously than many others.

Costing is now a much more important element in the management of public services such as the National Health Service (NHS). For example, the UK government undertook a major consultation in 2014/15, 'Improving the costing of NHS services' in England. The aim of the proposals was to 'deliver significant improvements in the accuracy and comparability of cost information. This would lead to cost savings through efficiencies that could be reinvested to improve the quality of care for patients'. Although costing of services in the NHS has existed for many years, a review in 2012/13 noted that the costing processes used by different providers can vary significantly. The improvements planned for over a six-year period include the introduction of a single, national, system for costing. Given the size of NHS England, this is a hugely significant undertaking. The diagram in Figure 12.1 shows the proposed approach.

Figure 12.1 Improving costing of NHS services
This figure was provided by NHS Improvement and has been licensed for use under the Open Government Licence 3.0.

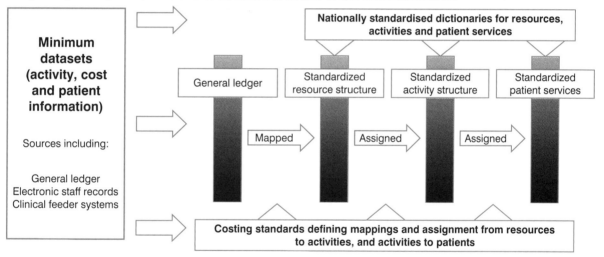

Data pulled from a range of sources is to be mapped and assigned to activities and then assigned to groups of patients in order to determine the costs of services at patient level. The idea of determining activities in a process is explained in greater detail in the next section of the chapter.

Private sector organizations are not required to make public their management accounting information, and so it is never used to compare one organization with another. By contrast, costing and management accounting information in the public sector can be made public, and comparison between different bodies engaged in similar activities is encouraged.

12.5 ACTIVITY-BASED COSTING (ABC)

Traditional absorption costing techniques, where overheads are 'absorbed' into products using a basis of, for example, machine or labour hours, were developed at a time when direct labour, materials and machine time constituted the most significant inputs into manufacturing processes. However, as processes in both manufacturing and many service business environments have become increasingly mechanized, direct labour inputs tend to be much less significant. In those cases where direct labour remains as a major product constituent the function is often exported to a country where low-cost labour is available. Machine-based processes have themselves often become more streamlined and efficient, using less energy and other types of resource. At the same time the relative importance of indirect overheads in many businesses' cost structures has tended to grow. The effect is that increasing amounts of overhead have been allocated to shrinking numbers of machine hours or direct labour hours. This results in questionable allocations of costs. For example, if the overhead absorption rate is £200 per direct labour hour, then every additional fraction of a minute spent on the production of a cost unit will result in a significant additional burden of overhead cost.

During the 1980s business managers and academics expended considerable effort in exploring alternative approaches to costing that offered more meaningful allocations of cost to products and services. A very important alternative to traditional costing emerged in the form of activity-based costing (usually referred to as ABC), the adoption of which has been widespread. The remainder of this chapter explains the principles of ABC, using examples to demonstrate its application in a practical context.

12.5.1 Principles of ABC

The fundamental principle of ABC is that overhead costs should be identified with cost objects as accurately as possible. Costs are caused or 'driven' by the various activities that take place in the business environment. Such activities in a manufacturing environment might include, for example:

- materials ordering
- materials storage
- setting up production runs
- testing the quality of production
- organizing production.

Although ABC was originally developed in the context of the manufacturing industry its use is by no means limited to that environment (see the comments about 'activities' in the context of NHS England in the previous section of the chapter). Activities in a service environment might include:

- appointments system (in, say, a medical or legal practice)
- transaction processing (in a bank).

Each activity can be identified with one or more **cost drivers**. (A cost driver is defined by CIMA as a 'Factor influencing the level of cost. Often used in the context of ABC to denote the factor which links activity resource consumption to product outputs.') So, for example, in the case of materials ordering, the cost driver might be the number of orders placed. The first part of the ABC process would require allocation of overheads to the identified activities in the form of **cost pools**. In the second part, overheads in the cost pool attributable to the materials ordering process would be divided by the number of orders placed to give a value for the cost of placing an order. Total product costs could be determined by aggregating the costs of all activities relating to the product, together with any direct elements of cost.

12.5.2 Applying ABC in a Manufacturing Business

The following example demonstrates the application of ABC in a simplified manufacturing context. The first part of the example costs products using overhead absorption based on direct labour hours. The second part uses the same data, but applies ABC principles.

Example 12.7

Sallis Weller produces two products: product X and product Y. Until now, it has adopted traditional absorption costing techniques, transferring overheads to production via an overhead absorption rate based on direct labour hours. The company's MD has recently read an article about ABC. He asks the finance director to organize a comparison by applying ABC alongside normal absorption costing for a month.

A – USING ABSORPTION COSTING

During November 20X7 the company produces 2 000 units each of product X and product Y, and incurs the following indirect production overhead costs:

	£
Factory cleaning	2 000
Power	16 000
Factory rental	23 000
Factory insurance	5 000
Supervisory salaries	12 000
Canteen charges	3 000
Machinery depreciation	21 000
Machinery maintenance	5 000
Production consumables	6 000
Other indirect labour costs	12 000
Other factory costs	8 000
	113 000

Total direct labour hours for the month are 5000, resulting in an overhead absorption rate of:

$$\frac{£113\,000}{5000} = £22.60$$

Relevant details for the two products are as follows:

	Product X	Product Y
Hours of direct labour (per unit)	1	1.5
	£	£
Direct materials (per unit)	17.50	12.00
Direct labour (per unit)	7.00	10.50
Prime cost	24.50	22.50
Overhead		
1 Direct labour hour × £22.60	22.60	—
1.5 Direct labour hours × £22.60	—	33.90
Production cost per unit	47.10	56.40

B – USING ACTIVITY BASED COSTING

ABC involves the identification of key activities and their drivers. The finance director examines the activity bases of the factory operations and establishes five basic activities which take place:

- machining
- finishing

- materials ordering
- materials issue to production
- scheduling, control and quality testing of production.

The fundamental cost driver for each activity, together with quantities, is established as follows:

Activity	Cost driver	Total	Product X	Product Y	£
Machining	Machine hours	3 000	2 000	1 000	45 000
Finishing	Direct labour hours	5 000	2 000	3 000	25 000
Materials ordering	Number of orders placed	25	16	9	4 000
Materials issue to production	Number of materials issues made	36	22	14	12 000
Scheduling etc.	Number of production runs	75	47	28	27 000
					113 000

This table shows that the production of X involves more activity in several respects than that of Y. Materials ordering appears more complicated (more orders have to be placed) and the number of production runs is far greater.

The final column of the table shows the results of the finance director's re-classification of the total of £113 000 indirect production overheads for the month into appropriate cost pools. The individual items for rental, insurance, supervision, etc. have been apportioned into cost pools relating to the five activities.

At this stage, all the information is in place to allocate overheads to each of the products by activity. An amount of cost per unit of cost driver can be calculated as follows:

Machining $\quad \dfrac{\text{Overhead}}{\text{Machine hours}} = \dfrac{45\,000}{3000} = £15$ per machine hour

Finishing $\quad \dfrac{\text{Overhead}}{\text{Direct labour hours}} = \dfrac{25\,000}{5000} = £5$ per labour hour

Materials ordering $\quad \dfrac{\text{Overhead}}{\text{Materials orders}} = \dfrac{4000}{25} = £160$ per order

Materials handling $\quad \dfrac{\text{Overhead}}{\text{Issues to production}} = \dfrac{12\,000}{75} = £160$ per issue

Scheduling etc. $\quad \dfrac{\text{Overhead}}{\text{Production runs}} = \dfrac{27\,000}{36} = £750$ per run

Then the overhead is allocated between products X and Y:

		Product X £		Product Y £
Machining	2 000 × £15	30 000	1 000 × £15	15 000
Finishing	2 000 × £5	10 000	3 000 × £5	15 000
Materials ordering	16 × £160	2 560	9 × £160	1 440
Materials handling	47 × £160	7 520	28 × £160	4 480
Scheduling etc.	22 × £750	16 500	14 × £750	10 500
Total		66 580		46 420
Per unit	66 580/2 000	33.29	46 420/2 000	23.21
Prime cost per unit (as before)		24.50		22.50
Production cost per unit: ABC		57.79		45.71
Production cost per unit: traditional		47.10		56.40

CONTRASTING ABC WITH TRADITIONAL ABSORPTION COSTING The example of Sallis Weller above illustrates the very large differences that can emerge when costing under the traditional method is compared with ABC. In the example, product Y appeared to cost more under the traditional method than product X. Following the application of ABC the positions reverse. Traditional methods of allocation ignore the detail of many of the activities that actually take place. Where production processes are more cumbersome because of, for example, the necessity for more frequent ordering of materials, such factors should be taken into account in costing.

12.5.3 Applying ABC in a Service Industry

Costing in the service industries usually entails the allocation, apportionment and absorption of a significant proportion of overhead. It is not surprising, therefore, that many businesses in the services sector have adopted variants of ABC systems.

Example 12.8 (Real-Life)

ABC IN BLOOD TRANSFUSION SERVICES

Health care involves complex systems with many variables. As explained earlier in the chapter, NHS England is currently working towards a costing system based upon the identification and costing of activities. The likely complexity of such a system is demonstrated by a study carried out to estimate the costs of blood transfusion services. Blood transfusion involves many levels of technical and human interactions. ABC used in this context involves identifying the many activities involved in blood transfusion and applying cost data to them to generate a cost per unit of blood. The study used real data from four hospitals, two in Europe and two in the USA, to estimate, retrospectively, the cost per unit of red blood cells. The study found that blood costs had been significantly underestimated previously. The average cost of a unit estimated in the study was US$761. This compared with previous estimates ranging from US$332 to US$717.

(Shander, A. and five others, (2010) 'Activity-based costs of blood transfusions in surgical patients at four hospitals'. *Transfusion*, Vol. 50)

12.5.4 ABC: Benefits and Problems

Supporters of ABC argue that its application results in significant improvement in the quality of information obtained from the costing system, and consequently, in better control and planning of activities. However, success ratings by the people who are deeply involved in implementing new systems may be biased, whether consciously or not. But some research evidence does suggest that a net improvement in financial performance tends to result when ABC is adopted.

On the other hand, ABC, as even the relatively straightforward manufacturing example earlier in the chapter showed, is a system of considerable complexity. The problems that have been identified in using ABC include the following:

EXPENSE A great deal of information has to be collected and administered, and the system is costly to implement. Costs might include the buying in or development of software, payments for consultancy time, reorganization and perhaps redundancy costs. Such costs may not be perceived as outweighing the benefits to be derived from a more sophisticated costing system.

RESISTANCE BY STAFF Staff may be suspicious of the implementation of ABC systems if they are concerned that new approaches to costing are likely to change the priorities of a business. They may fear redundancy or at least change because of the likely disruption to their working lives. If senior managers force through the types of changes required to introduce ABC they risk alienating the workforce, and staff resistance could result in deliberate attempts to sabotage the new system.

IDENTIFICATION AND SELECTION OF COST DRIVERS Typically, in the large and complex organizations that tend to adopt ABC, a large number of separate activities and cost drivers can be identified. Using a very high number of cost drivers might well produce more accurate cost allocation, but would be expensive and complicated to administer and understand. However, if the number of cost drivers in a system is to be kept to manageably low levels, the process of selection of appropriate drivers is very important. If the selection is made badly, the results of the ABC system may be erroneous and misleading.

CONTINUING FOCUS ON QUANTIFIABLE COSTS ONLY ABC involves the identification of a broader range of cost pools and cost drivers, but in essence, it can be argued that it does not differ very radically from traditional costing systems. In establishing costs for decision making purposes ABC fails to encompass the qualitative, non-financial factors that are almost always significant in taking decisions.

Chapter Summary

This chapter, together with Chapter 11, should provide a sound understanding of the basic principles and practices of costing. Although the overhead absorption techniques explained earlier in the chapter are generally regarded as quite old-fashioned, surveys of management accounting practice show that they continue to be used in a significant number of businesses in the developed economies of the world. ABC, since its early development in the 1980s and 1990s, has been adopted in a significant proportion of organizations, including service businesses which may never previously have had highly developed management accounting systems. It is noticeable, too, that many public sector organizations have adopted ABC techniques in response to the demand for increased accountability for the resources they consume.

Internet Resources

Book's companion website summary
The website contains the following resources in respect of Chapter 12:

Students' section
 A multiple quiz containing five questions
Two additional questions with answers

Lecturers' section

Answers to end-of-chapter exercises 12.9 to 12.14
Two additional questions with answers
Case study
Testbank
Instructor's Manual

Exercises: Answers at the End of the Book

12.1   Jersey Brookfield & Co is a manufacturer of soap powders and detergents.
       Each of the products moves through two stages: bulk production and then packaging.
       In the year ended 31 December 20X8 Jersey Brookfield & Co incurred production overheads which it plans to allocate and apportion as follows between the two departments:

	£	Basis of apportionment
Factory building depreciation	5 670	Floor area
Factory rates	11 970	Floor area
Factory insurance	7 980	Floor area
Canteen costs	18 876	No. of employees
Supervisory salaries	29 480	No. of employees
Other indirect labour	18 275	Machinery net book value
Machinery depreciation	21 500	Machinery net book value
Cleaning	17 850	Floor area

	£	Basis of apportionment
Electricity	30 290	Actual
Building maintenance	5 040	Floor area
Total	166 931	

The following information is relevant for the apportionment of overheads:

	Total	Bulk production	Packaging
Floor area	10 500 sq. m.	6 000 sq. m.	4 500 sq. m.
Employees	22	10	12
Machinery value	215 000	146 000	69 000
Electricity	30 290	18 790	11 500

Produce a schedule apportioning the overheads between the two departments (cost centres).

12.2   Barley Brindle produces a single product, Product B. One unit of Product B has a prime cost of £6.20, which includes one hour of direct labour @ £9.20, and each unit uses 0.5 hours of machine time.
Estimated production of Product B in 20X3 is 60 000 units.
Total production overheads are estimated at £218 000.
Calculate the overhead recovery rates (to the nearest penny) for 20X3, based on:

   i) direct labour hours

   ii) machine hours

   iii) units of production.

12.3   WGB produces two types of metal shelving in their factory – one for domestic use, and one, which is produced to a higher quality standard, for commercial use (in factories and hotel kitchens, for example).
Each shelf unit passes through two processes – first, metal machining and second, painting and finishing (P&F). Commercial shelving is made of stronger material, has extra bracing bars and is given an additional coat of paint in the painting and finishing department.
Cost structures for the two products are as follows:

Domestic shelves

	Dept	£
Materials	Machining	18.00
	P&F	3.30
		21.30
Direct labour	Machining	
	0.75 hours × £10.00	7.50
	P&F 1 hour @ £9.00	
		9.00
		16.50
Prime cost		37.80

Commercial shelves

	Dept	£
Materials	Machining	27.00
	P&F	4.60
		31.60
Direct labour	Machining	
	1 hour @ £10.00	10.00
	P&F 1.5 hours @ £9.00	
		15.00
		25.00
Prime cost		56.60

Production overheads are estimated at the following apportioned amounts for next year:

Machining	£172 490
Painting and finishing	£116 270

The company plans to produce 6000 units of each product next year, 20X6.

Calculate overhead absorption rates for 20X6 based upon:

i) percentage of direct materials cost

ii) percentage of direct labour cost.

Discuss which basis of overhead absorption might be preferable for each cost centre.

12.4 Identify the cost object that is likely to be used in an architect's practice which employs 15 architects and 15 support staff. List the principal costs that are likely to be incurred by the practice and explain how the costs might be identified with the cost object for management accounting purposes.

12.5 David has recently been elected as a local councillor for an area in England served by two primary schools (note: English primary school education usually lasts for six years). The council has threatened to close the smaller of the two schools (School A) on the grounds that it provides poor value for money compared with the larger school (School B). The biggest single item of cost is teaching staff salaries. Both schools employ a full-time head teacher and a full-time deputy head teacher. David has asked for, and has received, a summary of the salary costs for both schools for the 20X8/X9 financial year (see below). There is substantial local opposition to the threatened closure. David has asked you, as a preliminary step in his investigation of the issue, to:

i) tell him whether or not, on this evidence, School A does appear to provide poor value for money

ii) suggest possible reasons for any discrepancy in salary costs between the schools.

Appendix: Data on Schools A and B for 20X8/X9

	School A	School B
School roll	75	132
Average numbers of teaching staff	4.3	6.2
Teaching staff salary cost	£166 200	£210 000

12.6 ABC is a costing system that was developed in the 1980s as a result of an increasing awareness in businesses of the deficiencies of traditional approaches to production overhead absorption.

i) Describe the principal deficiencies in the traditional product costing system which ABC seeks to correct.

ii) Describe the key features of ABC.

iii) Identify and comment upon a significant advantage *and* a significant disadvantage associated with the typical implementation of an ABC system.

12.7 Arbend is a web-based bookseller which uses an ABC system. The chief management accountant and his team have produced the following information about expected annual overhead cost pools, activities and cost drivers:

Activity	Cost driver	Total for year	Total overhead pool per cost driver £000
Receipt of books, unpacking and shelving	Number of book orders received from publishers	250 000 orders	1 000
Storage	Number of books	12 million books, each spending on average 1 month in storage	6 800
Customer order processing, packaging	Number of orders received from customers	4 million orders	2 400
Inventory picking	Number of items on picking list	12 million items	800
Total			11 000

Each book order to a publisher comprises on average 48 books.

Using the above information, calculate the overhead cost associated with an order of four books from a customer.

12.8 Hallett Penumbra Systems produces a range of building products at several factories. The company's directors have decided to pilot an ABC system at one of its factories. The factory produces products C and D. After a substantial amount of preliminary work, the finance controller at the factory produces the following list of cost drivers, with overhead cost pool allocations to each driver, and an estimate of the relevant quantities involved for the 20X0 financial year:

Activity	Cost driver	Total	Product C	Product D	Total cost per cost driver £
Planned units of production			6 000	5 000	
Machining	Machine hours	6 000	2 500	3 500	148 200
Finishing	Labour hours	12 000	7 200	4 800	136 440
Materials ordering	No. of orders	186	124	62	12 183
Materials issues	No. of issues	120	70	50	11 592
Machine setup	Number of hours used in setup	70	26	44	19 915
Total					328 330

One unit of product C uses one machine hour. One unit of product C has a prime cost of £28.50. One unit of product D uses 1.4 machine hours. One unit of product D has a prime cost of £32.70.

i) Calculate the overhead absorption rate based on the company's traditional system of using machine hours as a basis for overhead absorption.

ii) Calculate the overhead per unit of product C and product D using the data provided for the new ABC system.

iii) Calculate the production cost of one unit of product C and one unit of product D under the old and new costing systems.

iv) Explain the principal reasons for the difference in the product costs produced by the old and the new costing systems.

Exercises: Answers Available on the Lecturers' Section of the Book's Website

12.9 Christine Bedford is managing director of the family business, Bedford Bowler. The company manufactures children's wooden trainsets. Recently Christine has been on a course about costing and she is keen to apply his new knowledge to the business. Thinking through the production process, she can identify three principal cost centres: machining, assembly and painting, and packaging.

Christine's accountant supplies the following summary of production overheads incurred by the business to the most recent year-end, 31 December 20X4. Christine adds a note of what she thinks is the most appropriate method of apportionment between cost centres.

	£	Basis of apportionment
Factory rental	21 105	Floor area
Packaging machine leasing charges	5 500	Actual (see note)
Cleaners' wages	17 991	1/3 to each cost centre

	£	Basis of apportionment
Factory rates	6 930	Floor area
Electricity: factory	8 280	Actual
Supervision	21 456	No. of employees
Machinery maintenance and repair	4 472	Call-outs
Machinery depreciation	12 250	Net book value
Total	97 984	

Note: the packaging machine leasing charges relate only to machinery used in the packaging cost centre. There is no other machinery in the packaging department.

The following information is relevant for the apportionment of overheads:

	Total	Machining	Assembly	Packaging
Floor area	6 300 sq. m.	2 500 sq. m.	1 700 sq. m.	2 100 sq. m.
Employees	18	5	9	4
Machinery value	61 250	35 000	26 250	–
Electricity	8 280	3 905	1 892	2 483
Call outs	8	5	3	–

Produce a schedule apportioning the overheads between the two departments (cost centres).

12.10 A manufacturing business, Oakshield Carver Limited, organizes its production into four cost centres. In the coming financial year the company plans to produce 115 000 items of product. Further details of its plans are included in the following table:

Cost centre	Production overhead £	Machine hours	Direct labour hours
Machining	297 000	80 000	3 000
Assembly	136 000	20 000	6 000
Finishing	121 500	15 000	9 000
Packaging	76 000	5 000	2 000
Totals	630 500	120 000	20 000

Calculate the overhead recovery rate for each department on the following bases:

 i) machining: machine hours

 ii) assembly: units of production

 iii) finishing: direct labour hours

 iv) packaging: units of production.

12.11 Facts as in 12.10.

The prime cost and timing details for one unit of production are:

	£
Materials	14.20
Direct labour	18.00
Prime cost	32.20

Each unit uses two hours of machine time in the machining department.

Each unit uses 1.5 direct labour hours in the finishing department.

Calculate the total production cost for one unit of the company's product, using the overhead absorption rates calculated in exercise 12.10.

12.12 Bushey Travel is an online travel agent. Clients can book online or by telephoning the company's head-quarters which are located in a business park. Bushey Travel operates as an agency only (ie. it does not provide holidays itself). It obtains commission on the cost of the holiday from the supplier of the holiday. Identify the principal categories of cost involved in Bushey Travel's operations.

12.13 Combe Cullen Systems manufactures two products in its Oldfield division. Traditionally the company has used an overhead absorption system based on machine hours. However, following a management consultancy exercise in which outside consultants reviewed the management information systems, the directors have decided to pilot an ABC system at the Oldfield division. For the coming year, 20X3, Oldfield's production overheads are estimated as follows:

	£
Factory rent and rates	42 200
Heat and light to factory	23 950
Factory insurance	7 100
Supervisory salaries	38 540
Other indirect labour	18 030
Canteen charges	6 100
Machinery depreciation	18 000
Machinery maintenance	5 520
Production consumables (eg. machine oil)	2 050
Other factory costs	7 480
Total	168 970

Following a detailed review of the production processes, the finance director and the divisional accountant identify a set of key cost drivers, together with cost allocations to each, and estimates of the relevant quantities involved for products A and B in the 20X3 financial year:

Activity	Cost driver	Total	Product A	Product B	Total cost per cost driver £
Planned units of production			6 000	5 000	
Machining	Machine hours	11 000	6 000	5 000	63 030
Assembly	Labour hours	9 000	3 000	6 000	43 020
Packing	Labour hours	4 000	2 000	2 000	31 000
Materials ordering	No. of orders	111	86	25	9 990
Materials issues	No. of issues	150	103	47	12 000
Machine setup	Number of hours used in setup	33	25	8	5 940
Quality inspection	Number of inspections	35	10	25	3 990
Total					168 970

Each planned unit of production of both product A and product B uses one machine hour. One unit of A has a prime cost of £12.50, while one unit of B has a prime cost of £16.00.

i) Calculate the overhead absorption rate based on the company's traditional system of using machine hours as a basis for overhead absorption.

ii) Calculate the overhead per unit of product A and product B using the data provided for the new ABC system.

---

iii) Calculate the production cost of one unit of product A and one unit of product B under both the old and the new costing systems.

iv) Comment on the difference between the production costs for each product under the old and the new costing systems.

Work to two decimal places (ie. the nearest penny).

12.14 Queen's Move plc is a company listed on the London Stock Exchange that specializes in household removals and storage services. The business runs its own fleet of removal vehicles and also has freehold premises used for storage in many major towns and cities. The directors are undertaking an exercise to identify the principal cost drivers in both aspects of the business with a view to implementing ABC on a two-year trial basis.

Identify the principal cost pools and activities and related cost drivers in both the removals and storage sides of the business.

13 Pricing

Aim of the chapter

To understand the principal factors involved in the price-setting decision by reference to a broad range of industry examples.

Learning outcomes

After reading the chapter and completing the related exercises, students should:

- Understand the interaction between supply and demand and the interdependence of price and quantity.

- Understand the various additional factors which play a part in pricing decisions.

- Understand the interface between pricing and costing, with especial reference to cost-plus pricing.

- Be able to apply knowledge of pricing issues across a range of industries and commercial activities.

Introduction

The two previous chapters examined methods of cost accumulation which are employed to determine, with a reasonable degree of accuracy, the total cost of a product or service. In both chapters references were made in passing to the potential usefulness of cost information for determining prices. This chapter will examine the pricing decision in much more detail. The issue of pricing is sufficiently important to merit a chapter to itself: after all, if prices are set too low a business will experience sub-optimal levels of profitability, and in the medium to long term may even fail. Conversely, where a business sets its prices too high, its revenue is likely to fall as its competitors gain market share at its expense. The chapter starts by examining some relevant economic theory.

13.1 THE RELATIONSHIP BETWEEN PRICE AND QUANTITY

In fundamental economic terms, supply and demand are critical elements in the determination of prices. In a pure market environment, scarcity of supply of a commodity pushes up prices. Conversely, plentiful supply results in lower prices. There is, therefore, a theoretical interaction between quantity and price, which can be illustrated graphically (see Figure 13.1).

Three sets of lines have been drawn on the graph. Set #1 describes the supply of a lower quantity of goods; the relative scarcity is reflected in a higher price. Sets #2 and #3 describe position of progressively higher supply which results in a relatively lower price. If a large number of price/quantity relationships are plotted the price/quantity relationship emerges. This is usually referred to as the **demand curve**.

The relationship described in the graph is an economist's representation of reality; it is an economic model of the relationship between price and quantity. How well does this neat graphical representation relate to reality? In practice, much depends upon the nature of the commodity traded, the degree of competition in the market, and the context in which it is supplied. It is possible to observe, in general terms, examples of such a relationship in the real world. For example, in the UK the price of strawberries in the summer months (when strawberries grown in the UK are available in large quantities) tends to be lower than in the winter months when the supply is smaller (because the only available strawberries are imported). However, it is usually quite difficult to observe the classic relationship between price and quantity in operation.

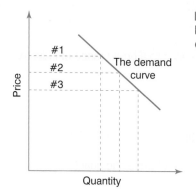

Figure 13.1
Price and quantity: the demand curve

13.1.1 Elasticity and Inelasticity

Demand is described by economists as elastic where:

- customers are relatively indifferent about the product (because, for example, there are many identical or close substitutes in the market)
- the demand is highly sensitive to changes in price.

Products for which demand is elastic would include, for example, most household commodities (washing up liquid, soap, tea, and so on).

By contrast, demand is inelastic where:

- customers place a high value on the product
- demand is relatively insensitive to price (ie. it takes a substantial increase in price to have any effect on demand).

Luxury goods and services tend to demonstrate inelastic demand. For example, if a customer shopping for a new suit has the resources and inclination to buy one from Armani, he is not likely to be satisfied by a cheap substitute from a chain store. The price of the Armani suit would have to increase by a substantial margin in order to deter such a customer.

13.1.2 Problems in Applying the Economic Model to the Real World

The model represented by the graph above takes account of only two variables – price and quantity. However, in the real world other complexities frequently come into play. For example, the effects of:

- *advertising*: if advertising is effective it can affect both demand and the price that people are willing to pay for a commodity or service
- *novelty*: a new product on the market can often command higher prices initially simply because of its novelty value
- *fashion*: an item that is widely perceived as more fashionable may be able to command a premium price
- *reputation*: a good brand name may command a premium price.

Sometimes, in practice, several of these factors interact.

In addition to the complex combinations of factors which affect price, there are other problems which arise in real-world attempts to apply the simple economic model such as:

- *lack of information:* in most cases, it is very difficult to obtain accurate information as to the effect on prices of a change in demand, because these are theoretical effects. The model may be useful in helping to broadly predict the direction of price movements, but it is difficult to know with any degree of precision how much a change in price, for example, will affect demand.
- *product range:* as noted, it is very difficult to obtain accurate information about the interaction of price/ quantity/demand. This becomes even more difficult where large numbers of products are concerned. Most businesses produce a range of products or services, some of which may differ only slightly from each other. Management, in most cases, will simply lack the huge resources which would be required to accurately estimate demand over a range of conditions.
- *State of competition in the market:* the number and nature of competitors in the market will affect prices. These effects are examined in more detail below.

Complete the following sentences with one of these words:

- elastic
- inelastic.

Demand for luxury goods tends to be _____.
Demand for soap powder tends to be _____.

Self-test question 13.1 (answer at the end of the book)

13.2 COMPETITION IN THE MARKET

The more suppliers in the market, the more competitive the environment. In such conditions, a state approaching 'perfect competition' is likely to exist. Perfect competition describes the hypothetical economic condition where no player in the market, whether provider or purchaser, has the power to change prices. Where there are many suppliers, no individual supplier can set prices at a significantly higher level. Prices and supplies will easily reach an equilibrium state in which dramatic movements are unlikely to take place.

There may be special competitive conditions, however, in the markets for some products:

- *Monopoly:* a **monopoly** exists where only one supplier supplies the market with a particular good or service. The monopolist can take advantage of this unique position in raising prices to a high level. Regulation by the state often seeks to ensure that a monopoly position cannot arise. For example, proposed mergers between businesses are often carefully examined by regulatory authorities who have the authority to block any merger which would lead to a single monopoly supplier in a market.
- *Oligopoly:* an **oligopoly** exists where there are few suppliers (between, say, three and five) in the market for the supply of a particular good or service, and where market shares are fairly evenly spread out. An example of oligopoly exists in the provision of accounting services. Although there are many accounting firms in the UK and worldwide, most of them are very small practices. There are only four major international firms which can genuinely compete for the business of accountancy advisory services to multinational corporations. Where oligopoly exists, there is a danger of reduced competition in the market, and stagnation of prices. Regulators often take a keen interest in oligopolistic market conditions, and will carefully assess the competitive implications of proposed mergers between members of an oligopoly. Nevertheless, oligopolies are found in many industries.
- *Cartel:* a **cartel** is a price-fixing arrangement where a few major suppliers in a market agree between themselves to keep prices high. This is widely regarded as anti-competitive and in most market economies regulations exist to outlaw cartels. Currently, in the UK the law allows for very substantial fines to be levied

on companies involved in price-fixing arrangements. The Competition and Markets Authority (CMA) is the agency in the UK responsible for consumer and competition issues. One of its functions is to enforce legislation with a view to eliminating anti-competitive behaviour and unfair trading. (The work of the CMA is described in detail on its website: www.gov.uk/cma.) A recent example of a CMA investigation is described below.

Example 13.1 (Real-Life)

RETAIL BANKING

In 2014 the CMA launched an investigation into the supply of retail banking services to personal current account (PCA) customers and to small- and medium-sized enterprises (SMEs). There has been concern for many years about the low level of competition in retail banking, and the CMA was looking for evidence that competition in this sector was restricted or distorted. One problematic aspect of competition which was thoroughly explored in the investigation is that PCA customers tend to be reluctant to switch their account to another provider, even where there is clear evidence of financial gains to be made by switching.

Competitive pricing and higher quality of services should result in increased market share for lower cost providers. But in the case of retail banking, customers' reluctance to switch accounts has meant that market share changes very slowly and poorer-quality providers are not necessarily penalized in the market.

The CMA concluded its investigation with a range of recommendations for improvements in the markets for PCAs and accounts for SMEs. These include measures to increase customer engagement, to advertise bank charges more prominently and to publish service quality indicators.

13.2.1 Price Setters and Price Takers

The position of an individual business in the market may determine whether or not it has any control over prices. In an intensely competitive market with many suppliers of goods or services, there may be little scope for an individual supplier to separate from the pack. Sometimes markets are dominated by a few large suppliers, trailed by a large number of smaller providers. In such cases, a small provider of goods or services is unlikely to be able to influence prices; this type of provider is known as a **price taker**; they have to take the prices determined by the more powerful players in the market. By contrast, a **price setter** does not have to accept the prices set by other people.

13.3 HOW DO PRODUCERS DECIDE ON PRICES?

As we have just seen, price takers have little scope for making decisions on prices. What about price setters? Theoretically, producers and suppliers of goods and services should have regard to demand and to market conditions. Some producers do examine the market, although many continue to rely upon cost-based pricing. This section of the chapter examines both market-based and cost-based pricing.

13.3.1 Market-Based Pricing

If market information is available or can be obtained at relatively low cost, businesses should use it. Sometimes pricing is based upon perceptions, and experience, of market demand which have little, if anything, to do with costs.

In some circumstances competition is important and pricing by competitors may be clearly visible. For example, supermarket businesses frequently compete with each other on price. It is, obviously, easy to determine what the competition is charging for a basket of products because prices are visibly displayed. There are relatively few supermarket businesses, and it is not clear that people will always go to the cheapest – other factors such as the range of goods on sale and the general brand identity matter, too. Nevertheless, the level of pricing in such markets is often an important factor in securing sales. Below is a real-life example.

Example 13.2 (Real-Life)

SUPERMARKET COMPETITION IN THE UK

In the early years of the 21st century, the market for groceries in the UK was dominated by four big companies: Tesco, Sainsbury's, Asda and Morrisons. Smaller players in the market included the German companies Aldi and Lidl. These companies are sometimes referred to as the 'discounters' because of the very low prices they charge for goods. Aldi and Lidl stores are very basic and they carry very few lines compared to the big market players. (A report in 2014 identified 1350 product lines in an Aldi store, compared to up to 25 000 product lines typically carried by Tesco stores). While both Aldi and Lidl had been growing slowly for several years, it was only in 2014 that they started to launch an effective assault on the market share of their largest competitors. This campaign was very successful indeed. At the beginning of 2014 Aldi and Lidl's share of the grocery market was just over 7%. By 2017, this figure had risen to 10.4%. The difference between 7% and 10.4% may not seem very big, but in terms of market share it is highly significant. Consumers appear to have become aware, as the result of effective marketing, that they were paying too much for groceries, and many of them have turned to Aldi and Lidl in order to cut the cost of their grocery shopping. In order to fight back the big four companies have had to cut their own margins. This reduction in margins appears to have produced a change across the market that could be permanent. Both Aldi and Lidl have ambitious expansion plans underway, so the competition is likely to remain intense.

13.3.2 Cost-Based Pricing

Cost-based pricing, as the term implies, is the fixing of the price for a product or service based upon the cost of providing it. However, cost-based pricing cannot usually be undertaken without any reference at all to the market, especially in the longer-term. If a cost-based price results in a product with a very much higher price than similar or identical products in the market, there is likely to be a problem. If the higher costs result from inherent inefficiencies or defects in the manufacturing process the business is likely to fail.

Sometimes international inequalities, very often in the price of labour, result in businesses either being priced out of a particular market, or having to change their source of supply. As noted in an earlier chapter, one of the reasons for the relative decline of manufacturing industry in the UK has been the availability of cheaper labour elsewhere. Firms have often moved their entire manufacturing operation into other countries where labour costs are lower.

COST-PLUS PRICING As the name implies, this approach to pricing first establishes the cost and then adds on a 'plus' factor – the required level of profit.

Example 13.3

Binnie Fairweather makes a range of commercial ovens for sale to hotels and restaurants. The company uses a cost-plus approach to pricing. Direct costs of producing an oven are:

	£
Direct materials	49.60
Direct labour	61.30
Other direct costs	21.50
	132.40

The company absorbs production overheads on the basis of machine hours used. Fixed production overheads for the current year are estimated at £695 000 and total machine hours are 25 000 for the year. Each oven uses 1.5 machine hours.

Binnie Fairweather requires a profit of 25% on total cost.

The fixed production overhead absorption rate is:

$$\frac{695\ 000}{25\ 000} = £27.80$$

Selling price is calculated as follows:

	£
Direct costs	132.40
Production overheads	
£27.80 × 1.5 machine hours	41.70
Total costs	174.10
Profit mark up: £174.10 × 25%	43.53
Selling price	217.63

Binnie Fairweather may be more or less flexible in relation to this calculated selling price. If the company looks around the other suppliers in the market it may see that selling prices for similar ovens are no more, generally, than £200. The company then has a choice: if it is in a price setting position it may decide to go ahead and market the product at approximately £218 or even higher, based upon factors such as:

- good brand name
- better quality (perceived or actual)
- a carefully targeted marketing campaign.

In fact, the selling price which is arrived at through application of cost-plus pricing may be simply a starting-off point in a long process of determining an appropriate price.

There are several disadvantages of cost-plus pricing:

- Absorption costing may not give a particularly accurate estimate of the overhead costs related to a product. As we have seen in Chapter 12, allocation and apportionment of costs can be quite arbitrary and may, therefore, lead to incorrect decisions.
- The absorption rate is set in advance; it may prove to be quite seriously inaccurate, in which case pricing decisions based on full cost-plus calculations may prove, in retrospect, to be less than optimal.
- The emphasis on costs may result in firms failing to consider market conditions properly. Where the market is highly competitive, even a small price differential could result in a large fluctuation in sales. Fluctuations in volume of sales and production could result in significant misallocation of **fixed costs**, thus adding to the absorption costing problem already identified.
- In industries where cost-plus pricing is widely accepted as a basis for establishing contractual arrangements, inefficiency may actually be rewarded. Under cost-plus pricing arrangements, the higher the cost, the higher the profit margin.

In order to address the problem of the unreliability of absorption costing for this type of decision making, a higher mark-up could be added to the variable elements of cost only, such as direct materials and labour. This approach is known as variable cost-based pricing. (Chapter 14 will examine the issue of **variable costs** in much more detail.)

Examples 13.3 and 13.4 illustrate cost-plus pricing in a manufacturing environment. This method is also commonly found in retail and service businesses. For example, a retailer may apply a standard mark-up to products in a particular category. In the case of service businesses a standard hourly charge is often applied to time spent on a particular customer's business. This is likely to be based upon an allocation of total costs of the business over the number of productive service hours available, plus a mark-up. Provided the resulting standard hourly charge is reasonably competitive, the cost-plus approach is likely to work well.

Example 13.4

The directors of Binnie Fairweather have concluded that cost-plus pricing on the basis of total cost is simply too unreliable. They have therefore decided to use variable cost as a base, with a mark-up of 55% of the variable cost total. This approach produces the following selling price:

	£
Variable costs	132.40
Add: profit mark up: £132.40 × 55%	72.82
Selling price	205.22

Whether or not this selling price is more realistic, given current market conditions for the company, would be a matter for the directors to decide. Again, this price might just be a starting point for the decision making process.

The management accountant clearly has a key role to play in pricing decisions, and especially where pricing is based upon cost. The determination of cost, as demonstrated in the previous two chapters, is far from straightforward in most business activities but it takes on an additional importance where it is used in making pricing decisions.

13.4 SPECIAL CASES

13.4.1 Tendering

Some types of commercial contracts for goods and services are arranged by tender. This is a process which involves several businesses competing for a contract; usually it involves the submission of sealed bids by a certain date and time. The customer opens the tenders on the same occasion, compares prices and conditions, and decides which tender to accept.

The sealed bid system is intended to allow for fair competition, and to give the customer the best opportunity of obtaining a fair price. In this situation, from the supplier's point of view, information about prices in the market is likely to be nonexistent or limited (unless the suppliers have banded together in an illegal cartel to artificially adjust prices). Tendering is, therefore, likely to be done on the basis of a cost-plus approach, using information derived from the business's costing system, together with some guesswork about the prices likely to be offered by the competition.

The customer is not obliged to choose the lowest tender price. Sometimes, a supplier will submit a price that is obviously underestimated, perhaps because they wish to obtain the business at very low cost (this may be worth doing, for example, if labour is underemployed at a slack period). Alternatively, they may simply have underestimated what is involved in the contract.

13.4.2 Highly Restricted Supply of Unique Products

Some products do not fit particularly easily into either the market-based or cost-based approaches to pricing.

Example 13.5

PRICING ORIGINAL WORKS OF ART

An original work of art is, by definition, unique. In a sense, each work of art creates its own demand because, until it is created, nobody can know with certainty that they want it or need it. However, once a certain class of works of art is established, a market of a sort may be created, and the market price is tied into intangible factors such as reputation and more obvious and quantifiable factors such as scarcity of supply. For example, the works of Vermeer, the 17th century Dutch artist are so scarce (there are only 36 definitively attributed paintings) that pricing become almost irrelevant; there is, effectively, no supply, although the demand would, presumably, be very high were one of his paintings to reach the market. Demand, in economists' terms, is highly inelastic.

The relationship between supply of works of art and prices does follow the classic economic model to some extent. When an artist with a reputation dies, the prices of his or her works will tend to increase because the supply has now definitively ceased.

Art pricing rarely has anything to do with cost, however great or small the reputation of the artist. A painting, for example, is a piece of stretched canvas, board or paper with pigments in some kind of medium applied to it; variable raw materials costs are unlikely in most cases to be very high. The labour required to produce it is rarely costed by the artist; if it were, the hourly rate would, for most sales, be laughably small. Cost-plus pricing in this case is hardly an option – information is lacking and the intrinsic cost of the product is rarely an issue in a decision to purchase in any case.

13.4.3 Target Pricing and Costing

This approach to pricing turns cost-plus pricing on its head. A target price is established by reference to the market, not cost. This may not be straightforward, especially where the product is highly differentiated, and will involve research into prices of similar products, consumer preferences and relative level of price elasticity. Once a target price has been established, the firm will then deduct the desired profit margin on selling price. The residual amount then represents the maximum amount of cost which the firm can incur in producing the product or service – the target cost. If this amount appears to be too small to accommodate all the associated costs, then the firm makes strenuous efforts to reduce those costs so that the target can be met. This may involve:

- engaging in general cost reduction programmes to reduce overheads to a minimum
- re-engineering a product
- investing to create additional production efficiencies
- making compromises on quality of materials
- planning for additional volumes of production so as to reduce unit costs (by means of, for example, taking advantage of discounts for large-scale purchases).

13.4.4 Discounting

Many businesses will give discounts on selling price to reward customer loyalty or to ensure early payment for goods or services supplied on credit. Usually, such discounting reduces the supplier's profit margin by a small amount, but the reduction is balanced by a commensurate benefit.

However, sometimes a business may make a rational decision to sell goods or services at less than the cost of producing them. On the face of it this strategy appears foolish; it would clearly lead to the rapid downfall of the business if done too often over too wide a product range. However, it can make sense where:

- there is a large quantity of inventory with a short shelf life to clear
- the goods or services are being treated as a **loss leader**.

Some inventory is, by its nature, perishable: food and soft drinks, for example. In other cases, the life of inventory is limited by fashion considerations. It usually makes sense for retailers to sell fashion items at the end of a season for whatever they can raise, so that room can be made for the new season's inventory.

A loss leader product or service is used to attract customer attention to a range of goods or to a particular supplier. Although it does not make long-term sense to provide goods or services at less than cost, a loss leader may help a business to break into a particular market.

13.4.5 Auction

Where prices are established at auction the seller abandons part of his or her control over price setting. For some types of commodity (eg. art, antiques, certain categories of real estate) selling at auction is the accepted method of contracting; it would not normally apply for new goods. Usually the seller can stipulate a reserve price. For example, a seller sends an antique vase to auction, setting a reserve on it of £1500. This means that if the bidding does not reach that price, the item will not be sold by the auctioneer.

13.5 MORE ISSUES IN PRICING DECISIONS

13.5.1 Product Life Cycle

The discussion and examples earlier in the chapter about cost-plus pricing took into account only direct and indirect costs of the current period. This approach is perfectly valid in some types of business. Sometimes, however, it is necessary to take a longer view of costs in order to determine an appropriate price. If a firm is to stay in business, the total revenue streams from a given product must normally exceed the total costs arising. This means that, where there has been a substantial upfront investment in developing a product or services, the cost of the investment must be taken into account when deciding on a selling price. Management accounting uses life cycle costing and pricing in order to ensure that all costs are taken into account, and that the level of pricing is capable of covering these costs. The example below illustrates the process.

Example 13.6

Glock Systems is a computer games developer. The company's management accountant is preparing for a meeting with the sales director in order to discuss the pricing of Glock's forthcoming game, codenamed XX23. The game has been in development for the last six months, and the following costs have been accumulated to date:

	£
Cost of games developers' time	503 000
Outsourced product and advertising design	177 000
Advertising agency billings	195 000
Allocation of general business overhead	138 000
	1 013 000

Sales projections indicate that the game is likely to sell around 1 500 000 copies over an 18-month period. At some time within the first 12 months of production Glock's directors will make a decision on whether or not to develop an updated version of the game.

Variable costs of production are estimated at £4.30 per copy. Further advertising costs will be incurred of around £100 000, and a further £115 000 is estimated as the future allocation of general overhead to this project.

What is the minimum price that should be charged for a copy of the XX23 game?

The total life cycle costs of this product are as follows:

	£
Already incurred	1 013 000
Variable costs of production (£4.30 × 1 500 000)	6 450 000
Additional advertising costs	100 000
Additional allocation of general overhead	115 000
Total	7 678 000

The minimum selling price that can be charged for each copy so as to cover the life cycle costs of the product is £7 678 000/1 500 000 = £5.12

13.5.2 Product Life Cycle Issues

Businesses are likely to take different approaches to pricing, depending upon the stage a product has reached in its life cycle. When a product is introduced to the market it is likely to have novelty value, and may even have some unique features that will make it prized by consumers until competitors catch up (such products are described as 'highly differentiated'). Examples are often found in computer and mobile phone technology.

Where a business has a genuinely new product, it can opt to adopt a price-skimming policy. This means it can charge relatively high prices for as long as the product's novelty endures. Once competitors start to produce rival versions of a new product, the first producer will be obliged to make price reductions. At the other end of the product life cycle the opposite effect may occur. Where a product ceases to be highly differentiated, is becoming outmoded and is likely to be replaced by more advanced versions, its producer may have to discount its selling price in order to continue to sell it. For example, fashion clothing reaching the end of its season, is likely to be heavily discounted in order to make way for new lines.

Which of the following statements is correct?
Price skimming is:

a) a rapid exercise in collection data about the prices charged by competitors

b) charging low prices, relative to competitors, in order to establish a presence in a market

c) offering discounted prices as an inducement to potential customers

d) charging high prices in the early stages of exploitation of a new product.

Self-test question 13.2 (answer at the end of the book)

13.6 PRICING IN CONTEXT

This section uses examples to illustrate a range of approaches to pricing in very different contexts.

13.6.1 Building Contractor

Aziz & Sons is a firm of building contractors. The firm has just been invited to submit a tender for constructing a very large office building. Aziz & Sons would like to get the business, if possible. Although the directors do not know the names of the other contractors on the tender list, they are likely to be able to make an educated guess; there are relatively few competitors which have the capacity to take on a job of this size.

How does the firm go about establishing a tender price? In practice, tendering for such contracts is an expensive and lengthy process. The cost of submitting the bid is wasted if the firm does not obtain the tender; this is an operating cost which has to be accepted by such businesses.

Aziz & Sons' management will have to study the architect's drawings in detail in order to understand what is entailed. Their management accountant will have to cost raw materials, subcontracted elements of the work (such businesses rarely employ directly all the different trades they need), direct labour, managerial time and, probably, an element of fixed overhead recovery. An estimate of the time taken and a programme of works will also be required. Once the costs are established, a tender price can be discussed, based, probably, upon a cost-plus approach where a mark-up is added. At the end of the process, an overall contract price is estimated. However, the senior management may feel at this point that the proposed bid price is simply too high – if it seems likely that competitors will bid less, the costs and the mark-up are likely to be re-examined. Sometimes, this may involve an element of target costing; working back from a bid price that looks feasible, management may look for ways of minimizing costs.

In this type of case, establishing a price is a lengthy and expensive process. While the basic approach is likely to involve cost-plus calculations, the price that is finally submitted in the tender will usually have been influenced by market-based considerations as well.

13.6.2 Toothpaste Manufacturer

Most people clean their teeth pretty regularly; therefore, toothpaste is a product that is sold in large quantities. It is a good example of a product to which people are relatively indifferent in the sense that they give the purchase little thought. Demand is elastic because purchasers do not place a high value on the product, will accept substitutes relatively easily, and are really not very interested in it. (For example, contrast the purchase of a tube of toothpaste with the purchase of a new car.)

Of course, we do not buy toothpaste direct from the suppliers, but almost invariably through the middleman, the retailer. As far as manufacturers are concerned their customers are retailers or wholesalers.

So, how do manufacturers price their product? If there are many competitors in the market, prices are likely to be kept at a stable level through competition. The manufacturer may not be able to exert very much influence on price. Provided the selling price covers costs and provides some profit, the manufacturer will, presumably, continue to manufacture and sell the product. However, they may not charge the same amount to all customers. Powerful purchasers (like the large supermarket chains) are likely to be in a position to exert influence on the manufacturer's price and to demand discounts for bulk purchases. Smaller purchasers will probably have to pay more.

In the case of a bulk manufacturer of a product for which demand is elastic, price is determined by the market. Some sectors of the market, moreover, are likely to be in a position to demand lower prices; thus, different prices may be paid for the same product depending upon the power and influence of the customer. Although cost is important, in the sense that costs must be covered in the longer term if the manufacturer is to survive, they are less relevant to the pricing decision than in some other types of business.

13.6.3 Writer

Minnie Tanner has just finished her first novel, 'Silver Moonlight', a 'romantic tale of love triumphing over adversity'. Like most writers, Minnie's dream is to have her book published in numerous editions, translated into many languages, with worldwide sales in at least seven figures. Mostly, of course, the dream does not come true. Suppose, for a moment, that Minnie's book is publishable (unlikely) and that she finds someone willing to publish it (highly unlikely).

How does Minnie set the price of the book?

The answer is that, although she is in a sense a producer, she does not set the price. In the unlikely event that a publisher accepts the manuscript, the publisher will have control over all the details of production and pricing. Minnie's earnings (if any) will be in the form of royalties dependent upon sales, at a royalty rate determined by the publisher. Her only hope of varying this arrangement is if she becomes a really successful author with very high sales. In such cases, which are rare, writers (or more likely, their agents) may be able to command large advances and better royalty deals. Minnie has a long way to go.

How does the publisher set the price of the book?

The decision on pricing in this case, is likely to have a lot to do with the market. Romantic novels are not exactly like toothpaste; there is more differentiation between products, but demand is relatively elastic. It becomes inelastic only once the author has established a faithful following of people who will go into a bookshop for 'the latest Minnie Tanner' book; at that point demand for the specific product is assured. However, demand is only relatively inelastic; if the publishers double the price of the book the market may not respond by buying it.

13.6.4 Solicitors

Haringey, Fisker and Blott is a firm of solicitors specializing in matrimonial and property conveyancing work.

How do solicitors establish their prices?

Solicitors and other professionals such as accountants, surveyors and business consultants, usually establish charge-out rates, which are used to charge clients on the basis of time spent.

Haringey, Fisker and Blott are all partners in the business; they also employ four full-time solicitors and two legal executives to assist in the conveyancing side of the business – a total of nine fee earners. Each year, the partners meet with their management accountant to discuss the charge-out rates to be employed in the practice in the coming year. The budget for 20X3 shows total costs of £625 000, which must be covered by income. In addition, of course, the partners wish to make a profit. Their desired mark-up on costs is 25%.

There are three grades of charge-out rate – for partners, staff solicitors and legal executives. During 20X2 the charge-out rates have been £90, £55 and £30 respectively. The partners work on the basis that they and staff are available for 46 weeks per year, 5 days per week, 7.5 hours per day. They aim to be able to charge 80% of available time to clients.

There are two questions to consider:

i) By what percentage do the partners need to increase charge-out rates for 20X3 to meet their desired mark-up?

ii) What other considerations should the partners take into account in deciding whether or not, and by how much, to increase charge-out rates?

Answers

i) At current rates, provided the estimates of time availability are accurate, accumulated charge-outs could raise the following fee income:

	£
Time available: 46 weeks × 5 days × 7.5 hours × 80% = 1380 hours per person	
Legal executives: 2 × 1380 × £30	82 800
Solicitors (staff): 4 × 1380 × £55	303 600
Partners: 3 × 1380 × £90	372 600
	759 000

The target total for fees for 20X3 is the budget costs plus a mark-up of 25%:

$$(£625\ 000 \times 25\%) + 625\ 000 = £781\ 250$$

The estimate of available fee income of £759 000 falls short of the target by £22 250 (£781 250 − 759 000). Charge-out rates would have to be raised by:

$$\frac{22\ 250}{759\ 000} \times 100 = 2.9\%$$

ii) The partners would need to take into account the following factors in determining prices:

- *Recovery*: although charge-out rates are very useful for management accounting purposes within many service businesses, they are sometimes used simply as a basis for establishing the amount of a bill. For various reasons, solicitors may not wish to charge the fees suggested by the bill, or may wish (and be able) to charge more. Usually, a percentage recovery figure will be calculated to indicate the extent to which the fees indicated by the charge-out rate have been recovered. If recovery falls much short of 100% the partners may need to rethink their rates.

- *Competition*: traditionally, solicitors' fees have been shrouded in mystery. However, with the advent of advertising by solicitors (it used to be prohibited in the UK) and a greater willingness on the part of the public to challenge solicitors' bills, competition has become more of a factor. Word of mouth is an important factor for professional practices in gaining new business; if word gets out that Haringey, Fisker and Blott's bills are much higher than average, they could lose business. So, to some extent, price affects demand, and market conditions should be taken into account.

Chapter Summary

The chapter began with a brief discussion of the classical economist's model of demand. The real-world application of the classical model is complicated by many different factors, including special competitive conditions such as monopoly, oligopoly and cartel. The disadvantages experienced by consumers and customers in such conditions are often addressed by regulation. In a UK context, the CMA seeks to ensure compliance with relevant legislation.

In practice, there are various approaches to the important decisions involved in price-setting. Market-based approaches are likely to be used in competitive conditions, but cost-based pricing, despite its several disadvantages, is also widely used in practice. There are many special cases of approaches to pricing decisions, including tendering, unique product pricing, target pricing, discounting and auction. Policies such as price skimming and price discounting may be adopted depending upon the stage a product has reached in its life cycle.

The management accountant is involved in many aspects of pricing. Prices must be set so that, in the long run, a product or service's revenue exceeds its costs. The role of the management accountant is to determine costs and to provide the information necessary for making pricing decisions

Pricing is a difficult area of management decision making. Despite the attractions of the simple demand model, it appears in practice that pricing in many industries is more of an art than a science.

Internet Resources

Book's companion website

The website contains the following resources in respect of Chapter 13:

Students' section

A multiple choice quiz containing five questions
Three additional questions with answers

Lecturers' section

Answers to end-of-chapter exercises 13.7 to 13.10
Three additional questions with answers
Testbank
Instructor's Manual
PowerPoint presentation

Exercises: Answers at the End of the Book

13.1 Which statement is correct? The demand curve plots the relationship between:
   a) selling price and cost
   b) quantity and cost
   c) quantity and selling price
   d) selling price and discounts.

13.2 Which statement is correct? Demand is described as elastic where it:
   a) is highly sensitive to changes in price
   b) seldom increases or decreases
   c) cannot be met
   d) increases only where there is a substantial change in price.

13.3 Which statement is correct? An oligopoly exists in cases where:
   a) one supplier controls the market
   b) about three to five suppliers control the market
   c) there are many suppliers of about equal size in the market
   d) new suppliers enter the market frequently

13.4 Auger Ambit Limited is a manufacturing company which sets prices based on total costs plus a mark-up.
   For the year ending 31 December 20X3 the company is forecasting total fixed costs of £788 000. Direct materials costs will be £18.00 per unit and direct labour costs will be £27.56 per unit. The company expects to produce 20 000 units, and normally looks for a profit mark-up of 25%.
   Suggest a suitable cost-based selling price per unit of product for 20X3.

13.5 Belvedere, Bharat & Burgess are in partnership together as accountants. They have recently enlarged their practice and have taken on extra staff. The partners meet to discuss charge-out rates, which currently stand at £110 per hour for each of the three partners, £85 per hour for senior staff and tax specialists and £50 per hour for all other grades of qualified accountant. The partnership operates on the assumption that 75% of hours worked will be chargeable to clients as fees, and that a 43-week year is worked, at eight hours per working day. Costs are expected to amount to £1 275 000 in the coming year, 20X4. In 20X4 the partners expect to employ a total of five senior staff, including tax specialists, and six other qualified accountants.

   i) If the partners' assumptions are correct, how much in fees could the partnership expect to bill in 20X4?
   ii) If hours are worked exactly as planned, the average recovery rate on billing is actually 94%, and total actual costs are 1% above the 20X4 budget figure how much profit or loss would the partnership make?

13.6 Discuss the key factors which would arise in determining selling prices for:

   i) a garden centre
   ii) a small grocery store which is open for 24 hours.

Exercises: Answers Available on the Lecturers' Section of the Book's Website

13.7 Ainsley Witt Limited manufactures old-fashioned dolls houses. The manufacturing process is labour intensive, and involves a cost of £54 per house. Materials costs are £22 per house, and in addition, the company pays a royalty per house manufactured of £1 to the designer.
   The company's usual level of overhead costs is £125 000 per year. In an average year about 2400 dolls houses will be produced. Ainsley Witt's sales manager has suggested that the company should carry out an exercise to compare the current selling price of £150 for a dolls house with a cost-plus calculation, based upon a target mark-up on cost of 23%.
   Calculate the difference between the current selling price and a selling price based upon the cost-plus calculation.

13.8 Burke and Harpur are solicitors who have recently set up in partnership together and are working hard to establish themselves in a town which already has several solicitors. Both have a charge-out rate per hour of £65. They are preparing a bill for Mrs Henrietta Higgs, for whom they have recently drafted a will.

The bill contains the following items:

	£
Fees for time: 43 hours @ £65	2 795
Taxation specialist's charges for advice	650
Other sundry charges	240
Total	3 685

The partners disagree about how much to charge. Burke thinks that £3685 is a ridiculously high amount to charge for drafting a will, and that if word gets out that the firm charges that much for the service, it will badly damage their chances of increasing business. He says they should charge £1500 and be prepared to take the loss.

Harpur worked the majority of the 43 hours noted on the bill. He defends the high charge on the grounds that it is only so high because Mrs Higgs wasted such a lot of time changing her mind about who should inherit her considerable wealth. Also, because she is so rich, she should be able to afford the charges. He adds that he personally does not care if Mrs Higgs decides not to use their services again because she was so difficult to deal with.

Discuss the points of view of the two partners on this pricing problem. Which partner do you think is correct?

13.9   Discuss the key factors which would arise in determining selling prices for:

   i) a plumber (sole trader)

   ii) a biscuit manufacturer.

13.10 Regulation exists in the UK to prevent the operation of cartels. It could be argued, however, that regulation against cartels interferes with the operation of a free market and the economists' demand/supply model.

   Discuss the pros and cons of this argument.

14 Marginal costing and decision making

Aim of the chapter

To understand some of the important elements in decision making with particular reference to marginal costing.

Learning outcomes

After reading the chapter and completing the related exercises, students should:

- Understand the principal factors involved in decision making, including the importance of relevant costs.

- Understand the nature and classification of costs as variable, fixed or semi-variable.

- Be able to use cost–volume–profit analysis to establish a break-even point and to assist in business decision making.

- Understand the issues involved in making decisions in special circumstances.

- Understand the limitations of marginal costing for decision making.

Introduction

The previous chapter examined the important decisions involved in setting product prices. This chapter expands the topic of decision making with particular reference to decisions about such questions as, for example:

- whether or not it is worthwhile to produce a particular product
- the amount of a product that must be sold in order to break even or to make a profit
- whether or not to accept contracts at special prices.

This type of decision is often referred to as 'short-term', by contrast with decisions that affect future periods such as the purchase of major items of equipment (decisions like the latter are generally referred to as 'long-term'; they are covered in Chapter 15 of this book). However, all such decisions are important and may have consequences that stretch far into the future. For example, the decision to cease manufacture of a particular product is not really short-term because a dropped product cannot necessarily be easily reinstated.

The type of decision making covered in this chapter relies upon a close examination of costs, in order to determine which costs are relevant to the decision. The first section of the chapter examines the idea of relevant costs and revenues, along with some other important factors such as risk and uncertainty, and varying attitudes to risk. The second section covers the issue of cost variability which is often important when determining relevant costs. The topic of **marginal costing** is introduced, together with cost–volume–profit analysis and break-even analysis which can be helpful to accountants and decision makers. The chapter then examines certain special cases of decision making, and then concludes with a review of the limitations of analysis based on marginal costing.

14.1 ISSUES IN DECISION MAKING

This first section of the chapter establishes some important principles in costing for decision making.

14.1.1 Relevant Costs and Revenues

Relevant costs and revenues are those that change as a result of a decision. Past costs cannot be relevant for decisions made now, because they have already been incurred; in the context of the type of decision making covered in this chapter, past costs are described as **sunk costs**. Future revenues may be, but are not always, relevant to a decision. For example, suppose that a decision is required as to the preferable production method (out of two possibilities) for 1000 units of product B which will sell for £100 each. There are two possible decisions in this case if production is to go ahead, but revenue will be the same under either decision and so is not a relevant factor.

The example below examines some aspects of relevant costs and revenues for decision making.

Example 14.1

Georgetown Systems is in business as a computer dealer. A recent inventory count showed that some of the business's inventory was becoming outdated. For example, there are five ATB2000 computers, purchased over two years ago at a cost of £1000 each. One of Georgetown's technical managers has been researching various possibilities for disposing of the computers. She has come up with three options:

1 Give the computers to a local school for disadvantaged children. The school is under-funded and is always pleased to receive gifts of money or equipment. Georgetown Systems' directors are well known supporters of local and national charities and the company's annual report always contains at least a page providing details of charitable activities during the year.
2 A discount trader has offered £200 each for the machines.
3 For an outlay of £400 each, the machines' processors could be upgraded. If this were done each machine could be sold for £700.

When considering this type of decision, it is easy to be distracted by the original outlay of £1000. For anyone who has absorbed and fully understood the techniques of financial accounting, it seems somehow wrong to ignore such a significant amount. However, it must be understood that the amount is not being ignored in the financial accounts; a total outlay of £5000 for the computers was no doubt properly recorded when the original transaction took place, and unless an allowance for loss of value has been made subsequently, the £5000 remains as an amount in inventory in the statement of financial position. But, for the purposes of the decision that now has to be made the historic cost of the machines is irrelevant; it represents an event that happened in the past and which remains the same whichever decision is made.

The relevant costs and revenues are shown in the table below:

	Option 1	Option 2	Option 3
Relevant revenues	0	5 × £200 = £1000	5 × £700 = £3500
Relevant costs	0	0	5 × £400 = £2000
Net revenue	0	£1000	£1500

Note that all relevant revenues and costs represent future outflows and inflows of resources. Which is the correct decision? On the face of it, the decision requires no thought at all: option 3 produces the best net revenue figure of the three. It is certainly preferable to the other commercial option, option 2. However, it is worth pausing to consider option 1 in the light of Georgetown's apparent objectives. It seems that the business does not exist solely to make profits, but that it also has charitable objectives, as evidenced by the nature and prominence of its reporting on charitable activities. The question in this case is whether the commercial objective outweighs the charitable objective. It is up to the business's managers to weigh up the factors involved. If they do decide to give the computers away, the management accounting procedures involved in determining relevant costs equip them with the knowledge of the value of the gift, which is the net potential revenue achievable under option 3.

B randade Ltd has an item of obsolete inventory which originally cost £1000. The item could be updated for a further outlay of £500, after which it could be sold to a customer for £700. Alternatively, the item of inventory could be sold for its scrap value of £300.

Identify any sunk costs and relevant costs and revenues in this scenario. What should Brandade do about the item of inventory?

Self-test question 14.1 (answer at the end of the book)

OPPORTUNITY COST A CIMA definition of opportunity cost is: 'The value of the benefit sacrificed when one course of action is chosen in preference to an alternative. The opportunity cost is represented by the foregone potential benefit from the best rejected course of action.' In the example above, if Georgetown decides to give the computers away, the opportunity cost of this action is the £1500 that could be realized if the computers were modified and sold.

In summary, the following principles are applicable when determining relevant costs and revenues:

- Past (sunk) costs are not relevant.
- Fixed costs are not relevant.
- Future costs and revenues are relevant where they vary under different decision scenarios.
- Costing for decision making is not the same as financial accounting for costs.
- Opportunity cost may be relevant to the decision.
- Non-financial factors may play an important part in decision making, especially where the business has objectives other than the making of profits.

14.2 COST VARIABILITY

In the discussion of relevant costs for decision making it was noted that future costs and revenues are relevant for decision making where they vary depending upon the decision scenario. With reference to costs, it is important to be able to distinguish between those costs that vary depending on such factors as level of output, and those that do not. Chapters 11 and 12 on costing introduced direct and indirect costs; it could be observed there that direct costs tend to increase proportionately with the level of output whereas indirect overhead costs are likely to remain unchanged. Full absorption costing (as explained in Chapter 12) is therefore not useful for decision making purposes.

This section of this chapter refines these initial observations by introducing variable, semi-variable and fixed costs.

14.2.1 Variable Costs

A fully variable cost is one that varies in line with the level of business activity. For example, direct materials costs tend to be fully variable. The relationship between level of activity and variable cost is shown in the graph in Figure 14.1.

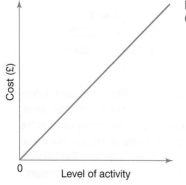

Figure 14.1
Graph of variable cost behaviour

Variable costs increase as the level of activity increases; the relationship between costs and activities is linear. As activity increases (eg. the number of units of production) variable costs increase. The line on the graph begins at 0 because at this point zero activity = zero variable cost. Example 14.2 demonstrates how a variable cost graph is created.

Example 14.2

S parks Kitchenware produces various types of kitchen equipment. A basic metal spatula requires 300 grams of metal at a cost of £1.00. The cost of metal to make two spatulas is exactly twice as much: 600 grams at a total cost of £2.00.

To make ten spatulas, 3 kg (300 grams × 10) of metal is required at a total cost of £10.00. For each additional spatula, the cost increases by £1 (ie. the same amount every time). This is an example of a fully variable cost.

Earlier we noted that direct materials costs tend to be fully variable. When might they not be fully variable? Well, in practice, it is usually possible to obtain lower prices per unit of material as volumes increase. In the case of Sparks Kitchenware, suppose that a quantity discount of 5% is available for purchases of metal in quantities over 100kg. This means that a higher volume of production will be relatively a little cheaper than a low volume. However, it is often quite realistic to make an assumption that direct costs are fully variable with the level of output.

We can plot the variable cost data onto a graph similar to that in Figure 14.2. The variable materials cost of the spatulas produced by Sparks Kitchenware is shown at three different levels of activity in the following table.

Number of units produced	Variable cost total (£1 × number of units produced)
0	0
10	£10
20	£20

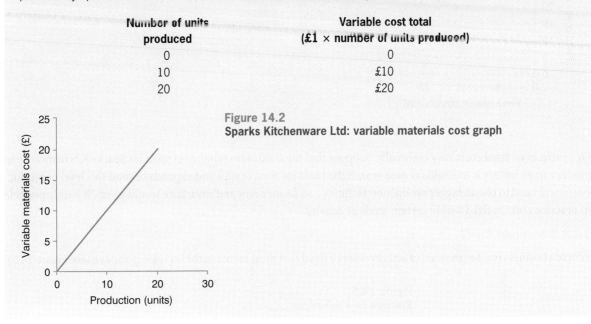

Figure 14.2
Sparks Kitchenware Ltd: variable materials cost graph

14.2.2 Fixed Costs

A fixed cost is one that does not vary with the level of business activity. The relationship between level of activity and fixed cost is shown in the graph in Figure 14.3.

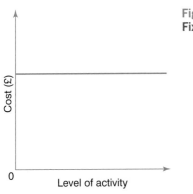

Figure 14.3
Fixed cost behaviour

Example 14.3

Sparks Kitchenware rents a factory unit. It pays rent of £28 000 each year for the unit, and insurance of £4360 each year. These are both examples of costs that do not vary with the level of output of the factory. Whether one or one million metal spatulas are produced, the cost of factory rent and insurance remains the same. We can plot the fixed cost of the factory rental (£28 000) onto a graph. See Figure 14.4.

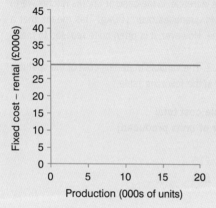

Figure 14.4
Sparks Kitchenware Ltd: fixed cost (factory rental) graph

Of course, even fixed costs vary eventually. Suppose that the maximum number of spatulas Sparks Kitchenware can produce in its factory is one million each year. If the business is successful and expands beyond this level of production it will need to obtain bigger production facilities – so factory rent and insurance would go up. It is only possible to describe costs as fixed within certain levels of activity.

14.2.3 Stepped Costs

Where a business reaches the level of activity where a fixed cost must increase, the increase is sudden (see Figure 14.5).

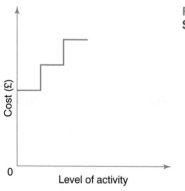

Figure 14.5
Stepped cost behaviour

Example 14.4

Sparks Kitchenware employs production supervisors at an annual salary cost of £12 500 each. The company's health and safety policy requires a certain level of supervision in the factory, and so the directors have decided that a supervisor must be employed for every ten machine operators. So, if the number of machine operators is 50, five supervisors will be employed at a total cost of £62 500 (5 × £12 500). If the number of machine operators rises to 51, the company's policy requires that six supervisors will be employed. The total cost rises to (6 × £12 500) £75 000. We can plot this stepped cost onto a graph. See Figure 14.6.

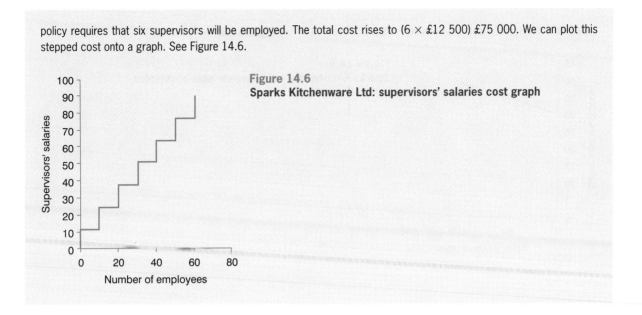

Figure 14.6
Sparks Kitchenware Ltd: supervisors' salaries cost graph

14.2.4 Semi-variable Costs

A **semi-variable cost** is one that varies to some extent with the level of business activity; it has both fixed and variable elements. For example, telephone bills have both fixed and variable elements. There is a line rental charge that is fixed; it remains the same regardless of the number of calls made. In addition to the fixed line rental, however, there is a variable element that depends upon the number of telephone calls made. The graph of a semi-variable cost (see Figure 14.7) shows that, even at a zero level of activity, some cost is incurred. That is why the cost line starts part way up the vertical axis.

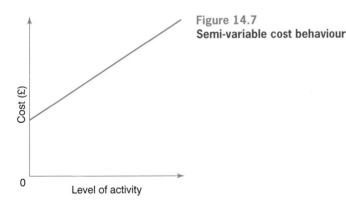

Figure 14.7
Semi-variable cost behaviour

Example 14.5

Sparks Kitchenware employs two sales staff. Each is paid a basic salary of £15 000 per year. In addition, each member of staff is paid a commission of 10% of sales value for every sale they make. Sales of £10 000, therefore, incur commission charges of £10 000 × 10% = £1000. Sales of £100 000 incur commission charges of £100 000 × 10% = £10 000. Total sales salaries costs:

- Sales level of 10 000: £30 000 (basic salary) + £1000 (commission) = £31 000
- Sales level of 100 000: £30 000 (basic salary) + £10 000 (commission) = £41 000

We can plot the semi-variable cost of sales salaries onto a graph. See Figure 14.8.

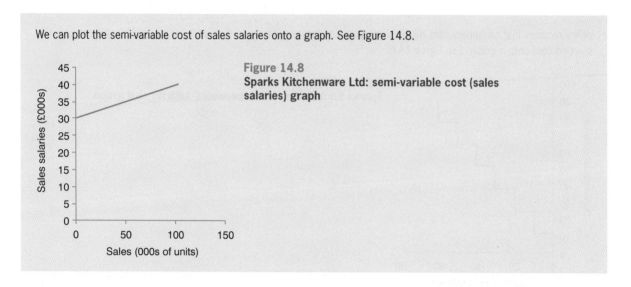

Figure 14.8
Sparks Kitchenware Ltd: semi-variable cost (sales salaries) graph

14.2.5 Typical Cost Behaviour in Different Business Sectors

In some types of business there are few, if any, variable costs. Even in businesses where a substantial proportion of cost is apparently variable with levels of activity, the reality may be that the costs are fixed in nature. We will look at some examples to illustrate these points.

A **MANUFACTURER** Usually, the direct materials used in manufacturing production tend to be variable; a progressively larger amount of material is used as the level of activity increases. By the same token, we would expect direct labour to be a variable cost. However, in practice, an employer's obligations to employees under employment regulations are often such that the labour cannot necessarily be regarded as variable. In many of the examples up to this point in the book, we have assumed that the supply of direct labour, like water from a tap, can be turned on or off at the convenience of management. This assumption may not be realistic. While a long-term downturn in an industry is likely to result in reductions in employees, short-term reductions in activity do not always result in workers being laid off.

Therefore, in determining whether or not labour is a variable cost, the circumstances must be examined carefully. For example, sometimes, especially in garment manufacture, workers are paid piece rates – ie. a sum for each completed item. Where this forms the whole of a worker's pay, the cost is truly variable. In some cases, however, there will be a basic, fixed level of wages plus a piece rate. This arrangement constitutes a semi-variable cost.

A **COMMERCIAL AIRLINE** Very few of the costs involved in running a commercial airline are variable. There are some very significant fixed costs, though:

- depreciation of aircraft
- employment of pilots and cabin crew
- aircraft maintenance and safety charges
- airport charges
- interest costs (on borrowing money to finance the purchase or lease of the planes).

A commercial aircraft service running scheduled flights must run the advertised flights even if there are very few passengers (in fact, because the planes have to be in certain places at scheduled times, a plane is likely to make the flight even if there are no passengers at all). Any variable costs are likely to be very minor indeed compared to the high level of fixed costs incurred. Variable costs would include, for example, the cost of any food and drinks supplied free during flights.

RESTAURANT Running a restaurant usually involves incurring a high level of fixed costs. For example:

- premises rental
- cost of employing staff
- depreciation of equipment.

What about food costs? To some extent these are variable, but because of the perishable nature of many food items there may be a fixed element of cost involved. If food is not sold to customers it will have to be thrown away sooner or later.

Labour costs may be variable to some extent, depending upon the basis of employment. If the restaurant proprietor expects a quiet evening he may be able to reduce the level of waiting and kitchen staff to some extent, but he will have to schedule at least some staff. Even if no customers at all turn up, he will still have to pay the staff for their time, and this basic minimum of staff time would represent a fixed cost.

HOLIDAY TOUR OPERATOR A holiday tour operator incurs fixed costs such as rental of offices, employment of staff to take bookings and deal with ticket administration, and so on. However, some of the costs are likely to be variable with the level of bookings taken from the public. A total of 37 couples booking a resort holiday will require 74 flight tickets and 37 rooms. There could, however, be some fixed elements to these costs; for example, where the contract with a hotel owner stipulates that, say, a minimum of 30 rooms will be paid for each week by the tour operator, regardless of whether or not they are used. In a case like this, the tour operator is being obliged to share with the hotel owner the risk of unused rooms.

Clearly, categorizing costs neatly into 'fixed' and 'variable' categories is not always as simple in practice as it may at first appear. In many businesses genuinely variable costs are rare.

14.3 MARGINAL COSTING FOR DECISION MAKING

A **marginal cost** in economics is the cost of one additional unit. If a factory produces 1000 units of a product, the marginal cost of the product is the cost that would be incurred in producing the 1001st unit. If fixed costs remain the same at a production level of both 1000 and 1001 units, the marginal cost of the 1001st unit comprises variable costs only. Marginal costing is an accounting term that describes an approach to costing that excludes fixed costs. It provides a superior basis for decision making, as the next example demonstrates.

Example 14.6

Modena Mayhew plans the following budget income and expenditure for May 20X5:

	£
Sales: 1000 units × £10 each	10 000
Costs	
Direct materials and labour	(4 000)
Production overheads, absorbed at £3 per unit	(3 000)
	3 000
Selling and administrative costs	(1 500)
Net profit	1 500

The business is not working to full capacity and it would be possible to produce more units of product. Modena Mayhew's sales director is approached by a contractor who wishes to order 100 units, to be produced and delivered for a special price of £8.50 per unit. In deciding whether or not to accept the order, the sales director needs information on the cost of a unit of product. What does it cost to produce one unit?

It might be tempting to take the total costs in the statement above (£4000 + £3000 + £1500 = £8500), divide by 1000 and come up with the figure of £8.50 per unit. However, this approach would be incorrect, unless all the costs were variable (and that is highly unlikely to be the case). Those costs that are fixed remain fixed unless the level of activity changes radically.

Really, the sales director needs to know the marginal cost of manufacturing one additional unit. Assuming that the production, selling and administrative costs are all fixed, and that all the direct costs are variables, this means that the business incurs £4000 of variable cost to produce 1000 units of product. The marginal cost of the 1001st unit of product is therefore £4 per unit.

If the sales director incorrectly calculated that the additional cost of the 100 unit order would be £850 (£8.50 × 100) he would conclude that it would not make sense to accept the order because the sales revenue from it would be no greater than cost. However, if he uses marginal cost, he may conclude that the order should be accepted.

14.3.1 Contribution

Contribution refers to the amount that remains after variable costs have been deducted from sales. Referring back to the information in Example 14.6, the additional contribution per unit of product that would be made on the special order for 100 units would be: £8.50 − £4.00 + £4.50 (Sales price per unit less variable cost per unit = contribution per unit).

If contribution is a positive figure it contributes towards meeting the fixed costs of the business. Once sufficient contribution is made to cover all of the fixed costs, any remaining amount contributes to net profits.

Contribution can be calculated per unit, and can also be shown as a total (number of units sold × contribution per unit).

14.3.2 Break-Even

The **break-even point** is the point at which no profit or loss is made in a set of business transactions. For example:

	£
Sales: 10 000 × £3	30 000
Less: variable costs: 10 000 units × £1	(10 000)
Contribution	20 000
Fixed costs	(20 000)
Net profit	Nil

B rinn Bartholomew sells municipal litter bins for £250 each. The bins cost £97 in direct materials (all variable cost) and £36 in direct labour (all variable cost). In June 20X7 the company plans to sell 1400 bins. Its budgeted fixed costs for the month of June are £120 400.

Self-test question 14.2 (answer at the end of the book)

- What is the company's budgeted contribution for June 20X7?
- What is the company's budgeted net profit for June 20X7?

14.4 COST–VOLUME–PROFIT ANALYSIS

It is important to understand the relationships between the level of business activity and the different types of cost and profitability. The analysis of the interaction of these factors is known as cost–volume–profit analysis (CVP analysis). We will examine CVP relationships further, firstly by charting cost, volume and profit in graphical form, and then by using formulae to express the relationships between the factors. First, we will look at the construction of **break-even charts**.

14.4.1 Break-Even Charts

STEP 1 Earlier in the chapter we constructed graphs for each different type of cost. Developing that approach further, we can show both fixed and variable costs on the same graph (see Figure 14.9). An alternative presentation is shown in Figure 14.10.

Fixed costs, as we have seen, are those that remain at the same level regardless of the volume of activity. Variable costs increase steadily as the volume of activity increases. Showing the two together on a graph gives the result illustrated. The upper sloping line represents total costs. Where there is zero activity (ie. no production or sales) the only costs incurred are fixed costs (which is why the total cost line starts part way up the vertical axis). As activity increases, so do total costs.

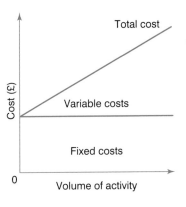

Figure 14.9
Graph of total costs, split into fixed and variable

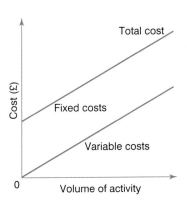

Figure 14.10
Graph of total costs, split into fixed and variable (alternative presentation)

Marshall Mexico Ltd has the following cost structure for 20X9:

Fixed costs: £50 000 up to 10 000 units of production
Variable costs: £5 per unit up to 10 000 units of production.

Using either graph paper or a spreadsheet program graphing facility, plot these costs onto a single graph, showing lines for fixed costs and total costs. Identify the areas of the graph that represent fixed costs and variable costs.

**Self-test question 14.3
(answer at the end of the book)**

STEP 2 We will now add a further line to the graph, this time tor sales revenue (see Figure 14.11). The addition of this line produces a break-even chart, which provides useful information about the activities of the business. The point at which the total revenue crosses the total cost line is the break-even point. We can see that the break-even point occurs where:

$$\text{Total sales revenue} = \text{Total costs}$$

By dropping a line down from the break-even point to the horizontal axis of the graph we can read off the volume at which the break-even point occurs; this is shown as a vertical dotted line on the figure.

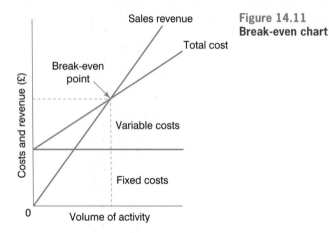

Figure 14.11
Break-even chart

Charting a line between the vertical axis and the break-even point, we can read off the sales value at which the break-even point occurs; this is shown as a horizontal dotted line on the figure.

The facts are the same as for self-test question 14.3. Marshall Mexico Ltd sells its product at £15 per unit. Taking the graph drawn for self-test question 14.3, draw a total revenue line and establish the break-even point. Drop a line down to the horizontal axis and find out the volume of activity at which the break-even point occurs. Draw another line from the break-even point to the vertical axis and find out the sales value at which the break-even point occurs.

Self-test question 14.4 (answer at the end of the book)

14.4.2 Break-Even Analysis Using Formulae

There are drawbacks to using graphs for establishing the break-even point of a business:

- The answer obtained tends to be approximate because of inaccuracies in drawing the graph.
- It would be unnecessarily time consuming to have to draw a graph each time analysis of break-even was undertaken.

Instead, we can work out the break-even points using the relationships between sales and costs that we established earlier.

$$\text{Selling price per unit} - \text{Variable costs per unit} = \text{Contribution per unit}$$

Remember that contribution per unit contributes towards meeting the fixed costs of the business. The point at which all the fixed costs of the business are met is the break-even point. Beyond the break-even point, the contribution contributes towards the net profit of the business. So, the break-even point occurs where:

$$\text{Sales revenue} = \text{Total costs}$$

and also where:

$$\text{Contribution} = \text{Fixed costs}$$

In order to calculate the number of units of sales required to break even, the following formula is used:

$$\text{Break-even point (in units)} = \frac{\text{Fixed costs}}{\text{Contribution per unit}}$$

The break-even point in sales value can be calculated by:

$$\text{Break-even point (in units)} \times \text{Selling price per unit}$$

Example 14.7

Mulberry Piggott Ltd manufactures and sells raincoats. It sells each raincoat for £30.00. Variable costs are £10.00 per coat. In the year ending 31 December 20X4 the company expects to incur fixed costs of £60 000. How many raincoats will it have to sell to break even?

$$\text{Sales revenue per unit} = £30.00$$

$$\text{Variable costs per unit} = £10.00$$

Contribution per unit is, therefore, £20.00.

$$\text{Break-even point (in units)} = \frac{\text{Fixed costs}}{\text{Contribution}}$$

$$= \frac{60\ 000}{£20} = 3000 \text{ units}$$

Break-even point in sales value:

$$3000 \text{ units} \times £30.00 = £90\ 000$$

Self-test question 14.5
(answer at the end of the book)

Neasden Northwich Ltd sells its products at £20 per unit. Variable costs per unit are £6. The company expects to incur fixed costs of £70 000 in 20X2. Calculate the break-even point (in units).

BREAK-EVEN IN PRACTICE Break-even is an important management accounting term, even in firms that do not calculate marginal costs. The following example gives a brief account of a business that is struggling to achieve the break-even point.

Example 14.8 (Real-Life)

CORK AIRPORT AUTHORITY

Cork Airport Authority (CAA) was established in 2003 as part of the break up of the state-owned Aer Rianta. The Irish transport minister made a promise that both CAA and the equivalent authority at Shannon (SAA) would begin their commercial lives as debt-free entities. This was a particularly important undertaking for CAA because Aer Rianta had borrowed over £150 million to fund the building of a new terminal at Cork. However, controversy ensued because, following a change in minister, the debt-free pledge was abandoned. CAA has proved to be unprofitable, and it met with controversy in 2006 when it increased its charges to airlines by very large amounts. Ryanair responded by cutting the number of its flights from Liverpool to Cork. Ryanair's deputy chief executive was quoted as saying that Cork Airport was 'massively uncompetitive against its peer airports throughout Europe'. By early 2007 CAA appeared to be indebted for a total of over £200 million. An *Irish Times* report in 2007 ('Cork airport must rise above its debt problem', J. McManus, 5th March) said: 'Cork Airport lost some £5.8 million last year and needs to increase its passenger throughput by 14% before it breaks even.... The losses at Cork Airport come before the company pays a penny towards servicing its debts...'.

14.5 FURTHER APPLICATIONS OF BREAK-EVEN IN PRACTICE

14.5.1 Target Profit

The break-even point, expressed in numbers of units or sales value, provides management with valuable information. However, managers may also want to know how many units they will have to sell in order to reach a specified target profit. We can apply marginal costing to this type of problem quite easily, as it is a logical extension to break-even analysis. Remember that, once sufficient contribution is made to cover all of the fixed costs of a business, any remaining amount contributes to net profits.

Example 14.9

Using data from the Mulberry Piggott Ltd example:

Sales revenue per unit = £30.00
Variable costs per unit = £10.00
Contribution per unit = £20.00
Fixed costs = £60 000.

The company's directors would like to know how many units would have to be sold to reach their target profit of £30 000. Applying the formula:

$$\text{Target sales in units} = \frac{\text{Fixed costs} + \text{Target profit}}{\text{Contribution per unit}}$$

$$\text{Target sales in units} = \frac{60\ 000 + 30\ 000}{20} = 4500 \text{ units}$$

Expressed in terms of sales value:

$$4500 \text{ units} \times £30 = £135\ 000$$

So, we can extend the break-even formula as follows:

$$\text{Target sales in units} = \frac{\text{Fixed costs} + \text{Target profit}}{\text{Contribution per unit}}$$

SHOWING PROFIT ON A GRAPH Up to now we have not focused specifically on the graphical representation of profit. Suppose that Mulberry Piggott Ltd can make and potentially sell up to 7000 raincoats per year without any change to fixed costs. We can plot the following points on a graph:

Production level	Fixed costs	Total costs	Total revenue
	£	£	£
0	60 000	60 000	0
7 000	60 000	130 000	210 000
		(£60 000 + [7000 × £10])	(7000 × £30)

The graph is shown in Figure 14.12. The areas of profit and loss are marked on the graph. Beyond the break-even point, as production increases, the area between the revenue and total costs lines is occupied by profit. The first dotted line shows sales in units and in revenue to produce profits of £30 000 (as calculated above).

The second dotted line shows the maximum activity level that is possible at expenditure on fixed costs of £60 000. Profits at this level (the difference between the total revenue and total costs lines) would be much higher than at a level of 4500 sales; we can prove this by doing the calculation of profit at the maximum activity level of 7000 units:

	£
Sales (7000 × £30)	210 000
Variable costs (7000 × £10)	(70 000)
Contribution	140 000
Fixed costs	(60 000)
Profit	80 000

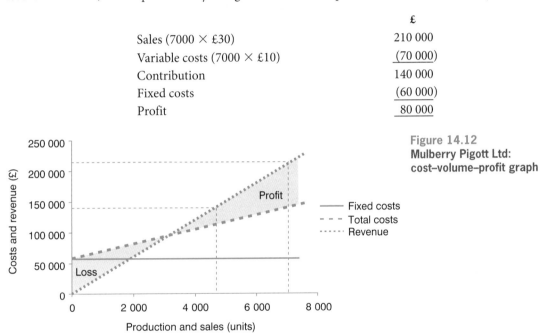

Figure 14.12
Mulberry Pigott Ltd: cost–volume–profit graph

14.5.2 Margin of Safety

Margin of safety is the excess of planned or actual sales above the break-even point. In Example 14.7 we calculated the Mulberry Piggott Ltd break-even point in units as 3000 raincoats. If we suppose that the sales of 4500 units targeted by the directors (as in Example 14.9) are a realistic target, the margin of safety, expressed both in units and in sales value, is as follows:

	Units of sales	Sales £
Actual sales estimate	4 500	135 000
Break-even point	3 000	90 000
Margin of safety	1 500	45 000

The margin of safety can also be expressed as a percentage of the sales estimate:

$$\frac{1500}{4500} \times 100 = 33.3\%$$

14.6 SPECIAL DECISIONS

14.6.1 Accepting Contracts

In this section we look more closely at business decisions involving acceptance or non-acceptance of contracts on special terms. Marginal costing analysis can be useful in reaching the appropriate decision.

If a contract at a special price would produce a positive contribution to fixed costs, then the business should accept the contract. However, there may be other factors to take into consideration. A business needs to have regard to factors such as maintaining its brand image and its position in the marketplace as, for example, a producer of high quality goods or as a firm with a serious commitment to minimizing its environmental impact. A special price contract could damage a business's image and its relationships with other organizations.

Example 14.10

Solidago Solanum Ltd manufactures sofas. Although the design details and fabric coverings vary, the basic design of the sofas is the same and they all sell for £1500 each. The company's factory can produce up to 1000 sofas per month, but in fact, production rarely exceeds 700 sofas per month.

The sales director has just received a query from a potential new customer, Cuttpryce Ltd. Cuttpryce is opening a chain of discount furniture stores and is examining potential sources of supply. The purchasing director of Cuttpryce offers to buy an initial consignment of 300 sofas at a price of £1200 each. The potential discount of £300 per sofa is so great that Solidago's sales director is tempted to refuse the order straight away. However, he consults his fellow directors over the decision.

The latest set of monthly management accounts shows the following summary:

Solidago Solanum: Management accounts for July 20X5

	£
Sales (655 × £1500)	982 500
Variable costs (655 × £895)	586 225
Contribution	396 275
Fixed costs	304 000
Net profit	92 275

What should the directors' decision be? Applying the basic decision rule: would the contract make a positive contribution to fixed costs?

Under the proposed contract:

	£
Selling price per sofa	1 200
Variable cost per sofa	(895)
Contribution per sofa	305

The contribution per sofa is positive, and so it appears that the contract should be accepted.

However, there are likely to be other relevant considerations. If it becomes generally known that Solidago sofas are available to Cuttpryce at £300 less than the normal price, why should anyone pay £1500? Acceptance of this new contract could have a significant impact on the rest of the company's business. If the company has a reputation for exclusivity and high quality, its brand image could be damaged by association with a discounter.

The marginal costing analysis provides a useful starting point for discussion, but the decision made by the directors will have to involve many other relevant factors.

In industries where the majority of the costs are fixed, the application of the decision rule explained in the example above can lead to some apparently absurd prices. Where variable costs are virtually non-existent, selling price is more or less the same as contribution. This means that, potentially, even a very low selling price can make a positive contribution to fixed costs.

14.6.2 Major Increases in Activity Levels

As we have seen, fixed costs remain fixed only up to certain levels of activity, within a relevant range of output. The concept of **relevant range** refers to the range of output that a business expects to be generating in the short-term. Once that range is breached a new set of cost relationships come into play. If a business is considering major increases in levels of activity, it must take into account any likely increases in fixed costs. The example below explains how this is done.

Example 14.11

Spindrift and Schooner Ltd is a small boat builder. It has operated successfully for many years from a boatyard that allows for production of 60 boats per year. In most years the company can sell all the boats it can produce. The selling price of each boat is £26 000. Variable labour and materials costs are £9850 per boat, and the fixed costs associated with running the business from the present boatyard are £482 000. Last year the company made a net profit of £487 000 on sales of £1 560 000.

The company's directors are meeting to discuss a proposal to increase the business's production capacity. A neighbouring property has become vacant and it would be possible to rent the additional space in order to produce more boats. The additional capacity in terms of production would be 20 boats. The sales director is confident that, with the growth in the leisure boating market, he will be able to sell the additional boats.

Variable costs per boat will remain the same. However, the expansion would produce an additional £265 000 in fixed costs. In a case like this, the increase in fixed costs has to figure in the decision making. The extra £265 000 is known as an incremental cost, and it must be compared with the incremental revenue that will be generated through higher sales. The basic decision rule is: if incremental revenue exceeds incremental costs, accept the project.

In this case we will assume that the sales director's confidence is justified and that he will be able to sell all of the additional 20 boats produced each year following the expansion:

	£
Incremental revenue	
Sales: 20 boats × £26 000	520 000
Incremental costs	
Variable costs: 20 × £9850	(197 000)
Incremental fixed costs	(265 000)
Incremental profit	58 000

Because the incremental profit is a positive figure it looks as though the business should increase its capacity. However, the directors might reflect that £58 000 is a relatively small increase in net profit, and that the net profit percentage on these additional sales at 11.1% is substantially lower than the existing net profit percentage of 31.2%.

14.6.3 Limiting Factors

So far, the only constraints on business activities which we have examined are the upper ceiling for production capacity and the restraint imposed by the market in terms of the amount of product or service that can be sold. However, there may be situations where other constraints operate. Such constraints are commonly known as limiting factors. For example, a product may require specialist labour for which there is a shortage, or a raw material which is in short supply.

Where a business produces more than one product, all of which require the input of resources whose supply is limited, management must come to a decision as to production priorities. The basic rule is that resources should be devoted to production of the products that produce the highest contribution per unit of limiting factor. This is not as complicated as it sounds, as the next example shows.

Example 14.12

Crosby and Crossthwaite Ltd use the same production line to produce their three principal products, A, B and C. All three products use the same grade of labour, which is in short supply because of a booming local economy that has ensured virtually full employment.

The products have the following sales and variable cost values per unit sold:

	A	B	C
	£	£	£
Selling price	50	55	48
Variable costs	(28)	(28)	(24)
Contribution per unit	22	27	24

On the face of it, it would appear that the company should concentrate production on product B because it produces the highest contribution to fixed costs. However, the picture alters when we look at the input to each of the products of the scarce labour resource:

	A	B	C
Number of labour hours used	2	3	3
Contribution per unit	£22	£27	£24
Contribution per labour hour	£11	£9	£8

When we calculate the contribution per unit of resource, we can see that product A comes out ahead because it uses only two of the limited labour hours. The ranking of the three products is first A, second B and third C.

If there is sufficient demand for product A, it appears that the company should switch production entirely towards product A. However, demand for product A may be insufficient. We will examine the additional factor of demand in the next example.

Example 14.13

Using the same information as in Example 14.12, suppose that Crosby and Crossthwaite Ltd can employ a maximum of 22 000 hours of labour in one year. Maximum annual demand for the three products is estimated at:

	A	B	C
Demand in units	8 000	6 000	8 000

How much of each product should the company plan to produce?

Taking product A first, 8000 units will use up 16 000 labour hours (at a rate of 2 hours per unit). The company should manufacture up to the maximum demand in respect of product A. This would leave 22 000 − 16 000 = 6000 labour hours available to manufacture something else. These hours should be used for the manufacture of product B, which is next in the limited resource rankings. Product B uses three labour hours per unit, so 6000 hours could produce 2000 units of product B.

The company's production plan is, therefore: product A 8000 units; and product B 2000 units.

14.7 LIMITATIONS OF ANALYSIS BASED ON MARGINAL COSTING

Analysis based on marginal costing can be useful to management as a source of information for decision making. However, it has several significant weaknesses and limitations:

1 This type of analysis assumes that variable costs increase at a steady rate in line with activity. This assumption may not be valid in practice. As the level of business activity increases, variable costs per unit may tend to fall as the business takes advantage of discounts for purchasing larger quantities.

2 As we have seen, very few costs are truly variable. In some businesses only relatively trivial costs vary with the level of business activity. Providers of services, in particular, usually incur a mixture of principally fixed and stepped costs. As developed economies become more and more dominated by service industries, as opposed to manufacturing, marginal costing analysis may become less and less relevant.

3 Fixed costs remain fixed only up to a point. Beyond a particular level of activity fixed costs will change. The level at which costs will change and the extent of that change may not be easy to estimate.

4 The examples used to illustrate the applications of cost-volume-profit analysis have all been based upon firms producing either a single product or a very limited range of products. In fact, most businesses provide a mixture of products or services. While it may be possible to identify variable costs for each product with a fair degree of accuracy, identification of fixed costs with a particular product is likely to be based upon quite arbitrary apportionment between products and activities.

5 All business decisions involve a complex range of factors. Marginal costing may help to point the way towards a decision, but there may be very good reasons in practice for ignoring the signposts offered by analysis based on marginal costing, as demonstrated in some of the examples earlier in the chapter.

If the limitations of this type of analysis are not fully appreciated, it is possible for businesses to make serious mistakes in when faced with decisions.

Chapter Summary

The chapter began with a discussion of relevant costs and revenues for decision making. However, it was noted that decisions may be influenced by non-financial factors, and by the firm's attitude towards risk and uncertainty. Individuals do not necessarily make completely rational decisions, and besides, in many if not most cases, perfect information is not available to assist them.

However, marginal costing analysis is sometimes useful in reaching decisions. In order to use it, it is necessary to understand the classification of costs into variable, fixed and semi-variable. Much of the central section of the chapter was devoted to explanations of these cost classifications and of the principles and practices of analysis based on marginal costing. The chapter proceeded to address break-even analysis, and then decision making under a range of special conditions, in which marginal costing can be useful. However, the techniques explained in the chapter should be understood in conjunction with the chapter's final section where several limitations of analysis based on marginal costing were explained.

Internet Resources

Book's companion website

The website contains the following resources in respect of Chapter 14:

Students' section

A multiple choice quiz containing ten questions
Six additional questions with answers

Lecturers' section

Answers to end-of-chapter exercises 14.15 to 14.25
Seven additional questions with answers
Case study
Testbank
Instructor's Manual
PowerPoint presentation

Exercises: Answers at the End of the Book

14.1 Bubwith Girolamo Ltd has been asked by one of its regular customers to supply goods for a special contract. The order is for 1000 units of metal casing, for which the contract price is £27 per unit. Direct labour input per unit is 2 hours, and direct materials input is 4 kg of metal. Bubwith Girolamo's direct labour employees are all paid at a rate of £12.50 per hour. The cost of metal is £4.50 per kg. None of the material is currently in stock.

The company currently has spare capacity following the cancellation of a major order earlier in the month. Direct labour employees are paid for a full working week of 37.5 hours, regardless of the state of the company's order book, but they are currently working only about 60% of the time. Consequently, there would be ample time available to fulfil the special contract.

Identify the relevant costs and revenues that Bubwith Girolamo should consider in making the decision, and advise whether or not the special contract should be accepted. Are there any non-financial factors that should be taken into consideration?

14.2 Wetwang Ltd owns a piece of machinery that is now surplus to requirements following changes in its production systems. The machinery was bought for £24 000 and since purchase a total of £6000 has been charged in depreciation. An offer of £12 000 for the machinery has been received from a local firm. Wetwang's directors would like to be sure that they receive the best price for the machinery. They could advertise the machinery in a trade magazine for £500.

If the directors decide to advertise the machinery what is the minimum price they should accept for it?

14.3 Billericay Ashworth Ltd makes tennis racquets. In an average month it produces about 3000 racquets. The following are some of the costs the company incurs:

- Cost of raw materials. Each racquet uses £13.00 of raw materials.
- Factory insurance. The cost for a month is £800.
- Telephone charges. The company has several telephone lines. Its line rental charges per month are £1000. If no calls are made, the call charge is £0. On average 500 calls cost a total of £250 and 1000 calls, on average, cost £500. In most months about 1500 calls are made in the company.

You are required to:

i) Classify each of the above costs as one of the following:

- variable
- fixed
- stepped
- semi-variable.

ii) Using either graph paper or a spreadsheet program graphing facility, plot each of these costs onto a separate graph. Activity levels should be on the horizontal (x) axis and costs on the vertical (y) axis.

14.4 Classify each of the following costs as:

- variable
- fixed
- stepped
- semi-variable.

i) Sales staff members' mobile telephone charges. There is a basic rental cost irrespective of the number of telephone calls made, plus a charge for each telephone call made, based on the number of minutes the call lasts.

ii) Factory machine oil.

iii) Metered water charges. The bill comprises a charge per unit for the number of units consumed.

14.5 For each of the following types of business, list at least two fixed and two variable costs that might typically be incurred:

- self-employed taxi driver
- solicitor
- shirt manufacturer
- beauty salon.

Try not to repeat the same examples of costs for the different businesses.

14.6 Porton Fitzgerald Ltd manufactures wardrobes. The selling price of a wardrobe is £210. Each wardrobe costs £52 in direct materials (all variable) and £34 in direct labour (all variable). In April 20X3 the company expects to sell 450 wardrobes, and it has budgeted for fixed overheads of £43 200.

What is the company's budgeted contribution for April 20X3?
What is the company's budgeted net profit for April 20X3?

14.7 Fullbright Bognor Ltd, a manufacturing business, has the following cost structure:

Selling price per unit: £85
Variable costs per unit: £41

The company's directors expect to incur fixed costs of £62 000 in the year ending 31 December 20X6. The maximum level of production which the company can reach is 3000 units per year. You are required to:

i) Draw a break-even chart recording: fixed costs; total costs; total revenue.

ii) From the chart estimate the break-even point in units and in sales value for Fullbright Bognor Ltd for the year ending 31 December 20X6.

iii) Use the break-even formula to find the break-even point in units and in sales value for Fullbright Bognor Ltd for the year ending 31 December 20X6.

14.8 Foster Beniform Ltd makes mannequins for shop window displays. The company's directors are meeting to discuss sales budgets for 20X8. The business has struggled to make a profit in recent years, but the finance director has made strenuous efforts in the last year or so to reduce the level of fixed costs and the directors hope to be able to make a profit in 20X8. The production facilities can produce a maximum of 2000 mannequins per year.

The selling price of a mannequin is £55, with variable costs of production of £25 per unit. In order to be able to make plans for 20X8 the directors would like to know the break-even point in units if (a) fixed costs in 20X8 are £40 000; (b) fixed costs in 20X8 are £50 000.

You are required to:

i) draw two break-even charts, one for each estimate of fixed costs, recording:

- fixed costs
- total costs
- total revenue.

ii) From the charts estimate the break-even point in units and in sales value for Foster Beniform Ltd for 20X8 at each projected level of fixed costs.

iii) Use the break-even formula to calculate the break-even point in units and sales value at each estimated level of fixed costs for Foster Beniform Ltd for 20X8.

14.9 Gropius Maplewood Ltd manufactures a single product that it sells for £150 per unit. Variable costs of each unit are £62, but are expected to rise at the beginning of 20X5 to £63; because of severe competition the company will not be able to pass on this increase in costs to its customers. Fixed costs for 20X5 are expected to be £90 000.

What is the break-even point for 20X5 estimated as (to the nearest whole unit)?

a) 1023 units
b) 1429 units
c) 1452 units
d) 1034 units

14.10 Gimball Grace Ltd manufactures a single model of electric fan heater. Each heater sells for £21. Variable costs of manufacture are £7.50. Fixed costs of the business are estimated at £54 000 for the 20X9 financial year. The net profit of the business in 20X8 was £36 500, and the directors hope to increase that by 10% in 20X9. How many fan heaters will they have to sell to reach their target net profit (to the nearest whole unit)?

a) 6974 units
b) 4000 units
c) 6704 units
d) 7374 units

14.11 Garbage Solutions Ltd makes wheelie bins. In the 20X1 financial year each bin will sell to local authorities for £25, with variable labour costs of £3.20 per bin and variable raw materials costs of £4.20. Fixed costs are budgeted at £178 900. The company's directors have budgeted net profit of £83 150 in 20X1.

What is the company's margin of safety in units (to the nearest whole unit)?

a) 10 165 units
b) 9448 units
c) 5441 units
d) 4724 units

14.12 Hubert and Hix Ltd makes rucksacks. It has developed and patented a highly effective waterproof material and a revolutionary design. These make the company's products very much sought after, and the rucksacks sell at a premium price of £68.50 to camping shops and hiking organizations. Annual sales are 20 000 rucksacks. Variable costs of manufacture are £29.00. The company's current level of fixed costs is £382 420.

Most of the company's sales are within France and the UK, but there has been growing interest in Scandinavia and last financial year export sales to Norway and Sweden accounted for 10% of total sales.

The company has just received an enquiry from a Moroccan hiking organization. The director of the organization, Raoul, tried out one of the company's rucksacks on a recent hiking trip in the Atlas mountains, and is convinced that it is the best rucksack he has ever used. He would like to start supplying the rucksack in Morocco. However, he knows that there will be very few buyers in Morocco at the premium prices charged by retailers in western Europe for the company's products. Raoul suggests that a reasonable price would be £50.00 and that the specification could perhaps be lowered, as the weather conditions are rather better in Morocco than in many parts of Europe. He estimates that annual sales in Morocco would be around 1000 units. Hubert and Hix's production director modifies the design slightly, and estimates that the variable costs of the new design would be £26.30. You are required to advise the directors on whether or not they should accept the order, taking into consideration both financial and non-financial factors.

14.13 Inez & Pilar Fashions Ltd is a fashion manufacturing and wholesale business operating from rented premises. The business is well established and has operated successfully for several years. However, Inez and Pilar, the company's directors, realize that they have reached maximum production capacity in their present building. They have an opportunity to expand into neighbouring premises. This would involve some minor reorganization of production but could be achieved quite easily. Inez and Pilar have worked out that given extra production capacity their sales could increase, at an optimistic estimate, from the existing level of £310 000 per year to as much as £345 000. However, if there is a downturn in the economy the increase might be only £20 000.

Inez and Pilar estimate that variable production costs constitute 30% of sales value. If they take over the neighbouring premises there will be additional fixed costs of £15 000 per year.

You are required to advise Inez and Pilar on whether or not they should expand their production facilities, using calculations to support your arguments.

14.14 Juniper Jefferson Ltd manufactures two models of baby buggy: the deluxe and the super deluxe. There is currently a shortage of the special grade of aluminium required for the buggy frame. This is unlikely to be a long-term problem, but it will affect production over the next three months. The cost and selling price information for each model is as follows:

	Deluxe £	Super-deluxe £
Selling price	150	165
Variable cost of raw materials	38.25	42.50
Aluminium (at £8.50 per kg)		
Other raw materials	12.50	15.00
Variable cost of labour	13.65	15.60

The company has 350 kg of aluminium in stock and expects to be able to buy no more than a further 1000 kg per month for the next three months. You are required to:

i) Calculate the contribution per unit of limiting factor for both models of buggy.

ii) Advise the directors on the production plan they should follow, assuming that:

 a) demand for the deluxe will be 800 units over the next three months, with demand for the super-deluxe at 300 units over the same period; or

 b) demand for the deluxe will be 600 units over the next three months, with demand for the super-deluxe at 400 units over the same period.

Exercises: Answers Available on the Lecturers' Section of the Book's Website

14.15 The directors of Darlene Fabrik are considering whether or not to start up a new production process. The process would use a machine that is no longer required for the purpose for which it was originally bought. It cost £45 000 four years ago, and accumulated depreciation at the decision date was £13 000. Similar machines of the same age can be sold for £38 000. The same model of machine would now cost £50 000 if purchased new.

What is the opportunity cost for input into the decision process?

14.16 A tour operator, Colby Overland, is organizing a coach trip to Russia as one of its new season's forthcoming attractions. Two of the major costs incurred are described as follows:

- Coach costs. Each coach holds up to 40 passengers. The total cost of hiring a coach for the fortnight long trip is £14 000. The company will book only as many coaches as it needs. When the 41st holiday reservation is made, another coach is booked (and a further coach is booked upon receipt of the 81st holiday reservation, and so on). Because of constraints imposed by the limited availability of hotel rooms in Omsk, no more than four coachloads of passengers would be taken on the trip.

- Hotel costs. Each time a holiday reservation is made the company emails the hotel in Omsk to make the extra booking. If no more rooms are available, the hotel refuses the booking and the tour is regarded as full. The hotel cost per passenger is £280.

 i) Using either graph paper or a spreadsheet program graphing facility plot each of these costs onto a separate graph. The number of holiday reservations should be shown on the horizontal (x) axis and cost on the vertical (y) axis.

 ii) Classify each of the costs as one of the following:

 - variable
 - fixed
 - stepped
 - semi-variable.

14.17 For each of the following types of business, list at least two fixed and two variable costs that might typically be incurred:

- milk delivery business
- coffee bar
- stationery manufacturer
- cross-channel ferry operator.

Try not to repeat the same examples of costs for the different businesses.

14.18 Vernon Ltd is a xylophone manufacturer. The direct materials cost of a xylophone is £300; the direct labour process is intensive and costs £450 per xylophone. Both direct materials and direct labour are fully variable. Each xylophone sells for £1500. In August 20X7 the company expects to sell 120 xylophones, and it has budgeted for fixed overheads of £54 000.

    i) What is the company's budgeted contribution for August 20X7?

    ii) What is the company's budgeted net profit for August 20X7?

14.19 Finch Fletcher Ltd manufactures trumpets. Each trumpet sells for £350, and has variable costs of manufacture of £120. The company can produce no more than 1200 in a year. In the year ending 31 March 20X3 the company's directors expect to incur fixed costs of £172 000.

You are required to:

  i) Draw a break-even chart recording:
- fixed costs
- total costs
- total revenue.

  ii) From the chart estimate the break-even point in units and in sales value for Finch Fletcher Ltd for the year ending 31 March 20X3.

  iii) Use the break-even formula to calculate the break-even point in units and in sales value for Finch Fletcher Ltd for the year ending 31 March 20X3.

14.20 Fallon Frodsham Ltd manufactures and installs small prefabricated building structures that are sold to people who want to establish a home office using part of their gardens. Each prefabricated building sells at £13 000, including installation costs. The variable costs of manufacture are £7300 per building. The company's directors have set a sales target of 150 buildings for the 20X6 accounting year.

  i) Using a break-even chart, estimate the maximum level of fixed costs the company can incur in 20X6 without making a loss, on the assumption that the sales target is met.

  ii) Apply the break-even formula to calculate the maximum level of fixed costs.

    Note: This question may require some thought. Known factors are total revenues sales revenue per unit × number of units sold, and total variable costs variable costs per unit × number of units sold). The point on the horizontal (x) axis at which the break-even point is reached is also known (150 units). The line must be drawn from that point upwards to the point where it intersects with the total revenue line.

14.21 Gulf Gadgets Ltd manufactures chess sets. Each chess set sells for £185. Variable costs of manufacture are £78. The company's directors are currently setting the budget for 20X4. Fixed costs are expected to be £65 000. The selling price of a chess set will rise to £187 and the variable costs of manufacture are expected to increase by 10%.

The break-even point for 20X4 is estimated (to the nearest whole unit) at:

a) 607
b) 655
c) 642
d) 596

14.22 Gecko Grimsby sells specialist aquaria. In the 20X2 financial year each aquarium sold for £1320. The variable costs of manufacture were £321 per aquarium and the total fixed costs incurred were £85 750.

If the selling price, variable costs and fixed costs are all expected to increase by 10% in the 20X3 financial year, how many aquaria (to the nearest whole unit) will the company have to sell to make net profits of £50 000?

a) 131
b) 144
c) 136
d) 124

14.23 Gospodin Grimshaw Ltd manufactures hiking boots for sale which it sells principally in Russia and other parts of eastern Europe. Each pair of boots sells for £15. Variable costs are £5.50 per pair. Fixed costs are budgeted at £87 900 for the 20X7 financial year. The company expects to sell 15 000 pairs of boots in 20X7. What is its margin of safety in pounds (to the nearest pound)?

a) £54 597

b) £86 205

c) £138 795

d) £62 520

14.24 Ince Pargeter Ltd manufactures padded carrying cases for laptop computers. The market is currently buoyant, and the company's factory is working to capacity. The company has been offered the opportunity to compete for a contract for 10 000 cases per year at a selling price of £15 per case. This is below the company's usual selling price of £17.25. Variable costs of manufacture would be the same as for existing cases, ie. £5.63. However, in order to be able to take on the contract the company would need to expand its production facilities. For technical reasons it would be impossible to expand production to increase capacity to produce exactly 10 000 additional units. The expansion of facilities would increase capacity to the point where 20 000 additional units could be manufactured. Ince Pargeter's sales director thinks it is possible that he may be able to obtain additional orders that will use up the spare capacity. If production facilities were expanded, fixed costs would rise from £283 000 to an estimated £390 000.

You are required to advise the company on whether or not it should expand its production facilities.

14.25 Jackson Demetrios Ltd manufactures three different types of office desk. Type A has extra drawers, type B has a printer shelf and type C has a moveable footrest.

In the company's present factory, production facilities are limited and there is a restriction on the number of machine hours available. The directors have considered moving to larger premises, but they are unwilling to make the move just at the moment because of fears of a downturn in the office furniture market.

Cost and selling price information for each type of desk is as follows:

	Type A	Type B	Type C
	£	£	£
Selling price per unit	175	160	165
Variable materials costs			
Wood	37	35	35
Plastics	16	15	18
Screws and fixings	2	2	2
Variable labour costs	18	16	16
Machine hours required per unit	2.5 hours	2.0 hours	2.1 hours
Sales demand for 20X5	1 400	1 600	1 550

Machine hours available are 4000 hours during 20X5. You are required to:

i) Advise the directors on the most profitable production plan available to them without further expansion of the premises.

ii) Calculate the overall contribution to fixed costs (to the nearest pound) if your recommended production plan is followed.

15 Capital investment decisions

Aim of the chapter

To understand some of the techniques used in longer-term decision making on capital investment.

Learning outcomes

After reading the chapter and completing the exercises, students should:

- Understand the need for control over capital investment decision making.

- Understand and be able to apply two simple methods of capital investment appraisal: payback and accounting rate of return.

- Understand the time value of money.

- Understand and be able to apply more complex methods of capital investment appraisal: net present value and internal rate of return.

- Understand some of the limitations of capital investment appraisal techniques.

Introduction

The two previous chapters have examined various aspects of decision making relating to pricing and short-term decisions about production, undertaking contracts, and so on. This chapter continues the decision-making theme by examining the methods and techniques used by businesses to decide on longer-term investment decisions. Managers are frequently called upon to make important decisions, often involving large sums, about expenditure on capital items. Capital expenditure involves investment in items such as tangible non-current assets, investment in other businesses, and the acquisition of holdings in the form of financial instruments that will be held for the longer term. Capital expenditure decisions involve the appraisal of profits and cash flows that will be generated into the future, usually over a relatively long time period.

This chapter examines a range of techniques used in practice to appraise capital investment projects. The early part of the chapter explains the use of two relatively straightforward techniques: accounting rate of return (ARR) and payback. The chapter then proceeds to consider the issue of the valuation of cash flows that may extend well into the future. The time value of money and the techniques used for estimating it are explained in the context of two more advanced appraisal techniques: **net present value (NPV)** and **internal rate of return (IRR)**. The chapter's concluding sections examine the limitations of these techniques and the problems that arise in applying them.

15.1 CAPITAL INVESTMENT IN CONTEXT

All businesses are likely at some time or other to be involved in decisions about the deployment of resources in longer-term investments. The operations of some businesses are capital intensive in that they require substantial investment in premises and machinery in order to facilitate production of goods. However, even in service industries it is common to find that some level of capital investment is required. Because of the relatively long-term impact of such investments it is important that they should be made in conformity with the strategic objectives of the business. It is part of the role of senior management to ensure that sufficient resources are made available in order to achieve their objectives. They must decide on the amount of capital expenditure that is appropriate and feasible. The process referred to as **capital budgeting** is, according to CIMA's Official Terminology, 'concerned with decision making in respect of the choice of specific investment projects and the total amount of capital expenditure to commit'. Below is an example of how a real business's capital budget is affected by competition in the marketplace.

Example 15.1 (Real-Life)

TESCO'S CAPITAL BUDGET

Example 13.2 in Chapter 13 examined the effects of Aldi and Lidl's effective strategy of increasing market share in the UK. This successful strategy has had significant adverse effects on the other players in the UK grocery market. Tesco's market share remains by far the largest (reported at 28.2% in the 12 weeks to the end of 2016). Pressure to reduce grocery prices and the struggle to maintain market share have had consequences in the form of reductions in Tesco's capital investment programme. An article in 2014* reported that Tesco would be reducing its annual capital spending from £3 billion to £2.5 billion for the three years to 2017. Capital spending by Tesco had peaked at £6.6 billion in 2009. Also, the nature of Tesco's capital spending has changed over time. Rather than opening new stores on out-of-town sites, it has tended recently to concentrate upon smaller city centre stores.

(*Baird, R. (2014) 'Budget rivals force Tesco to think smaller as it cuts its capital spending further for next three years', available at www.thisismoney.co.uk, 26 February.)

15.1.1 Capital Rationing

Because resources are limited, there may be significant levels of competition for funds within organizations. For example, divisions within the organization may have to compete with each other in order to win funding for capital projects. If funds are employed for a particular capital project they cannot, clearly, be used for anything else: each potential use of funds involves an opportunity cost. In conditions of **capital rationing** it is important that management has clear criteria, linked to overall strategic objectives, in order to make the best possible investment decisions. Capital rationing is defined by CIMA as follows: 'Restriction on an entity's ability to invest capital funds, caused by an internal budget ceiling being imposed on such expenditure by management (soft capital rationing), or by external limitations being applied to the company, as when additional borrowed funds cannot be obtained (hard capital rationing).'

In order to ensure that scarce capital resources are deployed as effectively and as efficiently as possible, senior managers should establish their decision-making criteria in advance. Some, although not necessarily all, of these criteria are likely to be expressed in quantitative terms. For example, a firm's board may say to its middle managers that it will consider any potential investment project that is projected to exceed certain cash flow or profitability criteria. The criteria may be set in terms of some of the investment appraisal techniques set out in this chapter: for example '. . .we will consider any project that is budgeted to generate an IRR in excess of 8.5% . . .'.

The next section examines some simple techniques that can be used to appraise potential capital investments.

15.2 SIMPLE APPRAISAL TECHNIQUES

Two techniques will be explained in this section of the chapter: ARR and payback. A single example will be used to explain both these and the more complex techniques later in the chapter. The example contains, necessarily, quite a lot of detail and this is explained first.

Example 15.2

Proctor Hedges manufactures a wide range of gardening equipment. It has recently developed a new design of compost bin. A market research project costing £20 000 was undertaken in which the prototype was demonstrated to a large number of gardeners at show gardens around the country. Results of the market research have been very promising. In addition, the company's marketing director has used his contacts to have the new design prominently featured in a prime time television gardening programme. The programme is due to appear in three months' time, and the company expects to receive a large number of orders very soon afterwards. The directors have decided that they must gear up production to be ready for the anticipated demand for the new product. The principal capital expenditure involved would be the purchase of an advanced plastics moulding machine. The existing factory site has ample spare room for the machine, and no significant additions to fixed costs are anticipated.

The production director has investigated the available machines, and has decided that the choice comes down to two alternatives, Machine A and Machine B. Information about the two machines is as follows:

	Machine A £	Machine B £
Capital outlay	450 000	600 000
Residual value at end of five years	50 000	100 000
Straight-line depreciation per year	80 000	100 000
Machine hours per year	80 000	120 000

Each compost bin takes two machine hours to manufacture; therefore the maximum capacity available is:

Machine A = 40 000 units per year
Machine B = 60 000 units per year.

The sales director estimates that demand will be greatest in the first couple of years. After that, it is likely that sales will tail off, as other new composting products are introduced to the market by competitors. After five years the product will probably have reached the end of its commercial life and will be discontinued. The machine could then be sold for its residual value, or, possibly, be transferred at its carrying amount into some other line of production.

Demand figures are estimated as follows for the five-year production cycle:

Year	Demand
1	60 000
2	48 000
3	42 000
4	25 000
5	25 000

Machine A could not produce sufficient items to meet demand in the first three years. However, the directors decide that they would, nevertheless, like to consider the purchase of Machine A because it requires only three-quarters of the capital outlay of Machine B.

The costings prepared by the finance director show that compost bins produced by Machine A would be expected to make a profit per unit (before depreciation) of £4.00. Machine B is a more efficient user of raw materials and so would be expected to make a profit per unit (before depreciation) of £4.10.

ESTABLISHING RELEVANT INFORMATION FOR THE APPRAISAL

Relevant revenue and expenses

The criteria for determining relevant revenue and expenses that were explained in Chapter 14 are also applicable in the context of long-term decision making. Even in a simple example like the one given, there is a great deal of information. Note that the cost of the market research project (£20 000) is not relevant to the decision. This may seem odd at first sight: why should it not be taken into consideration? Remember that past costs cannot be relevant for information made now, because they have already been incurred. The cost of the market research project is regarded for decision-making purposes as a sunk cost.

The directors must take into account only those costs and revenues that are relevant to the decision between the machines. Any costs or revenues that would have occurred in any case are irrelevant to the project appraisal. In real life, taxation is often a significant consideration, especially in private sector organizations. In this chapter we will ignore the effects of taxation, as being outside the scope of the book; however, in any subsequent study of this topic, or indeed in appraising projects in real life, tax will be an important element of the calculations.

Timing

There are widely accepted conventions in respect of timing for capital investment appraisal. The first event that would take place is the outflow of cash involved in acquiring the machine. Capital investment appraisal techniques make the assumption that the cash is spent now, immediately, and 'now' is referred to as Time 0. The capital investment would generate costs and revenues in future over a period that is assumed, in this example, to be a five-year period. A further simplifying assumption is conventionally made that all costs and revenues are incurred on the last day of the year, at Time 1, Time 2, Time 3, and so on. These assumptions about timings are necessary in order to keep the calculations manageable, but of course they do introduce further elements of imprecision and estimation into the appraisal calculations.

Assembling information for the appraisal

First, it will be helpful to establish an estimated production and sales schedule for each of the two machines. It is assumed that revenue and expenses approximate to cash flows.

Year	Demand	Machine A production and sales	Machine B production and sales
1	60 000	40 000	60 000
2	48 000	40 000	48 000
3	42 000	40 000	42 000
4	25 000	25 000	25 000
5	25 000	25 000	25 000

Because Machine A has a maximum production capacity of 40 000 units per year, it cannot meet demand. It will produce up to capacity for the first three years (120 000 units as opposed to demand of 150 000). It is assumed that dissatisfied customers will not wait for a compost bin (people are not likely to put their name down on a waiting list for this type of product) and will simply buy another type.

Once we have established sales and production figures, we can estimate profits before depreciation for each of the five years, as follows:

Year	Machine A	Machine B
1	40 000 × £4.00 = £160 000	60 000 × £4.10 = £246 000
2	40 000 × £4.00 = £160 000	48 000 × £4.10 = £196 800
3	40 000 × £4.00 = £160 000	42 000 × £4.10 = £172 200
4	25 000 × £4.00 = £100 000	25 000 × £4.10 = £102 500
5	25 000 × £4.00 = £100 000	25 000 × £4.10 = £102 500
Total profit	**£680 000**	**£820 000**

Before moving on, try self-test question 15.1 which tests understanding of relevant costs for decision making.

Bright and Darke Limited intends to invest in machinery for a new product line. It has a choice of two machines, Machine X costing £3 million, and Machine Y costing £3.5 million. The company has already undertaken a project to research demand for the new product; this cost £100 000 last year. The administration costs of a new production department will be £400 000 per year, whichever machine is bought.

Which of the following statements is correct?

Relevant costs for the decision about which of the two machines to buy include:

a) cost of machine purchase, cost of project to research demand, and administration costs of the new department
b) cost of machine purchase
c) cost of machine purchase and cost of project to research demand
d) cost of machine purchase and administration costs of the new department.

Self-test question 15.1 (answer at the end of the book)

15.2.1 Accounting Rate of Return

The accounting rate of return (ARR) method uses projections of accounting profit to calculate the expected rate of return on capital invested into an asset or project. It is calculated as follows:

$$\frac{\text{Average expected return (accounting profit)}}{\text{Average capital employed}} \times 100 = \text{ARR\%}$$

CALCULATING AVERAGE EXPECTED RETURN (ACCOUNTING PROFIT) Accounting profit, as we have seen earlier in the book, takes depreciation into account. Therefore, we must deduct depreciation from each of the annual profit figures calculated earlier, before calculating the average profit over five years:

Year	Machine A £000	Machine B £000
1	160 − 80 = 80	246 − 100 = 146
2	160 − 80 = 80	196.8 − 100 = 96.8
3	160 − 80 = 80	172.2 − 100 = 72.2
4	100 − 80 = 20	102.5 − 100 = 2.5
5	100 − 80 = 20	102.5 − 100 = 2.5
Total profit	280	320

The average profit per year generated by Machine A is:

$$\frac{280\ 000}{5} = £56\ 000$$

The average profit per year generated by Machine B is:

$$\frac{320\ 000}{5} = £64\ 000$$

CALCULATING AVERAGE CAPITAL EMPLOYED The capital employed figure to be taken into account is the capital employed by the project or investment (not the capital employed by the whole business).

In this particular example, because the straight-line method of depreciation is adopted, the capital investment is assumed to be depleted by the same amount each year (£80 000 for Machine A and £100 000 for Machine B). Therefore, we take initial capital employed (at Time 0) and capital employed by the end of the final year of operation (Time 5) and average the two figures, as follows:

	Machine A	Machine B
Time	**£000**	**£000**
0	450	600
5	50	100
Average	$\dfrac{450 + 50}{2} = £250$	$\dfrac{600 + 100}{2} = £350$

We now have both elements necessary for the calculation (average accounting profit and average capital employed) of ARR.

For Machine A:

$$\text{ARR} = \frac{56\,000}{250\,000} \times 100 = 22.4\%$$

For Machine B:

$$\text{ARR} = \frac{64\,000}{350\,000} \times 100 = 18.3\%$$

The ARR calculation shows Machine A as the better of the two options. Although Machine B is estimated to produce more profit, the average investment is considerably higher. If the directors were only to use this one method of investment appraisal they might very well opt for Machine A. Note, however, that the comparison of ARR ignores the fact that Machine B actually produces a higher absolute profit (£64 000) than that produced by Machine A (£56 000). This is a notable weakness of the ARR technique.

Students may well have spotted the similarity between the calculation of ARR and that of ROCE which was examined in Chapter 9. When calculating ROCE we looked at figures for the business as a whole. Proctor Hedges will, of course, have a ROCE figure for the business as a whole. If ROCE is substantially in excess of the ARR of 22.4% the directors may wish to think again about the whole project. If a project is undertaken that produces an ARR that is lower than ROCE, the ROCE percentage will be reduced overall.

The Proctor Hedges example requires comparison between two investments. However, sometimes only one possible investment is appraised (because the choice is simply between making the investment and not making the investment). In such cases it is common to find ARR being judged against a yardstick or target return percentage. If the proposed investment's ARR is less than the target then the investment may well be rejected.

15.2.2 Payback

Payback is a simple and unsophisticated investment appraisal technique that involves estimating the length of time it will take for cash inflows to cover the initial investment outflow. This can be a useful technique where one of management's principal criteria is the ability of a project to 'pay for itself quickly, so that proceeds can be reinvested in other projects.

Note that payback appraises investments in terms of cash inflows and outflows. Because depreciation is neither an inflow nor an outflow (remember: depreciation is an accounting adjustment) it is not taken into account.

Payback is relatively simple to calculate:

Time	Machine A £000	Machine B £000
Initial outflow		
0	−450	−600
Inflows		
1	+160	+246
2	+160	+196.8
3	+160	+172.2
4	+100	+102.5
5	+100	+102.5
5*	+50	+100

*Note that at the end of year 5 the machine will be sold, or transferred into alternative production at carrying amount. An inflow of the carrying amount is therefore included.

Payback is calculated by taking cumulative cash flows into account, and identifying the point at which the net cumulative cash flow reaches zero. For Machine A:

Time	Cash flow £000	Cumulative cash flow £000
0	−450	−450
1	+160	−290
2	+160	−130
3	+160	+30
4	+100	+130
5	+100 + 50	+280

Cumulative cash flow reaches the zero position some time during year 3. We can estimate a figure for payback expressed in years and months as follows:

Payback = 2 years + (130/160 × 12 months) = 2 years and 10 months
(to the nearest whole month)

For Machine B:

Time	Cash flow £000	Cumulative cash flow £000
0	−600	−600
1	+246	−354
2	+196.8	−157.2
3	+172.2	+15
4	+102.5	+117.5
5	+102.5 + 100	+320

Cumulative cash flow reaches the zero position some time during year 3 (as for Machine A). Estimating a figure for payback expressed in years and months:

Payback = 2 years + (157.2/172.2 × 12 months) = 2 years and 11 months
(to the nearest whole month)

Comparing the payback measures, we can see that Machine A pays back only slightly more quickly than Machine B. Payback, then, is unlikely to play a major part in this particular investment decision.

Payback is a popular method of appraisal in practice, but it has a major limitation in that it concentrates attention on only one important aspect – the ability of an investment to pay back quickly. As we can see from the Proctor Hedges example, cash flows beyond the point of payback are completely ignored. Surely these later cash flows should be taken into account in investment appraisal?

Net present value, which we examine next, does take into account all of the cash flows associated with an investment.

> I dentify and briefly describe a weakness in respect of each of the two appraisal techniques (ARR and payback) explained so far in the chapter.
>
> **Self-test question 15.2** (answer at the end of the book)

15.3 MORE COMPLEX APPRAISAL TECHNIQUES

In order to understand the more complex appraisal techniques, it is first important to gain an appreciation of the factor of time in longer-term investments.

15.3.1 The Time Value of Money

The principle of the time value of money rests on the observation that, because of interest, £1 now is not the same as £1 in a month's time or a year's time, or ten years' time. The effect of interest is illustrated below.

COMPOUNDING A saver puts £100 in the bank on 1 January 20X0. The bank's interest rate is 10% throughout the whole of the year which follows (unrealistically high, but let us keep the example straightforward). Consequently, when the interest is paid on 31 December 20X0 the saver now has £110 in the account. If £110 is kept in the account for the whole of the next year following – 20X1 – and the interest rate remains stable at 10%, by 31 December 20X1 the saver has accumulated:

$$£110 \text{ (at 31 December 20X0)} + \text{Interest for 20X1 } (10\% \times £110) = £121$$

Each year, provided the saver keeps both the original investment and the accumulated interest in the bank, the interest compounds. The amount of interest earned each year gradually increases. The five-year effect, assuming a constant interest rate of 10%, is as follows:

Year	Balance at start of year	Interest for year	Balance at end of year
1	100.00	10.00	110.00
2	110.00	11.00	121.00
3	121.00	12.10	133.10
4	133.10	13.31	146.41
5	146.41	14.64	161.05

So, £1 at Time 0 (the beginning of year 1) is the equivalent of £1.61 at the end of five years.

The compounding effect can be expressed via a formula derived as follows. Using 10% as an example:

$$£1 + (£1 \times 10\%) = £1.10$$

So, the initial sum invested $\times$ (1 + the rate of interest) = amount at the end of year 1. That is:

$$1 \times (1 + i)$$

where i = the interest rate (expressed as a decimal, eg. 0.10 rather than 10%).

What about a formula for year 2? For the total at the end of year 2 we take the amount at the end of year $\times$ (1 + the rate of interest) = amount at the end of year 2. That is:

$$1 \times (1 + i) \times (1 + i)$$

or:

$$1 \times (1 + i)^2$$

Test this out by reference to the example of £100 invested at a rate of 10% per year for two years:

$$£100 \times (1 + 0.10)^2 = £100 \times (1.21) = £1.21$$

The formula for year 3 adds another compounding factor:

$$1 \times (1 + i) \times (1 + i) \times (1 + i)$$

or:

$$1 \times (1 + i)^3$$

And so on. The formula for the compounding factor is expressed as follows:

$$(1 + i)^n$$

where i = the rate of interest and n = the number of years. For each combination of interest rate and number of years, we can work out a compounding factor. For example, what is the compounding factor for £1 invested at a constant rate of 4% over three years? Answer:

$$(1 + 0.04)^3 = (1.04) \times (1.04) \times (1.04) = 1.125$$

So £1 invested at a constant rate of 4% over three years will result in a balance at the end of year 3 of £1.125, rounded to £1.12.

---

1 Write down the formula for £1 invested at a constant rate of 8% for four years and work out the compounding factor.
2 Write down the formula for £1 invested at a constant rate of 7% for five years and work out the compounding factor.
3 Write down the formula for £1 invested at a constant rate of 6% for six years and work out the compounding factor.

Self-test question 15.3 (answer at the end of the book)

DISCOUNTING   In the discussion of compounding above we noted that, at a constant rate of 10%, £1 invested now (at Time 0) is the equivalent of £1.61 by the end of year 5. Conversely, we could say that £1.61 at the end of year 5 is the equivalent of £1 now. In order to have £1.61 at the end of year 5 we would need to invest £1 now. How can this be expressed in a formula?

Discounting formulae are the reciprocals of compounding formulae. So, we noted earlier that, at a constant rate of 10%, the initial sum invested $\times$ (1 + the rate of interest) = amount at the end of year 1. That is:

$$1 \times (1 + i)$$

We can turn this round to discount back from the end of year 1:

$$\text{Amount at the end of the year 1} \times \frac{1}{(1 + i)} = \text{amount of the initial sum invested}$$

Similarly, taking the reciprocal of the year 2 compounding formula:

$$\text{Amount at the end of the year 2} \times \frac{1}{(1 + i)^2} = \text{amount of the initial sum invested}$$

The formula for the discount factor is:

$$\frac{1}{(1 + i)^n}$$

where i = the rate of interest and n is the number of years.

For each combination of interest rate and number of years, we can work out a discounting factor. For example, what is the discounting factor for £1 at the end of year 3, which has been invested since Time 0 at a constant rate of 4%? Answer:

$$\frac{1}{(1 + 0.04)^3} = \frac{1}{(1.04) \times (1.04) \times (1.04)} = 0.88$$

This means that £1 at the end of year 3, which has been invested since Time 0 at a constant rate of 4%, is equivalent to:

$$£1 \times 0.88 = £0.88\text{p at Time 0}$$

To use the accepted terminology: £0.88p is the **present value** of £1 at the end of year 3 at a discount rate of 4%.

A table showing the value of the discount factors at a range of interest rates and time periods is set out in the appendix on the book's companion website.

Self-test question 15.4 (answer at the end of the book)

1 State the formula that shows the present value at Time 0 of £1 at the end of year 3 at a discount rate of 2%. Work out the discounting factor.
2 State the formula that shows the present value at Time 0 of £1 at the end of year 5 at a discount rate of 4%. Work out the discounting factor.
3 State the formula that shows the present value at Time 0 of £1 at the end of year 2 at a discount rate of 9%. Work out the discounting factor.

15.3.2 Net Present Value (NPV)

NPV is a method of investment appraisal that uses the technique of discounting in order to express all future estimated cash flows in the same terms. It takes into account the time value of money and ensures that the appraisal compares like with like. As with accounting rate of return and payback, the same example will be used to demonstrate the technique.

ESTABLISHING A DISCOUNT RATE First of all, though, some additional information is required. In order to recalculate the estimated future cash flows associated with a project, it is necessary to know the applicable rate at which to discount. So far, compounding and discounting have been explained in terms of interest rates. However, the discount rate that is applicable for investment appraisal is likely to be different from the interest rates payable by, for example, high street banks. Suppose that the generally available interest rate for money deposited in a well-known and respectable bank is 2%. In the absence of major political or economic instability, the depositor can be almost entirely sure that the interest will be paid and that the amount of both the original deposit and the interest on it can be withdrawn in the future. A business can therefore make at least a 2% return by placing funds on deposit, and that return is almost risk-free. The shareholders or investors in the business can themselves make 2% by making their own deposits into risk-free investments. If they wish to make a greater return they will have to be prepared to take on more risk. Exposure to risk should, all other things being equal, result in a premium rate of return to the investor. This means that businesses must invest in projects that will yield a better rate of return than that generally available for risk-free investment.

The appropriate discount rate for investment appraisal, therefore, includes a premium for risk. The appropriate rate may not be easy to establish but it will involve consideration of such factors as known interest rates for risky investments, the possibility of monetary inflation in the future, and the perceived riskiness of the business's operations. It may be helpful when determining the appropriate rate to consider the opportunity cost of investing. If there is an alternative use for the funds that will yield, say, 12%, the appropriate discount rate must be at least this rate. The cost of investing funds for a particular business is known as its **cost of capital**.

CALCULATING NPV Returning to the Proctor Hedges example: it will be assumed that the business's directors use a discount rate of 10% for investment appraisal. In order to express all the cash flows in the same terms (ie. in terms of the present value at Time 0 of future pounds of cash flow) we take each anticipated cash flow for each of the machines and calculate present value using the appropriate discount factor.

15.3.3 Machine A

The first cash flow is assumed to arise at Time 0, ie. the original investment of £450 000. Because this is already at Time 0 the effective discount factor is 1:

$$£450\ 000 \times 1 - \text{cash outflow of £450 000 at Time 0}$$

The next cash flow event is at the end of year 1. From the table in the Appendix we can see that the discount factor at 10% for 1 year is 0.909. Applying the discount factor to the year 1 cash flow (remember that all of the cash inflow is assumed to arise at the end of year 1):

$$£160\ 000 \times 0.909 = £145\ 440$$

We continue to discount the cash flows using discount factors that decrease as the cash flow events recede into the future. Setting the figures out neatly in a table:

Time	Cash flow £	Discount factor (from table)	Discounted cash flow £
0	(450 000)	1	(450 000)
1	160 000	0.909	145 440
2	160 000	0.826	132 160
3	160 000	0.751	120 160
4	100 000	0.683	68 300
5	150 000	0.621	93 150
Total			109 210

The total of £109 210 is known as the NPV; it is the total of the cash inflows and outflows associated with the investment (hence 'net'), all discounted and expressed in terms of pounds at Time 0 (hence 'present value').

15.3.4 Machine B

Time	Cash flow £	Discount factor (from table)	Discounted cash flow £
0	(600 000)	1	(600 000)
1	246 000	0.909	223 614
2	196 800	0.826	162 557
3	172 200	0.751	129 322
4	102 500	0.683	70 008
5	202 500	0.621	125 752
Total			111 253

The net present value of the investment in Machine B is estimated at £111 253.

The basic decision rule that is employed in respect of NPV is:

If NPV > 0 accept the project or investment

Or, where there is more than one alternative project or investment:

Accept the project or investment with the larger (largest) NPV

In this case, Machine B produces a slightly larger NPV, and so looks preferable to the investment in Machine A. (Remember that both ARR and payback indicate that Machine A is the better investment!)

RATIO OF CASH INFLOWS TO INITIAL INVESTMENT In deciding between investment projects it can be helpful to look at the relationship between the discounted cash flows generated by a project against the initial outflow of cash.

15.3.5 Machine A

Total positive discounted cash flows generated = NPV + initial investment:

$$= £109\ 210 + £450\ 000 = £559\ 210$$

(If this step seems complicated, just add up all the positive present values of cash flows from years 1 to 5 inclusive – it will give the same answer.) The ratio of the positive cash flows to the initial investment is:

$$\frac{£559\ 210}{450\ 000} = 1.24$$

15.3.6 Machine B

Total positive discounted cash flows generated = NPV + initial investment:

$$= £111\ 253 + £600\ 000 = £711\ 253$$

The ratio of the positive cash flows to the initial investment is:

$$\frac{£711\ 253}{600\ 000} = 1.19$$

Machine A gives the higher ratio. This means that it produces more positive cash inflow relative to the initial investment. Although the NPV of Machine B is, overall, slightly higher, the calculation of this ratio points towards Machine A as a better investment.

15.3.7 Internal Rate of Return (IRR)

The final investment appraisal technique to be examined in this chapter is the IRR. This technique is closely related to the NPV technique that we have just examined. The IRR of an investment or project is the expected yield (expressed as a percentage). IRR is the discount rate, which, applied to expected cash flows, produces an NPV of zero.

This is easier to understand if presented graphically. Using the example of Machine A, we can see that at a discount rate of 10%, a positive NPV of £109 210 results. What happens if we calculate NPV using, say, 12%, 14%, 16%, 18% and 20%? The following NPVs have been calculated at each of these rates:

Interest rate	NPV
	£
10%	109 210
12%	82 790
14%	58 410
16%	35 960
18%	14 990
20%	(4 540)

Note: the workings for NPV at 10% are shown in the previous section of the chapter. The workings for the discount rates 12% to 20% are not shown. Use the tables to obtain the discount factors and calculate the NPV at each discount rate. Make sure that you can confirm the NPV results in the table above. (To save time, use a spreadsheet.)

We can see that, as the discount rate used in the calculation increases, the total NPV of the project decreases to the point where it becomes negative. The internal rate of return lies somewhere between 18% and 20%. Plotting these points onto a graph produces the result shown in Figure 15.1. The points plotted show a gentle curve. The point at which the curved line passes through the x-axis (discount rate %) is the point of IRR. The graph confirms the observation we have already made from the figures: the IRR of Machine A lies just below 20%.

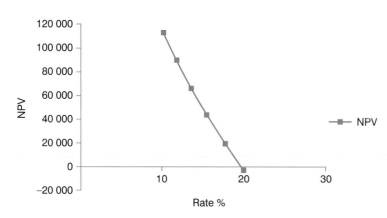

Figure 15.1
Net present value of Machine A cash flows at various discount rates

How can we arrive at a more accurate figure for IRR? There are two principal methods: (a) linear interpolation; and (b) using a computer.

LINEAR INTERPOLATION We take the two figures from the series that are closest to zero:

Using a discount rate of 18% NPV = £14 990.
Using a discount rate of 20% NPV = (£4540).
The total distance between these two figures is £14 990 + 4540 = £19 530.

This total of £19 530 represents the whole range possible between 18% and 20%. Expressed diagrammatically:

The distance between 18% and IRR is:

$$\frac{14\ 990}{19\ 530} \times 2\% = 1.54\%$$

The distance between IRR and 20% is:

$$\frac{4540}{19\ 530} \times 2\% = 0.46\%$$

IRR is 18% + 1.54% = 19.54% + (or alternatively: IRR is 20% − 0.46% = 19.54%, it amounts to the same).

USING A COMPUTER This is so much easier than linear interpolation! IRR can be calculated easily via a spreadsheet program such as Excel.

List the times and cash flows in consecutive descending columns in the spreadsheet and then execute the IRR command. In Excel the command is:

$$CDTX = IRR \ (Range)$$

For the Machine A data, the IRR calculated by the computer is 19.53%. This is slightly different from the result arrived at by linear interpolation; usually there will be a small difference. However, where the estimation of cash flows into the future is so imprecise (and it always is imprecise) there is not much point in getting too concerned about precision in calculating IRR.

MACHINE B We will repeat all of the above steps for Machine B. The following NPVs have been calculated at each of the same discount rates as for Machine A:

Interest rate	NPV £
10%	111 253
12%	79 142
14%	49 093
16%	21 625
18%	(4 083)
20%	(27 989)

We can see that the IRR lies somewhere between 16% and 18%. Plotting these points onto a graph, Figure 15.2 confirms the observation we have already made from the figures: the IRR of Machine B lies about three-quarters of the way between 10% and 20%.

Linear interpolation: Machine B

We take the two figures from the series that are closest to zero:

Using a discount rate of 16% NPV = £21 625
Using a discount rate of 18% NPV = (£4083)

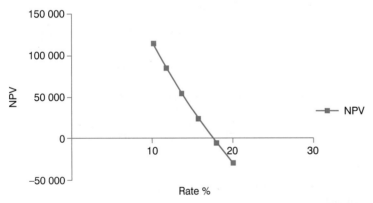

Figure 15.2
Net present value of Machine B cash flows at various discount rates

The total distance between these two figures is £21 625 + £4083 = £25 708.

This total of £25 708 represents the whole range possible between 16% and 18%. Expressed diagrammatically:

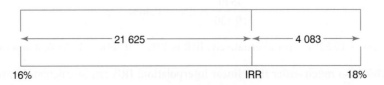

The distance between 16% and IRR is:

$$\frac{21\ 625}{25\ 708} \times 2\% = 1.68\%$$

The distance between IRR and 20% is:

$$\frac{4083}{25\ 708} \times 2\% = 0.32\%$$

IRR is 16% + 1.68% = 17.68% (or alternatively: IRR is 18% − 0.32% = 17.68%, it amounts to the same).
Using a computer: Machine B
For the Machine B data, the IRR calculated by the computer is 17.68%.

SIGNIFICANCE OF IRR FOR DECISION MAKING Where IRR is greater than the business's cost of capital the project is acceptable. If, as in the example, a choice has to be made between two possible projects, the one with the higher IRR is preferable.

In the Proctor Hedges example, the Machine A project produces an IRR of 19.53%, whereas the Machine B project produces an IRR of 17.68%. Both are well in excess of the 10% used by the company and so both projects would be acceptable. However, Machine A produces the better IRR rate, and so is preferable.

15.4 CHOOSING BETWEEN PROJECTS

The application of the four methods of investment appraisal to the example of Proctor Hedges produces the following results:

Method	Machine A result	Machine B result	Choice
ARR	22.4%	18.3%	Machine A
Payback	2 years 10 months	2 years 11 months	Machine A
NPV	£109 210	£111 253	Machine B
IRR	19.54%	17.68%	Machine A

Three out of the four sets of results point towards the choice of Machine A (but note that there is little to choose between them in terms of payback). NPV is the exception but in this case the results for the two machines are very similar.

It would seem that Machine A may be the better choice. However, as with all business decisions, the solution indicated by the figures may not be preferred once other factors are taken into consideration. A key point for consideration by the directors is that Machine A does not have sufficient capacity to meet demand in the first three years or so of the project. This means that a significant part of customer demand will be unfulfilled. Possible consequences include loss of customer goodwill, bad publicity and a knock-on effect on sales of the company's other products.

On the other hand, if demand for the compost bins proves to have been overestimated, Machine A will emerge, with the benefit of hindsight, as a very much better choice. None of the investment appraisal techniques we have examined in the chapter take account of the relative riskiness of the alternatives. This is a weakness that needs to be recognized by decision makers.

Which of the four techniques provides the most reliable results? The strengths and weaknesses of each of them are examined in the following section.

15.5 STRENGTHS AND WEAKNESSES OF THE COMMON INVESTMENT APPRAISAL TECHNIQUES

There are some weaknesses common to all four of the techniques examined. As noted above, the relative risk attached to future cash flows is not taken into account. Also, all of the appraisal techniques are based upon future estimates. As the estimates of cash flow recede into the future they become progressively less reliable. It is possible to accept, for example, that experienced managers are able to make a reliable prediction of the coming year's sales figures, but can they really predict sales figures five years from now with any degree of reliability? The imprecision that inevitably surrounds future figures means that they are open to manipulation by unscrupulous managers.

A further problem about attaching apparently precise values to future predictions is that managers may give the figures more credence than they really merit. The figures can only ever provide a guide to decision making.

The principal strength of all of the techniques described is that they are better than nothing. Managers sometimes make decisions based on 'gut feeling' or 'instinct' or 'experience'. These may not be reliable qualities upon which to base decisions; at least by making some effort to formally appraise projects, managers may be able to avoid making really big mistakes.

In addition to these general points, each of the techniques has its own strengths and weaknesses.

15.5.1 Accounting Rate of Return (ARR)

STRENGTHS

- Calculation of ARR is very straightforward.
- ARR is a widely used measurement (in the form of ROCE); it is easy to compare the ARR of a particular project with the overall ROCE for a business.
- It is a measurement that non-financial managers can readily understand.

WEAKNESSES

- ARR treats all future cash flows as equal in weight; it takes no account of the time value of money.
- ARR is calculated on the basis of accounting profits rather than cash flow. It includes the effect of depreciation, an accounting adjustment the nature and timing of which is determined by management.
- As noted earlier in the chapter, ARR fails to take into account the relative size of competing projects.

15.5.2 Payback

STRENGTHS

- Calculation of payback is very straightforward.
- It can be useful where rapid recovery of funding is a priority.
- It is a measurement that non-financial managers can readily understand.

WEAKNESSES

- Payback treats all future cash flows as equal in weight; it takes no account of the time value of money.
- Where rapid recovery of funding is not a major priority, payback provides little useful information.
- All cash flows beyond the payback point are simply ignored.

15.5.3 Net Present Value (NPV)

STRENGTHS

- NPV builds the time value of money into calculations.
- Unlike payback, NPV takes all of the future projected cash flows into account.
- NPV is very useful for ranking different projects as it deals in absolute values rather than percentages (which, as in the case of ARR, can give unreliable results).

WEAKNESSES

- It can be difficult to explain NPV to non-financial managers.
- There are significant practical difficulties in determining an appropriate discount rate.

15.5.4 Internal Rate of Return (IRR)

STRENGTHS

- IRR builds the time value of money into calculations.

WEAKNESSES

- It can be difficult to explain IRR to non-financial managers.
- Because IRR is expressed in percentage terms it ignores absolute values: 15% return on an investment of £100 000 is fine (£15 000), but not as good in absolute terms as a 12% return on £1 000 000 (£120 000).

- There are significant practical difficulties in determining an appropriate target discount rate.
- It is not always possible to calculate IRR.

The last point perhaps needs explanation. In the Proctor Hedges example, the pattern of cash flow was an initial major outlay of cash, followed by several years of inflows. Where the pattern of cash flows is more irregular (for example, a net inflow in years 1 and 2 followed by a net outflow in year 3, followed by another inflow in year 4) IRR cannot be used.

15.5.5 The Best Technique?

Of the four techniques examined in the chapter, NPV appears to have the fewest significant weaknesses and the most obvious strengths.

Chapter Summary

The focus of this chapter has been on decision making in the longer term. Capital budgeting and capital rationing were explained in order to set the scene for the explanation of appraisal techniques which occupied most of the chapter. Businesses need to have clear criteria upon which to base capital investment decisions, especially where capital is rationed.

Two relatively straightforward techniques are often used: accounting rate of return and payback. After explaining some of the factors involved in establishing relevant information for the appraisal, the chapter turned to an explanation of two relatively simple techniques: the accounting rate of return and payback. There are many significant drawbacks to both of these techniques: for example, they rely upon accounting measurement of profits, they ignore cash flow beyond the end of the payback period, they do not take into account the time value of money, and are economically non-rational. Discounted cash flow techniques, which have become more widely used in recent years, are more sophisticated approaches which do take time value into account. After a brief consideration of the importance of selecting a suitable discount rate, net present value and internal rate of return were explained.

As with other areas of accounting, it is important to appreciate the limitations of the information presented. The strengths and weaknesses of the common appraisal techniques were listed and explained.

Management accountants and managers should of course be alert to the possible misuse and misrepresentation of information used in investment appraisal. Provided that managers thoroughly understand the information, the techniques explained in this chapter can be used to improve the quality of decision making.

Internet Resources

Book's companion website

The website contains the following resources in respect of Chapter 15:

Students' section

A multiple choice quiz containing ten questions
Four additional questions with answers

Lecturers' section

Answers to end-of-chapter exercises 15.10 to 15.17
Five additional questions with answers
Two case studies
Testbank
Instructor's Manual
PowerPoint presentation

Exercises: Answers at the End of the Book

15.1   A business is considering whether or not to invest in a new building. The managers have incurred expenditure of £15 000 on an initial land survey. For capital investment appraisal purposes, what is this expenditure?

a) a fixed cost
b) a relevant cost
c) a sunk cost
d) an estimated cost.

15.2   Mellor & Ribchester Limited, a health drinks company, is considering whether or not to invest in a project to develop and sell a new range of fruit teas. Initial expenditure on a range of development expenses will be £150 000 at Time 0 to get the project up and running. Sales of the products will start in year 2, and it is anticipated that annual net cash inflows will be as follows:

	£
Year 2	68 000
Year 3	71 000
Year 4	54 000
Year 5	28 000
Year 6	10 000

Demand for the product is expected to decline after year 6 to the point where it will not be worth continuing production. The £150 000 of initial expenditure is treated as a non-current asset, to be depreciated on a straight-line basis over six years, with an assumption of nil residual value at the end of six years.

i) Calculate ARR for the project.
ii) Calculate the payback period for the project.

15.3   The compounding factor for an investment over four years at 3% per year is (to three decimal places):

a) 0.888
b) 1.093
c) 0.915
d) 1.126

15.4   At the end of year 4, £312 invested now at an annual rate of 6% interest over four years will be worth (to the nearest £):

a) £394
b) £387
c) £372
d) £418

15.5 The discounting factor for an investment over three years at 10% is (to three decimal places):

a) 0.700
b) 0.751
c) 0.100
d) 1.093

15.6 Assuming a constant discount rate of 12%, the present value of £1300 receivable at the end of year 5 is (to the nearest pound):

a) £563

b) £520

c) £2293

d) £737

15.7 Naylor Coulthard Limited is considering investing in a major advertising promotion of one of its skincare products. The advertising campaign would cost £250 000, all of which is assumed to be spent at Time 0. The effectiveness of the advertising would be short-lived; it would produce incremental cash inflows only in years 1 and 2. The year 1 net cash inflow is estimated at £196 000. The net cash inflow for year 2 is estimated at £168 000. After the end of year 2 another major advertising campaign would probably be needed to produce further incremental revenues.

The company's cost of capital is 9%. What is the NPV of the advertising promotion project? Does the NPV suggest that the project should be accepted or rejected?

15.8 A company estimates the following net cash inflows and outflows for a capital investment project that is currently under consideration:

Time	£000
0	(680 000)
1	180 000
2	200 000
3	240 000
4	350 000

The company's cost of capital is 12%.

i) Calculate the NPV of the project.

ii) Calculate the IRR of the project.

15.9 Outhwaite Benson Limited runs a chain of hairdressing salons. The company's directors, Linda Outhwaite and David Benson, are considering a proposal to add sunbed facilities to their salons. They have surveyed staff and customers and have found that 55% of their existing customers would consider using the facilities. On the basis of this finding they have constructed a set of costings and revenue projections. The sunbeds would cost £180 000 in total to buy and install; they would have an estimated useful life of five years after which they could be sold for £15 000 in total. Linda and David estimate that the net cash inflow arising each year from the sale of time on the sunbeds would be £46 000.

The £180 000 will be lent to the company by the two directors; it is the proceeds of sale of their second home in Italy. If the money is not put into the sunbed project it would be invested in the opening of a new salon. The average yield from a salon is 14% per year, and the directors decide to use this as the cost of capital in appraising the proposed sunbed investment.

i) Calculate the NPV of the sunbed investment project.

ii) Calculate the IRR of the sunbed investment project.

iii) Advise the directors on whether or not they should make the investment, considering any other relevant factors that might have a bearing on the decision.

Exercises: Answers Available on the Lecturers' Section of the Book's Website

15.10 Montfort Spelling plc operates a chain of health clubs. Each year the company opens a club in a new location. For 20X7, the company is examining two possible locations: Broughton Town and Carey City. The directors have collected information about costs and local demographics, and have come up with the following summary of the initial investment required, and cash flows for the subsequent five years. The company's normal policy is to completely refurbish its clubs every five years; it remodels and redecorates the clubs and sells off all the old equipment.

Initial outlay includes the cost of taking out a five-year lease on premises, buying in all the equipment and paying architects and builders to remodel the premises. The net cash inflows from years 1 to 5 include estimated takings in annual subscriptions and joining fees, less the costs of employing staff, and various other fixed costs of running the club.

The table below summarizes the cashflows for the two locations:

	Broughton Town £000	Carey City £000
Time 0: initial investment	(630)	(540)
Time 1: net cash inflows	250	242
Time 2: net cash inflows	275	250
Time 3: net cash inflows	280	260
Time 4: net cash inflows	295	270
Time 5: net cash inflows	310	280
Time 5: inflow from sales of equipment	35	30

The initial capital expenditure less the anticipated residual values is to be depreciated on a straight-line basis, in accordance with the company's policy, over five years.

i)   Calculate ARR for each project.
ii) Calculate the payback period for each project.
iii) Advise the directors of Montfort Spelling as to which location should be preferred.

15.11 What is the compounding factor for an investment over six years at 8% per year (to three decimal places)?

a) 1.587
b) 0.627
c) 1.595
d) 0.630

15.12 What will £1900 invested now at an annual rate of 17% interest over six years be worth (to the nearest pound) at the end of year 6?

a) 838
b) £741
c) £4874
d) £2223

15.13 What is the discounting factor for an investment over five years at 19%?

a) 0.419
b) 0.190
c) 0.950
d) 0.810

15.14 Assuming a constant discount rate of 14%, what is the present value of £85 000 receivable at the end of year 4 (to the nearest pound)?

a) £50 320
b) £47 600
c) £49 045
d) £73 100

15.15 Nuria Collezione Limited is a fashion clothing company. Nuria, the chief executive, regularly attends major fashion events in order to spot trends in the market. She has recently returned from a show that featured fake fur waistcoats and she thinks these could be next season's big fashion story. Unfortunately, fake fur tends to clog up the production machinery used in the company's factory, and it will be necessary to make an additional investment of £28 000 in new cutting and sewing machinery. Nuria thinks it quite likely that sales of 6000 waistcoats are achievable in the first year, and possibly up to 2000 in the second year. Her knowledge of fashion trends tells her that after that point the waistcoats will probably be unsaleable except at very heavy discounts. The first 5000 waistcoats will almost certainly sell at full price, and should produce a net cash flow of £4 each. The final 3000 of production may have to be sold at a discount and it is safest to assume that net cash flow will be only £3 per waistcoat. The machinery will be saleable at the end of the second year for around £10 000.

i) Assuming that the company's cost of capital is 13%, what is the NPV of the project?
ii) If Nuria's initial projections were wrong, and only 5000 of the waistcoats could be sold, all in the first year and producing net cash flow of £4 each, what would be the NPV of the project? Assume in this case that the machinery is saleable at the end of the first year for £13 000.

15.16 A company estimates the following net cash inflows and outflows for a capital investment project that is currently under consideration:

Time	£000
0	(1 650 000)
1	480 000
2	450 000
3	390 000
4	360 000
5	450 000

The company's cost of capital is 8%.

i) Calculate the NPV of the project.
ii) Calculate the IRR of the project.

15.17 Oppenheim Orgreave Limited sells sofas, armchairs and other furniture items from its premises in a retail park. Customers often ask for home delivery to be arranged, and the company has contracted out the service to a series of small delivery firms. The delivery services are of inconsistent quality; customers often ring Oppenheim's to complain that the delivery was late, or that the goods were damaged in transit. Oppenheim's directors have decided that the delivery problem must be properly addressed because the company is losing sales and acquiring a reputation for unreliability. The company's finance director has examined three options:

- Option 1. Buy three new delivery vehicles and employ full-time drivers. The initial outlay for the vehicles would be £76 000, and the annual incremental costs of employment, fuel and other motor expenses would be £82 000. At the end of their five-year useful life the vehicles could be sold for £9000.
- Option 2. Contract the service out to a single, high quality provider who would take on full responsibility for van purchase, maintenance and other costs, including the employment of drivers. Quotations for the service have been obtained; a good quality service can be purchased under a five-year contract for £105 000 per year.
- Option 3. Lease the three vehicles required for the service at a cost of £10 000 per year per vehicle for a term of five years. Fuel and other running costs, and the costs of employing three drivers, would be incurred direct under this option at a total cost of £77 000 per year.

The finance director estimates that an improved service would boost sales. Incremental sales of £113 000 per year would be made under all three options. Oppenheim's cost of capital is 12%.

i) Calculate the NPV for each option.
ii) Advise the directors on the most appropriate course of action, taking into account any other relevant factors.

16 Budgets

Aim of the chapter

To understand the reasons for, and the processes involved in, setting a budget for a business organization, and to be able to prepare and evaluate budget statements.

Learning outcomes

After reading the chapter and completing the exercises, students should:

- Understand the role of budgeting in business organizations.

- Know about the stages involved in setting a budget.

- Be able to prepare straightforward budget statements.

- Understand the issues involved in evaluating actual outcomes against budget plans.

- Be able to discuss some of the behavioural and other issues involved in budgeting.

Introduction

A **budget** is a plan, expressed in financial and/or more general quantitative terms, which extends forwards for a period into the future. Budgets are widely used in organizations of all types and sizes for planning, controlling and evaluating outcomes.

The three chapters preceding this one were principally concerned with assessing alternative courses of action and then making a decision. Once the decision is made, the following activities are undertaken:

- Planning: management formulates plans to help carry out the action using relevant information such as forecasts.
- Control: having set the plans in motion, managers then need to control activities in order to ensure that the plan is followed: this involves management information such as short-term monitoring reports.
- Evaluation: managers then need to assess the extent to which the plans have succeeded and the business objectives have been met. This involves performance reports, comparisons with forecasts and plans and explanations of variations between planned and actual outcomes. It may be necessary to redefine objectives and plans on the basis of actual outcomes.

This chapter proceeds as follows: first the relationship between strategic, longer-range, planning and short-term budgets is explored, using an example as an illustration of the type of thinking and processes involved in turning strategic plans into feasible short-term budgets. The different possible approaches to budgeting are then discussed, followed by an example that illustrates the stages that are likely to be involved in setting a budget in a manufacturing business. The chapter then proceeds to examine, using a detailed numerical example, the work involved in setting a budget. This is followed by a consideration of some of the issues involved in monitoring outcomes. Finally, the chapter examines the benefits and drawbacks of budgeting with particular reference to behavioural issues.

16.1 THE RELATIONSHIP BETWEEN STRATEGY AND BUDGET SETTING

In order to be able to meet the key objectives of their business, managers need to determine the appropriate long-term strategies to adopt. Some organizations formulate a strategic plan that reaches forwards into the future over a period of, say, three to five years. Using the strategic plan as a framework, managers will then set budgets, most probably on an annual basis. The rest of this section of the chapter uses an example to illustrate what might be involved in such a process.

Budgeting is not a simple process. But if the business sets its strategic objectives sensibly, the budget, to some extent, emerges naturally from higher level management decisions.

Example 16.1

Calder Calloway Cards Ltd, a greetings card manufacturer, was established several years ago by two brothers who continue to hold the majority of the shares in the company. The company has grown steadily, but its management information systems have remained rudimentary, mostly because of resistance from one of the founders who has been Managing Director (MD) throughout the company's life.

Following pressure from junior managers and the company's two non-executive directors the MD has finally become convinced, during the 20X2 financial year, that a more formal planning and management control process is required. The directors have met several times with a view to deciding upon a set of strategic objectives for the business. They have also decided to recruit a management accountant to help in the formal process of budget setting and evaluation.

The directors determine the following key strategic objectives:

- To grow the company to the point where it is a credible competitor with the largest producers in the greetings card market.
- To produce cards of high quality with a distinctive company design identity.

Out of these two key objectives a long-term plan develops. The directors decide that the plan should cover the next five years. It is a written document that identifies the strategy for achieving the key objectives. An extract from it includes the following principal actions (together with more detailed actions for achieving the key action):

- Increase sales by at least 30% per annum
  - recruit new members of the sales team
  - encourage and motivate by use of commission and reward schemes
  - identify new sales outlets.

- Reduce unit costs and increase gross profitability to 45% within five years
  - improve and expand production facilities by investment in the latest printing machinery
  - implement a system of capital expenditure control and evaluation
  - improve production logistics.

- Improve, and keep improving, the quality of the product
  - recruit quality supervisor
  - improve supervision
  - implement a Total Quality Management system to motivate all staff.

- Create a distinctive design identity for the company's products
  - recruit a design team under the strong leadership of a design director who will be a full member of the board of directors
  - identify and recruit staff at an appropriate level and remuneration
  - identify key elements of design policy in conjunction with design director.

Some of the points are likely to be acted upon within the next 12 months; others will produce action over the longer term.

The directors, working together with the new management accountant, will produce a budget for the next 12 months. This will identify financial and other quantitative measurements that represent the changes proposed. The immediate financial implications of the plan will be recognized in the budget. For example:

- Personnel budget: it seems likely that recruitment of the design team will take place within the next 12 months. Costs of recruitment and of the new salaries will be included in the budget. Consequential savings (for example, in respect of the payments made to freelance card designers) will also be estimated and taken into account. The personnel budget will be expressed both in terms of numbers of staff and financial costs.
- Capital expenditure budget: a detailed budget taking account of the effects of likely short-term decisions will be required. For example, if the production director decides that a printing machine should be scrapped and should be replaced during the year with a new machine costing around £20 000, the decision has an impact on production speed and quality, volume of production, cash (£20 000 has to be found) and depreciation.
- Sales budget: if the company aims to increase sales by at least 30% the budget should reflect this aim. The planned increase involves extra costs (for example, in recruiting additional staff, in creating and implementing a commission scheme and in planning a campaign to expand into new sales outlets).

All of these implications (and more) must be reflected in the budget for the following financial year.

16.2 PRINCIPAL TYPES OF BUDGET

Budgets are often prepared for a budget period of one year, coinciding with the business's annual reporting period. However, the budget period can extend over a shorter or even, occasionally, a longer period. The annual budget is usually further split into shorter periods of quarters, months, four-week periods, or even single weeks.

Some organizations use a system of rolling budgets. The budget is initially prepared for a period, probably of one year. With each month that elapses, another month is added on to the end of the budget so that at any given point in time, there is a full 12-month budget ahead. For example, a company sets a budget for the 12 months between 1 September 20X2 and 31 August 20X3. At the end of September 20X2 another month (September 20X3) is added. And so on.

16.2.1 Approaches to Budgeting

It is common to find organizations using an incremental approach to budgeting. Incremental budgets involve the establishment of a new budget using a previous budget as a base upon which to work. So, for example, in setting a new budget a business might simply increase all expenditure headings by 5% in line with the general rate of inflation in the economy. This approach is simple and cuts down on the amount of time spent on the budgeting process.

However, it may have disadvantages, too:

- Where a uniform level of increment is made across many budget headings, as in the example given, it may be less applicable to some than to others. A 5% general increase might be quite appropriate in some areas but other types of expenditure may be subject to greater or less than average inflation. Some departments or activities might be disadvantaged by such a broad and general approach.
- An incremental approach continued over more than one budget period can result in some parts of the budget being seriously out of kilter with real world conditions.
- This approach involves very little scrutiny of the budget, and may result in inefficiencies being perpetuated over several years.

By contrast, **zero-based budgeting (ZBB)** ignores any previous budgets and requires that budgetary allocations must be justified by managers. So, for example, if a manager has had a budget allocation for business travel and entertaining expenses in the past, an incremental approach would simply reallocate the expense, with possibly an additional increment to take account of inflation. A ZBB approach, on the other hand, would require the manager to justify an allocation. ZBB has the significant benefit of requiring managers to think carefully about expenditure, but of course there are some drawbacks too:

- The process of justifying expenditure is likely to take up the resource of managerial time, and there is an opportunity cost attached to that time. It could be argued that managers could more usefully employ their time elsewhere.
- ZBB can produce adverse reactions from managers who view the process as a threat to their authority or status.

There is no reason, of course, why some combination of the two approaches could not be used – perhaps a thorough budget overhaul every two or three years from a ZBB perspective, with a less challenging and time-consuming approach being adopted in the interim.

ZBB was first adopted in the USA and was widely used during the 1970s. However, it has not been much used outside the USA and, generally, its importance has diminished.

16.3 THE BUDGET PROCESS

The starting point for budgets in most commercial organizations is the sales budget, because sales volume is usually the principal factor that determines the scale of the business's activities. In a manufacturing organization the production, direct materials, direct labour and production overheads budget are directly dependent upon projected sales volumes and inventory levels. Budgets are also likely to be required for research and development, administration expenses, capital expenditure and marketing and advertising. Figure 16.1 sets out some of the principal budgets that are likely to be required in a manufacturing business.

The diagram presents the sales budget in the centre at the top, signifying its importance to all other budgets. The sales budget links in directly to the production budget which, in turn, drives budgets for raw materials, direct labour and production overheads. The link with other costs is a little more tenuous, as denoted by the broken lines. However, all of these costs are related to some extent to the general volume of activity generated by the business. All functional areas may have capital expenditure requirements: a capital budget is shown separately below. Finally, all of the budget information (sales, production, expenses and capital expenditure) is brought together in the form of three principal budget statements: budget statement of cash flows, statement of profit or loss and statement of financial position.

16.3.1 Who Sets the Budget?

The principle underlying much of the budgeting that takes place in commercial organizations is that of **responsibility accounting**. Managers are held to be answerable for the performance against budget of the areas and functions for which they are responsible. Broadly, two approaches to budget setting can be taken: the budget can be imposed from above, or a more participative approach can be taken in which managers are involved in the budget setting process at a detailed level. There are advantages and drawbacks to both approaches.

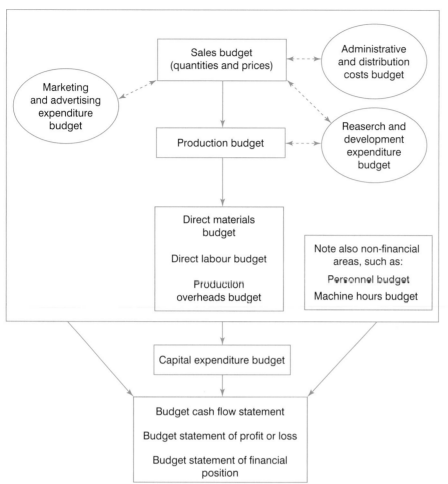

Figure 16.1
**Principal budget areas
within a manufacturing
business**

16.3.2 Imposition of Budgets

The process of imposing budgets from above is likely to be less time consuming than a more participative approach. Senior managers are able to impose their view of the best way to achieve the organization's objectives and they do not have to spend time on detailed consultation with lower levels of management. Junior managers may prefer this approach because it saves their own time, and also gives them a validated target to work for. If bonus levels are directly linked with managerial performance against budget it is probably preferable from the organization's perspective to have the budget imposed from above – where budgets are participative, there is a risk that managers can set themselves targets that are too easy to achieve. But the key drawback of an imposed budget is that it can create resentment if it is felt to be unachievable or if it fails to take into consideration real-world complexities.

16.3.3 Participative Approach

If junior managers and staff are invited to participate in the budget-setting process they are more likely to feel that they have 'ownership' of the budget, and to work towards meeting it. Also, they may have a more realistic awareness than senior managers of relevant constraints and limitations. But there are some potential drawbacks: junior managers may be motivated to keep their budget targets manageable, especially if their bonus payments are dependent upon meeting targets. A further problem is that participative processes take time, and the budget process may absorb too much managerial attention at the expense of other activities. This is especially likely to be the case where managerial status is perceived as depending upon the resources controlled.

To be successful, a participative budgeting process must be genuine. Sometimes, especially in large bureaucratic organizations, the process is one of pseudo-participation. Staff are apparently encouraged by senior managers to participate in decisions about the budget, but the process is a sham: all the real, important, decisions will be taken at a senior level. Pseudo-participation fools no one and serves only to antagonize staff.

16.3.4 Stages Involved in Setting a Budget

The principal stages that are typically involved in setting the budget will be illustrated by means of an example. Example 16.2 is set in a complex manufacturing environment that is organized into departments. It illustrates the participative style of budgeting where departments are asked to propose their own budgets.

Example 16.2

Arbel Limited manufactures and sells cosmetics and skincare products. It operates in a competitive market with a culture of constant scientific development. Arbel's strategic objective is to improve market share by the development of better products, innovating more quickly and effectively than the competition. Each year the research and development department finds new ways of improving products (for example, by changing the feel and consistency of a skin makeup).

STAGE 1: DISCUSSING THE SALES BUDGET

As is the case for most commercial organizations, the most significant constraint on Arbel's activities is the level of sales. Therefore, the budget process starts here.

In June 20X2 work starts on setting the budget for the accounting year that runs from 1 March 20X3 to 28 February 20X4. The directors meet to talk about the sales budget. Their discussion is influenced by the fact that a newly improved face cream has recently been introduced by a competitor. Arbel has responded to this by changing the advertising and packaging of their equivalent product, emphasizing the scientific soundness of the formula. The directors feel that the advertising is likely to prove effective, and they are optimistic about the sales projections for the coming year. They agree that the budget volume of sales (ie. number of items sold in the various categories of product) should increase by an average of 5%, and that prices can be increased by 3%. They are aware, however, that their competitors are working on anti-ageing products for both men and women; in order to keep up with the market Arbel is going to have to increase its research and development activities.

STAGE 2: THE PRODUCTION BUDGET

The next stage is that the detailed analysis of the sales budget is used to project production requirements. If sales volumes are expected to increase by 5% a corresponding increase in production will be required. But other factors can influence the production budget; for example, if a special product promotion is planned, linked to an advertising campaign, it will be necessary to plan for additional production. The optimum levels of inventory must be determined, and this decision may well impact on production targets.

STAGE 3: COMMUNICATION OF BUDGET GUIDELINES

At this point it is probably appropriate to broaden the scope of the budget process. The directors have made the strategic decisions relating to objectives and they have decided upon the broad general approach to be taken in the next following year's budget (eg. an increase of 5% in sales volume, some price increases, and so on). Budgeting guidelines will then be communicated to the various departments around the company.

STAGE 4: SUBMISSION OF DEPARTMENTAL BUDGETS

Individual departments or divisions can now be asked to submit their budgets for approval. These should be prepared in accordance with the corporate objectives, and so it is important that Arbel's directors communicate these effectively. The research and development department, for example, is clearly being directed to expand its activities; the head of R&D

will probably revise personnel requirements and may start work on presenting a proposal for an expansion of laboratory facilities. The marketing department may respond to the call for a 5% increase in sales volume by planning additional marketing campaigns.

STAGE 5: APPROVAL OF BUDGETS

A well-organized budget process will have a range of submission deadlines for parts of the budget. Once the departmental budgets have been submitted they can be coordinated and considered together to judge the extent to which they are reasonable and achievable given the inevitable operational constraints that apply to all businesses. For example, suppose that the head of R&D submits an ambitious budget based upon a planned expansion of numbers of personnel by 30%. He also requests capital expenditure of £1.5 million. These proposals may be quite reasonable in the context of management expectations (or not: the head of R&D might be trying to build up his personal prestige and organizational status). Senior managers will accept, reject or modify such proposals and then return them to the originator. In some processes, budget proposals may be discussed and modified several times before the final budget is agreed.

STAGE 6: AGREEMENT OF BUDGET

Once the budget has been extensively negotiated and discussed, the final agreed version can be drawn up, together with the projected statement of profit or loss, statement of financial position and statement of cash flows (sometimes referred to as the master budget). The budget is then disseminated across the business and then people can get on with the business of implementing it. If the process has been genuinely participative and a feeling of 'ownership' has been achieved, the budget may prove to be a very useful coordinating and motivating tool.

The process described above mainly describes the planning aspect of budgeting. Control is principally achieved by close monitoring of actual outcomes against budget. Monitoring is discussed later in the chapter.

16.4 SETTING THE BUDGET: A PRACTICAL EXAMPLE

This section of the chapter examines the mechanics of budget setting using a simple illustrative example based on a company that manufactures one product only. The budget period is reduced from the more usual 12 months to six months. Even though the setting is deliberately simplified the example produces many interlinked numbers. It works from the initial sales budget through to the production of master budget statements.

Example 16.3

Macey Nelson Limited manufactures a single product: kitchen blenders. The company is in the process of preparing a budget for the six months ending 30 June 20X8. The statement of financial position at 31 December 20X7 is as follows:

	£	£
ASSETS		
Non-current assets		
Machinery at cost	96 000	
Less: accumulated depreciation	(38 400)	
		57 600
Office fixtures and fittings and computer	15 000	
Less: accumulated depreciation	(3 000)	
		12 000
Current assets		
Inventories: finished goods (200 units)	15 000	
Inventories: raw materials	3 750	

Receivables (December 20X7 sales, all on credit)	40 000	
Cash at bank	8 000	
		66 750
		136 350

EQUITY AND LIABILITIES

Equity

Share capital	20 000	
Retained earnings	93 350	113 350

Current liabilities

Payables for raw materials (one month's purchases)	10 000	
Payables for production overheads (one month's purchases)	9 000	
Payables for administrative expenses (one month's purchases)	4 000	
		23 000
		136 350

At the end of every month the figure for receivables equals the total sales for the month just ended (eg. receivables at the end of December are December's sales). At the end of every month payables equals the total purchases for the month just ended (eg. payables at the end of December are December purchases).

Macey Nelson's selling price and cost structure for one kitchen blender is as follows:

	£
Selling price	100
Raw materials	25
Direct labour	20
Prime cost	45

The business uses full absorption costing based upon the number of units planned for production.

The company's sales director produces a forecast for sales (in units) for the first six months of 20X8 on the basis of discussions he has held with fellow directors and with his sales team. The production director then works out projected production in numbers of units. Projections for sales and production in units, together with opening and closing inventories of finished goods for each month are as follows:

Month	Opening inventories in units	Number of units: sales	Number of units: production	Closing inventories in units
January	200	250	300	250
February	250	280	280	250
March	250	280	330	300
April	300	300	350	350
May	350	300	350	400
June	400	300	350	450
Total		1 710	1 960	

Production in July is estimated at 350 units.

Production is planned in such a way as to build up inventories of finished goods towards the autumn; this is to ensure that the company has sufficient inventory to respond to a potential increase in demand following a major advertising campaign that is planned for the latter half of the year. At the beginning of each month the production director plans to have half of the raw materials in inventory which will be required for the coming month's production schedule. In order to simplify the budgeting exercise it is assumed that there is no work-in-progress at each month-end.

Production overheads forecast for the first six months of 20X8 are:

	£
Factory rental	16 000
Supervisory salaries	12 450
Other direct labour	6 250
Cleaning	3 900
Insurance	2 600
Power	5 800
Depreciation of machinery	4 800
Maintenance	1 000
Canteen costs	2 500
Business rates	2 800
Other factory expenses	700
Total	58 800

Production overheads accumulate evenly over the six-month period.

Monthly administrative costs total £4000, plus £250 of depreciation of office fixtures and fittings and computer. Each month's expenses are paid in the next following month (remember that this does not include depreciation, which is a non-cash adjustment).

No capital expenditure is planned for the six months ending 30 June 20X8 and there will be no disposals of non-current assets.

The requirement is to prepare the following budgets for the first six months of 20X8:

a) raw materials purchases budget
b) budget overhead absorption rate
c) budget statement of profit or loss for each of the six months ending 30 June 20X8 and a summary statement of profit or loss for the six-month period
d) budget statement of financial position at 30 June 20X8
e) budget statement of cash flows for each of the six months ending 30 June 20X8.

A) RAW MATERIALS PURCHASES BUDGET

Each unit of product uses £25 of raw material, and we need to ensure that raw material sufficient for half of each month's production is available in inventories at the beginning of the month. We can work out the opening and closing inventories for each month, the utilization of raw materials in production and hence (by means of a balancing figure) the amount of raw materials purchases each month:

First, opening inventories:

		£
January	Given in statement of financial position at 31 December 20X7	3 750
February	50% × 280 (Feb. production) × £25	3 500
March	50% × 330 (Mar. production) × £25	4 125
April	50% × 350 (Apr. production) × £25	4 375
May	50% × 350 (May production) × £25	4 375
June	50% × 350 (June production) × £25	4 375

Each month's opening inventories are the closing inventories of the previous month. A figure for closing inventories in June is still required. We know that July production is estimated at 350 so the opening inventories for July will need to be 50% × 350 × £25 = £4375 (remember that opening inventories for July are the same as closing inventories for June).

Utilization of raw materials in production:

		£
January	300 units × £25	7 500
February	280 units × £25	7 000
March	330 units × £25	8 250
April	350 units × £25	8 750
May	350 units × £25	8 750
June	350 units × £25	8 750

Bringing all this information together we can calculate the expected level of raw materials purchases.

Opening inventories + Purchases of raw materials − Raw materials used
in production = Closing inventories

This formula contains four pieces of information; we now know three of them so we can calculate the fourth. Purchases of raw materials is the balancing figure, which we can calculate for each month as follows

Closing inventories + Raw materials used in production − Opening inventories

	Opening inventories of raw material	Purchase of raw material (bal. fig.)	Raw materials used in production	Closing inventories of raw materials
	£	£	£	£
January	3 750	7 250	(7 500)	3 500
February	3 500	7 625	(7 000)	4 125
March	4 125	8 500	(8 250)	4 375
April	4 375	8 750	(8 750)	4 375
May	4 375	8 750	(8 750)	4 375
June	4 375	8 750	(8 750)	4 375

b) BUDGET OVERHEAD ABSORPTION RATE

Total production overheads for six months: £58 800
Total number of units to be produced: 1960

Therefore the budget overhead absorption rate per unit is:

$$\frac{£58\ 800}{1960} = £30 \text{ per unit}$$

We now know the total budgeted production cost per unit:

	£
Prime cost	45
Production overhead absorbed	30
Total production cost per unit	75

We need this information in order to calculate the budget statement of profit or loss for each of the six months in the budget period.

c) STATEMENT OF PROFIT OR LOSS

Macey Nelson: Budget statement of profit or loss for each month January–June 20X8

	Jan £	Feb £	Mar £	Apr £	May £	June £
Sales	250 × £100 = 25 000	280 × £100 = 28 000	280 × £100 = 28 000	300 × £100 = 30 000	300 × £100 = 30 000	300 × £100 = 30 000
Cost of sales (= Production cost)	250 × £75 = (18 750)	280 × £75 = (21 000)	280 × £75 = (21 000)	300 × £75 = (22 500)	300 × £75 = (22 500)	300 × £75 = (22 500)
Gross profit	6 250	7 000	7 000	7 500	7 500	7 500
Admin expenses (incl. dep'n)	(4 250)	(4 250)	(4 250)	(4 250)	(4 250)	(4 250)
Net profit	2 000	2 750	2 750	3 250	3 250	3 250

Macey Nelson: Summary budget statement of profit or loss for the six months ending 30 June 20X8

		£
Sales	1710 units @ £100 each	171 000
Cost of sales	1710 units @ £75 each	(128 250)
Gross profit	1710 units @ £25 each	42 750
Admin expenses	6 months × £4250	(25 500)
Net profit		17 250

d) BUDGET STATEMENT OF FINANCIAL POSITION AT 30 JUNE 20X8

Workings are as follows:

1 Non-current assets

	At 31 December 20X7 £	Depreciation – six months to 30 June 20X8 £	At 30 June 20X8 £
Machinery			
Cost	96 000		96 000
Acc. depreciation	(38 400)	(4 800)	(43 200)
Net book value	57 600		52 800
Office equipment			
Cost	15 000		15 000
Acc. depreciation	(3 000)	6 × £250 = £1 500	(4 500)
Net book value	12 000		10 500

2 Inventories

Raw materials closing inventories at 30 June 20X8 has already been worked out – £4375. Finished goods closing inventories in numbers of units at 30 June 20X8 is 450 units. The production cost of each unit is £75, therefore closing stock of finished goods is:

$$£75 × 450 = £33\ 750$$

3 Receivables

Receivables at the end of June 20X8 equal the amount of sales for June: £30 000

4 Retained earnings

Retained earnings at 31 December 20X7	93 350
+ Budget net profit for six months to 30 June 20X8	17 250
	110 600

5 Payables

Payables for raw materials purchases at the end of June 20X8 equal the amount of raw material purchases for June: £8750

Payables for expenses included in production overheads equal the production overheads incurred in June.

Total production overheads for six months:	58 800
Less: depreciation (not a purchased item)	(4 800)
	54 000

$$\frac{£54\ 000}{6} = £9000$$

Payables for administration expenses at the end of June 20X8 equal the administrative expenses incurred in June which will be paid in July 2013: £4000 (excluding depreciation which is not a purchased item).

We do not know the figure for cash at bank (until we have done the cash flow budget which is the next stage), but we know all the other figures in the budgeted statement of financial position at 30 June 20X8.

Macey Nelson: Budgeted statement of financial position at 30 June 20X8

	£	£
ASSETS		
Non-current assets (working 1)		
Machinery at cost	96 000	
Less: accumulated depreciation	(43 200)	52 800
Office fixtures and fittings and computer	15 000	
Less: accumulated depreciation	(4 500)	
		10 500
Current assets		
Inventories: finished goods (working 2)	33 750	
Inventories: raw materials (working 2)	4 375	
Receivables (working 3)	30 000	
Cash at bank (balancing figure)	20 925	
		89 050
		152 350
EQUITY AND LIABILITIES		
Equity		
Share capital	20 000	
Retained earnings (working 4)	110 600	
		130 600

Current liabilities

Payables for raw materials (working 5)	8 750
Payables for production overheads (working 5)	9 000
Payables for administrative expenses (working 5)	4 000
	21 750
	152 350

e) BUDGET STATEMENT OF CASH FLOWS FOR EACH OF THE SIX MONTHS ENDING 30 JUNE 20X8

We have already calculated most of the information we need. However, we still require calculations for payments made in respect of direct labour. Each unit produced requires direct labour valued at £20. Therefore, for each of the six months, payments for direct labour will be made as follows:

Month	Production (units)	Production × £20
January	300	6 000
February	280	5 600
March	330	6 600
April	350	7 000
May	350	7 000
June	350	7 000

	Jan £	Feb £	Mar £	Apr £	May £	June £
Opening balance at bank	8 000	19 000	18 150	18 925	18 425	19 675
Add: sales receipts	40 000	25 000	28 000	28 000	30 000	30 000
Less: payments for raw materials purchases	(10 000)	(7 250)	(7 625)	(8 500)	(8 750)	(8 750)
Less: payments for direct labour	(6 000)	(5 600)	(6 600)	(7 000)	(7 000)	(7 000)
Less: payments for overheads	(9 000)	(9 000)	(9 000)	(9 000)	(9 000)	(9 000)
Less: payments for admin expenses	(4 000)	(4 000)	(4 000)	(4 000)	(4 000)	(4 000)
Closing balance at bank	19 000	18 150	18 925	18 425	19 675	20 925

Notes:

1 Each month we start with the opening balance of cash at bank. On 1 January 20X8 this is the amount of cash at bank in the statement of financial position at 31 December 20X7.

2 We add in sales receipts (which, in this case, are the amount of the sales made in the previous month).

3 We take away payments for direct labour (which are made within the month in which they are incurred so there is no opening or closing creditor balance in respect of this item).

4 We take away payments for overheads and administrative expenses, which, in this case, are the amounts from the previous month.

5 At the end of each month we can calculate a budgeted closing balance at bank. This, in turn, becomes the opening balance of cash at bank in the following month.

DISCUSSION

This has been a very long, complicated example, with lots of calculations. Most students will need to work through this several times before they are completely familiar with the idea of the various budgets and the figures used to illustrate them.

The directors of Wilma Sewing Machines Limited have budgeted sales of 350 sewing machines in January 20X8. Opening inventory of sewing machines at 1 January 20X8 is expected to be 280 units, and the directors are budgeting for a closing inventory level of 310 units at the end of January 20X8. What is the production budget, in units, for January 20X8?

Self-test question 16.1 (answer at the end of the book)

The type of budget calculations shown in Example 16.3 can be done more easily and speedily on a spreadsheet, once a basic model is set up. Use of a spreadsheet facilitates 'what if' type questions, and allows budget setters to consider the effect of changes in assumptions. It is recommended that students set up the information above into a spreadsheet in order to understand the calculations and the way in which the figures work together.

There are some numerical examples of budget setting (none of them are as complicated as the Macey Nelson example) at the end of the chapter. Students can try these examples on paper, using spreadsheets, or, preferably, using both methods in order to gain understanding of the calculations.

16.5 MONITORING OUTCOMES

In order to control operations effectively, budgeting systems should incorporate procedures for monitoring outcomes on a regular and timely basis. It is important that managers build into their work patterns a regular, disciplined routine of monitoring outcomes and taking any necessary action. Provided the information is collected and acted upon quickly, problems can be addressed before they get out of hand. As we have seen earlier in the chapter, building a budget requires a very significant input of resource in the form of managerial time spent and the opportunity cost of such time. This would be largely wasted if managers then failed to complete the process by regular monitoring of outcomes.

It should be noted too, that monitoring itself is a costly process. Business organizations should ensure that procedures do not get out of hand; there is a danger that managers spend too much time looking backwards in order to provide explanations for past events.

To summarize, if monitoring is to be effective, some basic principles should be followed:

1 Frequency: monitoring should be carried out regularly. If the budget is subdivided into months, as is commonly the case, actual data should be collected monthly for comparison with budget.

2 Timeliness: actual data should be collected and reviewed against budget as soon as possible so that effective action can be taken quickly.

3 Understandable reporting: comparisons of budget and actual information should be clearly presented in a summary form that is likely to be read, and that can be understood, where necessary, by non-financial managers.

4 Proper accountability: managers should be held accountable only for those variations between actual and budget that they can control. If managers feel that they are taking the blame for outcomes beyond their control, demotivation and resentment are likely to result. This is particularly important where the managerial reward structure is linked to performance against budget.

16.6 BUDGETING: ITS BENEFITS AND DRAWBACKS

16.6.1 Benefits

The principal benefits of budgeting include the following:

PLANNING AND COORDINATION OF OPERATIONS AND ACTIVITIES Setting a budget concentrates the minds of all the personnel involved on the objectives of the organization and how they might best be achieved. This allows for coordinated, planned actions to take place, and should minimize the number of opportunities for 'off the cuff' decisions that are not necessarily in the best long-term interests of the organization. The effective coordination of activities becomes particularly important in a large organization where individual departments or divisions may not have a sufficiently broad perspective on the overall objectives of the organization.

Decision making at a divisional level may make sense within the context of that individual division but may not be optimal within the context of the business operation as a whole (later in the book Chapter 18 examines some of the problems associated with divisional control and performance).

PROVIDING MOTIVATION If properly handled, the budget process may help to promote a sense of ownership of targets and objectives. Staff may feel motivated to work harder and more effectively in order to achieve strategic and short-term objectives.

CONTROL OF OPERATIONS AND ACTIVITIES Because a budget is (or should be) a carefully thought out plan, it should allow managers to control business activity. If monitoring of actual outcomes against budget is timely and effective, action can be taken quickly in order to correct any aspects of the operations that are not functioning as planned.

BASIS FOR PERFORMANCE EVALUATION A budget can provide a yardstick by which group or individual performance can be judged. For example, each division in a major company may have sales targets set for it. Those divisions that regularly exceed targets can be rewarded by opportunities for new investment, by bonuses for staff, or at least, by not being closed down or sold off. High levels of attainment by individuals can be rewarded on the basis of evaluated budget out-turn.

16.6.2 Drawbacks

The budget process comprises the means of planning and controlling activity within organizations. This means influencing human behaviour, by getting people to maximize their performance in order to achieve organizational objectives. However, in the real world it is by no means a simple matter to influence people to behave in certain ways. Systems do not always work in the ways intended by their designers, and it is not uncommon to find that the desired outcome is not achieved because people do not behave in the predicted fashion. Many of the drawbacks to budgeting relate to behavioural issues and problems.

DEMOTIVATIONAL BUDGETS Although the budgeting process as described earlier in the chapter is often intended to encourage participation and 'ownership', the actual effect may be quite different to that intended. If the intention to encourage participation is not genuine, staff are likely to see through the pretence to the underlying reality. If budgeting is essentially authoritarian and top down in nature, employees are likely to feel resentful and disinclined to work to achieve the budget.

UNREALISTIC TARGETS Sometimes budgets are set in line with realistic expected outcomes, but sometimes senior management may decide to use the budget figure as a motivational tool by setting a target figure in excess of the realistic outcome. This approach may be useful if the target is achievable and if an appropriate reward system is in place. But if the target differs significantly from the most likely achievable outcome it may serve to demotivate: staff, faced with an apparently hopeless task, may simply decide that it is not even worth trying to achieve the target.

BUDGETARY SLACK In a budgeting process that is perceived by participants as hostile and threatening to their own interests, managers and staff may try to protect themselves by building an element of 'slack' into the budget. **Budgetary slack** would result where, for example, sales targets were set at a relatively low level and/or cost targets were set at a relatively high level. The budget thus becomes fairly easy to achieve. If individual managers or groups of managers wish to impress senior management they can exceed budget targets without too much additional effort.

INCREMENTAL BUDGETING In respect of costs, where an incremental budgeting approach is adopted, it is desirable to have as large a budget figure as possible so that the budget will grow from a large base. Unless there are penalties for exceeding cost budgets, managers may deliberately exceed the budget expenditure so as to provide a larger base for the following year's incremental budget calculation.

USE IT OR LOSE IT In many organizations managers feel it necessary to spend every last penny of the budget expenditure allowance, because they know that any unused amount will be taken away from them in future years. Unless the budget is calculated on a rolling basis, this approach can lead to a frenzy of spending towards the end of the budget year. Such spending may well not be congruent with the organization's objectives.

INFLEXIBILITY If the budget setting process is unresponsive to short-term change, its application may lead to undesirable results. In very rigid systems, and where the budget is set a long time in advance, this may mean that managers are unable to respond to unexpected events. Take the example of a business that has decided to substantially increase its sales targets. It achieves an even higher than expected level of growth in the first six months of the budget year, but a knock-on effect is that production is put under pressure. As a result the incidence of faulty products increases sharply. The department that handles complaints from customers is put under pressure. But budgetary restrictions mean that it cannot hire any additional staff in the short-term to deal with complaints. A backlog builds up, goodwill is lost, and customers start to look for an alternative source of supply.

DEPLETION OF ETHICAL STANDARDS In many of the drawbacks mentioned above, the consequence of strictly applied budgetary rules is to encourage staff to behave unethically. In order to protect their positions, they may be tempted to lie, to manipulate or to falsify records. This cannot be in the best long-term interests of the organization, and tends to create a dysfunctional business culture.

COST Last, but by no means least, budgeting is a very expensive exercise. Computers can make the processes of calculation of budgets and their reiteration through several versions easier. However, they cannot cut down the amount of valuable managerial time that is spent on thinking about, discussing and manipulating the budget. The opportunity cost of this application of the resource of time is rarely calculated, but it must often be substantial. Ideally, firms should weigh up the cost of conducting the budget exercise against the benefits to be derived from it, but in a complex world with multiple variables such an exercise is likely to be impossible.

Identify and explain two reasons why business managers might be motivated to build an element of 'budgetary slack' into their departmental budgets.	**Self-test question 16.2** (answer at the end of the book)

16.7 A RADICAL ALTERNATIVE

There are some obvious and fairly major drawbacks to budgeting, as set out in the previous subsection. Some people suggest that the most obvious way to avoid these problems is to take the radical alternative of scrapping the budget altogether. The case of Svenska Handelsbanken is frequently cited in this context: in the late 1970s its management decided to do away with budgeting altogether. It was followed by other major companies, mostly in Scandinavia at first, although the movement away from budgeting has become more widespread.

16.7.1 Beyond Budgeting

Example 16.4 (Real-Life)

In recent years there has been a growing interest in moving away from budgeting in the UK. The 'Beyond Budgeting' organization (www.bbrt.org) has been a leading proponent of change. Its description of what is involved is as follows:

'"Beyond Budgeting" means beyond command-and-control toward a management model that is more empowered and adaptive.

Beyond Budgeting is about rethinking how we manage organizations in a post-industrial world where innovative management models represent the only sustainable competitive advantage. It is also about releasing people from the burdens of stifling bureaucracy and suffocating control systems, trusting them with information and giving them time to think, reflect, share, learn and improve... The word "budgeting" is not used in its narrow sense of planning and control but as a generic term for the traditional command and control model (with the annual budget process at its core)'

A survey of the Beyond Budgeting membership, in which over 80 respondents participated, produced some interesting findings, among them:

- On average respondents work in organizations with six layers of management, although the Svenska Handelsbanken, with over 12 000 employees, manages with only three layers.
- Bureaucratic chores take up a lot of time – on average 27% of management time available. The problem of bureaucracy is more significant in larger organizations where managers are using around one-third of their time in unproductive tasks.
- The budgeting process is deemed the least valuable out of all management processes.
- 'Bureaucratic wrangling' (eg. blame shifting, resource hoarding, internal haggling and organizational power politics) is a major problem.

However, it should be recognized that budgeting continues to be widely used in all types of organization.

Chapter Summary

In many organizations, budgeting is an important activity which assists management in planning and in controlling activities. This chapter explored the relationship between strategic planning, which provides a framework for the business's activities over a period of years, and budgeting, which tends to be concerned with shorter-term planning, usually over a period of 12 months. The budget process involves several different stages, and can be very complex and time-consuming, especially in manufacturing organizations where production planning involves many different variables. The chapter illustrated the process with a simple example set in a manufacturing business, but even a straightforward one-product example involves many calculations. Budgeting is an area that engages a great deal of time and attention in organizations. If it is not carefully controlled it can elicit dysfunctional behaviours from participants, and the potential effects on human behaviour should be carefully weighed up by senior management to ensure that the benefits of the budgetary process outweigh the various costs involved.

Although there are benefits to be gained from effective budgeting, managers should be aware of the long list of detrimental behaviours and other drawbacks as explained in this chapter. Some managers have now become convinced that traditional budgeting is not worth the very considerable effort involved and are moving 'beyond budgeting'.

Internet Resources

Book's companion website

The website contains the following resources in respect of Chapter 16:

Students' section

A multiple choice quiz containing ten questions
Three additional questions with answers.

Lecturers' section

Answers to end-of-chapter exercises 16.9 to 16.16
Five additional questions with answers
Case study
Testbank
Instructor's Manual
PowerPoint presentation

Exercises: Answers at the End of the Book

16.1 You are the newly appointed management accountant of Brewster Fitzpayne Limited, a small manufacturing company. The management accounting information used in the company has previously been at a low level in terms of both quantity and quality. The finance director of the company was himself appointed only a few months ago, and he has decided that, as a priority, the management information system should be improved. He is planning, with your assistance, to install a budgeting system, but he needs to persuade his fellow directors that this innovation will be of benefit to the company. He has asked you to draft a briefing paper to the board setting out the principal benefits of a system of budgetary control.

16.2 Pirozhki Products Limited uses a rolling budget system. The company's directors are currently preparing a sales and production budget for the month of March 20X6, which is just over one year away.

They have decided that sales of their single product should be budgeted at 12 000 units for March 20X6, with 14 800 units budgeted for April 20X6. The company's policy is to hold closing inventory of finished goods at 75% of the next following month's sales level.

What is the production budget in units for March 20X6?

a) 8100
b) 14 100
c) 9900
d) 12 000

16.3 Luminant Productions produces light fittings from a small factory unit. The company's directors have just met to discuss the sales budget and related matters for the next quarter, and have come up with the following figures for projected sales:

	Units
July 20X5	8 600
August 20X5	8 200
September 20X5	9 000

Opening inventory of finished goods at 1 July 20X5 is expected to be 6000 units. The directors feel that they keep too many units in inventory and they intend to reduce it to more reasonable levels over the next few months. They plan to reduce opening inventory by 500 units each month after July 20X5.

Each light fitting unit uses £2 of raw materials. Raw materials inventory at 1 July is estimated to have a value of £2800. The directors wish to increase that inventory level slightly over the next few months, as there is a danger of running out of inventory to transfer to production.

	£
Opening inventory at 1 August should be:	3 000
Opening inventory at 1 September should be:	3 100
Opening inventory at 1 October should be:	3 200

Calculate for each of the three months:
 i) the production budget (in units)
 ii) the raw material purchases budget (in pounds).

16.4 Barfield Primrose is the manufacturer of the renowned 'Primrose' ice cream maker, which retails at £199. Barfield Primrose sells to wholesalers at £145 per unit. The prime cost structure of the ice cream maker is as follows:

	Per unit
Direct materials	37.00
Direct labour	24.00
Prime cost	61.00

For the year ending 31 December 20X9, the finance director of Barfield Primrose estimates that production overheads will be incurred totalling £312 390. He plans to use an overhead recovery rate based upon budgeted machine hours. The budget for machine hours is 17 355 hours for the year, and each unit produced uses up 1.5 machine hours.

Administrative and selling cost budgets have been prepared and the directors have recently decided on the sales forecasts for the coming year. The forecasts for the first three months are as follows:

	Sales forecasts: units	Administrative and selling costs: £
January	620	18 400
February	610	19 250
March	640	18 900

Calculate a budget overhead recovery rate for use by the company during 20X9. Then prepare a budget statement of profit or loss for each of the three months January to March 20X9.

16.5 Reinhart has his own wholesale business selling goods to retailers. His sales are made entirely on credit. In respect of the sales in any given month he expects 75% to be paid for in the next following month, and 25% in the month after that. (So, for example, sales made on credit in March would be paid for in April as 75% and May as 25%.) Budget data relating to four months of Reinhart's sales are as follows:

	£
November 20X1	25 000
December 20X1	26 800
January 20X2	21 000
February 20X2	21 300

Reinhart is preparing his cash flow forecast for the month of February 20X2. How much should he include as sales receipts?

a) £21 000
b) £21 250
c) £22 450
d) £21 225

16.6 Skippy is about to set up in business as a tour operator, after several years of working in the travel industry. He is starting out on a small scale, working from a room in a friend's office. The friend has agreed to let him have the room rent-free for six months in order to get him started.

In his first quarter of operations, January to March 20X5, Skippy plans two tours, both coach trips to Austria. He advertises the trips in November and December 20X4, paying the cost of £3000 out of his own money. He also pays £2000 for a computer. He intends that both of these amounts should constitute his initial capital contribution to the new business. The computer will be depreciated over its estimated useful life of five years on the straight-line basis.

The revenue and cost structure of each trip is as follows:

	£
The trip will cost £530 per person. The coach carries a maximum of 60 people and Skippy expects an 80% load factor – that is, 48 people. So 48 × £530 = sales revenue per trip	25 440
Hotel costs = £42.50 per person per night for seven nights half board	14 280
Coach travel costs	2 600
Insurance bond	1 500

Notes:

- The first trip is planned for 17 February, and the second for 15 March. The sales revenue from the trips will be received in advance – receipts from trip one will be received in January, and from trip two in February.
- The hotel requires a non-returnable deposit of 50% in advance, with the remainder paid at the end of the stay. Advance payments will be made in January for trip one and in February for trip two.
- The coach costs must also be paid in advance: trip one will be paid for in January and trip two in February. The insurance bond for both trips will be paid in January.
- Other costs are: telephone: the bill for an estimated £360 will be paid in March; and sundry office costs: £200 paid in cash each month.

Prepare for Skippy:

i) a budget statement of cash flows for the three months of January, February and March 20X5.

ii) a budget statement of profit or loss for the three months ending 31 March 20X5.

iii) a budget statement of financial position at 31 March 20X5.

16.7 Referring to the information given in exercise 16.6: at the beginning of April 20X5 Skippy reviews the past three months. Bookings on the first coach trip to Austria were not as good as planned: he sold only 42 places on the coach. However, the second trip was very popular with sales of 50 places. The hotel charged Skippy based upon the actual, not the budgeted number of people. Coach and insurance costs remained the same.

Actual office costs were higher than budgeted: in January Skippy paid £230, in February £350 and in March £270. The telephone bill of £455 was paid in March. Prepare a statement of profit or loss for the three months ending 31 March 20X5 showing columns for actual results, budgeted results and the variation between the two. Also prepare an actual statement of financial position at 31 March 20X5 showing an extra column for the budgeted figures. Overall, has Skippy's business performed better or worse than budget?

16.8 Lamar Bristol plc is a large trading organization with retail stores in most major towns and cities in the UK. The key budget factor is sales; the company's main board sets the sales budget by agreeing an annual fixed percentage increment which is applied to all of its retail stores. The increment varies from year to year and is dependent upon the directors' assessment of current economic conditions and competitors' published sales figures. Generally it varies between 2% and 4%.

Discuss the likely effectiveness and efficiency of this method of setting a sales budget, identifying strengths and weaknesses of the approach.

Exercises: Answers Available on the Lecturers' Section of the Book's Website

16.9 It is widely recognized that budget setting can be mishandled in organizations and may result in some undesirable effects that work against an organization's best interests. Write a short report that describes potential problems that may arise if budgeting is not handled properly.

16.10 Hildebrandt St. Martins Limited manufactures a single product. Its budget sales (in units) for December 20X4 are 9350. Opening inventory of finished goods for the month is budgeted at 12 360 units and closing inventory is budgeted at 13 475 units.

Each unit of finished goods inventory uses 2kg of a raw material that is forecast to cost £3 per kilo. Opening inventory of raw material at the beginning of December 20X4 is forecast at 18 000 kilos, but closing inventory for the month should fall to 16 000 kilos.

What is the budget amount in pounds of purchases of this raw material for December 20X4?

a) £56 790
b) £68 790
c) £49 410
d) £55 410

16.11 Colney Brighouse Limited makes office furniture. The company's directors are preparing sales and production forecasts for January, February and March 20X3 Sales forecasts in units for its two principal products, tables and office chairs, are as follows for the relevant months:

	Tables	Chairs
January 20X3	13 000	28 000
February 20X3	15 000	31 000
March 20X3	16 000	35 000
April 20X3	18 000	36 000

Opening inventory at 1 January 20X3 is forecast at 7500 (tables) and 19 000 (chairs). The directors have decided to aim for closing inventory at the end of each month amounting to exactly 50% of the following month's sales requirements. Prepare the production budget for tables and chairs for January to March 20X3 (inclusive).

16.12 Corby Thirlwell Limited manufactures ornamental birdbaths made out of reconstituted stone. The company works on a rolling budget system, and its senior management is currently examining forecasts for the month of June 20X7. June is a big month for sales in the birdbath business, and the directors are optimistically forecasting sales of 3250 units. They intend to launch a sales incentive scheme to encourage the sales staff to sell more birdbaths; from the beginning of 20X7 each birdbath sold will result in a payment of £1.50 to the salesperson. The selling price of each birdbath is £65. The production cost structure of one birdbath is as follows:

Per unit	£
Direct materials	18.00
Direct labour	12.57
Production overhead recovery	13.86
Production cost	44.43

Administrative overheads for June 20X7 are forecast at £12 479, and selling and distribution overheads (excluding the cost of commission) are forecast at £10 220.

i) Identify two advantages of the system of rolling budgeting.

ii) Prepare a budget statement of profit or loss for the month of June 20X7.

16.13 Discuss the advantages and drawbacks of a participative approach to budgeting.

16.14 Roxanne's budgeted year-end accounts at 31 December 20X8 include a figure for receivables of £23 600. This represents:

	£
20% of November sales of £28 000	5 600
60% of December sales of £30 000	18 000
	23 600

This calculation is based upon the normal pattern of receipts for the business: 40% of sales on credit are paid for within the same month, and 40% are paid for in the following month, with the remaining 20% paid for in the month after that.

If January 20X9 sales are budgeted at £28 000, how much will be included for sales receipts in the cash flow forecast in January 20X9?

a) £28 800
b) £23 600
c) £24 000
d) £19 520

16.15 Silas is starting out in business on his own, running a shop selling scuba diving gear. He has gained a lot of free publicity for his new venture by writing articles in specialist trade and enthusiasts' magazines, and he is well known as a leading expert on scuba diving. He is therefore fairly confident that he will be able to start selling in reasonable quantities straight away.

Silas is renting shop premises, and his principal start-up cost has been the cost of equipping the shop with inventory. He has also invested in an electronic till, a computer for keeping track of stock and dealing with correspondence, and some general shop fixtures and fittings. His expenditure just prior to start-up is:

	£
Inventory	42 000
Computer	2 500
Till	1 000
Fixtures and fittings	3 500
Total	49 000

Silas also transfers £6000 from his own bank account into a new business bank account. He has sold his house to finance the new venture and is currently living in the flat above the shop.

In his first year in trading Silas plans the following sales and purchases of inventory:

	Sales	Purchases
	£	£
April	1 500	2 250
May	4 500	3 750
June	8 250	6 750
July	9 000	7 500
August	12 000	7 500
September	12 000	7 500
October	12 000	6 750
November	10 500	6 750
December	12 000	6 375

	Sales	Purchases
	£	£
January	7 500	6 375
February	9 000	5 625
March	10 500	6 000
	108 750	73 125

It is expected that most sales will be for cash, but 25% are planned to be made on credit to scuba diving organizations. Credit sales are expected to be settled in full in the month after invoicing.

Purchases of inventory will be on credit, with payment made in full in the month following purchase. Closing inventory at the end of March is budgeted at £42 045.

Silas has budgeted for the following expenses:

Expense item	£	Payment details
Rent	6 000	Payable in quarterly instalments in April, July, October and January
Insurance	1 200	Payable in April
Telephone	600	Quarterly bills of £150 to be paid in June, September, December and March
Water rates	750	Payable in May
Business rates	1 500	Payable in April
Wages	1 800	£150 to be paid each month
Subscriptions	300	£150 in May and £150 in November
Sundry admin and other expenses	2 400	£200 to be paid each month

Silas plans to draw £1000 from the business in cash each month.

The computer will be subject to depreciation on a straight-line basis over four years. Fixtures and fittings and the electronic till have an estimated useful life of ten years and will be depreciated on a straight-line basis. No residual values are expected at the end of the assets' useful lives.

Prepare the following statements for Silas:

i) budget statement of cash flows showing the cash movement in each of the first 12 months of business.

ii) budget statement of profit or loss for the 12 months ending 31 March.

iii) budget statement of financial position at 31 March.

16.16 Working with the information from question 16.15, put the cash flow information into a spreadsheet. Use the spreadsheet to perform 'what if' calculations to answer Silas's questions as follows:

i) 'What would happen to my estimated cash at bank balance at the end of March if my receivables took two months, instead of one month, to be settled? Would the bank account go overdrawn at any point in the year?'

ii) 'I think I may have underestimated my sundry admin expenses. What would happen to the cash at bank balance at the end of March if my expenses each month were £400 rather than £200?'

iii) 'What would happen to the end of March cash at bank balance if both of these things happened – ie. debtors take two months to pay me, not one, and admin expenses increase to £400 each month? Would I have an overdraft at any point, and if so, what would be the maximum budget overdraft figure?'

17 Accounting for control

Aim of the chapter

To establish a context for the understanding of control in organizations, and to examine in detail one specific approach to accounting control in the form of standard costing, flexible budgeting and variance analysis.

Learning outcomes

After reading the chapter and completing the exercises, students should:

- Know about a classification of control mechanisms in organizations.

- Know about some of the problems of control in firms.

- Understand the use of a standard costing system in a manufacturing environment.

- Be able to compare actual results against flexed budgets.

- Understand and be able to analyze some of the possible reasons for variances that emerge from the comparison of actual with standard costs.

- Understand the pros and cons of standard costing systems.

Introduction

The previous chapter on budgeting referred to the use of budgeting in controlling as well as planning and monitoring business activity. This chapter continues the theme of control by examining a widely used technique: standard costing. Most of the chapter is devoted to an examination of the mechanisms of standard costing, flexible budgeting and variance analysis. Naturally, there are advantages and drawbacks to this particular approach to control, and these are briefly discussed towards the end of the chapter.

17.1 STANDARD COSTING, FLEXIBLE BUDGETING AND VARIANCE ANALYSIS

The previous chapter examined the setting of budgets and the comparison of actual with budgeted results. Often the identification and analysis of the difference between actual and budgeted performance is quite straightforward. For example, suppose that a business budgets to spend £10 500 on business insurance, on the basis that the previous year's charge was £10 000 and the general level of price inflation suggests that 5% would be a likely level of increase. But in fact, the business's insurers, in common with the rest of the insurance industry, raise charges by 10%. The actual bill for insurance totals £11 000, £500 more than was budgeted. Investigation of other insurers shows that it is not possible to obtain cover for less than £11 000.

The **adverse variance** of £500 against budget in this case can be easily explained. It is a general price increase, not attributable to any internal factor such as poor purchasing or failure to control expenditure properly. In this example, it is easy to establish the reasons for the variance against budget. But in a relatively complex manufacturing environment, it can be difficult to track down the reasons for variances unless some quite detailed analysis is carried out.

Example 17.1

S ugden Harkness Limited, a manufacturing business, sets a budget based upon a sales forecast for July of 5000 units. Each unit of product is budgeted to use 3 metres of raw material (15 000 metres in total) at a cost of £4.20 per metre (15 000 × £4.20 = £63 000). The actual business performance statement for July shows that, although exactly 5000 units were sold, the total cost of the raw material element of cost of sales was £68 000.

What has happened here?

Clearly, raw material costs have increased; there is an adverse variance of £68 000 − £63 000 = £5000. The reasons, however, are not clear, unless further analysis is undertaken. It could be that:

- the price has increased to a level higher than the £4.20 budgeted
- the production process has been less efficient than expected and has used more than 3 metres of raw material per unit of product
- both of these factors are present in some combination.

The management accountant of Sugden Harkness needs to be able to analyze the variance in more detail in order to be able to:

- find out if there is a problem that needs attention
- attribute responsibility for the adverse variance to the appropriate department or person.

The process of responsibility accounting ensures that problems are tracked to their source. Having correctly identified the source, it is then the responsibility of management to ensure that problems are dealt with via appropriate corrective action. As we saw in the previous chapter, one of the possible adverse consequences of a budgeting system arises where responsibility is incorrectly attributed, leading to resentment and demotivation. Sometimes, the reason for the occurrence of a problem seems obvious, but further investigation may be required to look beyond the apparently obvious and to uncover true causes and effects.

Taking the example of Sugden Harkness a little further, suppose that the adverse variance were found to be attributable to extra usage of the raw material. This looks, on the face of it, as though it should be the responsibility of the production manager and his team. It may well result from inefficiencies in the use of raw materials (too much wastage, for example). However, the picture changes if we find out that the regular supplier of the raw material had increased prices, and that, in response to the increase, the purchasing manager had purchased inferior quality material but at the budget price. The poorer quality resulted in more wastage as the material was put through the production process. The adverse variance now appears to be attributable to the purchasing manager rather than the production manager.

Despite problems of this type in attributing responsibility for variances, variance identification and analysis are very common procedures in the manufacturing industry. Variances are often identified and quantified by using a **standard costing** system.

17.2 STANDARD COSTING

Standard costing is a system of costing which can be used in business environments where a repetitive series of standardized operations are carried out. In such systems each element of production involves a consistent input of resources at prices that can be predicted with a fair degree of accuracy.

Standard costs are the budgeted costs of individual units of production. The standard cost is compared with actual cost in order to calculate an overall variance. This overall variance can then be broken down further in order to identify:

- the effects of variation in volume of the resource inputs
- the effects of variation in price of the resource inputs.

Standard costing and variance analysis are widely used in industries where mass production is carried out. Managers in such industries are frequently presented with financial reports including information about variances, and it is important even for non-financial managers to understand something about the fundamentals of standard costing systems.

17.2.1 Establishing Standard Costs

Establishing budget information can be a time-consuming and expensive task. Standard costs may also require a substantial investment of time in research and observation. For example, in order to establish standard costs for the direct materials component of a product, it is necessary to examine two aspects:

- the purchase price of the material inputs
- the expected rate at which material is used in the product.

The purchase price may be variable depending upon the supplier used, quantities available, movements on commodities markets, and so on. The standard cost will probably reflect a price which can be obtained with a reasonable amount of effort on the part of those responsible for materials purchasing. If too low a standard price is set purchasers will not have to make much of an effort to better it. On the other hand, if the standard price set would be obtainable only rarely, then purchasers may become demotivated.

Establishing the rate of usage will require careful observation of the manufacturing process, probably on a number of separate occasions. Again, the rate of materials consumption which is adopted as the standard is likely to reflect a realistic achievable target, set neither too low nor too high.

However, standard cost setters need to be wary of relying upon too many established precedents and practices. There may be a need to challenge lax and wasteful production procedures in setting standards.

Each element of cost of production is broken down and costed. Even for an apparently simple product, there may be many different elements of cost. Take a tin of beans, for example. Materials input per batch includes: beans, tomatoes, salt, sugar, flavourings, tins and labels. Each part of the processing involves labour and machine times which must be timed to the second in order to produce accurate costs and forecasts.

For each product a standard cost card is built up, as shown in the comprehensive demonstration example which follows.

Example 17.2

A comprehensive example will illustrate the application of variance identification in a standard costing system. Although the basic facts in the example are straightforward there are several calculations. The whole example takes up several pages, because each step is explained in full. Students should work through it slowly and ensure that each point is understood before moving on. It will seem difficult, if not impossible, at first, but it does all hang together quite logically.

Zamboni & Zeuss Limited manufactures a specialized metal component which is sold to manufacturers of heavy lifting machinery.

The standard cost card for one component is as follows:

	£
Selling price	150.00 per unit
Costs:	
Direct materials	35.00 (7 kg of metal @ £5 per kilo)
Direct labour	15.00 (3 hours @ £5 per kilo)
Prime cost	50.00

The company's budget for January 20X3 is as follows:

	£
Sales: 1000 units @ £150	150 000
Costs:	
Direct materials: 1000 units × (7 kg × £5)	(35 000)
Direct labour: 1000 units × (3 hours × £5)	(15 000)
Production overheads	(50 000)
	50 000
Selling and administrative overheads	(20 000)
Net profit	30 000

The production overheads, as we have seen in previous chapters, are usually absorbed via an overhead absorption rate. For the purposes of this particular demonstration we will assume that the overheads are simply recorded, and also, that they remain at the same level regardless of changes in the level of production, ie. they are **fixed overheads**. Later in the chapter we will examine overhead variances in more detail, but for the moment, we will simplify the overheads aspects of the question.

SIMPLE COMPARISON OF BUDGET WITH ACTUAL RESULTS

After the end of January 20X3, the management accountant identifies the variances between the budget and actual results. Actual results are as follows:

	£
Sales: 1100 units @ £145	159 500
Costs:	
Direct materials: 1100 × (7.5 kg × £4.50)	(37 125)
Direct labour: 1100 units × (2.8 hours × £5.50)	(16 940)
Production overheads	(52 000)
	53 435
Selling and administrative overheads	(21 250)
Net profit	32 185

A very brief comparison of the statements shows us that the company has produced higher profits than expected. Good news, surely? Well, yes, but has the business made as much extra profit as might be expected, given that it has sold an extra 100 components? The answer to the question is not immediately obvious; it requires further analysis of the variances.

FLEXING THE BUDGET

One problem with comparing the two statements shown above is that we are not really comparing like with like. The initial budget was produced on the assumption that 1000 units would be sold. The actual outcome is that 1100 units were sold. In order to make a more useful comparison, we need to adjust the budget to reflect the additional volume of sales. This is known as flexing the budget.

The flexed budget statement of profit or loss (flexed to reflect the actual level of activity of 1100 units sold) is as follows:

	£
Sales: 1100 units @ £150	165 000
Costs:	
Direct materials: 1100 × (7 kg × £5)	(38 500)
Direct labour: 1100 units × (3 hours × £5)	(16 500)
Production overheads	(50 000)
	60 000
Selling and administrative overheads	(20 000)
Net profit	40 000

The flexed budget shows the sales revenue that would have been expected from sales of 1100 units, and all the costs adjusted for the additional volume of sales. Remember that we are working on the assumption that production overheads do not increase in line with the volume of sales. Selling and administrative overheads, also, are not assumed to increase in line with the volume of sales; they are also regarded as fixed overhead costs. (Note: The distinction between variable costs and fixed costs will be examined in more detail later in the chapter.)

We now have three statement of profit or loss the original budget, the flexed budget and the statement of actual results. It will help at this point to place them side by side:

	Original budget £	Flexed budget £	Actual £
Sales	150 000	165 000	159 500
Direct materials	(35 000)	(38 500)	(37 125)
Direct labour	(15 000)	(16 500)	(16 940)
Production overheads	(50 000)	(50 000)	(52 000)
	50 000	60 000	53 435
Selling and administrative overheads	(20 000)	(20 000)	(21 250)
Net profit	30 000	40 000	32 185

CALCULATING VARIANCES

The original budget net profit was £30 000. Actual net profit is £32 185. The overall variance is a **favourable variance** of £2185. We will break this figure down into its constituent variances which will allow us to identify possible problem areas.

SALES PROFIT VOLUME VARIANCE

A key element of the difference is the sale of more units than originally anticipated. This variance is the difference between the original budget profit and the flexed budget profit: £40 000 − £30 000 = £10 000. It is clearly in the interests of the company to sell more components, and so this is a favourable variance.

SALES PRICE VARIANCE

The actual profit is affected by the fact that, although extra sales have been made, the selling price is actually lower than budgeted.

This variance is calculated as follows:

	£
Actual volume of sales at actual selling price: 1100 × £145	159 500
Less: actual volume of sales at budget selling price: 1100 × £150	165 000
Sales price variance	5 500

This represents an undesirable outcome for the firm; it would have been better to sell at the higher, budgeted, price, so this is an adverse variance.

At this stage refer back to the three statements presented side by side, and note that we are comparing the flexed budget statement with the actual statement in order to calculate this variance.

DIRECT MATERIALS VARIANCES

Comparing the figure for direct materials in the flexed budget statement with the figure in the actual statement:

Flexed budget for direct materials	£38 500
Actual direct materials	37 125
	1 375

The actual amount is less than budget; this is a good outcome and so this is classified as a favourable variance.

We can analyze this variance further by looking at the budget input of resources against actual input. Management accountants are able to calculate two direct materials variances: direct materials price variance and direct materials quantity variance. These relate, respectively, to price effects and volume effects.

DIRECT MATERIALS PRICE VARIANCE

We compare:

- the actual quantity of raw materials used at the price actually paid (actual price)
- the actual quantity of raw materials used at the price budgeted (standard price).
  Using the same measure of quantity (actual) ensures that we isolate the price effect.

Actual quantity at actual price
7.5 kg was used for each of 1100 components: actual quantity used is
    7.5 kg × 1100 = 8250 kg

8250 kg × price actually paid (£4.50)	37 125
Actual quantity at standard price 8250 kg. × standard price (£5.00)	41 250
Direct materials price variance	4 125

The business has paid less per unit for direct materials than it expected; this is therefore a favourable variance.

DIRECT MATERIALS QUANTITY VARIANCE

We compare:

- the actual quantity of materials used at standard price
- the standard quantity of materials used at standard price.

Actual quantity at standard price
Actual quantity used (already worked out): 8250 kg
Standard price per kg: £5

Actual quantity at standard price = 8250 × £5	41 250

Standard quantity at standard price
Standard quantity: 7 kg × 1100 components = 7700 kg
Standard price per kg: £5

Standard quantity at standard price = 7700 × £5	38 500
Direct materials quantity variance	2 750

The business has used more materials per component than budgeted; this is therefore an adverse variance.

In summary, the direct materials variances are:

Direct materials price variance	4 125 (F)
Direct materials quantity variance	2 750 (A)
Direct materials variance	1 375 (F)

Note: 'F' stands for 'Favourable'; 'A' stands for 'Adverse'.

DIRECT LABOUR VARIANCES

Comparing the figure for direct labour in the flexed budget statement with the figure in the actual statement:

Flexed budget for direct labour	£16 500
Actual direct labour	16 940
	440

The actual amount is more than budgeted; this is not a good outcome and so is classified as an adverse variance.

As with direct materials, we can break down this overall variance into two variances, one quantifying the price effect and the other quantifying the volume effect. These are traditionally known as the direct labour rate variance, and the direct labour efficiency variance, respectively.

DIRECT LABOUR RATE VARIANCE

We compare:

- the actual hours of direct labour used at the wage rate actually paid (actual rate)
- the actual hours of direct labour used at the wage rate budgeted (standard rate).

Using the same measure of hours (actual) ensures that we isolate the rate effect.

Actual hours at actual rate
Actual hours was 2.8 hours for each of 1100
components: $2.8 \times 1100 = 3080$ hours
3080 hours × Rate actually paid (£5.50)   16 940
Actual hours at standard rate
3080 hours × Standard rate (£5.00)   15 400
Direct labour rate variance   1 540

The business has paid more per hour for direct labour than it budgeted; this is therefore an adverse variance.

DIRECT LABOUR EFFICIENCY VARIANCE

We compare:

- the actual hours of direct labour used at standard rate
- the standard hours of direct labour used at standard rate.

Actual hours at standard rate
Actual hours used (already worked out): 3080 hours
Standard rate per hour: £5
Actual hours at standard rate = $3080 \times £5$ 15 400
Standard hours at standard rate
Standard hours: $3 \text{ hours} \times 1100 = 3300$
Standard rate per hour: £5
Standard hours at standard rate = $3300 \times £5$ 16 500
Direct labour efficiency variance   1 100

The business has used fewer hours per component than budgeted; this is therefore a favourable variance.

In summary, the direct labour variances are:

Direct labour rate variance	£1 540 (A)
Direct labour efficiency variance	1 100 (F)
Direct labour variance	£ 440 (A)

PRODUCTION OVERHEAD VARIANCE

Budget figure for production overhead:	50 000
Actual figure for production overhead:	52 000
Production overhead variance	(2 000) (A)

The company appears to have spent more than initially planned; therefore, this is an adverse variance.

SELLING AND ADMINISTRATIVE OVERHEAD VARIANCE

Budget figure for selling and administrative overhead:	20 000
Actual figure for selling and administrative overhead:	21 250
Selling and administrative overhead variance	(1 250) (A)

Having calculated this long list of variances, they can now be presented in the form of a standard cost operating statement, as follows:

Zamboni & Zeuss: Standard cost operating statement for January 20X3

	Favourable £	(Adverse) £	Total £
Original budgeted net profit			30 000
Sales profit volume variance			10 000
Flexed budget net profit			40 000
Other variances			
Sales price variance		(5 500)	
Direct materials price variance	4 125		
Direct materials quantity variance		(2 750)	
Direct labour rate variance		(1 540)	
Direct labour efficiency variance	1 100		
Production overhead variance		(2 000)	
Selling and administrative overhead variance		(1 250)	
Total	5 225	(13 040)	(7 815)
Actual net profit			32 185

What does this statement tell us? Remember that we started out with the simple observation that there was an overall favourable variance between budgeted profit and actual profit of £2185. The standard cost operating statement above allows us to identify the component parts of that overall variance, and to pinpoint the areas where problems may have arisen. There are several adverse variances:

- Sales price variance: although the volume of sales has increased, the beneficial effect on profit is not as great as it might have been because the selling price has fallen. Of course, these two factors may very well be related; it could be that the company has made a deliberate attempt to boost sales by setting a lower selling price. If that was the intention, the objective appears to have been met.

- Direct materials quantity variance: it appears that the production process is less efficient in terms of usage of materials than was originally intended. There may be good reasons why this has happened; indeed, the problem may be that the original standard set for quantity was too ambitious. Further investigation of the variance would probably be necessary. This adverse variance, however, is more than offset by a favourable direct materials price variance. Perhaps a special purchase of materials has been made, but, of course, if the quality is slightly poorer, it may be more difficult to use the materials efficiently.
- Direct labour rate variance: production staff appear to have been paid at a higher rate than allowed for in the standard cost calculations. If this is a permanent change, the standard cost needs changing. If it is a temporary change, the reasons for it should be investigated. It is noticeable, however, that the direct labour efficiency variance is positive; perhaps higher-paid staff are working more quickly, or perhaps the supervision process is more effective than originally anticipated.
- While the standard cost operating statement certainly provides management with more information than a simple statement like 'profits have gone up', it does not, clearly, answer all the questions. However, it serves a useful purpose in directing management's attention to areas which may require investigation and in suggesting the kind of questions which should be asked.

Before moving on try this self-test question which runs through the same variance calculations as the demonstration example above.

Self-test question 17.1 (answer at the end of the book)

Bridge and Blige Ltd make metal casings for lawn mowers in one standard size. In February 20X4 the company's budget for sales and related costs is as follows:

	£
Sales: 800 units @ £35	28 000
Costs:	
Direct materials: 800 units × (2 kg × £6)	(9 600)
Direct labour: 800 units × (1 hour × £7.50)	(6 000)
Production overheads	(4 000)
	8 400
Selling and administrative overheads	(2 300)
Net profit	6 100

The actual figures for February 20X4 are as follows:

	£
Sales: 900 units @ £36	32 400
Costs:	
Direct materials: 900 units × (1.9 kg × £5.50)	(9 405)
Direct labour: 900 units × (1.2 hours × £7.00)	(7 560)
Production overheads	(4 400)
	11 035
Selling and administrative overheads	(2 450)
Net profit	8 585

i) Prepare a flexed budget for 900 units for February 20X4.
ii) Calculate the full range of variances demonstrated in the Zamboni & Zeuss example.
iii) Prepare a standard cost operating statement which reconciles the difference between the budget net profit and the actual net profit figures shown in the statements above.

17.3 OVERHEAD VARIANCES

The Zamboni and Zeuss example contained only very simple overhead variances. However, it can be useful to management to have access to rather more detailed analysis. It is customary in manufacturing businesses to draw a distinction between variable overheads and fixed overheads in the calculation of variances relating to production overheads.

Variable overheads are those that increase or decrease corresponding to increases and decreases in production. For example, the following costs would all tend to vary as production levels vary:

- machine cleaning and repair costs
- machine oil and consumables costs
- quality inspection costs.

Many overheads, however, will be fixed. A production supervisor's salary, for example, is likely to stay the same whether he/she is supervising the production of 100 units per day, or 95, or 105. It would be a different matter if production changed radically and the number increased to, say, 1000. More production supervisors would have to be employed. However, it is safe to say that, provided variations in production levels are relatively small, many costs remain the same.

In the next section we will examine variable and fixed overhead variances by means of a demonstration. It is possible to break down overhead variances for activity and expenditure effects (as for materials and labour) but such a level of complexity is regarded as being beyond the scope of this book. We will, therefore, calculate only one overall variance for variable production overheads and one overall variance for fixed production overheads.

Example 17.3

Goldman Le Saint produces a single product. Its budget for March 20X6 is as follows:

	£
Sales: 1000 units @ £80	80 000
Costs:	
Direct materials: 1000 units × (4 kg × £3)	(12 000)
Direct labour: 1000 units × (3 hours × £5.00)	(15 000)
Variable production overheads: 1000 units × (4 machine hours × £2.00)	(8 000)
Fixed production overheads: 1000 units × (4 machine hours × £6.00)	(24 000)
	21 000
Selling and administrative overheads	(4 000)
Net profit	17 000

Note that in this example, production overheads are split into variable and fixed production overheads – the first time that we have encountered such a split.

Both variable and fixed production overheads are recovered via overhead absorption rates based upon machine hours. The budget machine hours for March 20X6 are 4000 hours (1000 units × 4 machine hours per unit).

The actual figures for March 20X6 are as follows:

	£
Sales: 900 units @ £80	72 000
Costs:	
Direct materials: 900 units × (4 kg × £3.00)	(10 800)
Direct labour: 900 units × (3 hours × £5.00)	(13 500)
Variable overheads	(9 600)
Production overheads	(25 500)
	12 600
Selling and administrative overheads	(4 000)
Net profit	8 600

The first stage in calculating variances, as before, is to flex the budget for the actual level of sales activity:
Flexed budget for 900 units

	£
Sales: 900 units @ £80	72 000
Costs:	
Direct materials: 900 units × (4 kg × £3.00)	(10 800)
Direct labour: 900 units × (3 hours × £5.00)	(13 500)
Variable overheads: 900 units × (4 hours × £2)	(7 200)
Fixed production overheads: 900 units × (4 hours × £6)	(21 600)
	18 900
Selling and administrative overheads	(4 000)
Net profit	14 900

As in the previous example, it will be helpful to set the original budget statement, the flexed budget statement and the actual statement side by side:

	Original budget	Flexed budget	Actual
	£	£	£
Sales	80 000	72 000	72 000
Direct materials	(12 000)	(10 800)	(10 800)
Direct labour	(15 000)	(13 500)	(13 500)
Variable production overheads	(8 000)	(7 200)	(9 600)
Fixed production overheads	(24 000)	(21 600)	(25 500)
	21 000	18 900	12 600
Selling and administrative overheads	(4 000)	(4 000)	(4 000)
Net profit	17 000	14 900	8 600

The overall variance is

Original budget net profit	17 000
Actual net profit	8 600
	8 400 (A)

SALES PROFIT VOLUME VARIANCE

This variance is the difference between the original budget profit and the flexed budget profit: £17 000 − 14 900 = 2100(A). The variance is adverse because the flexed budget profit is lower than the original budget profit.

Anyone who has managed to keep up so far will see that there are no variances for sales price, direct material, direct labour and selling and administrative overheads. Once the budget is flexed, it becomes clear that sales prices, direct material and direct labour costs are exactly as would have been predicted if 900 units had been budgeted for. The example therefore isolates the changes in variable and fixed production overheads.

VARIABLE PRODUCTION OVERHEAD VARIANCE

The variance can be calculated in the same way as, say, the total direct materials variance: by comparing the totals in the flexed budget statement with the actual statement:

Flexed budget for variable overhead	£7 200
Actual variable overhead	9 600
	£2 400 (A)

FIXED PRODUCTION OVERHEAD VARIANCE

The overall variance can be calculated in the same way as, say, the total direct materials variance: by comparing the totals in the flexed budget statement with the actual statement:

Flexed budget for fixed overhead	£21 600
Actual fixed overhead	25 500
	£ 3 900 (A)

We can now produce a standard cost operating statement:

Goldman Le Saint: Standard cost operating statement for March 20X6

	Favourable £	(Adverse) £	Total £
Original budgeted net profit			17 000
Sales profit volume variance			(2 100)
Flexed budget net profit			14 900
Other variances			
Sales price variance	–	–	
Direct materials price variance	–	–	
Direct materials quantity variance	–	–	
Direct labour rate variance	–	–	
Direct labour efficiency variance	–	–	
Variable overhead variance		(2 400)	
Fixed overhead variance		(3 900)	
Selling and administrative overhead variance	–	–	
Total	–	(6 300)	(6 300)
Actual net profit			8 600

Before moving on, try self-test question 17.2 which isolates the calculation of the variable and fixed production overheads variances.

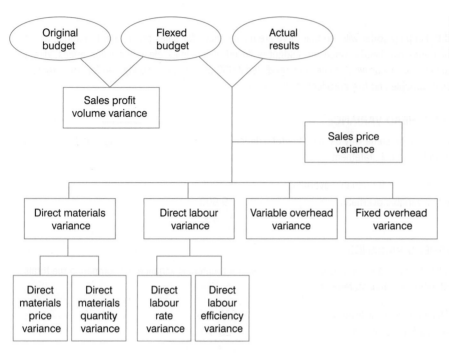

Figure 17.1
Summary of the variances covered in the chapter

S ingh and Waterhouse manufacture one style of storage shelving. The company's budget for April 20X8 is as follows:

Self-test question 17.2 (answer at the end of the book)

	£
Sales: 1800 @ £45	81 000
Costs:	
Direct materials: 1800 units × (16 metres × £1.00 per metre)	(28 800)
Direct labour: 1800 units × (2 hours × £5.00 per hour)	(18 000)
Variable production overheads: 1800 units × (2 machine hours per unit × £1)	(3 600)
Fixed production overheads: 1800 units × (2 machine hours per unit × £6)	(21 600)
Profit before other overheads	9 000

The actual figures for April 20X8 are as follows:

	£
Sales: 2000 units @ £45	90 000
Costs:	
Direct materials: 2000 units × (16 metres × £1)	(32 000)
Direct labour: 2000 units × (2 hours × £5.00)	(20 000)
Variable overheads	(3 800)
Production overheads	(23 400)
Profit before other overheads	10 800

i) Flex the budget for a sales level of 2000 units.
ii) Calculate all variances.
iii) Prepare a standard cost operating statement for the company for April 20X8.

17.4 INVESTIGATING THE REASONS FOR VARIANCES

Implementing a standard cost system represents a major investment of time and other resources for most businesses. The benefits of this investment will outweigh the costs only if full use is made by management of the information conveyed by variances. It is important, too, that the investigation of variances is carried out promptly. The examples in this chapter have all assumed that standard costs are being compared with actual on a monthly basis; this is a realistic assumption which reflects actual practice in industry. If the comparison were to be done annually or even quarterly, any underlying problems would persist for far too long. In order for management to be able to exert full control, frequent and timely action is required.

17.4.1 Deciding which Variances Merit Investigation

It is a matter of management policy to decide the level at which a variance becomes significant and worthy of further investigation. The following criteria will probably be important in deciding which variances merit investigation:

- Significance in percentage or monetary terms: for example, management may decide to investigate any variance, favourable or unfavourable, which is greater than 5% of the flexed budget total. Or they may use a monetary criterion, for example: 'investigate any variance greater than £5000'.
- Frequency of occurrence: variances may be individually minor, but cumulatively significant. For example, if there is a persistent adverse materials price variance across a range of different materials items, this may point to lax purchasing management.

17.4.2 Principal Reasons for the Occurrence of Variances

SALES VARIANCES Actual sales volume may differ from budget volume because of such factors as:
- greater than expected success of an advertising campaign
- improved efficiency and effectiveness of sales staff
- failure of a competitor
- entry of a new competitor into the market
- loss of sales staff, or loss of morale and motivation through poor management.

  Sales prices may differ because of such factors as:

- lowering of prices to increase volume
- lowering of prices to respond to new competition
- increasing prices to take advantage of exit of competitor from the market
- fashion trends (it may be possible to charge higher prices for fashionable items).

DIRECT MATERIALS VARIANCES Price variances may arise because of any, or a combination, of the following factors:
- successful negotiation for lower prices
- obtaining quantity discounts for large orders
- variation in material quality
- volatile market for material, leading to unexpected increases or decreases in price.

  Quantity variances may arise as follows:

- better or worse quality of material than expected
- employment of higher or lower skilled workers than anticipated
- level of supervision/number of quality checks
- poor functioning of machinery.

DIRECT LABOUR VARIANCES Rate variances may arise in the following circumstances:
- the mix of labour differs from plan; for example, using more higher paid staff in production because of under-employment elsewhere in the factory
- unexpected increase in rate arising from the conclusion of negotiations over wage levels.

Efficiency variances may arise as follows:

- better or worse quality of material than expected
- employment of higher or lower skilled workers than anticipated
- level of supervision/number of quality checks
- poor functioning of machinery.

OVERHEAD VARIANCES Overhead variances may arise because of any of the following:
- non-controllable price changes because of events in the wider economy
- poor management control over costs
- improved management control over costs.

Last, but not least, variances may occur simply because the standard cost was incorrectly set. For example, if the standard cost for a particular item reflects the best possible cost achievable only in ideal circumstances, then it is unlikely to be met. The existence of variances may signal no more than the need to alter the standard cost. However, before this step is taken the variance should be thoroughly investigated to ensure that there is no other cause.

17.5 STANDARD COSTING: ISSUES AND PROBLEMS

Standard costing continues to be widely used in practice, a fact which suggests that it continues to be a useful management control tool. Despite its continued use, though, standard costing has its critics. Problems include the following:

- Lack of timeliness: the reporting system may produce variances only once a month, with a time lag of, possibly, several days between the end of the month and the report. By the time managers have an opportunity to absorb the information and make decisions on actions to address variances, the problems causing the variances may have become much worse.
- Expense: all systems of gathering information for management control and decision making have a cost. As can be inferred from the detailed description of standard costing earlier in the chapter, assembling and recording the information is likely to involve much time and expense. It may not be easy to discern whether or not the costs outweigh the benefits.
- Top-down control: the emphasis on top-down accounting control is perceived by some to be a stultifying influence on the business.
- Danger of manipulation: managers and others may be tempted to manipulate the system in order to, for example, achieve personal targets or avoid blame.
- Danger of misinterpretation: unravelling cause and effect in the examination of variances is fraught with difficulty in practice. Managers must be able to identify the true cause of a variance in order to take appropriate action.

The real-life example below identifies some of the motivational issues in standard costing.

Example 17.4 (Real-Life)

STANDARD COSTING IN PRACTICE

In 2010, the Chartered Institute of Management Accountants (CIMA) in the UK, and KPMG, the accounting firm, published a research report: 'Standard costing: insights from leading companies'. KPMG carried out the research, which involved interviews with 12 major manufacturing groups. The research identified several key themes, one of which is the extent to which standard costs are aspirational targets. The research found that: 'A number of participants use their standard costing to drive performance improvement, choosing to set standards at a target "best ever achieved"'. Using standard costing in this way is clearly an attempt to influence participant behaviour to improve performance.

However, this approach can be taken too far. One participant in the research found that once workers had achieved an aspirational target they relaxed their efforts and made no further attempt to improve performance. This example illustrates the importance in management (and in management accounting) of taking into consideration the effects of human behaviour.

Chapter Summary

Standard costing systems are complex, and the description of variance calculations necessarily occupies a substantial proportion of this chapter. Many other variances can be, and sometimes are, calculated, but they are regarded as being beyond the scope of this text.

Despite the criticisms made of standard costing, it continues to be widely used as a control mechanism.

Internet Resources

Book's companion website summary

The website contains the following resources in respect of Chapter 17:

Students' section

A multiple choice quiz containing ten questions
Four additional questions with answers

Lecturers' section

Answers to end-of-chapter exercises 17.12 to 17.20
Five additional questions with answers
Case study
Testbank
Instructor's Manual
PowerPoint presentation

Exercises: Answers at the End of the Book

17.1 Denholm Pargeter Ltd is an engineering company producing a wide range of component parts for the aerospace industry. Its component XP04/H has the following budget sales and prime costs for March 20X9:

	£
Sales: 1200 units @ £30	36 000
Direct materials: 1200 units × (3 kg × £1.20)	4 320
Direct labour: 1200 units × (2 hours × £8.50)	20 400
Prime cost	24 720

The production manager wishes to assess the change to the budget on the basis that 1300 units are produced and sold.

Flex the budget for component XP04/H for 1300 units.

17.2 Darblay Harriett Ltd produces a single product – a wooden cabinet. The company's budget for November 20X1 is as follows:

	£
Sales: 2000 units @ £19.50	39 000
Direct materials: 2000 × (2 metres × £2.00)	(8 000)
Direct labour: 2000 × (1 hour × £6.00)	(12 000)
Production overheads	(10 000)
	9 000
Selling and administrative overheads	(3 000)
Net profit	6 000

Darblay Harriett Ltd does not absorb production overheads using an overhead absorption rate. It may be assumed that all of its overheads are fixed in nature.

If the company flexes its budget for 2600 units, what will be the revised net profit figure?

a) £14 700

b) £8700

c) £11 700

d) £17 700

The following information is relevant for questions 17.3 to 17.8.

Edwards and Sheerness Ltd is in the motor parts industry. Its budget for July 20X8 is as follows:

	£
Sales: 2500 units @ £29	72 500
Direct materials: 2500 × (3 kg × £3.00)	(22 500)
Direct labour: 2500 × (1.5 hours × £4.40)	(16 500)
Production overheads	(17 000)
	16 500
Other overheads	(3 500)
Net profit	13 000

Edwards and Sheerness Ltd does not absorb production overheads using an overhead absorption rate. It may be assumed that all of its overheads are fixed in nature.

The company's actual results for the month are as follows:

	£
Sales: 2650 units @ £28	74 200
Direct materials: 2650 × (2.8 kg × £3.30)	(24 486)
Direct labour: 2650 × (1.7 hours × £4.20)	(18 921)
Production overheads	(16 900)
	13 893
Other overheads	(3 600)
Net profit	10 293

17.3 What is the sales profit volume variance for the month?

a) £2707 (A)

b) £2010 (A)

c) £2707 (F)

d) £2010 (F)

17.4 What is the sales price variance for the month?

a) £640 (F)
b) £640 (A)
c) £2650 (F)
d) £2650 (A)

17.5 What is the direct materials price variance for the month?

a) £2226 (F)
b) £2226 (A)
c) £2385 (F)
d) £2385 (A)

17.6 What is the direct materials quantity variance for the month?

a) £1749 (F)
b) £1749 (A)
c) £1590 (F)
d) £1590 (A)

17.7 What is the direct labour rate variance for the month?

a) £901 (A)
b) £795 (A)
c) £795 (F)
d) £901 (F)

17.8 What is the direct labour efficiency variance for the month?

a) £2332 (F)
b) £2332 (A)
c) £2226 (F)
d) £2226 (A)

17.9 Ferguson Farrar Ltd is a manufacturing company. For the month of April 20X5 it budgeted for 4000 units of production, each to use 1.5 hours of machine time. Production overhead absorption rates were budgeted as follows:

| Variable production overheads: | £4 per machine hour |
| Fixed production overheads: | £8 per machine hour |

The actual level of production in the month was 4200 units.

The original production overhead budget, the flexed budget and the actual expenditure are shown in the following table:

	Original budget £	Flexed budget £	Actual £
Variable production overheads	24 000	25 200	26 250
Fixed production overheads	48 000	50 400	48 750
	72 000	75 600	75 000

i) Calculate the total variable production overhead variance.

ii) Calculate the total fixed production overhead variance.

17.10 Grindleton Gears Ltd is a manufacturing business which uses a standard costing system. If a variance exceeds 5% of the flexed budget total for that item, the management team investigates it, whether it is favourable or adverse. The company's flexed budget for February 20X6 is:

	£
Sales	123 470
Direct materials	(28 250)
Direct labour	(29 900)
Variable production overheads	(8 640)
Fixed production overheads	(19 780)
Profit	36 900

The management team is presented with the following standard cost operating statement for the month:

	Favourable £	(Adverse) £	Total £
Original budgeted net profit			30 900
Sales profit volume variance			6 000
Flexed budget net profit			36 900
Other variances			
Sales price variance	1 030	–	
Direct materials price variance	–	(1 650)	
Direct materials quantity variance	–	(106)	
Direct labour rate variance	–	–	
Direct labour efficiency variance	200	–	
Variable overhead variance	1 400	–	
Fixed overhead variance	339	–	
Total	2 969	(1 756)	1 213
Actual profit			38 113

i) Using the company's own criterion, decide which variances should be examined.

ii) List reasons why the variances you have identified may have arisen.

iii) Calculate the actual figures for sales, direct materials, direct labour, variable overheads, fixed overheads and profit.

17.11 The directors of Bellcraft are due to meet to discuss a proposal to implement a standard costing system to control their manufacturing operations. One of the directors has been reading a book about management systems which contains a chapter about the drawbacks of standard costing systems. He has circulated a paper in advance of the meeting suggesting that the proposed system would be excessively expensive and bureaucratic. He says that standard costing systems fail to produce information on a sufficiently timely basis, so that variance investigation is bound to be ineffective. You are the management accountant of Bellcraft, and you are due to attend the directors' meeting as an adviser.

Make notes to take into the meeting which address the criticisms of standard costing in the director's paper.

Exercises: Answers Available on the Lecturers' Section of the Book's Website

17.12 Dorchester Slugg Ltd manufactures plastic refuse bins. Its monthly budget for August 20X8 is as follows:

	£
Sales: 4000 units @ £18	72 000
Direct materials: 4000 × (7 kg × £1)	(28 000)
Direct labour: 4000 × (0.5 hours × £6.00)	(12 000)
Production overheads	(10 000)
	22 000
Selling and administrative overheads	(4 000)
	18 000

Dorchester Slugg does not absorb production overheads using an overhead absorption rate. It may be assumed that all of its overheads are fixed in nature.

Flex the budget for a sales and production level of 4500 units.

17.13 Dillinger Thompson Ltd produces a line of leather bags. Although they vary slightly in design the cost structure is the same for each bag. The company's budget for January 20X9 is as follows:

	£
Sales: 4000 units @ £22	88 000
Direct materials: 4000 × (1 sq. m. × £6.50)	(26 000)
Direct labour: 4000 × (0.5 hours × £7.80)	(15 600)
Production overheads	(24 000)
	22 400
Selling and administrative overheads	(6 000)
Net profit	16 400

Dillinger Thompson Ltd does not absorb production overheads using an overhead absorption rate. It may be assumed that all of its overheads are fixed in nature.

If the company flexes its budget for 3600 units, what will be the revised net profit figure?

a) £1760

b) £7760

c) £4160

d) £600

The following information is relevant for questions 17.14 to 17.19.

Estella Starr Ltd produces garden sheds which are sold direct to the public in kit form. March is one of the company's best months for sales, and in March 20X2 the directors have set some ambitious targets. These are summarized in the following budget for the month.

Estella Starr Ltd does not absorb production overheads using an overhead absorption rate. It may be assumed that all of its overheads are fixed in nature.

	£
Sales: 900 units @ £217	195 300
Direct materials: 900 × (16 metres × £4.00)	(57 600)
Direct labour: 900 × (4 hours × £6.30)	(22 680)
Production overheads	(62 300)
	52 720
Other overheads	(10 600)
Net profit	42 120

The company's actual results for the month are as follows:

	£
Sales: 830 @ £214	177 620
Direct materials: 830 × (15 metres × £4.10)	(51 045)
Direct labour: 830 × (4.1 hours × £6.00)	(20 418)
Production overheads	(61 400)
	44 757
Other overheads	(8 950)
Net profit	35 807

17.14 What is the sales profit volume variance for the month?

a) £6313 (A)
b) £8946 (A)
c) £8946 (F)
d) £6313 (F)

17.15 What is the sales price variance for the month?

a) £2490 (F)
b) £2490 (A)
c) £15 190 (F)
d) £15 190 (A)

17.16 What is the direct materials price variance for the month?

a) £6555 (A)
b) £1245 (A)
c) £6555 (F)
d) £1245 (F)

17.17 What is the direct materials quantity variance for the month?

a) £3320 (F)
b) £3320 (A)
c) £7800 (A)
d) £7800 (F)

17.18 What is the direct labour rate variance for the month (to the nearest pound)?

    a) £360 (A)
    b) £360 (F)
    c) £1021 (F)
    d) £1021 (A)

17.19 What is the direct labour efficiency variance for the month (to the nearest pound)?

    a) £523 (A)
    b) £523 (F)
    c) £340 (F)
    d) £340 (A)

17.20 Feltham Finch Ltd is a manufacturing company. For the month of August 20X9 it budgeted for 780 units of production, each to use four hours of machine time. Production overhead absorption rates were budgeted as follows:

Variable production overhead: £2.80 per machine hour
Fixed production overhead: £7.60 per machine hour
The actual level of production in the month was 760 units.

    The original production overhead budget, the flexed budget and the actual expenditure are shown in the following table:

	Original budget £	Flexed budget £	Actual £
Variable production overheads	8 736	8 512	8 476
Fixed production overheads	23 712	23 104	24 160
	32 448	31 616	32 636

    i) Calculate the total variable production overhead variance.

    ii) Calculate the total fixed production overhead variance.

18 Performance measurement

Aim of the chapter

To develop an understanding of ways in which performance is measured, managed and reported within the firm.

Learning outcomes

After reading the chapter and completing the exercises, students should:

- Understand why large organizations often use divisional structures.

- Be able to argue the advantages and drawbacks of divisionalization.

- Understand the nature of financial performance measurement in divisions.

- Appreciate the importance of non-financial performance measures within organizations.

- Understand the 'Balanced Scorecard' approach to financial and non-financial performance measurement.

Introduction

As discussed in earlier chapters most large businesses in most jurisdictions are required by law or regulation to produce periodic financial statements for use by interested parties, such as lenders and shareholders. But for most organizations, the internal reporting of performance has equal, and often greater, prominence. Internal performance reporting allows business managers to:

- assess the impact of their decision making
- monitor the performance of different parts of the business
- make better informed decisions about future courses of action
- control the activities of the business
- make decisions about reward and incentive structures
- plan for the future.

This chapter examines some important aspects of internal performance reporting in business, with particular emphasis on reporting issues in businesses that are split into divisions. The earlier part of the chapter is concerned with ways of measuring and reporting performance in quantitative (principally financial) terms. In recent years, though, the importance of reporting using a combination of financial, other quantitative and non-quantitative measures has been increasingly appreciated, and this type of reporting occupies the latter part of the chapter.

18.1 PERFORMANCE REPORTING AND ORGANIZATIONAL OBJECTIVES

The first section of the chapter examines an example of performance reporting in a service sector organization. This illustrates some important features of performance reporting within a fairly large organization. The larger a business becomes, the greater the complexity of its internal accounting and reporting processes. Very large businesses are likely to employ many full-time staff in a management accounting department with a responsibility to produce reports useful for management.

Activities should be orientated towards achieving organizational objectives, and, similarly, the reporting of activities should demonstrate the extent to which those objectives have been met. Most organizations, whatever their size, find it useful to develop key performance indicators (sometimes referred to as KPIs) which help to measure the extent to which objectives are being achieved.

Example 18.1 indicates some of the performance indicators, and reports, that might be useful in an estate agency business.

Example 18.1

Wisharts is a national firm of estate agents, with 180 branches around the country. The market for estate agency services is highly competitive in most locations, with several national and local firms competing for business. At the company's head office a small team of management accountants collates information submitted via the firm's intranet in a standard form. Each time a new instruction is received, or a property is sold, details are logged onto the computer system.

Senior managers at head office require weekly updates on the following key performance indicators:

- number of new instructions
- number of houses/flats sold, in total, and by each agent
- value of sales made
- average turnover of instructions in days (ie. the average length of time a house remains on the books of the agency).

Each Saturday at close of business, the branch manager enters the information into standard formats that are submitted to head office via the intranet. Senior managers at head office meet on the following Monday afternoon to discuss the results for the week which are presented on hard-copy report forms, summarized into 14 regions. The management accounting team also updates a set of graphs showing the movement over a rolling 12-month period of indicators such as average house price in each region and number of sales made per region. Where a region appears to be under-performing, managers are able to drill down into the regional data to identify individual office performance. The performance of individual agents is accumulated and a national ranking is produced at the end of each month. The top five agents in the country receive a substantial financial bonus and an allocation of points towards Wisharts's annual agents awards. Where branch or individual performance gives cause for concern, a member of the senior management team calls or visits the branch to determine the reasons and to take remedial action.

At the end of each four-week period, senior managers are presented with monthly management accounts showing total revenue and expenditure for the month, together with the totals for the key regional indicators of new instructions, number of houses/flats sold and average selling price. The Wishart management accounting system is designed to be flexible and responsive so that managers are able to request special purpose reports which they normally receive within 24 hours. Recently, for example, the chief executive requested a special report listing the details of all individual house sales in excess of £300 000 for region 12.

Hardly any of the information reported internally to the senior managers in the example above would be reported in the external annual report to stakeholders. Important indicators such as new instructions received are for internal use only.

Internal performance reports can take any form: they might be a one-page monthly summary in a small business, or, for a large business, could run to many pages of detail. The key point, as always with management information, is that they should provide information that is useful to managers in their planning, controlling, monitoring and decision-making functions. Information reported to managers should ideally have the following characteristics:

- It should be produced quickly so that managers can respond rapidly to it.
- It should be easily comprehensible, useful, accurate and reliable.
- The costs of producing it should not outweigh its benefits.

Also, the lines of responsibility within an organization should be clearly set out and understood by all concerned, and they should be orientated towards achieving the objectives of the business. For example, in the Wishart organization described in the example above, senior managers are likely to be concerned most with growing their market share in a highly competitive market. Having determined that growth in market share is a key objective, they must communicate the objective clearly to all the business's employees so that every individual understands their role in achieving it. Internal reporting should be orientated towards measuring the organization's success in pursuing its key objectives.

Self-test question 18.1 (answer at the end of the book)

Dreamstay runs a chain of eight luxury hotels, all located in prime city centre sites throughout Great Britain. One of its key business objectives is to maximize the revenue from both sale of rooms and additional value-added services such as in-house hairdressing and beauty salons. Suggest three key performance indicators linked to this objective.

18.2 DIVISIONAL RESPONSIBILITY IN LARGE BUSINESS ORGANIZATIONS

In some cases the sheer size and complexity of a business organization may make it difficult for a single management team to control all of the operations of the business. Where this is the case, part of the control can be devolved to divisional managers, leaving the most senior level of management free to deal with issues of major strategic importance (for example, a decision to launch a takeover bid). Divisions may be established, for example, by reference to the nature of their function or their geographical location, or both. A business that produces four major product groups might organize their activities into four divisions: one for each group. A major multinational car maker such as Nissan or Volkswagen might organize its activities into geographical groups such as North America, Asia-Pacific and Europe. The next example shows how a manufacturing business might organize its operations into divisions.

Example 18.2

Popps is a manufacturer and bottler of soft drinks operating in France and Spain. The French operations comprise the bottling of naturally sourced mineral water, and, at a separate location, the manufacturing and bottling of fizzy cola drinks. The Spanish operation is based at one location, manufacturing and bottling a similar range of cola drinks to those produced in France.

It would be possible to create two simple geographical divisions – one based in France and one in Spain. However, the two French operations differ somewhat from each other; they operate at different locations and are probably selling in slightly different markets. Therefore, Popps might find it advantageous to split operations into three divisions: Spain, France (cola) and France (water).

Divisions operate with varying degrees of autonomy. Highly decentralized organizations devolve a great deal of control to divisions, whereas, by contrast, in centralized organizations control is retained at the centre. There are advantages and disadvantages to both approaches.

18.2.1 Centralization and Decentralization

The advantages of decentralization include the following:

- Managers of decentralized parts of a business are likely to be given a high level of autonomy in decision making. This is likely to lead to a more flexible and rapid response to problems.
- Managers in decentralized businesses may be highly motivated if they are given sufficient responsibility in the running of their divisions.
- The comparisons made by senior management between the performances of different divisions in a decentralized business can help to generate a healthy level of competition between divisional managers.

However, there are some drawbacks, too. Healthy competition, if left unchecked, can result in a short-termist approach to decision making. Managers may take decisions that are not in the best overall interests of the organization for the sake of gaining some short-term advantage for their own division. Also, decentralized organizations can be more expensive to run where, for example, a separate sales department is required for each division. It would probably be cheaper and might be more efficient to run a single centralized sales department.

The advantages of a centralized approach to organizational management are:

- The operations of the business remain under close scrutiny and control by senior managers.
- There are none of the interdivisional rivalries that can lead to sub-optimal decision making.
- By centralizing functions such as accounting, marketing and selling, cost savings can be made.

However, highly centralized operations are very demanding of senior management time, and may operate relatively inefficiently as a result. The opportunity of motivating staff by assigning divisional responsibilities to them is lost.

Self-test question 18.2 (answer at the end of the book)

Identify each of the following statements about centralization and decentralization as TRUE or FALSE.

1 Interdivisional rivalries can lead to sub-optimal decision making.
2 Decentralization means that divisional managers are always motivated to make decisions that are in the best interests of the organization as a whole.
3 By decentralizing, senior managers may be able to concentrate more on the overall strategy of the organization.
4 Decentralization is likely to result in a more flexible and rapid response to problems in specific parts of the business.

18.3 ASSESSING DIVISIONAL PERFORMANCE

The nature of divisional performance assessment varies depending upon the degree of autonomy assigned to the division. A key principle is that divisional managers should be assessed only in respect of elements of performance that are under their control. A highly autonomous division will be responsible for virtually all aspects of its operations within a general framework of overall business strategy. Such responsibilities would include, for example, determining the level of investment in assets, the nature and direction of marketing strategies and fixing selling prices. By contrast, divisional control might be limited to minor issues.

Broadly, three levels of autonomy can be recognized under the following descriptions (and see Figure 18.1):

1 Cost or revenue centre: at cost-centre level, divisional managers are responsible for controlling costs, but not revenue or investment. Decisions on matters such as fixing selling prices, determining sales mix targets and making capital investments would be made by more senior managers at a higher level in the organization. Revenue centre managers are responsible for revenue and possibly sales-related expenses, but not for the costs of making the product or providing the service, or for capital investment decisions.

2 Profit centre: divisional managers have more autonomy than in a cost centre; they decide on selling strategies and fix their own prices. Also they are responsible for managing assets assigned to them by head office in the most cost-effective way. They are not, however, responsible for determining capital investments.

3 Investment centre: this describes the highest level of autonomy where divisional managers are responsible for costs, revenue and capital investment decisions.

Division Beta is part of the Glenpool organization. Beta division manufactures kit radios for export. The divisional management team is able to set prices for its products. An allocation of capital expenditure funds is made from head office each year, and the divisional managers are able to spend this as they choose.

Is Beta a profit centre, a cost centre, a revenue centre or an investment centre?

Self-test question 18.3
(answer at the end of the book)

The method of assessment of divisional performance varies, depending upon whether the division is a cost/revenue, profit or **investment centre**.

18.3.1 Cost/Revenue Centre

In a cost centre, divisional performance should be assessed only in respect of costs, because revenue is beyond the control of managers at a divisional level. Reporting in such divisions would therefore focus principally upon analyses of costs that can be controlled by divisional managers. This would exclude any depreciation charges (because depreciation is controlled at head office level) and probably any sales-related costs because the division has no autonomous control over sales strategies. In a revenue centre such as, for example, a regional sales office, performance would be assessed in terms of sales and sales-related costs.

18.3.2 Profit Centre

Divisional performance in a **profit centre** is likely to be assessed by using a statement of profit or loss which shows the profit or loss made for the period under review. Remember, though, that a statement of profit or loss used for

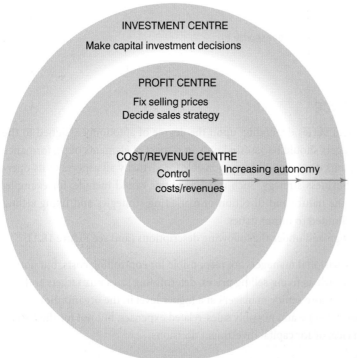

Figure 18.1
Scope of divisional control

INVESTMENT CENTRE
Make capital investment decisions

PROFIT CENTRE
Fix selling prices
Decide sales strategy

COST/REVENUE CENTRE
Control   Increasing autonomy
costs/revenues

reporting within an organization may not bear a very close resemblance to the financial accounting statements that are produced for use by people outside the business organization.

A divisional performance statement should distinguish clearly between the categories of costs controllable at divisional level and those that are controllable at head office level.

Divisional performance statement for a profit centre

	£000
Sales	X
Less: variable costs	(X)
Contribution	X
Less: Controllable fixed costs	(X)
Controllable profit	X
Less: Non-controllable fixed costs	(X)
Divisional profit before allocation of head office costs	X
Head office cost allocation	(X)
Divisional profit before tax	X

Some of the terminology in this statement should be familiar from earlier chapters. There are, though, some new elements in the form of the distinction between controllable and non-controllable costs, and in the allocation of head office costs. The following example illustrates the nature of some of the important figures.

Example 18.3

Delta division is a profit centre of Otranto plc, a listed company with a diverse range of manufacturing activities. The controllable profit of all the company's divisions is required to be at least 35% of sales. The division's accountant has summarized the following performance figures for the year ended 31 December 20X2:

	£000
Variable costs of production	3 588
Sales	6 782
Depreciation of non-current assets	982
Head office charge for central training, administration and IT costs	1 033
Delta's administration costs (all fixed)	433

If we arrange this information into the form of a divisional performance statement we will be able to assess Delta's performance, and to see whether or not it has achieved the required performance criteria for the year.

Delta: Divisional performance statement for a profit centre

	£000
Sales	6 782
Less: variable costs	(3 588)
Contribution	3 194
Less: Controllable fixed costs	(433)
Controllable profit	2 761
Less: Non-controllable fixed costs	(982)
Divisional profit before allocation of head office costs	1 779
Head office cost allocation	(1 033)
Divisional profit before tax	746

Note that the depreciation charge for the year has been treated as a non-controllable fixed cost. Delta is a profit centre, not an investment centre, and its managers have no authority over investment decisions. It would therefore be unfair to treat depreciation as a controllable item.

Has Delta met the group criterion for controllable profit? Controllable profit (£2 761 000) as a percentage of sales (£6 782 000) is 40.7%. So we can see that the division has returned a controllable profit well in excess of the target. This result is beneficial to the division, its managers (whose reputation within the business is likely to be enhanced) and to the business as a whole.

The above example is very straightforward so as to illustrate the principles involved in preparing a divisional performance statement. In practice, however, the distinction between controllable and uncontrollable costs may be difficult to determine. Taking training costs as an example: suppose that the head office of Otranto is responsible for organizing and running training courses. Divisions can choose whether or not to participate in training activities: if divisional staff wish to attend training courses they must ask their manager if the division is prepared to bear the cost. The courses are not charged at full cost; the element of cost that is not covered by fees paid is treated as part of the head office cost allocation. In this case, some element of training cost is controllable at a divisional level, but some of it is not. The amount of head office allocation depends upon the popularity of the training courses, and the willingness of divisional management to fund attendance by staff. If a division's managers decide that their staff will not participate in centrally organized training activities, an element of controllable cost is saved, the overall amount of head office training cost allocation increases and other divisions are penalized (even if only marginally).

Depreciation may be another grey area. In practice, divisional managers may be able to influence head office allocations and decisions on investments. Where this is the case, depreciation expense is, to some extent at least, controllable at divisional level.

The allocation of costs may be highly significant to managers, where their own performance appraisal is based upon divisional results. Where, for example, managerial bonuses are paid on the basis of controllable profit, senior managers at head office should carefully scrutinize the divisional performance statements to ensure that costs have been fairly allocated under the different headings in accordance with group policy.

18.3.3 Investment Centre

The managers of an investment centre control both costs and the level and nature of capital investment. Therefore it is possible to assess divisional performance in this case on the basis of **Return on Investment (ROI)**. This is a commonly used form of divisional performance measurement in cases where the divisions operate as investment centres. ROI is calculated as follows:

$$\frac{\text{Divisional net profit}}{\text{Investment in net assets}} \times 100$$

The advantages of using this type of simple measure are that it:

- relates net profit to the resources used to produce it
- is easy for managers to understand
- provides a benchmark for comparison across corporate divisions.

However, as with most measurements based on the relationship between accounting numbers, there are problems in ensuring that ROI provides a valid and consistent measure of divisional performance. Each of the components of ROI is examined in turn below.

18.3.4 Determining Investment in Net Assets

Where ROI is used for comparison purposes, it is important to ensure that investment in net assets is calculated on a consistent basis across divisions. Also, the investment in net assets should represent those resources involved in generating divisional profit that are controllable by divisional management. Investment in net assets may not always provide a useful basis for measurement; in service businesses, the principal 'asset' often comprises the members of staff who provide the service and their value is not usually quantified for reporting purposes.

Another problem is that the working of the ROI calculation contains, potentially, an incentive to divisional management to delay investment, as the following example illustrates.

Example 18.4

Scala Main plc conducts most of its business activities via five operational divisions. Division Gamma manufactures a well-established range of laboratory benches and other equipment. Investment strategy is determined at divisional level. The three principal managers of Gamma division are rewarded partly in salary and partly in bonuses that are dependent upon year-on-year improvements in ROI. The three managers have met to discuss a proposal to replace a significant piece of machinery. The proposed investment will cost £1.3 million, to be depreciated on a straight-line basis over ten years, with an assumed residual value of nil. The existing machinery is ten years old and has reached the end of its originally estimated useful life. In the year ended 31 December 20X3, the depreciation charge relating to the existing machine was £80 000, and its carrying amount at that date was £0. Normally, machinery is replaced when it reaches the end of its useful life. However, one of the managers suggests that the division should defer the investment. He points out that the machine is still working fairly well. Repair costs of £20 000 were incurred in the year ended 31 December 20X3, and it is reasonable to suppose that repair costs in 20X4 probably would not be any higher. A new machine would not incur repair costs during the first three years of ownership because it would be covered by a repair warranty.

Divisional profits were £1 600 000 for 20X3 (before taking into account depreciation and repair costs relating to the machine), and are likely to be at the same level in 20X4. Investments in net assets at 31 December 20X3 totalled £12 000 000. If the new machinery is purchased, investment in net assets at 31 December 20X4 is forecast to be £13 470 000. If the purchase is deferred, investment in net assets is forecast to be £12 580 000. ROI in the division is calculated as follows:

$$\frac{\text{Divisional net profit}}{\text{Investment in net assets at year-end}} \times 100$$

Assess the effects on ROI, and upon the business, of

i) replacing the machine
ii) deferring its replacement.

We can compare the effects of the alternative strategies as follows:

	20X3 Actual	20X4 (replacing machine)	20X4 (deferring replacement)
Profits before depreciation and repair of the machine	1 600 000	1 600 000	1 600 000
Depreciation	(80 000)	(130 000)	0
Repairs	(20 000)	0	(20 000)
Divisional profits	1 500 000	1 470 000	1 580 000
Investment in net assets	12 000 000	13 470 000	12 580 000
ROI	12.5%	10.9%	12.6%

Deferring the replacement of the machine is forecast to produce a significantly higher level of divisional profits, and a small increase in ROI over the 20X3 figure. If the investment is made, however, the ROI decreases. The divisional managers are likely to be tempted to defer investment so as to earn additional rewards in the form of bonuses. In 20X4, the strategy is likely to work reasonably well, provided that the machine continues to function at the required level of reliability. However, in one year's time the managers are likely to be tempted to adopt the same strategy in respect of this machine, and possibly other assets. If this approach is taken consistently, the efficiency of the asset base is likely to decline. All other things being equal, ROI is likely to increase, and managers will be rewarded for failing to keep the non-current asset base up to date.

ROI can be a useful measure, but it needs to be treated with some caution, especially where divisional managers' rewards are based on achieving a specified ROI performance. Divisionalization can lead to a lack of goal congruence in the organization, where divisions compete against each other, divisional managers spend too much time and effort on internal politics, and sub-optimal decisions are made.

18.3.5 Determining Divisional Net Profit

Often, divisions within a company sell to each other, and these interdivisional sales and purchases have an impact on the profits of the divisions involved. A suitable selling price for such transactions has to be agreed between the divisions, and this can have a significant impact on the level of profits in the divisions involved.

Example 18.5

B artolemi plc divides its operations into various divisions. Division P produces components that are used in the production process of Division R - these components are sold by P and by other companies for £20.00 per unit, and are readily available at all times. Up till now, R has purchased these components from other companies, but Paul, the divisional manager of P, has suggested that the profit from the sale of these components might as well stay within Bartolemi, so as to boost overall corporate profit, rather than being earned elsewhere. R's manager, Rosie, agrees, but argues that a discount on the market price would be appropriate given that P will have a captive market and will not have to expend any effort on marketing the components to R. She suggests that a price of £18 per unit is more appropriate. Variable costs per unit are £10, and fixed costs would not be affected by the extra production in Division P. The number of units purchased annually by R is 16 000. What will be the effect on the profit of the two divisions if P sells at:

i) £20 per unit?
ii) £18 per unit?

Because fixed costs would not change, the additional profit made by division P would be the contribution from the sales of 16 000 extra units. Depending on which selling price is used, the additional profit could be either:

$$16\ 000 \times (20 - 10 \text{ variable costs}) = £160\ 000$$
$$16\ 000 \times (18 - 10 \text{ variable costs}) = £128\ 000$$

There is a difference of £32 000 between these profit figures. If P sells to R, an additional profit of £160 000 is made for the company, Bartolemi, as a whole, and a profit of at least £128 000 for division P. But the key question to be resolved is which division obtains the benefit of the £32 000 profit figure. Clearly, Paul would prefer to sell at £20 so that the additional £32 000 remains in his division. Equally, Rosie wants to buy at £18, thus saving £2 per unit on the market price, and therefore adding £32 000 to her division's profit. The discussion between the two managers would have added importance for them if their personal bonuses depended upon divisional performance.

The danger for Bartolemi is that Paul and Rosie fail to reach an agreement, and that Rosie continues to source the component from outside. From Rosie's point of view as a divisional manager, if she sources the component at a price of £20, it doesn't actually matter whether the supplier is division P or an outsider. If Paul and Rosie fall out over this issue, she may decide to continue to source from outside, in order to deny Paul's division the opportunity to make profits (and perhaps to deny him the opportunity for personal gain in the form of bonus).

The scenario outlined in Example 18.5 illustrates what is usually known as the **transfer pricing** problem. More detailed consideration of transfer pricing is outside the scope of this book, but students should be aware of the nature of the problem because it is often an important issue in practice. The example also illustrates a problem of divisionalization: divisional managers may identify closely with their divisions to the detriment of the company as a whole. Senior management at head office level need to be aware of this type of problem, and should take all possible steps to minimize interdivisional rivalries. The company should aim for **goal congruence**, which means that all divisions should be working together to maximize returns for the company as a whole.

Divisionalization can lead to a lack of goal congruence in the organization, where divisions compete against each other, divisional managers spend too much time and effort on internal politics and less than optimal decisions are made. Also, there is a danger that divisional managers will focus upon short-term gains and will neglect longer-term strategic considerations. Senior managers in the organization need to be sensitive to the factors that affect divisional performance, and should be aware of the problems that may arise because of divisionalization.

18.4 NON-FINANCIAL PERFORMANCE MEASURES

Some of the drawbacks of financial performance measures such as ROI can be addressed by assessing performance using a set of non-financial measurements. Example 18.1 early in the chapter demonstrated how a range of performance measures, including both financial and non-financial, can be used to provide valuable management information in the form of KPIs. The rest of this chapter examines the use of a combination of measures in performance evaluation.

Some examples of non-financial performance indicators at a divisional level are given in the example that follows.

Example 18.6

Tony has recently been appointed to head the Light Aircraft division of a major aeronautical manufacturer, Lipp & Smeeton plc. Lipp & Smeeton's other principal divisions manufacture passenger aircraft and corporate jets, and build engines for the defence industry. The company's stated aims are to grow market share, and to maintain outstanding levels of quality and service to customers. The activities of the Light Aircraft division comprise manufacture of small aircraft for sale to private owners and clubs, and of powered gliders and hang-gliders. Whereas the other divisions have been consistently good performers, Light Aircraft has turned in losses for the last three years under poor quality divisional management, despite buoyant market conditions. Although the basic engine quality of the products has remained high, there have been complaints from customers about the long lead time for delivery, high prices and poor quality interior finish. Tony's task is to turn the division around, returning it to profit within 18 months.

What performance measures are likely to be appropriate in assessing both divisional performance and Tony's own performance?

Financial performance measures will be of importance in assessing how quickly the division can be returned to profit. Measures such as ROI, gross profit margin and sales revenue growth will be useful. The measures should correspond, as far as possible, with the aims of the company as a whole. Its first stated aim is to grow market share, and so it is important to ensure that the Light Aircraft division, and Tony, as its head, are assessed on market share measurement.

The division has maintained reasonable quality standards, but has failed on several aspects of customer satisfaction. The second stated aim of Lipp & Smeeton is to maintain 'outstanding levels of quality and service to customers'. Tony needs to ensure that the division first achieves those levels, before he need worry about maintaining them. The measurement of quality and service standards is likely to involve the following:

CUSTOMER SERVICE

Post-sales questionnaires to elicit customer satisfaction levels in respect of:

- competence of sales staff
- availability of sales staff
- effectiveness of staff in dealing with complaints (if any)

- delivery schedules
- product finish and quality
- product pricing compared to competitors.

QUALITY

- number of defects detected during quality inspection
- number of defects detected post-delivery
- customer satisfaction levels in respect of quality
- number of customer complaints per month/year.

The most appropriate non-financial measurements to use naturally vary from one organization to another. In the aircraft business, the safety and quality characteristics of the product are of surpassing importance, and measures of performance are likely to focus heavily on quality issues. In another context, for example, online rail travel booking, performance measures are likely to focus upon ease of use and accessibility of the service, efficiency and speed of information processing, and the appearance and design of the website. Where customers are being provided with a face-to-face service, for example, rail travel booking at a train station ticket office , other factors come into play. Customers are likely to value not only efficiency, but also the friendliness and helpfulness of the staff and their competence in making bookings. Performance measures are likely to reflect these factors.

> **Self-test question 18.4 (answer at the end of the book)**
>
> HB is the handbag division of a luxury goods manufacturer, BYPH. HB's business objective is to lead the market in the sales of very high quality, exclusive leather handbags. Each season HB changes most of its designs, apart from a small number of classic items.
> Discuss whether or not the following performance indicators are likely to be appropriate non-financial measures of success:
>
> 1 market share
> 2 number of defective products
> 3 volume of sales by product line
> 4 customer perceptions of exclusivity
> 5 competitiveness of product pricing.

18.5 THE BALANCED SCORECARD

As noted in the previous section of the chapter, the best way of assessing the performance of an organization or division is likely to be via a combination of financial and non-financial measures. In this section, we examine a popular method of performance measurement and reporting using financial and non-financial measurements that can be tailored to individual organizations.

The 'balanced scorecard' is an idea developed by two US academic researchers, Robert Kaplan and David Norton. The term describes an easily understood set of performance measures that can be used to provide managers with a relevant and thorough summary of complex information about the business. Kaplan and Norton likened the scorecard to the dials and indicators in an aeroplane cockpit:

> 'For the complex task of navigating and flying an aeroplane, pilots need detailed information about many aspects of the flight. They need information on fuel, air speed, altitude, bearing, destination, and other indicators that summarize the current and predicted environment. Reliance on one instrument can be fatal. Similarly, the complexity of managing an organization today requires that managers be able to view performance in several areas simultaneously.'

(Kaplan, R.S. and Norton, D.P. (1992) The balanced scorecard: measures that drive performance', *Harvard Business Review,* Jan–Feb, pp. 71–79.)

The balanced scorecard uses both financial and non-financial measures to examine the performance of the business. Kaplan and Norton identify four fundamental perspectives that can be applied to any business, in the form of questions:

- How do customers see us? (Customer perspective)
- What must we excel at? (Internal perspective)
- Can we continue to improve and create value? (Innovation and learning perspective)
- How do we look to shareholders? (Financial perspective)

These four perspectives are represented on the balanced scorecard as set out in Figure 18.2.

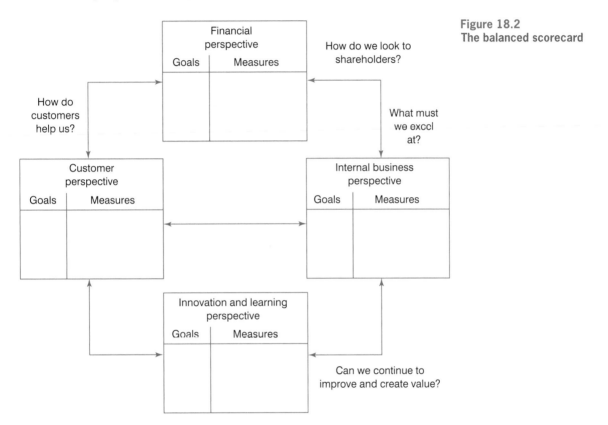

**Figure 18.2
The balanced scorecard**

In order to use the balanced scorecard managers must be able to identify the key performance measures under each of the four perspectives. It is important that these should be linked in to the overall business strategy, and, as suggested in the figure, to each other. The balanced scorecard emphasizes the interdependence of the measurements in its four perspectives. Kaplan and Norton illustrate the chain of cause and effect using the example of a real business: growth in employee morale was correlated to customer satisfaction which was linked to faster settlement of invoices, resulting in improvements in financial perspective indicators such as return on capital employed. In principle, a virtuous circle is established, where improvements in one perspective result in improvements elsewhere. Certain other advantages are claimed for the balanced scorecard:

- It minimizes information overload by limiting the number of performance measures used, ensuring that only really important measurements are reported.
- It brings key aspects of a business's performance together into a single management report.
- It ensures that managers are obliged to consider all of the really important measurements together, so that if good performance in one area has been achieved at the expense of diminishing performance in another area, the trade-off should be obvious.

18.5.1 The Four Key Perspectives of the Balanced Scorecard

CUSTOMER PERSPECTIVE Customer satisfaction is a critical area for all businesses. Kaplan and Norton observe in their paper that customers' concerns tend to relate to time (for example, time taken to fulfil orders), quality, performance and service and cost. In putting the balanced scorecard into operation, a business might, for example, identify two key goals: increasing market share and improving the delivery schedule. In this case relevant performance measures are likely to include:

- number of new customers gained
- percentage of sales from new customers
- percentage of total market share
- average time lapse between order and delivery.

INTERNAL BUSINESS PERSPECTIVE In order to achieve the goal of customer satisfaction, a business's managers must be able to identify the key internal processes that contribute to success or failure. Taking the same example as above, increased market share might hinge upon the business's relative success in introducing new products into a competitive market. If this is the case, business goals might include meeting a schedule of planned product innovations. The relevant performance measurement might be performance against this schedule.

INNOVATION AND LEARNING PERSPECTIVE As Kaplan and Norton point out, the intense nature of global competition means that businesses must continually innovate in order to survive and to create value for customers and shareholders. If a business is to grow, it needs to invest in its infrastructure in order to create the right conditions. This could involve investment in people (in the form of recruitment and training), organization of the business in order to maximize creativity and motivation amongst staff and investment in systems (such as computer systems) that will help to achieve the business's strategic objectives. A specific business goal could be, for example, to create the conditions necessary for first-class product innovation and development. Relevant performance measures might include:

- retention rate of employees in key areas
- number of new appointments in relevant departments
- satisfaction levels amongst key employees.

(Note that the 'innovation and learning' perspective identified by Kaplan and Norton is referred to in some subsequent writings as the 'learning and growth' perspective.)

FINANCIAL PERSPECTIVE The way in which shareholders see the business from a financial perspective is heavily influenced by the contents of the important financial statements such as the statement of financial position, statement of cash flows and statement of profit or loss. Such statements provide a summary of the financial effects of decisions made by managers in pursuing the goals they have identified for the business. The financial statements can be viewed as the acid test of success or failure. It may take time for the effects of innovative strategies to filter through and to be evidenced in the financial statements presented to shareholders. However, the success or failure of the strategies must eventually be judged by financial measurements. As Kaplan and Norton put it:

'A failure to convert improved operational performance, as measured in the scorecard, into improved financial performance should send executives back to their drawing boards to rethink the company's strategy or its implementation plans.'

Relevant performance measures might include some of the measurements explained earlier in the chapter and other widely used accounting ratios such as earnings per share and ROCE.

18.5.2 The Balanced Scorecard in Practice

The balanced scorecard idea has proved to be very pervasive and influential. Kaplan and Norton published their first paper in 1992, and followed it with several others and a couple of books. Around the world, many organizations, in both the private and public sector, use the balanced scorecard as an essential management tool: research evidence indicates that it is used by approximately 50% of the companies in the US Fortune 1000 listing, and by about 40% of companies in Europe. The balanced scorecard is used across a range of sectors, including education, healthcare, consumer electronics, hospitality and tourism. Some well-known examples of companies using it successfully are Philips Electronics and Unilever. The balanced scorecard is widely used in both the public and private sectors.

Example 18.7 (Real-Life)

VEOLIA WATER NORTH AMERICA

The Balanced Scorecard Institute (www.balancedscorecard.org) features several examples of successful balanced scorecard implementations over a range of industries and activities. One successful implementation was at Veolia Water North America. The business identified its overall strategic themes and then used them as a basis for developing a set of strategic objectives. This broad approach was further refined into a set of measures and targets: Key Performance Indicators (KPIs). Veolia, at the time of the balanced scorecard development, employed around 2700 employees at over 300 sites in the USA and Canada. Communication of the targets and measurements was therefore a complex process. Despite such logistical challenges, the business has successfully implemented its balanced scorecard programme, and has experienced significant improvements in measures such as operating cash flow, safety and environmental impacts.

18.5.3 Is the Balanced Scorecard Successful?

Since its introduction in the 1990s, the balanced scorecard has attracted a great deal of attention and has been the subject of many academic and professional journal articles. Many large businesses, as discussed above, have adopted it enthusiastically, but the scale of adoption does not necessarily prove success. Business managers are as likely as anyone else to take up the latest fad. So, is the balanced scorecard more than a passing fad? Of course, it is not easy to prove a causal link between the adoption of any new measure and improved (or deteriorated) performance. However, some studies have suggested that adoption of the balanced scorecard has been successful.

Chapter Summary

This chapter has explained a range of approaches to measuring and reporting performance within the firm. The early part of the chapter stressed the importance of linking performance measurement to the strategic objectives of the business. The topic of divisional responsibility was introduced in order to explain how larger organizations might monitor performance across a range of different activities. Students should by now understand the advantages and drawbacks of decentralization.

Three levels of divisional autonomy were identified and discussed: cost/revenue centre, profit centre and investment centre. Appropriate methods of performance assessment were identified in respect of each level of autonomy. Problems in determining the performance of individual divisions were also discussed.

Non-financial performance measures should not be overlooked; these can play a very important role in performance assessment. The chapter explained some of the non-financial measures that might be appropriate in the context of a particular firm, and then briefly outlined the key features of one of the most important recent developments in performance measurement: the balanced scorecard.

Internet Resources

Book's companion website summary

The website contains the following resources in respect of Chapter 18:

Students' section

A multiple choice quiz containing ten questions
Three additional questions with answers

Lecturers' section

Answers to end-of-chapter exercises 18.8 to 18.13.
Three additional questions with answers
Case study
Testbank
Instructor's Manual
PowerPoint presentation

Exercises: Answers at the End of the Book

18.1 Identify three key characteristics of management information.

18.2 Golfstore Retail plc was established five years ago by a small team of golf enthusiasts in Scotland. The company retails a range of quality golfers' clothing and equipment from stores around Scotland. Last year it expanded its stores into the north of England and into Wales. The management team has ambitions to open stores throughout the UK and Ireland, with the ultimate aim of expanding into Western Europe within the next eight years. The board has met to discuss the best way of managing the expansion, and to consider a proposal to establish relatively autonomous divisions based on geographical areas so that eventually, for example, there will be a Golfstore France with its own divisional management team.

Explain to the directors the principal advantages of divisionalization within the context of their business.

18.3 The managers of division Alpha of Burntwood and Down Holdings determine selling prices for the division, and control almost all costs. Decisions on non-current assets purchases are made at head office level. How would you classify Alpha?

a) A profit centre
b) A cost centre
c) A revenue centre
d) An investment centre

18.4 Perkora Bains manufactures household fittings. The company uses a system of divisional management, with divisions split by product type. All divisions are treated as profit centres. The accountant in the bathroom division (BD) has gathered the following data for production of the quarterly performance statement which is due for submission to head office:

	£000
Direct materials cost	280
Direct labour cost	311
Sales	1 671
Depreciation of non-current assets	112
Fixed costs excluding depreciation	580
Head office cost allocation	337

Of the fixed costs, £37 000 is non-controllable at divisional level. The head office cost allocation relates to research and development and marketing expenditure.

i) Prepare a quarterly divisional performance statement for BD.
ii) Identify the amount of profit that should be used as an indicator of divisional performance.

18.5   Identify and explain two reasons why Return on Investment (ROI) may be an unreliable measurement of divisional performance.

18.6   Tripp and Hopp Limited is a booking agency that specializes in selling London theatre tickets via its website. The company's objective is 'to provide a competitive, efficient and secure service to London's theatregoers'.

Draw up a list of six appropriate non-financial performance indicators that will help Tripp and Hopp's management to assess the extent to which the company is meeting its objectives. For each indicator, suggest a way of measuring it.

18.7   Your company is considering the introduction of a Balanced Scorecard system. Your head of department has attended a briefing session on the new system and has circulated the following email:

To: Marketing department staff
From: Head of department

BALANCED SCORECARD
You may have heard by now that our chief executive wants to introduce a so-called 'Balanced Scorecard' system for performance measurement. Frankly, even after attending the briefing I am still a bit clueless on the subject. I do not think it involves any figures, which would be good news, but we would have to measure things like customer satisfaction. Brian, the accountant, said that 'lots of companies have tried this system and it is well known'. I think he also said 'it is like flying an aeroplane' but perhaps I had dozed off at that point. Have any of you heard of it? I would like to hear from anyone who can provide me with a brief, comprehensible account of the Balanced Scorecard.
    Reply to the memo, explaining the Balanced Scorecard as concisely as possible.

Exercises: Answers Available on the Lecturers' Section of the Book's Website

18.8   Identify and briefly discuss the principal drawbacks to divisional organization within large businesses.

18.9   The management team of Florian Space Products plc is meeting to discuss a proposal to divide the company's operations into three divisions. Each division will deal with one of the business's three principal products. The finance director proposes that the divisions should be given cost centre status. The marketing director, however, argues that if divisionalization is to be effective, the divisions should operate on a fully decentralized basis as investment centres.
    Identify and explain two arguments supporting each of the directors' views.

18.10 Identify one from each list of words given below to fill in the missing words in the following sentence:
    A divisional performance statement for (1) ____ centre identifies contribution, (2) ____ profit, divisional profit before allocation of (3) ____ costs and divisional profit before tax.

List 1	List 2	List 3
A profit	Non-controllable	Interest
A cost	Operating	Divisional
An investment	Controllable	Head office

18.11 Spall Spelling plc operates several manufacturing divisions, with each division treated as a profit centre. Division D's accountant has drawn up the following list of data prior to preparing the monthly performance statement for submission to head office.

	£
Sales	272 600
Fixed costs	72 400
Depreciation	36 000
Variable materials	47 000
Variable labour	63 700

Of the depreciation charge for the month, 25% relates to non-current assets over which the division has complete control. Of the fixed costs, 15% are non-controllable. The accountant has been notified that the head office cost allocation for the month is £43 200.

Prepare a divisional performance statement for Division D.

18.12 Answer TRUE or FALSE to the following statements about the Balanced Scorecard method of performance measurement.

1. The Balanced Scorecard is helpful to managers who are not accountants because it uses only non-financial measurements of performance.
2. The Balanced Scorecard can help managers by cutting down information overload.
3. A problem with the Balanced Scorecard is that it uses the same performance measurements across all companies, and sometimes these are not appropriate.
4. In order to use the Balanced Scorecard effectively, managers must be able to link performance measurement to the overall business strategy.

18.13 As part of its implementation of the Balanced Scorecard method of performance appraisal, the directors of Bretton Tallis plc have met to discuss the key question: 'Can we continue to improve and create value?' The company, which is engaged in the manufacture and sale of replacement windows and doors, faces tough competition: recent entrants to the market have introduced a range of innovative product improvements, with the result that Bretton Tallis's product range is starting to look out of date. The directors conclude that the company can continue to improve and create value only if it takes urgent steps to improve the quality and design of its product ranges. Two specific goals are identified: to promote the rapid development of new plastics (in order to produce better and more distinctive products), and to create conditions in which innovative design can flourish.

For each of these goals suggest four performance measurements that could assist the company's directors in assessing progress towards the goals.

Financial Management

19 The management of working capital

Aim of the chapter

To know about the components of a business's working capital, and to understand some of the key principles and practices involved in managing each of the working capital components.

Learning outcomes

After reading the chapter and completing the exercises, students should:

- Be able to identify the principal components of working capital and to understand the potential consequences of the mismanagement of each of the components.

- Understand and be able to apply simple techniques used in the management of inventory.

- Understand the problems and opportunities involved in offering credit to customers, and the techniques involved in managing trade receivables.

- Understand some of the important issues relating to the management of cash, and of trade payables.

Introduction

Earlier chapters in this book have referred extensively to the components of working capital in a range of accounting contexts. The amount of a business's working capital can be identified easily from its statement of financial position; it is the total of current assets less current liabilities, and therefore the components of working capital are the principal elements included under current assets and current liabilities:

- inventories
- trade receivables
- cash (if any)
- trade payables
- bank overdraft (if any).

Cash circulates around the business as a result of routine transactions such as the purchase of new inventories, the receipt of amounts of cash owed by debtors, and the payment of amounts owed, for example, to suppliers, employees and the government. Cash is the fundamental business resource. Without sufficient cash, any business will, sooner or later, fail.
　　Sources of cash include:

- cash resources placed in the business by its owner(s)
- cash borrowed from individuals, other businesses or lending institutions
- cash generated by the business itself through the sale of goods or services at a profit.

A business must ensure that its sources of cash ultimately exceed the amounts of cash expended on the purchase of inventories, non-current assets and other goods and services involved in running the business. This chapter looks at the management of the principal working capital components. It will examine some of the problems and issues that arise in respect of the elements of working capital, and some management techniques that assist a business in keeping control over inventories, trade receivables, and so on.

19.1 ELEMENTS OF WORKING CAPITAL

As explained in the introduction to the chapter, cash circulates around the business. Figure 19.1 shows in the form of a diagram the inflows and outflows of cash that take place in a typical business environment where inventories are purchased, or manufactured. The diagram for a service business would look similar but would exclude inventories.

19.1.1 Management and Mismanagement of Working Capital

The principal elements of working capital must be carefully controlled so that the vital resource of cash is not misapplied. Problems can occur at any point in the cycle. For example, if too much inventory is bought, trade payables will rise. In order to pay the amounts owing in good time, additional pressure will be put on the cash resources of the business. In the following subsection we consider some of the consequences of mismanagement of the various elements of working capital.

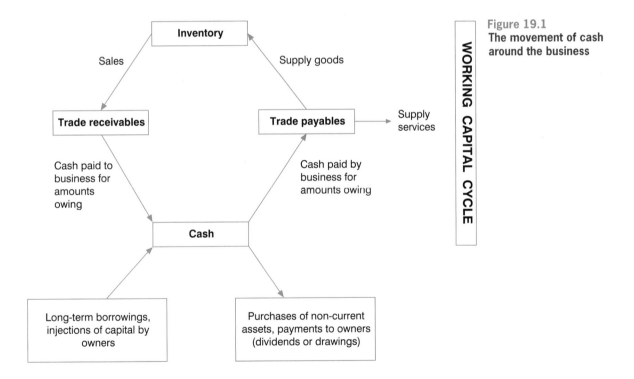

Figure 19.1
The movement of cash around the business

TOO MUCH INVENTORY A fairly common error in business is to tie up too much cash by over-purchasing inventory. This can lead to some of the following problems:

- If the inventory comprises items that go out of fashion rapidly, it may lose most or all of its value before it can be sold.
- If the inventory is perishable it may reach the end of its shelf life before it can be sold.
- It costs money to store inventory safely. Additional costs may be incurred for no obvious benefit.
- If too much cash is tied up because of over-purchasing of inventory, it is not available for other uses in the business. This could lead to a situation where the business is obliged to borrow cash, thus incurring finance costs.

TOO LITTLE INVENTORY There may not be sufficient inventory to fulfil orders and customers will go elsewhere. The business may have missed opportunities to purchase inventory at special prices or to obtain discounts for bulk purchases.

TRADE RECEIVABLES TOO HIGH Where the level of trade receivables is too high, the business is not collecting cash quickly enough. This may result in a bottleneck in the working capital cycle, causing a shortage of cash, with knock-on effects on other parts of the business.

TRADE RECEIVABLES TOO LOW A low level of receivables may indicate the possibility that the business is not allowing sufficient credit to its customers. Potential customers may be buying from a competitor who can offer superior credit terms.

TRADE PAYABLES TOO HIGH If trade payable amounts are not paid promptly there may be a consequent loss of goodwill towards the business. In extreme cases, suppliers may refuse to supply any further goods or services on credit, and will demand cash payments in advance, or upon delivery.

TRADE PAYABLES TOO LOW People and businesses like to have amounts due to them paid promptly, but in many types of business it is normal practice to allow credit. Credit terms are typically expressed as 'payment due within 30 days following invoice'. It usually makes good business sense to pay towards the end of the time allowed, and thus to take advantage of what is effectively a source of interest-free credit.

CASH TOO LOW If working capital is mismanaged, the consequence may be that the cash level in the business is too low. It may become necessary to borrow cash which will incur additional finance costs. Also, opportunities to earn interest by short-term investment of surplus cash are lost. If mismanagement also involves poor record keeping, businesses run the risk of running up unauthorized overdrafts and incurring penalty bank charges. Good cash management involves anticipating any cash shortages and making appropriate arrangements in advance - this is just as true for businesses as it is for individuals.

CASH TOO HIGH It may seem surprising that a business can suffer from the problem of too much cash, but it can happen. One of the reasons people go into business is to make profits in the form of a return on their investment. The return (or 'profit') made out of the initial investment in the business has to be greater than the return that can be made by leaving the money in a simple bank deposit account. Putting money into a bank account is easy, and requires virtually no effort on the part of the investor. By contrast, starting up a business requires a great deal of effort and skill, and the investor expects a much greater reward as compensation for the additional risk and work involved.

If there is surplus cash in the business, what can be done with it? The simple, short-term, answer is to place the money on deposit where it can earn interest. However, as noted above, this is unlikely to provide a sufficient return. Sometimes, if the cash surplus is more or less permanent, it makes sense to return the money in the form of a repayment of capital so that the owner can invest in another business venture.

Example 19.1 (Real-Life)

Tech companies, such as Microsoft, Apple and Google are frequently cited as examples of companies that have very high levels of cash. In 2013 a hedge fund manager, David Einhorn, brought a legal action against Apple in an attempt to get the company to return the bulk of its cash reserves (at that time $137 billion) to shareholders. The action was dropped shortly afterwards, but it served to emphasize the extraordinarily large amount of cash held by Apple.

19.2 ASSET AND LIABILITY COMPONENTS IN PRACTICE

The relative size and importance of the components of working capital (and other assets and liabilities) vary a great deal in practice, depending upon the nature of the business. This section of the chapter examines the statements of financial position of three listed businesses in order to illustrate and explain the point. The activities of the three selected businesses are diverse in nature: a service business, a retailer and a pharmaceuticals manufacturer.

Example 19.2 (Real-Life)

1 Experian plc is a global information services company. Amongst other activities it allows individuals to check their own credit ratings for a small fee.
2 Sainsbury plc is one of the largest UK supermarket groups
3 AstraZeneca plc is a very large pharmaceuticals business which researches, develops and manufactures pharmaceutical products.

The most recent (at the time of writing) statements of financial position for the three businesses are presented below. For ease of understanding some of the information has been summarized under headings such as 'other current assets'. Note that Experian plc and AstraZeneca plc both present their financial statements in US$. The figures have been analysed vertically, showing each asset figure as a percentage of total assets, and each liability figure as a percentage of total liabilities. (See Chapter 8 earlier in the book as a reminder of what is involved in vertical analysis). This analysis provides some further insight into the relative size and importance of the components of working capital and other areas of the statement of financial position.

	Experian plc US$ million 31 March 2016	%	J Sainsbury plc £ million 12 March 2016	%	AstraZeneca plc US$ million 31 December 2015	%
ASSETS						
Non-current assets						
Intangible assets	5 629	76.0	329	1.9	34 514	57.4
Property, plant and equipment	352	4.8	9 764	57.5	6 413	10.7
Investments and other non-current assets	297	4.0	2 436	14.4	3 190	5.3
	6 278	84.8	12 529	73.8	44 117	73.4
Current assets						
Inventories	1	0.0	968	5.7	2 143	3.6
Trade and other receivables	902	12.2	508	3.0	6 622	11.0
Other current assets	70	0.9	1 825	10.8	1 002	1.6
Cash	156	2.1	1 143	6.7	6 240	10.4
	1 129	15.2	4 444	26.2	16 007	26.6
TOTAL ASSETS	**7 407**	**100.0**	**16 973**	**100.0**	**60 124**	**100.0**
EQUITY	2 438		6 365		18 509	
LIABILITIES						
Non-current liabilities	3 626	73.0	3 884	36.6	26 746	64.3
Current liabilities						
Trade payables	1 124	22.6	3 077	29.0	11 663	28.0
Loans and borrowings	52	1.0	223	2.1	916	2.2
Other current liabilities	167	3.4	3 424	32.3	2 290	5.5
	1 343	27.0	6 724	63.4	14 869	35.7
TOTAL LIABILITIES	4 969		10 608		41 615	
EQUITY AND LIABILITIES	**7 407**	**100.0**	**16 973**	**100.0**	**60 124**	**100.0**

What does this table tell us?

Comparing the non-current assets section of the statement of financial position, we can see that the bulk of Sainsbury's assets comprise property, plant and equipment with relatively small amounts of intangible assets. This makes sense: Sainsbury's principal assets are likely to be its store premises and related assets. Experian, on the other hand, has a relatively low figure for property, plant and equipment. As a knowledge-based business, it requires little investment in tangible non-current assets. However, it does have very substantial amounts of intangible assets, which is also consistent with a knowledge-based business. AstraZeneca's largest asset category is intangible assets. This is expected to be the case in a pharmaceutical business, because the costs relating to potentially or actually successful drugs are treated as intangible non-current assets, amortized over the expected life of the product.

Turning to the current asset section of the statements we can see the composition of the working capital assets for each business. Experian plc, as a service provider, has negligible amounts of inventory. Its current assets comprise principally receivables and cash. Sainsbury's inventory figure comprises 5.7% of total assets which may seem relatively low. However, it should be noted that some of Sainsbury's inventory is perishable (many food items) or subject to fashion trends (clothing). Sainsbury's receivables figure represents only a low proportion of total assets. Again, this is to be expected, as most of the company's sales are paid for by cash or debit card. A striking feature of AstraZeneca's current assets is the large amount of cash which accounts for over 10% of total assets.

Turning to current liabilities we can see that Sainsbury's has a high level of trade payables. It has net current liabilities of £2280 million (current assets of £4444 million less current liabilities of £6724 million), but this is often the case for retailers: they tend to have high levels of current liabilities and negligible amounts of trade receivables. Experian plc, too, has net current liabilities of $214 million (current assets of $1129 million less current liabilities of $1343 million). AstraZeneca plc has a net current assets position of $1138 million (current assets of $16 007 million less current liabilities of $14 869 million), with trade payables and other current liabilities being significant figures.

SUMMARY

It can be seen from the above analysis that the composition of the statement of financial position varies substantially depending upon the nature of the business. Service businesses tend to have low levels of non-current tangible assets and very low levels of inventory. A retail business such as a supermarket operates with high levels of tangible non-current assets, virtually no trade receivables, and relatively high levels of trade payables. A pharmaceuticals business can be expected to have high levels of intangible non-current assets, and also substantial amounts of working capital under all the principal headings.

Moldova Mellish plc has relatively high levels of inventory and trade payables, but a very low level of trade receivables. It also has high levels of tangible non-current assets, but hardly any intangible assets.

Which type of business is the company most likely to be engaged in?

a) Architect's practice
b) Electrical goods retailer
c) Building construction
d) Pharmaceuticals

Self-test question 19.1 (answer at the end of the book)

19.3 THE MANAGEMENT OF INVENTORIES

The fundamental challenge in inventory management is ensuring that the optimal level of inventory is available at any given time. It is important to be able to fulfil customer orders quickly and efficiently, but equally, the business must ensure that it does not incur unnecessary holding costs.

19.3.1 Holding Costs

Holding costs include any incremental costs involved in storing inventory, such as additional costs of insurance, incremental premises costs and staff costs incurred in checking and moving inventory around. For decision making about the level of inventory to hold it is important to distinguish between variable and fixed holding costs (see Chapter 14 for a reminder of the classification of costs between fixed and variable). For example, if three people are employed by a business to store and move inventory, the acquisition of an additional few units of inventory will make no difference to overall employment costs. However, if inventory increases substantially then it may be necessary to employ more people in the warehouse, in which case the cost is stepped, and an incremental holding cost is incurred.

19.3.2 Economic Order Quantity

It is possible to calculate the optimum size of an inventory order by using the economic order quantity (EOQ) model. If inventory is ordered infrequently, the total costs incurred in the ordering process are lower than if there are frequent orders. On the other hand, if inventory is ordered more frequently, the average inventory level is higher than if there are infrequent orders, and holding costs tend to increase. The relationship between the order quantity and total incremental costs of ordering and holding inventory can be demonstrated in graphical form, as shown in Figure 19.2.

Ordering costs include items such as the clerical time involved in placing an order, and receiving and recording inventory receipts. The graph shows a fall in ordering costs the greater the quantity ordered (which means that fewer orders are placed). Holding costs move in the opposite direction: as inventory quantities increase so do incremental holding costs. There is an optimal ordering point where total costs are at the lowest point, shown by the dotted line on the graph.

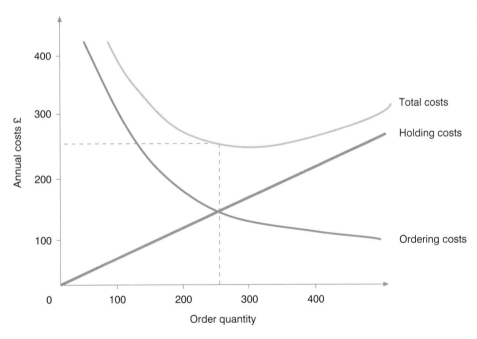

Figure 19.2
Economic order
quantity: graph

USING A FORMULA FOR ECONOMIC ORDER QUANTITY (EOQ) The EOQ can be calculated by using the following formula:

$$Q = \sqrt{\frac{2 \times D \times O}{H}}$$

where: Q = Economic order quantity
D = Demand for inventory item in the period
O = Cost per order
H = Holding cost per unit

Example 19.3 shows the application of the formula.

Example 19.3

Bullfinch Supplies Ltd uses the EOQ formula to determine the optimal size of inventory orders. For one of its most popular lines, the following information has been established by the company's management accountant:

Demand for the item in the period = 5000 units
Cost per order = £25
Holding cost per unit = £17

Applying the EOQ model, the economic order quantity (Q) is as follows:

$$Q = \sqrt{\frac{2 \times 5000 \times £25}{£17}}$$

$$Q = 121$$

So, if the business orders 121 units of inventory total costs (holding costs and order costs) are minimized.

The management accountant of Froggie Feltham Ltd has decided to start using the EOQ model in order to try to reduce inventory costs to their optimal level. For inventory item AA34Q he works out demand for the period at 16 000 units. The holding cost per unit is estimated at £1.50, and the ordering cost at £12. What is the EOQ?

Self-test question 19.2 (answer at the end of the book)

DRAWBACKS OF THE EOQ MODEL There are several significant drawbacks to the EOQ model. First, it assumes that holding costs are constant, but this may not be realistic. For example, if another member of staff is required once inventories exceed a certain level, there is a stepped increase in costs, rather than a smooth progression as assumed in the graph earlier in this section of the chapter. Also, the process of establishing both holding and ordering costs involves many assumptions and approximations. A further problem is that it overlooks fluctuations in demand throughout an accounting period. If demand is seasonal, application of the model may not provide sufficiently frequent ordering to guarantee an adequate level of inventory at times of peak demand.

19.3.3 Other Approaches to the Management of Inventories

LIMITING MANAGEMENT INPUT A business may have many thousands of different types of inventory, but only a relatively restricted number of lines in which there is a high level of turnover. Where this is the case, intensive management of all lines of inventory would be an inefficient use of management resources. Therefore, it makes sense to categorize the lines of inventory into, for example, high-level, mid-level and low-level usage. Management techniques such as EOQ can then be applied to the relatively few lines of high level usage inventory.

JUST-IN-TIME (JIT) JIT describes a radically different approach to the management of production, inventory and purchasing which originated in the Toyota company in Japan. JIT is sometimes described as a 'philosophy' of management. This system aims to completely eliminate waste in production, and is driven solely by demand for the finished product. Finished goods are produced in exactly the quantities required at exactly the right time for shipping to the customer. This means that finished goods inventory is kept to an absolute minimum, with a target level of zero. The precise demand for finished goods 'pulls' the material requirements through the production system, applying techniques and processes in a systematic and predictable manner. JIT extends to arrangements for materials and components purchased. Relationships with suppliers are organized so that when demand arises, the exact quantity of goods required can be delivered immediately by the supplier. This may mean delivery in small quantities very frequently. Order costs are likely to be relatively high, although the system should be highly automated in order to minimize costs, but holding costs under this approach should be virtually zero as materials received are put straight to work in the production system. In summary, inventory management under JIT is achieved by, as far as possible, the elimination of inventory.

Clearly, JIT demands a very high level of organization and cooperation from all those involved, including management, employees and, not least, suppliers. There is no slack time, and constant effort is required to make the system work. The system has been widely adopted outside Japan, sometimes under other names such as World Class Manufacturing or Lean Manufacturing.

19.4 THE MANAGEMENT OF TRADE RECEIVABLES

In many types of business, customers expect to be offered credit facilities: that is, they receive goods or services some time before being obliged to pay for them. Typically, the credit terms are that payment is required within a certain number of days after the issue of the invoice. A common arrangement is to require payment within 30 days. From the point of view of the seller, this represents a disadvantage in that it would be more beneficial to receive the cash straight away. However, if custom and practice within a particular business sector are to offer credit terms, any business that does not do so is likely to be at a disadvantage. In effect, it may be impossible to insist on payment in advance or upon delivery. A business that is obliged to offer credit terms to its customers is therefore placed in the position of having to manage its receivables carefully, to make sure that they do not become overdue, or in the worst case, fail to pay at all.

The benefits and drawbacks of offering credit terms to customers are summarized below:

Benefits of offering credit terms	Drawbacks of offering credit terms
1. Can increase revenue, especially if the terms are favourable and attractive to customers.	1. The risk of non-payment. 2. Administrative costs associated with the management of trade receivables. 3. Reduces the cash resources potentially available to the business. The business may have to borrow to finance receivables. 4. Loss of potential interest receivable.

19.4.1 Addressing the Risks of Offering Credit to Customers

The management of trade receivables largely relates to managing the various risks and drawbacks identified above.

NON-PAYMENT RISK The risk of non-payment can be minimized by careful vetting of potential customers. It would be unwise to offer credit terms without some investigation. The vetting process usually involves obtaining credit references (ie. one or more references from other businesses with whom the potential customer has a relationship and a track record of payment on time), information from a credit rating agency and any publicly available information, such as financial statements filed with Companies House. An example of a credit rating agency is Dun & Bradstreet. Its website (www.dnb.co.uk) provides a description and examples of the types of service it offers.

ADMINISTRATIVE COSTS Managing receivables inevitably incurs costs. A business has the choice of whether to incur the costs directly by managing its own receivables, or alternatively, to buy **factoring** services. When receivables are factored, a factor adopts the responsibility for collecting the amounts due, as in the following example which illustrates the typical costs of the arrangement.

Example 19.4

The directors of Busby Barton plc have decided to enter into a factoring arrangement in respect of the company's receivables. At the start of the agreement, the company's trade receivables total £166 000. The factoring company, Nene Factors Limited, pay Busby Barton plc 80% of the amount due, ie. £132 800, immediately. Nene Factors Limited takes over the responsibility of collecting the amounts due. At the end of each month it pays Busby Barton plc 80% of the total amount of sales invoices raised during the month, plus the balance (20%) of the amount of sales invoices from previous periods that have been paid, less a fee of 1.5% of total invoice value. The fee covers Nene Factors' own costs, including the cost of providing the finance for the 80% immediate payment.

The details of factoring arrangements can vary from that shown in the example above. The amount of the initial payment is usually somewhere between 70% and 90% of total invoice value, but the factor often excludes old or hard-to-collect balances from the total invoice value. The fee of 1.5% in the example is typical, but it may vary between 1% and 3%.

Factoring arrangements can be very helpful as a source of business finance, and also as a means of avoiding the complications of trade receivables management. However, there are some drawbacks. Factors usually avoid the most difficult elements of receivables collection by taking on only those invoices that relate to low-risk customers. The business is therefore left with the problem of collecting the difficult outstanding items. Also, there is the matter of the factor's fee. If the business can collect its receivables for less than the factor's fee, then it would be advisable to do so.

REDUCTION IN CASH RESOURCES AND POTENTIAL LOSS OF INTEREST Factoring provides a means of advancing payment for a substantial part of the total value of trade receivables, and helps to address the problem of reduced cash resources. Businesses that choose to keep trade receivables collection in-house are at a comparative disadvantage in terms of cash resources. They must perform a balancing act with the various elements of working capital to ensure that cash is not depleted more than absolutely necessary. Good quality business forecasting and budgeting can help in ensuring that any cash shortfalls are foreseen and provided for in advance by, for example, arranging short-term overdraft facilities.

19.4.2 The Credit Control Function

Where businesses keep the process of collecting trade receivables in-house, they need in almost all cases (except for the smallest businesses) to run a credit control function. The credit controller is typically responsible for:

1 running credit checks on potential customers
2 setting credit limits for each customer, and reviewing them regularly in the light of changing circumstances
3 reviewing the list of outstanding invoices, and chasing up overdue items
4 advising on bad and doubtful receivables which may require adjustment in the financial statements (see Chapter 4).

Credit control is effective only where good quality information is available. Customers' accounts must be kept up to date, and recording of sales invoices and receipts from customers must be done promptly and accurately. It should be possible to see at any time exactly how much a customer owes to the business.

A useful control mechanism is an age analysis of receivables which summarizes receivables according to how long they have been owed. The age analysis is prepared at least monthly in most businesses. The next example illustrates an age analysis of receivables for a business, and demonstrates the way in which the credit controller would typically review and act upon it. The data used in the example is limited, for obvious reasons. However, in real life a credit controller may be looking at age analysis reports with hundreds or thousands of lines of data.

Example 19.5

Perceval Holland Limited supplies goods on credit to its customers. The company offers credit terms of payment within 30 days of receipt of invoice. At 31 March 20X4, an age analysis of the company's receivables shows the following summary information:

Category	£	%	Last month %	March 20X3 %
0–30 days	76 500	65.4	66.7	70.3
31–60 days	32 000	27.3	27.2	22.3
60–90 days	7 500	6.4	5.2	7.0
Over 90 days	1 000	0.9	0.9	0.4
TOTAL	117 000	100.0	100.0	100.0

What are the key points arising from the summary age analysis?

Generally, the position has deteriorated compared to the previous year. The percentage of seriously overdue balances (ie. those outstanding for over 60 days) is similar (a total of 6.4 + 0.9 = 7.3% in March 20X4 compared to 7.0 + 0.4 = 7.4% in March 20X3). However, in March 20X4 there is a larger proportion of moderately overdue balances than in the previous year; in March 20X3 balances outstanding between 30 and 60 days accounted for 22.3% of the total, but this has risen quite significantly to 27.3% by March 20X4. These figures suggest that there has been a loss of control over trade receivables. The figures have deteriorated slightly between February 20X4 and March 20X4.

Beamish Mellon Limited produces a monthly age analysis of its receivables. The company offers credit terms of payment within 30 days of invoice. At 31 May 20X7 the summary was as follows:

Self-test question 19.3 (answer at the end of the book)

Category	£	%	Last month %	May 20X6 %
0–30 days	180 625	57.8	57.4	52.7
31–60 days	113 125	36.2	36.7	39.3
Over 60 days	18 750	6.0	5.9	8.0
TOTAL	312 500	100.0	100.0	100.0

What are the key points arising from the summary age analysis?

While the summary age analysis is useful for identifying general trends in the control of receivables, it does not provide sufficient detail to allow identification of specific problem areas. A detailed age analysis is required; data about individual amounts due allows the credit controller to identify problems and the actions required to address them. The next example expands the information given by the summary in the previous example. Remember that this is a very simple example that uses a limited set of data. In real life, an age analysis for most businesses is likely to be a much more complex document.

Example 19.6

Perceval Holland's detailed age analysis of trade receivables at 31 March 20X8 shows the following:

Customer name	Total outstanding £	Credit limit £	0–30 days £	31–60 days £	61–90 days £	Over 90 days £
A Ahmed	2 500	4 000			2 500	
B Burton	20 000	20 000	10 000	10 000		
C Clark	11 500	15 000	500	6 000	5 000	
D Delft	22 500	30 000	22 500			
E Edwards	32 500	40 000	18 000	13 500		1 000
F Faroukh	28 000	40 000	25 500	2 500		
TOTAL	117 000		76 500	32 000	7 500	1 000

What are the key points arising from the credit controller's review in respect of each trade receivable balance?

The detailed age analysis provides sufficient information about each customer to allow the credit controller to identify areas where action is required. The following points should be noted in respect of each of the balances outstanding.

A Ahmed: The whole amount of this receivable is seriously overdue, and therefore gives cause for concern. The credit controller must take action immediately to find out why this amount has not been paid. If it has not been paid because of a dispute over, eg. the amount or the quality of the goods received, then the dispute must be resolved without delay. Although the credit limit shows that this customer could obtain more goods on credit from the company it would be unwise to allow him or her to trade until the outstanding balance is paid or otherwise resolved.

B Burton: this customer has reached his or her credit limit, and no further trading can be permitted until some or the entire overdue amount is paid.

C Clark: a significant proportion of this customer's balance is seriously overdue, and almost all of it is over 30 days old. Action should be taken without delay to recover the overdue amounts. Clark still has £3500 of credit available but it would be unwise to allow the customer to continue to trade with the company until the overdue amounts have been paid off. A 'stop' should be put on this account to prevent further trading.

D Delft: there are no apparent problems with this account.

E Edwards: this customer is comfortably within the credit limit. However, an amount of £1000 is now very seriously overdue. There may be a specific problem with this outstanding amount, and any dispute should be resolved immediately. Part of the balance outstanding (£13 500 out of a total of £32 500) is overdue, although it may only just have exceeded the 30 day limit. The balance should be investigated further, and the payment record of Edwards should be investigated to see if there have been previous problems.

F Faroukh: This customer is well within the allotted credit limit. A small proportion of the total balance due has exceeded the 30-day limit. A further check should be done to see how long the £2500 has been outstanding. If it is only slightly in excess of 30 days there is unlikely to be any difficulty in recovering the amounts due.

19.5 THE MANAGEMENT OF CASH, OVERDRAFTS AND TRADE PAYABLES

A fundamental goal of business management is to ensure that the business does not run out of cash. In order to avoid unexpected cash shortages, managers must plan carefully in advance. In many businesses, the pattern of trade results in cash shortages from time to time. For example, in a highly seasonal business, such as the provision of goods for Christmas, revenue can be expected to be high in the period before Christmas, and, if sales are on credit, high cash inflows will result in and around December and January. Conversely, during the period of building up inventory there are likely to be substantial cash outflows. If the business cannot fund all of these outflows from its reserves of cash it must ensure that sufficient borrowing facilities are in place.

19.5.1 The Operating Cycle

An essential piece of management information used for planning cash and borrowing needs is the length of the business's operating cycle. This is the average length of time that elapses between the acquisition of inventory and the receipt of cash for its eventual sale. A long operating cycle indicates high working capital and a high requirement for cash; a short operating cycle indicates the opposite.

The components of the operating cycle are as follows:

Average inventory turnover period

+

Average trade receivables turnover period

−

Average trade payables turnover period

These components are all calculated using the formulae already explained in Chapter 9. The example should help as a reminder of what is involved in these calculations.

Example 19.7

F ennell Barnet Limited has the following relevant data for its financial year ended 31 December 20X6 (with comparative figures for 20X5)

	20X6	20X5
Opening inventory	125 700	113 400
Closing inventory	128 300	125 700
Opening trade receivables	93 300	94 200
Closing trade receivables	97 700	93 300
Opening trade payables	86 600	84 400
Closing trade payables	93 300	86 600
Cost of sales	709 600	685 500
Revenue	965 500	929 600
Purchases	667 700	662 400

Calculate the company's operating cycle for 20X6 and 20X5 and comment on any differences arising.

	20X6 £	20X5 £
Workings: Average inventory	$\dfrac{125\,700 + 128\,300}{2} = 127\,000$	$\dfrac{113\,400 + 125\,700}{2} = 119\,550$
Average trade receivables	$\dfrac{93\,300 + 97\,700}{2} = 95\,500$	$\dfrac{94\,200 + 93\,300}{2} = 93\,750$
Average trade payables	$\dfrac{86\,600 + 93\,300}{2} = 89\,950$	$\dfrac{84\,400 + 86\,600}{2} = 85\,500$

Operating cycle:

	20X6 £	20X5 £
A. Average inventory turnover period	$\dfrac{127\,000}{709\,600} \times 365 = 65.3$ days	$\dfrac{119\,550}{685\,500} \times 365 = 63.7$ days
B. Average trade receivables turnover period	$\dfrac{95\,500}{965\,500} \times 365 = 36.1$ days	$\dfrac{93\,750}{929\,600} \times 365 = 36.8$ days
C. Average trade payables period	$\dfrac{89\,950}{667\,700} \times 365 = 49.2$ days	$\dfrac{85\,500}{662\,400} \times 365 = 47.1$ days
Operating cycle: A + B − C	**52.2 days**	**53.4 days**

Comment: the operating cycle has improved slightly from 20X5 to 20X6, and therefore it is likely that slightly less financing is required. The average trade receivables period has increased by a little over two days, which means that the company is taking advantage of the credit terms offered by its suppliers to a greater extent in 20X6 than in 20X5.

As with all accounting ratios, it is impossible to give any precise indication of what constitutes a reasonable or an unreasonable figure. For this company, an operating cycle of around 52 to 54 days might be relatively low compared to other companies in the same industry sector, or it might be quite high. If credit terms in the industry are around 30 days, both the trade receivables and trade payables averages look quite reasonable, but more information would be needed about the business's activities in order to know whether the inventory turnover period was relatively high or low.

19.5.2 Managing Cash and Overdrafts

The operating cycle calculated in Example 19.7 gives a general indication of the requirement for working capital financing, based on information at two year-ends. This is not likely to be a sufficiently good guide for cash management purposes, and in practice it is likely that any business that uses operating cycle information will calculate it more frequently. Year-end information could be unrepresentative in a business that experiences significant seasonal fluctuations in trade. Estimates of maximum financing required can be calculated by the use of a budgeted cash flow forecast (see Chapter 16). Using operating cycle and cash flow budget information a business can calculate the extent to which it requires short-term financing in the form of limited period borrowing or overdraft facility. If no short-term financing is required, the business can plan for the utilization of any short-term cash surplus that is likely to arise, perhaps by placing some of the surplus cash on short-term deposit to earn interest.

19.5.3 Managing Trade Payables

Trade payables are generally regarded as a type of free financing. Exceeding the credit limit offered by suppliers by a relatively small amount is unlikely to lead to adverse consequences, and where businesses are short of cash, they are often tempted to take advantage of free credit by delaying payments to their suppliers by a few days. However, problems can arise where this financing device is abused. Suppliers may threaten to cut off supplies until their earlier invoices are paid, and important business relationships may suffer in consequence.

It is also important to clearly identify and to be aware of conditions of trade. Suppliers' credit terms may vary, with one offering 30 days credit and another 60 days credit. Also, there may be valuable discounts available for early settlement of amounts due. A business needs to have systems in place to identify instances where it is financially advantageous to take the discount rather than delay the payment to the supplier.

Sometimes, especially where there are many suppliers, it is helpful to produce an age analysis of payables, similar to the one produced for receivables. This can help to ensure that no supplier's credit terms are exceeded to the point where adverse consequences are likely.

Chapter Summary

Careful management of working capital is important in businesses of all sizes. This chapter has explained many of the issues and techniques related to the management of inventory, trade receivables, trade payables and cash. Management must balance all the elements of working capital to ensure, above all, that there are no unexpected shortages of cash but also in order to avoid the problems of deficiencies or excesses in the various elements, as explained early in the chapter.

Internet Resources

Book's companion website summary

The website contains the following resources in respect of Chapter 19:

Students' section

A multiple choice quiz containing ten questions
Three additional questions with answers

Lecturers' section

Answers to end-of-chapter exercises 19.13 to 19.21
Three additional questions with answers
Testbank
Instructor's Manual
PowerPoint presentation

Exercises: Answers at the End of the Book

19.1 Which of the following is NOT an element of working capital?

a) Inventory
b) Property, plant and equipment
c) Trade receivables
d) Cash

19.2 Which of the following is a possible consequence to a business of keeping its trade payables at too high a level?

a) A loss of goodwill on the part of suppliers, who may cease to supply goods to the business.
b) The business's overdraft may increase with a consequent increase in finance costs.
c) Inventory levels will be too high, thus incurring additional holding costs.
d) The operating cycle will increase.

19.3 Companies A and B have the following assets in their statements of financial position:

	A £m	B £m
Non-current assets	76.0	2.1
Current assets		
Inventories	10.6	5.0
Trade receivables	1.1	13.7
Cash	2.0	4.3
	13.7	23.0
ASSETS	89.7	25.1

Which of the companies is most likely to be a supermarket business? Explain the reasons for your choice.

19.4 Explain the interaction between inventory holding costs and ordering costs.

19.5 Prestbury Hannah Limited uses the EOQ formula to determine the optimal size of inventory orders. The company's management accountant has identified the following information in respect of inventory item BXC:

Annual demand for BXC = 7000 units
Holding cost per unit of BXC = £28.50
Cost per order = £37.00

What is the economic order quantity?

19.6 You are the management accountant of Bright Sigmund Limited, which imports garden furniture for sale to retailers. Most of the business's sales occur between March and September. The company's directors are concerned about the rising level of average inventory turnover in the business. Sales revenue and most categories of costs have been static for the last two or three years, but inventory levels have increased by over 30%. Costs of inventory storage and insurance have risen. One of the directors has heard about the economic order quantity formula, and has suggested to the Board that the company should use it to try to control its inventory levels.

You have been asked to prepare a briefing paper for the Board which describes the economic order quantity model, and to comment upon its suitability for use in Bright Sigmund Limited.

19.7 Sims & Aktar Limited currently offer 30-day credit terms to their customers. The company's most recent monthly figures show that trade receivables have been outstanding on average for 67 days. The managing director has asked you, the management accountant, to prepare a summary of the advantages and disadvantages of using a factoring service to collect the company's receivables. Prepare a brief paper providing the requested information.

19.8 You are the newly-appointed credit controller of Mohinder Benton Limited, which produces a summary age analysis of its outstanding trade receivables at each month-end. The company allows 30 days credit. The summary for April 20X4 shows the following information:

Category	£	%	Last month %	April 20X3
0–30 days	333 644	34.9	36.9	40.2
31–60 days	309 744	32.4	32.7	28.6
60–90 days	150 092	15.7	14.2	19.6
90–120 days	98 468	10.3	9.7	3.4
Over 120 days	64 052	6.7	6.5	8.2
TOTAL	956 000	100.0	100.0	100.0

In addition, the following information is available:

1   In total at the end of April 20X4 123 customers owed the company money. Of the 123 customers, 14 had been permitted to exceed their credit limits, and a further 26 had reached their credit limits.

2   In the company's financial year ended 31 December 20X3, the company had written off £36 650 of outstanding receivables.

3   Sixteen customers are currently in dispute with Mohinder Benton Limited because of disagreements about faulty goods, incorrect deliveries and failure to correctly record amounts received.

Write a report analyzing the information given above.

19.9 Which of the following statements is correct?
   The operating cycle is calculated as:

   a) average trade receivables turnover period − average inventory turnover period − average trade payables turnover period.

   b) average trade receivables period + average trade payables turnover period − average inventory turnover period.

   c) average trade payables period + average inventory turnover period − average trade receivables period.

   d) average inventory turnover period + average trade receivables turnover period − average trade payables turnover period.

19.10 Burstein Lyall Limited has an operating cycle for the year ended 31 December 20X9 of 78.4 days. The comparative figure for the year ended 31 December 20X8 was 75.3 days. The industry average operating cycle at 31 December 20X9 was 66.4 days.

   Briefly describe the significance of a company's operating cycle, and comment on the operating cycle statistics given above.

19.11 Skipholt Limited has the following efficiency ratios at 31 March 20X3:

Average trade payables period: 43.7 days
Average inventory turnover period: 49.6 days
Average trade receivables period: 39.4 days

Calculate Skipholt's operating cycle from the information given above.

19.12 Linwood Lees Limited's 20X5 financial statements were as follows:

Linwood Lees Limited: Statement of profit or loss for the year ended 31 January 20X5

	20X5	20X4
	£	£
Revenue	662 550	651 440
Cost of sales	(477 400)	(435 100)
Gross profit	185 150	216 340
Expenses	(150 690)	(187 590)
Profit for the year	34 460	28 750

Note: purchases for the year were £396 600 (20X4: £377 440)

Linwood Lees Limited: Statement of financial position at 31 January 20X5

	20X5	20X4
	£	£
ASSETS		
Non-current assets	1 126 330	1 044 770
Current assets		
Inventory	99 400	91 650
Trade receivables	86 700	89 400
Cash	16 070	18 850
	202 170	199 900
	1 328 500	1 244 670
EQUITY AND LIABILITIES		
Equity	791 630	757 170
Long-term liabilities	436 340	400 000
Current liabilities		
Trade payables	67 530	65 500
Short-term borrowings	33 000	22 000
	100 530	87 500
	1 328 500	1 244 670

Calculate Linwood Lees' operating cycle for the year ended 31 January 20X5. Prepare a brief report to the company's directors about the company's working capital management.

Exercises: Answers Available on the Lecturers' Section of the Book's Website

19.13 Which of the following is a possible consequence to a business of keeping its inventory levels too low?

a) Too much cash is tied up, which could lead to adverse consequences for the business.

b) Trade payables are likely to be too high, leading to problems in obtaining further credit from suppliers.

c) There may not be sufficient inventory to fulfil orders, with the result that potential customers go to another supplier.

d) The operating cycle is longer than it should be.

19.14 Companies X and Y have the following assets in their statements of financial position:

	X £m	Y £m
Non-current assets		
Intangible assets	136.0	—
Property, plant and equipment	25.7	189.6
	161.7	189.6
Current assets		
Inventories	0.4	136.3
Trade receivables	96.3	100.7
Cash	36.7	—
	133.4	237.0
ASSETS	295.1	426.6

Which of the companies is most likely to be a manufacturing business? Explain the reasons for your choice.

19.15 Tutbury Limited uses the EOQ formula to determine the optimal size of inventory orders. The company's management accountant has identified the following information in respect of inventory item X2275:

Annual demand for X2275 = 4000 units
Holding cost per unit of X2275 = £13.75
Cost per order = £32.00

What is the economic order quantity?

19.16 Wells Xavier Limited uses the EOQ formula to determine the optimal size of inventory orders. The company's management accountant has identified the following information in respect of inventory item SP36:

Annual demand for SP36 = 10 000 units
Holding cost per unit of SP36 = £12.70
Cost per order = £23.50

What is the economic order quantity?

19.17 Identify and explain the benefits to a business of employing a credit controller.

19.18 Identify and explain the ways in which the risk of non-payment of trade receivables can be minimized by a business.

19.19 Snaresbrook & Debden Limited produces a monthly age analysis of trade *payables*. The age analysis at 30 June 20X4 is as follows:

Category	£	%	Last month %	June 20X3 %
0–30 days	283 432	66.8	69.9	64.9
31–60 days	67 040	15.8	16.3	20.4
60–90 days	58 129	13.7	12.2	14.7
Over 90 days	15 699	3.7	1.6	0.0
TOTAL	424 300	100.0	100.0	100.0

You are the recently appointed financial controller of Snaresbrook & Debden Limited. Your assistant has presented you with some notes explaining various issues arising from the analysis.

Notes

1 The average credit period permitted by the company's suppliers is 45 days.
2 No information is available on the amount of payables that have been outstanding for longer than the credit period permitted by the company's suppliers.
3 The balance of trade payables outstanding for more than 90 days includes an amount of £4300 which is currently disputed with the supplier. There is a record of the goods having been received, but also a despatch note recording their return to the supplier because they were sub-standard. The supplier has no record of receiving the goods back again, and is threatening to sue Snaresbrook & Debden Limited for non-payment of the amounts due.

Produce a brief report on information conveyed by the age analysis, identifying any unsatisfactory aspects of both the report format and the information reported.

19.20 Theydon Limited has the following efficiency ratios at 31 January 20X7:

Average inventory turnover period: 77.8 days
Average trade receivables period: 66.4 days
Average trade payables period: 108.4 days

Theydon Limited supplies fashionable women's clothing to retail outlets. On average its suppliers allow the company 37 days credit. The company's policy in respect of trade receivables is to allow 30 days credit.
    Calculate Theydon's operating cycle from the information given above, and analyze its working capital management as evidenced by the figures.

19.21 Tucker & Ali Limited's 20X8 financial statements were as follows:

Tucker & Ali Limited: Statement of profit or loss for the year ended 31 December 20X8

	20X8	20X7
	£m	£m
Revenue	37.6	38.3
Cost of sales	(30.7)	(30.8)
Gross profit	6.9	7.5
Expenses	(5.7)	(5.2)
Profit for the year	1.2	2.3

Note: purchases for the year were £24.6m (20X7: £25.8m)

Tucker & Ali Limited: Statement of financial position at 31 December 20X8

	20X8	20X7
	£	£
ASSETS		
Non-current assets	42.3	40.8
Current assets		
Inventory	3.2	3.1
Trade receivables	4.4	4.2
Cash	0.8	0.2
	8.4	7.5
	50.7	48.3

	20X8	20X7
	£	£
EQUITY AND LIABILITIES		
Equity	24.1	22.9
Long-term liabilities	18.7	17.2
Current liabilities		
Trade payables	5.2	5.0
Short-term borrowings	2.7	3.2
	7.9	8.2
	50.7	48.3

Calculate the company's operating cycle for 20X8 and for 20X7. Prepare a brief report to the company's directors about the company's working capital management, identifying any problems or potential problems.

20 Financing the business

Aim of the chapter

The aim of this chapter is to know about and understand the principal sources of finance available to businesses of all sizes.

Learning outcomes

After reading the chapter and completing the exercises, students should:

- Understand the key issues involved in financing a business start-up.

- Know about some of the most important sources of small business finance.

- Understand the problems and opportunities presented by business growth, and some of the financing issues related to growth.

- Know about sources of finance for larger business.

- Know how the UK stock market operates, and the advantages and disadvantages of operating as a listed company.

Introduction

Chapter 1 provided an introduction to types of business organization, their financing, and the role of accounting in business. This chapter provides more detailed information about the sources of business finance. The availability of finance is often dependent upon the size of the business organization. Very large, well-established companies have access to a level and type of funding that is not normally available to people starting up businesses.

The chapter provides a progression through different businesses' stages. The early sections concentrate upon financing issues relating to business start-ups. The problems and opportunities of growth are then examined before, finally, the chapter examines the particular types of financing that are available to larger businesses.

20.1 FINANCING THE SMALL BUSINESS

All businesses have to start somewhere. They mostly start small and are usually based upon a bright idea which occurs to one person, or sometimes, to a small group of people. The idea may be brilliant but impractical in business terms. It may have occurred to lots of other people so there will be a high level of competition in the market. Or it may be so good and original that it is going to make its owner a millionaire.

The basic business idea may arise out of a need for a product or service which cannot, apparently, be found, or cannot be found at the right price.

20.1.1 Sources of Finance for a New Business Start-up

In Chapter 1 we examined sources of business finance in outline. Below we look in more detail at some typical sources of finance which might be used to finance the start-up of a new business. Money will be required for some or all of the following:

- purchase of equipment
- supporting the owner and family while the business gets going
- paying for premises
- paying for staff
- expenses like business rates, insurance, running costs of cars, etc.

Where does the money come from?

EXISTING CASH RESOURCES Existing cash resources may be available in the form of savings and windfalls. In fact, the arrival of an unexpected windfall, such as a lottery win, a convenient legacy, or a big redundancy pay-off, may even provide the impetus for the starting up of a business.

Also possible, depending upon the nature of the business, is self-financing through part-time work. In practice, many small businesses are financed in this way.

Example 20.1

S asha completes her degree in fine art, producing several very good pieces of work at her degree show. Two of the pieces sell, and Sasha is offered an exhibition at a local art gallery. However, even though she may be comparatively successful in her working life as an artist, it is highly unlikely that she will ever earn enough from her work to be able to provide herself with a decent living. Sasha takes a job for 15 hours per week in an art materials shop. This employment subsidizes her 'business' which is selling her own art work.

FAMILY OR FRIENDS If the prospective business person has no resources it is possible that his or her family may be prepared to support the business in its early stages. Sometimes this can be through an injection of cash, or the loan or gift of an item of equipment. Or sometimes, a supportive partner will agree to cover living costs from his or her salary during the early stages of the business.

Even if finance can be obtained in this way, there may be a downside. If the businessman borrows from his nearest and dearest, and then loses the lot in a reckless business start-up, family relationships can be scarred or even terminated. Business failure can, and often does, contribute to the breakdown of long-term relationships.

CROWDFUNDING Crowdfunding has grown very rapidly in popularity over the last few years. It is typically used to finance creative, quirky and unusual projects, but can also be used to raise seed capital for small businesses. Popular sites such as Kickstarter and Crowdcube have been used to finance a wide range of projects, as illustrated by Example 20.2.

Example 20.2 (Real-Life)

- A revamp of the main stand of Worthing FC: £15 000 was raised from 57 backers.
- Rice n Spicy curry suppliers: over £3000 raised from 65 backers.
- Research into the invasive lionfish in Honduras: £570 raised from 14 backers.

Typically, rather than a cash return in the form of interest or dividends, a reward is offered in the form of tickets, food vouchers, regular project updates, etc.

GRANT FINANCE Grants can be an excellent source of start-up finance, as they usually do not need to be repaid. However, they are available only for quite specific purposes (such as employment of local people in areas of high unemployment), and almost never serve to finance all of the expenses of a start-up. Also, once a grant is given, the granting authority will normally keep quite a close check on the progress of the business.

PEER-TO-PEER LENDING It is often impossible for a business start-up to obtain funding in the form of traditional bank loans. However, in recent years, new borrowing opportunities have arisen in the form of peer-to-peer lending websites such as Zopa. These sites put potential borrowers in touch with potential lenders. Rather than funding an individual project (which could be very risky), lenders put money into the fund. The loan is split into many small units and is lent to many different borrowers to spread risk. Each month borrowers pay back capital and interest which is spread over the loan units. This form of lending has proved popular with lenders who, in recent years, have received only very low interest rates on bank deposits. Interest rates earned on peer-to-peer lending are often much higher than bank rates. For example, Funding Circle, a peer-to-peer lender typically offers a return to investors (at the time of writing) of 7.5%. However, peer-to-peer lending must be treated with caution by lenders. If a lender places up to £75 000 on deposit with a high street bank, the deposit is protected by law, and its replacement will be funded by the UK government if the bank fails. There is no such protection for peer-to-peer lending.

COMMERCIAL BORROWINGS As noted above, it is unlikely that a new business startup will obtain traditional bank finance in the form of loans. However, the bank's reluctance to lend is often matched by the potential borrower's reluctance to get involved in this kind of borrowing. There are several sound reasons for this reluctance:

- Banks charge commercial rates of interest on loans. This can add substantially to the costs of a business start-up and can make the difference between potential success and failure.
- Bankers want to know that their loans will be repaid. They will maximize the likelihood of repayment by insisting upon **security** for the loan. This means that an arrangement is made so that, if the loan is not repaid on time, the bank can take an item, or items, of at least equal value from the business or the individual in settlement of the debt. The bank will usually insist upon a legally binding agreement known as a **charge**, to ensure that the loan gets repaid.

Example 20.3

Des starts up in business with a bank loan of £50 000. The bank stipulates a legal charge over Des's house. The business goes bust after two years, still owing the bank the original £50 000 plus £3000 in unpaid interest. Because the bank has the legal charge, the house must be sold to meet the debt, and Des and his family will, effectively, be evicted and may be made homeless. This may seem harsh but the charge is a legal document, and the bank is quite within its rights to insist upon repayment via the sale of the house.

If security is not available in any other form, bankers may ask for a guarantee from someone who is sufficiently wealthy to repay the loan if the business fails. This type of arrangement is fine, provided that the guarantor (ie. the person giving the guarantee) thoroughly understands the possible consequences if the business fails. There have been unfortunate cases where the guarantor has not understood that he or she stands to lose a very large sum of money if the business goes bad.

A secured loan is less risky, from a bank's point of view, than an unsecured loan. The nature of the loan and the value of the security tend to affect the interest rate. The greater the risk, the higher the rate of interest. Therefore, a loan made by a bank on good security will have a lower interest charge than an unsecured loan.

20.1.2 The Business Plan

When seeking finance in the form of a loan or a grant, it is usually necessary to produce a **business plan**. Even if the production of a business plan is not strictly necessary (because external finance is not being sought), it is worth producing one because the process of writing down plans and projections for a new business can help to clarify ideas. The business plan normally includes most or all of the following elements:

- description of the business concept
- detailed description of the product or service which the business will offer
- the market for the product or service; market research; analysis of the competition.
- profile of entrepreneur: a personal profile detailing relevant experience (including possibly a CV) and an analysis of personal strengths and weaknesses
- initial investment required; type and cost of equipment, premises and similar items
- details of other people involved; if the plan is to employ people straight away, details are required of how they will be recruited, and how much it will cost to employ them
- insurance requirements; any relevant legal issues.
- professional advisers; details of the type of professional advice that may be required, and how much it is likely to cost
- detailed financial projections; a budget will be required for at least the first year, showing the projected profit and cash flow (see Chapter 16 as a reminder of what is involved in the budgeting process).

20.1.3 Why Do Businesses Fail (and Why Do Some of Them Succeed)?

It can be quite difficult to estimate the failure rate for businesses. A statistic that is often quoted is that, of every ten new business start-ups, only one or two will remain in business after five years. During recessions, the rate of business failure increases, as might be expected. For example, the number of company liquidations increased in 2009 to 19 077 from 15 535 in 2008, an increase of 22.8%.

The Association of Business Recovery Professionals in the UK (www.r3.org.uk) provides a lot of useful information. For example, they cite the most common reasons for corporate insolvency as follows:

- loss of market: where companies have not recognized the need to change in a shrinking or changing marketplace, because their margins have been eroded or because their service has been overtaken technically
- management failure to acquire adequate skills, either through training or buying them in, over-optimism in planning, imprudent accounting, lack of management information
- fraud
- loss of long-term finance, over-gearing, lack of working capital/cashflow
- other reasons include excessive overheads, new venture/expansion/acquisition.

This is all very depressing, especially for anyone who is seriously thinking about setting up a business. However, many businesses do succeed and prosper. The factors which tend to lead to success include: adequate financing, a cautious approach to risktaking, existing management experience and experience and sheer good luck.

> **B**riefly describe the advantages and drawbacks of obtaining the following types of finance for a business start-up:
>
> i) grant finance
> ii) borrowing from family or friends.

Self-test question 20.1 (answer at the end of the book)

20.2 STAGES IN BUSINESS GROWTH AND EXPANSION

This section of the chapter examines the problems and opportunities that may arise in the growing business. It then examines sources of finance for the growing business.

20.2.1 Employing People

Many businesses do not grow past the point where they generate an income for one person and his or her dependants. A self-employed tradesperson, such as a plumber, small builder or garden designer may have no particular need or wish to expand the business to the point where employing another person becomes necessary. However, some business people will see the need for expansion, and employing another person is often the first step towards expansion.

ADVANTAGES OF EMPLOYING PEOPLE IN A SMALL BUSINESS There is an opportunity to increase the skills base of the business. One of the reasons why businesses fail is because of poor management. A sole trader is particularly vulnerable to this type of problem; he or she has to marshal a range of skills including selling abilities, financial management skills, organizational ability, self-discipline, and so on. If any one of these is missing the business may fail. One way around the problem of missing skills is to go into partnership with someone whose skills are complementary. Another way is to employ a person who can contribute skills lacking in the proprietor.

Employing people is likely to increase the volume of trade in goods or services. Two pairs of hands can achieve more than one. If the right person is employed, he or she may be able to contribute to the profitability of the business.

Example 20.4

Kingsley is a self-employed furniture designer who undertakes commissions for the provision of original, well-designed furniture for businesses. He started up in business two years ago, and he has been very successful in generating work. He now has more than he can easily cope with. He is working seven days a week from early morning until late at night and his relationships with friends and family are suffering. Also, he has received some unpleasant letters recently from suppliers, including a threat from the electricity utility company to cut off his supplies unless he pays his bill within seven days.

It is clear that Kingsley needs help. Administering a small business can take a disproportionately large amount of time. While Kingsley may not be ready to take on a full-time administrator he should examine the possibility of employing a part-timer who can keep control of the paperwork. This would, presumably, free up part of Kingsley's time so that he could get on with more productive work.

The other area in which he probably needs help is in the design work. This is a much more difficult issue to resolve than the administration. People award Kingsley design commissions because they like his work. If he delegates some of the work to an assistant the design values may suffer. Unless Kingsley is prepared to carry on working all hours, he will have to make a decision on whether he keeps the business very small by turning down any commissions which he cannot manage himself, or, alternatively, whether he is prepared to share the design work with someone else. The first course of action involves a risk; if he turns down too much work, the supply of commissions may dry up altogether. The second course of action also involves a risk; will the quality of work suffer? And does Kingsley have the necessary management skills to control the work of one or more designer employees?

DISADVANTAGES OF EMPLOYING PEOPLE IN A SMALL BUSINESS There is a very significant risk attached to employment. If a poor choice of employee is made, the mistake can threaten the survival of the business. Mistakes can be made in employing someone with whom there is a personality clash, or someone who is less competent than they appeared from their CV and the interview. Many employers will make an employment decision which, sooner or later, they come to regret.

Employing people costs money. Many successful small businesses pass through an awkward stage where there is too much work for the sole trader or partners to handle by themselves but where the financial risk of taking on an employee is unacceptable. The business proprietor(s) must be sure that they have the financial resources to pay for employment.

Employing people involves a great deal of paperwork. If staff are employed, the business becomes involved in the administration of Pay As You Earn (PAYE) and National Insurance Contributions (NIC) on behalf of the employee. Detailed records must be kept, and these are liable to be inspected periodically by HMRC. Business people often complain bitterly about the amount of work they have to undertake as tax collectors on behalf of the government. The amount of administration which is involved acts, potentially, as a disincentive to employing people (although it should be noted perhaps, that the administrative burden in the UK is probably less than in some other countries.

France, for example, imposes a far heavier administrative burden on the employer). The example below illustrates some of the practical financial considerations involved in the decision about whether or not to employ somebody.

Example 20.5

Recently, Kelly started a business importing and selling ornamental lamps, vases and similar items to retailers. The business has been successful, making profits of £35 000 in its first year and £38 000 in its second. Kelly has realized that, if the business is going to be able to grow, she will have to employ someone to assist her in selling goods to retailers. The ideal employee would have a good track record in selling and would be able and willing to travel four or five days a week visiting retailers' stores.

What financial factors does Kelly need to consider in making a decision about employing an assistant?

- *Salary.* Kelly needs to look carefully at how much she will have to pay in order to ensure the right employee. She needs someone with experience and who is prepared to act on his or her own initiative. Part of Kelly's annual profits will have to go to paying the employee. In addition to the annual salary, there will be the cost of providing transport (presumably an additional car will be required).
- *Employer's National Insurance and administration costs.* The employer must pay employer's National Insurance Contributions, and the cost of administering the payroll must be taken into account. Kelly may be able to do this herself (the cost of doing this is the time taken up which could be used on something else), or may have to pay her accountant a little extra to do it.
- *Balancing costs and benefits.* If Kelly succeeds in employing someone who is good at selling, the benefits could far outweigh the costs of employment. Suppose the total cost of employment is £30 000 per year; provided the employee can generate additional business which makes more than this amount in profit then it makes good business sense for Kelly to employ him or her. There may be other less obvious benefits – if Kelly gets flu and has to spend a week in bed the business, at the moment, grinds to a halt until she is better. If she could depend upon an employee, the business could be kept going more or less as normal.

20.2.2 Developing the Business Organization

As a business grows and starts to employ more people, the way in which it is organized becomes more of an issue. There is a tendency in most business organizations to establish manageable units according to the functions they carry out. For example, in a typical manufacturing organization, it may be appropriate to establish separate departments for marketing, production, despatch, design, personnel, accounting and general administration. In the early days of the business only one or two people will be employed in each function, and the business proprietors are likely to retain firm control over all of the operations of the business. However, as the business grows, it becomes increasingly difficult for its owners to control every aspect of its functions. It is important for proprietors to be able to recognize when this stage has arrived, and to be prepared to delegate control to others.

PROFESSIONAL MANAGEMENT People who have started up successful businesses are often very reluctant to concede any part of their control to others. However, in most cases, it eventually becomes necessary to employ professional managers – people who have the experience and knowledge to manage functions such as marketing and personnel. Conflict sometimes ensues between the managers and the original founders of the business as they disagree about the right way to manage change and growth.

COMMUNICATION ISSUES As the business grows and departmental structures emerge, a range of communication problems can arise. Departments develop their own identities, and can, if not properly managed, become narrow in outlook, fighting territorial battles with other departments to protect their own status. Where this type of 'in-fighting' occurs, the overall objectives of the business tend to be forgotten.

GROWTH IN BUREAUCRACY As we have already noted in this chapter, a certain amount of unavoidable record keeping and administration is imposed on businesses by government regulation. As businesses grow and organizational functions separate, the business itself starts to require more complex records. An accounting department is usually required in order to keep the financial records straight. Some kinds of authorization and control procedures are, inevitably, required, but a great deal of management skill is required to make sure that the generation of paperwork does not get out of hand. Organizations with excessive administration procedures may ultimately fail because they have become too inwardly focused. For example, staff become demotivated by the requirement to produce what they see as excessive paperwork. Perhaps the need for prompt and thorough organizational reporting starts to take priority over activities such as production quality control and establishing new sales contacts.

20.2.3 Sources of Finance for the Growing Business

Expansion and growth of a successful business usually involves moving into new areas. Sometimes, this involves expanding the range of products and/or services on offer. Or, new opportunities may arise to expand the market that the business serves. Expansion requires finance, which sometimes has to be sought from sources outside the business.

The sources of finance mentioned earlier in the chapter as suitable for the small business may also be appropriate for this stage, although some are likely to be more appropriate than others. For example, commercial borrowing is unlikely to be obtainable for a business start-up, but is more likely to be available to a growing business with a sound record of profitable trading. Conversely, finance from family and friends (unless they are wealthy) is less likely to be available for an established, growing business. A source of finance that may be appropriate, and which has not been mentioned so far in the chapter, is venture capital.

VENTURE CAPITAL Venture capital is funding provided by institutional investors and/or individuals who wish to invest in growing companies with very good prospects for the future. Venture capital investors typically set up a dedicated venture capital firm or fund which seeks to invest in particular types of business, often within a restricted industry sector. These firms are sometimes referred to as 'private equity' providers.

The type of funding provided by venture capitalists is typically for the medium- to long-term (often between five and ten years). The funding is provided in exchange for an equity stake in the business, and the venture capitalist(s)/private equity investor(s) will typically take an active role in the management of the business. The 'hands-on' management role of the venture capitalist is often one of the most attractive aspects of the deal for the managers of the growing business as it can give them access to experience and contacts that would not otherwise be available to them.

Venture capital is usually provided for a fixed term, after which the venture capitalists withdraw from the business, perhaps by selling their equity stake back to the original founders of the business, or by realizing their investment when the successful business is floated on the stock market (the next section of this chapter contains more information about stock market flotation).

INDIVIDUALS: 'ANGELS' AND 'DRAGONS' Individual investors may become involved in the provision of finance to growing businesses via an intermediary like a venture capital organization, as described above or via peer-to-peer lending (such as Zopa and Funding Circle) as described earlier in the chapter. Alternatively, they may provide finance to a business without an intermediary, by direct investment. Traditionally, such investors have often been referred to as 'business angels'. A relatively new piece of terminology is the business 'dragon', a term which refers to a very successful television format – 'Dragons' Den' that originated in Japan but which has been exported successfully around the world. The format in the UK involves people with business start-ups or established businesses that require new funding pitching their business idea to five 'dragons' who are successful and often well-known entrepreneurs. Most of the pitches fail miserably, thus providing much entertainment value, but a few are successful. Those who are successful are rewarded with an input of cash in exchange for an equity stake in the business from one or more of the dragons, plus their direct management input into the business.

LEASING The acquisition of non-current assets may require a significant outflow of cash. One way of acquiring assets without a large cash outflow is to lease them. There are, broadly, two types of lease. Operating leases are for relatively short periods, and involve regular rental payments for the use of an asset. Operating lease arrangements are often used for assets such as photocopiers and motor vehicles. Finance leases cover most or all of the life of an asset, and are in essence a way of purchasing an asset in instalments. The business that leases the asset (the lessee) pays the provider of the lease (the lessor) regular amounts of cash, agreed in advance. Finance lease arrangements, as the name implies are arrangements for financing the acquisition of an asset. The regular payments include an element both of capital payments in respect of the asset acquisition, and interest payments (the finance cost related to the lease).

Leasing can be an appropriate way of financing asset acquisitions for businesses of any size. However, they may be particularly helpful for the growing business which must carefully balance working capital requirements with its need to acquire assets.

Briefly outline the principal features of venture capital financing.

Self-test question 20.2 (answer at the end of the book)

20.3 SOURCES OF FINANCE FOR LARGE BUSINESSES

There are many possible sources of finance available to large businesses, including commercial borrowing, leasing, issues of new shares, flotation on the stock market and investment by venture capitalists. Some of these are possible only where the business is structured as a company. Financial reporting by limited companies was covered in Chapter 7, and some of the information below should be familiar.

20.3.1 Issue of Shares

Upon the initial formation of a company, ordinary share capital is issued to the first shareholders of the company. In the case of small businesses, the number of shareholders is usually low, often no more than one or two people. As companies grow, they may issue more shares to other people. Private companies in the UK (companies with 'limited' after their name) are not permitted to issue shares to the general public, or to have their shares quoted on a stock market. Public limited companies in the UK (companies with 'plc') after their name, on the other hand, are permitted to issue shares to a wider public. Some plcs are quoted on a stock market and so are able to issue their shares widely to the general public. It is important to note that not all plcs are quoted companies, but that only plcs (and not private companies) may have their shares quoted on the stock market.

The ordinary shares of companies are often referred to as **equity shares**. They have a nominal value such as £1.50 or 25p; this is the basic denomination of the share. Shares that are quoted on a stock market have a share price – a market value which is, usually, greater than the nominal value. For example, a listed company has 5 000 000 shares with a nominal value of 50p each and a market value of £3.75. This gives the company a total nominal value of 5 000 000/50p = £2 500 000; this is the nominal value of its issued share capital. The total market value (its market capitalization) of the company is: 5 000 000 × £3.75 = £18 750 000.

20.3.2 Rights of Shareholders

Ordinary (equity) share capital entitles its owners (shareholders) to a vote which they can exercise at the general meetings of the company. The other principal right of shareholders is to receive dividends. Dividends are paid out to shareholders, often on a regular basis; dividends constitute the income received by shareholders on their investment. Very large companies usually have two regular payment dates each year for dividends (an interim dividend and a final dividend). The company's directors decide upon the level of dividend to be paid out; it is usually expressed as an amount in pence per share, for example: 'the directors have declared an interim dividend of 5p per ordinary share in issue'.

20.3.3 Benefits of Limited Companies

The liability of shareholders in companies is limited. That means that, even if the company fails, the shareholders cannot be called upon to contribute any further cash.

Because the capital of limited companies is split up into many shares, it is possible for a shareholder to sell a very small proportion of the total share capital of the company to another person. This can be useful where, for example, the original shareholders of a company have decided that they wish to spread the share ownership more widely, perhaps to other family members.

Usually, if a business becomes really large, a limited company is the only realistic business vehicle for it. It allows for multiple shareholders, each owning, perhaps, a very small proportion of the total business. Sole traders, for obvious reasons, usually own very small businesses. Similarly, partnerships, except in a few special cases, tend to be small or medium-sized businesses. The special cases tend to be professional firms (such as firms of accountants, lawyers, architects or other professionals) where very large partnerships do exist. In most cases, however, if a business grows to be very large, it will be in the form of a company.

Sometimes, the directors of a company may choose to raise finance by obtaining a listing on the Stock Exchange. This involves selling shares to a wider public than family, friends and business associates. In the next two subsections we look at various aspects of the operation of the UK stock market.

20.3.4 The London Stock Exchange (LSE)

A stock market is a place where stocks are traded. So, what are the stocks referred to in the term 'stock market'? The LSE is the UK's stock market. It trades in, principally, the shares of quoted companies. Quoted companies comprise both UK-based companies, and overseas companies which have a quotation in the UK. The market also trades in British Government bonds (these are known as 'gilts' or 'gilt-edged stock'), other types of shares and company bonds (also known as **loan stock** or **debentures**).

So, where is this 'place' where stocks are traded? In former times the principal stock market location in the UK was the trading floor of the LSE. This was a place in the City of London where the agents of people and organizations which wished to trade in stocks and shares met in person to arrange transactions. This physical location is no longer necessary following the far-reaching reforms and reorganization of trading which took place in the 1980s and 1990s. Transactions in shares are now arranged and dealt with electronically, so the 'place' occupied by the stock market is, nowadays, a virtual location.

The LSE is a powerful organization which regulates the trading in shares and organizes their listing. The LSE operates in two principal capacities: as a 'primary market' and as a 'secondary market'.

PRIMARY MARKET The primary market function allows companies to raise capital via the LSE. In order to exploit the capital-raising potential of the LSE new entrants to the market apply for a listing and, if successful, float the company on the stock market. This means that they are entitled to offer shares, either newly issued or existing shares, to the public.

Companies which already have a stock market listing may decide that they need to raise more finance. Such companies can issue more shares and sell them for cash.

SECONDARY MARKET The secondary market function allows trading in shares to take place between willing buyers and sellers. This is an extremely useful function which allows for easy liquidity in shares. Liquidity means, in this context, that shares can be bought and sold easily. High liquidity is extremely attractive to investors; it means that they are not tied into their investment over long periods, but can liquidate (turn into cash) their investment whenever it suits them to do so. One of the problems of investing in unquoted companies can be that it can be difficult (or downright impossible) to sell the investment to anyone else.

20.3.5 Organization and Operation of the LSE

The LSE's market is split into two: the main market and the Alternative Investment Market (AIM).

THE MAIN MARKET The main market is the most important element of the market provided by the LSE. Companies on the main market have a full listing and are subject to the full range of regulation applicable to listed companies. In order to obtain a listing on the main market companies normally have to have been in business for at least three years and to have a full record of accounts for that period.

THE ALTERNATIVE INVESTMENT MARKET (AIM) The AIM is a market which deals in shares of smaller and/or newer companies than those which are eligible to obtain a full listing. Many relatively small companies choose to obtain a quotation on this market. Investing in these companies is potentially riskier than investing in companies with a full listing because: (a) the business venture may be inherently riskier; and (b) the shares of AIM companies are often quite illiquid – that is, they may not be traded very often or in very large volumes. This could make a holding of shares in an AIM company more difficult to sell than a holding listed on the main market. However, some AIM companies are highly successful; they may move on to a full listing once they have built up a trading record.

SHARE PRICES There are over 2000 UK companies quoted on the LSE at any one time, plus several hundred overseas companies. Although many companies have been listed for years, the list is constantly changing as new companies come to the market (at a rate of some 200 to 300 per year), and existing companies leave (because they have failed and go into liquidation, or because they are taken over, or because their directors decide to de-list).

Shares in quoted companies have a market price which can fluctuate a great deal. Shares in the larger, better-known companies, are traded very frequently, and their price can change from minute to minute. It is possible to obtain share prices with a delay of only a few minutes from many sources nowadays. One of the best and most reliable is the LSE's own website (www.londonstockexchange.com).

Shares in smaller companies, especially those on the AIM, may be traded infrequently, ie. their trading volume is low. Prices for such shares may remain quite static with long periods of inactivity.

Share prices will tend to rise when a company is doing well, or when some piece of good news is announced (for example, the company has obtained new business or it has sacked an incompetent director). Conversely, bad news often results in a fall in share price. However, sometimes movement in share prices has relatively little to do with individual companies' activities and is the result of a general market sentiment. For example, there was a huge general drop in share prices following September 11, 2001. This affected all companies, but those involved in aerospace, insurance or tourism were particularly badly affected.

STOCK MARKET INDICES: THE FTSE Anyone who watches television news, or who listens to radio news, will have heard the (usually) brief reports about the financial markets which sound something like: 'Bad news on the financial markets. The Footsie 100 fell 54 points to close at 5729.2.' While the first sentence makes sense, the second sounds like gibberish to the financial novice. We can pick the important pieces out of the statement:

'Footsie' is the usual verbal reference for 'FTSE' which stands for 'Financial Times Stock Exchange'. The FTSE organization, which is owned by the LSE and the Financial Times newspaper, runs a series of indices both for the UK stock market and worldwide. The FTSE 100 is an index which relates to the changes in value of the top 100 listed UK companies. The index started originally with a value of 1000. Each of the 100 constituent companies figures in the index according to the relative size of its capital. The minute-by-minute changes in the value of the 100 companies' share prices are fed into the index calculations. For most interested observers, daily tracking of the index value tells them all they need to know, but it is possible for people and organizations who are deeply involved in investing, to find the current value at any time during the LSE trading hours.

So, if the index falls by 54 points, it reflects an overall, average, fall for the day in the share prices of those companies which make up the index. Some of the companies' share prices may have gone up; some have fallen, and overall, the average movement for the day is slightly downwards.

The reported index total (5729.2) is only really helpful to a person who keeps a regular eye on the movements in share prices. The index figure on its own means very little.

WHICH COMPANIES ARE IN THE FTSE? At regular intervals the FTSE committee reviews the membership of the FTSE 100; the principal criterion for membership is size which, of course, fluctuates. The FTSE 100 account for over 80% of the market capitalization of companies listed on the LSE. The committee also reviews membership of the other principal stock market company classifications:

There are indices for the following:

- FTSE 250 – these are the 250 companies which are next in order of size after the FTSE 100. They account for around 15% of the total market capitalization of companies listed on the LSE.
- FTSE All-Share – the FTSE 100 and FTSE 250 plus a group of smaller, but still significant companies classified as FTSE SmallCap.
- FTSE Fledgling – these are fully listed companies which do not qualify in size terms for the FTSE SmallCap.

Information about the current values of all of these indices, and the rules which operate for their calculation, can be found at the FTSE website: www.ftserussell.com

20.3.6 Flotation and Other Types of Share Issue

FLOATING A COMPANY As noted earlier, between 200 and 300 companies become publicly quoted each year. The process is time consuming (it can easily take up to a year to organize and carry out), and may deflect directors' attention from running the business. A great deal of professional advice is required in order to conduct a successful flotation. Corporate finance advisers, stockbrokers (usually referred to simply as 'brokers'), lawyers and professional accountants are involved in ensuring that the process is successful.

Flotation for most companies involves a placing of the shares. This means identifying prospective buyers (usually institutional investors such as pension schemes, life assurance companies, venture capitalists, investment trusts and asset managers), and arranging to sell a portion of the shares. In the case of a placing, there is no invitation to the general public to buy into the new shares. An offer for sale, by contrast, does involve a general invitation to the general public and the institutions to buy shares in the company. It involves preparation of a detailed prospectus which contains a great deal of information about the history and prospects of the company.

In either case, once the shares are floated they can be bought and sold in the secondary market. However, in most cases of smaller companies coming to the market for the first time, the principal or only buyers of the new shares are likely to be half a dozen or so of the well-known institutional investors.

OTHER TYPES OF SHARE ISSUE

New issues. Once a company has been floated successfully it may issue further blocks of shares in order to raise new capital. If there is sufficient demand for the shares, the new issue is likely to be successful.

Rights issues. It is commonly the case that, where a listed company wishes to raise cash via a new issue of share capital, it will do so via a rights issue. A rights issue is an offer to existing shareholders to purchase additional shares. It is usually expressed in such terms as 'a one for three rights issue'. This would mean that for every three shares already held in the company, the shareholder could buy one additional share. Taking up the rights issue allows an individual shareholder to retain the same percentage shareholding as before, as the following example illustrates.

As in the Wendover example (see example 2.6 below), it is usually the case that the rights issue price will be pitched below the current market value of the share, in order to make it attractive to shareholders. If the rights issue fails (in that existing shareholders do not take up the issue) then it would be possible to try to raise additional capital by a placing or an offer for sale. However, existing shareholders could be assumed to have a particular interest in the company; if they aren't interested in investing more money in the company, it is even less likely that outsiders will wish to do so. A real-life example of a rights issue is described in example 20.7.

Example 20.6

Wendover Household Goods plc has a total issued share capital of 1 000 000 £1 shares whose current market price is £5.30 each. It requires a fresh injection of capital to finance the building of a new factory. Wendover's corporate finance advisers tell the directors that the best way of raising the money is via a rights issue. They suggest an issue of 1 for 4 at £4.40. How much cash will this rights issue raise for the company? An issue of one share for every four held will result in the issue of an additional 250 000 £1 shares. Each of these will be sold for £4.40, resulting in a cash inflow of £1 100 000.

Jeannie Lemmon is one of Wendover's principal shareholders. She holds 170 000 of the issued shares. How much will Jeannie have to pay if she takes up the rights issue? Jeannie's holding is 170 000 shares. She will have the opportunity to buy 170 000 ÷ 4 = 42 500 shares. Therefore, she will have to pay 42 500 × £4.40 = £187 000 if she decides to take up the rights issue.

Example 20.7 (Real-Life)

LLOYDS BANKING GROUP (LBG)

Following the financial crisis in 2007, the UK government persuaded Lloyds TSB to merge with the failing Halifax banking group. Subsequently, in 2009, LBG sought to refinance itself, partly by launching the largest rights issue ever to take place in the UK. The group's 2.8 million shareholders were asked to buy up a rights issue. The terms of the issue were 1.34 new shares for every existing share held, at a price of 37p each. This price was deeply discounted, compared to the quoted price of an LBG share at the time, by around 60p per share. In December 2009, it was announced that the issue had been successful.

MERGERS AND ACQUISITIONS Where a full-scale effort is made by one company to purchase a majority of another company's shares, this is referred to as a **takeover bid**. What happens is that the bidding company offers to purchase shares from existing shareholders at a stated price. The existing shareholders do not have to accept the offer; the offer has to be pitched at a price which will make it sufficiently attractive to induce a large number of the existing shareholders to sell. Takeovers are a common feature of the stock market environment. A **hostile bid** refers to a bid by one company which is rejected by the target company's directors. Not all takeovers, however, are hostile.

The consequences of a successful takeover bid are often far-reaching. The purpose of a takeover, in principle, is to allow a better quality management to take on the control of the operations of the target company. Ideally, takeovers should lead to improved efficiency and better returns for shareholders of the company which is taking over the other. In practice, it appears that takeovers do not always have the desired effect.

Mergers and acquisitions (M&A) is a general term which refers to any bringing together of companies either by agreement or as a result of a hostile bid. (Note that both 'mergers' and 'acquisitions' have specific meanings for accountants, but it is beyond the scope of this book to examine those meanings.)

Identify the following statements as either TRUE or FALSE:

1 All takeover bids are hostile bids.
2 A rights issue is an offer to sell shares to existing shareholders in proportion to their existing holdings.
3 An offer for sale of shares is limited to a few major financial institutions.
4 The LSE trades in corporate bonds, as well as shares.

Self-test question 20.3 (answer at the end of the book)

20.3.7 To List or Not to List?

It may not be easy for the directors of a limited company to decide on whether or not to list. There are advantages and drawbacks.

ADVANTAGES OF LISTING

- The principal advantage of listing is that the company can raise more finance for new projects and investments.
- Listing increases a company's general profile and credibility and may enhance its reputation.

- Listing may allow the founder members of a company to turn their hard work in the past into cash by selling part or all of their holding of shares.
- Listed companies shares can, in most cases, be liquidated easily. Listing is, therefore, likely to increase the pool of potential investors, and may increase the value of the company.

A survey carried out jointly in 2001 by the LSE and Eversheds (a firm of business lawyers) found that the most popular reason cited for seeking flotation was 'to raise funds' (mentioned by 64% of respondents), followed by 'to increase the company's profile and credibility' (mentioned by 23% of respondents).

DRAWBACKS OF LISTING

- A listed company is in the public spotlight. Financial journalists are likely to become much more interested in a company's activities once it is listed. This may work to the company's advantage when everything is going well and the publicity is welcome. However, if the company is struggling, or if it is engaged in some controversial activity, publicity may be a major drawback.
- A listed company may become a 'takeover target'. A company can take over another company by buying up a majority of the shares in order to obtain control over it. The directors of the target company usually find themselves in a difficult position in these circumstances and they often lose their jobs.
- There is increased pressure on companies' management to produce consistent and ever-improving results. This pressure may result in short-termism, where investment in the long-term future of the company may suffer in order to produce the kind of short-term results that satisfy City commentators.
- Obtaining a listing is not cheap. A great deal of accounting and legal work must be paid for, plus underwriting costs. The total costs usually amount to at least 10%, and occasionally as much as 20%, of the amounts of cash raised by the flotation.
- The additional layers of regulation are onerous and compliance with them can be very expensive. It is usually necessary to employ additional staff.
- Movements in the company's share price can be worryingly difficult to explain or predict.

In the LSE/Eversheds survey referred to earlier, the principal drawbacks to being a public company were identified as 'additional reporting requirements and associated costs' (mentioned by 57% of respondents) and 'volatility of share price, often with little correlation to business fundamentals' (mentioned by 18% of respondents).

Chapter Summary

There are many different potential sources of finance for businesses of all sizes, but the financing options available are more numerous and more flexible for larger and more successful businesses. The financing of very large businesses, such as the FTSE 100 companies, often involves complex arrangements such as the LBG's rights issue mentioned in the real-life example in the chapter. However, the more well-known a business is, the more likely it is that information about it, and its financing arrangements, will be publicly available in the form of newspaper articles, blogs and other commentaries.

It is worth following up some of the internet resources listed below in order to develop knowledge of the types of finance available.

Internet Resources

www.ftserussell.com – the website of the FTSE and Russell organizations which are responsible for the indices used on the LSE. The website explains in detail the composition and operation of the indices.

www.londonstockexchange.com – the LSE's own website contains information about all companies currently listed, including news items, current share prices, hyperlinks to companies' own websites, information about what is involved in listing, and a great deal besides.

www.bvca.co.uk – the website of the British Venture Capital Association

www.bbc.co.uk/dragonsden – the BBC's Dragons' Den website includes videos of pitches by hopeful entrepreneurs and an online version of the series.

www.zopa.com – the website of one of the leading peer-to-peer lending companies

www.kickstarter.com – the website of a key crowdfunding organization

Book's companion website summary

The website contains the following resources in respect of Chapter 20:

Students' section

A multiple choice quiz containing ten questions
Four additional questions with answers

Lecturers' section

Answers to end-of-chapter exercises 20.10 to 20.15
Four additional questions with answers
Case study
Testbank
Instructor's Manual
PowerPoint presentation

Exercises: Answers at the End of the Book

20.1   Erika is planning to become a self-employed graphic designer working from a small one-room office in a new development in the middle of town. You are a small business adviser and she has asked you for help in producing her business plan.

Prepare a list of questions to ask Erika at your first meeting, based upon the major headings which you would expect to see covered in the business plan.

20.2   Ben has a degree in public relations and a huge list of useful contacts in the aerospace business which he has established over a period of several years while working for Amis & Lovett, a large PR agency. He would like to set up his own PR agency. He plans to employ a new graduate and a secretary immediately in order to avoid being regarded as a 'one man band'. He is confident that his savings (£45 000) will tide him over the first couple of months while he finds enough work to get started.

List the main risks which you see in Ben's plan for the new business start-up.

20.3   Nancy is a self-employed hairdresser. She runs a salon with the assistance of one untrained employee who takes bookings, tidies and sweeps up, and makes tea and coffee for the clients. Nancy would like to expand the business; this would involve employing a fully trained stylist. There is sufficient space in Nancy's existing premises for another person to work.

Advise Nancy on the costs, risks and potential benefits involved in employing a stylist.

20.4 Oleander Enterprises Limited is a small holiday company run by its two principal directors and shareholders, Libby and Lisa. The company organizes exclusive (and expensive) holiday tours of French chateaux. During the four years since it was set up the company has gone from strength to strength. It now employs six people and it makes substantial annual profits. The company has a cash surplus and the directors have been considering ways of using the surplus to expand the business, possibly by starting up operations in new countries. Recently, the directors have been approached by Loretta, the managing director of another holiday company, Oxus Orlando Limited, which organizes holiday tours in Turkey. Loretta is the principal director and shareholder of Oxus Orlando. She would like to sell her company and retire on the proceeds.

Advise Libby and Lisa on:

i) the advantages and drawbacks of expanding by buying into another company
ii) the type of information they will require in order to be able to make a decision on whether or not to buy Oxus Orlando.

20.5 Ashton Longton plc, a listed company, has issued share capital of £8 000 000 comprising shares of £1 nominal value. The current quoted price per share is £3.85.

What is the company's market capitalization?

20.6 What is the Alternative Investment Market a market for?

a) Companies that do not currently wish to proceed to full listing.
b) Companies that promote alternative lifestyles.
c) British Government securities.
d) Overseas companies without a trading history.

20.7 Warminster Toys plc has a total issued share capital of £3 000 000 in 50p shares. The company decides to make a rights issue of 1 for 5 at a price of £5.42 per share. How much will the holder of 50 000 shares have to pay to take up the rights?

a) £27 100
b) £135 500
c) £54 200
d) £271 000

20.8 Yolande Brighton is the managing director of Brighton Bestwines plc, a company which supplies the licensed trade. The company has been very successful but has now reached the point where it needs to expand its warehousing capacity if it is to continue growing. The directors have been contemplating applying for a listing on the AIM. The company will issue a further 500 000 shares (it already has 1 000 000 shares in issue). It hopes to be able to sell the shares at around £2.50 each.

The directors have invited you to their board meeting to discuss the flotation. They are keen to raise the finance, but one or two of them are wondering about potential drawbacks to being quoted on the AIM, and they would like you to give them an outline of any possible problems they face.

Prepare a list of potential drawbacks for discussion at the meeting.

20.9 Speke Septima Limited was started up three years ago to market a range of designer kitchen products. The company has been very successful, but now needs finance to expand into overseas markets. The directors have discussed a range of financing options, and have reached the tentative conclusion that they should approach a venture capital firm. In outline, they propose to sell 30% of the company in exchange for an equity investment of £3 million, and a seat on Speke Septima's board. They have asked you, a financial adviser, to identify any potential drawbacks in entering into a venture capital arrangement of the type proposed.

Identify and describe drawbacks to the proposed venture capital arrangement.

Exercises: Answers Available on the Lecturers' Section of the Book's Website

20.10 Norman and Naylor Partners is a business which runs corporate events. Sam Norman and Sally Naylor founded the business about five years ago, and it has been very successful. The partners share profits equally. It now employs five full-time staff and calls upon a pool of up to 40 additional staff who can be employed part time for specific events. Sally is several years older than Sam, and would now like to pull out of the business. She plans to take out her share of the value of the business with a view to buying and running a vineyard in Italy.

Identify the business problems and risks which Sam must deal with as a result of Sally's decision. What are the financial implications (in broad terms) for the partners?

20.11 Lionel is an experienced chartered surveyor with many years of experience. He is employed by a large property company where he receives a good salary and a performance-related bonus. He has recently been approached by an old friend, Leo, who is one of three partners in a firm of surveyors. The other two partners are nearing retirement age, and they have decided that they need to bring in some 'new blood'. The partnership has been in operation for nearly 20 years and has carved out a sizeable niche in commercial property management. Leo tells Lionel that the partnership has been valued by a business valuation specialist at £1 200 000. If Lionel accepts the invitation to join the partnership he will be required to pay £300 000 in cash for a quarter share of the business. In exchange he will be entitled to one-quarter of the profits made by the partnership in the future.

i) Advise Lionel on the type of information he will need to examine in order to be able to make a decision on whether or not to buy into the partnership.
ii) Identify possible sources of finance which might be available to Lionel to fund his investment in the partnership.

20.12 Lucinda and Lister are sole (and equal) shareholders and directors of L&L Limos Limited, a company which runs a small fleet of limousines for hire for weddings and parties. Each year the company has gradually increased its revenue and has developed a reputation for reliability. There is no direct competitor for their service in their own town, and increasingly often the company is asked to undertake business in neighbouring towns and cities. Quite often these days the directors have to turn business away because all of the available cars are booked. The option of expanding the fleet and taking on new drivers looks increasingly attractive.

i) Describe the sources of finance that might be suitable to finance the proposed expansion.
ii) Identify the additional costs which might be involved in the expansion.
iii) Briefly identify and describe any risks associated with the expansion and its financing.

20.13 Amery Chorlton plc, a listed company, has issued share capital of £4 000 000 comprising shares of 25p nominal value. The current quoted price per share is 98p.
What is the company's market capitalization?

20.14 Willoughby Wooster plc has a total issued share capital of £1 000 000 in 25p shares. The company decides to make a rights issue of 1 for 2 at a price of £2.70 per share. How much will the holder of 30 000 shares have to pay to take up the rights?

a) £40 500
b) £10 125
c) £20 250
d) £7500

20.15 Tatiana, a friend of yours, has recently been left approximately £50 000 of listed company investments in her grandmother's will. She has been trying to read the Financial Times in order to see what is happening to her investments. She has found some information about three of them:

i)   Turtlehammer plc rose to 215p on speculation of a hostile bid from a competitor, but fell back to 210p by the end of the day's trading.
ii) The share price of Teddington Tilmain plc has risen by 26 pence following the announcement that it has obtained an important new export contract.
iii) Tolson Tortellini plc has announced today that it is making a rights issue of 1 for 4 at £2.30.

Tatiana frankly admits that she doesn't understand any of this. She asks you to explain each of the pieces of news in terms that she can understand. She would like to know if any of it is likely to be good news for her.

Answers to self-test questions

CHAPTER 1

Answer to self-test question 1.1

a) Setting up a partnership does not involve any particular legal considerations. FALSE
b) A sole trader is liable personally for all losses made by the business. TRUE
c) A director of a company cannot hold shares in that same company. FALSE
d) Partners are responsible in law for the consequences of each other's actions. TRUE

Answer to self-test question 1.2

The correct answer is c. An issue of shares is not an appropriate source of finance for a sole trader.

Answer to self-test question 1.3

The correct answer is a. The profit on the sale of the building is taxed as a capital gain.

Answer to self-test question 1.4

Sole traders, partnerships and smaller limited companies are not required by law to have an audit. Only larger companies have an absolute legal requirement to have their financial statements audited. However, there is nothing to prevent smaller businesses from having an audit.

CHAPTER 2

Answer to self-test question 2.1

Bank overdraft = Liability
Computer and printers used to keep the administrative records of the business = Asset
Plates and cups available for sale to customers = Asset
Cash float kept in the till: £100 in various notes and coins = Asset
Loan of £20 000 from George's brother = Liability

Answer to self-test question 2.2

1   The total of assets in Saqib's business is £30 000 (Non-current assets) + £5000 (Inventory) + £4000 (Trade receivables) + £3000 (Cash held in business bank account) = £42 000
2   There is only one category of liability in the business: trade payables of £6000. Therefore total liabilities are £6000.
3   Saqib's capital is stated in the question as £36 000.
4   Applying the accounting equation to Saqib's business: Assets (£42 000) = Capital (£36 000) + Liabilities (£6000).

Answer to self-test question 2.3

Assets − Liabilities = Capital
Therefore, Amy's capital can be calculated as: £58 000 − £30 000 = £28 000.

CHAPTER 3

Answer to self-test question 3.1

Jules

Trading account for the month ended 31 December 20X4	
Revenue: 66 bags @ £23	1 518
Cost of sales: 66 bags @ £14.50	957
Gross profit	561

Note: the heading specifying the name of the business and the period covered by the trading account is essential information and must not be omitted.

Answer to self-test question 3.2

Jules (continued)

Jules: Inventory movement account for January 20X5

	Units	£
Opening inventory: 36 bags @ £14.50	36	522
Add purchases: 68 bags @ £14.50	68	986
Less: items of inventory sold: 42 bags @ £14.50	(42)	(609)
Closing inventory: 62 bags @ £14.50	62	899

Note that this account is part of Jules's business records. It is not shown in his financial statements.

Jules: Trading account for the month ended 31 January 20X5

	Units	£	£
Revenue			
42 bags @ £23	42		966
Cost of sales			
Opening inventory: 36 bags @ £14.50	36	522	
Add: purchases: 68 bags @ £14.50	68	986	
	104	1 508	
Less: closing inventory: 62 bags @ £14.50	(62)	(899)	
Cost of sales: 42 bags @ £14.50	42		(609)
Gross profit for month*			357

*Check: each bag sold gives a gross profit of £23 − £14.50 = £8.50. If Jules sells 42 bags he expects to make a profit of 42 × £8.50 = £357.

CHAPTER 4

Answer to self-test question 4.1

Konstantin

Cost of sales is calculated as follows:

Cost of sales:		
Opening inventory		35 500
Add purchases:		
Purchases	177 200	
Add: import duties	700	
Less: purchase returns	(5 000)	
		172 900
		208 400
Less: closing inventory		(36 600)
Cost of sales		171 800

Answer to self-test question 4.2

Peter

The rental expense for the year is charged on the accruals basis of accounting. This means that rent in respect of the first six months of the year was 6/12 × £150 000 = £75 000. Rent for the second six months of the year (from 1 July 20X5 to 31 December 20X6) was 6/12 × £165 000 = £82 500. The total rental charge in the business's statement of profit or loss for the year ended 31 December 20X6 was therefore £75 000 + £82 500 = £157 500. A prepayment of £82 500 is carried forward as an asset in the statement of financial position at 31 December 201X6.

CHAPTER 5

Answer to self-test question 5.1

	£
Cost of Salvatore's new vehicle	65 000
Estimated sale proceeds after four years of use	(25 000)
Estimated total depreciation over four years	40 000

Spread evenly over four years, this produces a straight-line annual depreciation charge of £10 000.

Answer to self-test question 5.2

Year ending 30 April 20X2

Car depreciation expense in the statement of profit or loss will be £17 209 × 30% = £5163. The statement of financial position will show the following amounts:

	£
Car at cost	17 209
Less: depreciation	(5 163)
Carrying amount of vehicle	12 046

Year ending 30 April 20X3

Car depreciation expense in the statement of profit or loss will be £12 046 × 30% = £3614. The statement of financial position will show the following amounts:

	£
Car at cost	17 209
Less: depreciation (5163 + 3614)	(8 777)
Carrying amount of vehicle	8 432

Year ending 30 April 20X4

Car depreciation expense in the statement of profit or loss will be £8432 × 30% = £2530. The statement of financial position will show the following amounts:

	£
Car at cost	17 209
Less: depreciation (5163 + 3614 + 2530)	(11 307)
Carrying amount of vehicle	5 902

Answer to self-test question 5.3

To calculate Sergio's profit or loss on sale of the machine, first the carrying amount after five years' depreciation must be calculated:

	£
Machine at cost	15 000
Year 1 depreciation (30% × £15 000)	(4 500)
Carrying amount at end of year 1	10 500
Year 2 depreciation (30% × £10 500)	(3 150)
Carrying amount at end of year 2	7 350

	£
Year 3 depreciation (30% × £7350)	(2 205)
Carrying amount at end of year 3	5 145
Year 4 depreciation (30% × £5145)	(1 544)
Carrying amount at end of year 4	3 601
Year 5 depreciation (30% × £3601)	(1 080)
Carrying amount at end of year 5	2 521

Sale proceeds are greater than carrying amount and so a profit on sale has been made of £489 (£3010 − £2521 = £489).

CHAPTER 6

Answer to self-test question 6.1

Transaction	Impact on cash	Impact on profits
Purchase of inventory for cash for £1800.	Cash is immediately reduced by £1800.	No immediate effect on profit. A sale of the inventory items will probably take place in due course. When that happens the cost of inventory sold is set off against revenue in the form of cost of sales.
Sale of old delivery van for £360.	Cash is immediately increased by £360.	A profit or loss on sale (see Chapter 5) will be calculated by setting off the proceeds of sale (£360) against the carrying amount of the asset. The effect on profit would be an increase of £360 only if the carrying amount of the asset at the date of sale was nil.
Long-term loan from brother of £5000.	Cash and long-term liabilities are both immediately increased by £5000.	The loan itself has no effect on profit. Any interest paid on the loan will reduce profits.
Payment of interest of £150 on bank overdraft.	Cash is reduced by £150 (or, more likely, the overdraft is increased by £150).	The interest paid reduces profits.
Amortization charge of £8000 relating to patent rights.	No effect on cash.	Profits are reduced by £8000.

Answer to self-test question 6.2

	Statement of profit or loss	Non-cash item: depreciation	Non-cash items: trade receivables and trade payables	Cash outflow: inventory purchase	Total cash inflow (outflow)
	£	£	£	£	£
Revenue	89 300		(8 500)		80 800
Operating costs*	(78 800)	4 500	9 000	(6 900)	(72 200)
Operating profit/cash flow	10 500	4 500	500	(6 900)	8 600
Interest paid	(1 000)				(1 000)
Net profit/cash flow	9 500	4 500	500	(6 900)	7 600

*Operating costs = cost of sales (£56 200) + operating costs (£22 600) = £78 800

Amy Binyon: Statement of cash flows for the year ended 31 December 20X2

	£	£
Cash flows from operating activities		
Operating profit		10 500
Depreciation		4 500
		15 000
Less: increase in inventory	(6 900)	
Less: increase in trade receivables	(8 500)	
Add: increase in trade payables	9 000	
		(6 400)
Cash generated from operations		8 600
Interest paid		(1 000)
Net cash inflow from operating activities		7 600

Answer to self-test question 6.3

	Statement of profit or loss	Non-cash items: depreciation	Non-cash items: trade receivables and trade payables	Cash outflow: inventory purchase	Total cash inflow (outflow)
	£	£	£	£	£
Revenue	109 300		(200)		109 100
Operating costs total*	(86 500)	5 000	700	(700)	(81 500)
Operating profit/cash flow	22 800	5 000	500	(700)	27 600

*operating costs total = cost of sales + operating expenses (£62 700 + 23 800 = £86 500)

Inventory: there has been an increase in inventory between the two year-ends: £7600 − 6900 = £700. This difference is the total additional cash outflow for the accounting period.

Trade receivables: the amount of cash received in respect of sales revenue in the period is:

	£
Opening trade receivables	8 500
Revenue	109 300
Less: closing trade receivables	(8 700)
Cash received	109 100

The adjustment for non-cash items is the difference between the closing and opening balances: £8700 − 8500 = £200, ie. an increase in trade receivables.

Trade payables: The amount of cash paid in respect of operating costs and expenses in the period is:

	£
Opening trade payables	9 000
Operating costs total	86 500
Less: closing trade payables	(9 700)
	85 800

The adjustment for non-cash items is the difference between the closing and opening balances: £9700 − 9000 = £700, ie. an increase in trade payables.

Amy Binyon: Statement of cash flows for the year ended 31 December 20X3

	£	£
Cash flows from operating activities		
Operating profit		22 800
Depreciation		5 000
		27 800
Less: increase in inventory	(700)	
Less: increase in trade receivables	(200)	
Add: increase in trade payables	700	
		(200)
Cash generated from operations		27 600

CHAPTER 7

Answer to self-test question 7.1

Since 2005 all listed companies in the European Union are obliged to comply with international accounting standards; this, of course, includes UK listed companies. The Companies Act 2006 allows other companies (unlisted) a choice between setting out their financial statements in a UK format (and by implication complying with UK accounting standards) or using international accounting formats and standards.

Answer to self-test question 7.2

Workings

1   Selling and distribution costs

	£
Selling costs	63 477
Distribution costs	54 460
	117 937

2   Tangible non-current assets: property, plant and equipment

	£
Premises at carrying amount	65 700
Vehicles at carrying amount	44 430
Fixtures and fittings at carrying amount	17 260
	127 390

Uppingham Telephones Ltd: Draft statement of profit or loss for the year ending 31 March 20X3

	£
Revenue	717 216
Cost of sales	(509 582)
Gross profit	207 634
Selling and distribution costs (working 1)	(117 937)
Administrative expenses	(24 512)
Profit before tax	65 185
Tax on profit	(19 500)
Profit for the year	45 685

Uppingham Telephones Ltd: Draft statement of changes in equity for the year ended 31 March 20X3

	Share capital £	Retained earnings £	Total equity £
At 1 April 20X2	20 000	161 479	181 479
Profit for the year		45 685	45 685
Dividend		(5 000)	(5 000)
At 31 March 20X3	20 000	202 164	222 164

Uppingham Telephones Ltd: Draft statement of financial position at 31 March 20X3

ASSETS

Non-current assets

Intangible assets		30 866
Property, plant and equipment		127 390
		158 256

Current assets

Inventories	42 370	
Trade receivables	82 026	
Cash at bank	13 222	
		137 618
		295 874

CAPITAL AND LIABILITIES

Equity

Share capital		20 000
Retained earnings		202 164
		222 164

Long-term liabilities

Loan		15 000

Current liabilities

Trade payables	39 210	
Other payables: taxation	19 500	
		58 710
		295 874

CHAPTER 8

Answer to self-test question 8.1

Horizontal trend analysis: Jamal's sales 20X1–20X8

Year	£	Percentage increase (decrease) on previous year
20X1	250 031	–
20X2	347 266	38.9
20X3	441 179	27.0
20X4	531 150	20.4
20X5	523 622	(1.4)
20X6	545 331	4.1
20X7	590 942	8.4
20X8	679 244	14.9
20X9	771 485	13.6

Since the start of the business sales have increased each year, apart from 20X5 when there was a small drop. Jared claimed at interview that he would be able to increase sales by 15% each year, but it is only in 20X8 and 20X9 that the increase has approached 15%. In the early years of the business there was very rapid sales growth, but this had clearly stopped by the time Jared was appointed. It is possible that Jared has made a major contribution to the improvements in sales, but the figures alone do not prove this conclusively.

Jamal's decision on Jared's salary increase will depend on the answers to some of the following:

- To what extent has Jared been responsible for the recent improvements in sales trends?
- Are there other market factors at work (for example, has demand in the market for pre-packaged foods strengthened)?
- Has Jamal set performance targets for Jared, and have these been met?

Answer to self-test question 8.2

a) The increase in the revenue figures for the companies are:

$$\text{Barnes \& Jack Ltd} = \frac{(2\,044\,032 - 1\,743\,906)}{1\,743\,906} \times 100 = 17.2\%$$

$$\text{Carleen Baker Ltd} = \frac{(1\,850\,490 - 1\,564\,774)}{1\,564\,774} \times 100 = 18.3\%$$

Carleen Baker's revenue growth is slightly higher.

b) The additional information allows for a more detailed breakdown of Barnes & Jack Ltd's revenue, as follows:

	Barnes & Jack Ltd		
	20X5	20X4	Percentage change
	£	£	%
Domestic and shop market	1 555 725	1 293 106	20.3
Zoos	488 307	450 800	8.3
	2 044 032	1 743 906	17.2

From this analysis, it appears that Barnes & Jack Ltd have done slightly better in terms of revenue growth than Carleen Baker Ltd, in the areas of their business that are directly comparable.

CHAPTER 9

Answer to self-test question 9.1

Augustus Algernon Ltd

$$\text{Pre-tax ROE (return on equity)} = \frac{\text{Profit before taxation and after interest}}{\text{Equity (ie. share capital and retained earnings)}}$$

$$= \frac{162}{120 + 1000} \times 100$$

$$= 14.46\%$$

$$\text{Post-tax ROE (return on equity)} = \frac{\text{Profit after taxation}}{\text{Equity}}$$

$$= \frac{114}{120 + 1000} \times 100$$

$$= 10.18\%$$

$$\text{ROCE (return on total capital invested)} = \frac{\text{Profit before interest and tax}}{\text{Equity + long-term borrowings}}$$

$$= \frac{186}{120 + 1000 + 480} \times 100$$

$$= 11.63\%$$

Answer to self-test question 9.2

Arbus Nugent Ltd

$$\text{Current ratio} = \frac{\text{Current assets}}{\text{Current liabilites}}$$

$$\text{Quick ratio} = \frac{\text{Current assets} - \text{inventory}}{\text{Current liabilites}}$$

For Arbus Nugent Ltd for 20X4 and 20X3:

	20X4	**20X3**
Current ratio	$\frac{87\ 620}{31\ 450} : 1 = 2.8{:}1$	$\frac{74\ 850}{32\ 970} : 1 = 2.3{:}1$
Quick ratio	$\frac{87\ 620\ -\ 34\ 300}{31\ 450} : 1 = 1.7{:}1$	$\frac{74\ 850\ -\ 31\ 600}{32\ 970} : 1 = 1.3{:}1$

Both the current ratio and the quick ratio have improved.

Answer to self-test question 9.3

Armitage Horobin Ltd

		20X1	**20X0**
Non-current asset turnover	$\dfrac{\text{Revenue}}{\text{Non-current assets}}$	$\dfrac{283.4}{289.2} = 0.98$	$\dfrac{271.1}{275.3} = 0.98$
Inventory turnover	a) $\dfrac{\text{Cost of sales}}{\text{Average inventory}}$		
	Average inventory $= \dfrac{23.7\ +\ 25.9}{2} = 24.8$		Average inventory $=\dfrac{21.2\ +\ 23.7}{2} = 22.5$
	$\dfrac{\text{Cost of sales}}{\text{Average inventory}}$		
	$\dfrac{182.6}{24.8} = 7.36$		$\dfrac{175.0}{22.5} = 7.77$
	b) Inventory turnover in days $= \dfrac{\text{Average inventory}}{\text{Cost of sales}} \times 365$		
	$\dfrac{24.8}{182.6} \times 365 = 49.6$ days		$\dfrac{22.5}{175.0} \times 365 = 46.9$ days
Trade receivables turnover	$\dfrac{\text{Trade receivables}}{\text{Sales on credit}} \times 365$		
	$\dfrac{33.0}{283.4} \times 365 = 42.5$ days		$\dfrac{28.2}{271.1} \times 365 = 38.0$ days
Trade payables turnover	$\dfrac{\text{Trade payables}}{\text{Purchases}} \times 365$		
	$\dfrac{24.5}{184.8} \times 365 = 48.4$ days		$\dfrac{20.6}{177.5} \times 365 = 42.4$ days

Non-current assets turnover has hardly changed. Inventory turnover has worsened, in that inventory is now held on the premises for an average of 49.6 days compared with 46.9 days in the previous year. Trade receivables turnover has worsened in that it is now taking debtors, on average, 42.5 days to pay, compared with 38 days in the previous year. Trade payables turnover has improved, in that Armitage Horobin is taking advantage of the interest-free credit offered by creditors to a greater extent than in the previous year. However, 48.4 days may be regarded as too long a period to wait, on average, for payment, and there may be a loss of goodwill on the part of creditors towards the company.

Tutorial note: average inventory has been used in the calculations because there was sufficient data available. In the case of trade receivables and trade payables there was insufficient data, and so closing trade receivables and trade payables have been used in the calculations. Although, ideally, averages should be used in the calculations it is often not possible to obtain them.

Answer to self-test question 9.4

Armley Regina plc

$$\text{Dividend per share} = \frac{220\,000}{1\,000\,000} = 22\text{p per share}$$

$$\text{Dividend cover} = \frac{680\,000}{220\,000} = 3.09\text{ times}$$

$$\text{Earnings per share (EPS)} = \frac{680\,000}{1\,000\,000} = 68\text{p per share}$$

$$\text{Price/earnings (P/E) ratio} = \frac{508\text{p}}{68\text{p}} = 7.5$$

$$\text{Market capitalization} = £5.08 \times 1\,000\,000 \text{ shares} = £5\,080\,000$$

CHAPTER 11

Answer to self-test question 11.1

Beeching Plumstead

Canvas material	Direct materials
Metal spokes for wheels	Direct materials
Spare parts for sewing machine repairs	Indirect production overheads
Advertising expenditure	Other indirect overheads
Machine oil	Indirect production overheads
Electricity bill for factory	Indirect production overheads
Wages of assembly line workers	Direct labour
Wages of factory canteen staff	Indirect production overheads
Wages of assembly line supervisor	Indirect production overheads
Secretary's salary	Other indirect overheads
Delivery vehicle depreciation	Other indirect overheads

Answer to self-test question 11.2

Gonzalez Perez

a) *FIFO*

	Deliveries into inventory			Transfers to production			Balance	
Date	Units	£	£	Units	£	£	Units	£
1 Mar							55	165.00
10 Mar	160	3.20	512.00				215	677.00
12 Mar				35	3.00	105.00	180	572.00
25 Mar				20	3.00	60.00	160	512.00
				50	3.20	160.00	110	352.00

Tutorial note: the 110 items remaining in inventory after the transfer to production on 25 March are all assumed to belong to the batch of items delivered on 10 March, and so are valued at £3.20 each (110 × £3.20 = £352.00).

b) *AVCO*

Date	Deliveries into inventory			Transfers to production			Balance		
	Units	£	£	Units	£	£	Units	AVCO £	£
1 Mar							55	3.00	165.00
10 Mar	160	3.20	512.00				215	3.149	677.00
12 Mar				35	3.149	110.21	180	3.149	566.79
25 Mar				70	3.149	220.42	110	3.149	346.37

Answer to self-test question 11.3

Harvey & Cork

Batch No: 30453A

	£	£
Direct materials		
Metal: 100kg @ £4.50 per kilo	450.00	
Paint: 2 litres @ £6.80 per litre	13.60	
Glass: 500 pieces @ 30p per piece	150.00	613.60
Direct labour		
Grade A: 22 hours @ £8.00	176.00	
Grade B: 19 hours @ £9.00	171.00	
		347.00
Prime cost		960.60

$$\text{Cost per picture frame} = \frac{£960.60}{500} = £1.92 \text{ (rounded)}$$

CHAPTER 12

Answer to self-test question 12.1

Swift Metals Ltd: Apportionment of production overheads – year ended 31 December 20X3

		Total	Preparation	Cost centre Tooling	Finishing
	Basis	£	£	£	£
Factory costs	Floor area	700 000	245 000	315 000	140 000
Canteen costs	Employees	18 496	8 704	6 528	3 264
Machinery depreciation	Net book value	17 650	2 600	11 200	3 850
Machinery maintenance and repair	Call-outs	2 961	658	1 974	329
Supervisory salaries	Employees	23 358	10 992	8 244	4 122
Totals		762 465	267 954	342 946	151 565

Tutorial note: note that, by contrast with the Choremaster example, supervisory salaries for Swift Metals are apportioned on the basis of the number of employees supervised. Remember, there are no fixed rules about the way in which costs are apportioned – the basis of apportionment is whatever is most appropriate for the business.

CHAPTER 13

Answer to self-test question 13.1

Demand for luxury goods tends to be inelastic.
Demand for soap powder tends to be elastic.

Answer to self-test question 13.2

The correct answer is d. Price skimming is charging high prices in the early stages of exploitation of a new product.

CHAPTER 14

Answer to self-test question 14.1

Brandade Ltd

The initial outlay on the item of inventory (£1000) is a sunk cost.

Relevant costs for the decision are the additional outlay of £500. Relevant revenues are those arising under the two alternatives.

Option 1, to update the inventory, has relevant costs of £500 and relevant revenues of £700, giving a net revenue figure of £200 (£700 − 500).

Option 2, to sell the inventory for scrap, has no relevant costs. Relevant revenue of £300 is the same therefore as net revenue: £300.

Option 2 appears to be the preferable option.

Answer to self-test question 14.2

Brinn Bartholomew: Budget for June 20X7

	£
Sales: 1400 bins × £250 each	350 000
Variable costs	
Direct materials: 1400 bins × £97	(135 800)
Direct labour: 1400 bins × £36	(50 400)
Contribution	163 800
Fixed costs	(120 400)
Net profit	43 400

The company's budgeted contribution is £163 800.
The company's budgeted net profit is £43 400.

Answer to self-test question 14.3

Marshall Mexico Ltd.

The following points can be plotted onto the graph:

Level of production	Fixed costs	Total costs
	£	£
0	50 000	50 000
10 000	50 000	100 000

We do not need to plot any other points in order to draw the graph, because variable costs increase at a steady rate in line with the level of production. The data produces the graph shown in Figure 1.

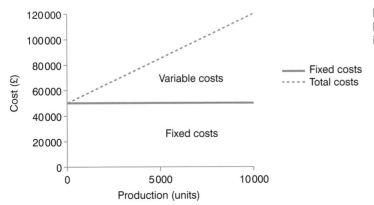

Figure 1
Marshall Mexico Ltd: total costs, split into fixed and variable, for 20X9

Answer to self-test question 14.4

From Figure 2 below we can see that the break-even point is 5000 units. In terms of sales value this is between £60 000 and £80 000 on the vertical axis – probably at approximately £75 000.

We can check this answer by working out a profit statement at a production and sales level of 5000 units:

	£
Sales (5000 × £15)	75 000
Variable costs (5000 × £5)	(25 000)
Contribution	50 000
Fixed costs	(50 000)
	0

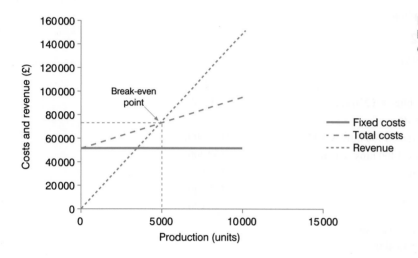

Figure 2
Marshall Mexico Ltd: break-even chart for 20X9

Answer to self-test question 14.5

Calculating Neasden Northwich Ltd's break-even point (in units):

Sales revenue per unit = £20.00
Variable costs per unit = £6.00

Contribution per unit is, therefore, £14.00 (sales minus variable costs).

$$\frac{\text{Break-even point}}{\text{(in units)}} = \frac{\text{Fixed costs}}{\text{Contribution per unit}}$$
$$= \frac{70\,000}{£14} = 5000 \text{ units}$$

CHAPTER 15

Answer to self-test question 15.1

The correct answer is b) cost of the machine purchase. The cost of the project to research demand for the new product is a sunk cost, and is not relevant. The administration costs of the new department are the same, regardless of which machine is purchased. Therefore the only relevant cost to take into account in making the decision is the cost of the machine.

Answer to self-test question 15.2

Because the ARR is a percentage measurement, it ignores the absolute value of the return, which may result in a project with a higher profit being rejected.
Payback has a major limitation in that it concentrates only on one aspect of an investment, ie. the rate at which it pays back its initial investment. Cash flows after the point of payback are ignored.

Answer to self-test question 15.3

1 Formula for £1 invested at 8% over four years:

$$£1 \times (1.08)^4$$

Compounding factor $= (1.08) \times (1.08) \times (1.08) \times (1.08) = 1.360$

2 Formula for £1 invested at 7% over five years:

$$£1 \times (1.07)^5$$

Compounding factor $= (1.07) \times (1.07) \times (1.07) \times (1.07) \times (1.07) = 1.403$

3 Formula for £1 invested at 6% over six years:

$$£1 \times (1.06)^6$$

Compounding factor $= (1.06) \times (1.06) \times (1.06) \times (1.06) \times (1.06) \times (1.06) = 1.419$

Answer to self-test question 15.4

1 Present value (PV) at Time 0 of £1 at the end of year 3 at a discount rate of 2%:

$$PV = £1 \times \frac{1}{(1.02)^3}$$

$$\text{Discounting factor} = \frac{1}{(1.02)} \times \frac{1}{(1.02)} \times \frac{1}{(1.02)}$$

$$= 0.942$$

2 Present value (PV) at Time 0 of £1 at the end of year 5 at a discount rate of 4%:

$$PV = £1 \times \frac{1}{(1.04)^5}$$

$$\text{Discounting factor} = \frac{1}{(1.04)} \times \frac{1}{(1.04)} \times \frac{1}{(1.04)} \times \frac{1}{(1.04)} \times \frac{1}{(1.04)}$$

$$= 0.822$$

3 Present value (PV) at Time 0 of £1 at the end of year 2 at a discount rate of 9%.

$$PV = £1 \times \frac{1}{(1.09)^2}$$

$$\text{Discounting factor} = 1 \times \frac{1}{(1.09)} \times \frac{1}{(1.09)}$$

$$= 0.842$$

CHAPTER 16

Answer to self-test question 16.1

Opening inventory	280
Production (balancing figure)	380
Transfers out of production	(350)
Closing inventory	310

The production budget is 380 units $(310 + 350 - 280)$.

Answer to self-test question 16.2

First, if managers build in some slack, their budget is likely to be easier to achieve, and so they will not have to work so hard. Second, managers would be motivated to build in some slack if there is any performance pay or bonus payable for achieving budgets.

CHAPTER 17

Answer to self-test question 17.1

Bridge and Blige Ltd

i) Flexed budget for 900 units

	£
Sales: 900 units @ £35	31 500
Costs:	
Direct materials: 900 units × (2 kg × £6)	(10 800)
Direct labour: 900 units × (1 hour × £7.50)	(6 750)
Production overheads	(4 000)
	9 950
Selling and administrative overheads	(2 300)
Net profit	7 650

ii) Calculation of variances

Summary of budget, flexed budget and actual statements

	Original budget £	Flexed budget £	Actual £
Sales	28 000	31 500	32 400
Direct materials	(9 600)	(10 800)	(9 405)
Direct labour	(6 000)	(6 750)	(7 560)
Production overhead	(4 000)	(4 000)	(4 400)
	8 400	9 950	11 035
Selling and administrative overhead	(2 300)	(2 300)	(2 450)
Net profit	6 100	7 650	8 585

The overall variance is:

Original budget net profit	6 100
Actual net profit	8 585
	2 485 (F)

Sales profit volume variance

This variance is the difference between the original budget profit and the flexed budget profit: £6100 − £7650 = £1550. The flexed budget profit is greater than the original budget profit, so this is a favourable variance.

Sales price variance

	£
Actual volume of sales at actual selling price: 900 × £36	32 400
Less: actual volume of sales at budget selling price: 900 × £35	31 500
Sales price variance	900 (F)

Direct materials variances

Comparing the figure for direct materials in the flexed budget statement with the figure in the actual statement:

Flexed budget for direct materials	£10 800
Actual direct materials	9 405
	£ 1 395 (F)

Direct materials price variance
We compare:
The actual quantity of materials used at the price actually paid (actual price).
The actual quantity of materials used at the price budgeted (standard price).

Actual quantity at actual price	
1.9 kg was used for each of 900 casings: actual quantity	
used is 1.9 kg × 900 = 1710 kg	
1710 kg × price actually paid (£5.50)	9 405
Actual quantity at standard price	
1710 kg × standard price (£6.00)	10 260
Direct materials price variance	855 (F)

Direct materials quantity variance
We compare:

The actual quantity of materials used at standard price.
The standard quantity of materials used at standard price.

Actual quantity at standard price	
Actual quantity used (already worked out): 1710 kg	
Standard price per kg: £6	
Actual quantity at standard price = 1710 kg × £6	10 260
Standard quantity at standard price	
Standard quantity: 2 kg × 900 casings = 1800 kg	
Standard price per kg: £6	
Standard quantity at standard price = 1800 kg × £6	10 800
Direct materials quantity variance	540 (F)

In summary, the direct materials variances are:

Direct materials price variance	£855 (F)
Direct materials quantity variance	540 (F)
Direct materials variance	£1 395 (F)

Direct labour variances
Comparing the figure for direct labour in the flexed budget statement with the figure in the actual statement:

Flexed budget for direct labour	£6 750
Actual direct labour	7 560
	£ 810 (A)

Direct labour rate variance
We compare:

The actual hours of direct labour used at the wage rate actually paid (actual rate).
The actual hours of direct labour used at the wage rate budgeted (standard rate).

Actual hours at actual rate	
Actual hours was 1.2 hours for each of 900 casings:	
1.2 × 900 = 1080 hours	
1080 hours × rate actually paid (£7.00)	7 560
Actual hours at standard rate	
1080 hours × standard rate (£7.50)	8 100
Direct labour rate variance	540 (F)

Direct labour efficiency variance
We compare:

The actual hours of direct labour used at standard rate.
The standard hours of direct labour used at standard rate.

Actual hours at standard rate	
Actual hours used (already worked out): 1080 hours	
Standard rate per hour: £7.50	
Actual hours at standard rate = 1080 × £7.50	8 100
Standard hours at standard rate	
Standard hours: 1 hour × 900 = 900	
Standard rate per hour: £7.50	
Standard hours at standard rate = 900 × £7.50	6 750
Direct labour efficiency variance	1 350 (A)

In summary, the direct labour variances are:

Direct labour rate variance	£540 (F)
Direct labour efficiency variance	1 350 (A)
Direct labour variance	£ 810 (A)

Production overhead variance

Budget figure for production overhead:	4 000
Actual figure for production overhead:	4 400
Production overhead variance	(400) (A)

Selling and administrative overhead variance

Budget figure for selling and administrative overhead:	2 300
Actual figure for selling and administrative overhead:	2 450
Selling and administrative overhead variance	(150) (A)

iii) Bridge and Blige: standard cost operating statement for February 20X4

			Total
			£
Original budgeted net profit			6 100
Sales profit volume variance			1 550
Flexed budget net profit			7 650
Other variances	Favourable £	(Adverse) £	
Sales price variance	900		
Direct materials price variance	855		
Direct materials quantity variance	540		
Direct labour rate variance	540		
Direct labour efficiency variance		(1 350)	
Production overhead variance		(400)	
Selling and administrative overhead variance		(150)	
Total	2 835	(1 900)	935
Actual net profit			8 585

Answer to self-test question 17.2

Singh and Waterhouse

a)   Flexed budget for 2000 units

	£
Sales: 2000 × £45	90 000
Costs:	
Direct materials: 2000 × (16 metres × £1)	(32 000)
Direct labour: 2000 × (2 hours × £5.00)	(20 000)
Variable production overheads: 2000 units × (2 machine hours per unit × £1)	(4 000)
Fixed production overheads: 2000 units × (2 machine hours per unit × £6)	(24 000)
Profit before other overheads	10 000

ii)   Variance calculations

First of all, we will set the original budget, flexed budget and actual side by side:

	Original budget £	Flexed budget £	Actual £
Sales	81 000	90 000	90 000
Direct materials	(28 800)	(32 000)	(32 000)
Direct labour	(18 000)	(20 000)	(20 000)
Variable production overhead	(3 600)	(4 000)	(3 800)
Fixed production overhead	(21 600)	(24 000)	(23 400)
	9 000	10 000	10 800

The overall variance is:

Original budget net profit	9 000
Actual net profit	10 800
	1 800 (F)

Sales profit volume variance

This variance is the difference between the original budget profit and the flexed budget profit: £9000 − 10 000 = £1000 (F). The variance is favourable because the flexed budget profit is higher than the original budget profit.
There are no variances for sales price, direct material, direct labour and selling and administrative overheads. Once the budget is flexed, it becomes clear that sales prices, direct material and direct labour costs are exactly as would have been predicted if 2000 units had been budgeted for.

Variable production overhead variance

The overall variance can be calculated in the same way as, say, the total direct materials variance: by comparing the totals in the flexed budget statement with the actual statement:

Flexed budget for variable overhead	£4 000
Actual variable overhead	3 800
	£200 (F)

Fixed production overhead variance

The overall variance is calculated in the same way as by comparing the totals in the flexed budget statement with the actual statement:

Flexed budget for fixed overhead	£24 000
Actual fixed overhead	23 400
	£600 (F)

iii) Singh and Waterhouse: standard cost operating statement for April 20X8

	Favourable £	(Adverse) £	Total £
Original budgeted net profit			9 000
Sales profit volume variance			1 000
Flexed budget net profit			10 000
Other variances	Favourable £	(Adverse) £	
Sales price variance	–	–	
Direct materials price variance	–	–	
Direct materials quantity variance	–	–	
Direct labour rate variance	–	–	
Direct labour efficiency variance	–	–	
Variable overhead variance	200	–	
Fixed overhead variance	600		
Selling and administrative overhead variance	–	–	
Total	800		800
Actual net profit			10 800

CHAPTER 18

Answer to self-test question 18.1

- Average price per room sold as a percentage of rack rate (NB rack rate is the full published price of a hotel room, before deduction of any discounts).
- Occupancy rate (number of rooms actually occupied as a percentage of the total rooms available).
- Average revenue per customer from provision of additional services.

Answer to self-test question 18.2

Statements 1, 3 and 4 are TRUE.
Statement 2 is FALSE.

Answer to self-test question 18.3

The divisional management of Beta appears to have considerable autonomy over its operations, including control over investment strategy. This indicates that Beta is an investment centre.

Answer to self-test question 18.4

In any business, appropriate non-financial measures of success are those that relate to the overall business strategy. There is a contradiction hidden in HB's business objective: it wants to lead the market, which implies a greater market share than its competitors. On the other hand, it also aims to provide exclusive products – that is, luxury products that people can own, safe in the knowledge that they belong to an elite. This contradiction epitomizes the luxury goods business. Of the five performance indicators listed, all except the fifth are likely to be appropriate. Market share (1) and sales volume (3) relate directly to the strategic objective of leading the market. Defective product items (2) relates to the objective of supplying high quality items. Customer perceptions of exclusivity (4) again links directly to the business strategy. However, competitive pricing (5) is not really an issue. In the luxury goods business, the perception of exclusivity is likely to be assisted by high prices.

CHAPTER 19

Answer to self-test question 19.1

The fact that the business has hardly any intangible assets means that it is unlikely to be engaged in pharmaceuticals production and sale. High levels of tangible non-current assets mean that it is unlikely to be an architect's practice.

The low level of trade receivables suggests a business that sells principally for cash, and therefore (b) the electrical goods retailer is the most likely identity for this company.

Answer to self-test question 19.2

Froggie Feltham Ltd.
Applying the EOQ model, the economic order quantity (Q) is as follows:

$$Q = \sqrt{\frac{2 \times 16\,000 \times £12}{£1.50}}$$

$$Q = 506 \text{ units}$$

Answer to self-test question 19.3

Beamish Mellon Limited

Key points arising from the summary age analysis at 31 May 20X7

The company's credit control appears to be improving gradually. Although 6% of receivables are over 60 days old, this is an improvement from the previous year's figure of 8%. Also, 57.8% of receivables are within the 30 day limit, a slight improvement from the previous month, and significantly better than a year previously. However, there is still room for improvement. The 6% of outstanding receivables over 60 days old should be investigated to see if they are the subject of dispute and, if so, whether the disputes can be resolved. Further profiling of amounts over 30 days old would probably be helpful to see if the balances relate to a few or to many customers, and if there are any consistent patterns in late payment.

CHAPTER 20

Answer to self-test question 20.1

i) The principal advantage of grant finance is that it does not normally require repayment. Also, unlike borrowings, there is no interest charge. However, there are usually quite stringent conditions attached to grant finance. If conditions are breached, the grant may even become repayable. Once the grant is given, a period of careful monitoring often follows during which the business is under scrutiny.

ii) The principal advantage of obtaining finance from family or friends is its availability. If other potential sources of finance have proven to be unfruitful, this type of finance may be the only feasible way to start the business. It may be interest-free and with no fixed repayment date. However, there may be significant drawbacks, too. If the business fails, the unhappy entrepreneur may not be able to repay amounts borrowed, and relationships are likely to suffer as a result.

Answer to self-test question 20.2

Venture capital financing is typically provided for growing businesses, usually for the medium to long term (periods of, say, five to ten years). The venture capital firm, funded by institutional investors and wealthy individuals, provides finance and takes an equity stake in the business. Usually, there is some element of active involvement in management of the business. At the end of the agreed period of financing, the venture capital firm will sell its stake in the business. If the arrangement has been successful, the sale will be at a substantial profit.

Answer to self-test question 20.3

1 All takeover bids are hostile bids – FALSE.
2 A rights issue is an offer to sell shares to existing shareholders in proportion to their existing holdings – TRUE.
3 An offer for sale of shares is limited to a few major financial institutions – FALSE.
4 The London Stock Exchange trades in corporate bonds, as well as shares – TRUE.

Answers to exercises

CHAPTER 1

1.1 The only correct statement is c) The sole trader is entirely responsible for the management of the business.

1.2 The only correct statement is d) Partners are personally liable for the debts of the business.

1.3 The only correct statement is a) A limited company is a separate person in law.

1.4 The most appropriate form of finance for purchasing a new office building, out of those listed, is a) ten-year mortgage loan.

1.5 The most appropriate form of finance for the new office photocopier, out of those listed, is c) a lease.

1.6 **Advice to Arnold Tapwood:**

It is not difficult to set up in partnership. By contrast with the establishment of a limited company, there is no requirement to submit information to the authorities. However, the partners would be well advised to consider drawing up a partnership agreement, for which they would require legal advice. Although the provisions of the Partnership Act 1890 apply where there is no partnership agreement, in most circumstances it is preferable to have a formal agreement. This would cover areas such as profit sharing and arrangements in the event of a dispute between the partners.

1.7 **Advice to Geoffrey:**

Geoffrey will probably find it difficult to finance this business start-up because of its risky nature. He appears to be quite sure that lots of people will want to pay a subscription to his website, but he appears to have nothing but optimism to support this view. It is highly unlikely that a bank would be at all interested in making a loan in the circumstances.

Geoffrey has no existing resources to draw upon and his family has refused to put money into the business. It is remotely possible that grant finance might be available from a specialist organization, and Geoffrey should explore every possibility, however remote, for grant aid.

Another possibility is to join forces in partnership with another dangerous sports enthusiast who does have some resources to draw upon.

This appears to be a business proposition which will be very difficult to finance. If Geoffrey cannot find a business partner who is prepared to put some money into the venture, he may have to shelve the idea for the time being. If he gets a job, pays off his debts and saves some cash he might be able to finance the start-up himself at some point in the future.

1.8 The only correct statement is d) A sole trader must submit a tax return annually.

1.9 The only correct statement is b) Partnerships must prepare annual financial statements as the basis for the calculation of tax.

1.10 The only correct statement is b) A limited company must send annual accounts to all of its shareholders.

1.11 Podgorny & Weaver Limited

List of amounts owed by retail businesses: the directors would be able to see if any of the retailers owed very large amounts. If the list also contained details of the length of time the amounts had been outstanding, the directors would also be able to see if the amounts owing were significantly overdue for payment.

Summary of the value of goods held in inventory: it is important for a fashion goods business not to carry excessive inventories of goods which may be about to go out of fashion. The business will lose money if the inventory cannot be sold. The directors need this statement to assess the risk of having excess inventories.

Summary of the value of orders received in the last month: the directors need to assess whether the orders received meet their expectations. If the value of orders received is less than expected, the directors need to take action to address the problem.

Statement of profit or loss for the last month: the directors will be able to assess the performance of the business compared to their expectations, and perhaps, compared to the same month in the previous financial year.

1.12   Burnip Chemicals plc
        The activist group would probably be looking for the following type of information:

i)   details about the amounts of emissions
ii) details of the amounts which the company has paid in fines
iii) details of plans for improvements to the factory which will minimize the emission of toxic waste.

A company's financial statements principally contain information about the financial performance and condition of the business. Details about the amounts of emissions during the year are not financial items, and it is quite possible that the company would make no reference to the matter.

The amount of fines paid might be evident from the financial statements. However, the expenses listed in the statement of profit or loss are summarized information (it would not be feasible to list each individual payment), and the amount paid in fines might well not be evident.

Details of planned improvements, similarly, may not be evident from the financial statements.

Although annual financial statements can be of interest to activist groups, they do not necessarily provide a full picture.

Tutorial note: some companies voluntarily publish information about their environmental policies and performance in addition to their financial statements, but they are not obliged by law to do this.

CHAPTER 2

2.1

Cash kept in a tin in the office	ASSET
Oven	ASSET
Bank loan, repayable over five years	LIABILITY
Plastic packaging for biscuits	ASSET
Flour and sugar	ASSET
Amounts payable to supplier of dried fruit	LIABILITY

2.2

Amir

Value Added Tax (VAT) payable to HMRC	CURRENT LIABILITY
Office computer	NON-CURRENT ASSET
Amount due from Lomax plc for consultancy work carried out by Amir	CURRENT ASSET
Bank overdraft*	CURRENT LIABILITY
Bank loan to be repaid in three years' time	NON-CURRENT LIABILITY
Amount payable to stationery supplier	CURRENT LIABILITY

*Tutorial note: some businesses have an almost permanent bank overdraft, which they effectively use as long-term finance. However, a bank overdraft is technically 'repayable on demand' – that means that the bank is entitled to demand repayment at any time. Because of this, bank overdrafts are always classified as current liabilities in the business statement of financial position.

The accounting equation is:

$$\text{ASSETS} = \text{CAPITAL} + \text{LIABILITIES}$$

Applying the equation to the information given in questions 2.3 to 2.10

2.3

	£
ASSETS	83 000
LIABILITIES	36 500
CAPITAL (missing figure)	46 500
	83 000

Brian's capital is £46 500.

2.4 In this case we turn the accounting equation around to find liabilities:

$$\text{ASSETS} - \text{CAPITAL} = \text{LIABILITIES}$$

	£
ASSETS	188 365
Less CAPITAL	(43 650)
= LIABILITIES	144 715

The liabilities in Basil's business total £144 715.

2.5 In this question assets are split into non-current and current assets. However, the basic principle remains the same: total ASSETS = CAPITAL + LIABILITIES.

Non-current assets	12 000
Plus Current assets	8 500
= ASSETS	20 500
LIABILITIES	17 300
CAPITAL (missing figure)	3 200
	20 500

Brenda's capital is £3200.

2.6 In this question four pieces of information are given. However, the basic accounting equation still holds good.

Total assets = £27 000 (non-current assets) + £16 000 (current assets) = £43 000
Total liabilities = £12 000 (current liabilities) + £10 000 (non-current liabilities) = £22 000.
Brigitte's capital in the business is ASSETS − LIABILITIES, ie. £43 000 − £22 000 = £21 000.

2.7 Bryony's capital is d) £34 340.
Explanation:

Total assets = £35 840 (non-current assets) + £16 500 (current assets) = £52 340
Total liabilities = £12 000 (current liabilities) + £6000 (non-current liabilities) = £18 000
Bryony's capital in the business is ASSETS − LIABILITIES, ie. £52 340 − £18 000 = £34 340

2.8 Reminder: the accounting equation (ASSETS = CAPITAL + LIABILITIES) can be expressed as

ASSETS − LIABILITIES = CAPITAL
or
ASSETS − CAPITAL = LIABILITIES

ASSETS = £39 497 (Non-current assets) + £26 004 (Current assets) = £65 501 CAPITAL = £33 058

Total LIABILITIES therefore = £65 501 − £33 058 = £32 443
Total LIABILITIES = Current liabilities + Non-current liabilities
therefore:
£32 443 = £16 777 + Non-current liabilities.
The missing figure for non-current liabilities is therefore £15 666.

2.9 The missing figure for long-term liabilities is b) £9276.
Explanation:

Total ASSETS = £36 609 (Non-current assets) + £38 444 (Current assets) = £75 053
CAPITAL = £39 477
Therefore:
Total LIABILITIES = £35 576 (£75 053 − £39 477)
Current liabilities are £26 300, therefore non-current liabilities = £9276 (£35 576 − £26 300).

2.10   i) Total assets = £18 337 (Non-current assets) + £12 018 (Inventory) + £365
           (Trade receivables) + £63 (Cash) = £30 783
        ii) Total current assets = £12 018 (Inventory) + £365 (Trade receivables) + £63 (Cash) = £12 446
        iii) Total liabilities = £3686 (Bank overdraft) + £2999 (Creditors) = £6685
        iv) Callum's capital can be found by using the accounting equation:

$$£30\ 783\ (\text{Total assets}) - £6\ 685\ (\text{Total liabilities}) = £24\ 098.$$

2.11 **Ciera's business: Statement of financial position at 31 December 20X1**

	£	£
ASSETS		
Non-current assets: Premises		39 000
Current assets		
Inventory	18 600	
Trade receivables	6 500	
Bank	13 000	
		38 100
		77 100
CAPITAL AND LIABILITIES		
Capital		29 600
Non-current liabilities		
Long-term loan		20 000
Current liabilities		
Trade payables	23 700	
Amounts owed to HMRC	3 800	
		27 500
		77 100

2.12 Explanation:
     In transaction 1, Dan is using up £1500 of the amount in the business bank account, but at the same time is
     increasing non-current assets.

     Increase non-current assets by £1500
     Decrease bank account by £1500

     In transaction 2, Dan is using up £3000 of the amount in the business bank account, but at the same time is
     decreasing trade payables.

     Decrease trade payables by £3000
     Decrease bank account by £3000

     Dan's business: Statement of financial position at 3 May 20X3

	£	£
ASSETS		
Non-current assets (30 000 + 1500)		31 500
Current assets		
Inventory	15 000	
Trade payables	5 000	
Bank account (18 000 − 1500 − 3000)	13 500	33 500
		65 000

	£	£
CAPITAL AND LIABILITIES		
Capital		52 000
Current liabilities		
Trade payables (16 000 − 3000)		13 000
Net assets		65 000

Note that the capital in the business has not changed at all between 1 and 3 May.

2.13 1 Ernest's business: Statement of financial position at 31 December

	£	£
ASSETS		
Non-current assets		
Gallery premises		68 000
Office equipment		2 260
		70 260
Current assets: cash at bank		18 600
		88 860
CAPITAL AND LIABILITIES		
Capital		70 700
Current liabilities		
Payable to artists	16 560	
Payable to printers	1 600	
		18 160
		88 860

2 Once Ernest has paid the artists and the printers (and, presumably, he will have to in the very near future) he will be left with only £440 in the bank. This will not leave him with enough money to pay the costs which are estimated at £4000 of the exhibition in January. He may be able to obtain the goods and services needed to put on the exhibition on credit (that is, he will not pay for them straight away), but he would be taking the risk that the exhibition is a failure. If it produces no money, or less than the £4000 or so needed to cover essential costs, then Ernest will be in a very difficult position.

He may be able to borrow some money to put the business on a better footing. The only substantial asset the business owns is the art gallery premises. It may be possible to secure a mortgage loan on the property so as to obtain some much needed cash.

2.14 The business entity concept expresses the idea that the business exists separately from the person or people who have contributed capital to it. They are treated as separate entities, and the capital contribution made by the owner is treated as an obligation that the business owes.

2.15 Financial information should have the quality of timeliness. That means it should be produced and communicated to users within a reasonable timeframe to allow them to make appropriate decisions. If information is not produced on a timely basis it may be useless for decision-making purposes.

CHAPTER 3

3.1 i) The answer is b) Jackie has purchased 47 sets during June.

Explanation:

	No. of sets
Opening inventory	30
Add: purchases (missing figure)	X
Less: closing inventory	(42)
=Sets sold in June	35

The missing figure is 47.

ii) The answer is c) Jackie's cost of sales is £2625. Explanation:

	No. of sets	£
Cost of sales:		
Opening inventory at 1 June 20X9	30	2 250
Add: purchases during month	47	3 525
	77	5 775
Less: closing inventory at 30 June 20X9	(42)	(3 150)
	35	2 625

An even easier calculation is to take the number of sets sold (35) and multiply by the cost price (£75). This gives the answer of £2625.

iii) Jackie's gross profit for the month of June is d) £1995. Explanation:

	£
Revenue (£132 × 35 sets)	£4 620
Less: cost of sales (see answer 3.1 ii)	2 625
Gross profit	1 995

Another way of calculating this is to work out the gross profit on one set (£132 − £75 = £57) and multiply it by the number of sets sold (£57 × 35 = £1995).

3.2 The revenue raised through selling the special purchase trainers is as follows:

	£
750 pairs @ £15.50 per pair	11 625
200 pairs @ £12.50 per pair	2 500
50 pairs @ £5 per pair	250
Total revenue	14 375

The cost of sales was the purchase price of £8500. There is no opening or closing inventory. Gross profit is therefore: £14 375 − £8500 = £5875.

If Jay had managed to sell 1000 pairs at £15.50 the revenue would have been £15 500. £15 500 less the cost of sales figure of £8500 = £7000.

3.3 We can construct Jake's trading account and use it to find the value of the missing figure of opening inventory.

First we put in the total value for revenue, and for gross profit. The difference between these two is cost of sales, ie. £340 000 − £140 000 = £200 000.

Then we can work in reverse order through the cost of sales calculation. Because closing inventory is £17 400, the total value of opening inventory + purchases must be £217 400 (ie. we deduct closing inventory of £17 400 to get cost of sales of £200 000).

If the total value of opening inventory + purchases is £217 400 and we know that purchases for the year = £197 300, then opening inventory is the difference between these two figures:

$$£217\ 400 − £197\ 300 = £20\ 100.$$

The missing figure of opening inventory is £20 100.

Jake: Trading account for the year

	£	£
Revenue: 8000 units @ £42.50		340 000
Cost of sales:		
Opening inventory: missing figure	20 100	
Add: purchases	197 300	
	217 400	

	£	£
Less: closing inventory	(17 400)	
		(200 000)
Gross profit: 8000 units @ £17.50		140 000

3.4 Jethro: Trading accounts for October, November and December 20X4

	October	November	December
	£	£	£
Revenue	39 370	48 998	56 306
Cost of sales:			
Opening inventory	30 863	43 258	53 190
Add: purchases	37 085	40 830	6 250
Less: Closing inventory	(43 258)	(53 190)	(23 980)
	24 690	30 898	35 460
Gross profit	14 680	18 100	20 846

3.5 Leon's trading results are as follows for the two years under review:

	20X7	20X6
	£	£
Revenue	295 993	287 300
Cost of sales	(242 085)	(235 920)
Gross profit	53 908	51 380

i) Gross profit margin in 20X7 $= \dfrac{£53\,908}{£295\,993} \times 100 = 18.2\%$

Gross profit margin in 20X6 $= \dfrac{£51\,380}{£287\,300} \times 100 = 17.9\%$

ii) The amount of the increase in revenue is £295 993 − £287 300 = £8693.

iii) The percentage increase in revenue is: $\dfrac{£8693}{£287\,300} \times 100 = 3\%$.

iv) The amount of the increase in gross profit is £53 908 − £51 380 = £2 528.

v) The percentage increase in gross profit is: $\dfrac{£2528}{£51\,380} \times 100 = 4.9\%$.

3.6 The table shows the gross and net profit margins for Louis's business for three years:

	20X2	20X1	20X0
	£	£	£
Gross profit margin	$\dfrac{£77\,402}{£291\,318} \times 100 = 26.6\%$	$\dfrac{£75\,980}{£282\,400} \times 100 = 26.9\%$	$\dfrac{£73\,269}{£269\,340} \times 100 = 27.2\%$
Net profit margin	$\dfrac{£25\,008}{£291\,318} \times 100 = 8.6\%$	$\dfrac{£24\,260}{£282\,400} \times 100 = 8.6\%$	$\dfrac{£23\,999}{£269\,340} \times 100 = 8.9\%$

Louis's revenue figures have increased in each of the three years, as have gross profit and net profit. However, the gross and net profit margins have fallen. Gross profit margin has declined from 27.2% in 20X0 to 26.6% in 20X2. Net profit margin is stable in the latest two years, but has declined from 8.9% in 20X0.

3.7   Madigan & Co: Statement of profit or loss for the year ended 31 March 20X8

	£	£
Fees from clients		95 311
Expenses		
Salaries: assistant	19 300	
Secretary	11 150	
Office rental	10 310	
Office service charge	3 790	
Insurance	794	
Pil	1 250	
Subscriptions etc.	952	
Business travel	1 863	
Entertainment	342	
Telephone and broadband	1 103	
Other administration expenses	1 575	
Stationery	761	
Sundry expenses	715	
Charitable donations	120	(54 025)
Net profit		41 286

3.8   Working: categorizing the items

	£	Category
Delivery vehicle	5 020	Statement of financial position: non-current assets
Revenue for the year	351 777	Trading account
Staff costs: storeman's wages	12 090	Statement of profit or loss
Electricity	2 821	Statement of profit or loss
Cash at bank	3 444	Statement of financial position: current assets
Capital at 1 April 20X2	18 011	Statement of financial position: capital
Administrative costs	3 810	Statement of profit or loss
Opening inventory at 1 April 20X2	20 762	Trading account
Non-current assets in warehouse and office	3 900	Statement of financial position: non-current assets
Drawings	25 219	Statement of financial position: capital
Sundry expenses	1 406	Statement of profit or loss
Warehouse and office rental	10 509	Statement of profit or loss
Insurance	3 909	Statement of profit or loss
Trade receivables	36 623	Statement of financial position: current assets
Water rates	1 226	Statement of profit or loss
Security services charge	2 937	Statement of profit or loss
Purchases	255 255	Trading account
Bank charges	398	Statement of profit or loss
Trade payables	31 950	Statement of financial position: current liabilities
Delivery expenses	8 630	Statement of profit or loss
Part-time admin assistant's wages	3 779	Statement of profit or loss
Closing inventory	22 446	Trading account AND statement of financial position: current assets

Norbert: Statement of profit or loss for the year ended 31 March 20X3

	£	£
Revenue		351 777
Less: cost of sales		
Opening inventory	20 762	
Add: purchases	255 255	
	276 017	
Less: closing inventory	(22 446)	
		(253 571)
Gross profit		98 206
Expenses		
Staff costs: storeman's wages	12 090	
Warehouse and office rental	10 509	
Insurance	3 909	
Electricity	2 821	
Water rates	1 226	
Security services	2 937	
Delivery expenses	8 630	
Administrative costs	3 810	
Part time admin assistant's wages	3 779	
Sundry expenses	1 406	
Bank charges	398	
		(51 515)
Net profit		46 691

Norbert: Statement of financial position at 31 March 20X3

	£	£
ASSETS		
Non-current assets		
Delivery vehicle	5 020	
Non-current assets: warehouse and office	3 900	
		8 920
Current assets		
Inventory	22 446	
Trade receivables	36 623	
Cash	3 444	
		62 513
		71 433
CAPITAL AND LIABILITIES		
Capital		
Opening capital balance 1 April 20X2	18 011	
Add: net profit for the year	46 691	
	64 702	
Less: drawings	(25 219)	
Closing capital balance 31 March 20X3		39 483
Current liabilities		
Trade payables		31 950
		71 433

3.9 There will be relatively few users of Mary's accounting information. She herself, as the proprietor of the business, is likely to be the principal user. However, if she needs to borrow money at some point in the future, potential lenders are likely to be interested in seeing her financial statements in order to assess the ability of the business to make repayments of loans and to meet regular interest payments.

Tax collecting agencies such as HMRC will be interested in Mary's accounts as a basis for assessing the amount of income tax due on her profits. The only other group of users likely to have an interest in Mary's accounts is the supplier group. If other businesses supply goods to Mary on credit they are likely to be interested in the likelihood of being paid promptly.

3.10 Calculations and comparisons, of course, depend upon the businesses selected. Where there are differences between the businesses, these could be attributable to some of the following reasons:

1   Loss of market share which would reduce revenue but would not necessarily reduce all of the costs, leading to a drop in profit margins.
2   Exceptional costs, such as business reorganization. The narrative sections of the Annual Report may well describe and quantify such costs.
3   Especially good, or bad, performance in one part of the business. The notes to the financial statements in an Annual Report contain 'segment reporting' where a more detailed breakdown of figures such as revenue is given for different segments of the business. It should be possible to identify from this information those segments of the business that are performing particularly well or badly.
4   Information not fully comparable.

See if you can identify other reasons for differences between the figures from different businesses.

3.11 There is no standard answer to this question, because it all depends upon the company selected.

CHAPTER 4

4.1   **Oscar: Extract from statement of profit or loss for year ended 31 December 20X1**

	£	£	£
Revenue			72 411
Less: returns			(361)
Cost of sales			72 050
Opening inventory		4 182	
Add: purchases	53 005		
Less: returns	(1 860)		
		51 145	
		55 327	
Less: closing inventory		(5 099)	
			(50 228)
Gross profit			21 822

The correct answer is a) £21 822.

4.2   **Omar: Extract from statement of profit or loss for year ended 30 April 20X4**

	£	£	£
Revenue			347 348
Less: returns			(2 971)
Cost of sales			344 377
Opening inventory		43 730	
Add: purchases	240 153		
Add: import duties	6 043		
Less: returns	(1 800)		
		244 396	

	£	£	£
		288 126	
Less: closing inventory		(41 180)	
			(246 946)
Gross profit			97 431

The correct answer is a) £97 431.

4.3   Poppy: Statement of profit or loss for the year ended 28 February 20X3

	£	£	£
Revenue			220 713
Less: returns			(3 997)
			216 716
Cost of sales			
Opening inventory		7 140	
Add: purchases	123 057		
Import duty	9 911		
		132 968	
		140 108	
Less: closing inventory		(7 393)	
			(132 715)
			84 001
Expenses			
Rental		17 211	
Staffing costs		9 777	
Insurance		8 204	
Delivery van expenses		2 107	
Discounts allowed		716	
Telephone charges		1 227	
Electricity		1 604	
Marketing		1 888	
Administrative expenses		922	
			(43 656)
			40 345

4.4   Telephone expense for inclusion in Pookie's accounts for the year ended 31 August 20X2:

	£
$1/3 \times £9760$ relating to September 20X1	3 253
October–December 20X1	12 666
January–March 20X2	8 444
April–June 20X2	9 530
July and August 20X2: $(9760 + 12\,666 + 8444 + 9530) \times 2/12$	6 733
	40 626

The correct answer is b) £40 626.

4.5   The prepayment at 28 February 20X1 is $7/12 \times 644 = £376$.
The prepayment at 28 February 20X2 is $7/12 \times 796 = £464$.
The correct answer is b) 20X1: £376 20X2: £464.

4.6 **Simon: Statement of profit or loss for the year ended 31 July 20X6**

	£	£	£
Revenue			317 342
Cost of sales			
Opening inventory		38 888	
Purchases		230 133	
		269 021	
Less: closing inventory		(39 501)	
			(229 520)
Gross profit			87 822
Discounts received			377
Income from curtain-making service		6 519	
Costs of curtain-making service		(2 797)	
			3 722
			91 921
Shop rental		18 750	
Assistants' wages	22 379		
Add: accrued commission	3 173		
		25 552	
Business rates		3 510	
Insurance	4 478		
Less: prepaid	(501)		
		3 977	
Electricity	2 064		
Add: accrual	377		
		2 441	
Telephone		1 035	
Travelling expenses		603	
Delivery expenses		2 490	
Trade subscriptions		165	
Charitable donations		500	
Accountant's fees		800	
Legal fees		350	
			(60 173)
Net profit			31 748
Total accruals:			
Assistants' commission		3 173	
Electricity		377	
Accountant's fees		800	
Legal fees		350	
		4 700	
Prepayment: insurance		501	

4.7 Ted: Extract from statement of profit or loss for the year ended 31 December 20X6

	Closing inventory at cost	Closing inventory at cost/ net realizable value
	£	£
Revenue	599 790	599 790
Cost of sales		
Opening inventory	49 071	49 071
Add: purchases	379 322	379 322
Less: closing inventory	(62 222)	–
Less: closing inventory*	–	(50 472)
	366 171	377 921
Gross profit	233 619	221 869
Gross profit margin	38.9%	37.0%

*Closing inventory at cost	62 222
Less: pink items at cost	(17 750)
Add: pink items at net realizable value	6 000
Closing inventory adjusted to net realizable value for pink items	50 472

4.8 Ulrich will require a general allowance of 1% of trade receivables outstanding for over three months:
1% × £67 400 = £674.

The amount due from Gayle will be treated as irrecoverable and will no longer appear in trade receivables. Trade receivables will be stated at £397 700 − 17 000 = 380 700.

Extract from Ulrich's statement of financial position at 31 July 20X5:

Trade receivables	380 700
Less: allowance	(674)
	380 026

Ulrich's profit for the year is reduced by:

a) the amount of the bad trade receivable: £17 000
b) the allowance made for the first time this year: £674

In total, Ulrich's profit is reduced by £17 674.

4.9 Ursula: Statement of profit or loss for the year ended 31 December 20X8

	£	£	£
Revenue			326 620
Cost of sales			
Opening inventory		31 090	
Add: purchases		239 285	
		270 375	
Less: closing inventory		(30 048)	
			(240 327)
Gross profit			86 293
Discounts received			361
			86 654
Expenses			
Warehouse rental		11 070	

	£	£	£
Business and water rates		3 899	
Electricity	4 850		
Add: accrual	338		
		5 188	
Insurance	3 414		
Less: prepayment	(622)		
		2 792	
Assistant's wages		10 008	
Telephone		2 663	
Delivery costs		4 490	
Administration charges		3 242	
Bad trade receivable written off		672	
Allowance for doubtful trade receivables		1 098	
Accountant's fee accrual		700	
Discounts allowed		1 046	
			(46 868)
Net profit			39 786

Ursula: Statement of financial position at 31 December 20X8

	£	£
ASSETS		
Non-current assets		23 360
Current assets		
Inventory	30 048	
Trade receivables*	49 682	
Less: allowance	(1 098)	48 584
Prepayment	622	
Cash at bank	361	
		79 615
		102 975
CAPITAL AND LIABILITIES		
Capital		
Opening capital balance 1 January 20X8	70 219	
Add: net profit for the year	39 786	
	110 005	
Less: drawings	(33 988)	
Closing capital balance 31 December 20X8		76 017
Current liabilities		
Trade payables	25 920	
Accruals	1 038	
		26 958
		102 975

*The bad trade receivable of £672 disappears completely from the records. The total of trade receivables in the accounts list was £50 354 but this total is reduced for presentation in the statement of financial position to £49 682 (ie. £50 354 − 672).

4.10 a) Recognition occurs when items are brought into the financial statements. For example, when a business proprietor concludes that he is unlikely ever to recover the amount of a trade receivable, a bad trade receivable expense will be recognized in the statement of profit or loss.

b) The underlying assumption of accruals in accounting requires that the effects of transactions should be recognized in the accounting period in which they occur. This may not necessarily be the accounting period in which the transactions are invoiced or paid. For example, where a business receives a shipment of goods on the final day of its accounting year, the increase in purchases (and inventory) should be recognized within that accounting year. This is despite the fact that an invoice for the inventory will not be received until after the year-end.

c) Net realizable value refers to the amount for which an asset can be sold, net of any incidental expenses of sale. For example, an item of inventory may be able to be sold for a gross sum of £13 000. However, shipping and insurance costs would have to be borne by the seller if the inventory were sold. The net realizable value of the inventory is therefore £12 500. If this amount is lower than the cost of the inventory, accounting convention requires that the inventory is recognized at £12 500.

d) Going concern is the fundamental assumption underlying the preparation of financial statements. It assumes that the business will continue to operate into the future, and assets and other elements of the financial statements should be valued on the basis of this assumption. If the business cannot be assumed to continue as a going concern, the assets and other elements of the business must be valued accordingly. For example, the value of inventory in a business at its year-end is £100 000 on a going concern basis. However, if the going concern assumption does not apply, inventory must be valued at the amount it is likely to realize (net realizable value) if the goods have to be sold quickly when the business ceases to exist.

CHAPTER 5

5.1 The correct answer is d) £2615. Explanation:

Cost of the new van	£14 460
Less: expected sale proceeds in four years' time	(4 000)
Depreciable amount	10 460

Spread evenly over four years this gives an annual depreciation charge of £10 460/4 = £2615.

5.2 The correct answer is a) £70. Explanation:

Cost of new exercise bike	£450
Less: expected sale proceeds in three years' time	(30)
Depreciable amount	420

Spread evenly over three years this gives an annual depreciation charge of £420/3 = £140. However, in the year ended 31 August 20X5, Victoria owned the bike for only six months out of the twelve.

The depreciation charge for the bike for this year is £140/2 = £70

5.3 The correct answer is c) £1956.
Explanation:

Depreciation on machine 1

$$\frac{10\ 300}{5\ \text{years}} = £2060 \text{ each year}$$

This is a full year's depreciation, but Vinny would calculate depreciation only for the part of the year he had owned the asset. Therefore the charge for the year ended 31 December 20X8 would be: £2060 × 9/12 = £1545.

Depreciation on machine 2

Cost of new machine	£8 580
Less: expected sale proceeds in four years' time	(2 000)
Depreciable amount	£6 580

Spread evenly over four years, this gives an annual charge of £ 6580/4 = £1645. However, the charge for the year ended 31 December 20X8 would be for the three months of ownership only: £1645 × 3/12 = £411 (to the nearest pound).

The total depreciation charge for these two assets is £1545 + 411 = £1956.

5.4 Violet has purchased an intangible asset in the form of mineral extraction rights. She has a licence to extract gold (if she can find it) from the land for 3.5 years only. At the end of that period she has no further rights over the land unless she renegotiates them. The initial payment of £273 000 will be spread over the 3.5-year period of ownership of the rights. As noted in the chapter, amortization is almost invariably calculated on the straight-line basis.

In the first year of ownership Violet will charge amortization in her statement of profit or loss of:

$$\frac{£273\ 000}{3.5\ \text{years}} = £78\ 000$$

The statement of financial position at 31 December 20X5 will show the following in respect of mineral rights:

	£
Intangible non-current assets	
Mineral rights at cost	273 000
Less: accumulated amortization	(78 000)
Carrying amount	195 000

5.5 i) The total charge for depreciation for the year ended 31 August 20X4 is as follows:

	£
Buildings: £306 000 × 2%	6 120
Motor vehicles: £32 300 × 25%	8 075
Fixtures and fittings: £12 720 × 10%	1 272
	15 467

ii) The presentation of non-current assets in Vincenzo's statement of financial position at 31 August 20X4 is as follows:

	£	£
Non-current assets		
Buildings at cost	306 000	
Less: accumulated depreciation (18 360 + 6120)	(24 480)	
		281 520
Motor vehicles at cost	48 770	
Less: accumulated depreciation (16 470 + 8075)	(24 545)	
		24 225
Fixtures and fittings at cost	12 720	
Less: accumulated depreciation (6360 + 1272)	(7 632)	
		5 088
Total		310 833

5.6 The correct answer is b) £3780. Explanation:

Basic cost of new wedding car	£24 400
Additional cost of white spray	800
Total cost	25 200

First year's depreciation on reducing balance basis: £25 200 × 15% = £3780.

5.7 The correct answer is b) £9319. Explanation:

	£	£
Carrying amount of cars at 1 January 20X9	£22 830	
Depreciation for the year: £22 830 × 25%		5 707
New car added on 1 January 20X9	£14 447	
Depreciation for the year £14 447 × 25%		3 612
Total depreciation for the year		£9 319

There is another, quicker, way of doing the calculation:

	£
Carrying amount of cars at 1 January 20X9	£22 830
Add: new car purchased on 1 January 20X9	14 447
Total depreciable value at 31 December 20X9	37 277

Depreciation: £37 277 × 25% = £9 319.

Tutorial note: in William's statement of financial position at 31 December 20X9 the presentation will be as follows:

	£
Non-current assets	
Tangible non-current assets	
Cars at cost (38 370 + 14 447)	52 817
Less: accumulated depreciation (15 540 + 9319)	(24 859)
Carrying amount	27 958

5.8

	£
Sale proceeds	£2 380
The carrying amount of the van is £8300 − £6330	(1 970)
Profit on sale	410

Tutorial note: this is a profit on sale because Xenia receives more for the van than the value (carrying amount) at which it is recorded in her accounts.

5.9 First, we need to work out the carrying amount of the van at 1 June 20X4.

	£
Cost on 1 June 20X1	10 100
Year 1 depreciation: £10 100 × 30%	(3 030)
Carrying amount at 1 June 20X2	7 070
Year 2 depreciation: £7070 × 30%	(2 121)
Carrying amount at 1 June 20X3	4 949
Year 3 depreciation: £4949 × 30%	(1 485)
Carrying amount at 1 June 20X4	3 464

Comparing the carrying amount with the sale proceeds of £3000 results in a loss on disposal of £464.

5.10 By the time Ying disposes of them, Ying has owned the computers for exactly 2 years and 6 months (1 January 20X4 to 1 July 20X6). The annual charge for depreciation is: £3672/4 = £918.

2.5 years of charges = 2.5 × £918 = £2295

The carrying amount of the computers at the date of disposal is:

	£
Cost	£3 672
Less: accumulated depreciation	(2 295)
Carrying amount	1 377

Sale proceeds	£550
Less: carrying amount	(1 377)
Loss on sale	£827

In effect, Ying has underestimated the depreciation appropriate to these assets. Their value has dropped more quickly than she initially supposed.

5.11 i) Working for depreciation:

Machinery at cost	£28 760
Depreciation straight line over four years:	
28 760/4	£7 190

Zoe's Snacks: Statement of profit or loss for the year ended 31 December 20X2

	£	£
Revenue		132 614
Less: cost of sales		
Opening inventory	–	
Purchases	83 430	
Less: closing inventory	(1 209)	
		(82 221)
Gross profit		50 393
Expenses		
Staffing	15 030	
Premises rental	7 400	
Electricity	2 961	
Telephone	1 806	
Insurance	1 437	
Sundry expenses	981	
Accountant's fees	600	
Depreciation (see working above)	7 190	
		(37 405)
Net profit		12 988

Zoe's Snacks: Statement of financial position at 31 December 20X2

	£	£
ASSETS		
Non-current assets		
Machinery and fixtures at cost	28 760	
Less: accumulated depreciation	(7 190)	
		21 570
Current assets		
Inventory	1 209	
Cash at bank	3 406	
		4 615
		26 185
CAPITAL AND LIABILITIES		
Capital		
Capital introduced		20 000
Add: profit for the year		12 988

	£	£
Less: drawings		(8 453)
		24 535
Current liabilities		
Trade payables		1 650
		26 185

ii) If Zoe were to use a period of seven years over which to depreciate the machinery and fixtures, the depreciation charge would be:

$$\frac{\text{Cost £28 760}}{\text{7 years}} = £4109 \text{ (to nearest £).}$$

Effect on profit:

Net profit as stated in the statement of profit or loss above:	£12 988
Add back: depreciation over four years	7 190
Net profit before depreciation	20 178
Less: depreciation over seven years	(4 109)
Net profit adjusted for change in depreciation	16 069

Net profit is £12 988 if machinery and fixtures are depreciated over four years.

If the depreciation period is increased to seven years, net profit increases to £16 069 (an increase of nearly 24%).

iii) Net profit percentage is net profit as a percentage of sales revenue.
Net profit percentage with depreciation over four years:

$$\frac{£12 \; 988}{132 \; 614} \times 100 = 9.8\%$$

Net profit percentage with depreciation over seven years:

$$\frac{£16 \; 069}{132 \; 614} \times 100 = 12.1\%$$

Note: a change in the method of depreciation can make a large difference to net profit and to the net profit percentage.

5.12 Depreciation and the accounting equation
The accounting equation is as follows:

$$\text{ASSETS} - \text{LIABILITIES} = \text{CAPITAL}$$

Depreciation does not affect liabilities, but it does affect both assets and capital. Depreciation is a way of matching the using up of a non-current asset over its useful life with the revenue generated by the asset. The carrying amount of the asset gradually reduces, as the asset is used up. Each year the reduction in asset value is the same as the amount that is set against the business's revenue. Both profit and assets are therefore reduced by the same figure. A reduction in profit results in a reduction in capital.

5.13 The answer to this question depends, of course, upon the football club selected. You are likely to find that player registrations are treated as intangible assets in the statement of financial position, and you should be able to see how amortization of registrations has been accounted for. In addition, you are likely to find some discussion of the club's player transfers during the season in the chairman's report and possibly in other sections of the annual report. If you are a football fan, the annual report should give you some useful insights into how well your club is doing financially, and will help you to see, for example, how much the club has had to borrow in order to pay transfer fees. Unfortunately, if the club is privately owned, rather than being a listed company, its financial statements are probably not easily available.

CHAPTER 6

6.1 Impact of transactions on Fergus's business:

	Impact on cash etc.	Impact on profits
Introduction of additional capital of £10 000 in cash.	Cash and capital are both increased by £10 000.	No impact on profits.
Purchase on credit of goods for resale for £8000.	Inventory and trade payables are both increased by £8000. There is no immediate impact on cash, but there will be an outflow of cash when the goods are paid for.	No immediate impact on profits. When the goods are sold, they will form part of cost of sales.
Payment received from customer for £1800.	The asset of trade receivables is reduced by £1800 and there is a corresponding increase (inflow of cash) in cash of £1800.	No impact on profits. The sale to which the trade receivable relates would already have been recorded.
Purchase of a new machine for use in the business.	There is an outflow of cash of £12 000 and non-current assets are increased by £12 000.	No immediate impact on profits, but there will be an additional depreciation charge for the year of £1200 (ie. £12 000 over ten years).
Sales returns of £1000 in exchange for a cash refund.	There is an outflow of cash of £1000.	Sales returns are increased by £1000. Sales returns are deducted from revenue in the statement of profit or loss and thus, reduce profit.
Drawings of £1300.	Cash and capital are both reduced by £1300.	There is no impact on profit. Effectively, Fergus is taking £1300 of his own capital out of the business.

6.2 The correct answer is b) 2, 3 and 5. Explanation:

	£
Non-current asset at cost	20 700
Less: accumulated depreciation	(18 210)
Carrying amount	2 490

The asset is sold for £1300; that is less than it is recorded in the accounts. A loss is thus incurred on sale of £2490 − 1300 = £1190.

Profits are reduced by £1190 (statement no. 2), cash is increased by £1300 (statement no. 3) and non-current assets are reduced by £2490 (statement no. 5).

6.3 The correct answer is a) £23 040. Explanation:

The net cash outflow from operating activities in Ketchup & Co for the year ended 31 March 20X6 is calculated as follows:

	£	£
Operating loss		(38 650)
Add back: depreciation		12 750
		(25 900)
Add: Decrease in inventory (32 250 − 34 400)	2 150	
Less: Increase in trade receivables (26 770 − 25 360)	(1 410)	
Add: Increase in trade payables (25 500 − 23 380)	2 120	
		2 860
Net cash outflow from operating activities		(23 040)

6.4 The correct answer is c) (10 500). Explanation:

Gayle's net cash outflow from financing activities for the year ended 31 August 20X7 should exclude any cash flows relating to investing activities because these are presented under the investing heading in the statement of cash flows.

Financing cash flows include the following:

	£
Repayment of bank loan	(5 000)
Loan received from brother	1 000
Drawings	(6 500)
	(10 500)

6.5 The correct answer is c) £33 925. Explanation:

The net cash inflow from operating activities in Gaston's business for the year ended 31 December 20X2 is calculated as follows:

	£	£
Operating profit		36 027
Add back: depreciation		4 585
		40 612
Less: Increase in inventory (37 669 − 31 470)	(6 199)	
Less: Increase in trade receivables (21 777 − 19 303)	(2 474)	
Add: Increase in trade payables (18 250 − 16 264)	1 986	
		(6 687)
Net cash flow from operating activities		33 925

6.6 **Spicer & Co: Statement of cash flows for the year ended 31 March 20X3**

	£	£
Operating profit		76 496
Add back: depreciation		12 471
		88 967
Increase in inventory (40 747 − 36 600)	(4 147)	
Increase in trade receivables (50 661 − 48 730)	(1 931)	
Increase in trade payables (36 644 − 35 191)	1 453	
		(4 625)
Cash generated from operations		84 342
Interest paid		(230)
Net cash inflow from operating activities		84 112
Cash flows from investing activities		
Purchase of non-current assets (£175 630 − 128 547)	(47 083)	
Net cash outflow from investing activities		(47 083)
Cash flows from financing activities		
Capital returned to owner (drawings)	(45 800)	
Net cash inflow from financing activities		(45 800)
Net decrease in cash		(8 771)
Cash at beginning of period		7 423
Cash at end of period: overdraft		(1 348)

6.7 i) Ishmael: Statement of cash flows for the year ended 31 July 20X5

	£	£
Operating profit		17 043
Add back: loss on disposal of non-current asset		627
Add back: depreciation		36 900
		54 570
Increase in inventory $(61\,650 - 59\,900)$	(1 750)	
Increase in trade receivables $(83\,360 - 80\,410)$	(2 950)	
Increase in trade payables $(79\,950 - 76\,640)$	3 310	
		(1 390)
Cash generated from operations		53 180
Interest paid		(3 700)
Net cash inflow from operating activities		49 480
Cash flows from investing activities		
Purchase of non-current assets $(£543\,720 - (£501\,120 - 5200))$	(47 800)	
Proceeds of sale of non-current assets	1 073	
Net cash outflow from investing activities		(46 727)
Cash flows from financing activities		
Increase in bank loan	20 000	
Capital returned to owner (drawings)	(53 693)	
Net cash inflow from financing activities		(33 693)
Net decrease in cash		(30 940)
Cash at beginning of period		12 440
Cash at end of period: overdraft		(18 500)

ii) **Explanation of Ishmael's overdraft at 31 July 20X5**

Cash at the beginning of the period of £12 440 has, by the end of the year, become a sizeable overdraft. The statement of cash flows is useful for identifying where the outflows of cash have arisen. The business is generating positive net cash flows from its operating activities, which is reassuring. The outflows arise in respect of investing and financing activities. Investment has been made in non-current assets. This is necessary in most businesses to ensure that the ability to generate positive operating cash flows is maintained. Overall, the carrying amount of non-current assets has not increased by very much $(£402\,600 - £393\,400)$, which suggests that the investment that has taken place in the year is to replace worn out assets, rather than a sign of expansion in the business.

The most significant item in the financing section of the statement is the amount of cash that has left the business in the form of drawings. This has been offset to some extent by an increase in the business bank loan. Drawings for the year are higher than the net operating cash flow generated by the business which is a worrying sign, suggesting that Ishmael may be taking too much out of the business. The increase in business bank loan is likely to mean increased interest costs in future years.

CHAPTER 7

7.1 It is true that directors take complete responsibility for the preparation of accounts, but they do not have to actually prepare the accounts themselves. They may delegate the preparation to others, but the directors take ultimate responsibility for ensuring that the accounts present a true and fair view, and that they are filed on time. It is not a criminal offence to produce accounts that fail to present a true and fair view. However, directors can be subject to criminal sanctions for failing to prepare and file accounts, and they may be guilty of a criminal offence if it can be proven that they have deliberately defrauded creditors.

The answer is b): statements 2 and 4 are correct.

7.2 The correct answer is c) £240. Bayliss Chandler Limited has 40 000 shares in issue (£20 000/50p). Ambrose owns 10% of the issued capital, ie. 4000 shares. He is entitled to a dividend of 6p per share:

> 4000 × 6p = £240.

7.3 The correct answer is d) Carina received £150; Cathy received £50. A holding of 8000 shares in Peachey plc is equivalent to a nominal value of 8000 × 25p = £2000. The total dividend payable for the year is 10% of nominal value, therefore the holder of 8000 shares will receive 10% × £2000 = £200, half on 31 March 20X2 and half on 30 September 20X2.

At 31 March 20X2 Carina owns all 8000 shares and will receive £100 in dividend.

At 30 September 20X2 Carina owns 4000 of the shares and her sister Cathy owns 4000. Therefore, they share the dividend, receiving £50 each.

In total for the year, Carina receives £150 in dividend and Cathy receives £50.

7.4 The correct answer is c) £6400. Explanation:

80 000 ordinary shares × 5p per share =	£4 000
Preference dividend for 20X3:	
£20 000 × 6%	1 200
Arrears of preference dividend for 20X2	1 200
Total	£6 400

7.5

Workings

1 Cost of sales

Opening inventory	51 240
Add: purchases	603 493
	654 733
Less: closing inventory	(57 210)
Cost of sales	£597 523

2 Selling and distribution costs

As stated in the list of balances	80 714
Add: accrued commission	6 000
	£86 714

3 Administrative expenses

As stated in the list of balances	73 959
Less: prepaid insurance	(1 270)
	£72 689

4 Finance costs

Interest payable as stated in list of balances	1 977
Preference dividend (£100 000 × 8%)	8 000
	£9 977

Solar Bubble plc: Draft statement of profit or loss for the year ended 31 January 20X8

	£
Revenue	975 420
Cost of sales (working 1)	(597 523)
Gross profit	377 897
Selling and distribution costs (working 2)	(86 714)
Administrative expenses (working 3)	(72 689)

	£
	218 494
Finance costs (working 4)	(9 977)
Profit before tax	208 517
Tax on profit	(60 625)
Profit for the year	147 892

7.6 Workings

1 Administrative expenses

	£
Secretarial costs	51 498
Electricity (admin. office)	12 491
Office rental	42 704
Administration office: telephone charges	6 964
Depreciation of office computer equipment	8 390
Office manager's salary	21 704
Directors' remuneration	59 200
Other administrative expenses	36 075
	239 026

2 Selling and distribution costs

	£
Salespersons' salaries	64 299
Delivery van depreciation	12 000
Other selling and distribution costs	5 911
Salespersons' commission	12 270
Delivery van expenses	24 470
	118 950

Note: it is often a matter of judgement as to how expenses are allocated between selling and distribution cost and administrative expenses.

3 Tangible non-current assets: property, plant and equipment

	£
Factory and plant at carrying amount	2 518 000
Delivery vans at carrying amount	120 000
Office equipment at carrying amount	151 020
	2 789 020

4 Other payables

	£
Taxation	216 470

Brighton Magnets Limited: Statement of profit or loss for the year ended 31 August 20X9

	£
Revenue	3 796 842
Cost of sales	(2 712 350)
Gross profit	1 084 492

	£
Selling and distribution costs (working 2)	(118 950)
Administrative expenses (working 1)	(239 026)
Other operating income	12 900
Operating profit	739 416
Interest receivable and similar income	644
Interest payable and similar charges	(1 207)
Profit before tax	738 853
Tax on profit	(216 470)
Profit for the year	522 383

Note: this statement of profit or loss contains an extra line, for the sub-total of operating profit. This line does not appear in IAS 1 *Presentation of financial statements*, but it is quite often found in practice. It is quite permissible to provide additional information in financial statements, over and above the information that is absolutely required by law or by regulations such as international standards.

Brighton Magnets Limited: Statement of changes in equity for the year ended 31 August 20X9

	Share capital	Retained earnings	Total equity
	£	£	£
At 1 September 20X8	800 000	1 597 172	2 397 172
Profit for the year		522 383	522 383
Dividend		(40 000)	(40 000)
At 31 August 20X9	800 000	2 079 555	2 879 555

Brighton Magnets Limited: Statement of financial position at 31 August 20X9

ASSETS	£	£
Non-current assets		
Property, plant and equipment (working 4)		2 789 020
Current assets		
Inventories	186 420	
Trade receivables	321 706	
Cash at bank	18 290	
		526 416
		3 315 436
CAPITAL AND LIABILITIES		
Equity		
Share capital		800 000
Retained earnings		2 079 555
		2 879 555
Current liabilities		
Trade payables	219 411	
Other payables: taxation	216 470	
		435 881
		3 315 436

7.7   Statement 1 is false: listed companies are not obliged to produce a social responsibility report as part of their annual report

Statement 2 is true: consolidated financial statements do bring together the results and the assets and liabilities of all group companies

Statement 3 is true: compliance with the UK Corporate Governance Code is compulsory for all listed companies. Statement 4 is false: XBRL International is a non-profit independent consortium.

The answer is b): statements 2 and 3 are correct.

7.8 The principal objectives of the Strategic Report are to:

- provide insight into the entity's business model and its main strategy and objectives (strategic management)
- describe the principal risks the entity faces and how they might affect its future prospects (business environment)
- provide an analysis of the entity's past performance (business performance).

7.9 Since 2005 listed companies in the UK have been obliged to use international accounting standards. Unlisted companies can choose which set of standards to use; both conventions are acceptable in company law (CA 2006). However, most UK unlisted companies use UK accounting standards. These have recently changed and most companies adopt FRS 102 *The Financial Reporting Standard*. However, those companies that meet the criteria for classification as micro-entities can choose to adopt FRS 105 *The Financial Reporting Standard Applicable to the Micro-Entities Regime*.

CHAPTER 8

8.1 The correct answer is a) higher than average increase in revenue, and lower than average increase in gross profit. Ronald's percentage increase in revenue:

$$\frac{110\,450 - 95\,544}{95\,544} \times 100 = 15.6\%$$

His increase in revenue is, therefore, higher than average.
Ronald's percentage increase in gross profit:

$$\frac{38\,392 - 33\,469}{33\,469} \times 100 = 14.7\%$$

His increase in gross profit is, therefore, lower than average.

8.2 The correct answer is c) A gradually inceasing percentage of revenue growth and a gradually decreasing percentage of gross profit growth.
Horizontal analysis of Rory's statement of profit or loss data shows the following percentage changes:
Percentage increases over previous year:

	20X4	20X3	20X2
	%	%	%
Revenue	4.2	3.6	3.0
Gross profit	3.3	3.4	3.5

Revenue growth percentage is gradually increasing.
Gross profit growth percentage is gradually decreasing.

8.3 **Horizontal analysis of annual changes in selected items from Larsen Locations Limited's statement of profit or loss 20X4 to 20X7**

	20X7	20X6	20X5
	%	%	%
Sales of services	0.5	5.4	0.1
Administrative expenses	20.1	8.5	0.9
Operating profit	(10.1)	5.8	1.0

Larsen Locations has experienced more volatile change in revenue, administrative expenses and operating profit than The Wilton Group plc. Sales in 20X6 increased by a greater amount than Wilton's sales, but there was a negligible rate of sales growth in 20X5 and 20X7. However, the most obvious difference is in the greatly increased level of administrative expenses in Larsen Locations' 20X7 accounts. Presumably this increase arises because of the move to larger premises and taking on more staff. The increase in costs in 20X7 does not appear, as yet, to have produced a similar level of increase in sales. The higher costs appear to have resulted in a lower level of operating profit – a 10.1% decrease in 20X7 compared to the previous year.

8.4 **Vertical analysis: Chapter Protection Limited's statement of profit or loss for the year ended 31 December 20X4**

	£	%
Revenue	188 703	100.0
Cost of sales	(115 863)	(61.4)
Gross profit	72 840	38.6
Administrative expenses	(14 260)	(7.6)
Distribution and selling costs	(20 180)	(10.7)
Operating profit	38 400	20.3
Finance costs	(1 200)	(0.6)
Profit before tax	37 200	19.7
Tax	(7 450)	(3.9)
Profit after tax	29 750	15.8

8.5 **Causeway Ferguson plc: Horizontal trend analysis of statements of profit or loss: 20X2–20X6**

Percentage changes over previous year

	20X6	20X5	20X4	20X3
	%	%	%	%
Revenue	(2.6)	(0.3)	9.4	3.6
Cost of sales	(2.5)	–	11.0	4.5
Gross profit	(2.8)	(0.8)	7.2	2.3
Administrative expenses	4.0	0.2	4.3	1.8
Selling and distribution costs	4.2	1.2	0.3	1.1
Profit before tax	(25.8)	(5.6)	25.6	5.5
Tax	(25.7)	(5.6)	25.8	5.4
Profit after tax	(25.8)	(5.5)	25.5	5.6

Causeway Ferguson plc: Common size analysis of statements of profit or loss: 20X2–20X6

	20X6	20X5	20X4	20X3	20X2
	%	%	%	%	%
Revenue	100.0	100.0	100.0	100.0	100.0
Cost of sales	(60.7)	(60.6)	(60.4)	(59.5)	(59.0)
Gross profit	39.3	39.4	39.6	40.5	41.0
Administrative expenses	(16.5)	(15.5)	(15.4)	(16.2)	(16.4)
Selling and distribution costs	(15.8)	(14.7)	(14.5)	(15.9)	(16.3)
Profit before tax	7.0	9.2	9.7	8.4	8.3
Tax	(2.1)	(2.8)	(2.9)	(2.5)	(2.5)
Profit after tax	4.9	6.4	6.8	5.9	5.8

Commentary

The following key features emerge from the horizontal and the common size analysis:

1 In each of the five years from 20X2 to 20X6 there has been a fall in the gross profit percentage. The falls from year to year are not dramatic but decline gradually.

2 There was some growth in revenue until 20X4. The last two years show decreases. The decline in revenue together with the steady decline in gross profit margin suggest that the company has some problems to address.

3 Administrative expenses and selling and distribution costs have increased each year. Usually the increases are small, but they represent significant amounts over a five-year period. In 20X6 both categories of cost increased by over 4%, and contribute significantly to the overall substantial drop in operating profit for the year.

4 While it might be premature to announce the 'withering away' of the company, some aspects of its performance would cause concern to a shareholder. The fact that there are new competitors in the market would explain the declining revenue performance of the last two years. The gradual decline in gross margin, however, goes right back to the beginning of the five-year period and could not be completely attributable to competitive effects if the competitors have emerged only recently.

8.6 Report on Marks & Spencer plc's five-year trading record extracts: 2012–2016.
Although sales have grown over the five-year period in the UK, the rate of growth has slowed. Similarly, the rate of growth in international sales has slowed, and sales internationally have actually fallen in 2016. Profitability has fallen, especially in respect of international activity. It is particularly striking that international sales have produced a significant operating loss in 2016. This follows several years of declining profitability internationally.

It is possible that the business is curtailing some of its international operations, or that it is about to do so. The Annual Report would provide more information on this point.

Overall, the business appears to be going through a period of slow decline. Shareholders may be concerned about the direction in which the business is heading. Although revenue overall has risen, the business may be having difficulty in controlling its costs, especially in respect of international activities.

Appendix

Percentages of total: UK retail and international retail

	2016 %	2015 %	2014 %	2013 %	2012 %
Revenue:					
UK retail	89.7	89.4	88.8	89.2	89.3
International retail	10.3	10.6	11.2	10.8	10.7
Total	100.0	100.0	100.0	100.0	100.0
Operating profit					
UK retail	107.4	91.3	86.4	84.0	88.1
International retail	(7.4)	8.7	13.6	16.0	11.9
Total	100.0	100.0	100.0	100.0	100.0

Operating profit as a percentage of revenue

	2016 %	2015 %	2014 %	2013 %	2012 %
UK retail	6.6	6.9	6.6	7.1	7.4
International retail	(4.0)	5.6	8.2	11.2	8.3
Total	5.5	6.8	6.7	7.5	7.5

Percentage increase (decrease) from previous year

	2016 %	2015 %	2014 %	2013 %
Revenue				
UK retail	2.7	0.7	2.3	0.9
International retail	0	(5.7)	7.3	0.8
Total	2.4	0	2.8	0.9
Operating profit				
UK retail	(2.1)	6.7	(5.1)	(3.8)
International retail	–	(35.6)	(21.6)	35.8
Total	(16.7)	1.0	(7.8)	0.8

CHAPTER 9

9.1   The correct answer is d) pre-tax return on equity is 11.7%.

$$\frac{\text{Profit after interest and before tax}}{\text{Equity}} = \frac{267.8}{2290}$$
$$= 11.7\%$$

9.2   The correct answer is b) post-tax return on equity is 8.2%.

$$\frac{\text{Profit after interest and tax}}{\text{Equity}} = \frac{189.8}{2290}$$
$$= 8.2\%$$

9.3   The correct answer is b) return on capital employed is 11.5%.

$$\frac{\text{Profit before interest and tax}}{\text{Equity} + \text{long-term borrowings}} = \frac{302.8}{2290 + 350}$$
$$= 11.5\%$$

9.4   The correct answer is a) Ambit Limited.
The pre-tax return on shareholders' funds is calculated as:

$$\frac{\text{Profit before tax and after interest}}{\text{Equity}}$$

For each company:

Ambit Limited	**Bolsover Limited**	**Carcan Limited**	**Delphic Limited**
$\dfrac{803.6}{80.0 + 4550.0} \times 100$	$\dfrac{540.8}{95.0 + 3881.0} \times 100$	$\dfrac{575.8}{86.0 + 3928.0} \times 100$	$\dfrac{855.4}{60.0 + 7000.0} \times 100$
$= 17.4\%$	$= 13.6\%$	$= 14.3\%$	$= 12.1\%$

The company with the highest return is Ambit Limited.

9.5   The correct answer is a) 1.95:1

Total current assets = 18 370 + 24 100 + 70 = £42 540
Total current liabilities = 15 450 + 6400 = £21 850

$$\text{Current ratio} = \frac{\text{Current assets}}{\text{Current liabilities}}$$
$$= \frac{42\,540}{21\,850} = 1.95:1$$

9.6   The correct answer is b) Trimester Tinker Limited's current ratio is higher than the industry average but its quick ratio is lower.

Current assets = 108 770 + 94 300 + 1600 = £204 670
'Quick' assets = 94 300 + 1600 = 95 900
Current liabilities = 110 650

$$\text{Current ratio} = \frac{204\,670}{110\,650} = 1.85:1$$

$$\text{Quick ratio} = \frac{95\,900}{110\,650} = 0.87:1$$

Trimester Tinker's current ratio of 1.85:1 is higher than the industry average of 1.62:1
Trimester Tinker's quick ratio of 0.87:1 is lower than the industry average of 0.93:1

9.7   The correct answer is d) 2.98.
Non-current asset turnover is calculated as follows:

$$\frac{\text{Revenue}}{\text{Non-current assets}}$$

The correct figure to take for non-current assets is carrying amount, ie. £170 000 + 59 985 = £229 985.

$$\frac{686\,430}{229\,985} = 2.98$$

9.8   Sole trader

Opening inventory   405 000

Closing inventory   405 000 + 10% = 445 500

Average inventory for the year: $\dfrac{£405\,000 + 445\,500}{2} = £425\,250$

Inventory turnover in days:

$$\frac{425\,250}{1\,506\,700} \times 365 \text{ days} = 103.0 \text{ days}$$

9.9   The correct answer is c) 66.9 days. Only credit sales are taken into account when calculating the trade receivables turnover ratio.

Credit sales for the year: £1 703 698 × 70% = £1 192 589

    Trade receivables turnover ratio:

$$\frac{218\,603}{1\,192\,589} \times 365 \text{ days} = 66.9 \text{ days}$$

9.10   The correct answer is c) 1 and 4 could be valid explanations.

1   The absence of the credit controller on sick leave is likely to result in a slowing up of trade receivables recovery. Many trade receivables will be paid on time as a matter of routine, but some always need chasing. Unless a credit controller is chasing this latter group for payment, they will delay or defer settling their debts. This is a valid reason.

2   An increase of 4% in revenue is not likely to make any difference to the collection of debts. A very large increase might put pressure on administrative systems, but 4% is not likely to matter.

3   Early settlement discounts should have the opposite effect: trade debtors should pay up more quickly in order to take advantage of the settlement discount.

4   It is important to state the company's terms on the invoice stationery. If this is not done, new and occasional customers will simply not know the terms of trade, and may be inclined to take longer to pay. Other customers may use the absence of stated terms as an excuse to take longer to pay.

Reasons 1 and 4 could be valid explanations.

9.11   The correct answer is a) 42.9 days. The calculation of the trade payables turnover period ratio should include only purchases made on credit.

Purchases made on credit = 90% × £1 952 278 = £1 757 050.

Trade payables turnover in days:

$$\frac{206\,460}{1\,757\,050} \times 365 \text{ days} = 42.9 \text{ days}$$

9.12   The dividend per share is b) 5p.

$$\frac{\text{Dividend}}{\text{Number of shares in issue}} = \frac{300\,000}{6\,200\,000}$$
$$= 5\text{p per share}$$

9.13   The dividend cover ratio is a) 3.77.

$$\frac{\text{Earnings after tax attibutable to ordinary shareholders}}{\text{Dividend}}$$
$$= \frac{1\,131\,400}{300\,000} = 3.77$$

9.14 The earnings per share are a) 18.86p.

$$\frac{\text{Earnings after tax attibutable to ordinary shareholders}}{\text{Number of shares in issues}}$$

$$= \frac{1\ 131\ 400}{6\ 000\ 000} = 18.86\text{p per shape}$$

9.15 Market capitalization is the share price $\times$ the number of shares in issue.
Waldo Wolff's market capitalization at 31 December 20X5 is £3.11 $\times$ 6 000 000 = £18 660 000.

9.16 The company's P/E ratio was c) 8.4.
First, calculate earnings per share:

$$\frac{\text{Earnings attibutable to ordinary shareholders}}{\text{Number of shares in issue}}$$

$$= \frac{750\ 090}{3\ 300\ 000} = 22.73\text{p}$$

P/E ratio = price divided by earnings per share:

$$\text{Price per share} = \frac{\text{market capitalization}}{\text{number of shares}}$$

$$= \frac{6\ 303\ 000}{3\ 300\ 000}$$

$$= £1.91$$

$$\frac{\text{Price}}{\text{Earnings per share}} = \frac{191\text{p}}{22.73\text{p}} = 8.4$$

9.17 i) Gearing ratio

$$\frac{\text{Debt}}{\text{Equity}} = \frac{2\ 000\ 000}{3\ 739\ 400}$$

$$= 53.4\%$$

ii) Interest cover

$$\frac{\text{Profit before interest and tax}}{\text{Interest}}$$

$$= \frac{646\ 750}{200\ 000}$$

$$= 3.23\text{ times.}$$

9.18 **Report to the directors of The Cuttlefish Biscuit Corporation Limited**
Gross profit margin for Cuttlefish is better than the industry average, but net profit margin is worse. This suggests that the business is incurring higher costs on average, such as administration, selling and marketing costs, than its competitors. There may be good reasons in the short term why this should be so, but if business costs continue at a relatively high level the directors may wish to consider a range of possible cost reductions. In the meantime, it would be helpful to examine costs in detail to identify areas where savings are possible.

The trade receivables turnover ratio shows that Cuttlefish collects its receivables more quickly than average in the industry. Given that most businesses will automatically take 30 days credit, 36 days is very good. There may be room for some improvement, however, and the directors may wish to consider, for example, introducing discounts for early settlement if they have not already done so.

Inventory turnover is slightly worse than the industry average. It may be advisable to look more closely at the level of inventory held in the business and look for ways of managing inventory more efficiently.

On average the industry takes a lot longer to pay trade payables than Cuttlefish. 31.4 days would usually be considered a low turnover ratio where the industry trading terms are settlement within 30 days. The directors might consider extending this period by a few days; it would release some cash into the operating cycle, and could probably be done without endangering relationships with suppliers.

Cuttlefish's gearing ratio is low, compared to others. No particular action is recommended on this point, but if directors are looking for long-term finance for business expansion, they should bear in mind that the business is not currently regarded as highly-geared. Further long-term loans, within reasonable limits, would therefore be an option for consideration.

Generally, Cuttlefish appears to be doing well compared to industry averages.

9.19 Confidential report to the board of Cryer Roussillon Limited

Executive summary:

The implementation of the range of new strategies has been very successful. The company is now more profitable than it was a year ago, and its statement of financial position is healthy. The company should now concentrate on consolidating its position, and should seek to expand revenue volume.

Note: The appendix to this report sets out a set of relevant ratio calculations.

Detailed report:

The company's revenue has dropped by almost 2% since last year. However, gross profit has improved by almost 24%, and the gross profit margin is now 41.3% compared to only 32.7% in 20X5. The company's strategy of pursuing higher margin revenue appears to have paid off. It should now concentrate on increasing revenue volume in those higher margin products. Operating expenses appear to be well under control; some effective cost cutting appears to have taken place in 20X6.

The company has made a major investment in non-current assets. Carrying amount has increased by 88% in the year. It is possible that the benefits to be obtained from these assets have not fed through into revenue volumes and profits yet. The non-current asset efficiency ratio is notably poorer in 20X6 but could be expected to improve in 20X7 as the assets are utilized throughout the whole year.

Liquidity is not a problem. Liquidity ratios in both 20X5 and 20X6 are good, and the amount of cash at bank has increased very substantially. The directors' decision not to propose a dividend has helped, and means that spare cash is now available for extra investment.

Inventory turnover has worsened to 43 days (from 37.5 in 20X5). The company must ensure that it is not building up too much inventory, and controls in this area may need further attention. Trade receivables, on the other hand, appear to be better controlled in 20X6: trade receivables turnover has reduced, and appears to be at a quite satisfactory level.

The company has taken on long-term debt resulting in a relatively modest level of gearing. The level of gearing does not appear to be a cause for any concern at the moment.

Appendix

	20X6	20X5
Performance		
Gross profit margin	$\frac{85\,272}{206\,470} \times 100 = 41.3\%$	$\frac{68\,830}{210\,619} \times 100 = 32.7\%$
Operating profit margin	$\frac{43\,813}{206\,470} \times 100 = 21.2\%$	$\frac{21\,220}{210\,619} \times 100 = 10.1\%$
Return on shareholders' funds	$\frac{40\,813}{129\,783} \times 100 = 31.4\%$	$\frac{21\,220}{97\,070} \times 100 = 21.8\%$
Liquidity		
Current ratio	$\frac{45\,763}{15\,470} = 2.96$	$\frac{44\,610}{16\,290} = 2.74$
Quick ratio	$\frac{20\,693 + 10\,792}{15\,470} = 2.04$	$\frac{29\,420 + 640}{16\,290} = 1.85$
Efficiency		
Non-current assets turnover	$\frac{206\,470}{129\,490} = 1.59$	$\frac{210\,619}{68\,750} = 3.06$
Inventory turnover (days)	$\frac{14\,278}{121\,198} \times 365 = 43.0$	$\frac{14\,550}{141\,789} \times 365 = 37.5$

	20X6	20X5
Trade receivables turnover (days)	$\dfrac{20\ 693}{206\ 470} \times 365 = 36.6$	$\dfrac{29\ 420}{210\ 619} \times 365 = 50.1$
Gearing Debt/Equity	$\dfrac{30\ 000}{129\ 783} = 23.1\%$	Nil

9.20 *Tesco plc*

Report on the performance of Tesco plc in 2016

The performance figures show that Tesco in 2016 has returned to profitability, after a very poor performance in 2015. Revenue for 2016 is 4.4% below revenue in 2015, but the business is making profits again in 2016, showing that costs are being more tightly controlled than in the previous year.

A brief examination of the narrative sections of Tesco's 2016 Annual Report shows that the company is still in the process of turning around its operations. The report clearly states that Tesco had lost the trust of its stakeholders (shareholders, customers, suppliers) and that it has had to take drastic action in its 2016 financial year to restore that trust. It has simplified its operations, cutting the range of products offered by 18%. This simplification has helped to reduce costs. It has also taken steps to rebuild and improve relationships with its suppliers.

The performance ratios in the table below are unimpressive, but at least they show significant improvement since 2015.

	2016	2015
Gross profit margin	5.24%	(3.87)%
Operating profit margin	1.92%	(10.1)%
Net profit margin (before tax)	0.3%	(11.13)%
Net profit margin (after tax)	0.4%	(9.95)%

CHAPTER 10

10.1 Cueline Limited's directors are looking at two options: renewal of the lease and purchase of freehold premises. They need to examine projected financial information for both options in order to ensure that they reach the right decision.

Renewal of the lease

The following items of information would be useful:

- The estimated cost of any lease premium (a lease premium is a capital sum payable at the start of a lease).
- The regular annual rental and any service charges that will have to be paid over the lease term.
- If a large sum has to be paid at the start of the lease, the directors need to examine financing options. Does Cueline Limited have the cash available? Will it need to borrow? If it does have the cash available are there better uses to which it can be put?
- If a loan has to be taken out, how much will the regular charge for interest be?

Purchase of freehold premises

The directors need to identify a range of possible properties for purchase by contacting local commercial property agents. By doing this, they will be able to estimate an approximate capital outlay for the purchase. They need to plan any necessary financing, taking into consideration the following points:

- Will a mortgage loan be available for this type of property?
- What effect will a loan have on the company's gearing?
- How much will the regular charge for interest be?
- What are the implications of the loan and interest repayments for the company's cash flow?

10.2 Putt's directors need to make a thorough assessment of the consequences of a change in strategy. They should obtain information on the following:

- The state of the market for golf-related items and the outlook for sales over the next few years. This may involve commissioning specific market research.

- An estimate of the impact of the change on the future performance of the company. How profitable is the company likely to be in the future? Will future performance be an improvement on past performance? How big a difference will the change in strategy make?
- An assessment of the competition. How successful have competitor businesses been in obtaining market share? Are there any new entrants to the market who are likely to pose a threat to Putt plc?
- The likely effects of the proposed change on the need for selling space. Would the existing shops expand their range of golf-related items if more space were to be made available? Would shops need to move (for example, nearer to golf courses)? Are there any implications for staffing (for example, would some staff need to be made redundant)?
- Disposal of existing non-golf inventory items. Would these items need to be sold quickly, and would they have to be sold at a loss? If so, what is the projected effect on the company's statement of profit or loss?

10.3 a) The obvious financial impact of employing another member of staff is the cost of the salary, plus other costs such as employer's national insurance, employer's contributions to the pension scheme (if any) and any other incidental costs of employment such as health benefits. It would appear to make sense to employ another person if the department's income would, in consequence, increase by enough to cover the additional costs, and the partners would require information about the effect on both income and costs.

However, there are other relevant considerations. If the conveyancing department is genuinely short-staffed, either or both of the following effects could occur:

- Existing staff will be overworked and may become disgruntled. If sufficiently dissatisfied they may seek to change employment.
- There might be an adverse effect on quality. If a serious mistake is made in conveyancing, the firm could lay itself open to legal action, or to criticism from regulators. If it acts inefficiently in dealing with client business, the consequence could be a loss of reputation. Prospective clients may take their business elsewhere.

b) This involves a significant strategic decision. The existing partners will seek information on:

- The likely cost of bringing in another partner. The new partner would be entitled to a share of the profits of the business, although this could be made dependent upon performance to some extent. She would also expect the same range of benefits (health benefits, pension scheme and so on) as the existing partners. There would, presumably, also be other knock-on effects on staffing (for example, she would almost certainly need some secretarial assistance).
- The expected benefits in terms of increased fees. How much extra business could a divorce specialist be expected to generate? Would she be able to contribute any capital to the business?
- How many solicitors experienced in divorce law actually operate in the area? Is there really a gap in the market for another one? Are there any cross-selling opportunities (for example, people who are getting a divorce often sell property jointly, and there may be new opportunities for generating extra conveyancing work)?
- It is important that partners (as joint proprietors of a business) are able to agree among themselves. Would the proposed new partner be an easy person to work with?

CHAPTER 11

11.1

Expense	*Classification*
Plastic moulding machine depreciation	Indirect production overheads
Sales office fixtures and fittings depreciation	Other indirect overheads
Plastic materials	Direct materials
Advertising expenditure	Other indirect overheads
Depreciation of factory building	Indirect production overheads
Electricity bill for factory	Indirect production overheads
Wages of assembly line workers	Direct labour
Wages of factory canteen staff	Indirect production overheads

Expense	Classification
Wages of assembly line supervisor	Indirect production overheads
Secretary's salary	Other indirect overheads
Delivery vehicle depreciation	Other indirect overheads
Factory consumables	Indirect production overheads
Royalty payable per item produced to telephone designer	Direct expenses
Mobile telephone bill – sales director	Other indirect overheads

11.2   ArtKit Supplies Limited: Cost statement for the year ended 31 August 20X2

	£	£
Direct materials		
Metal	18 006	
Lacquer paint	1 600	
Hinge fittings	960	
		20 566
Direct labour		
Machine operators' wages	27 250	
Finishing operative's wages	19 270	
		46 520
Prime cost		67 086
Production overheads		
Rental of factory	6 409	
Machine repair	176	
Depreciation: machinery	1 080	
Electricity: factory	1 760	
Factory cleaning	980	
Sundry factory costs	2 117	
		12 522
Production cost		79 608
Other overheads		
Secretarial and administration salaries	22 460	
Salesman's salary	28 200	
Office supplies	2 411	
Office telephone	1 630	
Sundry office costs	904	
Delivery costs	1 920	
		57 525
Total costs		137 133

11.3   The correct answer is d) £132. Because Porter Farrington adopts a FIFO policy for inventory valuation, the 40 items left in inventory at the end of November 20X2 are deemed to be those most recently delivered. The most recent delivery before the end of the month was the 50 items delivered on 2 May at a cost of £3.30 per unit. The correct valuation is:

40 units @ £3.30 = £132.00

11.4   Scenario A: Batch costing
Scenario B: Product costing
Scenario C: Job costing

CHAPTER 12

12.1   Jersey Brookfield & Co: Apportionment of production overheads for the year ended 31 December 20X8

	Basis	Total £	Bulk production £	Packaging £
Factory building depreciation	Floor area	5 670	3 240	2 430
Factory rates	Floor area	11 970	6 840	5 130
Factory insurance	Floor area	7 980	4 560	3 420
Canteen costs	No. employees	18 876	8 580	10 296
Supervisory salaries	No. employees	29 480	13 400	16 080
Other indirect labour	Machinery value	18 275	12 410	5 865
Machinery depreciation	Machinery value	21 500	14 600	6 900
Cleaning	Floor area	17 850	10 200	7 650
Electricity	Actual	30 290	18 790	11 500
Building maintenance	Floor area	5 040	2 880	2 160
		166 931	95 500	71 431

12.2   Barley Brindle

i) *Overhead absorption rate for 20X3 based on direct labour hours*

Each unit uses one hour of direct labour; production of 60 000 units is planned, therefore 60 000 direct labour hours will be used.

Overhead absorption rate: $\dfrac{£218\,000}{60\,000} = £3.63$

ii) *Overhead absorption rate for 20X3 based on machine hours*

Each unit uses 0.5 hours of machine time. Anticipated total machine time is, therefore 60 000 × 0.5 = 30 000.

Overhead absorption rate: $\dfrac{£218\,000}{30\,000} = £7.27$

iii) *Overhead absorption rate for 20X3 based on units of production*

Overhead absorption rate: $\dfrac{£218\,000}{60\,000} = £3.63$

12.3   WGB

Totals for direct materials based on production of 6000 of each product

	£
Metal machining dept.	
Domestic shelves: £18.00 × 6000	108 000
Commercial shelves: £27.00 × 6000	162 000
	270 000
Painting and finishing dept.	
Domestic shelves: £3.30 × 6 000	19 800
Commercial shelves: £4.60 × 6 000	27 600
	47 400

Totals for direct labour based on production of 6 000 of each product

	£
Metal machining dept.	
Domestic shelves: $0.75 \times £10 \times 6000$	45 000
Commercial shelves: $1 \times £10 \times 6000$	60 000
	105 000
Painting and finishing dept.	
Domestic shelves: $1 \times £9 \times 6000$	54 000
Commercial shelves: $1.5 \times £9 \times 6000$	81 000
	135 000

i) *overhead absorption rates based on % of direct materials:*

$$\text{Metal machining dept:} \frac{172\,490}{270\,000} = 63.9\%$$

$$\text{Painting and finishing dept:} \frac{116\,270}{47\,400} = 245.3\%$$

ii) *overhead absorption rates based on % of direct labour:*

$$\text{Metal machining dept:} \frac{172\,490}{105\,000} = 164.3\%$$

$$\text{Painting and finishing dept:} \frac{116\,270}{135\,000} = 86.1\%$$

Materials are relatively much more significant than labour hours in the machining department. Therefore, it would probably make sense to use an overhead absorption rate based on the percentage of direct materials consumed.

By contrast, in the painting and finishing department, direct labour is relatively more important than the input of materials. Therefore, it would probably make sense to use an overhead absorption rate based on the percentage of direct materials consumed.

Because the machining department probably involves use of a relatively high level of machine hours it may be worth considering the calculation of an overhead absorption rate based on machine hours.

12.4   The cost object with which costs are identified in an architects' practice is likely to be a job for a specific client. The principal costs incurred by the practice are likely to be:

- architects' and support staff salaries and related benefits such as health insurance, travel allowances, car parking
- premises costs, including rental, power, business rates, water rates, service charges
- sundry supplies such as paper, computer consumables, magazines
- depreciation of capital items such as premises (if owned not rented), computer equipment, desks, tables, chairs.

Architects' salaries and the salaries of any ancillary staff directly associated with a particular job can be identified with the cost object using a record-keeping system that records time spent on a particular job. Salaries of staff that are not specifically identified with particular jobs plus all other expenses would fall into the general category of overheads. These might be allocated on a 'direct labour hour' basis according to the amount of time directly spent by the professional staff on particular jobs.

12.5   David

i) Does School A, on this evidence, provide poor value for money?

The average salary cost per child taught in 20X8/X9 was £2216 in School A whereas in School B it was £1591. The average salary per member of staff was £38 651 in School A, and £33 871 in School B. Salary costs in school A are certainly relatively higher than in School B. However, on its own, this information says little about relative value for money.

The ratio of staff to children is 17.4 (75/4.3) in School A and 21.2 (132/6.2) in School B. This suggests that School B is somewhat more efficient. However, it would be necessary to look at other costs and educational outcomes before being able to draw any firm conclusions.

ii) Possible reasons for the discrepancy between salary costs in the two schools. Both schools employ a full-time head teacher and a full-time deputy head teacher. These are senior posts for which higher salaries are payable. However, the burden of higher salaries is proportionately greater in School A because it has fewer staff. Nearly half of the average teaching staff number is accounted for by the head teacher and deputy.

It is quite possible that the higher average salary in School A is entirely accounted for by the head teacher/deputy issue. However, differences can arise between schools in this respect where one employs more newly and recently qualified teachers who are at the lower end of the standard salary scales.

Where schools allocate their own budgets (as is the case in England) they can choose, within certain parameters, to spend more on some categories of expenditure than others. It is possible that School A is able to spend more on salaries because of spending less on another category of spending. For example, it may be better supported by charitable contributions than School B and therefore perhaps spends less on computer equipment and books.

12.6 i) The traditional product costing system is based upon a rather outdated industrial model of labour intensive production processes allied to the use of large, relatively slow machinery. Overhead absorption rate calculations are typically based upon either machine hours or direct labour hours. However, in modern industry, both of these factors may be relatively insignificant. At the same time, indirect overheads have tended to increase in importance. The use of high-technology machinery, for example, may result in high annual depreciation charges and staff may be used in a supervisory rather than a direct labour capacity.

The effect has been that increasing amounts of production overheads have been allocated to a steadily shrinking base of labour or machine hours. This results in very high absorption rates which are highly sensitive to very small changes in labour or machine time spent.

ii) The basic principle of ABC is that cost units should bear the cost of the activities which they cause. A much higher level of investigation into the nature of production activities and related costs is undertaken in the application of ABC. Costs are seen as 'driven' by activities, and so it is clearly important to establish what those activities are. Activities include:
- materials ordering, handling and control
- testing and supervising quality
- preparing machinery for production runs.

A cost driver is established for each activity; for example, in the case of materials ordering it is likely to be the number of orders placed. A production activity that involves high levels of materials ordering will, under the application of ABC, bear a higher proportion of ordering costs than a production activity which involves relatively few materials orders.

iii) In a modern production environment, ABC, properly applied, is likely to result in a more realistic way of allocating overheads to products. It may help to avoid some of the incorrect decisions which can easily result where traditional product costing is used. However, a significant disadvantage of ABC is that it is costly and complicated to implement. Firms must be sure that the potential benefits of installing ABC outweigh the substantial costs of implementing it properly.

12.7 Overhead cost for a customer order of four books:

Activity		Cost £
Receipt of books	$\frac{£1\,000\,000}{250\,000} \times 4/48$	0.33
Storage	$\frac{£6\,800\,000}{12\,000\,000}$	0.57
Customer order processing	$\frac{£2\,400\,000}{4\,000\,000}$	0.60
Inventory picking	$\frac{£800\,000}{12\,000\,000} \times 4$	0.27
Total		1.77

12.8 Hallett Penumbra Systems
i) Overhead absorption rate based on machine hours
Estimate of production overheads for 20X0: £328 330
Total machine hours = 6000

$$\text{Rate per machine hour} = \frac{£328\ 330}{6000} = £54.72 \text{ per hour}$$

ii) Overhead per unit using ABC system
   Cost per unit of cost driver:

Activity				Cost £
Machining	$\dfrac{\text{Overhead}}{\text{Machine hours}}$	=	$\dfrac{148\ 200}{6\ 000}$	£24.70 per machine hour
Finishing	$\dfrac{\text{Overhead}}{\text{Labour hours}}$	=	$\dfrac{136\ 440}{12\ 000}$	£11.37 per labour hour
Materials ordering	$\dfrac{\text{Overhead}}{\text{No. of orders}}$	=	$\dfrac{12\ 183}{186}$	£65.50 per order
Materials issue	$\dfrac{\text{Overhead}}{\text{No. of issues}}$	=	$\dfrac{11\ 592}{120}$	£96.60 per issue
Machine setup	$\dfrac{\text{Overhead}}{\text{No. of hours}}$	=	$\dfrac{19\ 915}{70}$	£284.50 per hour

Allocation of overhead between product C and product D:

	Product C £		Product D £	
Machining	2 500 × £24.70	61 750	3 500 × £24.70	86 450
Finishing	7 200 × £11.37	81 864	4 800 × £11.37	54 576
Materials ordering	124 × £65.50	8 122	62 × £65.50	4 061
Materials issues	70 × £96.60	6 762	50 × £96.60	4 830
Machine setup	26 × £284.50	7 397	44 × £284.50	12 518
Total		165 895		162 435

iii) Production cost of one unit of each product under ABC system
   Number of units planned for production:
   C uses 1 machine hour per unit, so 2500 units are planned for production
   D uses 1.4 machine hours per unit, so 3500/1.4 = 2500 units are planned for production

	C	D
Total production overhead	£165 895	£162 435
Number of units planned for production	2 500	2 500
Production overhead per unit	£ 66.36	£ 64.97
Prime cost per unit	28.50	32.70
Production cost per unit	94.86	97.67

Production cost of one unit of each product under the old costing system

Prime cost per unit	£28.50	£32.70
Production overhead for 1 machine hour	54.72	

Production overhead for 1.4 machine hours

1.4 × £54.72		76.61
Production cost per unit	83.22	109.31

iv) Product D uses significantly more (1.4 compared to 1) machine hours per unit than product C. So, any system of overhead absorption based on machine hours will result in a disproportionately larger charge to product D than to Product C. It can be argued that, in this case, ABC produces a more equitable result that is more appropriate for decision making than the old system of overhead absorption.

CHAPTER 13

13.1 The correct answer is c) the demand curve plots the relationship between quantity and selling price.

13.2 Demand is described as elastic where it is a) highly sensitive to changes in price.

13.3 An oligopoly exists in cases where b) about three to five suppliers control the market.

13.4 Auger Ambit Limited

Fixed costs per unit: $\dfrac{£788\,000}{20\,000} = £39.40$

Cost-plus calculation:

	£
Variable materials cost per unit	18.00
Variable labour costs per unit	27.56
Fixed costs per unit	39.40
Total costs per unit	84.96
Profit mark-up: £84.96 × 25%	21.24
Selling price	106.20

13.5 Belvedere, Bharat & Burgess

i) The partnership could expect to bill fees as follows:

	£
Time available: 43 weeks × 5 days × 8 hours × 75% = 1290 hours per person	
Accountants: 6 × 1290 × £50	387 000
Senior staff and tax specialists: 5 × 1290 × £85	548 250
Partners: 3 × 1290 × £110	425 700
	1 360 950

ii) If the average recovery rate on billing is 94% this means that the partnership has not been able to recover all of the hours charged by its staff and partners.

	£
Billed: £1 360 950 × 94%	1 279 293
Costs: £1 275 000 × 101%	1 287 750
Loss for 20X4	(8 457)

13.6 i) The managers of a garden centre will have regard to local competition in setting selling prices. If there is little competition it may be possible to charge higher prices. In the long run, of course, the business must be able to cover all of its costs. It would be normal practice for the management of such a business to apply a standard mark-up on cost.

Probably, cost-based pricing will be the principal price-setting strategy, but management will also keep an eye on the competition. Even if competitors are charging lower prices, management may feel justified in charging more if, for example, it offers complementary services such as garden design, a coffee shop and a bookshop.

ii) Generally, convenience stores are able to charge relatively high prices, simply because of the additional convenience they offer. Much depends upon the competition, of course. Now that many large supermarkets are offering 24-hour service, a small grocery store may find that it has to bring down prices in order to be able to compete.

There is a cost element to take into account in setting pricing; in a 24-hour business labour must be employed at highly unsocial hours, and there may be a wage premium to pay (although the extent of this depends upon the local employment market, availability of hard-up students to work through the night, and so on). Additional costs have to be met either by increasing selling prices or reducing profit margins.

CHAPTER 14

14.1 Bubwith Girolamo Limited

Relevant revenues = 1000 units × £27 = £27 000

Relevant costs = direct materials cost (4 kg × £4.50 × 1000) = £18 000.

Relevant revenues less relevant costs produces a positive figure, and so it appears that the special contract should be accepted. Note: the direct labour cost is not relevant to the decision because the direct labour force is currently under-utilized but is paid for a full working week.

The staff will be paid whether or not the contract is accepted.

A relevant non-financial factor might be the relationship with the regular customer. It might even be worth taking unprofitable work on occasion in order to maintain goodwill.

14.2 Wetwang Limited

The information about original purchase cost and depreciation is irrelevant. If the Wetwang directors decide to try to sell for more than the existing offer, the opportunity cost of that decision is £12 000. Any new offer must at least meet the £12 000 plus the cost of advertising of £500. The minimum acceptable price is £12 500 on the information given.

14.3 Billericay Ashworth Limited

i) The cost of raw materials is a variable cost; the cost of factory insurance is a fixed cost; telephone charges are a semi-variable cost.

ii) For the graph of raw materials cost, two points are plotted:

- cost of raw materials at zero production: £0
- cost of raw materials at 3000 production level: 3000 × £13 = £39 000.

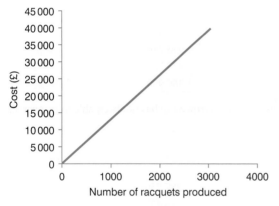

Figure 1
Billericay Ashworth Limited: Raw materials cost

For the graph of factory insurance, two points are plotted:

- cost of factory insurance at zero production level: £800
- cost of factory insurance at 3000 production level: £800.

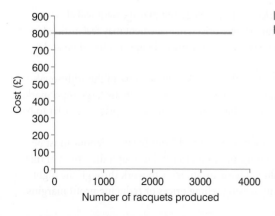

Figure 2
Billericay Ashworth Limited: Factory insurance

For the graph of telephone charges, three points are plotted:

- Telephone charges where no calls are made: £1000 (ie. basic rental charge).
- Telephone charges where 500 calls are made: £1250 (ie. basic rental charge of £1000 + £250 in call charges).
- Telephone charges where 1000 calls are made: £1500 (ie. basic rental charge of £1000 + £500 in call charges).

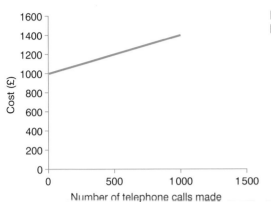

Figure 3
Billericay Ashworth Limited: Telephone charges

Note that the activity level in this case is the number of calls made: we have no information that links call charges with the level of production or any other measurement of activity.

14.4   Cost classification

i) Sales staff members' mobile telephone charges: semi-variable cost.
ii) Factory machine oil: it depends! This would probably be a relatively minor cost and would, in practice, be treated as part of fixed factory costs. However, the more the machines are used, presumably the more oil they consume, so it could be argued that this cost is variable with production. It would depend upon the particular circumstances.
iii) Metered water charges: this is a variable cost based upon the number of units consumed.

14.5   Examples of fixed and variable costs

Type of business	Examples of fixed and variable costs
Self-employed taxi driver	*Variable costs*
	Petrol or diesel
	Replacement parts for cab
	Fixed costs
	Accountancy and tax advisory services
	Cab licence
Solicitor	*Variable costs*
	Stationery costs (eg. files for holding documents)
	Overtime payments to staff called out to attend clients in police custody
	Fixed costs
	Rental of office premises
	Employment costs of secretarial staff
Shirt manufacturer	*Variable costs*
	Cost of shirt material
	Labour costs (if variable such as piece rates)
	Fixed costs
	Sewing machine depreciation charges
	Factory heating charges

Type of business	Examples of fixed and variable costs
Beauty salon	*Variable costs*
	Cost of beauty products
	Stationery costs (eg. cost of appointment cards)
	Fixed costs
	Staff salaries
	Business rates

Note how difficult it is, especially in service businesses, to think of significant variable costs.

14.6   Porton Fitzgerald

Porton Fitzgerald Limited: Budget statement for April 20X3

	£
Sales: 450 wardrobes × £210 each	94 500
Variable costs	
Direct materials: 450 wardrobes × £52	(23 400)
Direct labour: 450 wardrobes × £34	(15 300)
Contribution	55 800
Fixed costs	(43 200)
Net profit	12 600

The company's budgeted contribution for April 20X3 is £55 800 and the budgeted net profit is £12 600.

14.7   Fullbright Bognor Limited

i)   For the break-even chart for the year ending 31 December 20X6 the points plotted are:

Production level	Fixed costs £	Total costs £	Total revenue £
0	62 000	62 000	0
3 000	62 000	185 000	255 000
		(£62 000 in fixed costs + [3000 × £41])	(3000 × £85)

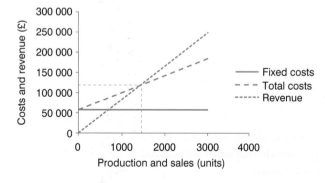

Figure 4
Fullbright Bognor Limited: Break-even chart

ii)   Reading from the chart, the break-even point in units lies somewhere between 1000 and 2000 units, at around 1400 to 1500 units. The sales value appears to be around £120 000. (Note: the larger the scale chosen for the graph, the more accurate the estimate of break-even is likely to be.)

iii)

	£
Selling price per unit	85.00
Variable costs per unit	41.00
Contribution per unit	44.00

$$\text{Break-even point (in units)} = \frac{\text{Fixed costs}}{\text{Contribution per unit}}$$

$$= \frac{62\,000}{44.00} = 1409 \text{ units (to nearest whole unit)}$$

The break-even point in sales value = 1409 units × £85 = £119 765.

14.8   Foster Beniform

a)   Where fixed costs are £40 000

    i)   For the break-even chart for 20X8 (fixed costs at £40 000) the points plotted are:

Production level	Fixed costs £	Total costs £	Total revenue £
0	40 000	40 000	0
2 000	40 000	90 000	110 000
		(£40 000 + [2000 × £25])	(2000 × £55)

    ii)   Reading from the chart, the break-even point in units appears to be around 1300 units; the break-even point in sales value appears to be around £73 000.

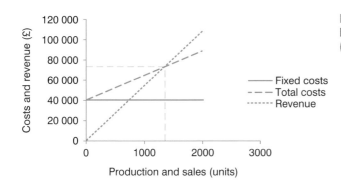

Figure 5
Foster Beniform Limited: Break-even chart (fixed costs at £40 000)

    iii)

	£
Selling price per unit	55.00
Variable costs per unit	(25.00)
Contribution per unit	30.00

$$\text{Break-even point (in units)} = \frac{\text{Fixed costs}}{\text{Contribution per unit}}$$

$$= \frac{40\,000}{30.00} = 1333 \text{ units (to nearest whole unit)}$$

Break-even point in sales value = 1333 units × £55 = £73 315.

b)   Where fixed costs are £50 000

    i)   For the break-even chart for 20X8 (fixed costs at £50 000) the points plotted are:

Production level	Fixed costs £	Total costs £	Total revenue £
0	50 000	50 000	0
2 000	50 000	100 000	110 000
		(£50 000 + [2000 × £25])	(2000 × £55)

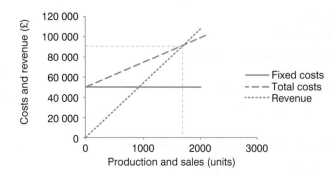

Figure 6
Foster Beniform Limited: Break-even chart (fixed costs at £50 000)

ii) Reading from the chart, the break-even point in units appears to be around 1700 units; the break-even point in sales value appears to be around £90 000.

iii) Formula calculations

	£
Selling price per unit	55.00
Variable costs per unit	(25.00)
Contribution per unit	30.00

$$\text{Break-even point (in units)} = \frac{\text{Fixed costs}}{\text{Contribution per unit}}$$

$$= \frac{50\ 000}{30.00} = 1667 \text{ units (to nearest whole unit)}$$

Break-even point in sales value = 1667 units × £55 = £91 685.

14.9   Gropius Maplewood Limited

	£
Selling price per unit	150
Variable costs per unit	(63)
Contribution per unit	87

$$\text{Break-even point (in units)} = \frac{\text{Fixed costs}}{\text{Contribution per unit}}$$

$$= \frac{90\ 000}{87} = 1034 \text{ units}$$

The break-even point for 20X5 is estimated as d) 1034 units to the nearest unit.

14.10   Gimball Grace Limited

Target net profit for 20X9: £36 500 × 110% = £40 150.

Contribution per unit = £21.00 (selling price) − £7.50 (variable costs) = £13.50.

$$\text{Target sales in units} = \frac{\text{Fixed costs} + \text{Target profit}}{\text{Contribution per unit}}$$

$$= \frac{54\ 000 + 40\ 150}{13.50} = 6974 \text{ units}$$

The correct answer is a) 6974 fan heaters.

14.11   Garbage Solutions Limited

Contribution calculation:

	£
Selling price per unit	25.00
Less: variable labour costs	(3.20)
Variable raw materials costs	(4.20)
Contribution per unit	17.60

$$\text{Break-even point} = \frac{\text{Fixed costs}}{\text{Contribution per unit}}$$
$$= \frac{178\ 900}{17.60} = 10\ 165 \text{ units}$$

$$\text{Target sales in units} = \frac{\text{Fixed costs} + \text{Target profit}}{\text{Contribution per unit}}$$
$$= \frac{178\ 900 + 83\ 150}{17.60} = 14\ 889$$

The margin of safety is the difference between target sales and break-even sales:
$$14\ 889 - 10\ 165 = 4724$$

The correct answer is d) 4724 units.

14.12 Hubert and Hix Limited

The contribution per unit from the rucksack designed for the Moroccan market would be:

	£
Selling price per unit	50.00
Variable costs per unit	(26.30)
Contribution per unit	23.70

The contribution per unit is a positive figure, therefore the advice to management, based solely upon the accounting figures, would be to accept Raoul's order. This advice would be appropriate provided that spare production capacity was available and provided the level of fixed costs would not increase. What non-financial factors should be taken into consideration?

The sales of this special order are all to Morocco; therefore it is quite likely that French and British buyers would not find out that similar rucksacks were available at a substantially lower price. The fact that the specification is lower also helps; if Western European buyers were to ask why the rucksacks were priced so much lower in Morocco, it would be quite reasonable to point out that the product was of a different quality (although the difference in variable costs is only £2.70 between the two grades of product, suggesting that the quality difference is not very great).

Would the company suffer if it became known that it was offering a product of lesser quality? This is a factor that needs to be borne in mind by producers of high quality goods. However, as noted above, the quality differential is not likely to be very noticeable.

In the circumstances, the company should consider seriously accepting Raoul's order, although the sales director might like to investigate Raoul's assertions regarding the Moroccan market. Is it really true that there would be few buyers in Morocco at the company's normal prices? Or is Raoul just saying this to beat the company down on price?

14.13 Inez & Pilar Fashions

Because fixed costs increase with the increase in production capacity, it is necessary to look at the level of incremental profits that could be made. We can examine these at two levels:

Optimistic incremental sales forecast

	£
Sales (£345 000 − 310 000)	35 000
Incremental variable costs: £35 000 × 30%	(10 500)
Incremental fixed costs	(15 000)
Incremental net profit	9 500

Pessimistic incremental sales forecast

	£
Sales	20 000
Incremental variable costs: £20 000 × 30%	(6 000)
Incremental fixed costs	(15 000)
Incremental net loss	(1 000)

Clearly, if the pessimistic forecast is accurate, a net loss will be incurred by expanding the production facilities. However, at most levels of incremental sales some profit would be made. Unless the directors are very averse to taking risks, and/or they feel that the pessimistic forecast is the most likely outcome, it is probably worth expanding production facilities.

Other factors to take into account would be:

- Could the additional capacity be used to produce new product lines?
- Is the current constraint on production capacity causing problems with customers? (If customers are becoming impatient because of delays in production there may be a loss of goodwill; this could be an argument in favour of expanding the facilities even if there is a small risk of an incremental loss.)

14.14 Juniper Jefferson Limited

i) Contribution per unit of limiting factor

	Deluxe	Super deluxe
	£	£
Selling price	150	165
Variable cost of raw materials		
Aluminium (at £8.50 per kg)	(38.25)	(42.50)
Other raw materials	(12.50)	(15.00)
Variable cost of labour	(13.65)	(15.60)
Contribution per unit	85.60	91.90
Kilos of material used		
Deluxe (£28.25/8.50)	4.5	
Super-deluxe (£42.50/8.50)		5
Contribution per unit of limiting factor	85.60/4.5 = £19.02	91.90/5 = £18.38

ii) Production plan

The directors should follow a production plan that produces the deluxe model in preference to the super-deluxe, where possible.

The availability of the raw material in the next three months is:

	kg
Already in stock	350
Three month's purchases	3 000
	3 350

If all of this material were to be used in the production of deluxe buggies, it would be possible to make 3350/4.5 = 744 deluxe buggies (rounded down to the nearest whole number).

a) If demand for the deluxe is 800 units, then it makes sense to turn production over completely to the production of the deluxe (800 > 744).

b) If demand for the deluxe is 600 units, then the maximum 600 should be produced. This would mean using 600 × 4.5 kg = 2700 kg of the scarce raw material, leaving 3350 − 2700 = 650 kg for producing super-deluxe buggies.

So 650 kg would produce 650/5 = 130 super-deluxe buggies at a rate of usage of 5 kg per buggy. The production plan would thus be:

   Deluxe = 600
   Super-deluxe = 130.

CHAPTER 15

15.1 The £15 000 spent on the initial land survey is irrelevant to the business decision because the expenditure has already been made. This is an example of a sunk cost; the correct answer, therefore, is c.

15.2   Mellor & Ribchester Limited

i)   ARR calculations

$$\frac{\text{Average expected return (accounting profit)}}{\text{Average capital employed}} \times 100 = \text{ARR\%}$$

£150 000 of non-current asset expenditure, depreciated over six years on a straight-line basis, results in an annual depreciation charge of £150 000/6 = £25 000. This must be taken into account in calculating accounting profit.

The average profit per year generated is:

Year	£000
1	$0 - 25 = (25)$
2	$68 - 25 = 43$
3	$71 - 25 = 46$
4	$54 - 25 = 29$
5	$28 - 25 = 3$
6	$10 \quad 25 = (15)$
Total profit	81

$$\frac{\text{£81 000}}{6} = \text{£13 500}$$

Time	£000
0	150
6	0
Average	150/2 = 75

$$\text{ARR} = \frac{\text{£13 500}}{75\,000} \times 100 = 18\%$$

ii)   Payback period

Cumulative cash flow reaches the zero position sometime during year 4. Payback to the nearest month is:

Time	Cash flow £000	Cumulative cash flow £000
0	(150)	(150)
1	0	(150)
2	68	(82)
3	71	(11)
4	54	43
5	28	71
6	10	81

3 years + (11/54 × 12 months) = 3 years and 2 months (to nearest whole month).

Note: the cash inflows in this example do not start until year 2. This does not change the methods of working out ARR or payback.

15.3   The compounding factor for an investment over four years at 3% per year is:
$(1.03)^4 = (1.03) \times (1.03) \times (1.03) \times (1.03) = 1.126$. The correct answer is d.

15.4   The compounding factor is: $(1.06)^4 = 1.263$
$1.263 \times £312 = £394$ (to the nearest £). The correct answer is a.

15.5 The discounting factor is:

$$\frac{1}{(1.1)^3} = 0.751$$

The correct answer is b.

15.6 The correct discount factor (from tables) is: 0.567.

PV of £1300 receivable at the end of year 5, assuming a constant discount rate of 12% is:

$$£1300 \times 0.567 = £737 \text{ (to nearest £)}.$$

The correct answer is d.

15.7 Naylor Coulthard Limited

Calculation of NPV of the advertising promotion project

Time	Cash flow £	Discount factor (from table)	Discounted cash flow £
0	(250 000)	1	(250 000)
1	196 000	0.917	179 732
2	168 000	0.842	141 456
TOTAL			71 188

The NPV is positive which suggests that the project should be accepted.

15.8 i) NPV at 12% cost of capital

Time	Cash flow £	Discount factor (from table)	Discounted cash flow £
0	(680 000)	1	(680 000)
1	180 000	0.893	160 740
2	200 000	0.797	159 400
3	240 000	0.712	170 880
4	350 000	0.636	222 600
			33 620

ii) IRR

12% cost of capital produces a positive NPV. The IRR (the point at which NPV = 0) must therefore be higher than this. Calculating NPV at 16%:

Time	Cash flow £	Discount factor (from table)	Discounted cash flow £
0	(680 000)	1	(680 000)
1	180 000	0.862	155 160
2	200 000	0.743	148 600
3	240 000	0.641	153 840
4	350 000	0.552	193 200
			(29 200)

IRR must, therefore, lie somewhere between 12% and 16%.

Using a discount rate of 12% NPV = £33 620

Using a discount rate of 16% NPV = £(29 200).

The total distance between these two figures is £33 620 + 29 200 = £62 820.

Expressed diagrammatically:

The distance between 12% and IRR is $\dfrac{33\,620}{62\,820} \times 4\% = 2.14\%$

IRR is 12% + 2.14% = 14.14%

(NB: the IRR according to computer calculation is 14.07%.)

15.9   Outhwaite Benson Limited
Sunbed investment project

i) NPV at 14% cost of capital

Time	Cash flow £	Discount factor (from table)	Discounted cash flow £
0	(180 000)	1	(180 000)
1	46 000	0.877	40 342
2	46 000	0.769	35 374
3	46 000	0.675	31 050
4	46 000	0.592	27 232
5	46 000 + 15 000	0.519	31 659
			(14 343)

ii) IRR

14% cost of capital produces a negative NPV. The IRR (the point at which NPV = 0) must therefore be lower than this. Calculating NPV at 10%:

Time	Cash flow £	Discount factor (from table)	Discounted cash flow £
0	(180 000)	1	(180 000)
1	46 000	0.909	41 814
2	46 000	0.826	37 996
3	46 000	0.751	34 546
4	46 000	0.683	31 418
5	46 000 + 15 000	0.621	37 881
			3 655

IRR must, therefore, lie somewhere between 10% and 14% (but much nearer to 10% than to 14%).
Using a discount rate of 10% NPV = £3655
Using a discount rate of 14% NPV = £(14 343).
The total distance between these two figures is £3655 + 14 343 = £17 998

The distance between 10% and IRR is $\dfrac{3655}{17\,998} \times 4\% = 0.81\%$

IRR is 10% + 0.81% = 10.81%
(NB: the IRR according to computer calculation is 10.77%)

iii) On the basis of the results of the NPV and IRR calculations it appears that the directors should not make the investment in the sunbeds. The company's cost of capital is 14% and this investment falls well short of that target.

However, the directors may consider other factors in making their decision. For example:

- How important is it to the future of the business that it diversifies its range of services? Will the hairdressing business continue to produce strong returns? If there is some uncertainty, it may make sense to diversify.
- Are competitors offering sunbeds? If they are, the existing hairdressing business could be damaged if Outhwaite Benson does not do the same.
- Is it possible that the provision of the sunbed service will attract new customers who may also use the hairdressing services? If so has this potential for additional sales been taken into account in the projected cash flow figures?

Finally, how reliable are the estimates? If the projected cash flows are put into a spreadsheet the directors can perform a series of 'what if' calculations to test out various levels of projection (optimistic, pessimistic, average).

CHAPTER 16

16.1 Subject: Summary of the benefits of effective budgeting
To: The directors of Brewster Fitzpayne Limited
From: Management accountant
A budgeting system assists senior management in its tasks of planning and controlling business activity by ensuring that a detailed plan is laid out and quantified for a specified period (usually one year). The budget should help the company to attain its longer-term objectives, and it is important to ensure that there is a clear relationship between the budget and the longer-term business strategy determined by the directors.

Budgets allow for coordinated efforts on the part of all personnel and departments. Once the key elements of the budget have been determined (usually starting with the sales budget) budget guidelines can be issued to all departments and managerial staff. They will then be required to submit draft budgets for their own areas. Senior management must then ensure that these drafts are amended where necessary to ensure proper coordination of plans. Senior staff have an overview of the business objectives and should be able to ensure that individual budgets mesh together to achieve optimal outcomes.

If properly used, budgets can inspire and motivate staff to greater efforts. It is important that staff lower down the hierarchy feel a sense of 'ownership' of the budget so that they will be more inclined to make the extra effort to achieve targets.

Actual business performance should be monitored carefully against budget. If this is done properly and on a timely basis, senior managers are able to control operations much more effectively than is possible without a budget. Timely and effective control allows for higher quality decision making.

Finally, it is possible to use budgets as a basis for individual and group performance evaluation. For example, sales staff could be rewarded by means of bonuses or extra commission for exceeding budget targets. This use of budgets must be handled carefully, however. If targets for achievement are set too high then dissatisfaction and demotivation may well result.

16.2 Pirozhki Products Limited
The correct answer is b) 14 100. Explanation:
The forecast for opening inventory at 1 March 20X6 is 75% of forecast sales in March:

$$75\% \times 12\,000 \text{ units} = 9000 \text{ units}$$

The forecast for closing inventory at 31 March 20X6 is 75% of forecast sales in April:

$$75\% \times 14\,800 \text{ units} = 11\,100 \text{ units}$$

Transfers out of finished goods inventory will be 12 000 units in March (ie. the quantity sold), so production required is:

	£
Opening inventory	9 000
Production (bal. fig.)	14 100
Transfers out of inventory	(12 000)
Closing inventory	11 100

16.3 Luminant Productions

i) Production budget July–September 20X5

	Opening inventory units	Production: units	Transfers out of production (for sales): units	Closing inventory units
July	6 000	8 100	(8 600)	5 500
August	5 500	7 700	(8 200)	5 000
September	5 000	8 500	(9 000)	4 500

ii) Raw materials purchases budget: July–September 20X5

Closing inventory + Raw materials used in production − Opening inventory = Raw materials purchases

	Opening inventory of raw material £	Purchases of raw materials (bal. fig.) £	Raw materials used in production £	Closing inventory of raw material £
July	2 800	16 400	£2 × 8 100 = £16 200	3 000
August	3 000	15 500	£2 × 7 700 = £15 400	3 100
September	3 100	17 100	£2 × 8 500 = £17 000	3 200

16.4 Barfield Primrose

Budget overhead recovery rate, based on machine hours:

$$\frac{\text{Budget production overheads}}{\text{Machine hours}} = \frac{312\ 390}{17\ 355} = £18.00 \text{ per machine hour}$$

The total production cost of one ice cream maker is, therefore:

	£
Prime cost	61.00
1.5 machine hours × £18.00 per hour	27.00
Production cost	88.00

Barfield Primrose: Budgeted statement of profit or loss for the three months ending 31 March 20X9

	Jan £	Feb £	March £
Sales	620 × £145 = 89 900	610 × £145 = 88 450	640 × £145 = 92 800
Cost of sales (= production cost)	620 × £88 = (54 560)	610 × £88 = (53 680)	640 × £88 = (56 320)
Gross profit	35 340	34 770	36 480
Admin and selling	(18 400)	(19 250)	(18 900)
Net profit	16 940	15 520	17 580

16.5 The correct answer is c) £22 450. Explanation:

In February Reinhart's budget sales receipts will be estimated as follows:

	£
In respect of sales made in January: 75% × £21 000	15 750
In respect of sales made in December: 25% × £26 800	6 700
Total	22 450

16.6   Skippy's tour operating business

i) Skippy: Budget statement of cash flows for January–March 20X5

	January £	February £	March £	Total £
Receipts				
Trip 1	25 440	–	–	25 440
Trip 2	–	25 440	–	25 440
	25 440	25 440		50 880
Payments				
Hotel: Trip 1	7 140	7 140	–	14 280
Trip 2	–	7 140	7 140	14 280
Coach	2 600	2 600	–	5 200
Insurance bond: 2 × £ 1500	3 000	–	–	3 000
Telephone bill	–	–	360	360
Office expenses	200	200	200	600
Total payments	12 940	17 080	7 700	37 720
Opening balance	0	12 500	20 860	
Add: receipts	25 440	25 440	–	
Less: payments	(12 940)	(17 080)	(7 700)	
Closing balance	12 500	20 860	13 160	

ii) Skippy: Budget statement of profit or loss for the three months ending 31 March 20X5

	£
Sales	50 880
Expenses	
Hotel costs (£14 280 × 2)	28 560
Coach	5 200
Insurance bonds	3 000
Telephone	360
Office costs	600
Advertising	3 000
Computer depreciation:	
£2 000 × 20% = 400: for 3 months (3/12)	100
	40 820
Net profit	10 060

iii) Skippy: Budget statement of financial position at 31 March 20X5

	£
Computer at cost	2 000
Less: accumulated depreciation	(100)
Carrying amount	1 900
Cash at bank	13 160
	15 060
Capital introduced	5 000
Profit	10 060
	15 060

Note that capital introduced by Skippy consists of the advertising expenditure paid for before January 20X5 (£3000) and the computer (£2000).

16.7   Skippy's tour operating business
Working 1: Actual sales

	£
Trip 1: 42 × £530	22 260
Trip 2: 50 × £530	26 500
	48 760

Working 2: Hotel costs

	£
Trip 1: 42 × 7 nights × £42.50 per person	12 495
Trip 2: 50 × 7 nights × £42.50 per person	14 875
	27 370

Skippy: Actual and budgeted statement of profit or loss for the three months ending 31 March 20X5

	Actual £	Budget £	Variance £
Sales (working 1)	48 760	50 880	(2 120)
Expenses			
Hotel costs (working 2)	27 370	28 560	1 190
Coach	5 200	5 200	–
Insurance bonds	3 000	3 000	–
Telephone	455	360	(95)
Office costs (£230 + £350 + £270)	850	600	(250)
Advertising	3 000	3 000	–
Computer depreciation: £2000 × 20% = 400, so for 3 months = £100	100	100	–
	39 975	40 820	845
Net profit	8 785	10 060	(1 275)

* Variance is the term used in costing for differences between actual and budget figures. Adverse variances are shown in brackets in the comparison and favourable variances are shown without brackets. Variances are examined in more detail in Chapter 17.

Skippy: Actual and budgeted statement of financial position at 31 March 20X5

	Actual £	Budget £
Computer at cost	2 000	2 000
Less: accumulated depreciation	(100)	(100)
Carrying amount	1 900	1 900
Cash at bank (see working 3)	11 885	13 160
	13 785	15 060
Capital introduced	5 000	5 000
Profit	8 785	10 060
	13 785	15 060

Working 3: Actual cash at bank

	£	£
Receipts (same as sales revenue)		48 760
Payments	39 975	
Less: depreciation (non-cash item)	(100)	
Less: advertising paid for by Skippy	(3 000)	(36 875)
		11 885

Overall, Skippy's business has performed slightly worse than budget: actual sales are 95.8% of budget, but there has been a related saving on hotel costs which helps to offset the variance. Office and telephone costs are higher than budgeted. However, overall, the differences are fairly minor and Skippy is likely to be quite pleased with his first three months in business.

16.8   Lamar Bristol plc

This is a relatively efficient approach to budget setting. While some external research into competitors' sales figures and general economic conditions is required, the resource input to the research process is unlikely to be extensive. Because the budget is market-led it is based upon economic reality, and is therefore quite likely to provide a realistic target for stores.

However, there are some problems with this approach. It is incremental in that it builds upon the sales budget for the previous year. However, if this budget amount was less than could have been achieved with greater effort, the directors' approach to budgeting does not question or challenge it.

It ignores differences between stores. Some stores will struggle more than others to achieve this across the board target because of, for example, local competition which is stronger in some locations than others. A percentage increase that is easily achievable by one store might be impossible for another. A further problem is likely to arise if store managers' remuneration is linked to performance. If a store manager is set a target that is impossible to achieve, resulting in no bonus payment, he or she is likely to feel resentful and demotivated.

CHAPTER 17

17.1   Denholm Pargeter Ltd

March 20X9: budget for XP04/H flexed for 1300 units

	£
Sales: 1300 units × £30 per unit	39 000
Direct materials: 1300 units × (3 kg × £1.20)	4 680
Direct labour: 1300 units × (2 hours × £8.50)	22 100
Prime cost	26 780

17.2   Darblay Harriett Ltd

The correct answer is c) £11 700. Explanation:

November 20X1: budget flexed for 2600 units

	£
Sales: 2600 units × £19.50	50 700
Direct materials: 2600 × (2 metres × £2.00)	(10 400)
Direct labour: 2600 × (1 hour × £6.00)	(15 600)
Production overhead	(10 000)
	14 700
Selling and administrative overhead	(3 000)
Net profit	11 700

Edwards and Sheerness Ltd: general information for the answers to questions 17.3 to 17.8: Comparison of original budget, flexed budget and actual:

Flexed budget for 2650 units

	£
Sales: 2650 units × £29.00	76 850
Direct materials: 2650 × (3 kg × £3.00)	(23 850)
Direct labour: 2650 × (1.5 hours × £4.40)	(17 490)
Production overhead	(17 000)
	18 510
Other overheads	(3 500)
Net profit	15 010

Comparison of original budget, flexed budget and actual:

	Original budget £	Flexed budget £	Actual £
Sales	72 500	76 850	74 200
Direct materials	(22 500)	(23 850)	(24 486)
Direct labour	(16 500)	(17 490)	(18 921)
Production overhead	(17 000)	(17 000)	(16 900)
	16 500	18 510	13 893
Other overheads	(3 500)	(3 500)	(3 600)
Net profit	13 000	15 010	10 293

17.3 Sales profit volume variance
The correct answer is d) £2010 (F). Explanation:

Flexed budget net profit	15 010
Original budget net profit	13 000
	2 010 (F)

17.4 Sales price variance
The correct answer is d) £2650 (A). Explanation:

Actual volume of sales at actual selling price: 2650 × £28	74 200
Actual volume of sales at standard selling price: 2650 × £29	76 850
	2 650 (A)

17.5 Direct materials price variance
The correct answer is b) £2226 (A). Explanation:

Actual quantity of materials used at actual price:	
2650 × 2.8 kg = 7420 × £3.30	24 486
Actual quantity of materials used at standard price: 7420 × £3.00	22 260
	2 226 (A)

17.6 Direct materials quantity variance
The correct answer is c) £1590 (F). Explanation:

Actual quantity of materials used at standard price: 7420 × £3.00	22 260
Standard quantity of materials used at standard price:	
2650 × 3.0 kg = 7950 × £3.00	23 850
	1 590 (F)

17.7 Direct labour rate variance
The correct answer is d) £901 (F). Explanation:

Actual hours at actual wage rate: 2650 × 1.7 hours = 4505 × £4.20	18 921
Actual hours at standard wage rate: 4505 × £4.40	19 822
	901 (F)

17.8 Direct labour efficiency variance
The correct answer is b) £2332 (A).
Explanation:

Actual hours at standard wage rate: 4505 × £4.40	19 822
Standard hours at standard wage rate: 2650 × 1.5 hours = 3975 × £4.40	17 490
	2 332 (A)

17.9   Ferguson Farrar Ltd

i) Total variable production overhead variance

	£
Actual variable production overhead	26 250
Flexed budget variable production overhead	25 200
	1 050 (A)

ii) Total fixed production overhead expenditure variance

	£
Actual fixed production overhead	48 750
Flexed budget fixed production overhead	50 400
	1 650 (F)

17.10   Grindleton Gears Ltd

i) The variances which are regarded as significant according to the company's 5% criterion are:

Direct materials price variance (£1 650 000 (A): 5.8% of flexed budget)

Variable production overhead variance (£1 400 000 (F): 16.2% of flexed budget).

ii) Possible reasons for the direct materials price variances are:

● unexpected price rises across the industry
● failing to obtain quantity discounts for large orders
● variation in material quality
● volatile market for material, leading to unexpected increases or decrease in price.

Possible reasons for the variable production overhead variances are:

● price changes because of events in the wider economy
● improved management control over costs
● some items of expense have simply gone unrecorded (possible in this case as the variance is so large).

iii) Actual figures can be derived from the information given by adding the flexed budget amount to the variances, as follows:

	£
Sales 123 470 + 1030	124 500
Direct materials: 28 250 + 1650 + 106	(30 006)
Direct labour: 29 900 − 200	(29 700)
Variable production overheads: 8640 − 1400	(7 240)
Fixed production overheads: 19 780 − 339	(19 441)
Actual profit	38 113

17.11   Bellcraft

Expense and bureaucracy

It is undeniably the case that standard costing systems involve some expense. However, the benefits of any good system should outweigh the costs. It will be important to monitor the costs of implementing the system to make sure that they do not get out of hand. Quantifying the benefits of the system is not easy, but better control should ultimately result in benefits such as improved profitability, less wastage and reduced storage costs. The system is bureaucratic in that it involves the production of reports. However, the quantity of information could be reduced by using an exception reporting basis.

Lack of timeliness

This has traditionally been a problem associated with standard costing systems, especially where reporting is normally done on a monthly basis. However, reporting can be done much more frequently than that, especially now that computer capacity has increased so much. We could aim for weekly, or even more frequent, reporting of variances so that timeliness is not a problem. Even if there is a passage of time between events and their reporting, it does not have to mean that variance investigation is useless. The cause of the variance can be identified, and remedial action taken to ensure that its causes are tackled.

CHAPTER 18

18.1 Three key characteristics of management information:

1   It should be produced quickly so that managers can respond rapidly to it.
2   It should be useful, and easily comprehensible.
3   The cost of producing the information should not outweigh its benefits.

18.2 Golfstore Retail plc

The advantages of divisionalization for this company include the following:

Divisions based on regions or (eventually) countries in Western Europe will ensure that management can exploit local opportunities that might not come to the attention of head office management. For example, a regional management team should be better aware of the trading conditions in their area, and if, say, a new golf course is planned for a particular town, they could ensure that a new store is opened in the area.

Divisionalization can result in better motivated managers. This can be enhanced if senior divisional managers are rewarded at least partly on the basis of results achieved. A degree of competition between divisions can be healthy and productive.

In this particular case, the company is beginning to expand. If divisionalization is instituted now along a geographical split within the UK, a pattern is established which could make the addition of future divisions within Europe relatively straightforward.

18.3 Division Alpha is a) a profit centre.

18.4 i) Quarterly divisional performance statement for BD

	£000
Sales	1 671
Less: variable costs $(280 + 311)$	(591)
Contribution	1 080
Less: Controllable fixed costs $(580 - 37)$	(543)
Controllable profit	537
Less: Non-controllable fixed costs $(37 + 112)$	(149)
Divisional profit before allocation of head office costs	388
Head office cost allocation	(337)
Divisional profit before tax	51

ii) The division's performance should be judged on the basis of the amount of profit over which it has control. Controllable profit is £537 000.

18.5 1   Transfer pricing can have an impact on divisional performance. Where divisions sell goods to each other, it is necessary to identify an appropriate price for the goods. The level of price affects the allocation of profit between divisions and so may affect profit-related remuneration. Where it is difficult to agree realistic transfer prices divisions have an incentive to source goods from outside the company and in this case the profit goes outside the company. If divisional performance is affected by transfer pricing agreements, there is a knock-on effect on the Return on Investment measurement.

2   The calculation of Return on Investment can also be affected by the valuation of net assets. Higher asset valuation results in a lower ROI. For this reason, managers may be reluctant to replace worn out non-current assets.

18.6 Tripp and Hopp Limited

Both financial and non-financial performance indicators should relate to the company's strategic plans. The company's objective relates to the provision of a service, so its performance indicators should be service-oriented.

There are many possible ways of measuring the company's progress in meeting its objectives. The table below suggests some possible performance indicators, and ways of measuring them.

Aspect of service	Performance indicator	Measurement
Competitive	Price of service (eg. commission charged)	Comparison with competitors' commission arrangements
Competitive	Customer satisfaction	Could be measured using a questionnaire on the website, or a follow-up survey
Efficient	Number of complaints	Website link to a complaints form. Monitoring number of complaints and outcomes
Efficient	Speed of transaction	Measure time taken for each transaction on the website and compare averages over time
Efficient	Ease of use by customer	Could be measured using a questionnaire on the website, or a follow up survey
Secure	Number of security breaches over a period	Cost of security breaches could be measured and compared over time

18.7   Memo
To: Head of Department
Balanced Scorecard

The Balanced Scorecard (BS) is a summary of management information that is used by managers to examine the performance of the business. The BS contains four dimensions relating to the fundamentals of a particular business. Any business that uses it has to ask the following questions:

● How do customers see us? (The customer perspective)
● What must we excel at? (The internal perspective)
● Can we continue to improve and create value? (The innovation and learning perspective)
● How do we look to shareholders? (The financial perspective)

The business needs to establish goals in respect of each of the four perspectives, and related performance measures that will help management in judging progress towards the goals. This may all seem fairly complicated, and it would certainly involve quite a lot of work up-front, but it results in a way of reporting useful and relevant performance measures concisely. Incidentally, some of the performance measures (although not necessarily all of them) would involve the use of figures.

Brian is quite right – the BS system has been adopted by very large numbers of US, European and Australian companies. The aeroplane analogy comes from the originators of the BS (two American academics: Robert Kaplan and David Norton). They compared running a business to flying an aeroplane: both pilots and managers need information about all sorts of measurements to be clearly set out in front of them.

I hope this explanation helps. There are several detailed sources of information on the subject of the BS – books, articles and websites. Let me know if you'd like any references.

CHAPTER 19

19.1   The correct answer is b), property, plant and equipment which is classified as non-current assets, and therefore does not comprise part of working capital.

19.2   The correct answer is a) a loss of goodwill on the part of suppliers, who may cease to supply goods to the business.

19.3   Company A is more likely to be a supermarket business. This conclusion is indicated by the low level of trade receivables and the relatively high level of non-current assets.

19.4   Holding costs comprise any incremental costs involved in the storage of inventory. Ordering costs include any costs of preparing orders and the costs involved in recording receipts of goods into inventory. There tends to be an inverse relationship between the two types of cost: where goods are ordered infrequently, ordering costs are low because there are relatively few orders, but holding costs tend to be high. Where there are frequent orders, ordering costs are high, but the frequency of orders means that relatively lower amounts of inventory are held and so holding costs tend to be lower.

19.5 Prestbury Hannah Limited
Applying the EOQ model, the economic order quantity (Q) is as follows:

$$Q = \sqrt{\frac{2 \times 7000 \times £37.00}{£28.50}}$$
$$Q = 135 \text{ units}$$

19.6 Bright Sigmund Limited
Briefing paper on the EOQ model

The Economic Order Quantity model (EOQ) is used as a means of minimizing total incremental inventory cost. It aims to strike a balance between holding costs and ordering costs and to ensure that the optimum quantity of inventory is held. Infrequent orders reduce ordering costs, but, because more inventory is held, tend to increase holding costs. The converse is true where there are frequent orders. Using the EOQ for important lines of inventory could help to reduce inventory levels overall, and to minimize incremental costs. The use of EOQ would require the company to estimate demand, item by item, and also to estimate holding costs per unit of inventory, and ordering costs.

There are some problems with the use of EOQ. It inevitably involves a great deal of estimation, and errors in estimation are likely to produce sub-optimal inventory levels. In a seasonal business like ours, estimating average annual demand is unlikely to produce sensible answers, and there would be a risk of running out of key items of inventory at busy times.

19.7 Sims & Aktar Limited
Factoring services

The principal advantages of using factoring services for the collection of trade receivables are, firstly, that there is a cash flow advantage. If we transfer our receivables to a factor, we will receive a significant percentage of the amounts outstanding straight away rather than having to wait, on average, 67 days to receive the cash. This immediate cash inflow will make a very significant difference to our operating cycle, and will reduce or eliminate the need to make up cash shortages by going into overdraft.

The second significant advantage is the saving in administrative costs. It might be possible to reduce the number of clerical staff involved in credit control, or to deploy them elsewhere.

There are, however, some disadvantages. The immediate cash flow arising from transferring our trade receivables to a factor is a one-off event that cannot be repeated. Also, there is a cost involved. Factoring is, essentially, a financing arrangement and there is a fee payable to the factor for financing and for administration. This fee is typically between 1% to 3% of the value of receivables factored. However, the costs involved could be outweighed by the benefits received including the savings in our own costs.

19.8 Mohinder Benton Limited

Overall, there has been a deterioration in the efficiency of trade receivables collection between April 20X3 and April 20X4. Although the percentage outstanding for over 120 days has improved slightly between the two years, the percentage outstanding for over 90 days $(10.3 + 6.7 = 17\%)$ is worse than it was a year ago $(3.4 + 8.2 = 11.6\%)$. Also, fewer amounts are paid within the 30-day limit – a year ago 40.2% of amounts due were in the 30 day category. This is not an impressive percentage, but it has declined still further in the year to 30 April 20X4.

The additional information is not encouraging. The news that over 10% of customers have been permitted to exceed their credit limits is disturbing, and suggests that controls in this respect are weak. Moreover, a large percentage of customers had reached their credit limit (21.1% of customers are in this category) suggesting that there may be significant problems with their accounts.

A substantial amount was written off at the most recent year-end date. The disappearance of these balances from the list may account for the apparent improvement in the seriously overdue balances (over 120 days).

A large number of customers (13%) are in dispute with the company over amounts due. This is a very worrying indicator. It suggests that the company's record keeping may be faulty and/or that disputes are not thoroughly investigated or promptly resolved.

In summary, the picture presented by this information provides several causes for concern, and suggests that immediate effective action is required to improve the collection of trade receivables.

19.9 The correct answer is d) Average inventory turnover period + average trade receivables turnover period − average trade payables turnover period.

19.10 Burstein Lyall Limited.

The operating cycle gives an indication of a business's cash and borrowing needs, and it is helpful in planning for the arrangement of any short-term borrowing requirements.

Burstein Lyall's operating cycle has lengthened between the two year-end dates. Without further information about the components of working capital it is impossible to say how this has arisen. However, a lengthening operating cycle means greater pressure on the company's cash resources. The operating cycle at both year-ends is significantly greater than the industry average. Although it is important always to be wary of this type of comparison – Burstein Lyall may not be representative of the industry for quite valid reasons – it may indicate that a significant proportion of the business's competitors are better at managing their working capital.

19.11 Skipholt Limited

Operating cycle = 39.4 days (trade receivables turnover) + 49.6 days (inventory turnover) − 43.7 days (trade payables turnover) = 45.3 days.

19.12 Linwood Lees Limited

Workings:

$$\text{Average inventory} = \frac{99\,400 + 91\,650}{2} = 95\,525$$

$$\text{Average trade receivables} = \frac{86\,700 + 89\,400}{2} = 88\,050$$

$$\text{Average trade payables} = \frac{67\,530 + 65\,500}{2} = 66\,515$$

$$\text{Average inventory turnover:} \frac{95\,525 \times 365}{477\,400} = 73.0 \text{ days}$$

$$\text{Average trade receivables turnover:} \frac{88\,050 \times 365}{622\,550} = 48.5 \text{ days}$$

$$\text{Average trade payables turnover:} \frac{66\,515 \times 365}{396\,600} = 61.2 \text{ days}$$

Linwood Lees' operating cycle is therefore 73.0 + 48.5 − 61.2 days = 60.3 days

Other ratios:

Current ratio

20X5: Current assets/current liabilities = 202 170/100 530 = 2.01 (including short-term borrowings).

20X4: Current assets/current liabilities = 199 900/87 500 = 2.28 (including short-term borrowings).

Gross profit margin

20X5: Gross profit/revenue × 100 = 185 150/662 550 × 100 = 27.9%
20X4: Gross profit/revenue × 100 = 216 340/651 440 × 100 = 33.2%

Report to directors

More information would be required about earlier periods, and about industry averages, to be able to say whether or not the operating cycle of the business is reasonable. The company's current ratio gives no cause for concern in either year.

Revenue has increased in the year, but gross profit margin has slumped from 33.2% to 27.9%. Inventory has increased. Reasons for this may include deliberate accumulation of inventory for a special sales promotion, or inefficiency in purchasing decisions, or a large one-off purchase of inventory to take advantage of discounts. However, a more positive sign is that expenses have decreased. It is possible that the 20X5 figures included a significant non-recurring item.

Trade receivables have decreased despite the increase in revenue, suggesting improved efficiency in collection of outstanding receivables. Trade payables have also increased from the previous year, which may be part of a deliberate effort to exploit this interest-free source of credit. However, the average inventory turnover figure is over 60 days and it is quite likely that suppliers are growing impatient with the company and there may be a resulting loss of goodwill. The absolute increase in payables is not, however, substantial, and it would be consistent with an especially large purchase of inventory, as noted above, to take advantage of favourable discounts.

A final point to note is that the company's cash resources have declined, at the same time as a large increase (50%) in short-term borrowings has occurred. Long-term liabilities have also increased from an already high level. Although this factor has no immediate significance as it will not fall due for more than one year, it contributes to a general picture of a company whose management of working capital has declined.

CHAPTER 20

20.1   Erika

The main points for the business plan, and the related questions, are as follows:

Description of the service to be offered

Is the service highly specialized, or is it a more general design service? For example, the design services offered may be principally focused on, say, company identity and logo designs, or alternatively upon graphic design input into advertising material. Or, Erika may be planning to cover a broad range of services, depending upon her talents and interests.

Market for the service

- Who will be the principal customers for the services offered?
- Has Erika investigated the market by carrying out any market research?
- Who are the principal competitors? Are they well established?
- How difficult will it be to break into the market for design services?

Profile of Erika

This will include training and education, relevant experience, age, an analysis of personal strengths and weaknesses, and a current portfolio of her best work.

- Does Erika have the appropriate profile of experience for the work she is planning to do?
- Is her portfolio up to date and does it contain examples of the type of work she will be undertaking to provide as a self-employed designer?

Initial investment required

This will be a particularly important section if Erika is planning to borrow money. Has she prepared a plan of her expenditure and income in the first year to 18 months following her business start-up? Relevant expenditure will probably include the following:

- office rental and business rates
- utilities bills (water, electricity, telephone)
- advertising and marketing
- office equipment and computer
- insurance.

Also, how will Erika support herself in the early months of her new business? In this type of business, Erika will need to find the work, do it, submit it and then invoice the client. Under normal commercial arrangements payment will follow about a month later. So, there is a time lag of up to several months between initially being commissioned for the work and finally receiving payment. In the meantime, Erika needs to live off something, and this element must be built into her initial plans.

Detailed financial projections

If Erika is looking for business start-up finance she will need to prepare detailed financial projections in the form of a budget, showing the projected profit (or loss) and cash flow in the business. Once the business starts she will need to keep business accounting records and submit tax returns. She may need to register for VAT.

- Does Erika have financial management or accountancy skills?
- Will she need an accountant to provide accountancy and tax advice?

Other issues

Will any other professional services be required in the first year or so of the business? For example, Erika may need legal advice in negotiating a lease on the office. Is Erika planning to employ any staff?

20.2   Ben

There are several risks attached to Ben's business start-up plan:

Risk of not obtaining work

Although Ben has a good contact list, all his contacts have been made through Amis & Lovett, his employers. Much will depend on whether or not any of Amis & Lovett's existing clients will give their work to Ben's agency. If their relationship with Amis & Lovett is good, and they are satisfied with the work, they may be quite happy to stay with the larger agency. Ben is taking a big risk.

Risk of running out of money

Even if the work does follow Ben, the nature of the type of service he offers means that he will not start receiving payment for his work for quite some time. He has £45 000 which sounds like a lot, but this may not keep him going for very long. If he has not already done so, he needs to make a realistic plan so that he can budget for the first year or so of his new business.

Risk of employing people

Ben is taking a risk by employing people straight away. He may not have enough work to justify employing anybody in the early months of the business. His employees will expect to be paid at the end of the month, whether or not Ben has much work. He would probably be well advised to get the work first, and only then employ staff.

20.3   Nancy

As regards costs, because there is sufficient space for another person to work on the premises, there will be no significant incremental cost involved. There will be a small additional cost in consumables such as hair products and electricity, but the main cost will be in paying the salary of the new stylist, plus any additional administrative costs. Nancy already employs one person, so presumably she or her accountant already operates a payroll system that makes sure that the employee and HMRC are paid the correct amount. There are two main risks:

1. That there will not be sufficient business to keep the new stylist busy. Employing another person does not make financial sense unless the new employee can generate enough additional business to cover the costs of employing him or her.
2. That the new stylist will prove to be unsatisfactory in some way. Perhaps there will be personality clashes with Nancy or the customers, or perhaps he or she will not produce work of sufficient competence. An employee who turns up late, or not at all, or who is unpleasant to clients will create problems.

There could be two additional benefits for Nancy and her business:

1. Additional profits could be generated that would increase Nancy's wealth. She could either draw down more money from the business or could invest the profits in further expansion, perhaps by moving to larger premises and employing more staff.
2. The range of services offered could be expanded and improved.

20.4   Oleander Enterprises Limited

i) Advantages and drawbacks of buying into another business

Buying into another company may be advantageous because Libby and Lisa will be buying up an established business with employees who have knowledge of holiday operations in Turkey. They will not need to start from scratch in finding out about a new country. However, Oxus Orlando is, essentially, a service business which is very dependent upon the quality of its employees. Loretta, the main director, plans to retire, so her expertise will be lost. If the key employees also choose to leave, there may not be much value left in the company, and Libby and Lisa may find that they have paid too much for the investment.

ii) Information needed.

Libby and Lisa need to know:

- The price of the investment in Oxus Orlando, which Loretta wishes to sell.
- What they would get in exchange for the investment (for example, does the business own its own premises)?
- How profitable Oxus Orlando is (they will be able to ascertain this information from the business's annual financial statements).
- Details about the employees of the business. How much are they paid, how long have they been in their current jobs and how likely is it that they will stay if the company changes ownership?

20.5   Ashton Longton

The company has 8 000 000 shares in issue, each valued at £3.85. Market capitalization is
8 000 000 × £3.85 = £30 800 000.

20.6   The correct answer is a. The Alternative Investment Market is a market for companies that do not currently wish to proceed to full listing.

20.7   Warminster Toys

The correct answer is c) £54 200. The rights issue gives the holder of 50 000 shares the right to buy
50 000/5 shares = 10 000 shares. Each new share costs £5.42, so the total amount payable to take up the rights is: 10 000 × £5.42 = £54 200.

20.8   Brighton Bestwines plc

Potential drawbacks of listing on the Alternative Investment Market include:

1 Additional regulation applies to listed companies, for example, they have to produce additional financial reports. The additional compliance often requires the employment of more staff.
2 There will be legal and other professional fees incurred in listing. These are likely to be around 10% or more of the total amount raised, which means that for every share sold at the target price of 2.50, at least 25p will be spent on fees.
3 Many directors are uncomfortable with the additional attention paid to listed companies by the media. They may incur additional costs in obtaining professional public relations advice.
4 The company's share price may fluctuate for reasons that are unconnected to the fortunes of the company.
5 There is a potential drawback in allowing other parties to buy shares in that the company may lay itself open to takeover bids. However, in this case the shares issued for sale will amount to only one-third of the total, so the company will be safe from the threat of takeover.

20.9   Speke Septima Limited

The principal drawback in the proposed arrangement is the risk that the relationship between the venture capital firm will not work out well. Much will depend upon the person who is appointed to the board by the venture capital firm. If he or she brings the right mix of skills and personality to the business, the arrangement could be very successful, but the relationship could turn out to be problematic. A related problem is that the existing directors may resent the loss of complete control over the activities of the business.

Glossary

Absorption costing The costing of products and services to include both direct and indirect costs of production.

Accounting policies Those principles of accounting that are selected by the managers of a business to be applied in the preparation of the financial statements.

Accounting standards Regulations containing detailed guidance and rules on the preparation of financial accounts. Internationally, International Financial Reporting Standards (IFRS) are issued by the International Accounting Standards Board (IASB). In the UK accounting standards are issued in the form of Financial Reporting Standards (FRSs) by the Accounting Standards Board (ASB).

Accruals An important accounting convention that involves the matching of revenue and expenses, so that all of the expenses incurred in making a sale are deducted from it. Also referred to as matching.

Acid test ratio The ratio of current assets, excluding inventories, to current liabilities (also known as the 'quick' ratio).

Adverse variance An unfavourable difference between a budget figure and an actual figure. (In terms of sales, an actual figure that is lower than budget; in terms of costs an actual figure that is higher than budget.)

Amortization A measurement of the amount of non-current asset value that has been used up during the accounting period (the term usually relates to intangible non-current assets).

Articles of association A document, required by company law, which sets out the constitution of the company.

Assets Resources controlled by a business that it will use in order to generate a profit in the future.

Audit An independent examination by a properly qualified professional auditor of the records and financial statements of a business. (Note that in the context of this book the entity is a business enterprise, but audits of charities, local government and central government, for example, also takes place.)

Audit report The report by an independent auditor on the financial statements of a business.

Bad trade receivable An amount owed to a business that cannot be recovered.

Balanced scorecard Developed by Kaplan and Norton, the balanced scorecard provides an easily understood set of key performance measures for an organization.

Batch costing The accumulation of costs relating to a batch of identical products.

Break-even chart A graph showing lines for costs and revenues, from which the break-even point can be estimated.

Break-even point The point at which neither a profit nor a loss is made – ie. where total costs equal total revenues.

Budget A statement, prepared in advance, usually for a specific period (eg. for one year), of a business's planned activities and financial outcomes.

Budgetary slack An adverse effect observable in some businesses where managers deliberately set themselves easily achievable targets.

Business entity concept The business is regarded as separate from its owner(s).

Business plan A detailed document produced to support an application for business finance.

Capital Amounts invested by the owners of the business to which they subsequently have a claim.

Capital budgeting The process of decision making in respect of selecting investment projects, and the amount of capital expenditure to be committed.

Capital introduced The resources in the form of money and other goods put into a business by its owner(s) when it starts up.

Capital rationing Where a shortage of capital available for investment requires prioritization of investment projects.

Cartel A price-fixing arrangement where a few major suppliers in a market agree between themselves to keep prices high.

Cash flow The movement of cash in and out of a business.

Cash flow statement See Statement of cash flows.

Charge A legal arrangement for security for a loan. A lender puts in place a charge over specified property of the borrower. If the borrower fails to repay the loan, the proceeds of sale of the property are used to reimburse the lender.

Common size analysis The application of vertical analysis across comparable figures for more than one accounting period.

Consolidated financial statements The financial statements for a group of companies, which combine together the financial statements of all the companies in the group.

Contribution The amount that remains after deducting variable costs from sales revenue.

Cost accounting The process of identifying and summarizing the costs associated with business operations.

Cost and management accounting Accounting orientated towards the provision of information resources that managers can use to run the business.

Cost centres Functions or areas into which costs can be organized.

Cost drivers In activity-based costing, the various activities that take place in the organization to which costs are attached.

Cost object Any product, activity or service that requires costing.

Cost of capital The interest rate that is applicable to a particular business.

Cost of sales The cost of buying in or manufacturing the goods that have been sold in an accounting period.

Cost unit An item of production or a group of products or a service for which it is useful to have product cost information.

Cost pools In activity-based costing, the accumulation of costs associated with particular activities in the organization.

Current assets Assets held in the business for a short period of time only (examples include inventories, trade receivables and cash).

Current liabilities Amounts that will have to be paid by the business in the near future.

Current ratio The ratio of current assets to current liabilities.

Debentures Company bonds that entitle their holder to eventual repayment of the value of the stock plus a regular annual rate of interest (debentures are sometimes referred to as 'loan stock').

Debt Finance in the form of loans.

Demand curve An economic model of the relationship between price and quantity demanded.

Depreciation A measurement of the amount of non-current asset value that has been used up during the accounting period (the term usually relates to tangible non-current assets).

Direct costs Those costs directly associated with the manufacturing process.

Direct expenses Direct costs other than direct materials and direct labour costs.

Directors The senior managers of a limited company. Directors have special responsibilities in law.

Dividend A payment periodically made by a limited company to its shareholders.

Dividend cover A ratio that calculates the number of times the current dividend could be paid out of available profits for the period.

Doubtful trade receivable An amount owed to a business in respect of which recovery is doubtful – it is not clear whether the amount can be recovered.

Drawings The taking of cash (or other resources) out of an unincorporated business by its owner(s).

Equity The ordinary shareholders' interest in a company, comprising their original contribution in share capital plus any profits retained in the business.

Equity shares The share capital in a company that entitles its owner(s) to a share of the business's profits (in the form of dividend) and to voting rights.

Expenses The amounts incurred by the business in purchasing or manufacturing goods sold, and other expenditure on items like rent and telephone charges.

Factoring An arrangement to obtain cash from a factoring company in exchange for trade receivables of the business.

Favourable variance An advantageous difference between a budget figure and an actual figure. (In terms of sales, an actual figure that is higher than budget; in terms of costs an actual figure that is lower than budget.)

Financial accountants Specialists in the provision of financial information orientated towards interested parties external to the business.

Financial accounting The processes and practices involved in providing interested parties external to the business with the financial information that they need.

Financial reporting Reporting financial information to interested parties external to the business.

Finished goods Inventory items that have been through a complete manufacturing process and that are now ready for sale.

Fixed cost A cost that remains the same, regardless of variations in the level of business activity.

Fixed overheads Those costs that do not tend to vary directly with increases and decreases in activity in a business.

Gearing The relationship between equity capital and loan capital in a company.

Gearing ratio The relationship between equity capital and loan capital expressed as a ratio.

Goal congruence Ensures that all divisions within an organization work together to maximize returns for the organization as a whole.

Goodwill The intangible factors that add value to a business, such as brand names and customer loyalty.

Gross profit The amount of profit after deducting cost of sales from total revenue.

Horizontal analysis Analysis of comparable accounting figures over a period of time.

Hostile bid A takeover bid which is not welcomed by the target company.

Incorporation The process of setting up a limited company.

Incremental budgets Budgets that are set by taking a previous period's budget total and adding a standard percentage increase.

Indirect costs Those costs that are not directly identifiable with a unit of production.

Input tax VAT on purchases of goods and services.

Intangible non-current assets Non-current assets that do not have a physical presence.

Interest cover A measurement of the number of times interest could be paid out of available profits.

Internal rate of return (IRR) The discount rate which, when applied to a set of cash flows related to an investment, produces an NPV of £0.

International financing reporting standards (IFRS) Accounting standards issued by the International Accounting Standards Board (IASB).

Inventory Items bought by a business to sell on to somebody else, or to process or transform in some way to make saleable goods (more usually known as 'stock' in the UK).

Inventory turnover ratio Measures the length of time, on average, that an item of inventory remains in the business before being sold.

Investment centre A method of divisional organization where managers are able to control costs, pricing strategy and investment strategy.

Issued share capital The number of shares actually issued by a company.

Job costing An accumulation of costs relating to one identifiable job or task.

Leasing A financing arrangement for obtaining the use of business assets without having to purchase them.

Lessee A person or business that obtains the use of an asset under a leasing arrangement.

Lessor A person or (usually) business that makes assets available to businesses under leasing arrangements.

Liabilities Amounts that the business is obliged to pay to other people or organizations.

Limited company A legal arrangement for regulating the ownership of business.

Limited liability The liability of the shareholders of a limited company is limited to the amount of their original investment.

Loan stock Company bonds that entitle their holder to eventual repayment of the value of the stock plus a regular annual rate of interest (loan stock is sometimes referred to as 'debentures').

Long-term liabilities Also referred to as non-current liabilities: those liabilities that fall due in over 1 year.

Loss The deficit which occurs when expenditure exceeds revenue

Loss leader A product or service that is used to attract customer attention to a range of goods or to a particular supplier.

Management accountants Specialists in the provision of financial information for use within the business.

Management accounting Accounting carried out within a business for its own internal uses, to assist management in controlling the business and in making business decisions.

Marginal cost The cost of one additional unit.

Marginal costing An approach to costing that excludes fixed costs.

Margin of safety The excess of planned or actual sales above the break-even point.

Market capitalization The total value obtained by multiplying the number of shares a listed company has in issue by the market value of one share.

Market value [of a share] The price at which the share can be traded on the stock market.

Matching An important accounting convention that involves the matching of sales and expenses, so that all of the expenses incurred in making a sale are deducted from it. Also referred to as accruals.

Memorandum of Association A document, required by company law, comprising a statement made by the company's original shareholders confirming their intention to start the company.

Monopoly A market condition where only one supplier supplies the market with a particular good or service.

Mortgage A loan secured on real estate.

Net present value The aggregate of a set of cash inflows and outflows forecast to take place at future dates, discounted to present values.

Net profit The amount of profit after deducting both cost of sales and other expenses from total revenue.

Nominal value The basic denomination of a share – for example, 50p or 25p.

Non-current assets Assets that remain in the possession of the business over a long period of time, almost always in excess of one year.

Non-current asset turnover ratio Expresses the efficiency with which non-current assets have been used in a business to generate revenue.

Non-current liabilities Also referred to as long-term liabilities: those liabilities that fall due in over one year.

Offer for sale A general invitation to both the public and financial institutions to buy shares in a company.

Oligopoly A market condition where there are few suppliers (about three to five) of a particular good or service. Typically, the market shares between the suppliers are fairly evenly spread.

Operating and Financial Review (OFR) A voluntary, largely non-financial, report providing the directors' analysis of the business and its prospects. Included as part of the annual report by many listed companies in the UK.

Ordinary share capital The shares in a company that confer the right to vote in company general meetings, and to receive a share of any dividend paid out by the company.

Output tax VAT on sales of goods and services.

Overhead absorption A method of allocating an appropriate portion of production overheads to cost units.

Overhead absorption rate A rate used to estimate the amount of production overhead incurred in manufacturing.

Partnership A business that is run by two or more people with a view to making a profit.

Period costs Costs incurred during the accounting period.

Placing Offering a limited group of prospective buyers the opportunity to buy new shares in a company.

Prepayment An item of expense that has been paid in advance at the end of an accounting period.

Present value The discounted value at the present time (ie. now) of a cash flow expected to arise in the future.

Price setter An influential supplier in a market with the power to influence the level of prices for a product or service.

Price taker A supplier in a market with little or no influence over the level of prices charged for a product or service.

Prime cost The total of all direct costs associated with manufacture.

Product costing The accumulation of costs relating to the production of a large number of identical units.

Product costs Those costs relating to the production of goods or services for sale by a business.

Profit The surplus that remains after deducting business costs from business income.

Profit and loss account The UK term for statement of profit or loss.

Profit centre A method of divisional organization where managers are able to determine pricing strategy and control costs, but do not determine investment strategy.

Prospectus A document produced in accordance with (in the UK) Financial Services Authority regulation. It is prepared by a company which offers its shares for sale to the general public, and contains a large amount of information about the history and prospects of the company.

Quick ratio The ratio of current assets, excluding inventories, to current liabilities (also known as the 'acid test' ratio).

Raw materials Materials that are bought in by a business and then put through a manufacturing process.

Recognition The inclusion of items of, for example, income and expense in the financial statements. Recognition is an important accounting convention.

Reducing balance method [of depreciation] A method of estimating depreciation which results in a higher charge in the earlier years of an asset's useful life, with the charge progressively reducing towards the end of the asset's useful life.

Registered auditors Professionally qualified auditors who are authorized to conduct the audits of businesses and other organizations.

Relevant range In decision making, the range of activity within which certain assumptions about cost behaviour remain valid.

Responsibility accounting Accounting within the business that identifies the person or department responsible for particular outcomes.

Retained profits The amount of profit left in a business (ie. profit not distributed to the owners of the business).

Return on Investment (ROI) A commonly used method of assessing divisional performance; it expresses divisional net profit as a percentage of the investment in divisional net assets.

Revenue The amount of goods and/or services sold in an accounting period by a business, expressed in terms of monetary amounts.

Rights issue An offer of shares made to existing shareholders in a company, in proportion to the number of shares already held (eg. a 1 for 7 rights issue involves offering one new share for every seven already held).

Rolling budget A budget that is updated on a regular basis as each period of time (usually one month) elapses.

Sales Referred to as revenue in international accounting terminology.

Security An arrangement between a lender and a borrower where specified items of property can be used to meet the loan if the borrower defaults (ie. does not repay the loan).

Semi-variable cost A cost that varies to some extent with the level of business activity; it has both fixed and variable elements.

Shareholders The investors in a limited company; each investor owns a share or shares in the company.

Sole trader A person who operates a business himself or herself, keeping any profits that are made.

Standard costing A system of costing that attributes consistent costs to elements of production.

Statement of cash flows A statement prepared periodically that summarizes the cash flows in and out of a business.

Statement of financial position A statement of the resources owned and controlled by a business at a single point in time.

Statement of profit or loss A statement prepared by businesses of all sizes, at least annually, which shows the total business revenue less expenses. The net total is the profit or loss of the business.

Stewardship Taking responsibility for the management of resources on behalf of somebody else. (The principal example in this book is that of company directors managing a company on behalf of its shareholders.)

Straight-line method [of depreciation] The method that charges depreciation evenly over all accounting periods that benefit from the use of a non-current asset.

Sunk costs Costs that are irrelevant to a capital expenditure decision, because they have already been incurred.

Takeover bid A move to take over a majority of shares in a target company so as to gain control of it.

Tangible non-current assets Non-current assets that have a physical presence (unlike intangible non-current assets).

Trade payables Amounts owed by a business to other people or organizations that have provided goods or services on credit.

Trade payables turnover ratio Assesses the length of time, on average, that a business takes to settle its payables.

Trade receivables Amounts owed to a business by other people or organizations.

Trade receivables turnover ratio Assesses the length of time, on average, that it takes to turn trade receivables into cash.

Trading account The upper part of the statement of profit or loss where gross profit is calculated.

Transfer pricing The method of pricing sales of goods or services between divisions in an organization.

Trend analysis The analysis of comparable accounting figures over a period of time sufficient to establish reliable tendencies and trends.

Variable cost A cost that varies in proportion to the level of business activity.

Vertical analysis An accounting analytical technique that involves expressing all of the figures in an accounting statement as proportions of a key figure (for example, sales).

Work-in-progress Items of part-completed inventory.

Working capital The elements of financing required for investment in items that move rapidly in and out of the business, for example, inventory.

Working capital cycle The movement of the elements of working capital (trade receivables, trade payables, inventories and cash) around the business.

Zero-based budgeting A budget process that ignores any previous budgets and requires that budgetary allocations must be justified in full by managers.

GLOSSARY

**APPENDIX - GLOSSARY OF INTERNATIONAL ACCOUNTING TERMINOLOGY
AND THE UK EQUIVALENT**

International	UK
Statement of financial position	Balance sheet
Statement of profit or loss	Profit and loss account
Revenue	Sales (or turnover)
Finance costs	Interest
Non-current assets	Fixed assets
Property	Land and buildings
Inventory (or inventories)	Stock
Trade receivables	Debtors
Trade payables	Creditors

Note: although, as listed above, there are some significant differences in terminology, many terms are identical, for example, current assets, current liabilities, cost of sales.

Index